METHODS IN SOCIAL SCIENCE
A Case Book

THE UNIVERSITY OF CHICAGO PRESS
CHICAGO, ILLINOIS

—

THE BAKER & TAYLOR COMPANY
NEW YORK

THE CAMBRIDGE UNIVERSITY PRESS
LONDON

THE MARUZEN-KABUSHIKI-KAISHA
TOKYO, OSAKA, KYOTO, FUKUOKA, SENDAI

THE COMMERCIAL PRESS, LIMITED
SHANGHAI

METHODS IN
SOCIAL SCIENCE

A CASE BOOK

COMPILED UNDER THE DIRECTION OF THE
COMMITTEE ON SCIENTIFIC METHOD IN THE SOCIAL SCIENCES
OF THE SOCIAL SCIENCE RESEARCH COUNCIL

EDITED BY
STUART A. RICE

Professor of Sociology and Statistics, University of Pennsylvania

THE UNIVERSITY OF CHICAGO PRESS
CHICAGO · ILLINOIS

COMMITTEE ON SCIENTIFIC METHOD IN THE
SOCIAL SCIENCES OF THE SOCIAL
SCIENCE RESEARCH COUNCIL

Committee

WALTER W. COOK, Johns Hopkins University
ARTHUR N. HOLCOMBE, Harvard University
WILLFORD I. KING, New York University
ROBERT M. MACIVER, Columbia University
EDWARD SAPIR, University of Chicago
HORACE SECRIST, Northwestern University
FREDERICK J. TEGGART, University of California
L. L. THURSTONE, University of Chicago
MARY VAN KLEECK, Russell Sage Foundation

Investigators

HUBERT R. KEMP, University of Toronto
HAROLD D. LASSWELL, University of Chicago
ROBERT M. MACIVER, Columbia University
STUART A. RICE, University of Pennsylvania

FOREWORD

This volume comprises a series of interpretations of the scientific methods employed by authors of significant contributions to social science. In most instances these interpretations are case analyses, that is, each relates to a specific piece of work by a specific individual author. Exceptions to this general criterion are frequent and have been allowed in a number of directions. In some instances it has seemed desirable to give attention to the work of two or more authors in a single analysis; this amounts in some cases to an elucidation of the work of an entire school. In other instances, the analysis has served as an occasion for the consideration of larger problems relating to the structure of social science or of one of its particular subdivisions. One paper, that by Professor Pirenne, is not even cast in the form of an analysis.

The contributions selected for analysis differ widely in character. Some are distinguished in the widest sense; they are among the great systematizing works of human thought. But since "method" has been regarded as a concept of variable meanings, and as such has been at times employed in a comparatively restricted sense, some of the contributions analyzed have been correspondingly restricted in scope and breadth of generalization.

While unique in plan, the volume is necessarily incomplete in accomplishment. Both the claim and the confession result from the varied meanings attached to the term "method," and the inclusive interpretation here employed. This interpretation is reflected in the nature and, to some extent, in the arrangement of the analyses; it grew out of an evolution in the project. The reader must be prepared at each point to take note of three methodologies: that of the committee and the investigators responsible for planning the study; that of the individual analysts in making their interpretations of authors' work; lastly, that of the authors themselves, as set forth in the case analyses. An explanation of the origin and development of the project is obviously required, for it will serve as the equivalent of an analysis of the method of the study as a whole. Such an explanation appears in Appendix A. An exposition of the problem of defining "method," however, together with an explanation of the arrangement of the analyses in accordance with the interpretation adopted, appear in the Introduction.

Numerous gaps and discrepancies will be disclosed to discerning read-

v

ers. Nevertheless, it is confidently believed that each of the case analyses has importance, and that, taken together, they will aid in producing a better understanding of the foundations and the present structure of social science. No attempt has been made by the editor to synthesize the interpretations of the individual analysts, or to draw conclusions from their findings with respect to the methodology of social science. If this task is attempted, it should form the subject of a separate volume.

A list of acknowledgments, if it were to be complete, would read, almost literally, like a catalogue of American social scientists. Through the kindness of Professor Ogg, the individual questionnaires on research returned to the American Council of Learned Societies in connection with a recent study[1] were made available. The projects reported upon by members of several of the constituent societies were canvassed, and in a considerable number of cases correspondence with the authors was undertaken. Moreover, correspondence went on with members of the faculties of many of the leading American universities. In the case of some of these, particularly Harvard, Chicago, Columbia, Princeton, Syracuse, Wisconsin, Northwestern, and Pennsylvania, personal conferences and group meetings were of much help. The number of persons to whom acknowledgments are due as a result of these contacts is much too large for individual mention.

The Committee on Scientific Method of the Social Science Research Council originated and sponsored the project,[2] and directed it to a point near completion. Authority and appropriations for the work were secured from the Council. Both bodies gave constant support, and individual members of each contributed generously of time and thought. Contributors of case analyses not infrequently were put to great sacrifice of other work and personal convenience. The authors of the works analyzed, whenever available and called upon, co-operated whole-heartedly. To the advisory committees appointed by the several social science societies special gratitude is due. The membership of these committees is recorded in Appendix A. Their appointment in some cases involved much labor by the presidents of the societies, in their endeavor to procure committeemen who would render the greatest service. Special thanks are due the Russell Sage Foundation and Northwestern University, which provided office facilities and innumerable courtesies to the Committee and its investigators.

To the foregoing general acknowledgments the editor desires to add his personal appreciation of the contribution made by a few persons: To the

[1] Frederic Austin Ogg, *Research in the Humanistic and Social Sciences*, New York: Century Co., 1928. Pp. viii + 454.

[2] Cf. Appendix A.

unflagging interest and labors of Professor Horace Secrist, chairman of the Committee on Scientific Method from its inception until July 1, 1928, is due, more than to any other individual, the development and the completion of the project. This appreciation should extend, however, to the entire Committee, and particularly to Miss Mary van Kleeck, its secretary, and to Professor Robert M. MacIver, who continued as chairman until its discharge. To Professor Harold D. Lasswell, the writer's coinvestigator, has primarily been due the expansion and development of the inquiry along the lines indicated by this publication. His optimism and clarity of perception became available at a time when the difficulties involved in the enterprise appeared insuperable.

In the final editing of the volume, invaluable help was given by several persons: At the request of the Social Science Research Council, Professor Lasswell, Professor Edward Sapir, and Mr. Robert S. Lynd accepted the time-consuming and important tasks of reading the entire manuscript, criticizing it in detail, and advising with respect to general editorial problems. Professor McQuilken de Grange served as editorial *alter ego* on a number of occasions, one of them during a continuous and extended period. Mrs. Amy Sellin, editorial assistant, assumed much of the burden which resulted from this co-operative reflection and criticism, and in addition contributed many helpful suggestions. All references were verified by Miss Rose Epstein, who also prepared the Index. Since numerous disagreements still persist even within this intimate circle of advisers, however, and since entire responsibility for the publication was lodged by the Social Science Research Council in the present writer, he alone is to be charged with the many defects of omission and commission to which critical readers are certain to take exception.

STUART A. RICE

TABLE OF CONTENTS[1]

INTRODUCTION

CASE ANALYSES

SECTION I. THE DELIMITATION OF FIELDS OF INQUIRY

ANALYSIS

[1] This table provides a classification of the analyses. Like any other classification its form is dependent upon the purposes and working concepts of the person making it. These are described in the Introduction and in Appendix A, the former containing (pp. 10–14) a detailed exposition of the section headings and their sequence. Cf. also Professor Harold D. Lasswell's classification (Appendix B) to which the present table is closely related. Since many methodological considerations may receive attention in a single analysis, some analyses might have been placed as readily in one section as another. Hence alternative classifications are presented elsewhere in the volume. In Appendix H analyses have been assembled into overlapping groups representing the special social sciences. In two indexes which follow Appendix H, analyses have been arranged alphabetically by names of analysts and alphabetically by names of authors. The General Index will also serve to bring many related topics together.

TABLE OF CONTENTS

INTRODUCTION

INTRODUCTION

BY THE EDITOR

The attitudes of scientists and scholars toward studies of method are conflicting. On the one hand there are those who regard methodological inquiry as a prerequisite to the further development of social science. A corrective is needed, they feel, for the immaturity and obscurity that have characterized that field. Generalizations in physical science are usually based on controlled observations which are described so explicitly that he who objects may repeat. Students of social science may look at the same phenomena and draw wholly divergent conclusions, which are tolerated as legitimate expressions of individual judgment. The distinctive characteristics of social phenomena are in dispute. The demarcation of social science from physical science is a matter of opinion, as is the question whether or not there can be social *science* in the sense that physics and chemistry are science. Must the social scientist break new paths toward the acquisition of knowledge, or may he have the aid of precedent from the older disciplines? Such problems as these retard our advance, and they are methodological problems.

There are scholars who contend, on the other hand, that a concern with questions of method is a mark of decadence in any science. A period of active development is initiated when some great mind perceives new or previously unseen relationships among things or ideas. The fertile imagination and creative insight behind this perception are intuitive in quality. As the implications of a new orientation are followed out and harvested by workers of lesser genius, a period of diminishing returns and comparative stagnation sets in.[1] Conscious of their relative unproductivity, these workers eventually resort to a study of method, like disappointed patients to a new quack remedy, hoping there to find a cure-all for the ailment. Erstwhile leaders in scientific progress sometimes contribute to the vogue. In declining years memoirs on their methods by great scientists are not unexpected, along with adumbrations on the secrets of their success from captains of industry. There are not, say the critics, any beaten roads to discovery, any means of teaching or emulating imagination and inspiration, any substitutes for hard work. These are the only "methods" that count for the extension of science.

[1] The state of physics a generation ago, the state of economics in the later "classical" period, and the state of "general" sociology today have been cited in illustration of this view.

3

The opposing attitudes toward methodological study set forth above are composite, hence possibly exaggerated. In illustration of the skeptical attitude there are quoted here statements by two eminent scholars concerning the methods of William Graham Sumner. Sumner is generally regarded, to employ the title of a recent collection of biographies, as one of the "masters of social science." His *Folkways* has been frequently acclaimed the greatest single contribution to sociology.[2] The late Charles H. Cooley wrote of him:

As regards his technical procedure there was, so far as I can see, nothing original or distinctive. Like Montesquieu or Darwin or a hundred others before him, he simply collected a great mass of relevant material and made what he could of it.

As regards concepts: any work that is at all original must have something distinctive in this way, but Sumner's work, considering its influence, had remarkably little. He merely enlarged, analyzed and interpreted the familiar idea of custom. What distinguishes him and makes the manner of his work a possible source of help to others is something inseparable from his personality—his ardor, his penetration, his faith in social science, his almost incredible power of work, his great caution in maturing and testing his ideas before publication.

A. G. Keller added:

In general I agree wholly with what Dr. Cooley says. . . . . Sumner used to laugh at "methodology." He had none, except of the sort that is exemplified in Darwin's works; he got myriads of facts and then performed inductions on them. His methodology consisted in toil. I may illustrate his attitude by the advice he gave to a young man about learning a new language: "The way to learn a language is to sit down and learn it." . . . . The case is one of utter simplicity: hard work plus saving common sense, with no talk about it.

The conflict of views that has been evidenced above is more apparent than real. It demonstrates the need for definition of terms. When Pearson, proceeding from the contention that "the field of science is unlimited," asserts that "the unity of all science consists alone in its method, not in its material,"[3] he leaves an inference that scientific method is a concept of elemental clarity and uniformity. His statement induces the impression that "everyone knows" what scientific method is. In fact, the expression is cloaked in ambiguity comparable to that surrounding such

[2] The two expressions which follow may be compared with Robert E. Park's discussion of Sumner's methods in analysis 8, pp. 154–175. They are excerpted from letters to the editor.

[3] Karl Pearson, *The Grammar of Science* (3d ed.; London: A. & C. Black, 1911), Part I, p. 12.

shibboleths as "justice," "liberty," and "democracy." No problem in the present study has offered greater difficulties than that of attaching to the terms "method" and "methods" consistent interpretations acceptable to all persons involved. The problem has been of the utmost practical importance to the study, because upon it has depended the purpose and the organization of the entire work.

One means of arriving at a definition of "method" might be an inductive examination of the uses given to the word in the literature of the social sciences. An enumeration of so-called "methods" was begun by the present writer, but its futility soon became apparent. The number of items in such an enumeration would be indefinitely large. Each subdivision of social inquiry, no matter how small, has its own "methods." Again, the items would be of differing degress of generality.[4] Sociologists and social workers make use of "case method," but they also use the "method of the interview" as a subordinate aspect of case method. "Statistical method" comprises among others the "method of least squares," while the latter may utilize the "method of logarithms." It seems clear that the units in the suggested compilation would have no consistent relationship to subject matter, and would lack co-ordinate relationship, in most instances, with each other.

A much-used distinction would designate most of the procedures just mentioned as "techniques," reserving the term "method" for the logical processes of inference from data. In this view techniques, or technical methods, are employed in fact-gathering, and in the manipulation or ordering of data prior to inference. That is, they are *aids* to observation or inference. Hence, they are almost infinitely varied, as the data to be dealt with are varied. Only the specialists in a given subject can master the techniques of that subject. Logical methods, on the other hand, since they refer to the reasoning process itself, are substantially the same in every field, varying only with their application.

This distinction leaves the student of method in a dilemma: If scientific method refers only to the nature and validity of the logical processes by means of which inferences are drawn from data, the methodologist is replaced by the logician. Methodological differences between social and

---

[4] For example, the methods of historical research have been adapted to the nature of the sources. Professor Pirenne in analysis 30 mentions the "auxiliary sciences of history," namely, epigraphy, paleography, diplomatics, archaeology, numismatics, sigillography, and heraldry. Professor Spier in an appendix to analysis 19 describes documentary method, typological method, distributional method, geological method, annual-deposit method, stratigraphic methods (three in number), and seriation method as commonly used methods of achieving chronology in archaeology, itself a type of method in history.

physical science are ruled out by definition. Analyses of methods in social, science can only provide new illustrations of the handful of deductive and inductive types of reasoning which John Stuart Mill and others have expounded. On the other hand, if techniques be admitted within the scope of the definition, complete acquaintance by any single individual with the methods of social science becomes impossible. This impossibility is demonstrated by the increasing specialization within the field.

The simplicity of the distinction between method and technique, moreover, disappears in practice. They are intertwined at every point. Detailed technical procedure in one problem achieves a co-ordinate, or indeed a principal, rôle in the solution of others. One may wish, for example, to infer the degree of relationship between two variables; he may employ the logical method of *concomitant variations*. But as an auxiliary thereto he may derive a Pearsonian *coefficient of correlation*, a technical device. Prior to the calculation of the latter there may have preceded an intricate series of steps designed to build up the two series that are to be statistically compared. These may include instrumental observation, or controlled experiment, or interviews to elicit information held by others, or statistical refinement of previously existing data. Each step not only involves technique, but must be carried out logically with respect to the elements involved at that point, and in relationship to the ends in view.

It is equally difficult to draw distinctions between "scientific methods" and "scientific problems." The latter have been defined as questions concerning relationships between or among variables, methods referring to the means whereby the questions are answered. But the statement of a problem concerning relationships necessitates definitions, explicit or implicit, of the variables involved. It would be difficult to exclude this question of definition from a study of scientific methods.

The origin of a problem or a hypothesis, moreover, involves further difficulty for one who seeks to discriminate method from the entire scientific process; for here are encountered elements which cannot be detached from the personality of the scientist. Darwin is said to have obtained the idea of natural selection from a reading of Malthus. His hypothesis might be termed a discovery or invention; it required capacity for insight. Twenty years were devoted to the collection of data before the final inductive logical processes could be completed. At what point did "method" enter in? Professor L. L. Thurstone has suggested that all scientific work starts and ends with something personal, equivalent to insight, but that it contains an intervening period of more or less mechanical manipulation of evidence. This central period can be subjected to rules of procedure. But can either extremity of the entire sequence, or the middle, be cut off by itself and regarded as method to the exclusion of other elements? Do all stages of the sequence represent method?

Some do not wish to exclude personal elements leading to invention or discovery from a discussion of scientific methods. These same persons are among the most insistent upon rigid scientific procedures in social science. This seeming paradox is resolved by the reflection that achievement of any kind is conditioned both by innate factors within the individual and by the cultural setting in which his activity is carried on. A degree of control over scientific progress might conceivably follow an examination of the psychological histories of scientists, and analyses of the cultural factors in their contributions.[5]

There are numerous other forms in which the term "method" appears in general use in addition to those already cited. The method of organizing a research enterprise, for example, while an essential part of scientific work, is method in a sense distinct from logical inference, or technique in a narrow sense, or discovery, or the formulation of the problem itself. Again, in educational and other circles, the term connotes the process of imparting knowledge. In this sense it is not infrequently confused with method as a scientific auxiliary.

In the face of all these conflicting usages method must be regarded as a term of variable meanings. In the present work it seemed desirable to employ whatever versions of the term would have utility for the interpretation and the further development of social science.

One version which will be stressed from this point onward has not been scrutinized in the foregoing discussion: namely, that view of method which identifies it with the concepts and assumptions underlying scientific inquiry, and in terms of which the major aspects of a problem are formulated. Method in this sense precedes, either explicitly or implicitly, the employment of methods in any more limited sense. The concepts and assumptions underlying scientific investigation are frequently undiscerned, in spite of their all-pervading and far-reaching consequences upon it. Differences in the formulations of investigators are more likely to

[5] A series of analyses interpreting scientific method in its personal and cultural aspects would have been a legitimate part of this volume. Two such inclusions have actually been made. In analysis 12, Ogburn examines some of the personal and cultural factors which were involved in a statistical invention. Following analysis 47 there is appended an intimate autobiographical account of the development of his research interests by the author of the work analyzed by Clark. Less extended or less explicit references of similar character are scattered throughout the book. A recent study of invention and discovery in a particular field, in which the author adopts the approach here suggested, is that of Bernhard J. Stern, *Social Factors in Medical Progress* (New York: Columbia University Press, 1927).

proceed from differences in their ways of conceiving problems and data than from any other methodological cause. Hence it would seem that what may be called the "conceptual" version of method refers precisely to those aspects of social inquiry whose clarification would be most beneficial. Moreover, since this interpretation of the term can be made to include the more limited interpretations, it seems to be the most general and the most fundamental that can be employed.

The hard-headed, factual-minded type of investigator, most akin among his fellows to the "practical man" among laymen, will remain skeptical of the value of this interpretation. He will ask his science for "facts," and be willing to "let the concepts go." He would like to build a social science out of such tangible units as bushels of wheat, votes of electors, birth-rates, and reaction times. By binding such units together in mathematical formulas, he thinks, social science may approach the solidity of the so-called "natural" sciences. But before quantitative methods can be employed it is necessary to identify and define the objects to be counted. Even prior to this it is necessary to formulate the problem with respect to which—and delimit the field within which—enumeration is to occur. In social science these steps offer peculiar difficulties. They are inseparable from the investigator's concepts and assumptions.

It is interesting that at the very moment when the social sciences are striving to become more factual, physical scientists are becoming less and less certain of the meaning of "facts," and more and more interested in the underlying concepts which have the power to make facts appear and disappear. The physicist, for example, changes his concepts concerning light, and with them his facts, according to his experimental convenience. It is a fact that the earth moves around the sun, according to the Copernican astronomical system. It is not a fact according to the Ptolemaic system, in which the sun moves around the earth. Either is "true" relatively; but apart from the element of simplicity, neither set of facts has any greater inherent validity than the other. It is impossible to answer the naïve human query which inevitably arises respecting such matters: "But which is *really* true?"[6]

The facts of human history—the raw material of social science—are even more dependent than the facts of physics upon the presuppositions of those who record and interpret them. Anthropologists have demon-

---

[6] For further elaborations of this viewpoint cf. such recent books as *The Anatomy of Science,* by Gilbert Newton Lewis (New Haven: Yale University Press, 1926; pp. ix + 221), and *The Logic of Modern Physics,* by P. W. Bridgman (New York: Macmillan Co., 1927; pp. xiv + 228).

strated the extreme difficulty of understanding the cultural forms of primitive people in terms of our own ideational systems. The enumeration of statistical units among such people must follow the interpretative process. All words are abstractions—generalized symbols of classes of experience. The classes and the class limits tend to vary from language to language. This is one reason why experience notoriously changes in accordance with the ideational system to which it is related.

Moreover, the flow of events in their entirety escapes the perception of the most gifted; the perceptions, in fact, of all human beings collectively.[7] If the events with which history and social science deal are to have any coherent meaning, they must be selected in accordance with some guiding point of view, some preconception, in other words, concerning the *kinds* of events that are of causative importance.[8] When someone contends that he merely "takes facts as he finds them," he is self-deluded. He is accepting without criticism generalized symbols of experience, already interpreted in such a way as to fit within the modes of a given ideational system, and selected in accordance with some one or more dominant views as to what is important.[9]

The set of ideas with which an investigator begins work will condition the formulation of his problem and whatever else he does. There would have been no search for Neptune had the Ptolemaic concept of astronomical arrangements continued among astronomers. Cultural anthropologists would not have discovered "stages" of social evolution had it not been for Darwinian theory. When Darwin was ejected from culture phenomena, culture "stages" disappeared. A large amount of detailed and careful scientific inquiry proceeded from the assumption by Lombroso that physical stigmata were associated with crime. The assumption was discredited,

[7] Cf. analysis 30 by Professor Pirenne on "What Are Historians Trying To Do?", Part II, *passim*.

[8] As Frederick J. Teggart has pointed out (*A Theory of History* [New Haven: Yale University Press, 1925]), the so-called "new history" represents a new conception concerning the relative importance of various types of events, and a reconstruction of the past in accordance therewith. As long as men are subject to change in the prevailing patterns of their thought, history will continue to be revised in accordance with new principles of selection. Without risking prophecy, it is possible to imagine a "new" psychological history superseding in the future the present "new," then old, "social" history of today.

[9] This is probably an inadequate statement of the extent to which selection is enforced upon the historian. He must not merely choose a view as to what is important, but also a view as to how these selected "important" data are to be treated. Cf. Professor Schevill's analysis of the work of Voltaire, analysis 29, where this point emerges with engaging clarity. Schevill's references to the "new history" may be compared with the editorial references in n. 7 above.

and the scientific results based upon it were scrapped. Karl Marx interprets history in economic terms; Carlyle, in terms of individual personality. Assume that Marx and Carlyle had set about the development and appropriate use of statistical "methods," each being similarly equipped with mathematical knowledge and intellectual capacity. The methods of Marx might have become something akin to modern economic statistics today. It is doubtful whether Carlyle could have developed and employed—compatible with his concepts—a statistical "methodology" at all. He might have evolved something like the mental and personality testing of modern psychologists. Numerous illustrations parallel to these are contained in the following papers.

To recapitulate, instead of saying that the concepts and assumptions of an author *predetermine* his methods, they are regarded in this volume as a *part* of his methods. They are regarded as *instruments* as well as *frameworks* of investigation. Moreover, in a majority of the analyses they have been emphasized as the most important part of a given author's methodology, although this emphasis has not precluded attention to method in any of its less extended meanings.

In setting up specific criteria for the selection of contributions to be analyzed and for the presentation of analyses, three broad objectives in social science were distinguished.[10] These are seldom found in isolation, and may not be mutually exclusive when subjected to logical analysis. In specific studies they may be discerned as differing modes of emphasis. They are:

A. Definition
B. Ascertainment of sequence and change
C. Discovery of relations

These objectives appear in the following section headings under which the various analyses have been grouped:

I. The Delimitation of Fields of Inquiry
II. The Definition of Objects of Investigation
III. The Establishment of Units and Scales
IV. Attempts To Discover Spatial Distributions and Temporal Sequences of Culture Phenomena
V. Interpretations of Change as a Developmental Stage

[10] Some of the problems encountered in establishing this classification, and the development of thought concerning them as the inquiry developed, are set forth in Appendix A. Alternative modes of classification are also presented in this appendix and in Appendix B, while suggested classifications within certain specific fields of subject matter in social science appear in Appendix C and Appendix D.

VI. Interpretations of Temporal Sequences with Consideration of Special Types of "Causation"

VII. Interpretations of Relationship among Unmeasured Factors

VIII. Attempts To Determine Relations among Measured but Experimentally Uncontrolled Factors

IX. Attempts To Determine Quantitative Relations among Measured and Experimentally Controlled Factors

Definition, implicit if not explicit, is an essential preliminary to observations of change or sequence and to the determination of relationships among factors. Phenomena which are relevant must be discriminated from phenomena which are irrelevant, whether the task be the delimitation of a general science, the identification of units for statistical enumeration, or the portrayal of entities having some intervening degree of inclusiveness. The unity possessed by the thing defined may seem to be "natural," as when human beings are distinguished from one another; or it may seem wholly conceptual, as when two economic systems are distinguished and compared. If one may accept the basis of classification here employed, the analyses grouped in Sections I, II, and III portray the work of men who viewed definition as their primary task.[11] But since the entities defined differ widely in degree of generality and in internal complexity, these tasks differ enormously in detail. It seems a far cry from the generalizations of Auguste Comte concerning a new science to the identifications by Sumner and Pareto of "folk ways" and "residues" and thence to the instruction book of a census enumerator. These first three sections have been distinguished from one another, therefore, according to the inclusiveness of the definitions of which they treat, proceeding in order from the more general to the more particular. The authors whose work is analyzed in Section I are concerned with problems of delimitation among fields of subject matter having an order of generality equivalent to that of a special social science. In Section II objects of investigation of less extensive but still of highly conceptual type receive attention. In Section III the establishment of units and scales of sufficient simplicity to receive statistical treatment are the center of interest.

Turning to the second general scientific objective, a distinction in terms must be noted. The term *sequence* refers to a succession among things which are regarded as different, such as particular historical events. *Change* refers to an alteration in what is regarded as the same thing, such as a civilization. The choice between these words depends on any occasion

[11] I.e., as these analyses are interpreted by the editor. Cf. Table of Contents, n. 1; also final paragraph of this Introduction.

upon one's concepts of the subject matter or object matter. A given flow of phenomena in time, for example, may be viewed as "a change in civilization" or as "a sequence of civilizations." Similarly, one might refer either to "changes in native North American culture" in various parts of the continent, or to "sequences of cultures" across the continent.

Sequence and change may be viewed as spatial or temporal. The notion of change merges into that of *correlation among variables*. Thus a variable may change from place to place, or over a period of time, or in accordance with changes in other variables to which it is related. It follows that Category B, in the preceding threefold classification of scientific objectives, is not clearly distinguished from Category C. The former, "Ascertainment of Sequence and Change," refers here to the work of men whose primary interests concerned the distribution of phenomena in space and time, and to whom questions of relationship among factors in change seemed to have lesser importance. Analyses of work of this sort will be found especially in Sections IV, V, and VI.

In Section IV have been grouped analyses in which particular significance is attached to the determination: first, of spatial patterns of distribution of culture data, second, of temporal sequences of culture patterns. These are hinged together, as it were, by analysis 17 in which both spatial and temporal distributions exhibit meaning in reference to each other. All of the contributions discussed have to do with sequences rather than with changes; and in each the order of the succession rather than its cause seems to be regarded as of immediate first importance.[12]

In Section V attention shifts from sequence to change. Correspondingly, the interest in determining a mere order of succession gives way to an interest in explanation. But the type of explanation differs considerably from that which is involved in the discovery of relations among factors. Change is viewed somewhat in the light of an unfolding within a particu-

[12] It will be a matter of opinion whether or not analyses 14, 15, and 16 have been properly included in this section. The contributions examined have to do with "human geography," and in particular with the concept of "region." It is the interpretation of the editor that the emphases of the authors have been upon the *distributions* of phenomena. On the other hand, the analysts have tended to emphasize the problem and the need of establishing *relationships* among regional phenomena. If relationship rather than distribution is placed in the foreground of attention, the three analyses named would more properly fall in Sec. VII. It is of interest that since the present classification of these analyses was editorially determined, Dr. Isaiah Bowman, of the American Geographical Society, has contended that a great deal of contemporary regional research consists in the juxtaposition of facts, without an attempt to say why they should be juxtaposed. His remarks were made at a conference called by the National Research Council and the Social Science Research Council to discuss the "region" as a research lead in science (Washington, April 11–12, 1930).

lar cultural entity itself. It represents, that is, a stage in development. The papers in this section will have particular interest to those who are concerned with the possibilities of *prediction* in social science. Analysis 21, for example, describes a foreseen discovery of linguistic forms which recalls to mind the predictions by astronomers of the discovery of Neptune and the newer trans-Neptune planet.

In Section VI interest reverts from change to sequence, as individual events are recorded. The subject matter is history, in the usual sense. The explanations advanced by the historians considered in the group are varied, but they rest upon specific isolable factors of "causation," which may be viewed as exterior to the events themselves. The notion of relationship definitely enters. The final paper of the section, that by Professor Pirenne (No. 30), sums up the aims and purposes of historical inquiry.[13]

The end result of scientific labors is usually regarded as the determination of relations among generalized factors in change.[14] By some this is regarded as the only type of endeavor that merits the name "science." Sections VII, VIII, and IX have to do with attempts to establish relations of this character. Attention to individual events is left behind, except as these events may appear as units or unitary factors in a problem of relationship. Within the confines of this third general objective of science problems center upon the degree of control over his data that the scientist is able to exercise. Upon this control rests the comparative validity and precision of his results. The three sections mentioned have reference, in order, to three increasing degrees of scientific control over data. In Section VII are placed analyses relating to work in which there is neither measurement of factors nor experimental control over them. In Section VIII appear analyses of work in which there is measurement but no experimental control. In Section IX appear analyses in which there is measurement and in which an approach, at least, is made to controlled experimental conditions.

All classifications are to some extent artificial. Any order in which the following papers might be presented would necessarily represent the imposition of an editorial point of view. Hence readers of the book are urged to reclassify its contents in accordance with their own methodological interests and aims. Since many will wish to visualize the collection from the standpoint of the special social sciences, a classification of analy-

[13] It was prepared independently of the preceding historical analyses, which Professor Pirenne had not seen.

[14] It is unnecessary to consider factors related to sequences, since the moment a problem is stated in this fashion the meaning becomes altered and we are in fact dealing with factors related to change.

ses by disciplines appears in Appendix H. This is likewise arbitrary, and overlapping among the various headings appears freely. Other appended tables present the titles of papers by names of analysts and by names of principal authors treated. None of these classifications and tables is intended to imply that any limitation was placed upon the treatment of his subject by any contributor. Nor will they, in any instance, indicate more than a part of the methodological interest of the analysis.

CASE ANALYSES

SECTION I
THE DELIMITATION OF FIELDS OF INQUIRY

ANALYSIS 1

THE METHOD OF AUGUSTE COMTE: SUBORDINATION OF IMAG-INATION TO OBSERVATION IN THE SOCIAL SCIENCES

By McQUILKIN DeGRANGE
Dartmouth College

I

To obtain an ordered view of knowledge as a whole; to allocate to each science its place in this synthesis; to study the spontaneous evolution of the sciences already in existence; to derive from this study the directive principles needed for the systematic development of sciences yet to be; in particular, to learn from the history of the physical sciences how consciously to accelerate the rise of social science—such were the essential aims of the philosophical effort of Auguste Comte (1798-1857).

II

Comte's education was, in its scientific aspects, unique. Distinguishing himself from the first in mathematics (1814), he was then, at the École Polytechnique, conducted through the physical sciences (1816). When the school was closed, he studied biology at the medical school of Montpellier (1817). His omnivorous reading had early brought him into contact with the Encyclopedists and the eighteenth century, with De Maistre and the conservative school. Finally, his association with Saint-Simon threw him, prematurely perhaps, into social speculation in its most active form. And back of all was the influence of the French Revolution, which had forced political reconstruction into the forefront of all men's minds.

With such a background, it is not surprising that Comte, from the first, was struck by the absence of the scientific spirit in the fields of inquiry beyond biology; that he felt from the beginning the need of importing into these fields the methods of the physical sciences; that he should have been far more deeply impressed by the imperfection of social science than attracted by grandiose schemes of reform.

It will be clear, then, why Comte was early impressed by Condorcet's remark that men who hesitated to make pronouncements in astronomy or chemistry were nevertheless ready to deal with the most complicated political problems. Evidently politics had to be raised from a theological to a positive level.[1]

But if politics once became positive, the entire range of human thought and interest would thereby become positive, and the end—and the beginning—of an era in human history would be reached. The making of a science of politics thus implied not only a new science but a new world. Obviously, so vast a project could be entered upon only after a profound study of the whole range of human investigation. No mere economic reforms could ever satisfy the mind upon which the greater vision had dawned. So Comte departed from Saint-Simon (1824) and went off to compose his *Positive Philosophy*, confident in the belief that intellectual regeneration had to come first, and that the rest would follow.

Before he did so, however, he had laid the foundations which were to support the structure of his later thought. In the years from 1818 to 1826, he was following that elementary precept of method which requires an investigator in any field to inform himself of the state of knowledge in that field before beginning active work therein. The result was the series of essays long lost sight of but revived and republished in 1854 as an appendix to the *Positive Politics*.[2]

The second of these essays makes "A Brief Estimate of Modern History" (1820). It rests on a historical distinction between the catholico-feudal system and the scientific-industrial system. Its main thesis is that industry must replace war and science take the place of theology. It is divided into two "series"; the first traces the decline of the old system, the second the growth of the new. The beginnings of the latter on the industrial side are traced to the enfranchisement of the commons, and on the scientific side to the introduction of the sciences of observation into Europe by the Arabs. These two elements in combination overcome the forces represented by feudalism and theologism, and out of the conflict arises the modern age.

Such was the outcome of the meditation upon the facts of history that Comte was to continue throughout his life. The second result came in 1822, when he presented his "Plan for the Scientific Operations Necessary for Reorganizing Society"—surely one of the most mature productions

---

[1] By "theological" Comte means those explanations which refer the causes of social phenomena to wills, especially divine wills; by "positive," those explanations of the same phenomena based upon observed sequences or laws.

[2] These essays were translated and published separately by Henry Dix Hutton, and are now to be had under the title *Comte: Early Essays on Social Philosophy* (London: Routledge & Sons, 1911). It is to this volume of *Early Essays* that reference is made in these pages.

ever achieved by a man of twenty-four, and by far the most important of Comte's early essays, for it contained in germ all his later works.

The "plan" begins by tracing the existing social anarchy to the conflict between an old social system and a new, whence comes the negative attitude that rejects all constructive thought. Only by the formation of a completely new system and its replacement of the old can the period of intellectual disorder be brought to an end. The destructive theories that served as the means to combat the expiring system cannot serve to direct the growth of the nascent one. Men, aided by acquired experience, must, with all the accumulated materials, construct a new edifice fitted for their needs and enjoyment.

Hitherto, wrong methods have been used in framing a plan of reorganization. "The pretension of constructing offhand, in a few months or even years, a social system in its complete and definitive shape, is an extravagant chimera, absolutely incompatible with the weakness of the human intellect."[3]

How, then, shall the task be performed? The history of science provides the answer.

When a science is reconstituted on a new theoretical basis, sufficiently prepared, in the first instance the general principle is announced, discussed and verified; subsequently, by a long series of efforts, all the parts of the science are worked out and their co-ordination established, which, at the outset, no one, not even its founder, could have conceived.[3]

The formation of any plan for Social Organization necessarily embraces two series of works, as distinct in their objects as in the kind of capacity they demand. One, Theoretical or Spiritual, aims at developing the leading conception of the plan—that is to say, the new principle destined to co-ordinate social relations, and at forming the system of general ideas, fitted to guide Society. The other, Practical or Temporal, decides upon the distribution of authority, and the combination of administrative institutions best adapted to the spirit of the system already determined by the Theoretical labors. Since the second reposes on the first, of which it is only the result and the realization, the general enterprise must necessarily begin with the former.[4]

These passages are the key to Comte's life-work. Since theory and practice must be separated, and theory must precede practice, the most urgent necessity for social welfare is the re-formation of thought throughout upon a new and homogeneous basis, so that it will at last become self-consistent. Once this work is done in a single mind, the results can be transmitted to others. Comte's was to be the mind in which this total reorganization should take place.

[3] *Early Essays*, p. 107. [4] *Ibid.*, pp. 109–10.

The source of guidance in this mental regeneration is easy to find.

Scientific Thinkers, occupied with the study of the Sciences of Observation, are the only men whose capacity and intellectual culture [as a class] fulfil the necessary conditions. It would be evidently abnormal, when the most urgent social needs call for a general work of the highest order of importance and difficulty, to entrust this work to any but the greatest intellectual forces we can command, and to men *who pursue a method whose superiority is universally recognized.*[5]

Further quotation is needless, even did space permit. The words just italicized explain Comte's labors for the twenty years to follow.

Already indeed he had long been meditating upon the work of the scientists of his own and earlier time. In his second essay he had said:

The sciences successively became positive in the natural order of sequence, that is to say, according to their degree of remoteness from Man. Thus, Astronomy first, then Physics, later Chemistry, and finally, in our own day Physiology, have been constituted as positive sciences. This revolution, then, has been completely accomplished for all special branches of knowledge and evidently approaches its consummation for Philosophy, Morals, and Politics.[6]

It need not be explained that the mind which put politics on a positive basis could at the same time be the mind which should regenerate thought, since it would have achieved homogeneity in the whole range of inquiry. Hence the ultimate expression of purpose in the third essay:

In the last resort, all resolves itself into establishing, through the combined efforts of European men of science, a positive Theory in Politics distinct from Practice, and one which shall bring our social system into harmony with the present stage of knowledge. Pursuing this course of reflection, we shall perceive that the above conclusions may be resumed in a single conception: *scientific men ought in our day to elevate politics to the rank of a science of observation.*[7]

To unify the system of scientific thought, then, was the first necessity. It could be done only by rendering positive the only domain of inquiry yet remaining beyond the bounds of science, namely, politics. The two tasks were ultimately one; the second could be achieved only by applying to the new domain the methods that had been successful in the older one. No wonder, then, that Comte had always been interested in science and that he had to a considerable degree concentrated upon the question of method.

The early essays put this point beyond doubt, and they need no further

[5] *Ibid.*, p. 122. (The italics are the analyst's, as is always the case throughout this discussion, except when otherwise noted.)

[6] *Ibid.*, p. 68.   [7] *Ibid.*, p. 130. (Comte's italics.)

comment in this direction; they should not be dismissed, however, without being examined to see how far Comte had already reached the positions he was to occupy in the *Positive Philosophy*.

In the first place, he had already made the generalization that was later to become the Law of the Three States: "From the nature of the human intellect, each branch of knowledge in its development has to pass through three different theoretical states: the theological or fictitious state; the metaphysical or abstract state; and lastly, the scientific or positive."[8] This position, here stated seemingly as a result of deduction, was in fact, as anyone can convince himself by reading the essays as a whole, an induction from the history of the sciences. "Men familiar with the progress of the sciences can easily verify the truth of *this general historical summary*."[9]

In the next place, the general course of thought in the development of the sciences had become clear.

The fundamental characteristic of these revolutions which have led the different sciences up to the positive state consisted in transferring to Observation the preponderance hitherto exercised by the Imagination.[10]

Further, the possibility of a general view of knowledge from a positive standpoint had been clearly envisaged, as well as the place of the new science in this synthesis.

In the natural series of phenomena, we evidently miss the Social point of view as regards beings which can be so treated, and especially Man. It is, however, equally clear that this omission is the only one. Thus we already possess Celestial Physics, Terrestrial Physics, Mechanical and Chemical; Vegetable Physics; Animal Physics. We still need an additional science— Social Physics—in order to complete the Natural Sciences. This condition once fulfilled, we can, summing up all our various conceptions, at last construct a truly Positive Philosophy.[11]

Again, the nature of the new domain had taken on a more definite form. Comte had advanced sufficiently far in his thinking to see that "social

---

[8] It is all too often forgotten that Comte never, at any time after this third essay, rested his explanation of social development upon a single law, the Law of the Three States. No; he always added to it another, which took various forms as Comte's thought developed. This second law was intended to explain the succession of ultimate purposes revealed from time to time by the organization of societies. In its final form this law reads as follows: "Activity passes through a succession of three states: conquest, defense, industry."

Comte's early discussion of this matter can be found in *ibid.*, pp. 182–84; the quotation just given is taken from *La politique positive*, IV, 177.

[9] *Early Essays*, p. 132.

[10] *Ibid.*, p. 139.   [11] *Ibid.*, p. 236.

organisation must be conceived of as intimately connected with the state of civilization and determined by it, and the progress of civilization considered as being subject to an invariable law based upon the nature of things."[12]

Positive Politics should no more seek to govern phenomena than the other sciences do. They have abandoned this ambitious chimera, which characterised their infancy, for the simple task of observing and correlating their phenomena. Political science should do the same. It should employ itself exclusively in co-ordinating all the special facts relative to the progress of Civilization, and in reducing these to the smallest possible number of general facts, the connection of which ought to manifest the natural law of this progress.[13]

Besides, he had arrived at an understanding of the relation of the new science to its nearest predecessor, as well as a clear conception of its basic phenomenon:

Social phenomena, as belonging to man, are no doubt included under Physiological phenomena. For this reason, *Social Physics must necessarily start from individual Physiology* and maintain continual relations with this science. Nevertheless, the former must be considered and cultivated as an entirely distinct science, by reason of *the progressive influence of human generations upon each other.* This influence, which in Social Physics is the preponderating consideration, cannot be rightly studied from the purely physiological point of view.[14]

And, in conclusion, Comte had arrived at a most important position in regard to method: In both organic and inorganic physics,

the human intellect proceeds from the Known to the Unknown; but in the first case it rises from the Special to the General, because the knowledge of details is more accessible to it than that of the whole; while in the second case, it begins by descending from the General to the Special, because it is more intimately acquainted with the whole than with the parts.[15]

In the study of Inorganic bodies, we find Astronomy, Physics, and Chemistry at first quite isolated from each other, and afterwards becoming mutually related to such an extent that they now tend to become a single science [whereas] only in consequence of the progress of positive Physiology have we succeeded in analysing with precision the different general points of view under which a living body can be considered, so as to found a rational divi-

[12] *Ibid.*, p. 143. Notice the echo of Montesquieu: "Laws are the necessary relations arising out of the nature of things" (*The Spirit of Laws,* p. 1).

[13] *Early Essays,* p. 157. The quotation continues: "leaving for subsequent appreciation the influence of the various causes that can modify its rapidity." What Comte had in mind is evidently what is today called the "growth of culture."

[14] *Ibid.*, p. 237 n.

[15] *Ibid.*, p. 211; and see Aristotle *Politics* i, 2.

sion of the science upon these distinctions.[16] [Hence] in studying the development of the Human Race, we must commence by co-ordinating the most General facts, descending from these to deductions of increasing specialty.[17]

The *Positive Philosophy*, as will be seen, was well under way.

III

The preliminary work was completed; the general law underlying intellectual evolution had been discovered; the successive development of the sciences had been accounted for; it remained, to construct a positive philosophy, only to make explicit the processes underlying the historical movement—processes that had up to then remained implicit.

For behind and underneath the sciences is of course a philosophy, a philosophy that differs from all other philosophies in that it rests upon the same epistemological positions as scientific inquiry itself, and seeks to go no farther into the "nature" of things than the methods of science can take it. That is to say, there is a "positive" type of philosophy.

Then, too, Comte understood philosophy in the Aristotelian sense, as an orderly view of all knowledge. A review of all the sciences would involve precisely such an ordered view of all knowledge. The relation here, between science and philosophy, is direct, and the two coincide so far as the ground covered is concerned. In this sense it is futile to attempt a distinction between science and philosophy. The two are coextensive.

When the task of making such a synthesis is approached from the side of the sciences, however, a preliminary difficulty presents itself: Several sciences, in the usual sense of the word, may and often do occupy themselves with the same set of phenomena; there is overlapping of the same subject matter. How is the philosophical mind to know which sciences must be dealt with in constructing a synthetic view of knowledge? Are there not, in this respect, sciences and sciences?

Comte's answer is clear: There are. Certain sciences are of primary interest for the philosophical mind and others only of secondary interest. To obtain a distinction between the two, Comte goes straight to the phenomena with which the various sciences are concerned and establishes a distinction there. This distinction is of primordial importance for any understanding of Comte's scientific or philosophical position, as well as for the comprehension of the views presented in the last pages of the *Positive Politics*.

There are, then, according to this analysis of Comte's, two classes of phenomena: events and beings. Beings are the seats of events or happen-

[16] *Early Essays*, pp. 212, 213.   [17] *Ibid.*, p. 214.

ings; events but aspects of beings. Either class, however, may be envisaged separately, and man has always done so, as the very existence of the two terms shows. When events are, by abstraction, envisaged apart from the beings in which they are manifested, the result is attributes or properties. Thus Gilbert began with the observation of what happened when amber was rubbed, passed on to the classifying of objects as electrics and non-electrics, and ended with the property of electricity. When, on the other hand, beings are envisaged as the seats of events, they become complexes of properties. Amber, to carry on the illustration, presents many other properties to the observer than electricity alone.

Hence there are two kinds of science, from this point of view: those that deal with specific abstract properties and those that deal with complexes of these qualities. Once the conception is clear, it becomes obvious that the first type of science is the only one of direct interest to the synthetic mind, for the second type will deal with nothing that is not already treated in the first type.

If, then, analysis could reduce all beings to manifestations of a small number of specific and irreducible properties, the philosophical mind would need to concern itself only with the sciences devoted to the study of such properties, for in so doing all the range of knowledge would be brought under review.

Now Comte's position is that such an analysis of phenomena has been in course of operation throughout the whole history of science; that science in general has always been seeking for and ultimately discovering new classes of abstract phenomena; and that a new science has historically arisen when abstraction has attained to a new property.

On the basis of his historical survey of scientific development, he therefore asserts that there are but two kinds of science between which the philosophical mind, in search of a universal synthesis, must choose: the abstract, dealing with fundamental abstract properties; and the concrete, studying complexes of properties. These might be termed the component and the composite sciences, to avoid the connotations that the terms "abstract" and "concrete" today carry to the mind of the reader.

On this distinction Comte built his *Positive Philosophy*. In this treatise he had obviously to discuss only the abstract or "component" sciences. His first task was, therefore, to determine the number and the nature of the specific and irreducible properties into which the whole range of human inquiry could be analyzed. Such an undertaking is beyond the powers of any human mind, however great, called upon to present an independent and unaided solution. Fortunately, the whole history and the sum of the efforts of humanity were within reach and able to give aid.

The entire development of the sciences was available to suggest the answer. The scientific evolution from the Greeks to the Arabs and from the seventeenth century to Comte's own time could be studied as one continuous attempt to attain to the desired and indispensable analysis.

The Greeks had begun with mathematics and astronomy; the Arabs had prepared the materials and the methods out of which had come physics and chemistry; Bichat and others in Comte's time had attained to an abstract biology, in which Cabanis and Gall had, it seemed, once for all incorporated the intellectual and moral life of man. There remained but one step to take: to carry on the scientific advance until it had covered the domain of the "political" as Comte called it, the "social" as it is termed today. Beyond this domain there could be nothing, for the whole range of human thought had been surveyed. A philosophy based on the results of the entire evolution of science would be both positive and encyclopedic.

One other problem remained to be solved before Comte could feel himself in a sure logical position: In what order must the abstract or component sciences follow one another, whether in history or logic? Had there, indeed, been any order imposed by the logic of facts? Once more, recourse to the history of science provided the answer; there Comte found the principle that had spontaneously guided the entire scientific development.

The various specific classes of phenomena, he discovered, differ as regards the generality and the complexity of their constituent materials. Some are more general and less complex than others, and they will therefore precede in reaching the scientific stage. There is, in other words, an order which has had to be followed in the development of the sciences, an order which explains why the sciences have successively arisen in time and dictates the sequence that must be traversed when they are treated philosophically.

This discovery of the principle that had spontaneously directed the scientific evolution made possible the conscious construction of an encyclopedic hierarchy of the sciences, a hierarchical encyclopedia covering the whole range of inquiry open to the unaided mind of man: encyclopedic because no domain was omitted, hierarchical because of the orderly subordination of group to group.

In this way, then, Comte's first great task had been completed. He had achieved a first survey of the entire domain of knowledge. He had brought order into the world of intellect. He had attained a standpoint whence he could see the task he had set himself as a whole in the light of all the developments in the world of science that had hitherto taken place. He was now in a position to follow in a strictly logical fashion the formation of one science after another, to understand the nature of the entire scientific achievement, to set forth one by one the main methods that had been employed, and finally to enter upon the deliberate construction of a new science.

To review the field of scientific inquiry from this central standpoint was the primary aim of the *Positive Philosophy*, which Comte wrote from 1830 to 1842. In regular succession he traversed the sciences from mathematics to and through biology, in each case seeking to make precise the domain, the method, and the systematic divisions of the general field. In this paper only the second of these inquiries will be examined, that dealing with the methods of the different sciences; and attention will, besides, be limited to what seems to throw light upon the social science which was Comte's ultimate point of arrival, the goal which he had always had in view.

In discussing the methods employed by an original mind in arriving at his conclusions, two points of view may be taken: first, the actual processes involved, regardless of logical standards; and, second, the degree to which these processes conform to those uniform procedures summarized under the term "scientific method." In Comte's case, the two points of view coincide so far as a man's conscious intentions can make them do so. He became a philosopher only because he wished to see the place in knowledge as a whole of the science he wished to create; he became a positive philosopher because he desired to give to his new science the same basis of stability that assured the existence of the sciences already in being; he constructed an encyclopedia because only so could it be made certain that the whole domain of knowledge open to man had been covered; he made this encyclopedia hierarchical because to do so rendered it possible to see the domain of each member and its relation to all the other members, and in particular the place and the nature of the science of social life. He was able to do all these things as the result of his profound study of the historical movement, the implications of which he did but make explicit: The evolution of science, that is, had reached the point by the end of the eighteenth century which enabled a synthetic mind to see the significance of the movement as a whole.

In precisely the same spirit he approached the study of method. Here only could he find the sure guidance that would enable him to attempt with confidence the ambitious task he had set himself. Hence the very first necessity that faced him was to determine the procedures that the makers of the sciences had employed, spontaneously or consciously, in the past. These procedures, once determined, were to be his guide. In short,

Comte's personal processes were to be, in his intention, strictly subordinate to scientific procedures as a whole; and when in his later life he found that he had to make a revision of his work, he attributed the necessity to his failure to adhere with sufficient fidelity to the basic principles he had laid down from the beginning.

It was induction, then, based on the history of the sciences that led Comte to the position that the sum of scientific methods is more or less applicable to all domains of science, but that certain classes of phenomena can be, and have been, better studied by one procedure than by another. In such a class is to be found, and out of it arose, the characteristic application of a given procedure. He says:

In general, our art of observing [and by this term he meant scientific method as a whole, for reliance on observation rather than on imagination is the distinctive mark of science] is composed of three different procedures: (1) observation properly so-called, *i.e.*, the direct examination of the phenomenon such as it is presented in nature; (2) experiment, *i.e.*, the contemplation of the phenomenon more or less modified by artificial circumstances, instituted by us expressly in view of a more perfect exploration; (3) comparison, *i.e.*, the gradual consideration of a series of analogous cases, in which the phenomenon is simplified more and more.[18]

It is quite impossible here to review Comte's interesting discussions of method as he rises, one by one, through the physical sciences: the clearest example of the use of observation proper is to be found in astronomy; experiment is best studied in physics; comparison in biology. Chemistry, subordinate to physics as an example of the use of experiment, yet affords the best example of the art of nomenclature, etc. Attention must be turned to and concentrated upon the treatment of "organic physics"; and first of "physiology" as an introduction to "politics," i.e., biology as an introduction to sociology.

In coming to the field of the organic Comte recurs with emphasis to a point he had already brought to attention in the essays.

An essentially empirical aphorism prescribes in every subject possible a constant procedure from the simple to the composite; but there is at bottom no other solid reason for it than that such a progress is in fact suited to the nature of the inorganic sciences, which by their superior perfection were inevitably destined to serve, up to the present, as the essential type for formulating precepts of universal logic.[19]

[18] *Cours de philosophie positive*, II, 13–14. The edition referred to is always the second edition, edited by Littré (Paris: Baillière et Fils, 1864).

[19] *Phil. pos.*, IV, 258.

But all that is required in any case is that the progress of the mind shall be from the known to the unknown, and this requirement may often be satisfied by passing from the composite to the simple. Now there is in this very respect a fundamental difference between the inorganic and the organic.

For in the first, where the solidarity is but slightly pronounced, and must but slightly affect the study of the subject, it is a question of exploring a system whose elements are almost always much better known than the whole, and ordinarily even are alone directly appreciable—which requires in fact that we proceed habitually from the less to the more composite case. But in the second, the opposite progress becomes most often the only truly rational one, by another necessary consequence of the same logical principle, since the whole of the subject is certainly there much better known and more immediately within reach than the different parts that will ultimately be distinguished in it.[20]

This position of Comte in regard to the movement from the composite to the simple in the case of the organic must not be understood to imply any a priori position in the dialectical sense. Although Comte does not deal with this objection explicitly, his answer to it would be a reference to a distinction, found throughout his work, between the spontaneous and the systematic periods in the development of all sciences. The sciences can become positive only in a definite order, the hierarchical; but the facts upon which the sciences are built have at all times been in process of collection. Inductions, of a primitive kind, have always been in the making. At a certain moment, historically, they can be gathered into a systematic theory—the moment, namely, when the preceding science in the hierarchy has become positive. Physical and chemical data, for example, long antedated the sciences of physics and chemistry. And all the more is the statement true for biology and sociology. In the spontaneous period of the history of biology and sociology a general body of inductions had gathered in regard to the physical organism and society. It is these spontaneous inductions that must, in Comte's view, provide the starting-point for the systematic study and not any dialectical position whatever. The known, in the case of the physical world, consists of inductions regarding the details, arrived at spontaneously at first and then colligated into a general theory, and so developed into an abstract science; in the case of the physical organism and of society, it is the whole, not the separate parts, that is the subject for the first spontaneous inductions, and with them the systematic study must begin.

[20] *Ibid.*, pp. 258–59.

Biology, then, moving from the whole to the parts, is the typical field for the employment of the method of comparison. There are five principal forms of the procedure: (1) comparison between the different parts of each determinate organism; (2) comparison between the sexes; (3) comparison between the various phases presented by the development as a whole; (4) comparison between the different races or varieties of each species; (5) finally, and most significant, comparison between all the organisms of the biological hierarchy.

It is always assumed that in any of these parallels, the organism will constantly be considered in its normal state. When the essential laws relative to this state shall have been suitably established, the human mind will be able to pass rationally to comparative pathology,[21] the study of which, still more detailed by its nature, will lead to the perfecting of these laws by extending their original scope.[22]

The essential spirit of the method, Comte further remarks,

consists always in conceiving all the cases envisaged as being of necessity radically analogous from the point of view from which they are considered, and in representing consequently their actual differences as simple modifications, determined in a fundamental and abstract type, by the whole of the characters proper to the corresponding organism or being.[23]

Out of comparison comes classification, an art which finds its happiest exercise in biology, whether in the formation of natural groups, or their rational co-ordination, or the sub-ordination of characters.

After all these preparations, the outcome of his whole previous life, Comte approached his project, unique in history, of consciously creating a new science. He does so with all the caution required by the occasion. First, he demonstrates the necessity and the opportuneness of the new inquiry. Then follows an account of the principal philosophical efforts to constitute social science in the past. In the course of this attempt to determine the contemporary state of knowledge in his subject, he changes "social physics" into "sociology."[24] Only after these preliminaries did he reach the question of what should be the fundamental character of the positive method to be employed in the rational study of social phenomena.

Comte begins by reiterating a thought he had already emphasized several times before—a thought which, because of its special importance to a science so new as sociology, is presented here rather than earlier—the thought, namely, that the most just notions in regard to method, when

---

[21] Freudians, and others, please note.
[22] *Phil. pos.*, III, 245–46.   [23] *Ibid.*, p. 247.
[24] The word "sociology" dates from 1839 (see *ibid.*, IV, 185 n.)

presented in isolation from any effective application, are always necessarily reduced to a few incontestable but very vague generalities, profoundly insufficient to direct with success the various researches of the intellect; the more complex and special phenomena become, the less is it possible usefully to separate method from doctrine. True as the statement is in regard to the lower sciences, it is even more applicable to the higher, so new and so complex. Here more than elsewhere the positive method can be appreciated only in the light of the rational consideration of its principal uses, in proportion to their gradually accomplished results. Hence no true preliminary treatise on method in sociology can be presented.

Nevertheless, some discussion of a general nature is permissible, although it can be only a review of the resources possible to the new science in the light of the sciences already in existence. This review Comte proceeds to make.[25]

In the first place, it should be repeated that positive method as a whole is marked by the systematic subordination of imagination to observation. Metaphysical idealities must be abandoned in favor of observed realities; the search for absolutes must be given up once for all.

In the second place, there must be a strict adherence to the rule that directs men, in other sciences, to seek for laws and to set aside permanently all chimerical notions as to the illimitable power of interference on the part of men with regard to social phenomena. Political conceptions must be considered as relative and not absolute—relative to the regularly varying state of human civilization.

Henceforward, no order nor agreement is possible in political philosophy except by subjecting social phenomena, in the same manner as all others, to invariable laws, the sum of which circumscribes, for each epoch, the fundamental limits and the essential character of political action in the proper sense.[26]

Finally, and in summary, the criterion of prevision, the most undeniable criterion of rational positivity, applicable to every one of the lower sciences, must be extended to the science of social phenomena, "within the limits of precision compatible with their greater complication."[27]

Once these preliminary counsels have been given, Comte proceeds to

[25] Hence the passage referred to constitutes no defense of the coquettish deprecation of the study of method exhibited by some investigators. Doctrine and method are inseparable, it is true; but to argue that therefore no thoughtful discussion of methods is of any avail is to take an untenable doctrinaire position.

[26] *Phil. pos.*, IV, 225.

[27] *Ibid.*, p. 226.

make a first division of social phenomena into two classes: the first concerning the conditions of existence of society, the second concerning the laws of its continuous movement—whence social statics and social dynamics. But in doing so he was careful to say that "it would be premature to attach any grave importance to this methodical distribution. . . . . Any division of the work of sociology is inopportune and even irrational so long as the whole has not been adequately conceived of." Such a distinction is not to be applied pedantically, but merely to be used in the analysis of social theories, which can always be envisaged from the two points of view, as indivisible in fact as are the ideas of organization and life in biology.[28]

Turning, then, in methodical order to the first of these divisions, Comte proceeded to advance from the known to the unknown, i.e., from the composite to the simple, and sought the general guiding conception from which investigation should at first proceed. Here he was following the guidance of ages of spontaneous observations of social phenomena. This age-long induction leaves no doubt that the characteristic fact of social phenomena from the statical point of view is the universal consensus they exhibit. Hence social statics

must have for its permanent object the study, at once experimental and rational, of the mutual actions and reactions that are continually exercised one upon the other by all the various parts whatever of the social system, abstraction being made as far as possible of the fundamental movement that always gradually modifies them.

Each of the numerous social elements should always be exclusively conceived of as relative to all the others, with which a fundamental solidarity intimately and unceasingly combines it.[29]

Instances of this consensus and solidarity are the relations between astronomy and abstract geometry, between a given art and other arts, between sciences and arts—hence, once the state of any given single element of society is known, the general corresponding state of all the other parts may to a certain degree be deduced.[30] Another and most important relation is that between social organization proper and the corresponding state of civilization—by which Comte at the time designated what today is called "culture"—the neglect of which relation leads to the gross exaggeration of the power of legislatures to influence the course of social life. Not only must political institutions and social mores, on the one hand, and general mores and ideas, on the other, be unceasingly solidary,

[28] *Ibid.*, pp. 231–32, 234.
[29] *Ibid.*, p. 235.   [30] *Ibid.*, p. 237.

but the two as a whole are integrally related to the corresponding state of mankind, considered in all its various modes of activity, intellectual, moral, and physical.[31] Hence

every truly rational political institution, to have a real and durable efficacy, must constantly rest upon an exact analysis, previously made, of the corresponding spontaneous tendencies, which alone can furnish sufficiently solid basis for its authority.[32]

Such being the essential general conception of the nature of the domain with which social statics has to deal, the proper method of dealing with it is apparent: Since social phenomena are thus profoundly connected, their real study can never be rationally separated. Whence results the permanent obligation always to consider simultaneously the various aspects of social life, whether in statics or dynamics. Each of these aspects can doubtless become, in isolation, the preliminary subject of special observations, and indeed to a certain degree must do so in order to provide the science with suitable materials; but this necessity is, in full rigor, applicable to the present epoch alone, when the first necessity is to make a first sketch of the science. Sociology, like other nascent sciences, must at the beginning use the incoherent observations which inevitably resulted, with quite other intentions, from the irrational researches of other days. When the foundation of the science is sufficiently advanced beyond this spontaneous stage, the fundamental correlation of phenomena will doubtless be the principal guide in their direct exploration.

Every isolated study of the various elements of society is then by the very nature of the science profoundly irrational and must remain essentially sterile.[33]

Those who strive to fragment the system of social studies still further, through a blind imitation of the methodical division proper to the inorganic sciences, fall involuntarily into the capital aberration of envisaging as an essential means of philosophical improvement an intellectual disposition radically antipathetic to the fundamental conditions of such a subject. No doubt social science will one day be able to be rationally subdivided in a useful way to a certain degree; but we can in no wise know today in what this ulterior division will consist, since its true principle must be the outcome only of the gradual development of the science, which can certainly not be founded now except in the light of a study which sees it as a whole. Even a permanent division today into statics and dynamics would present a philosophical danger. At any age whatever of the science, the partial researches which will become necessary will be suitably indicated and conceived of only in the light of the progress of studies in their entirety, which will spontaneously call to attention

[31] *Ibid.*, p. 243.   [32] *Ibid.*, p. 252.   [33] *Ibid.*, p. 255.

the special points the illumination of which can really aid in directly improving the subject. Following any other route, there will essentially be obtained only a sterile and encumbering mass of irrational special discussions, badly instituted and worse pursued, destined much rather radically to hinder the formation of the true political philosophy than to prepare useful material for it.[34]

Even if experience were to show this methodological position badly taken, the positive philosopher, always sub-ordinating ideality to reality, would avoid vain logical controversies, engendered spontaneously only by the dialectical type of philosophical inquiry, as to the absolute value of this or that method; abstraction being made from every scientific application. The preferences, always relative, result from nothing but a better harmony between means and ends; and he would change methods at once, without any vicious obstinacy or the slightest philosophical inconsequence if effective application ultimately showed the inferiority of the method he had at first adopted.[35]

So much, then, for the general spirit and method of social statics. The same approach leads to the determination of the nature of dynamics. Here, too, centuries of spontaneous induction, quickened by the investigations of the eighteenth century, provided the starting-point, composite as before but even better known. The central conception here is the pregnant idea of continuous progress, or rather of the gradual development of mankind.

In a methodical treatise of political philosophy, it would doubtless be fitting to begin by analyzing the individual impulsions which are the characteristic elements of the progressive power of the human species; and to do this by relating these impulsions to that fundamental instinct (the eminently complex result of the necessary concourse of all our natural tendencies) which directly urges man to ameliorate his condition, whatever it may be, without ceasing and in every relation.[36]

Comte, however, assuming this notion to be sufficiently clear to advanced thinkers, preferred to consider only the elemental conception of dynamics, namely, the idea of continuous succession, envisaged in the whole of mankind. In order to present the idea more clearly, he begins by establishing an indispensable scientific abstraction, following the artifice judiciously instituted by Condorcet—the abstraction, namely, of the hypothesis of a single people, to whom would be ideally transferred all the consecutive social modifications observed in the concrete among distinct peoples. This rational fiction, he asserts, is much less distant from

[34] *Ibid.*, pp. 255–56.   [35] *Ibid.*, p. 261.   [36] *Ibid.*, p. 262.

the reality than is customarily assumed, for from the political point of view the true successors of this or that people are certainly those who, utilizing and continuing the primitive efforts of that people, have prolonged its social progress, whatever the soil they inhabit and the race whence they spring. It is therefore the idea of continuity that should underlie the discussion of sociological succession.[37] Hence

the true general spirit of dynamic sociology consists in conceiving of each of these consecutive social states as the necessary result of the preceding and the indispensable motor of the following, according to the luminous maxim of Leibnitz: The present is big with the future. The science then in this connection has for its object to discover the constant laws that this continuity follows—laws which in their entirety determine the fundamental advance of human development.[38]

Such a conception, he adds, makes it possible to set aside, once for all, the idle controversy concerning human perfectibility, by replacing this term with the word "development," which designates, without any moral judgment, a general and incontestable fact.[39]

That it is an incontestable fact, the physical, moral, intellectual, and social aspects of human existence all reveal. Of these, the most convincing and the most distinctly characterized of all is the intellectual, since it has had the fewest hindrances and the most rapid advance and so almost always has had to serve as the fundamental guide in inquiries such as this. Of this evolution, the principal part, the part that has most profoundly influenced general progress, consists no doubt in the continuous development of the scientific spirit, from the work of Thales and Pythagoras down to that of Lagrange and Bichat.

In studying this development, it is easy to see that the great progress in each epoch and even in each generation necessarily always resulted from the state immediately anterior; so that men of genius present themselves to us as essentially but the characteristic organs of a predeterminate movement which, in their absence, would have opened for itself other issues; as history often verifies in the most sensible fashion by showing several eminent minds quite prepared to make the same great discovery simultaneously.[40]

In the intellectual order, no accidental influence nor any individual superiority can, for example, transport to one epoch the discoveries truly reserved, in the light of the fundamental movement of the human mind, for a later

---

[37] *Ibid.*, p. 263.   [38] *Ibid.*

[39] *Ibid.*, p. 264. The term "development" "indicates the simple expansion [*essor*], gradually seconded by a suitable culture, of the always pre-existent fundamental faculties which constitute the whole of our nature, without the introduction of any new faculties whatever" (*Ibid.*, p. 278).

[40] *Ibid.* p. 269.

one, and reciprocally. The history of the sciences above all verifies, in the most undeniable manner, this intimate dependence of even the most eminent geniuses upon the contemporaneous state of human reason.[41]

And in the same way, "each of the fundamental modes of social existence determines a certain system of correlative mores, whose common physiognomy is easily to be found in all individuals, in the midst of their most characteristic differences."[42] In brief, the new science,

according to the aphorism of Pascal,[43] represents in a direct and continuous manner the mass of the human species, whether past, present, or even future, as constituting in all regards, and more and more either in order of time or of space, an immense and eternal social unity, whose various organs, individual or national, ceaselessly united by an intimate and universal solidarity, inevitably co-operate, each according to a determinate mode or degree, in the fundamental evolution of humanity.[44]

Such being the inductive basis of the dynamic section of sociology, what are the methods most applicable to the study of a composite of this nature? Here as elsewhere the three fundamental modes of observing will be applied: pure observation, experiment, and comparison. Each of these has its special contribution to make in developing the new science.

In sociology, better than elsewhere, can be appreciated the dependence of observation upon a theory previously arrived at—otherwise the observer could not tell what he should be looking at in what is going on under his eyes. The application of this first part of scientific method, for this very reason, is difficult, but its results are always subject to ulterior correction, based upon a greater mass of facts.

Experiment seems almost forbidden to the new science, but there are two sorts of experiment, direct and indirect. An experiment consists not only in the artificial institution of the circumstances of the phenomenon; every time that the normal accomplishment of the phenomenon undergoes in any manner whatever a determinate alteration, there is an experiment, at least of the indirect kind. In sociology this pathological analysis consists essentially in the examination of the cases where the fundamental laws, whether of harmony or filiation, undergo perturbations more or less pronounced from accidental or temporary causes,

---

[41] *Ibid.*, pp. 285–86.　　[42] *Ibid.*, p. 286.

[43] "The whole series of human generations during the course of the ages should be regarded as one man, ever living and ever learning" ("Fragment d'un traité du vide," *Pensées de Pascal* [introduction par E. Havet; Paris: Ch. Delgrave, 1881], II, 271).

[44] *Phil. pos.*, IV, 293.

whether special or general, as is seen especially in the various epochs of revolution.[45]

It is, however, from the use of the comparative method that the greatest assistance will be obtained. For example, all the various forms of the method, already pointed out in the case of biology, can be utilized. And in addition certain other modifications suggest themselves: Human societies may be compared with animal societies, at least from the statical point of view; or different states of human societies with one another as they exist in different localities on the globe, especially those that are independent of one another. "From the unfortunate inhabitants of Tierra del Fuego to the most advanced peoples of Western Europe, no social difference can be imagined which is not in fact realized at certain points of the earth and almost always even in several regions distinctly separate."[46] It must be remembered, however, that these uses of comparison make no allowance for the necessary succession of different social states, and so could lead to misunderstanding as to the fundamental order in which the different degrees of human evolution have had to result one from the other; and, besides, even if the positive order were known beforehand, these uses of the method would hardly permit of perceiving exactly the real filiation of the various systems of society.[47] Finally, their use could make it difficult to distinguish between simple secondary modifications and the principal phases of social development, which might thus be taken one for the other. In this fashion, it would be possible for investigators to attribute to race or climate differences that arise simply from an unequal rate of speed in the evolution of the two societies compared.[48]

All these considerations and others make more and more evident the fact that the comparative or any other method can be applied only in the light of a rational conception of the whole of the fundamental evolution of mankind, arrived at before the application of the method by means of a spontaneous induction. When this thought is kept in view as the various modes of comparison are reviewed, it becomes clear that the historical comparison of the different consecutive states of mankind constitutes for the new science of sociology the principal scientific artifice, which, because of its character, may be called the *historical method*.[49] Indeed, the rational development of this method will form the very basis of the new science in what it has most characteristic to offer.

[45] *Ibid.*, pp. 307–9.
[46] *Ibid.*, p. 318.   [48] *Ibid.*, p. 320.
[47] *Ibid.*, p. 319.   [49] *Ibid.*, p. 322.

It is at this point that social science becomes most distinct and clearly separated from biology; the positive principle of this indispensable separation residing in the necessary influence of the various human generations upon the generations following—an influence which, gradually accumulated, soon ends by constituting the preponderant consideration for the direct study of social development. So long as this fact is not recognized, the positive study of mankind must rationally appear as a simple, spontaneous prolongation of the natural history of man. Logically, too, the historical method has a special importance, for it constitutes the distinct contribution of the new science to the whole armory of positive method, to the common profit of all natural philosophy. And here also is revealed most clearly the tendency of sociological inquiry to move from the whole, the known, to the details, the unknown.

When the application of this new means of investigation shall have been sufficiently prolonged to allow its characteristic qualities to be adequately developed, it will be recognized as so distinct a modification of the fundamental art of observing as to be assigned to the position which brings to a close the series which, beginning with observation proper, passes from experiment to comparison. By its use alone will it become possible to foresee, to a certain degree, the movements of society and of the human mind, for each determinate epoch and in each essential aspect, since it alone will provide an exact knowledge beforehand of the uniform direction of the gradual modifications recorded by history.[50]

So terminates Comte's examination into the general spirit that should characterize sociology and the various fundamental means of investigation proper to it.

It would be interesting to pursue the subject into the remaining chapters of the *Positive Philosophy*, which deal successively with the relations between sociology and the other abstract sciences; with social statics or the general theory of the spontaneous order of human societies; with social dynamics or the general theory of the natural progress of mankind; with the whole dynamic aspect of human history that fills the last two volumes of the treatise. Space forbids; and except for the service of illustrating the use of the methods already described, such a review would, in rigorous logic, fall beyond the scope of the present discussion.

IV

The publication of the *Positive Philosophy* was completed in 1842. For some years thereafter Comte published no major treatise. Not until 1851

[50] *Ibid.*, pp. 323–31.

did the first volume of the *Positive Politics*[51] appear, to be followed in regular succession, year by year, by three other volumes, until the whole was finished in 1854.

In the interval between the composition of these two treatises Comte had passed through a crisis in his personal life which was to have far-reaching results upon his later thought. The episode in question was the brief but profoundly felt relation with Clotilde de Vaux (1845–46). Much has been written of the influence upon Comte's intellectual development of this deep affection,[52] which was to endure to the very end of his days. Suffice it to say, for the present purposes, that the experience afforded a release for the deep-seated emotions that had been repressed throughout practically all of Comte's mature life. On the inner aspects of this release only one remark may be made here, for it alone has a direct bearing upon the central thought of this section of the present discussion. That remark is the following: The effect upon Comte of this profound spiritual experience was to bring home to him in the most stirring emotional sense the full significance of a fact that he had hitherto comprehended in its intellectual aspects only—the fact, namely, of the primacy in human existence of the affective over the intellectual factor. He now felt that the reorganization of thought to which he had given the earlier part of his life was not adequate alone to bring about the regeneration of society that had ever been his aspiration; he now *knew* that a reorganization of feeling would have to be affected as well. The immediate consequence was the realization that he would have to advance in his own thinking from philosophy and science to religion. In his own words, the life of an Aristotle that he had been leading would have to be followed by that of Paul.

It will, then, be evident why the subtitle of the *Positive Politics* is the following: *A Treatise on Sociology, Instituting the Religion of Humanity.* These words clearly imply that Comte, at the moment of beginning his new effort, considered the philosophical and scientific foundations he had laid in the *Positive Philosophy* to be sufficiently solid and extensive to bear the weight of application. What he now set himself to do, on the intellectual bases already established, was to plan the main lines for a superstructure in which to shelter the affective life of man. He set out,

[51] *La politique positive* (4th ed.; Paris, 1912). (All editions in French have identical paging). Translated into English under the title *The System of Positive Polity* (now long out of print). For various reasons not here in point, the analyst prefers to translate the title as *Positive Politics* rather than *Positive Polity*. The references are all to the French text.

[52] The latest biography is that by Jane Style, *Auguste Comte: Thinker and Lover*, (London: Kegan Paul, 1928).

that is to say, upon the achievement of one of the most ambitious schemes of what is today called "social control" ever attempted or imagined.

This change in the direction of Comte's efforts has often been taken to be an abandonment of the high standards of intellectual endeavor set by the *Philosophy*. Many charges have been brought against Comte on grounds derived from the *Politics;* they may all be condensed here into the single accusation that at this period of his life Comte abandoned the scientific method. In other words, his personal processes at this point in his career had their way over the procedures approved by science.

On this charge two remarks will here be made. In the first place, the *Positive Politics* is essentially a work of application, and applications are deductions from theories. Hence there will be found in many chapters of the work a preponderance of deductive reasoning. Given the nature of his effort, how could it have been otherwise? Comte considered that he had in the *Philosophy* laid sufficiently sound premises to justify him in proceeding to draw conclusions in the *Politics* regarding action. The confidence he felt may have been unfounded, but no abandonment of scientific method is necessarily implied in the new orientation of effort.

But, in the second place, Comte, by virtue indeed of this very effort to apply conclusions already reached was led to develop certain of them in a perfectly logical and continuous manner,[53] and to correct certain others in a way demanding comment. Under the first head should be mentioned the steady evolution of his thought in such matters, for example, as his abstract conception of humanity. From the "artifice" of Condorcet he passed with unbroken continuity to the definition in the fourth volume of the *Politics:* "The continuous whole formed by all convergent beings."[54] If he does not, even here, reach the complete "theoretical abstraction indispensable to the generality of our positive conceptions,"[54] he is at least advancing along a perfectly straight line of scientific thought. Still other evidences of continued progress in theory could be adduced from such instances as the development in the *Politics* of the conceptions of sociological statics and dynamics tentatively proposed in the *Philosophy*, or the more elaborate use of the method of filiation as shown by the improvement made in the *Social Dynamics* over the last two volumes of the *Philosophy* in retracing the cultural evolution of man, or the continued meditations upon the nature and the scope of biology, or the advance in thought in-

[53] Pareto, among others, has inveighed against what he termed "the mania for applications" among social scientists. His objections are in great part well founded, but there is much to be said on the other side, especially when the "application" is of the nature of that attempted by Comte.

[54] *Pol. pos.*, IV, 30.

volved in the proposal to condense into one volume the second and the third volume of the *Politics,* or finally the gradual emergence of the "first philosophy"[55] that reached its full expression only in the fourth volume of the *Politics.*

If, then, the basic conceptions on which the *Politics* is constructed are those of the *Philosophy,* and if the thoughts of the latter steadily evolve in certain very important even though relatively minor aspects, and if, in the last place, the deductive aspects of the *Politics* are a normal consequence of an attempt to apply theories already elaborated, then the alleged departure from scientific method in Comte's later life must be found in the cases in which Comte effected radical changes in the ideas he brought from the *Philosophy* to the *Politics.*

That no such departure took place is the position here defended. On the contrary, it is asserted that the very effort to apply conclusions already reached regarding the nature of sociological data to the problem of "social control" brought Comte closer to the facts and phenomena with which he had been dealing, resulted in an improvement of his original views, and led him to formulate propositions whose contrast with received opinions is no objection to them if it can be shown that they were reached by advances along the methodological routes approved by science.

To defend the position just taken, it will be necessary to return to an early conception of Comte's, hitherto insufficiently emphasized here. No regression or repetition is involved; rather an illustration of another aspect of scientific method. The doctrine referred to is that to which Comte gave the name "law of classification." This law is seldom mentioned in discussions of Comte, for it is too often forgotten that his original law of the three states was accompanied almost from the beginning by his discovery of the regularity underlying the order in which the abstract sciences attained to the positive stage of law. This formulation is not only noteworthy in itself; it is an indispensable complement of the law of the three states, which, lacking the law of classification, has no more sociological significance than had Turgot's original formulation of the idea.[56]

From the point of view of method the law of classification illuminates Comte's conception of a hierarchy of the sciences and justifies his insistence

[55] Comte called "first philosophy" fifteen laws that differ from all others in that they apply indifferently to all phenomena whatever and not to certain orders only (*ibid.,* pp. 170–80).

[56] See Schelle, *Œuvres de Turgot* (Paris: Alcan, 1913), I, 313–16, or the Appendix to the translation of Turgot's discourse *On the Progress of the Mind* (Hanover, N.H.: Sociological Press, 1929).

upon the fact that there is a relation of subordination among the various abstract sciences. According to this position, then, there is a "natural" order which is followed by the various classes of phenomena in reaching the stage of law. That is to say: Scientific analysis results in the discovery of specific and irreducible classes among the whole mass of observable phenomena; but the recognition of these classes and their reduction to law has been no haphazard proceeding; it is not even a facultative operation; it reveals a regularity that Comte at an early stage in his thinking defined as follows:

The order in which our different conceptions become Positive corresponds to the degree of facility which the study of the corresponding phenomena presents. It is determined by their greater or less complication, their greater or less dependence, the degree of specialty, and their more or less direct connection with man—four grounds which, though each exerts its distinct influence, are at bottom inseparable. Here, then, we have the Classification which is dictated by the nature of the phenomena.[57]

And at the end of Comte's labors the formulation becomes the following: "Every positive classification must proceed on the principle of the increase or decrease of generality, whether subjective or objective."[58]

It is on this law that Comte's hierarchical arrangement of the sciences is based; to understand it is essential to a full comprehension of his thought. To understand it is indispensable for an appreciation of the changes that the *Politics* records in Comte's intellectual evolution. There need then be no apology for considering the law in some detail.

This law of classification, like the law of the three states, is an induction from the history of the sciences. It says in substance that the history of scientific development may be envisaged as the successive recognition and reduction to law of a series of specific and irreducible classes of abstract phenomena. These classes have been, and have had to be, recognized in turn because of the differences they present in the matter of generality. The recognition of each class has facilitated and accelerated the recognition of succeeding classes. When the abstract conception of number, for instance, had been reached, that of extension was in order, and both preceded the abstract conception of movement: whence calculation, geometry, and mechanics, which became positive sciences in that order.

Again, when the distinction between the physical and the chemical became clear, and each of these classes could be scientifically dealt with, it became possible to ask whether the sum total of observable phenomena had been exhausted or whether other classes yet remained. When the en-

[57] *Early Essays*, p. 233.   [58] *Pol. pos.*, IV, 179.

tire group now termed in general "physical" had been set aside from the mass, it was possible to reach the conception of the biological or vital in the abstract sense. When biology had thus arisen, it was again possible to account for and set aside the effects and the influences of this new homogeneous class of phenomena, and ask once more whether any specific classes remained. This question, in fact, Comte put to himself at the beginning of his career; his answer was the institution of a science of social physics or sociology on the basis of the existence of a specific class of phenomena that could not be dealt with by biology, and to which the name "social" had by common consent been given. The second half of his life may be envisaged from the point of view here in question as having been devoted to the investigation, under the spur of the need to apply his earlier theories, of the problem whether this class of "social" phenomena was in reality homogeneous and specific. The answer he found at last was that it was not an irreducible class, but that it was in fact a composite group, combining two distinct orders of phenomena, to each of which in the sequel had to be allotted a separate place in the hierarchy as a new and abstract science, each with its own concepts and methods.

Such was the idea underlying Comte's law of classification. It will be evident that a hypothetical investigator, proceeding *ab initio* into the field of science, would, in the light of Comte's law, have as his first methodological task to make a classification of the whole range of phenomena. If he came into the field after certain advances had already been made, his first duty would be to examine into the validity of the current and accepted classifications. Such an examination, then, in theory, Comte, as the discoverer of the law, should have made. Such a theoretical prescription of his own law he nevertheless failed to follow. He assumed —and in truth it was impossible in the face of views universally held from the time of Aristotle that he should have done otherwise—that the division of all phenomena above the chemical into two classes, namely, the individual (studied by biology) and the social (to be studied by his own new science of social physics), was beyond question; and so he never inquired into the finality of the division until he was compelled to do so, after years of investigation had forced him to see that something was wrong with the classifications he had been using.

Comte's failure to follow an implied prescription of his own principle of method was in no sense due to any impairment of his intellectual powers under emotional strain; on the contrary, it was this very affective disturbance, giving rise directly to an attempt to carry his thoughts into the field of application, that indirectly led to the discovery of the error in method, and so to a position which deserves to be critically examined. If sound, this position is in advance of the thought of today.

The remainder of this section is therefore the story of the way in which Comte, by the logic of the facts with which he was dealing, was compelled to abandon the personal processes[59] that had been guiding him and conform to the stricter methods he had himself laid down as the outcome of his own inductive study of the whole evolution of science. Is it not the justification of method that it puts the personal inclinations of inquirers under the direction of the cumulated experience of the race?

It will be advisable, then, in beginning this account of the way in which a mind of unusual power and originality finally liberated itself from the uncritically accepted tenets of generations preceding to mark clearly the starting-point. It is found stated without the least ambiguity in the words of 1825 already quoted on page 24: "Social Physics must necessarily start from individual Physiology." That is to say, the individual forms a class and the social a class, each a specific group of phenomena, and the hierarchical order is satisfied when the individual is studied before the social, and indeed dictates such an order of approach.

So far, the position is clear, and there is an inference that seems equally clear: The individual is equated with the biological. Hence the order of treatment of the two sets of phenomena should be first the individual or biological and then the social. That such was Comte's position there can be no doubt; the fact is put beyond doubt by another remark already referred to on page 35: "In a methodical treatise on political philosophy, it would doubtless be fitting *to analyze first the individual impulsions* which become the characteristic elements of the power possessed by the human species to progress." But Comte, "assuming this preliminary notion to be sufficiently clear to enlightened minds," made no effort to carry out the analysis and so lost the opportunity to avoid the error that he was later forced to correct.

It is important even at the expense of reiteration to restate the position—which is still the accepted one—for Comte's later work was to refute it, and all the importance of this later work is derived from the very fact of the refutation. It is this: The study of the individual is the business of biology; hence biology precedes sociology in the hierarchy of the sciences; and the study of the first is a necessary introduction to the study of the second. Of course a knowledge of the individual includes a knowledge of the intellectual and moral aspects of life (what is now called

[59] On certain aspects of the inner processes of Comte see Montmasson, *Le rôle de l'inconscient dans l'invention scientifique* (Paris: Alcan, 1928), pp. 181 and 391.

the "psychological," a term Comte rejected because of its associations at his period). These phenomena are at the very top of the biological scale, hence the true order of study must be first the biological, i.e., the vegetal, the animal, the intellectual, and moral, and then the sociological, i.e., the social.

It will be noticed that no essential logical improvement results from the separation of the intellectual and moral from the lower orders of the biological and their inclusion in a separate group, as in Spencer's scheme. The underlying logic of the original apportionment is unaffected by the modification just defined. In either case, the individual, whether bio- logical or psychological, precedes the social. The only improvement— a real one, it may be admitted, because it points the way to the ultimate solution—is the splitting of the biological phenomenon into two classes that the Spencerian position effects.

It was the position defined above that Comte was forced to reconsider as the result of his passing from the plane of philosophy to that of reli- gion. And this reconsideration in turn was to lead him to see that the identification of the individual with the biological was a first error; that the hierarchical subordination of the individual to the social was another; that both had resulted from the failure adequately to analyze the phe- nomena involved; that there were in reality three classes of phenomena in question instead of two; that the social was divisible; that the three were the biological, the collective, and the individual or moral; that no one of these was identifiable with either or both of the other two; that there were therefore above the chemical three specific and irreducible classes of phenomena; that the order of treatment of these three classes was, as a necessary consequence of the law of classification, the following: the biological or vital or organic; the sociological or collective; the individ- ual or moral; that, finally, the hierarchy of the sciences would have to comprise seven abstract sciences instead of the six it had originally been assigned.

In still other terms, what Comte was to have forced on his attention by his effort to create a positive type of religion was the specific and irre- ducible nature of the individual phenomena, and the logical position of these phenomena above and beyond the biological (granted) and the sociological as well (new and not admitted). The whole importance of the *Politics* and its superiority over the *Philosophy* may be said to lie in this reapportionment of the phenomena in the upper ranges of the hierarchy; and the new arrangement is full of implications of the utmost importance to the thought and the life of the future.

The first indication of the new orientation of Comte's thinking is to be found in the second volume of the *Politics*, the *Social Statics* (1852). In the first volume of the treatise his philosophical position is precisely the same it had been since 1825. In the *Statics*, however, Comte's increasing attention to the phenomena of religion had forced him to inquire more searchingly than he had ever done before into the nature of the relations between the individual and the social, a term that he now begins to find insufficiently precise. If the individual makes society, then his original scheme—biology, sociology—is correct; but what if the sociological so profoundly affects the individual as to make it possible to say that the latter is made by the former? Is not the puzzling logical situation thereby created symptomatic of error? Could the original classification be defective or erroneous? How can the "individual" phenomenon be at once cause and consequence of the "social"? The question is still being asked today. To Comte, however, it presented a dilemma: If the transmission of the acquired results of human experience produced such transformations as observation shows to be the fact, then either there was a phenomenon beyond the social or else the social was not a specific but a composite phenomenon.

Comte's evolution toward the second of these alternatives begins almost at the first page of the *Social Statics*, in the first chapter, in which he goes deeply into the nature of religion. Feeling becomes more and more the center of his interest. He sees, for example, that the exterior world radically modifies the affections, without doing so directly, however. It arouses certain of them and represses others, though never increasing or diminishing their number: "Despite the fundamental permanence of our propensities, their effective impulsions necessarily vary *with the natural course of our conceptions and our enterprises.*"[60] That is to say, there is something which is *beyond* the social, upon which the social works. The influences of the social world are transmitted to the individual only indirectly, through the humanity of which he is a part.

Hence Comte finds himself forced in the direction of a revision of his earlier views. The first clear statement of his conclusion, with an equally clear formulation of the methodological consequences, occurs about the middle of the first chapter of the *Statics:*

This indirect transmission would become fully *conformable to the fundamental law of natural classification* if the individual order were to be distinguished from the social order proper, *i.e. collective*, by adding a final degree to the general hierarchy of phenomena. Although this new degree would dif-

[60] *Pol. pos.*, II, 26.

fer much less from that which precedes it than in any other case,[61] nevertheless it would follow the other as in all prior cases, since it is the most particular and most independent of all.[62]

He goes on to speak of "this definitive improvement of my hierarchical encyclopedia." The starting-point of a new movement of thought, its rise from a consideration of the affective nature of religion, and the methodological reasons for the new departure are all evident. Comte, in fact, was on the way to distinguishing a new specific and irreducible property, though he did not, and of course could not, grasp the full significance of the fact at once; time alone could bring complete understanding.

The thought was maturing in his mind, however, and when occasion again was offered to elaborate the idea, as occurred in the logical development of the last chapter of the *Statics*, real progress in grasping its implications had evidently been made. At the point mentioned Comte is discussing the limits within which society, conceived of in the most general sense as all mankind, can be modified. After discussing the principles and limits of modifiability, he proceeds:

To apply to the human order these general principles, I must divide it first definitively into its two necessary modes: one, collective; the other, individual: which constitute respectively social existence and moral existence. The first chapter of this volume having introduced this normal complement of my hierarchical encyclopedia, the last should irrevocably establish this capital improvement, to the continuous application of which the remainder of this treatise will give rise, especially in an implicit fashion.[63] . . . . Man, properly so-called, considered from the point of view of his fundamental reality . . . . cannot be understood without a preliminary knowledge of humanity, on whom he necessarily depends.[64]

Henceforward, then, the seven essential degrees of the encyclopedia will be: mathematical, astronomical, physical, chemical, vital, social, and, finally, moral. And in order that the distinctive feature of individual life may be clearly marked, Comte gives the name of *la morale* ("morals") to what is essentially the science of individuality, abstractly considered.

In defending this new position Comte made a real advance in his conception of the science of biology, an advance that was to have rapid reaction upon his conception of the remaining members of the encyclopedia. *"True biology has in no wise the individual knowledge of man as its object, but only the general study of life, envisaged above all in the*

[61] *Ibid.*, p. 55.   [63] *Ibid.*, p. 432.
[62] *Ibid.*   [64] *Ibid.*, p. 433.

totality of beings that enjoy it."[65] In other words, biology ceases to occupy itself with life in general, and becomes the study of an abstract property, the irreducible phenomenon of vitality, "which consists in the continuous renewal of material substance, the sole attribute that universally separates living things from inert bodies."[66] Thus, an analysis lasting twenty-five years had finally resulted in so definitive a recognition of one class of phenomena proper to the higher ranks of the encyclopedia as to make of it once for all an irreducible and specific group, and its study an abstract science in the exactest sense. The same advance had still to be made for the remaining members of the hierarchy.

To make it was no easy task. In the first place, since the study of the intellectual and moral functions of man had been eliminated from biology by the same operation that had made that science the abstract science of vitality, the question at once arose: Where shall these functions be studied? The easy answer that they should go by themselves into a group of phenomena between biology and sociology has already been disposed of. The answer had to be sought in another direction—a direction that is indicated by the fact that Comte had come at last to speak of *orders,* the collective and the individual. He was in fact being driven, through continued analysis of the data, to see the significance of his own principles of method; his unconscious processes, that is, were being forced more and more into the paths prescribed by the conscious procedures of scientific method. He was indeed on the way to doing for the sciences above biology what he had just done for biology itself. In each of them he was advancing toward specificity and abstraction; and because of their intimate relationship, any change in the conception of one implied a correlative change in the conception of the other. This advance was to continue in the third volume of the *Politics,* the *Social Dynamics* (1853).

The *Dynamics* was to deal with the philosophy of history, not in the old dialectical and metaphysical sense of that phrase, but rather what might accurately be called the positive philosophy of history, i.e., an explanation of the facts of history on the basis of the scientifically established laws of sociological dynamics. Here, then, was an opportunity for a new definition of sociology and a reconsideration of the dynamical laws. Certain theoretical advances had been made in the course of the *Statics,* as has just been set forth; they could now be taken into account in a formal fashion. Especially in the reformulation of the definition of sociology is the effect of the new distribution of phenomena apparent. The intellectual and moral groups had once for all been excluded from biology.

[65] *Ibid.,* p. 437.   [66] *Ibid.,* I, 586.

Moreover, in the course of this exclusion, a definite stand had been taken in regard to them, a position that was greatly to influence their ultimate disposition. They had, that is, been divided into three classes: (1) the affective, (2) the intellectual, (3) the active.

In regard to these three classes, Comte, from the days of the *Philosophy*, had given the predominance to the affective group.[67] In deciding, then, as to the disposition of the phenomena once for all beyond the domain of biology, it was almost inevitable that he should—as he did—consider the phenomena of feeling as a class apart. This attitude was all the more rational in that the accumulations passed on from generation to generation seem to be exclusively intellectual and active in their nature, whereas feelings, though they may and do vary infinitely in intensity and object, do not augment and cumulate in any true sense. Moreover, as Comte clearly saw, the feelings are conditioned in their exercise by the social heritage; and they are, besides, the very spring of individuality.

No wonder, then, that Comte seized on this distinction and made it the basis of a new definition of sociology—a definition that marks another stage in his analysis of phenomena into specific classes. "All real appreciation of mental laws belongs to the positive study of the whole development of mankind," he said at this stage of his progress, "and this is the science of sociology"; "but, reciprocally," he continues, "sociology is reducible to the true science of the understanding." To it must be added the field of man's activity. "But though this complement is indispensable, it cannot prevent us from recognizing that sociology consists essentially in the study of the totality of the intellect."[68]

Now the allocation to sociology of the study of the laws, statical and dynamical, of the intellect and the activity[69] could, it will be realized after reflection, be only provisional, for without referring to any other difficulties raised by this theoretical position, it is sufficient to ask what becomes of the essential unity of the mind? How can functions essentially one, and divisible only for systematic purposes, be divided between two

[67] "Notre faible nature, où la vie affective l'emporte tant sur la vie rationnelle" (*Phil. pos.*, IV, 250).

[68] *Pol. pos.*, III, 47.

[69] This term has a special sense in Comte's philosophical vocabulary. It is constantly used in connection with the term "intellect" to which it is in fact completely parallel in meaning. The intellect for Comte comprised the cerebral organs whose purely general function it was to correlate and co-ordinate the sense impressions so as to produce ideas and thoughts. In a similar way, the "activity" comprised the cerebral organs whose purely general functions it was to co-ordinate muscular contractions so as to produce true acts. Of course the terms may denote either the organs or the functions; and it is the latter, functional, sense that Comte usually gives them.

distinct and independent sciences? The answer is that they cannot be so separated, and Comte was to discover the fact—by force once more of the direct study of the data.

The new advance is made in the fourth volume of the *Politics* (1854), in the third chapter of which occurs a final review of Comte's intellectual position as a whole. It should therefore be the starting-point of any comprehensive study of Comte's life-work; and its special importance here lies in the revisions it contains of the definitions already given, for they were changed once more, as the implications in Comte's new idea became explicit. His words must be quoted at some length at this point, for they completely validate the conclusions already reached in this section of the present discussion.

In the course of the third chapter of the fourth volume of the *Politics*, and the review of his whole system of thought that it contains, Comte comes in the regular course of the discussion to the science of biology, which he proceeds to consider as a whole for the third time in his career. In the original conception he had had of that science, there must, he says, be effected an *épuration;* the systematization of biology presented in an earlier work is in fact "placed between two expositions essentially foreign to biology, but which I *could not then introduce elsewhere and of which I was in need in order to institute sociology."*[70] It is these two expositions which are now to be removed; and the fact, as well as the words just italicized, throws a vivid light upon the tortuous intellectual path Comte had been forced to follow as he traversed an unexplored domain. Both these sections—one dealing with the problem of personal unity, the other with the nature of the cerebral synthesis—both connected directly with the question of individuality, found their permanent place in the seventh science in the hierarchy.

Continuing his review of his labors, Comte next came to the last two members of the encyclopedia, the *"irrevocable separation of which"* sums up the main points of superiority of the *Politics* over the *Philosophy.*[71] One of the first changes in his anterior labors involves the condensation into a single projected volume of the *Statics* and the *Dynamics* of the *Politics* he was completing. This condensation, he points out, will require no new idea; it will in fact be easy to carry out after having, from the two existing volumes, *"dissected out Morals, the rise of which, resulting from my labors, could not hold therein a sufficiently dominating position."*[72]

Going into the details of the future volume to contain the whole of his

[70] *Pol. pos.*, IV, 217.   [71] *Ibid.*, p. 228.   [72] *Ibid.*, p. 229.

sociological theories, Comte emphasizes the necessity of a special introduction and conclusion: an introduction to define the general constitution of sociology and its relation to biology; a conclusion to sum up the results and show how sociology prepares the way for morals, i.e., for what has here been called the science of individuality. These two appreciations are more urgent and more difficult in the case of the proposed sociological volume than elsewhere, he says,

since the approach to the goal leads to an attempt to overstep the degrees. When biology had been sketched out, an attempt was made to found morals without having instituted sociology; and the initiation of the individual will always tends to reproduce this spontaneous inclination of collective evolution. My career became decisive only through the construction of social science, the necessary interposition of which—between biology and morals—it will always be necessary to give the reasons for, although this explanation no longer requires the efforts and developments it demanded of me.[73]

The necessary revision of sociology indicated, Comte next passed to a discussion of his new science *la morale* ("morals"); and here once more is to be found an illustration of the continuous modification by Comte of his conceptions in the presence of the data as they became more sharply defined. After the lower sciences "have suitably sketched out the knowledge of the milieu, completed by that of the body," the higher sciences begin

the systematic study of the soul, by appreciating collective existence, first statical, then dynamical. But this necessary examination constitutes only a last preparation, the incomplete character of which is undeniable. From it arises the feeling that since the special study of the intellect and the activity are therein separated from feeling, *such special study permits only of an appreciation of Results,*[74] the source and destination of which belong to the science that follows it. If this false position of the mind is not manifest in the treatise I am completing, the fact is due only to the circumstance that *in it*

[73] *Ibid.*, pp. 228–9.

[74] Sumner and Keller reach an identical conclusion, but they seem never to have drawn the inevitable inference: "Any real science of society will obviously study what it professes to study, namely, a society. In so doing it must watch what really happens, that is, consequences as distinguished from purposes or motives" (*The Science of Society* [New Haven: Yale University Press, 1927], III, 2175).

Feeling is "the supreme motor of human existence." "The habitual service of feeling demands alternately the satisfaction of impulses and the communication of emotions. Its two ministers [intellect and activity], theoretical and practical, always concur in this double office, which constitutes their whole destination." Comte thus defines the source and destination of the *results* with which sociology deals (*Pol. pos.*, III, 48, 79).

the elaboration of "morals" is spontaneously mingled with the construction of sociology.

Despite the systematic superiority of the *Politics* over the *Philosophy*, the first

cannot exhibit the complete rationality to which I have always aspired. For the normal separation between sociology and "morals," *alone decisive from the synthetic point of view,* arose while I was executing an elaboration *that it should have dominated.*[75]

The story need be followed no farther. Comte had at last grasped all the implications of his own law of classification as it affects the grouping of the phenomena belonging to the higher ranks of the hierarchy. The working-out of these implications gave the following results: In the domain of organic physics (using the term employed in the *Philosophy* for the whole range of phenomena above the chemical) there are three classes of specific and irreducible phenomena. These are, respectively: (1) the biological or organic or vital, i.e., those dealing with life in the abstract, the property of "continuous renewal of material substance"; (2) the sociological or collective or societal (to use Sumner's word), i.e., those dealing with the accumulating "results" of the collective exercise of the intellect and the activity; (3) the moral or individual, i.e., those dealing with the affective, intellectual, and active sources of individuality, abstractly conceived.

Such was the point of arrival of Comte's entire intellectual evolution. In the whole mass of phenomena above the chemical—the group called, as a whole, the organic as opposed to the inorganic—he had at last discovered the existence of three groups, three orders, three specific and irreducible classes of phenomena—three and not two, as he had thought at the beginning. His final position might therefore be envisaged as a contradiction of the original arrangement of the hierarchy of the sciences.

There are, Comte said, it will be recalled, two sorts of sciences: the abstract and the concrete. The first deal with "events," which when considered abstractly give rise to attributes, properties, modes of being. The second deal with "beings," which in their manifestations are complexes of properties. Now Comte, when he constructed his hierarchy, followed the division—at least as old as Aristotle—which separates "individuals" from "societies" and asserts that the study of the first is the natural introduction to the study of the second. In accepting this division without subjecting it to analysis Comte made his original error. For, in Comte's language, the individual is a "being" and not an "event," i.e., a complex

[75] *Pol. pos.,* IV, 233.

of phenomena and not a specific property. So, too, is "society," however abstractly considered. The science, then, which deals with either of these two in their entirety does not belong in the encyclopedia as Comte defined it, for it would be concrete and not abstract, composite and not component.

The fact is evident, and Comte admits it both by implication and statement. Yet it is not too much to say that his error was unavoidable, seen from whatever point of view. No other position was possible when he began to write; practically no other is even yet considered to be tenable. There was no possibility of any other approach to the scientific study of the higher ranges of phenomena. Comte's whole career, from this point of view, might be considered as a sacrifice made to obtain a clearer and more systematic view of the upper limits of man's knowledge.

And it is easy, *now*, to see what the initial difficulty was. The "individual" in the inclusive sense of the word presents a wide range of phenomena to observation which must be assigned, each to its appropriate class; the "society," likewise, provides material for analysis and classification. Both "individual" and "society" when analyzed are found to be composed, in part, of the same classes of phenomena; and it was this circumstance which caused Comte so much difficulty in breaking out the path he was the first to traverse. What he ultimately discovered was that the "individual" is a composite of biological, sociological, and moral elements, i.e., is a bio-socio-moral phenomenon. The "society" too is a composite, a composite of two elements, the societal or collective and the moral or individual; i.e., is a socio-moral phenomenon.

It was the fact that two classes of phenomena are common to both the "individual" and the "society" that made, and make, it impossible to draw a clear line of demarcation between the two. Obviously a change in one of these component elements will at once exercise an influence upon the other; and so there will be a continuous reciprocal movement that will defy analysis so long as the existence of two distinct elements is not suspected. In other words, the "individual" and the "society" are inseparable correlatives and can no more be isolated than hills and valleys. Each influences the other by virtue of the fact that each contains elements that are common to both. So long as this fact is not recognized, the relations of one to the other is no real problem; it is but a pseudo-problem; the real problem is to analyze each member of the correlation into its constituent abstract elements and to discover what uniformities there are to be observed in their manifestations. The old conundrum regarding the relations of individual and society simply disappears; and its existence for so long a period is now seen to have been symptomatic of a faulty method.

The whole problem may be formulated in another fashion, answering a question that is often asked in this connection: What is the place, if any, of psychology in the hierarchy of the sciences? In the light of the foregoing discussion there can be no doubt as to the answer here to be given. Psychology has no place in the hierarchy. It is not, as it is generally understood, an abstract science at all; it is a concrete science, like meteorology or geology. It includes a biological, a collective, an individual element. Only when all three of these are combined can the "individual" in his concrete reality be understood. In this sense there is a "psychology." If the biological, i.e., physiological, element be omitted from the combination, then the "individual" in the sense just defined disappears, and the remainder is a combination of collective and moral or individual elements—which is still a psychology, but a "psychology" of the "society," i.e., a social psychology, in which the abstract phenomena termed collective or societal and individual or moral combine in infinitely varying proportions (usually following the whims or leanings of the writer) in order to explain the concrete manifestations of groups, collectivities, societies, on the one hand, or of individuals in social situations, on the other.

Up to the present point of this section, clear inference supported by Comte's own statements amending his earlier views, has in two cases shown the necessity of recognizing the existence of a body of phenomena beyond the sociological. The method by which this demonstration has been arrived at has, however, owing to the devious route of Comte's own progress, been mainly of a somewhat formal nature, from the viewpoint of logic. Such logical proofs are, however, held in suspicion by many, and so it will be well in conclusion to put the outcome of the foregoing discussion in another light by reviewing it twice briefly from the standpoint of the facts which were, in truth, at all times the underlying forces urging Comte onward to his final conclusion.

In the first place, then, a series of logically disturbing considerations more and more impressed themselves upon Comte's consciousness as he proceeded with his reorganization of thought. There was, to begin with, the attentive study he had made throughout his review of human culture in the last volumes of the *Philosophy* of the influence of art in the development of mankind. It was this historical examination of art which had first led him to study feeling, the source and the end of æsthetic effort, which has always the communication of emotion as its goal.[76] Again, he had noted in individual instances the failure to reveal the effects that might be expected to follow the normal influence of sociological factors. Individual men, that is, showed themselves recalcitrant in the presence of societal forces. More important than either was the personal change Comte underwent in his own life as the result of his profound affection for Clotilde de Vaux, which, coming late in life,[77] after many years of emotional repression, left him no possible doubt as to the primacy of feeling. And this moral transformation could in no way be traced to sociological conditions. Finally, and as an outcome of this experience, came his exhaustive study of the nature of religion. Here was the starting-point of his *Statics*, in which began the evolution of thought that has already been summarized. The end product was the recognition of a factor in human life that is neither biological nor sociological, and the consequent institution of a seventh science in the hierarchy.

The significance of this methodological result for the entire range of present-day thought cannot here be more than hinted at. It challenges the supremacy of sociology over the wide domain it has hitherto claimed; it opens a new field of investigation to science which is certain to be more and more developed;[78] it implies a reconsideration of the whole psychological position as held at present, for it implies that the forces that impinge upon the moral life of man do but condition it; they do not determine it. Moral phenomena, that is to say, like all other phenomena, manifest those uniformities that are called laws; but it is their *own* laws that they follow, not the laws of other classes of phenomena. In short, and to express the significance of the thought in its most implicit form, moral and individual phenomena form a specific and irreducible class; and the irreducibility of individual phenomena is the positive formulation of the metaphysical doctrine of free will.

The last aspect of Comte's thought that can be mentioned here is, for the investigator of phenomena from the objective point of view, the most important of all despite its incompleteness, for it alone gives a definite hint as to the precise nature of the concrete phenomena which will have to be included within the new domain. Comte, under the admitted influ-

[76] This is Comte's own statement (see *La synthèse subjective* [Paris: V. Dalmont, 1856], I, 44).

[77] Comte's friendship with Clotilde de Vaux began in 1845, when Comte was forty-seven. The episode came late in life, of course, but scarcely in the "old age" where it is often situated.

[78] If the sociologists do not reach this conclusion through the natural progress of their own researches, the psychiatrists are certain to force it upon them—not always in the most conciliatory fashion.

ence of Cabanis,[79] had always been cognizant of the importance of the reactions that occur between the physical and the moral in man. As time went on, his attention was increasingly drawn to a specific aspect of this relation, an aspect which he described in the following terms: Sociology essentially makes abstraction of the continuous reaction between the physical and the moral in man, in the light of the necessary relations of the vegetative viscera with the affective organs [of the brain]. In fact, *these individual perturbations* do not sensibly alter collective existence, and they do so less as it is further developed. Their mutual neutralization between various individuals leaves subsisting in sociology only the permanent influence of the truly collective attributes.[80]

Here, then, was a phenomenon *beyond* sociology, for social life, modifying the moral elements of the individual, thereby indirectly modifies the physical, and that in a way for which no biological explanation could by any possibility be adduced.

Once the starting-point was clear in Comte's mind, he went on steadily to develop the idea. No important quotations can be drawn from his works, for his thought was still in gestation even in the third chapter of the last volume of the *Politics* where he dealt with the matter for the last time. Occasional references in his letters show the scope of his meditations: once he speaks of his interest in the phenomenon of forgetting; several times he refers to the problem raised by the phenomena of the stigmata in the case of certain saints. From the latter point of view a hint can be had as to the implications contained in his statement, several times repeated, that the ancient domain of grace should become one of the most important fields of scientific inquiry. Nothing could be more suggestive to one who has once examined into the content of that old theological term. Yet all this speculation must remain, as regards Comte's own understanding of the matter, entirely without support from Comte's own words; never did he attain to the point of formulating a definition of the individual phenomenon that would compare with his definitions of the abstract biological or sociological phenomenon already quoted, for at the very moment when he was completing the meditation that was to have resulted in a volume devoted to the science of individuality in the abstract sense, a volume devoted to the seventh science in the hierarchy, *La morale,* he died (1857).

[79] P. T. G. Cabanis, *Rapports du physique et du moral de l'homme.*

[80] *Pol. pos.,* II, 438. See, for a very recent treatment of this aspect of Comte's work, Blondel, *Introduction à la psychologie collective* (Paris: Colin, 1928), where the same conclusions are reached as are presented in the paragraph above.

V

Order, precision, clarity of thought, architectonic vision, philosophical power, synthetic unity—such were some of the characteristic qualities that Comte brought to the task of consciously creating a new science. A lifelong progress, pursued with the most single-minded perseverance, brought him to a point beyond question in advance, in certain respects, of the thought of today. The full fruition of his labors was prevented by death. Only the guidance of his method remains.[81]

[81] [This analysis was first prepared in 1928 and was revised by the analyst in the summer of 1929.—EDITOR.]

ANALYSIS 2

RELATION OF UTILITY THEORY TO ECONOMIC METHOD IN THE WORK OF WILLIAM STANLEY JEVONS AND OTHERS

By FRANK KNIGHT

University of Chicago

I. THE UTILITY CONCEPT IN ECONOMIC THOUGHT

The following paper deals with the inspired idea which Jevons, far more than any other one man, originated and introduced into economic thought. Some references to particular features of Jevons' treatment of utility theory will be made in the course of the argument, but in the main it must suffice to remind the reader briefly of the place of the author and the doctrine in the development of economic science.

Following the publication of *The Theory of Political Economy* in 1871, and the near-contemporary and largely independent work of Menger, Walras, and Clark, the classical theory of price was revolutionized by the marginal-utility concept. It was a literal turning-upside-down, in that cost of production, instead of the cause of price, came to be viewed as its effect. After Wieser's *Natural Value* in 1889 and Marshall's *Principles of Economics*, Volume I, in 1890, conditions became fairly settled on the basis of the new ideas. Underlying differences in statement among economists, we find general agreement that the prices of (final) goods and services are caused or explained immediately by marginal utility, and in the long run by cost of production. That is, (relative) prices of goods are said to measure or reflect their relative marginal utilities to consumers, for each consumer distributes his expenditures (large or small) among the different commodities in such proportions as to establish this equality, and the competition of the market sets prices at the point where the forthcoming supplies can be disposed of. But marginal utility depends upon supply, and supply, while in the short run a "datum," tends in the long run to be so adjusted (through the allocation of production capacity between any one industry and all other industries) that the comparatively variable price of the single commodity is brought to equality with its comparatively fixed cost of production—the latter reflecting the yield of resources in industry at large. (The qualification for "rent" elements in money cost cannot be taken up here but does not change the essential principle.)

There is still much controversy regarding the precise interpretation of utility (as well as cost). The notion that utility causes or explains price rests on the view that it is the controlling principle of choice—specifically of the choices of consumers in expending their incomes. Jevons, and his contemporaries and successors in economic theory generally, followed Bentham in identifying it with pleasure, but that is an issue properly outside the field of economics. Utility in economics is simply the universal principle of motivation, quantitatively conceived; it is "that which" men act in order to get and to maximize. Thus, utility theory as a methodological principle may be said to rest on two assumptions or postulates: first, a factual assumption that men do uniformly act in such a way as to get the maximum of something, which we agree to call want-satisfaction or utility; and, second, a purely methodological assumption that this fact is the explanation of their actions.

The first or factual assumption is manifestly untrue. It is contrary to universally recognized facts, which are as well grounded as any facts whatever, that men "uniformly" so act. The most that can be contended is that they try or strive to do so, and *tend* to succeed in their endeavor. But it goes without saying that there is a varying, and on the average a considerable, margin of *error* in choosing. Assuming, for the present, that satisfaction is the universal motive of choice, we certainly have to distinguish between realized and anticipated satisfaction, and recognize that it is the latter which controls. Hence, if utility is to be treated as the cause of behavior, it should be defined as the power to *arouse* desire rather than the power to satisfy it.[1]

This introduction of *effort* and *error* as essential features of utility reasoning, making maximum utility define the goal of conduct which people try to reach, but not that which they actually realize, seems to differentiate it sharply from the sort of cause met with in the physical sciences —at least as the basic notions of science are dinned into our ears by the empiricist logicians. A scientific cause, we are told, is antecedent to the event, and its nature is antithetical to that of an end or aim. More strictly, it is not a cause at all, but simply a uniform antecedent. Causal laws are purely descriptive; they state the order in which events occur. They must under no circumstances be confused with ends or ideals, and,

[1] This difficulty did not greatly disturb Jevons. He recognized "the uncertainty of future events" (*op. cit.* [4th ed.; Macmillan & Co., 1911], pp. 34 ff.), but only in the sense of a known, mathematical probability, the sort of uncertainty which disappears in the average of a large number of cases. Elsewhere (pp. 13, 39) he seems to assert that at the moment of choice and under the conditions presented error is intrinsically impossible.

moreover, they exclude the possibility of error. Where there is not exceptionless uniformity, there is imperfect causality in the scientific sense; indeed, except in so far as the world of experience is reducible to exceptionless uniformity there can be no science at all.

Such is the accepted view. Yet certain queries at once intrude themselves upon the mind. Everyone knows that the laws of physics do not literally and exactly describe actual observations, that they also deal with approximations and tendencies. These, however, are not associated with effort and error in the materials and instruments under observation. When the physicist speaks of a perfect gas or a frictionless machine, he does not imply that gases strive to be perfect or machines frictionless, partly succeeding and partly failing, like the "economic man" in his effort to achieve maximum satisfaction.

But if effort and error are assumed to be absent from the behavior of the scientist's materials and instruments, they are certainly present in the scientist himself, and this fact is important. The student of physics approaches his problems with a wish or a bias, a literal "craving" for the simplest and the most general description of the phenomena. His generalizations are usually simplified in one of three ways: First, whenever observations approximately fit some simple pattern, and the divergences seem to be "at random," he assumes that the matter itself would fit perfectly and that the discrepancies represent error on his part. Or, second, if these discrepancies are greater, it may be argued that the data "would" fit the simple law or curve if "disturbing factors" could be eliminated, and that the law states a "fundamental tendency." The student is striving to purify some material or isolate the principal cause (sequence) in a complex, and has reason to believe that he has only in part succeeded. Third, a simple formula may be used arbitrarily to describe a relation which only approximately conforms to it, because a more accurate description would be too cumbersome to use.

Thus the element of approximation or tendency in physical laws is associated with striving and failure, but there is still the important difference that the striving and failure are assumed to pertain to the scientist and not to the matter under observation. Another important contrast between a physical law and the utility principle is the factual character of the discrepancies between the observations and the law. In physics it is a question of observed fact whether the observations do or do not fit the formula, or how and how much they diverge. But it is definitely and forever *not* a matter of observation (at least in the same sense) whether human beings so behave as to secure the maximum satisfaction for themselves. Here we are just as sure, in general, that there is a discrepancy, but we are dependent on the uncertain data of communication with the person himself or on inference of a very long-range and dubious sort, and there is no apparent possibility of reducing the facts to objective quantitative terms.

To escape from this ineradicable vagueness and uncertainty, the possibility of developing economics along the lines of the natural sciences naturally suggests itself; the possibility, that is, of using objective data exclusively and eschewing all questions of motivation as natural science does those of real cause. It is easy to understand the great stir resulting from efforts to rid economics of utility theory and to supplant it by an objective, quantitative science. With the positive part of this program the present analyst is in hearty accord. But it is the purpose of this paper to show that economics must also continue to develop the older type of theory. In fact, at least three notions which are confused in the current utility concept must be retained and used, though with a recognition, not always in evidence hitherto, of the distinct meaning and function of each.

II. FACT AND HYPOTHESIS IN PHYSICAL THOUGHT

The first step in the argument is to glance again at physical science and set down an emphatic reminder of the large and vital non-factual element it contains. In addition to simplified descriptive generalizations of the three sorts already pointed out, we meet with hypotheses which are not descriptive of any actual or, in some cases, any conceivable observations. A brief consideration of Boyle's Law will bring out the point.

Within wide limits, observations of the relation between pressure and volume of a given mass of gas at constant temperature conform closely to the simple curve $pv = C$, and the use of this statement as a "law" would be justified by the reasoning given above. But physics does not stop here; it goes on to raise and answer the question "why," and in giving us the kinetic theory of gases it goes completely outside the field of observed facts.[2] This kinetic theory is especially illuminating as to the nature of our intellectual cravings and processes. The random movements and impacts of the molecules postulated as an explanation of gaseous pressure are beyond direct observation, but they are the sort of phe-

[2] It may be said that the Brownian movements and various experiments come close to making molecular movements visible. But, in the first place, the theory is older than such observations and not essentially affected by them; and, in the second place, the experiments do not involve actual direct observation. A general discussion of the relation between observation and inference would at once annihilate the naïve contrast between them, and so would greatly strengthen the argument of this paper; but space limits exclude any development of this line of attack.

nomenon which we imagine *could* be observed with sense organs of the kind we possess but indefinitely multiplied in power and sensitiveness. The hypothesis contrasts sharply in this regard with other types of postulates, particularly with the forces and fields of force used to explain so many elementary phenomena, and which seem not to be susceptible of any interpretation of which a sensory picture can be formed. The kinetic type of theory evidently corresponds to a fundamental intellectual craving, and its nature and function deserve emphasis. Gaseous pressure is a type of phenomenon or experience which calls for explanation, which is not satisfactory as an ultimate; and the motion of small, inert particles in the common-sense Euclidian space is on the contrary a final resting-point for the mind. In our thinking we strive to get rid of force or cause, and reduce all processes to motion and the communication of motion by impact (conservation of momentum). The kinetic theories of gravitation and other forces, from Newton down, illustrate this intellectual urge.

In this sketch it is possible to mention only a few of the points at which the craving to eliminate the "Metaphysical" seems doomed to frustration in the field of physics itself.[3] Besides the fact that a kinetic theory itself is not descriptive of actual observations, physics is forced to employ other hypothetical entities which are not even imaginably perceptible to senses such as ours. The first example, of course, is the failure of kinetic theories to replace most of the fields of force, especially the electrostatic and electromagnetic; but that is not the end of the matter. Some forms of *potential energy* may be reduced to kinetic, or to motion plus force, but apparently

[3] Certain philosophical comments which must come to mind here are excluded by space limitations from the discussion: (1) The reduction of other forms of change to motion of particles in space does not really extricate us from conceptual embarrassment, as the history of thought from Parmenides to the ether-drift experiments makes clear. To the modern mind neither the particle nor the space is a satisfactory absolute. (2) There is an equally insistent original bias in favor of the reality of mind, freedom, and purposive activity. Common sense is dualistic, where the speculative intellect craves monism. At present, under the special sophistication of our scientific age, the tendency is toward mechanism; but at other times it has run toward subjectivism, and may well do so again with a change in fashion, since for abstract logic that is rather the more defensible of the monistic alternatives. (3) As Bergson in particular has shown, and as pragmatism clearly implies, it is easy to "explain" the mechanistic bias itself in terms of practical "reasons"—a strong consideration in favor of mind and purpose as "more ultimate" than matter and motion—if one is determined to be a monist "regardless." (4) Science itself has subjectivistic implications not sufficiently recognized, in that verification by different observers is required to establish objectivity. For verification is clearly dependent on communication of conscious mental content. (5) Most embarrassing of all is the question as to what properties of matter are really objective. One of the first achievements of the modern physical view itself was to resolve the "visible and tangible," the plain man's reality, into subjective experience.

some (chemical separation) involve no force or pressure conceivably accessible to our perceptive powers. And in addition there is the *ether,* or *radiant energy* in some form, and now we are told that we must add *spatial curvature.* And all this on the plane of physics, without raising any question about the various levels of life and mind. The point for emphasis is the vast gulf between the theoretical system of present-day physics and a mechanistic formulation of that science itself—a point which was admirably stated by Mach a couple of generations ago, and by numerous thinkers since. Interestingly enough, in the twentieth century it is not the physicist but psychologists and sociologists who accept a physical interpretation of nature; the latter are far enough from the basic facts to be able to do it.

III.   FACTUAL VERSUS EXPLANATORY ECONOMICS: UTILITY AS FORCE OR AS MOTIVE

In the humanistic and the social studies we meet with the same craving for monism, carried toward the pole of physical realism or mechanism by the temper of the age and the prestige of natural science. Its extreme manifestation is the vogue of behaviorism, which is less a psychology than a dogmatic repudiation of everything properly to be called by that name. In economics it finds expression in the emphasis on statistical study, associated with a restriction of the data to physical facts or what pass as such. The result is, or would be, to confine the study of economics to *commodity statistics;* that is, all distinctively human data would be excluded from consideration, whether on (*a*) a factual or (*b*) a critical and evaluative level. This will be discussed later. Specifically, there would be no place for the discussion of the motives of economic activity, and hence none for the utility concept. Our attitude toward this tendency has already been indicated. We admit, and indeed urge as much as anyone, the value of such work and the propriety of any particular worker pursuing the commodity-statistics type of economics exclusively. But, we also insist that this cannot be all of the science, that there is also an imperative need for other types of study, in which utility, in several forms which must be carefully distinguished, will take a central place.

In support of this view, the first consideration is the wide divergence of physics from this "behavioristic" ideal, as evidenced by the number and the variety of "metaphysical" entities it is compelled to recognize and use. But mere empirical laws are subject to far more serious limitations in connection with social data. In the first place, economic sequences and relations physically considered do not show a degree of uniformity comparable to that met with in physical nature. We know enough about them to be quite sure that there is in them nothing analogous to the unvarying properties of space, time, mass, momentum, energy, and the innumerable physical, chemical, and electrical "constants"; there are no corresponding invariable economic magnitudes. Economics deals with *commodities* indeed, but not as physically defined (a point which will receive further notice presently). Its physical ultimates are human reactions, which vary widely in time and in space.

Far more serious, however, than the question of the amount of uniformity in economic data is that of the *kind* of uniformity which really exists and which economics is interested in, the kind of valid generalizations regarding such data that are possible and relevant. A critical glance at economic literature will show that there is no worse source of confusion than conceiving of commodities as physical entities. It should go without saying that they are defined and classified on the basis of the *services* or *utilities* they render. It is a "fact" as certain as any physical sense datum that people do get the same utility or service from various goods. Conversely, they may obtain different utilities or services from the same good. This may be the case even at the same time and place, and it is far more likely to be the case at different times and places. There is more stability or uniformity in the human attitudes and interests from which the "things" derive all their significance than there is in goods and services physically specified (if one can speak at all of a service as a physical entity). So true is this and so potent the urge toward relevance in the subconsciousnesses of men that the effect of approaching economics with the physical-science bias frequently results in palpable error in statement. The writers think they are following physical likenesses and differences although the critical reader can see that they are not doing so consistently; the result is a complete *non sequitur*, or plain nonsense.

A crying example is the case of index numbers. Edgeworth and others have had an uphill task in getting the profession at large to see that there is no such thing, in any relevant sense, as an objective average of prices. When, for instance, change has taken place—that is, when there is any occasion at all for the computation of an index—it is utility magnitudes which must be measured and compared. "Institutional economics" ought to be a reaction in the direction of true realism, but the movement which goes by that name has largely shut itself away from its peculiar task by tying up with statistical method, the nearly irresistible bias of which is in the opposite direction. It should again go without saying that an economic institution is, like other institutions, a category of meaning. Language, for example, has its physical basis or aspect. One can plot the voice-waves with an oscillograph or take motion pictures of the vocal organs in action. Such study may be very useful in its place; but it is only an auxiliary to the study of language as an institutional fact.

It is not straining the point to say that the most general principles of economics have been vitiated by this general confusion of taking price as the measure of the magnitude with which the economist is really concerned. In the work of Marshall we have an ideal illustration of the power of the bias toward accepting the price measure of the burdens and the benefits of the production-and-consumption process. The error has long received something more than verbal recognition in connection with price as the measure of utilities to consumers in different circumstances; but, on the production side, where it is undoubtedly more important, one who stresses the question of the relation between the different entrepreneur outlays and real human costs is still in danger of being stared at as a sentimentalist or tagged as a "bolshevik." In an age of thought so dominated as ours by physical conceptions, it is hardly possible to place too much emphasis in the opposite direction. It is highly to the credit of Jevons that in his exposition of utility theory he stated most explicitly that utility theory involves no comparison between utility magnitudes for different minds.[4] In the explanation of price relations this is true and profoundly important, and it is depressing to see the standard treatises and textbooks still in the process of catching up with the founder in this regard.

However, it is here that we must begin to emphasize distinctions. The standpoint of criticism and evaluation and control is as important as that of explanation, and viewing the matter in the large, it is not clear that Jevons' statement is more nearly correct or less one-sided than those of our textbooks. For we inevitably compare the utilities of different individuals, and it is essential that we do so if we are to treat the phenomena in the most significant way. In one sense utility is an explanatory concept, more or less closely analogous to force in physics. It is the pressure or urge which "makes" people choose as they do. The objection that such a notion is "mystical" or "unscientific" has been sufficiently answered by reference to the actual procedure of physics.

Yet the treatment of utility as a force raises a methodological question, for the analogy with physics is not complete. Even in physics it seems likely that the *reason* behind the apparent necessity for using the concept of force lies in the fact of interrupted sequences or the storing-up of a *potentiality* of change without actual change. It is conceivable that we might think in terms of process alone, and thus gratify a deep-seated

[4] *Op. cit.*, p. 14.

intellectual craving, if it were not for the cases in which forces clearly "exist" without momentarily producing their effects. The point seems to have still greater weight in connection with utility and conduct. Much of the feeling of the reality of motives rests on the fact that there are urges toward acts which do not find expression in action. In physics it is possible within wide limits to speak of composition and resolution of actual motions and avoid reference to forces; but in the case of human choices this procedure is generally inapplicable, even in those choices which do not necessarily follow an all-or-none law, and still more clearly in that large proportion which do. Hence the certainty, *a fortiori,* that economics cannot dispense with the utility concept.

The difference between human and physical science arises out of the facts of consciousness and mental communication. In human behavior we have a kind of direct knowledge of motives, whereas we only infer the existence of physical forces from observation of the changes specific to each. Hence, the irresistible urge to treat motives as real. But furthermore, our knowledge of motives through personal experience and social intercourse shows that (in contrast with physical forces) they do not coincide with observed behavior. "Men do otherwise than they intend." The indubitable fact of error reinforces the necessity for giving motives recognition separately from behavior facts, and at the same time throws the student in quest of knowledge of motives themselves into the field of long-range and dubious inference already mentioned. It is a difficulty which must be faced, not evaded or ignored; error can be neither denied nor defined in physical terms. The aim or purpose of action is not perceptible to sense organs or laboratory instruments, but is as real as the action itself, and fully as important a datum to the economist. The method of our science must be fitted to the character of its data and problems.

In using utility as a concept to explain behavior this discrepancy between the "force" and its "effect" must not be lost sight of, or confusion and error will result. If one feels the need of postulating a force back of choice, in more strict analogy with physical concepts, one is of course free to do so, and several alternatives are open. One may delve into the subconscious or unconscious mind, or examine the purely physical history of the "organism" in its "environment." But it will not do to contend that mind and purpose, "effort and error," can be left out of account entirely as factors in the understanding of behavior. If assumed forces explaining error are employed, they ought not to be confused with utility, and still less should arbitrarily postulated forces exactly accounting for the behavior observed be adopted as the definition of utility, as B. M. Anderson and others have advocated.

IV. EXPLANATION VERSUS CONTROL: UTILITY AS VALUE

But there is another and equally vital distinction to be drawn. The picture of the human being as an "economic man" even in his motives (in contrast with his behavior), that is, as a creature whose *efforts* are directed solely toward maximum satisfaction of existing wants, still leaves out facts of which economic theory must take account. Again there is no question as to the propriety of adopting this picture as the basis for study at a certain stage, just as there is no question as to the legitimacy of objective, statistical economics. But the science cannot be restricted within either boundary. As previously observed, economists constantly make, and cannot avoid making, comparisons between utility magnitudes affecting different individuals. That is—passing over still finer distinctions which a more exhaustive study would have to make—they recognize differences in intrinsic importance between different want-satisfactions, as a matter apart from actual choices or from the motives to which an errorless choice would conform. The individual may err regarding ends as well as means; or more important ends may be procurable for other individuals (or possibly for "society") by a use of means different from any which he would freely choose.

In fact, the warp and woof of every practical issue of social policy is made up of just such questions as these. There can be no discussion of general policy which does not run in terms of values in a sense distinct from the factual personal desires of individuals. For economists to refuse to recognize such values and make statements involving them as data would be to deprive their science of all general significance. Questions of policy of every sort, taxation, monopoly and competition, capital and labor, relief of destitution, would be barred.[5]

Objections may be made on behalf of a more "scientific" conception of economics, that these questions of values should be left to specialists of a different type—the ethicist or social philosopher. The answer is that such a specialization is impracticable, and that there are sound reasons why it has not been and will not be carried out. It is true that in the physical-science field a division of labor along this line is the established custom, the pure scientist discovering cause-and-effect relations which the engineer applies by treating them as relations of means and end. But the situation in regard to social science (if it should be called "science") is different. The function of science generally is, no doubt, essentially

---

[5] We must pass over the important but somewhat subtle consideration that individual behavior aside from outside control cannot really be explained in terms of personal desires; "in fact" people do not treat their wants as ultimate data but are concerned about what to want as well as how to get what they consciously want.

pragmatic. The "purity" of pure science is largely an illusion—a useful one, since it happens in many cases that men accomplish more in the accumulation of useful knowledge if they work "as if" for the sake of truth alone and leave to others the application of their results.

But the relation of "theory" to "practice" is very different in the physical and the human fields. The function of natural science is to increase man's power over nature. This we may assume is a thing desirable and safe to promote. But in social science the maxim "knowledge is power" has no corresponding application. Power of man over man is another matter. In the first place, it has no clear meaning. It might mean individual self-control, but that is certainly not a very "scientific" conception, and however desirable it may be, it does not appear that objective scientific social study is designed to promote "power over man" in that sense. Whatever power results seems more likely to be power of some men or groups over other men or groups, and the question of "who's who" naturally arises. Are we laboring to increase the power of government over its subjects, or that of subjects over their government? How about different classes of subjects? And the relations between producers and consumers? sellers and buyers? laborers, managers, property-owners, and "experts"? And what of ourselves, the scientists, parties of the first part? Are we perfecting a technique to be used by ourselves, or for us, or rather to be used "on" us by the sort of people who do get into positions of power in modern political and economic society? There is no need to elaborate the reasons why social scientists will not devote themselves unquestioningly to the increase of knowledge, leaving the application to "others," but must insist on having something to say about policies and ends.

As to linguistic usage, it may be noted that in spite of the disclaimers of Jevons and innumerable successors it is this last meaning of "real value" which most obstinately adheres to the word utility. It is difficult for mere scientists to change usage, and it would probably be wise in this case for economists to give up the attempt. No visible harm or difficulty would result if we dropped the word from scientific discussion and spoke unambiguously of the demand curve, or of the social forces underlying it, or of the actual desires of individuals, or of "social importance," whichever is actually meant. At any rate, some terminology should be adopted which will clearly separate these notions, all fundamental to economic discussion, yet so different, and all so confused as to be fatal to accuracy of thought and clearness of exposition.[6]

[6] [This analysis was first prepared in 1928 and was revised by the analyst in the spring of 1929.—EDITOR.]

THE POSSIBILITY OF A SCIENCE OF POLITICS: WITH SPECIAL ATTENTION TO METHODS SUGGESTED BY WILLIAM B. MUNRO AND GEORGE E. G. CATLIN

By W. Y. ELLIOTT

Harvard University

"The sciences," says Schopenhauer, "in that they are systems of concepts, speak entirely of universals; history speaks of particulars. History would therefore be a science of particulars (a conception) which implies a contradiction."[1] Here is one ground for refusing the dignity of a science to politics, since like history it must concern itself with an undistorted picture of a concrete reality in which exceptions are apparently the only rule and in which events are unique. So far as it is descriptive and objective it must stick to particulars. Politics that goes beyond this, we are told, becomes philosophy. This is the first ground usually urged for denying the possibility of a political science.

A science, says Lēvy-Brühl, "cannot be a science in so far as it is normative."[2] Its theoretical constructions, that is, cease to be scientific whenever they introduce practical moral or æsthetic standards of value. For these subjective values are not and cannot be measured or demonstrated. In the subjective realm of value the claim to an a priori validity of standards in their own rights is the precise denial of the controlling method of the experimental sciences. Therefore, any theoretical constructions which involve presuppositions as to values—let us say those of the inherent worth of individual moral personality which are basic to citizenship in constitutional democracies, or of rights and duties, the conceptions of fraternity, equality, liberty, etc.—are part of a realm to which true science is a stranger.

These two assertions, and variations on the same themes, constitute the main grounds generally asserted for denying a scientific nature to the study of human activity in general—that is, to the so-called social sciences, anthropology, economics, ethics, history, jurisprudence, psychology, sociology, and others—and to politics in particular among them, as being along with sociology and social psychology the most inchoate and complex of all.

---

[1] A. Schopenhauer, *Die Welt als Wille und Vorstellung:* "Über Geschichte," in *Werke,* ed. Leipzig (1877), III, 502.

[2] Lēvy-Brühl, *La morale et la science des mœurs* (5 ème éd. révw.; Paris: F. Alcan, 1913), chap. ii, esp. pp. 11–14.

Students of political phenomena have in general taken two quite opposed attitudes toward this sweeping denial of all really scientific value to their branch of human study.

On the one hand, part of them have gone over to the philosophers and the artists and have taken the high ground that a proper study of politics shares the realm of ideal values with philosophy; and the practice of politics or its appreciation, with the arts. "It is quite true," say the metaphysically minded among our fellows in the study of politics, "that politics is not a science and cannot be. Any study of that rational creature man, endowed with the precious gift of a free will, must repudiate the deterministic calculus of the natural sciences. The study of human values is higher in the hierarchy of disciplines. Next to pure philosophy it stands." Where philosophy begins with an attempt at understanding the underlying fundamentals and the possibilities of the whole universe (including man), and then issues in the attempt to explain these after the sciences leave off, just so politics (philosophically conceived) attempts to focus the human understanding on man, the political animal, evaluating in their context his political purposes and the institution in which they are writ large. And just as philosophy (so conceived) has generally issued in a justification either of the ways of God to man or of man toward the universe, so has this metaphysical conception of the high rôle of politics generally issued in a justification either of the state to man or of the ways of man toward the state, as if they were—the one or the other—divinely authorized. Monistic idealism has taken the former attitude of justifying the state, with a classic illustration in *The Philosophical Theory* of the State of the late Dr. Bernard Bosanquet. Pluralistic idealism has generally put the apology for the individual against the state, or for individual associations such as churches, labor unions, etc., against the state. In spite of his claims to political realism, Mr. Laski stands here. Both are interested primarily in the question of value, and are but little concerned with facts except by way of illustration or of Procrustean bed-making. Their method has generally been to deduce a system of political ethics from a priori generalizations of political values with something of the same logical unfolding of premises as that of the pure mathematical sciences or the non-Euclidian geometries or symbolic logic.

On the other hand, the pure political scientists like to fancy that they are true scientists because they are concerned only with "facts." "God forbid," they agree with Lord Verulam, "that we should give out a dream of the imagination for a pattern of the world." And they follow their master, Francis Bacon, still further: *Est itaque quod gratias agamus*

Macciavello et hujusmodi scriptoribus, qui aperte et indissimulanter proferunt quid homines facere soleant, non quid debeant.[3] They are concerned only with the inductive explanation of the causal effects of certain acts. They insist on shunning the *idola fori, tribus, specus, theatri.*[4] They proclaim themselves scientists in method and they follow so far as they can, and sometimes farther than they ought, the methods and techniques of the physical and experimental sciences. An interesting example of this method is to be found in Vilfredo Pareto's *Trattato di sociolgia generale.* They have derived strength from the philosophic justification of their method afforded by the instrumentalism of John Dewey, and the prevailing current of positivistic and "scientific" methods in the other social sciences.[5]

On the whole, their main concern is to get as certain and as scientifically controlled understanding of political phenomena as of those to which the natural sciences have led in physics, chemistry, or astronomy, where observation of similarities and uniformities has been rewarded by the formulation of laws which permit prediction and even experimental verification. They have, through a natural envy, wished to steal some of the prestige that experimental science enjoys in the modern world.

If the political *theorists* as a group accept the denial of the possibility of a political *science* of the same nature as the experimental sciences, their positivistic confrères, the political scientists proper, will accept no such limitation. The latter maintain, with considerable justice, that any such description of science as that given by Schopenhauer is inadequate; that many of the really important conquests of modern science are due not to any primary interest in the mere manipulation of concepts, but to the fruitful linkage of manifold particulars. And some of them, even though accepting the necessity of turning those particulars into conceptual universals—or into the approximations called scientific laws and principles— would still claim that politics has its laws quite as much as other sciences.

---

[3] F. Bacon, *De augmentis scientiarum*, Liber Septimus, in *Works*, ed. 1864 (Boston), III, 31.

[4] One of the most typical statements of this point of view is given in Part II of Stuart A. Rice's *Quantitative Methods in Politics* (New York: A. A. Knopf, 1928).

[5] Pareto's chief sociological work has appeared in a revised French translation, *Traité de sociologie générale* (2 vols.; Lausanne, 1917–19) ; a revised Italian edition (3 vols.; Firenze, 1923). [Cf. analysis 7.—EDITOR.] In American political writing the best examples of this method are to be found in the work of Rice, *op. cit.*

John Dewey himself has recently turned his back upon the previous leads of his own philosophy in *The Public and Its Problems*, in which he terms this method "pseudo-scientific" so far as it is applied to social sciences.

The difficulty of formulating these laws, they admit. But that, they think, is due more to the complexity of the phenomena than to the lack of causal sequences of a scientifically determinable nature. Such a position is that of my distinguished colleague, W. B. Munro, who in his recent presidential address to the assembled political scientists and their fellows, the historians, asserted that politics had best heed the timely advice given to it in the last generation by Bagehot and go to physics for its method. He suggested quite trenchantly that politics must get a divorce from its "polygamous companionate marriage" with philosophy, law, and psychology, and leave off its philanderings with ethics. Apparently he thought that the only possible union that would not be a *mésalliance* would be a firm yoke with the physical sciences, admitting, perhaps, of platonic relations with economics and history.[6]

Such a conception of political science as absolutely divorced from ethics and philosophy seems to proceed from a skepticism of all fundamental ethical values in politics which my colleague would be the last to admit. He did, however, suggest that a scientific politics would discard the outworn fiction of absolute civic equality[7]—which, it is worth noting, is rather an ethical ideal of value than an attempt at describing facts. He was, however, quite right in pointing out that when equality was treated as if it were a scientific fact and not a legal approximation to equal civic status or a sort of mystic religious belief, it led science sadly astray. When, for instance, men's opinions are registered only by votes, their intensity and survival power are not always properly estimated.

In short, scientific politics would, he hoped, proceed to follow physics in getting at the subatomic forces in political action. Below the individual lie various component elements of political forces. These, he thought, were hardly to be afforded to us by contemporary psychology—individual or social—even though social psychology has acquired for itself the requisite jargon, of a degree of obscurity quite satisfactory. In fairness to psychology, one ought to note that behaviorism is trying precisely to apply his suggested method by ruling consciousness and purpose out of

[6] "Physics and Politics—an Old Analogy Revised," an address delivered before the American Political Science Association, Washington, D.C., December 28, 1927, and printed in the *American Political Science Review*, XXII, No. 1 (February, 1928), 1–11, esp. 8.

[7] *Ibid.*: "Both the science and the art of government still rest upon what may be called the atomic theory of politics—upon the postulate that all able-bodied citizens are of equal weight, volume and value; endowed with various absolute and inalienable rights; vested with equally absolute duties; and clothed with the attribute of an indivisible sovereignty" (p. 3).

the equation, and that physiological psychologists have gone even farther. But Pavlov in his study of conditioned reflexes has shown that man (and even the animals) cannot be reduced to a series of anything quite like tropisms, even in the simplest reactions to physiological stimuli.

Professor Munro, for his part, expressed the hope that politics might, by adopting the method of physics, ultimately establish laws of a really scientific nature, including the discovery of the "true reasons for the vast differentiation between good, bad, and indifferent citizenship which is perhaps the most obvious of all the phenomena of politics."[8] To do that it would be necessary to add to the hydrogen atom—the citizen—not only the group atoms which made his effective combinations but to get down to the electronic forces of ideas and imponderables upon whose stimulus the real diversity of citizenship depends.[9]

His speech, which very aptly summed up the prevailing currents among American Political Scientists and which was universally acclaimed by them, by a series of neat analogies left one with the impression that a political science, at least as reputable as the scatter-shot diagrams of meteorology, might be devised to explain the vagaries of electorates and the political reactions of public opinion and of forms of governments. In some interesting lectures delivered under the Jacob Schiff Foundation at Cornell he had already sketched the formulation of what he has called the "law of the pendulum" in politics: With appropriate historical citations, it is easy to observe that every great war has produced an infallible victory for social discipline and conservative reaction as its aftermath— a wave of autocracy and efficiency. Witness, after the last, Mussolini, Pilsudski, Stalin, Primo di Rivera, Poincaré in France, tranquillity in England, and normalcy in America. This in turn is followed in due course by a reaction toward radicalism. What the due course is, or the causes of it, does not appear, unless it be the eternal mutability of what Saint-Beuve called "the sea of human opinion," governed by cyclical phases as the ocean tides are by the moon—although with admittedly less chronological exactitude. The rough reckoning for these shifts appears to be between ten and fifteen years, according to Munro. It is not a mere matter of democracy against autocracy but of reaction in a swing from right to left, or from what is roughly called conservatism to what is roughly called radicalism.

The triumph of Toryism, which assumed international proportions during the dozen years which followed the close of the Napoleonic Wars, was bound

[8] *Ibid.*, p. 5. Obviously "good citizenship" is itself a concept of philosophic rather than of scientific discourse.

[9] *Ibid.*, p. 6.

to induce a reaction. It came during the early thirties in Europe and America alike. The law of the pendulum, rather than the influence of the frontier, would seem to furnish the right clue [in America]. It has the merit of recognizing, moreover, the essential unity of European and American history. When the world swings to the Right, America goes with it—and to the Left also.[10]

Now the theory of the pendulum, like the theory of the cyclical degeneration of governments, or of the organic rise and decline of civilizations, has an honorable history among historians. Many of them have traced the swing of what Lord Salisbury also termed the "pendulum of politics"; although most of them have found, as Dicey did in *Lectures on the Relation between Law and Public Opinion in England during the Nineteenth Century*, that the base of the pendulum had shifted considerably in one direction at the end of the longer period. For particular purposes it is possible to describe such a swing, as, for instance, the change in the attitude of the Supreme Court of the United States toward the restrictive force of "obligation of contract" over state laws under Chief Justices Marshall and Taney, compared to the Court's attitude under Chase and Waite. But the charting of directions as merely "right" and "left" is, it may be, a too great simplification of political history. Which two historians will agree upon the length of the time period or the tendencies involved, even when once they have selected a common base for their pendulum?

Under the English parliamentary system it is to be expected that the government will lose a majority of by-elections, as the result of the electorate's stored-up grievances against the party in power. But general elections come irregularly and by no means mark clear shifts "right" or "left" when they do come. The use of the terms *radical* and *conservative* for such purposes can hardly be allowed to be scientific. Too many issues are involved to permit a uniform shift even with such a simple machinery as that of British parliamentarism.

Aristotle's normal cycle of the degeneration of forms of governments, while it showed insight into the tendencies of the contemporary Greek city state, can hardly be taken as a scientific law even within this narrow context. The most ambitious of all the attempts at such a philosophy of political history is that of Oswald Spengler.[11] The tendencies which he

[10] William Bennet Munro, *The Invisible Government* (New York: Macmillan Co., 1928), pp. 76–77.

[11] *The Decline of the West* (2 vols.; New York: Alfred A. Knopf, Inc., 1926–28). A vulgarization of this thesis has been made by Goddard and Gibbons, *Civilization or Civilizations* (London: Constable & Co., 1926). These authors take as scien-

thought to descry in Roman civilization can hardly be accepted by historians as descriptively exact. To superimpose them, as he does, upon a block-concept of "European civilization" in turn declining toward Caesarism and false democracy is a poetic rather than a scientific analogy.

Such laws, if laws they be, are in any case astronomic rather than subatomic. Though that may ultimately amount to the same thing in physics, as Einstein's *Zur einheitlichen Feldtheorie* indicates, it can hardly be said to do so in politics without elaborating why. Furthermore, as a universal description of political phenomena such a law as that of the pendulum is subject to some suspicion. In which direction did the reaction go after the Greek fleet defeated the Persians at Salamis? The triumph of Athenian democracy has usually been attributed to the demands of the victorious sailors of the lowest class. A military interpretation of history, even that of von Delbrück—Tory that he is—has usually been given as the explanation of the rise of democracy: the leveling of the man on horseback by new strategy, new weapons, mass wars.[12] And it would be hard to call the growth of democracy a swing toward conservatism. For that matter what is one to say of our own War of 1812–15 or of the Civil War of 1861–65? Did they initiate *a swing to the right* or arrest "inefficient" democracy? Actually, in spite of some arrests in its development, universal suffrage, male and female, made ground in Europe, America, and Asia after the World War itself as never before. In England, the Labour party certainly represented the growth in power of a more real radicalism, if radicalism be defined in terms of an impatience with existing institutions. On the Continent, too, the left was certainly stronger than before the war. There were periods when it was manifestly directing the destinies of European governments. On any reading, it would be hard to balance the books against "radicalism" in Europe without admitting that its post-war position has been, on the whole, improved.

Professor Munro is on surer ground when he traces our "fundamentalism in politics" to a worship of shibboleths, but he who would manufacture a law for the use of shibboleths, after the fashion of advertising psychologists, must remember that shibboleths work both ways and are subject to some discount when used too much. Nor are we advanced very much by considerations on the part of our political scientists of the

---

tifically exact the time limits of Spengler's periods, dividing the fourteen hundred years up meticulously into appropriate fractions for the organic growth and decay of each civilization.

[12] *Geschichte der Kriegskunst* (3 vols.; 1907–9). See also the English translation by Roy McElwee, *Government and the Will of the People* (1923).

comparative "efficiency" of direct primaries and conventions, proportional versus single-member-district representation, parliamentary versus presidential, or unitary versus federal government. To all these arguments political scientists give and must give various answers, for in these arguments it is not a question simply of engineering technique, of efficiency, or of adjustment to a given context. It is a question of which is more valuable in the light of changing ethical, economic, geographic, cultural, and many other factors which are questions of reasonable (or more often of unreasonable) choice.

It is sometimes urged that for problems of a purely administrative nature the analysis of means toward given ends is all that is needed, and that here scientific technique, with an especial emphasis on statistical method, is particularly applicable. If the administrative problem is so conceived that would be true.[13] Political administration, as a whole, however, can never be divorced from policy. A tax program, even in its administrative and executive details, is a case in point. In sewage disposal and similar problems, the scientific element is exhausted when one has disposed of the engineering details. The where and how of disposal become embarrassingly political.

SCIENTIFIC LAWS IN POLITICS

Would we not be much nearer seeing which scientific laws, if any, are possible in politics by clearing up a little further the meaning of our terms? That is a bit of elementary wisdom in any discussion. First, What do *science* and *scientific* method mean to us? Second, What meaning do we attach to *politics*, and to *political* in the term *political science?*

Scientia, we are often and learnedly told, means only understanding or knowledge. Whenever facts are capable of being given an organized arrangement into an intelligible and a coherent structure, whatever the principle of arrangement, there we have a science. Science need mean only this classification plus a "rigorous weighing of all the evidence, including a full consideration of all possible theories." A historian

[13] A clear example of the use to which statistics may be scientifically put is the purely mathematical study of E. V. Huntington, "The Apportionment of Representatives in Congress," *Transactions of the American Mathematical Society*, XXX, No. 1, 85–110. On the other hand, the choice of a method of reapportionment involves, clearly, constitutional as well as mathematical considerations, although these also seem to the writer to favor Professor Huntington's method of "equal proportions" rather than the method of "major fractions" incorporated recently into law by Congress. That political considerations come into even such an issue was seen by the obvious determination of certain state delegations to block any method by which they would lose seats.

like Thucydides is also a scientist on this basis.[14] Social sciences can claim scientific respectability if this is the demand put upon them—and this only.

But let us carry the inquiry into the kinds of sciences a step farther. In the pure or mathematical sciences logical deduction is the essence of scientific method, and demonstration is in terms of an internal logical coherence or a self-completing system.[15] In the experimental sciences we find two major groupings, the inorganic (or physical) and the organic (or biological). In the former, scientific formulation of rules results in the explicit statement of general laws of scientific universality such as the periodic and Mozley's laws. The method of the physical sciences is both inductive and deductive. Experiment can verify causality so far as it is described merely in terms of behavior. The biological sciences aim at the same complete abstraction and proceed step by step toward biophysics, biochemistry, etc., without ever satisfactorily explaining development in these terms. Nevertheless, theories of heredity and variation do attempt a universality of statement in the manner of the deterministic physical sciences.

It is needless to say, after the confession of scientists like M. Jules Henri Poincaré, that the higher speculative frontier of all the natural sciences tends to become metaphysical if not æsthetic—sometimes both.[16] Creative artistry and creative philosophy come into the formulation of new hypotheses. But *quâ* scientist the observer is simply interested in extending his range of known relations between facts. Often the new facts found (as in the case of Pasteur's great discovery of the existence of bacteria are themselves the sufficient reward.

In the social sciences, the rules involved are rarely if ever capable of the same explicit statement as universalized abstraction. This is due

[14] Cf. Morris Cohen, "Social Sciences and Natural Sciences," in *The Social Sciences and Their Interrelations*, ed. W. F. Ogburn and A. Goldenweiser (New York: Houghton Mifflin Co., 1927), pp. 451 ff. This is the ablest critique of the subject yet published.

[15] See A. Wolf, *Essentials of Scientific Method* (London: G. Allen & Unwin, Ltd., 1925), for a rigorous definition of the meaning of method as it is common to all the sciences. So far as the essential attitude of science must be deterministic, many parts of social studies cannot be so treated! See Lawrence Hyde, *The Learned Knife: An Essay on Science and Human Values* (London: G. Howe, Ltd., 1928).

[16] See also A. N. Whitehead, *Science and the Modern World* (New York: Macmillan Co., 1925). For an estimate of the mathematically demonstrable elements in science see P. W. Bridgman, *The Logic of Modern Physics* (New York: Macmillan Co., 1927), and G. N. Lewis, *The Anatomy of Science* (New Haven: Yale University Press, 1926).

first of all to the nature of the facts involved. Social happenings have the historical character of unique events, and history does not, like physical nature, repeat itself. It does not submit itself to rigid deterministic laws because men are purposive and morally creative beings. What constitutes a political fact? Similarities between Mussolini and Caesar, Napoleon, the Kaiser, etc., have been suggested. All these figures are facts, as events in history are facts. But they are not capable of scientific comparison as if the similarities meant uniformity or identity. Each personality, each régime, is unique because it is historical, and that, it is claimed, is the case with all political facts, including political institutions. The *podestà* is a Fascist revival of a late medieval institution; but little similarity exists beyond the rough analogy suggested by the name. He would be a rash "scientist" who ventured to predict the future of Fascism on the basis merely of rough historical analogies. Some general suggestions might be ventured but they could hardly be called scientific.

In any science the essential thing is first to limit the field of scientific focus in order that abstraction may be possible. Then one must reduce the phenomena, which are to be handled, to statement in the simplest units—even if they cannot be stated in terms of measurable variables. If we succeed in carving out a field for politics less amorphous than that of sociology, it may still be that it is impossible to state the units in simple terms. Political science as a merely classificatory science must deal with forms of governments, subgroups such as parties and other associations of political import. It can hardly go as a descriptive science beyond the state of botany in the days of Linaeus. This is, and will remain, true of the comparative approach. The probability is that it has no single unit such as the atom or the light-year to deal with. Genus and species are never exactly similar. Is a science possible? How much light does mere classification throw upon the actual working of institutions? Have we not done too much grafting of institutions on to foreign trunks because of this too simple reasoning by analogy?

If we are to use the term *science* for our study of political phenomena, it will only be on the basis that prediction and experimental verification are not necessary predicates in the social sciences. The reasons for this do not depend alone upon the complexity of the processes involved. They come from the nature of the phenomena under discussion—the actions of beings who are capable of some degree of self-direction and of novelty in social adjustment. All that one can require of a *social* science is (1) that the phenomena observed are capable of intelligible statement in terms of their relations to a system of their own. In other words, social phe-

nomena must be capable of universally valid description, but not necessarily of description in measurable terms. (2) There must be the possibility of a logical detachment that permits objective judgment at least
to the degree of the "weather man," who doesn't permit his hopes of a
fine day to prevent his announcement of a blizzard brewing in the northwest. Our method to be scientific must be Baconian rather than scholastic.
It must not be prejudiced by fixed dogma of any sort. It is entirely
legitimate to attempt the reduction of human behavior to a completely
deterministic calculus. But it is not legitimate to proceed on such an
assumption when the facts have ceased to bear it out, merely in order
to be "scientific."

But if science be used in a wide sense, i.e., an objective description of
observable and describable external characteristics of human behavior,
there are at least as good grounds for calling politics a science as there
are for any of the other social sciences—including psychology. We may
even have as good right to catalogue the habits of kings as of cabbages,
allowing for the probability that more kings than cabbages behave with
eccentricity according to any standard of normality. If we are to apply
to these phenomena any scientific methods of an order like those of the
physical sciences, if we are to go beyond mere scientific detachment of
attitude and consider the *basis of the selection of our facts and the economy of their arrangement,* to say nothing of the logical bases of the
system of arrangement, we must carefully inquire how far politics permits the adoption of a methodological technique like that of the more
manipulable physical sciences.

In dealing with the nature of the *political* fact, what are its simplest
terms? Is it at all a measurable variable? What possibility of scientific
control exists in determining the relation between two or more such political variables? Is experiment altogether impossible? If not direct experiment, may we use the indirect method of Durkheim and other social
psychologists, of which even J. S. Mill was a little skeptical.[17]

For the purposes of definition I shall call "politics," *in the broadest
Aristotelian sense of the term,* a combination both of political philosophy
and of political science. As a theoretical study, it includes the formulation of ethical principles and a critique of the values historically incorporated in institutions; it also includes the special field of descriptive and
comparative political *science* which is concerned with the objective formu-

[17] For a description of this method see W. R. Dennes, *The Method and Presuppositions of Group Psychology,* "University of California Publications in Philosophy"
(1924). For J. S. Mill's comments on method see his *System of Logic* (New York,
1869), pp. 222–50.

lation of such uniformities as the facts may afford. The latter is properly called "political science"; the former, "political ethics" or "political philosophy." Their combination in the study of the whole range of political phenomena is politics or political theory in the terms of our modern curriculum.[18]

But what is the field of politics in its scientific aspect? What are its especial facts? It includes (I assume for purposes of defining its content) all *those actions of human beings that are aimed at supporting or resisting any attempt at an existing monopoly of force which claims the sanction of law.* Its focus is therefore on the activities of a particular association— the *state;* but it must consider the state as that affects and is affected by individuals, by other associations including other states, by its own institutional setting, and by its entire environmental as well as its cultural context.

Some of these separate elements like climate, geography, territory, economic resources, and population are capable of scientific description and analysis. Some of them are supplied by the variables which other sciences measure as they affect political action. Economics can offer us an objective basis for certain elements in our political equation. Psychology can offer yet others more dubious. Anthropology may be too suspect as a science to allow us to speak of "Nordic" institutions, but there is an observable psychology of peoples to which Wundt and others have drawn attention. The fact that its description requires as much of artistic insight as of "scientific" method may blind behaviorists to its importance. But they are blind by choice, in any case, to anything that requires interpretation in terms of conscious reflection.

There is, though, an observable and measurable regularity of recurrence in the behavior of certain interest groups that are of primary importance to politics. I cheerfully admit the fact that the limits of probable error would scandalize a physicist, even an astronomer, although, as Professor Munro says, "they ought not to annoy a meteorologist." These groups have a deep, although not an exhaustive, significance in the decision of some political issues. One must return to some degree to artistry to interpret these results, but so does many another type of scientist.

[18] See the author's *The Pragmatic Revolt in Politics* (New York: Macmillan Co., 1928), pp. 84–85. I am aware that this is not the conventional view of American political scientists. Mr. Gordon Dewey, in his interesting articles "On Methods in the Study of Politics," uses the term "political science" to include "politics." He is obviously, however, not using "politics" in the older Aristotelian sense of the English universities, and of the continental theorists. See *Political Science Quarterly,* XXXVIII, No. 4 (December, 1923), 636–37. See also the interesting comment of Mr. Stuart Rice, *op. cit.,* pp. 6–7. For a discussion of terminology see J. W. Garner, *Political Science and Government* (New York: American Book Co., 1928).

But where is our simple fact for politics itself? Is it the individual or the group? What sort of group? Or may each serve for different equations?

In commenting on the difficulty of finding the simple fact—either in the infinitely small or the infinitely great—Henri Poincaré in *Science and Method* notes the essential difficulty to which the social sciences are the peculiar heirs. Physics may track down the electron; astronomy may measure light-years. Even

the biologist has been led instinctively to regard the cell as more interesting than the whole animal, and the event has proved him right since cells belonging to the most diverse organisms have greater resemblances for those who can recognize them, than the organisms themselves. [But] the sociologist is in a more embarrassing position. The elements, which for him are men, are too dissimilar, too variable, too capricious, in a word, too complex themselves. Furthermore, history does not repeat itself; how, then, is he to select the interesting fact, the fact which is repeated? Method is precisely the selection of facts, and accordingly our first care must be to devise a method. Many have been devised because none holds the field undisputed. Nearly every sociological thesis proposes a new method, which, however, its author is very careful not to apply, so that sociology is the science with the greatest number of methods and the least results.[19]

If this is true of man in general, the proper prey of sociology, may we not at least as political scientists simplify our problem by taking a particular aspect of the creature—*political* man. That is, in effect, what Mr. G. E. G. Catlin proposes in his *Science and Method of Politics*.[20] By abstracting a political man, he thinks, we can limit our science to manageable proportions. Taking a leaf from the classical economists, and *remembering the limits of our method where they sometimes did not*, we can abstract a *political* man to match their *economic* man; or better, a *political act*, with the individual as the unit of behavior, to match the economist's *economic act*, with a similarly simple unit.

The difficulty here is that Mr. Catlin takes his abstraction straightway as if it were an order of fact. One might object to borrowing a method and a unit which modern economists hold to be thoroughly suspect. There never was a purely economic man and few theories were really built upon his hypostatization as a fact. Those that were, were vicious. Certainly

[19] *Op. cit.*, trans. Francis Maitland (London: T. Nelson & Sons, 1914), pp. 19–20.

[20] This is the only modern book in English that seriously sets itself to examine the presuppositions of political science as a science, whereas, of course, continental literature affords the formidable efforts of Alfred and Max Weber, of Michels and Pareto (Knopf, 1927). One must now add the modestly stated claims of Stuart A. Rice, *op. cit.*, Parts I and II.

the group is, as an order of fact, a more useful as well as more scientific variable in exchange relations and the production and distribution of wealth.[21]

But Mr. Catlin, for one, feels that some real use was got out of the economists' abstraction. Human nature for economic purposes is sufficiently uniform in its acquisitiveness to permit the utilitarian simplification. Can we not similarly simplify politics by treating as a *political* act "that [act] of man in his relation to the wills of his fellows in *control, submission,* and *accommodation,*" just as in economics we distinguish "man in his relation to 'things' " in "their production and negotiation?"[22]

If one raises Aristotle's objection that man is essentially a πολιτικὸν ζῷον or a polity-building being—and deduces from that further that *all* his acts are political in so far as they are social, Mr. Catlin contends that it is simply not true. Politics is not sociology.

Admitting a social situation determined, among others, by factors meteorological, geological, biological, by factors of natural wealth and of technical discovery, by factors of conservative tradition and established civilization, and admitting a human nature (i.e., common characteristics in human beings) of a certain, if imperfectly known, constancy, as distinct from inexplicable caprice, our problem is to examine how men have discovered and elaborated a *modus vivendi* in relation to each other without making life worthless to themselves, through restrictions and repressions, or worthless through oppression for others. This is a problem not chimerical, as is that of the "science of History"; it is less ambitious than that of the sociologist as usually propounded; it is less technological than the study of law or of government.[23]

What will be the process of this science? Mr. A. F. Bentley some years ago indicated the process of the applied science of politics as a matter of the study of group pressures.[24] That is not Mr. Catlin's solution. His

[21] See the presidential address before the American Economic Association of W. C. Mitchell, "Quantitative Analysis in Economic Theory," *American Economic Review,* Vol. XV (1925), and Allyn A. Young, *Economic Problems, New and Old* (New York: Houghton Mifflin, 1927), especially "The Trend of Economics," pp. 232–62.

[22] *Op. cit.,* p. 205.

[23] *Ibid.,* p. 204. Presumably the term "worthless" implies value judgments of some sort—ethical, economic, or other—although this is never made explicit. Indeed, it is implicitly denied by the context.

[24] *The Process of Government* (Chicago: University of Chicago Press, 1908). See also the recent work of P. Odegard, *Pressure Politics* (Columbia University Press, 1928), and of E. P. Herring, *Group Representation before Congress* (Baltimore: The Johns Hopkins Press, 1929), and in collaboration with the author, "Le rôle politique des associations aux Etats-Unis," *Révue des sciences politiques,* LII (1929), 52–78, 230–50.

basis is individualistic and Hobbesian. "To have their way with their fellows" is the basis of this psychology of politics[25] a natural legacy from his earlier study of Hobbes. It is an *individualistic* egotism that forms groups only to magnify the individual's ego. It is essentially the power theory of politics.[26] Now the interesting, and perhaps the fatal, thing is that Mr. Catlin does not feel called upon to answer the question "Powers for what?"[27] He assumes that the formal aspect of the will to power can afford us a science, without regard to content. But the only valid means of distinguishing the fields of the social sciences lies in their focus of fact-selection. The difference between human adjustment in a religious body and in a state is afforded precisely by the content of willing—the purpose of association. There is, in the largest sense, a political problem in church organization, as in every other group. But its focus is not upon those legal or political relationships which command the sanction of organized force. Or, if this is the case, the church tends to usurp the state's function in part or in whole—a theme elaborated in the Middle Ages with sufficient detail, and revived in modern issues in Mexico and Tennessee.

If political science is to study other phenomena than government, it can, nevertheless, hardly achieve simplification unless it focuses its study on associational activities where they become governmental. Group discipline, say of the church, the trade-union, or the professional association, partakes of the nature of government and is "political" in the broadest sense of that term. It becomes of interest to political scientists, however, only by way of comparison; or when it affects rights and duties general to citizenship; or when it infringes upon the sphere of other groups. Mr. Catlin's definition in this respect seems to be merely sociology with economics dubiously left out.

The examples which he produces may serve to test his method. He takes the study of voting as the focus of his problem. The vote serves literally as a means of counting heads to avoid the more painful breaking of them—all moral community being ruled out as unnecessary to scientific method. The fault of Aristotle lay, he thinks, in refusing to separate ethics from politics. The vote is a merely Hobbesian estimate of relative

[25] *Op. cit.*, p. 211. See Mr. Catlin's *Thomas Hobbes* (Oxford: B. Blackwell, 1922).

[26] Cf. W. E. Hocking, *Man and the State* (New Haven: Yale University Press, 1926), p. 325: "Briefly the state exists to *establish the objective conditions for the will to power* in human history." But to Professor Hocking these objective conditions also are in turn conditioned by ethical judgments. He rejects the purely egotistic basis of politics.

[27] *Science and Method of Politics*, p. 211 n.

strength. The constitutional morality of the minority is dictated by motives of prudence. "The study of the vote, where ascertainable, is very near to the heart of the political relationship."

But how to weigh votes? They suppose a political equality that is not realistic or scientific.[28] The answer is: By the power standards of present culture, since man-power is prevalent in industrial democracies—making due allowance, as Mr. Catlin does, for Mussolinis when they occur.

He thinks it possible to pursue the questionnaire method of sampling used by Merriam and Gosnell in the study of the reasons for non-voting;[29] supplemented by Allport's psychological graphs of atypical opinions;[30] or by Rice's "Some Applications of Statistical Method to Political Research."[31] Mr. Catlin offers only to supplement these methods in detail by a study of crimes,[32] or of degree of reputability, such as the compara-

[28] "In contemporary England, the right to vote is an indication of social value. The criminal classes have no vote, the ordinary citizen has one, the propertied and educated classes often have two. These votes indirectly affect legislation and the fashion in which men shall be governed and controlled. The vote of the peer directly affects it, his vote counting one in the Upper House to about 70,000 counting one in the Lower Chamber" (*ibid.*, p. 255). Of course the vote of the peer hardly does count on this scale since 1911.

[29] C. E. Merriam and H. F. Gosnell, *Non-Voting* (Chicago: Univeristy of Chicago Press, 1924). See also H. F. Gosnell, *Getting Out the Vote: An Experiment in the Stimulation of Voting* (Chicago: University of Chicago Press, 1927). B. A. Arneson, "Non-voting in a Typical Ohio Community," *American Political Science Review,* XIX (November, 1925), 816–25, proceeds by what I should regard as a far sounder method, i.e., by classifying voters and non-voters according to their affiliations with racial, social, religious, and economic groups. [Cf. analysis 50.— Editor.]

[30] F. H. Allport and D. A. Hartman, "The Measurement and Motivation of Atypical Opinion in a Certain Group," *American Political Science Review,* XIX (1925), 735–760.

[31] Rice, *op. cit.*

[32] Mme de Staël (the celebrated daughter of Necker) in *The Influence of the Passions upon Happiness* observes: "In the Canton of Berne . . . . it has been observed that every ten years nearly the same number of divorces took place; and there are several towns in Italy where an exact calculation is made of the number of murders that are regularly committed every year. Thus events which link with a multitude of various combinations have their periodical return, and preserve a fixed proportion, when our observations on them are the result of a great number of chances. Hence we may be led to believe that political science may one day acquire the force of geometrical evidence."

John Adams' comment: "Curious! Curious!" "The science of morals when applied to a particular individual, may be wholly erroneous with regard to him; but the organization of a constitution is invariably grounded on data that are fixed, as the greater number in everything afford results that are always similar and always foreseen." And again: "Sensible!" (Note taken from John Adams' marginal comments in his copy of the work cited, now in the Boston Public Library.)

tive numbers of honors bestowed upon bankers, newspaper proprietors, and landowners by the English crown in different periods, or the proportion of lawyers in Parliament. Only by such a technique can politics lift itself beyond description to abstraction. Can it go on to prediction? At least Mr. Catlin does not. He remains content, like Poincaré's sociologist, with having stated a method, using a footnote to promise a volume in application. We are left for the present with an interesting conception of political science as the measure of the "market for power," with no technique applicable to such phenomena as Fascism, revolutions, or dictatorships which reject voting as a measure. But it may well be that it is only when groups have "settled down" to a political stability that permits voting that they can be treated scientifically—in spite of Brooks Adams' *Theory of Social Revolutions* (New York: Macmillan Co., 1913).

My own view is that a better field for a scientific attempt at examining the political act is through the study of groups,[33] leaving individuals to the biographers, to the political artists, and to the psychologists.

My conclusions are: (1) scientific method in politics, in the sense of an objective and adequately detailed descriptive approach can readily be agreed to. When we cannot experiment, we can at least dispassionately observe and compare. (2) Scientific method in the sense of a critical basis or methodology of selecting facts must be at least understood sufficiently to prevent the foisting-off of pseudo-scientific "results" on us by psychologists, sociologists, economists, and statisticians. They are allies, but one must remember the old Italian proverb: "God protect us from our friends. We can take care of our enemies ourselves!" (3) In the field of political action it is necessary to simplify the technique used by resolutely renouncing any claim to discovering measurable variables in such a unit as political man (or woman). The grounds for this renunciation are those of scientific economy (in the case of political man); those of agreement with the poet: *varium et mutabile semper femina* (in the case of newly political woman). The individual—given our present lack of a definitive scientific psychology—is still too unexplored and uncharted a realm to permit quantitative treatment of motives.[34]

[33] This, if I am not mistaken in his meaning, is also the view of Professor Munro: "Hence the first problem of political science is not that of adjusting social control to the interests of the individual citizen but of securing and maintaining a fair balance between the various groups to which the individuals belong" ("Physics and Politics, etc.," *op. cit.,* p. 5).

[34] I cannot, up to the present, see any pragmatic results from hypothetical distribution-curves of opinion, particularly when they are based on the assumption of a normal curve. The statement of opinion does not permit the scientific exactitude of self-analysis, even were sampling possible in any adequate manner. The arrange-

The only realm of political behavior that seems to me to offer a valid opportunity for a method comparable to that of astronomy, where we can observe and verify, although we do not control the divine harmonies of the spheres, lies in the regularity which political response to typical issues assumes in certain groups of known political orientation: for example, the Catholic church, the American Federation of Labor, the National Manufacturers' Association, the National Anti-Saloon League. In these and in like groups of some permanence we get institutionalized behavior. We can even count on a lower limit of political solidarity in political parties, as Professor A. N. Holcombe has shown.[35] The analysis of the vote does disclose externals of behavior that we may sample roughly and usefully over a period of years. Even here sectional groupings, not mere aggregates of individuals, are our best units. Though the results will be too complex to permit statement as *laws* in any way analogous to the laws of physics, they may yet be intelligibly represented as the relation between two or more variables: namely, (1) sectional beliefs, about economic and political interests, and (2) party shifts in power. One must be advised here also not to mistake interesting leads for complete scientific analyses. Professor Holcombe's study of party shifts is only a partial picture of historical causality.

In the case of the groups like religious bodies, labor unions, and the like, we are not able to secure a scientific treatment of politics whenever there is a new adjustment of wills involved. The problem becomes too complex. For example, no one could predict in advance what attitude and what solidarity the Catholic population of this country would assume in regard to the candidacy of Governor Smith for the presidency. But the solidarity and political effectiveness of great interest groups are capable of scientific estimate as political forces focused on a certain question within a limited period. For example, we can get a very good idea of the political solidarity of organized labor in Massachusetts against a fifty-four-hour week by the previous records of its convention votes and by a sampling already afforded us through its past history in opposition to the law. We can form a useful and partially scientific estimate of the attitude of the Roman Catholic church on certain issues when its solidarity is fairly well known from a history of its effective control over its members, as in the case of opposition to state abolition of parochial schools in Oregon or

ment of opinions will produce mathematically interesting results, but the qualitative significance of such studies by any of the techniques yet proposed seems of slight scientific value.

[35] *Political Parties of To-Day* (New York: Harpers, 1924). See also W. Y. Elliott and E. P. Herring, *op. cit.*

elsewhere. The same thing might be said of the fundamentalism of Tennessee on the issue of public-school instruction in a biology not founded upon Genesis, although solidarity is not to be thought of as organically complete in either case.

But we could obviously not exhaust the possibilities of public opinion even when a large number of groups had expressed themselves pro and contra a particular issue. There would be defections in each group, for none is organic in the control of its members; and there are always conflicts and overlappings among groups.

Take such a case as the advisory referendum held in 1924 on the proposed Child Labor Amendment to the federal Constitution in Massachusetts. The alleged opposition of the Roman Catholic church may have been very powerful, but there is no scientific possibility of measuring it on an issue to which the church was not openly committed. Any sampling by the questionnaire method would be ridiculous. Motives would not be openly avowed even when they were clearly known. One could learn far more from a friendly Irish politician or from a Catholic priest, if either were willing to talk frankly.

An objective variable in most campaigns would quite certainly be the amount of the opposing campaign funds. Here too, however, no measurably scientific relation is to be uniformly expected, for large campaign funds are generally calculated to beat down more than the usual resistance. Another suggested method is that of polling "bosses" at a convention, national or state. This smacks more of the artistry of sampling opinion than of science, because one always wants to know which two out of three answers given are false—even if all are not—or what the true card up the sleeve is when all those laid upon the table are spurious. A "drift" might be shown, but there are too many unknown factors involved in the final outcome.

Nor is it of particular scientific value to have a poll of the nation like that conducted for presidential elections by the *Literary Digest*. The sampling is so extensive as to amount simply to a pre-election contest. On the other hand, its poll on the prohibition issue was of some value, since no election on such a scale can be legally held.

Interesting results may undoubtedly be had from such types of political problems as are shown by the studies of the effect of the direct primary upon the age and the social classes of candidates. Here the only essential is to have an area of sufficiently similar political habits which carries on without the direct primary in order to establish a control group. Similar studies in different methods of prohibition enforcement might be tried.

Generally the lack of control groups of this sort prevents the intelligent use of the method of concomitant variation. Without such controls one may attribute to the direct primary or to a particular type of prohibition enforcement factors that are part of a general economic and social change. The same thing could be said of comparisons of the effects of compulsory voting laws. Quite different political trends followed the introduction of compulsory voting in Australia and in Argentina, for example. But the political issues at the time of introduction may have had quite as much influence as the differences in national temperaments on the classes who had previously not voted.

When the utmost has been said for this sort of deterministic calculus we are left with the huge realm of political action which is motivated by choices of values. Included in this are most of the issues which attract the attention of legislative bodies when they have to form policies. While one may agree that the metaphysical theorists of the state are wrong in not considering the deterministic elements of a political equation, and that they are equally wrong in attributing to a single set of moral values universal validity in all human groups, it is certain that quite as much progress toward an adequate understanding of politics is to be made through the study of men's ethical beliefs as through the studies of geography, anthropology, history, and economics, or any of the other social sciences. Institutional studies in themselves are not enough. The knowledge of which "social myths" move man in given groups to hold a national loyalty, or a class loyalty, or a religious loyalty, is essential to any problem in the estimation of political values.

Plato was not wrong in thinking that men might be ruled by myths—"noble lies" he called them. He was wrong only in supposing that a transparent lie or a myth that could not stand criticism and ran counter to men's underlying desires—such a myth as that of his own caste commonwealth—might be imposed upon them successfully for any length of time.

It is assuredly not the business of the political scientist to attempt an ideal formulation of values. That is the proper job of the political philosopher. But just as the political philosopher will be more adequate to his normative task if he be reasonably acquainted, as was Aristotle, with historical and contemporary political institutions, so the political scientist will be less likely to drag in bad philosophy unconsciously or without acknowledging it to be philosophy at all if he knows something of political philosophy.[36] One is continually struck by the amount of half-baked

---

[36] For a more comprehensive statement of this thesis see the writer's *The Pragmatic Revolt in Politics*, esp. pp. 83–85.

philosophy current in so-called "scientific" studies in politics—values dragged in without criticism, and, what is worse, without consciousness that they are *values* and not the purest "facts."

The political scientist must necessarily employ abstraction in dealing with problems of technique, though he does so more perilously than any physical scientist—if only because the former is dealing with man, a bundle of active valuations, while the latter is dealing with materials of a known uniformity of makeup and of some rigidity of behavior. The atoms are not likely to turn on their discoverer to say, "Aha! Now that we know why we exploded we will no longer combine in that way!" Human beings, on the other hand, show a marked tendency to mistreat the scientist by using his laws to avoid his results. Peace pacts may not preserve us, but federal unions have over long periods in the past really "outlawed" war between the states composing them.

Allowing for this huge discrepancy between the two realms of phenomena, it seems probable that Hume was wrong in asserting in the essay "That Politics May Be Reduced to a Science": "So great is the force of laws, and of particular forms of government, and so little dependence have they on the humours and tempers of men, that consequences almost as general and certain may sometimes be deduced from them, as any which the mathematical sciences may afford." The context is too important. British parliamentarian forms cannot be imposed with similar results on a largely illiterate, superstitious and poverty-ridden community, such as that of the Hindus and Mohammedans in India, full as it is of caste lines and religious cleavages. Few scientists would care to accept Jeremy Bentham's *Theory of Legislation*, which held that a pleasure-and-pain psychology would "provide the elements of a moral calculus, and Legislation may thus become a mere matter of Arithmetic."[37] When it came to cases, Bentham himself, as Professor J. A. Fairlie has noted, could find nothing better to suggest than "registration of land titles, population, births, marriages, and deaths, publication of national accounts and lists of official fees, dues, and tolls, and fixing standards of quantity and quality."[38] How small a part of legislation would such a calculus exhaust!

Given for our comparisons political areas which have a cultural history of about the same general development, some useful approximations to laws may be offered. I take for an example parliamentary govern-

[37] *Op. cit.*, trans. and ed. Etienne Dumont (London: Oxford University Press, 1914), I, chap. viii, 43.

[38] J. A. Fairlie, "Political Science and Statistics," in *The Social Sciences*, ed. Ogburn and Goldenweiser, p. 291.

ment in the Great Powers of Continental Europe. One can say rather definitely that a two- or, at most, a three-party system of coherent groupings, which affords a constitutional and responsible opposition, is the best practicable means of maintaining a balance between executive stability and responsibility to representative control. In order to work, the Cabinet must have the power to dissolve the Lower House, as in the practice of most continental systems it has not. This one mechanical device would do more to force a coagulation of the multiparty coalitions into really effective opposing parties than any particular type of representation could. Yet the example of France has been consciously followed by other continental countries who prefer representation of minority opinion to stable ministerial responsibility, partly because, as is the case in France, history has multiplied the parties that represent deep-rooted social or religious cleavages which no mechanical devices can eradicate.

Some simple laws may be stated, too, from the experience of all governments. A constitutional form which is accepted by the citizens strengthens any régime. Mussolini tries to secure this element of consent by harping upon the sacred ideal (or myth) of the nation—organized into a corporative state with its syndicates for labor and its associations of employers. He knows his Aristotle on revolutions, for his master, Machiavelli, in *The Prince* at least, simply expanded Aristotle's fifth book of the *Politics*. I should offer Rousseau's declaration of this trite truth, also, as a statement of a law of politics: "The strongest is never strong enough to remain always master unless he transform obedience into duty and force into law."

One might go on with a catalogue of obvious verities like that which gave rise to the social-compact theory; simply stated, it meant only that political organization and a fixed process of making and administering law are necessary in order to avoid social anarchy. But prescriptions beyond this point must be made to fit a particular cultural context. Timbuctoo cannot be governed like the island of Britain—though its government may offer some amusing parallels to that of Chicago, if one goes behind forms to political realities.

To sum up, politics is what Aristotle declared it to be: an attempt to understand the whole complex of forces that affect government by men under institutions, laws, and organized force. But it is also an attempt, as Aristotle saw, to evaluate the ends of government. In the former relation, classificatory scientific activity and even rough laws within these classifications may be possible. In the latter relation one becomes a philosopher and deals with values in an ideal scale. It is no more possible for political science to leave out all considerations of these values than for the philosopher to abstract *in vacuo*. The political scientist must concern himself with the technique of government. He does so most fruitfully when his ends are already given by the adoption of a particular form of government. He may usefully study the behavior of groups when the groups have become highly institutionalized. Until psychologists succeed in turning man into an automaton, the political scientist can hardly abstract his political man out of the total context of human activity, remembering that man is (under any tenable philosophy) capable of foresight and of actively choosing the goods which he values.[39]

APPENDIX: COMMENTARY
BY GEORGE E. G. CATLIN

In order to make precise certain differences in point of view between Professor Elliott's entirely legitimate attitude and my own, it may be convenient to outline briefly the points of divergence.

a) The statement, "Political *science*, like history, concerns itself with a picture of concrete reality" (p. 70)[40]: On the contrary, the distinction between science and history, the writer would suggest, is fundamental. Political science is only concerned with "social happenings" as "unique events" in the sense in which economics is concerned with economic history. Political science, like every other science, makes abstractions of those aspects of reality which are relevant to its endeavor to co-ordinate phenomena. (The selection of the "political act" as the "simple fact for politics" is of more importance than the superimposed working hypothesis of a "political man.")

b) The statement, "No science can be built up when there are presuppositions of value" (p. 70): There is, it would seem, on the contrary, no objection to *supposing* that wealth is good. But the task of economic science is not to discuss this proposition taken from psychology or ethics but to work with it experimentally as a hypothesis. The distinction between the schematism of science and the ultimate discussions of metaphysics and ethics is fundamental.[41] It is not denied that "man is (under any philosophy) capable of foresight and of actively choosing the goods which he values." It is merely said that it is indifferent to the scientist

[39] [This analysis was first prepared in 1928 and was revised by the analyst in April, 1929.—EDITOR.]

[40] Professor Catlin attributes this argument to the analyst. It is, however, intended simply as one of the stock arguments against treating political phenomena as capable of scientific analysis. The same comment applies to (b). The analyst's own point of view is briefly summarized on page 86, paragraph 3.—W. Y. Elliott.

[41] See the writer's "Is Politics a Branch of Ethics?" *Monist*, July, 1927, pp. 384–403.

what goods a man may happen to value. The business of the scientist is to study those methods which a man must adopt to attain this or that end *if* he happen to choose it.

c) The statement, "Human beings use the laws of the scientist to avoid his results" (p. 90): This seems to savor of the anthropolatric dogma that to speak of "psychological laws" is self-contradictory—man having a soul is free. A man, as Professor Elliott urges, is "really" a part of society. Any human being is, therefore, subject to the laws of human nature working itself out under the conditions of a social structure which can be changed, not arbitrarily, but only effectively by certain *methods*.

d) The statement, " 'Institutionalized behavior' (discovered a *posteriori*) provides an instance of a 'deterministic calculus' " (p. 80): The determinism of politics is that of the forces which reach merely contingent equilibrium in particular (historical) conventions and institutions.

e) The statement, "The where and how of disposal becomes embarrassingly political" (p. 77): In such administrative questions the political-science element is not exhausted. It finds much profit in discussing the matter as a conflict of power, influence, support, and votes. *Non olet.*

f) The statement, "The study of the group or of fundamentalism in Tennessee or of the parliamentary system is an appropriate subject for primary study" (p. 88): The group is "real," as the atom (in chemistry or politics) is not. But groups, institutions, "particular forms of governments," are highly complex organic forms, but simple elementals. A sound methodology, it is suggested, starts with the elementals; it must distrust the obvious.

g) The statement, "The subject of study for politics is 'the institution of the state' " (p. 81): This is subsequently identified with "the attempt to understand the forces affecting government by men under institutions," a more Aristotelian use (p. 91). With the latter definition the writer partly agrees (regarding it as equivalent to "the forces affecting the control relations between men and the consequent conventions and institutions"), but the two phrases are not synonymous. The national-state group occupies in political studies a pre-eminent but not a prerogative position as against tribe, *polis*, papal system, religious order, trade-union executive, masonic order, international league, and other social forms involving primarily a co-ordination relation of men with men.

The writer especially *agrees* with Professor Elliott on the following points:

a) The case for a science of politics is on a par with that for a science of economics: If, as Professor Cassel holds, economics can assume, without discussing, values, there is no inherent reason why the same should not be true of politics. Politics must grow out of its pre-Adamite period of moral philosophy and of observations on practice. At present politics is not on the same systematic basis as economics.

b) No political scientist can afford to ignore what the political and ethical philosophers have to say about the "normative study" of society, and there can be no "absolute divorce" between ethics and any other subject whatsoever: Ethical indifferentism in the study of means does not imply moral callousness. But, although the motive for surgery may be philanthropy, a sincere contemplation of the healthy and good does not exempt the surgeon from the study of physiology.

c) "Quite as much progress toward an adequate understanding of politics is to be made through the study of ethics as through the study of geography, anthropology, history, and economics, or for that matter any of the other social sciences" (p. 89): A study of values is indubitably quite as valuable as a study of social forces and controls.

d) No satisfactory standard of measurement has, as yet, been worked out for such political phenomena as a dictatorial régime, although beyond question, this régime does depend upon a quantity of support: This admission, however, does not mean that we may overlook the crucial importance of discovering some unit of measurement in politics, as in economics and in the mechanical and electrical sciences. And, unsatisfactory though the unit of support arbitrarily named the "vote" (on any control issue) may be, it will be remembered that coinage supplies equally arbitrary units, and that money measurements break down in time of violent revolution or in an agricultural or a communistic economy. The unit here taken, it will be observed, is not the "person" as a psychological complex but the "unit of support," the will which behaves either to support, to oppose, or to remain passive.[42] The gender of this will may perhaps become a matter of speculation for political philosophers; it is indifferent to scientists. All beings able to enter into the control relationship as active wills are "political beings," and their ability is to be presumed from their behavior.

e) In political science, "rough laws" are possible: The writer would, however, prefer to call these laws "incompletely understood, deduced, and demonstrated" rather than "rough." There are no fringes of caprice in a law *quâ* law.

[42] By "will" is here meant a center of energies of measurable persistency displayed in behavior, not interpreted in terms of the energy of another. Whether philosophically it would not be better, as Professor Dewey thinks, to stop talking about will and to keep in mind the possibility of interpretation always in terms of extra-mental stimulus is a problem of fundamentals outside our province.

ANALYSIS 4

MARY RICHMOND'S FORMULATION OF A NEW SCIENCE[1]

By PHILIP KLEIN
New York School of Social Work

While *Social Diagnosis* is undoubtedly the outstanding written contribution thus far made by social work to the social sciences, it does not treat of the entire field of the former, but only of that division generally termed *social case work*. Moreover, the book limits itself still further to a part of social case work designated as social diagnosis. Only so much reference is made to social treatment, scientific recording, administrative technique, and research, as is necessary for orientation. However, the author sets forth or assumes a relation between social case work and the social sciences, which may be extended to the entire field of social work.[2] This relation requires some elaboration before a detailed examination of the book is attempted.

THE ANALOGY TO MEDICINE

The title of the volume summarizes the major idea in the author's thesis, namely, that social diagnosis in social case work[3] corresponds in nature and importance to medical diagnosis in the work of the physician. The word *diagnosis* is clearly borrowed from medicine: At first implicit, this parallel becomes in the course of the treatise decidedly explicit and undoubtedly intentional, even though the author does not pursue to the end its full implications. Moreover, there emerges from this parallel a more fundamental similarity, that serves to give an important orientation to social case work (and to all social work) in relation to the entire field of social science.[4]

[1] Mary E. Richmond, *Social Diagnosis* (New York: Russell Sage Foundation, 1917).

[2] The validity of *Social Diagnosis* as a partial formulation of principles of social case work has provided considerable stimulus for similar formulations in the other fields of social work, and upon these formulations work has been done in recent years.

[3] For the reader who is unfamiliar with the concept of social case work as here used, an extract from a statement by Porter R. Lee, summarizing its essentials, follows this analysis as an appendix.

[4] The concept of this underlying similarity, while nowhere expounded by Miss Richmond herself, is believed by the analyst to be not only in conformity with her ideas but to pervade them thoroughly and to describe the point of view of social

95

Strictly speaking, the existence of a separate *medical science* may be denied. Recognition as sciences may be given biology, physiology, anatomy, chemistry, physics, bacteriology, electrodynamics, histology, psychology, etc. Medicine may be regarded as merely drawing upon these constituent sciences for content. Only pathology and therapeutics might be regarded as strictly medical subjects and even these only as a scheme or system of special relations among the constituent sciences of biology, chemistry, etc. This view, however, overlooks the essential fact in medicine—its focus in the concern with *health*. This focus gives the conglomerate of constituent sciences a distinct and separate entity, and a point of view from which otherwise irrelevant phenomena become correlated and systematized. From this point of view, then, medicine is a system of knowledge of which the immediate body consists primarily of symptomatology and therapeutics, these depending upon, and consisting of, the more primary sciences enumerated in part above, and providing the means by which the art of the physician may be practiced for the purpose of maintaining or re-establishing the health of the human body.

Miss Richmond realizes that social case work, as well as all social work, is based on the findings of such social sciences as sociology, psychology, economics, ethnology, political science, law, pedagogy, and anthropology, to mention the most important only, and also on the unique composite sister-science of medicine. A new organization of these sciences is effected when focused on the need of dealing with individuals or groups of individuals who have become unable to maintain the burden of self-maintenance in their social environment. The author proceeds on the assumption that this new organization has already become sufficiently distinct, and sufficiently tested and established in practice, to be described, and for generalizations to be formulated. Her book crystallizes some of the material of a potentially separate science (and an already separate art) into actual recorded science.

One other generalization is pertinent to Miss Richmond's point of view and to the suggested parallel with medicine. In common usage, the word *science* is employed somewhat loosely. Two other terms are preferable: *scientific method* and *sciences*. For our purposes it is sufficient to regard *scientific method* as consisting, first, of an approximation to strict logic in our processes of thought—faulty as logic itself must inevitably be in view of the unattainable perfect major premise. Secondly, it consists of continuous strict mental discipline, which does not allow an unproved

---

workers who accept *Social Diagnosis* as at least a partial expression of their philosophy and as a guide for practice.

hypothesis to become an axiom or a conclusion, and holds even axioms and conclusions as somewhat tentative or, in a sense, as a higher order of hypotheses. *Sciences* are arbitrary divisions of human knowledge, possessing distinctness to the degree imposed by technical methods, subject matter, or utility. Whether this or that subject is a science and one of the sciences is, after all, determined arbitrarily and sanctioned only by common usage. Medicine *has* been so sanctioned as a separate science, and has made ample returns for that sanction by the progress in experiment, research, and service which it has made as a distinct discipline.

The eventual sanction for social work as a separate science will probably be given by common usage on the same conditions of showing progress in its own field.

THE CONTRIBUTION OF SOCIAL CASE WORK TO THE SOCIAL SCIENCES

While the chief task of *Social Diagnosis* is a detailed exposition of the process represented by the title, it would be a mistake to overlook the significance of Miss Richmond's contribution for general sociology and for the whole family of social sciences. Here again we must keep to the implications of her thesis rather than to clearly stated propositions— implications that are compelling and spread over almost every page of the volume. To state it briefly, Miss Richmond, representing the accumulated wisdom and practice of nearly a half-century of labor by social caseworkers, discarded the concept of the "poor" as one of economic connotation. In its place steps the "client," conceived as a person (or family) whose character, physical condition, or circumstances, or a combination of these, have made him incapable of full self-maintenance in his social setting. The problem, then, is one of character and environment; or more accurately it is psychological, physical, and sociological. The economic distress of the client is only one of the possible symptoms of his inadequacy though, admittedly, a pregnant one. In a less enlightened era it may have been an overshadowing symptom, perhaps the only one seen by the social agency; it may have been mistaken for the entire disease and its treatment attempted in the same category—by economic aid. This aid may have been charity—private, church, or fraternal; or it may have been public relief. At any rate, it was considered aid to the *poor*— economic readjustment to the economically unadjusted. The poor were thus conceptually distinct from the sick, the delinquent, the unemployed, and from the victims of domestic infelicity, parental neglect, or overindulgence; the wards of charitable agencies were regarded as distinct from those of hospital, court, sanatorium, and prison.

In Miss Richmond's mind this distinction disappears. By way of corollary, the distinctions between the clients of other agencies, such as courts and hospitals, also disappear or at least become insignificant. There remains the "client," unable for one reason or another to take care of himself, who appeals to one or another of the community's agencies for aid. The aid then given is called "case work," and social diagnosis is its essential first step. The author puts it this way:

> When a human being, whatever his economic status, develops some marked form of social difficulty and social need, what do we have to know about him and about his difficulty (or more often difficulties) before we can arrive at a way of meeting his need? The problem may be one of childhood or old age, of sickness, of exploitation, or of wasted opportunity, but insofar as it concerns some one individual in his social relationships it is not alien to social work as here understood. The effort to get the essential facts bearing upon a man's social difficulties has commonly been called "an investigation," but the term here adopted as a substitute—social diagnosis—has the advantage that from the first step it fixes the mind of the case-worker upon the end in view [p. 26].

In this paragraph the author is seen not only to disregard distinctions between *poverty* and other "social difficulties" as she calls them but even to assume that the need for case work appears *without regard to the economic* status of the individual. This new way of looking at those members of society that have been regarded during the entire history of our civilization as merely the economic burden of the community; the perspective by which they are brought into co-ordinate relationship in the social panorama with the sick, the delinquent, and with children; the new analysis of their difficulties in terms of psychological, physical, and sociological maladjustments and of possibilities of rehabilitation in the same terms—these together form a contribution of immeasurable consequence to the social sciences, and they are formulated comprehensively for the first time by Miss Richmond.

This conceptual change took on importance when it was carried over into the deliberate procedure of social case work; and it has given the latter, as it is known today, its characteristic form. To describe in detail the differences in procedure between that based on the old concepts and that which emerged from the new would require too much space. A brief but significant illustration may be found, however, in the "social history." This is now considered an essential tool in all case work, and practically no counterpart is found in its historical precursors. While a medical social worker or an attaché of the juvenile court may record additional data required by the special interests or legal demands of his agency, the body of information suggested by the sample outline reproduced here is considered essential by all case-workers. The following outline of the contents of the social history is quoted from a report prepared jointly by representatives of a number of separate fields of social case work:[5]

1. History

    Dates and places of births, marriages, deaths of individual members of family group, causes of death

    Date of coming to U.S., previous and present residences; citizenship; legal settlement

    Education: school grades reached; special training

    Social service exchange data; records of other agencies

    Court records

    Health records: statements from physicians, clinics, hospitals which have known any of group as to physical or mental illness or handicaps

    Developmental history, age of dentition, etc., of members of family

    Background

        family

        racial (national)

        cultural

        educational—school records past and present

        religious or church affiliation

        industrial—work records past and present

        recreation and special interests

    Analysis of social difficulties

    Previous plans of treatment

    Response to treatment activities

2. Current Personal Data

    Marital status

    Social status

    Income: sources

    Budget

    Debts

    Resources

    Usual occupation and weekly wage

    Relationships:

        within family group—husband and wife, parents and children to each other

        with relatives

        with employers and fellow workers

        with friends and neighbors

        with teachers and fellow pupils

[5] *Social Case Work, Generic and Specific: An Outline.* The Report of the Milford Conference. Vol. II of series, "Studies in the Practice of Social Work" (New York: American Association of Social Workers, 1929).

Radical changes in reaction to environment

Personality data:

habits of individual in day-to-day living, eating, sleeping, drinking, etc.

re: health

work

play

education

sex

religious observances

attitudes of individual

evidences of lack of social responsibility

evidences of lack of individual responsibility

ambitions

choice of companions

appearance

interests

abilities; disabilities

likes; dislikes

3. Current Environmental Data

Housing; number of rooms, rent; condition of house, sleeping conditions;
ventilation, light; cleanliness, etc.; condition of neighborhood

Community facilities or lacks

Church

Place of work, trade or occupation

School

Groupal relationships: clubs, labor unions, fraternal and other groups

Racial or national characteristics of neighborhood and conflicts

Standing in the community

Reversals in financial status

Radical changes in general environment

Significant changes in neighborhood or location

Standards of living

manners

general atmosphere

general attitudes of members of family toward one another

relatives—attitude toward family or individual

attitude toward discipline

presence or lack of family group activities

interest in housekeeping and home standards

Some noteworthy features suggested by the outline are: First, the range
of information covered as relevant and necessary; second, the fact that
institutions as varied in history and in stated purposes as family welfare

agencies, hospitals, and courts consider the same information as essential. Especially interesting is a comparison of the modern procedure indicated by the "social history" with that of the pre-case-work days of the same types of institutions. For example, the lineal ancestor of the family agency was the relief society, which is still represented among us by some institutional "contemporary ancestors", especially among the municipal or the county poor-relief bodies. The typical case records of some of these would, aside from names and addresses, be devoted largely to questions of legal residence and settlement, persons legally responsible for support, and similar matters chiefly concerning the limitations of material assistance. The latter—given in kind as often as in cash—was frequently attuned to the lowest practicable subsistence level. As to the use of the social history in medical social work there is no ancestor for comparison. The very existence of social case work in hospitals and dispensaries is a matter of about two decades. Or if we turn to the juvenile court, we find the social history to be an essential aspect of a procedure that tends to lift the case almost clear of former procedural technicalities. The recorded data bear only a skeletal resemblance to the court docket with its references centered about guilt or innocence, conviction or acquittal.

It should be clear, of course, that the author's material is derived in a setting of *modern conditions* of *Western civilization* in *pacific society.* Wars, famines, overwhelming disasters produce a social setting in which mass destruction demands mass handling; presumably, social diagnosis and social case work as a whole are applicable and have validity to the degree that the mass aspect disappears and individualization becomes possible. For the same reason those social imperfections that demand large educational campaigns or legislation are of interest to, but not directly part of, the author's discussion. She takes for granted, further, an economic sufficiency for the community as a whole, or what used to be called "a social surplus." Two other conditions or facts are predicated: one the author refers to as "power to get things done," that is, economic and institutional facilities, backed by a willing public opinion; the other, a specialized practitioner—the social worker. The separate existence of social work as a discipline or a science or even as a thesis has become possible, and can be understood only in connection with the social worker as its practitioner, just as medical science has become an entity only as the thing practiced by the physician. The volume is addressed first to social workers, for whom it essays "to make some advance toward a professional standard" (p. 26).

"SOCIAL DIAGNOSIS" IN DETAIL

The essential elements of the author's thesis built upon the considerations just discussed may' be stated in a brief paragraph:

Social case work is being practiced in the typical American community of our day under many auspices in apparently distinct fields and serves such seemingly different types as the widow, the paralytic, the neglected child, the unemployed, the tuberculous. Common to all these "types" is the fact that they are psychologically, physically, or socially unadjusted, and the purpose of social case work is to effect an adjustment. There is a common knowledge and a common procedure in case work for all types of clients. Complete and expert diagnosis is absolutely necessary for intelligent treatment.

The processes which lead up to social diagnosis and thence to the shaping of a plan of social treatment may be divided into—
  the collection of evidence and
  the drawing of inferences therefrom.[6]

A. COLLECTION OF EVIDENCE

The lion's share of the book is claimed by this topic. Attention will be directed here to four distinct phases of the subject, but these are not dealt with by Miss Richmond in strictly chronological order, nor is the material forced too rigidly into a corresponding framework. These phases are: (1) the nature of evidence; (2) the processes of obtaining evidence; (3) sources of evidence; (4) variations or special conditions determining the selection of evidence.

1. *The nature of evidence.*—The author first establishes the fundamental difference between social evidence and evidence in the legalistic sense. Inasmuch as the nature of any useful evidence is determined by the purpose for which it is used, social evidence for case work consists "of all facts as to personal or family history which taken together indicate the nature of a given client's social difficulties and the means to their solution." Cumulative rather than probative values are pertinent, and the issues are more complex than those in which legal evidence is sufficient or necessary. While, however, more general and circumstantial evidence is sought and admitted, each item of evidence must nevertheless be tested and weighed with the greatest rigidity and circumspection, for the chances of cumulative error increase with the multiplicity and the cumulative nature of the evidence.

Evidence is classified as *real* where "the very fact at issue is presented

⁶ P. 28.

to our senses"; *testimonial,* consisting of "assertions of human beings"; and *circumstantial,* which is everything else. In social case work by far the greatest amount of evidence comes from testimony. The first determinant of its validity is the *competence of witnesses;* the second is possibility of *bias of witnesses.* The emphasis upon all phases of the nature of evidence and the dangers attendant upon its collection is of fundamental importance in the author's conception of the practice of social diagnosis as a basis of treatment. The competence of the social case-worker to judge when facts obtained from various related fields of science are valid evidence is largely dependent upon his acquaintance with those fields. The special types of evidence to be sought from each are considered in some detail.

2. *Processes of obtaining evidence.*[7]—The *first interview* with the client is regarded as the most important single process in making the social diagnosis. The process of interviewing as a whole is the major means of obtaining testimonial evidence. The author also considers letter-writing, the use of documents, blank forms, telegraph, and telephone with respect to their technical merits and difficulties.

3. *Sources of evidence.*—The bulk of the book is devoted to a detailed discussion of the sources of social evidence; the principles governing the choice of sources; and methods of procedure. Space forbids more than a rough listing of those "sources": the family group, relatives, medical sources, schools, employers, documents, neighborhood sources, social agencies, public officials, fraternal orders, and business sources. Seven tentative principles are enumerated as governing the selection of possible sources. These deserve at least a brief summary:

First: Strike out boldly for history, and avoid . . . . those references whose point of view is most like our own. [Consult] the people who knew our client at his best, if he ever had a best. . . . .

[7] In the author's scheme of presentation, "Processes Leading to Diagnosis," constituting Part II of the volume, includes divisions that are here designated as the *processes of obtaining evidence* and as the *sources of evidence.* Developments in the theory and practice of social case work that have taken place since the publication of *Social Diagnosis* justify this slight divergence in presentation, which at any rate does no violence to Miss Richmond's thesis. The author's plan of organization depends on what she lists as the processes (different in some ways from what would now be listed by her successors) as follows:

"(1) The first full interview with a client.
(2) The early contacts with his immediate family.
(3) The search for further insight and for sources of needed co-operation outside his immediate family.
(4) The careful weighing in their relation to one another of the separate items of evidence thus gathered and their interpretation" (p. 103).

Second: Seek first those sources that are likely to be rich in history only and seek later those most likely to be rich also in co-operation.

Third: Seek out the witnesses who have been able to make first-hand observations in preference to those whose information is at second-hand.

Fourth: Bear in mind . . . . [to] recognize the special value of supplementary clues—of clues, that is, to sources of information not revealed in the first interview or in subsequent ones with the family group. . . . .

Fifth: See someone belonging to each of the groups able to view the client and the family from a different angle.

Sixth: Distinguish groups all of whose members are likely to see eye to eye, and in which consultation with one source may possibly suffice, from those in which there is likely to be diverse experience within the group.

Seventh: Recognize in contradictory evidence and in a total of evidence that reveals no plan of action, the need of further inquiry [pp. 170–76].

4. *Variations and special conditions.*—The chapters in Part III deal with variations in the nature and in the proportion of different kinds of evidence required by the case-worker when the client exhibits certain well-recognized types of problems. These problems bring into play to a more than usual degree the subject matter of special fields of science. Against a background of "what is true of everybody" and "of any family" the author gathers together the outline of special facts that may be true of a particular individual family exhibiting a special social difficulty. These tend to border upon other fields of knowledge. The immigrant family, desertion and widowhood, the neglected child, the unmarried mother, the blind, the homeless man, the inebriate, the insane, and the feeble-minded are each dealt with in an organized outline. This presents the pertinent special aspects of the problems considered, in the form of questions, which are not, however, truly questions, but guides to orientation in which the interrogatory form is merely a technical convenience.

B. DRAWING OF INFERENCES

Critically considered, the discussion of evidence as roughly classified in the foregoing four divisions constitutes the entire body of Miss Richmond's book. The collection of evidence and its interpretation by the drawing of inferences are so intimately tied up together, and the latter is so involved in the technique of the former, that the author deems it unnecessary to give the drawing of inferences an extended separate treatment. There is indeed one early chapter devoted to "Inference" as part of the discussion on social evidence, and a later chapter on "Comparison and Interpretation," but these are rather summary in their presentation, even though qualitatively in keeping with the rest of the volume. Particularly the pages dealing with the diagnostic summary give point and direction to the study.[8]

THE AUTHOR'S METHOD OF RESEARCH

No new methodological departure of importance to the social sciences has been made by Miss Richmond.[9] There is, however, a thoroughness in the collecting and the testing of material, evidence of intellectual power, breadth of knowledge, and a cultural comprehensiveness that are almost unique in a specialized study. For Part I, dealing with theoretical considerations chiefly in the fields of logic, law, and psychology, the author needed only the library. For Part II, treating mainly of the collection and interpretation of evidence, the long experience of the author herself contributed a large part of the material. Insomuch, however, as her own experience was chiefly in but one of the four or five larger subdivisions of case work, the author, in thorough appreciation of the meaning of the *scientific method,* sought to supplement and test the data of her direct experience by the following methods:

a) "Short papers" had, under the direction of Mr. Francis McLean, been prepared by a number of social case-workers, prior to the writing of *Social Diagnosis* "describing informally their methods and experiences in taking the step which, in their work, preceded the development of a plan of treatment. This group was added to later, ... on such subjects for instance as present neighborhood sources of information . . . . methods of conducting a first interview, etc. . . . ." The author made extended use of these papers which represented first-hand experience of many competent workers.

b) Two experienced social case-workers were employed—one in a family agency and one in a medical social work agency—to study case records in five different cities for one year. These records were used in the same way as the material obtained from the author's direct experience.

c) A number of records were printed informally and used by several different persons teaching case work in schools of social work. Criticisms

[8] Besides case work, other divisions of social work are also practiced with the aid of recognized techniques and by a professional group of practitioners but are not yet formulated to the same degree as social diagnosis; their generalizations are not yet accepted so commonly and the advantages of crystallization into part of a recognized science are therefore relatively lacking. These advantages are, for example, time-saving, transmissibility of knowledge and technique, and comparability of results.

[9] This statement depends, of course, upon the interpretation of the meaning of method held by Dr. Klein. It could, perhaps, be modified in the light of the wider interpretation adopted for the purpose of organizing the present collection of analyses as a whole. [Cf. the Introduction, pp. 7–10.—EDITOR.]

and comments based upon these in and out of the schoolroom were collected.

d) Through the co-operation of fifty-six social agencies in three cities, the "outside sources" of evidence were listed for fifty cases in each. These were carefully analyzed and statistical deductions utilized.

The "questionnaire" method used in Part III on "Variations in the Processes" was based on suggestions from many specialists in the fields covered, but was worked over in staffs and groups before adopted in the form finally used in the book. Nothing in these is striking but the evident thoroughness and conscientiousness and the pervading brilliance and wisdom of the author. It will be noted also that little of historical setting is included in the volume—barely enough to serve as introduction and to indicate a general sequence and a relation to continental progress in the same field. The author had set a self-imposed limit to the task and adhered to it throughout.

SUMMARY

Social Diagnosis is a descriptive study of that portion of the field of social work known as social case work. Social diagnosis is regarded by the author as analogous in social case work to the medical diagnosis in the work of the physician. The analogy with medicine, which is employed throughout the volume, is rooted in the implication that the same relationship exists between medical science and its constituent physical sciences as exists between social work and the social sciences, and the analogy is supported by the parallel between the task of the medical practitioner in the field of medicine and the social worker in his field of activity. The author takes pains to assure the representativeness of her selection of illustrations in the exposition of her thesis. Much of the material in the volume though applied strictly to social diagnosis appears to be intended to have a wider significance as representative of the entire field of social work. The specific contribution of the author to the social sciences is her clear acceptance of the concept of an individual or group of individuals suffering from the disability of social maladjustment. This replaces the older concepts, such as that of the "poor" as a term of economic connotation, and of the "sick," "delinquent," etc., as denoting groups essentially different from each other and presenting different social problems. As a corollary of this conceptual basis, the treatment proposed and described for all persons suffering from a social disability is individualized case work, calling upon a common procedure of which social diagnosis is a major part, and which is supplemented by movements for social reform by legislation, education, and administrative improvement.

APPENDIX: THE CONCEPT OF SOCIAL CASE WORK

The following statement is taken from an Introduction by Porter R. Lee to *Vocational Aspects of Medical Social Work*, a study published by the American Association of Social Workers. It serves to summarize the concept of social case work as used in the foregoing analysis, and may be regarded as a logical extension of footnote 3.

"Social case work deals with human beings who have found difficulty in the conditions of social life in making their way to acceptable organization of existence. The standards of our civilization do not demand that a man be completely self-sufficient. They demand only that he be able to secure for himself or his family the combination of opportunities, services, and expert advice with whose assistance he can work out what will be for him an acceptable organization of existence. When he succeeds in doing so, he is a self-maintaining individual. Self-maintenance is the product of a reasonably adequate human equipment adjusting itself to a reasonably favorable environment. There is no formula by which one can determine either a reasonably adequate human equipment or a reasonably favorable environment. Self-maintenance does not depend upon any such formula. Those who fail in self-maintenance present all degrees of human equipment and they are living in all varieties of social environment. Failure means nothing except that for a particular combination of circumstances representing an environment a particular human equipment is inadequate, or that for a particular human equipment a particular combination of environmental circumstances is unfavorable.

"The chief objective of social case work is to assist individuals who need such service to achieve what may be for them as complete a measure of self-maintenance as possible. This objective might be itemized as an attempt to develop within the individual his fullest capacity for self-maintenance and at the same time to assist him in establishing for himself an environment which will be as favorable as may be to his powers and limitations.

"Failure in self-maintenance presents itself in many forms. One may be unequal to the task of earning a living, one may be unequal to his responsibilities as a parent, student, employer, employee, or teacher. One may be incapacitated through sickness, helpless through lack of adult supervision, unable to withstand temptation, injuriously affected by the ordinary experiences of life. Failure does not necessarily imply fault. A large part of social case work is concerned with children who are not receiving the kind of care that for them is necessary to self-maintenance, as the term is used here, and to which the present standards of society entitle them. If any one or a combination of these and other factors prevent one from achieving an acceptable adjustment to life and its demands, there may be evidence of a greater or less degree of self-maintenance. The organizations through which social case work is carried on deal with human beings presenting problems such as these or others like them. . . . .

"Social case work, in other words, has become both a well-established form of expert service to human beings who have failed in the task of self-maintenance, and an important ally of other services, such as medicine, education, and the administration of justice which also deal with these human difficulties from different points of view. . . . .

"With reference to the problem of self-maintenance, social case work has developed a substantial body of knowledge and a wide range of methods and procedures for putting it into effect in individual cases. Neither this knowledge nor those procedures are in the aggregate as substantial as the knowledge or the procedures used by some of the older professions. They are, however, increasing both in substance and in the precision with which they can be used. . . . .

"It is possible to describe the processes of social case work as covering the assembling of data, diagnosis, and treatment. Each of these phases calls for a considerable degree of skill and the use of a wide range of specialized knowledge. In applying this procedure, every case worker finds himself using certain processes in which, if he is to achieve his professional objectives, he must develop a considerable degree of skill. Among these may be mentioned interviewing, diagnosis—which is the interpretation of assembled data in terms that make effective treatment possible—leadership as the capacity to establish and maintain a helpful, purposeful relationship with another person, and the organization, through an effective plan, of several different forms of service" (pp. 7–11).

STRUCTURAL PSYCHOLOGY AND THE PSYCHOLOGY OF *GESTALT:* THE METHODS OF E. B. TITCHENER COMPARED WITH THOSE OF K. KOFFKA, W. KÖHLER AND M. WERTHEIMER

By R. M. OGDEN
Cornell University

The structural psychology of the late E. B. Titchener and the psychology of *Gestalt* which has been developed by Koffka, Köhler, and Wertheimer offer as striking a contrast as one can readily imagine. While each is an outgrowth of German experimental psychology, the one follows the tradition of Wilhelm Wundt, while the other is more in line with the teachings of Wundt's rival, Franz Brentano.

Titchener, who was a pupil of Wundt, confined himself to the development of the experimental, observational side of Wundt's teaching. He made little or no use of the functional and integrative aspects of Wundt's doctrine. Neither did he undertake to discover the underlying physiology of sense organs and the nervous system, but was content to refer these important problems to the biologist. For Titchener, the field of psychology was limited to those phenomena of experience which are dependent upon the nervous system, and the business of the psychologist was to observe and describe these phenomena under experimentally controlled conditions. A psychological "fact" is any phenomenon, thus determined, which has been described. Experimental control means a definite experimental setting which permits a variation of the phenomenon with a corresponding variation of its conditions. Description requires an appropriate set of dimensional categories in accordance with which these variations can be recorded.

What has come to be known as "structural" psychology is essentially a method of analyzing "conscious" phenomena as they occur under experimental conditions. According to Titchener, as psychologists we need not concern ourselves with the physiological correlates of these conscious processes beyond their recognition; we have no concern with their value for the "mind in use"; and we need be at no special pains to establish such a continuity of phenomena from one event to another as a complete parallel of psychological with neurological processes would require. In a word, "structural" psychology is not "functional." It does nothing; it promotes nothing; it merely ascertains what is factual or existential in experience as determined by a nervous system. Other disciplines will treat of experience in other ways: trace its course from one thing to another, examine these things as physical beings and agencies, evaluate them as better or worse.

In order to define psychology as a science, one must first inquire what science is. Titchener has raised and answered this question in a posthumous work.[1] Unfortunately, this small portion of a large work which he had projected lay complete and untouched for nearly ten years prior to the author's death. Consequently, no attention could be paid to more recent developments in psychological theory, and no mention is made of *Gestalt* psychology, with which this analysis is also concerned.

In placing psychology as one of the three major sciences, the other two being physics and biology, Titchener approaches his problem as a positivist.[2] The man of science, he tells us, is a disinterested observer who

reads out all prior meaning, all interpretation, from the objects of his enquiry, and considers them for their sake, in their right, as they are. The data of science are in this sense meaningless; they are stripped of meaning, bare existences. It is true that they at once acquire a new meaning, a meaning for science; but this new meaning is, precisely, that they shall henceforth remain without meaning in the old sense, that their meaning shall be their mode of natural existence, their constitutional manner of being. If science is curiosity, therefore, it is the curiosity which pierces the overlay of interpretation to arrive at sheer existence; if it is love of truth, then truth is the face its objects wear to themselves and their kind and the man who identifies himself with them, and science seeks to know that face; if it is a passion for facts, then facts are the materials of a world scoured clean of belief and inference and all such evaluative accretion, and science aims to explore this world. The instinctive tendency of the scientific man is toward the existential substrate that appears when use and purpose—cosmic significance, artistic value, social utility, personal reference—have been removed.

---

[1] *Systematic Psychology: Prolegomena* (New York: Macmillan Co., 1929). Certain parts of this book were published in *American Journal of Psychology:* "Brentano and Wundt: Empirical and Experimental Psychology," *ibid.*, XXXII (1921), 108 ff.; "Functional Psychology and the Psychology of Act. I," *ibid.*, 519 ff.; Functional Psychology and the Psychology of Act. II," *ibid.*, XXXIII (1922), 43 ff. Cf. also in this connection H. P. Weld, *Psychology as Science* (New York: H. Holt & Co., 1928), esp. chaps. i–iv.

[2] I do not mean that Titchener committed himself to a definite theory of knowledge, but merely that he approached science by way of experience.

He responds positively to the bare "what" of things; he responds negatively to any further demand for interest or appreciation.[3]

In this fine passage Titchener draws a sharp line of demarcation between science and its applications—the "technologies," as he was wont to call them. He proceeds then to define science, both by point of view and by subject matter. The method of science is observation, for which, we are told, there is an older meaning of *observance* expressing the positive side of the scientific attitude. "The scientific enquirer wants to know how the facts, if they could see, would look to one another; he is not the indifferent detective, but the sympathetic witness; observation, like every first-hand acquaintance, is a sort of participation."[4] Observation leads to a description of facts, and "it is universally agreed . . . . that the first problem of science is analysis."[5] "The typical business of science, therefore, appears in the forms of elementary analysis, relational analysis and relational synthesis, classification, and the formulation of natural laws. Or we may say, still more briefly, that the man of science analyzes with a view to some later synthesis."[6]

We now come to the definition of the three major sciences:

Psychology is the science of existential experience regarded as functionally or logically dependent upon the nervous system (or its biological equivalent); biology is the science of existential experience regarded as functionally or logically dependent upon the physical environment; and physics (including chemistry and physical chemistry) is the science of existential experience regarded as functionally or logically interdependent.[7]

These are the three scientific points of view. But the things viewed are also capable of definition. The subject matter of psychology, since it correlates with a nervous system, is formally *systemic;* materially, it is *sensory* (qualitative). The subject matter of biology, since it deals with the organism, is formally *individuate;* materially, it is *behavioral.* The subject matter of physics, since it knows no bounds, is formally *universal;* materially, it is *energetic.*

These definitions show how completely Titchener accepted as his premise the radical empiricism of the positivist. Science is separated both from the logical method which it employs and from the practical world of everyday life. Thus the "existential" is limited to the experience of the man of science. Not only is there no place in science for "mind in use," but there appears to be, properly speaking, no place for a "social"

[3] *Systematic Psychology*, pp. 32–33.
[4] *Ibid.*, p. 39.   [6] *Ibid.*, pp. 61–62.
[5] *Ibid.*, p. 85.   [7] *Ibid.*, p. 142.

science. With reference to *behaviorism,* which was beginning to make its appearance at the time Titchener wrote, it is worthy of note that the attack of this discipline leaves Titchener's system quite untouched.[8] He has remarked in a footnote to his book, "logically . . . . a strict behaviorism can have no quarrel with an existential psychology, since there is no point of contact between the two disciplines." Although the behaviorist may not have realized it, this separation of "the two disciplines" as being the one a "science" and the other a "technology" is perhaps more deeply responsible for the revolt against "structural" psychology than the introspective method which it employs. According to positivism, experience furnishes the only data of science, whether physical, biological, or psychological. Consequently, there is nothing peculiar about introspection. It is merely a name given to the observation of that kind of experience which is dependent upon a nervous system.

The real force of the behaviorist's revolt is directed against the relegation of the study of individual and group behavior to the unscientific realm of technology. It is true, according to Titchener, that the material side of biology is "behavioral"; but it is the experience of "the man of science" who observes the individuate, organic processes that furnishes data for a scientific biology, and not the organic processes themselves. In other words, the behaviorist aims to be realistic in his study of the whole organism, to concern himself with the real processes of the total organism and not with the experiences that depend upon these processes. This concern is warrantable, as Titchener admits; but, if it is to be scientific, it must fall within the field of biology; otherwise it becomes a technology "which is always concerned to do something, to accomplish some practical end."

Into this controversy the *Gestalt* hypothesis introduces a revolutionary concept. Titchener's system derives from the teachings of Wundt, the philosophical postulates of which are positivistic, and in Wundt's hands idealistic. While it is less easy to trace the genesis of the *Gestalt* hypothesis, there can be no doubt of its affiliation with the psychology of Wundt's great rival, Brentano, whose postulates were those of Aristotelian realism.

Although in his book Titchener makes no reference to *Gestalt* psychology, he devotes a lengthy argument to the psychology of Brentano and his immediate followers. This psychology, which Titchener characterizes as the psychology of act, is, in brief, the psychology of *experiencing,* as

[8] Cf. E. B. Titchener, "On 'Psychology as the Behaviorist Views It,'" *Proceedings of the American Philosophical Society,* LIII (1914), 1 ff.

contrasted with the Wundtian notion of observed experience. It is not positivistic, but intentional. Experience always refers to something else: primarily, to an object or *real*; though, secondarily, one experience may refer to another. In this, rather than in the Wundtian tradition, three pupils of Stumpf—men who had also been influenced by Külpe, von Ehrenfels, and the Austrian school of psychology—have worked out the principles of *Gestalt* psychology. But the changes they have wrought in the empiricism of Brentano are more radical than any of those to which Titchener gave his meticulous consideration.

The system of *Gestalt* psychology, which is in process of development, is realistic; but it avoids the distinctions of the act psychologies between *experiencer, experiencing,* and *experienced.* Instead, the concept of *Gestalt* embraces all three. This means that one need not take into account either "the man of science" or the experiencing self. There are no "functions" of experience to be classified as Stumpf classifies them, and there are no "contents," elementary or complex, which a psychologist or any other scientist is called upon to discover, enumerate, or describe. Since, according to the *Gestalt* hypothesis, form and not content is the essential characteristic of the existential world, it is the business of science to describe and to state the conditions under which the events of life, and of the world at large, *take shape.*

The *Gestalt* is a definite structure; but it exists, not as a "content," strictly in its own right, but as a *figure* on a *ground.* The figure-ground relationship is very important, for whenever we treat of a figure as though it were completely self-contained, we come to erroneous conclusions. We put too high a premium on logical definition when we suppose that things exist as separate entities that remain constant throughout a manifold of combinations and recombinations into which they may enter. Instead of this "constancy hypothesis" the figure-ground relation demands that the conditions of the "ground" shall participate in the formation of the "figure," and that the *Struktur* of the "figure" shall, in turn, influence the "ground" upon which the "figure" appears.

As previously stated, the *Gestalt* is more in line with Brentano than with Wundt, for it is realistic rather than idealistic; and it is both functional and intentional within the realm of actuality. *Gestalt* psychology seems, however, to escape the just criticism to which Titchener has subjected the act psychologies by its refusal to make any fundamental distinction between act and content. Titchener has remarked that Brentano "made the Aristotelian method his pattern of scientific procedure," and *Gestalt* psychology has, no doubt, adopted a similar method. But it is possible that the *Gestalt* hypothesis will eventuate in a theory which is revolutionary even with respect to its Aristotelian origin. While Aristotle makes form "the essence or very nature of each thing," he also refers to *substance* as that which is formed. Brentano's psychology consists of acts or functions which refer to substances, while *Gestalten*, as we have pointed out, embrace both the acts and the things to which they refer. Furthermore, the dynamic events of changing *Gestalten* require no "mental acts" for their definition or existence. Consequently, no gap appears between the experiencing subject and the object of his experience.

What else may exist in this universe, apart from *Gestalten*, has not yet been precisely stated. But surely the "ground" exists as well as the "figure" which emerges from it; and if *Gestalten* are not merely self-inclosing forms, but also figure-ground patterns, this would suggest a monistic philosophy which, having abandoned the distinction of form and content, no longer requires a *substance* of body or mind, to which reference need be made.[9]

According to the *Gestalt* hypothesis, psychology deals primarily with those forms that are experienced. No psychologist of this school will deny Titchener's contentions that the point of departure in science is observation and that observation is perception. But it does not necessarily follow that the science of psychology must confine itself to "sensory" phenomena dependent upon a nervous system. This conclusion, which inevitably follows upon Titchener's positivistic postulates, is no longer warranted when realism replaces positivism. According to *Gestalt* theory, perceptual experience is the point of departure of "the man of science," and his observations are a formal participation with his surroundings. But his interest may lead him to describe one form or another; and, accordingly, he may call himself a physicist, a biologist, or a psychologist. Instead of commanding a variety of points of view, with correspondingly varied subject matter, "the man of science" has but a single point of view which envisages the shape of things and events. When these things and events are immediately perceived his description of them takes an experiential form. He "psychologizes" the situation and traces its pattern with special heed to its sensory aspect. But experience likewise reveals *gradients* which have their counterpart in the behavior of organisms. Accordingly, he can trace behavior, record its shape, and determine its conditions without perceiving what the organism perceives. Finally, he can perceive effort and can trace its counterpart in

---

[9] This does not necessarily mean that all forms reduce to one basic pattern. The *Gestalt* philosophy is more likely to appear pluralistic than monistic in that respect.

the physical world where organismic behavior gives way to energistic formations.

Regarded as figure-ground patterns, Titchener's definitions of the three major fields of science might be said to hold for the *Gestalt* hypothesis. But in so regarding them, a revolutionary change has been wrought in their implications. The sensory field of psychology is no longer cut off from, but instead interpenetrates, the fields of biology and physics. Where lines are drawn between these three sciences is largely a matter of convenience with respect to the problem upon which one is engaged. The psychologist is interested in the whole man, as the behaviorist contends that he should be. The phenomena of individual experience are but means of describing real events in which the whole man is engaged, by himself, with others, and with his environment. The world of experiential phenomena, considered apart from the physical and biological events in which the whole man participates, is an abstract and, therefore, an unreal world. But unreal though it is, the abstract world follows the formal patterns of the real world, and, by virtue of its self-imposed restrictions, is able to supply the tools of logic and the means of appraising the good, the beautiful, and the true. What, according to positivism, is existential—a "mode of natural existence"—becomes realistically nonexistential, abstract, and on a par with other derivative forms like those of logic, mathematics, and art. Form comes first; its qualities, intensities, and so on are secondary and contingent. The color *red*, for instance, is neither primary nor real, but an abstraction wholly dependent upon a figure-ground pattern of behavior. As Wertheimer has stated the case: " 'Elements' have no priority as fundamentals in 'plus-combinations,' appearing under conditions which in principle are alien to them; instead, they are to be understood as parts of wholes, determined by those wholes."[10] Köhler reaches a similar conclusion when he remarks that the analysis of "structural" psychology which reduces the sensory field to "sensations" has in no wise attained a structural unit, but only a *differential*, which "does not mean anything like a real unit but only signifies the small uniform part of a medium, field, or process which our thinking regards more especially in a certain moment of our theoretical consideration."[11]

We see, then, that Titchener's positivism and the *Gestalt* hypothesis are worlds apart. Whereas Titchener's science deals with the whole of experi-

[10] M. Wertheimer, "Untersuchungen zur Lehre von der Gestalt," *Psychol. Forschung*, I (1921), 53.

[11] W. Köhler, "An Aspect of *Gestalt* Psychology," *Pedagogical Seminary*, XXXII (1925), 695.

ence from different points of view, the *Gestalt* hypothesis embraces all reality in one point of view. So emphatic, indeed, is the realism of the *Gestalt* that even the phrase "point of view" is questionable and possibly misleading. Certainly, there is no "eye" requisite to see the *Gestalt* before it can exist. The principle of formation is simply assumed to be the all-embracing postulate of existence. Therefore, descriptive observation will and must follow this principle in recording facts, whether the facts be of experience, behavior, or energetics. There is no limbo to which technologies can be relegated, because all investigation employs the same method. How "scientific" the results may be depends not only upon a "point of view," but also upon the nature of the figure-ground pattern which is being investigated. With the aid of highly developed instruments of precision, certain figure-ground patterns can be accurately recorded and adequately described. Some results obtained in the physical sciences are exemplary in this respect. In biological research, the problems are usually under less exact control; and in psychological research, we are as yet on the threshold of adequate descriptions. The *Gestalt* hypothesis opens an avenue of approach to the science of experience which does not confine the psychologist to conscious phenomena. His problem may be behavioristic or experiential as he chooses. Furthermore, he is supplied with a postulate which embraces group behavior and suggests the possibility of a scientific conception of the "group mind."[12]

The present danger which lurks in the foreground of this new and intriguing conception is that of overhasty generalization. Nothing is more likely to hinder the advancement of any working hypothesis than the rapid crystallization of a theory. Arising, as the *Gestalt* hypothesis has, not from speculation—like Brentano's act psychology—but from experimental investigation, the demands for further experiment far outweigh those which lead to speculative inference. And yet it is impossible to contrast this hypothesis with another system of psychology without forcing the issue in ways which the factual results thus far achieved do not warrant. For all such overstatements, the writer can only crave the indulgence of his readers.

The system of Titchener may be regarded in one of two ways: To some it is the "swan song" of that positivistic philosophy which, especially in the hands of Ernst Mach and Richard Avenarius, sought to free science from the shackles of metaphysics. To others, like Titchener himself, the system of "pure science," while bound to retreat temporarily before

---

[12] Cf. the analyst's *Psychology and Education* (New York: Harcourt, Brace & Co., 1926), pp. 81–93, 339–45; also J. T. MacCurdy's *Common Principles in Psychology and Physiology* (New York: Macmillan Co., 1928), p. 259.

the onslaught of the more powerful forces of technology, will not suffer defeat. A later generation, he believed, will rise to its support when, at length, technology, having spent its force, requires such revitalization as only a pure and positivistic science can give.

Upon this field of controversy between "pure science" and technology the *Gestalt* hypothesis appears like a surd; for it is inexpressible in the language which Titchener employs in defending his own point of view and in opposing his enemies. Whether or not psychology and the other sciences will accept this surd, which does not so much modify as replace the hypotheses with which they hitherto have worked, time alone can tell.[13]

[13] [This analysis was first written in September, 1928, and was revised by the analyst in February, 1929.—EDITOR.]

ANALYSIS 6

PROBLEMS OF METHOD IN INTERNATIONAL LAW: ALFRED VERDROSS' CONCEPT OF THE UNITY OF THE LEGAL ORDER ON THE BASIS OF THE INTERNATIONAL CONSTITUTION

BY JOHANNES MATTERN

The Johns Hopkins University

STATEMENT OF PROBLEM AND METHOD OF APPROACH

As a first step in the direction of a scientific approach toward problems in the domain of law, analytical jurists have come to distinguish between positive and non-positive law. Positive law they define as the formal enactments of legislatures, decrees and ordinances of executive and administrative departments, decisions and rulings of courts, official boards, commissions, etc., actually enforcible by those organs upon the members of the body politic. All rules of conduct not so enforcible they hold to be law of a non-positive character, such as the law of God to man, known as natural or divine law, and social customs and traditions as far as they have not yet received formal recognition by judge or legislator.

Applying the same distinction to the sphere of international law, the extreme wing among the positivist school denies the positive character to all international law as not enforcible in the sense in which municipal law can be enforced. A more moderate section recognizes as positive international law the rules of conduct embodied in treaties, conventions, decisions of courts of arbitration, and codifications accepted and adhered to by all or at least the majority of nations. Positivists of all shades, however, deny the positive legal character to that body of general moral principles, often reverently avowed in treaties and conventions, but readily disregarded by the parties concerned as their particular interests suggest or demand. It is on the score of the denial of the positive character to the moral principles thus avowed and disregarded that Verdross throws down the gauntlet to the positivists, failing to distinguish, as he does, between the mere avowal of such principles and the positivists' condition of compliance or practical enforcibility.

In his first work, "Zur Konstruktion des Völkerrechts,"[1] Verdross endeavored to disestablish the dualism of constitutional and international

[1] *Zeitschrift für Völkerrecht*, VIII (1914), 329–59.

law by a construction of the law which would comprise both in a monistic legal order. Rejecting Jellinek's attempt to bridge the gap between constitutional and international law by a metalegal concept of the "will of the state," i.e., sovereignty, he sought to find a legal medium for the connection of the two. His search for this legal medium was carried on through two later studies: "Völkerrecht und staatliches Recht"[2] and "Grundlagen und Grundlegungen des Völkerrechts."[3] But while the concept of the unity of the legal order as evolved in his first effort still concedes the supremacy of constitutional law, the successive development in his two subsequent endeavors leads to the gradual dethronement of constitutional law and the corresponding elevation of the law of nations to the position of the ruling authority in the monistic legal order. In the interval between his earlier and later views concerning the relative position of constitutional and international law within a monistic legal system, Max Wenzel, Hans Kelsen, and Fritz Sander had proceeded in their own fashion to establish the unity of the legal order. For this purpose Wenzel considered international law as part of the fundamental law of the state;[4] Kelsen conceded the possibility of a choice between constitutional and international law as the supreme ruling authority;[5] Sander resorted to a kind of intertwining (Verschlingung) of the two.[6] In The Unity of the Legal Order on the Basis of the International Constitution (Die Einheit des rechtlichen Weltbildes auf Grundlage der Völkerrechtsverfassung)[7] Verdross proposes to utilize the results of his co-workers for "the reconstruction" and "a provisional conclusion" of his enterprise.

There have been earlier attempts similar to those of Verdross and his colleagues of the Viennese or Austrian School. But with them Verdross disclaims all kinship, at least so far as method is concerned. They were constructed on the basis of natural law as part of divine law. Conceding that he "would not recoil from the accusation of intending to warm over [wieder aufwärmen] the old law of nature," Verdross nevertheless denies such an intent. He confesses to the belief in natural law "in so far as it

[2] See his Die völkerrechtswidrige Kriegshandlung und der Strafanspruch der Staaten (Berlin: Hans Robert Engelmann, 1920), pp. 34-43.

[3] Niemeyers Zeitschrift für internationales Recht, XXIX (1921), 65-91.

[4] Juristische Grundprobleme (1920).

[5] Das Problem der Souveränität und die Theorie des Völkerrechts (Tübingen: J. C. B. Mohr [P. Siebeck], 1920).

[6] "Das Faktum der Revolution und die Kontinuität der Rechtsordnung," Zeitschrift für öffentliches Recht, I (1919), 132-64.

[7] (Tübingen: J. C. B. Mohr, 1923), pp. v-vii. References to Verdross which follow are to this work, except as indicated. His latest work, Die Verfassung der Völkerrechtsgemeinschaft (Wien and Berlin: Springer, 1926), will be considered briefly.

posits only a few fundamental principles [of conduct], all else being left
to positivist determination." He denies "the existence of any proof to the
effect that there are no unchangeable ethical (and as such natural law)
principles, or at least no scientific determination [*Erkenntnis*] of such
principles."[8] Regardless of this belief, however, Verdross insists that his
system of the unity of the legal order is based on the law as reality exhibits it to be and that he proposes to construct a system of law reversing
the fundamental position of the adherents of the positivist school by the
method heretofore claimed as theirs. Thus he declares war on the positivist school "not because we [Verdross] abandon the experience of law,
but because we believe that it [positivism] is committing this error."[9]

Enlarging upon the general statement concerning his method of approach, Verdross insists that the two concepts of "sovereignty" and "the
metalegal position of the state" constitute "the central points around
which all other problems revolve. . . . . Krabbe, Kelsen, and Sander have
demonstrated that the state can be considered only as a figure of law
[*Rechtsfigur*]. Nevertheless, the existence of the state before and beyond
the law is still insisted upon, though without a shadow of proof. For no
one has ever shown in which sphere of reality this thing of fiction has taken
form." And since "the burden of proof rests with the one who affirms and
not with the one who denies," Verdross feels justified in asserting that the
state can be considered only "as a definite legal status [*als ein bestimmter
rechtlicher Tatbestand*],"[10] as though this were not an affirmation requiring proof as much as the postulate of the positivist which it aims to deny.
The state, having thus been declared *incompos voluntatis,* is asserted to
be a manifestation, figure, or function of a law existing prior to the
state. In other words, the positivists' proffer of evidence for the reality
of sovereignty, conceived as the state's will, as manifested in every state
act, in every state constitution, in every agreement and treaty with other
states, in the insistence upon the opportunity to prevent by a single vote
in the Council of the League of Nations a decision incompatible with
the vital interests of the state concerned—all this evidence Verdross
sweeps aside in favor of the theoretical construction of a system of law in
which the state is reduced to an agency of the law. This, we are told, is
reality and genuine positivism.

SOVEREIGNTY AND INTERNATIONAL LAW

Although Verdross definitely states that from the point of methodological justification the alleged failure of the positivists to prove the
existence of a will of the state is equivalent to the proof of its nonexistence,

[8] *Ibid.,* p. viii.   [9] *Ibid.*   [10] *Ibid.,* pp. 1–2.

he nevertheless attempts a positive demonstration of the alleged fictitious character of the positivist doctrine. He proceeds to prove that sovereignty as conceived by Bodin, by the scholastic writers, by Ayala, Gentilis, Grotius, Pufendorf, Wolff, Leibniz, Zouch, Rachel, by the positivists, and by the doctrinarians of the French Revolution was anything but a concept from which the freedom of action of the state could be deduced.

And so he points out that the *summa potestas* claimed by Bodin for the prince was subject to the superior law of nature of which the law of nations was considered a part.[11] He holds that Bodin's definition of the sovereign state as a state *qui superiorem in terris non recognoscit* merely meant that Bodin did not recognize the pope and the emperor as organs of the universal world-order for the execution of international law, such execution being left to the organs of the sovereign states.[12] The same idea Verdross finds prevailing in the scholastic doctrine. According to Augustine,[13] "the right to declare war . . . . rests with the princes as a prerogative derived from the law of nations as part of the law of nature." Thomas Aquinas[14] declares that the prince is one not subject to the authority of another prince. Cajetan,[15] the Dominican, defines the prince or the sovereign state as *civitas perfecta*, such as the pope, the emperor, a king, a free city, i.e., all who do not have another superior equal to a prince above them. Victoria[16] denies the *potestas temporalis* of both emperor and pope, conceding to the latter only the *potestas spiritualis*. In the opinion of Victoria, sovereignty of the state implies not supremacy in all things but only in most matters pertaining to temporal affairs. Sovereignty of the state is therefore quite compatible with a subordination to the pope in spiritual things. Suarez[17] distinguishes between the *civitas perfecta* and the *civitas imperfecta*. The *civitas perfecta* is one which is not subject to the superior authority of any other worldly power; the *civitas imperfecta*, one which is subject to such authority. Verdross continues to show that the scholastic doctrine forms the starting-point of the later non-scholastic authorities. Ayala[18] and Gentilis[19] define as sovereign that organ which is not subject to a superior judge and which is endowed with the authority to make war. But the right to make war, Verdross remarks, is a right derived from international law. Grotius[20]

---

[11] *Ibid.*, pp. 14–15.   [12] *Ibid.*, p. 17.

[13] "Ordo naturalis mortalium paci accommodatus hoc poscit, ut suscipiendi belli auctoritas atque consilium penes principes sit" (*ibid.*, pp. 18–19).

[14] Quoted *ibid.*

[15] *Ibid.*

[16] Quoted *ibid.*, p. 20.

[17] *Ibid.*, pp. 20–21.

[18] *Ibid.*, pp. 23–24.

[19] *Ibid.*

[20] *Ibid.*, p. 24.

explains that the *summa potestas* is called supreme (*summa*) because it is not subject to annulment by the decision of another human will. As Verdross adds, this means that the *summa potestas* signifies a definite legal authority (*bestimmt qualifizierte Rechtsinstanz*); it does not mean that the *summa potestas* stands above the law.

There is something quite subjective in this interpretation of the doctrine of the scholastic and later non-scholastic writers. According to the prevailing opinion it was the object of these writers to substantiate the rising claim to sovereignty on the part of the slowly evolving national states by the attempt to harmonize that claim with the fictitious suzerainty of the Emperor and the supreme authority of the papacy in spiritual matters. What they aimed to show was that whatever limitation there was to the sovereignty of these states was to be found in the law of nature, including the law of nations. According to Verdross, they meant to prove that the sovereign state, being subject to natural and international law, was a sovereign state only by virtue of such law. The non-subjection of the state to pope and emperor is, according to Verdross, proof merely that international law requires no international agency for its application and enforcement.

It is quite apparent that Verdross is here ascribing to the authorities concerned intentions similar to those held by a later school which sought to demonstrate the reality and supremacy of international law by proving the subjection of the state to natural law. Thus Pufendorf, Wolff, Leibniz, Zouch, and Rachel, while defining the sovereign state as the state which does not recognize the superior authority of another state or of any legislative authority above or outside, agree that even such sovereign states are subject to natural law.[21] According to this doctrine, sovereignty is a certain legal competence, derived from natural law or the law of nations, to act in such matters as the making of war and peace, or, as Zouch expresses it, the supreme authority to decide those affairs which pertain to the intercourse of nations.[22] Even Moser,[23] the father of the positivist school, and the doctrinarians of the French Revolution serve Verdross to demonstrate that sovereignty was considered by them as a legal qualification derived from the superior law of nations.

[21] *Ibid.*, pp. 25–27.

[22] "Summa potestas decernendi de iis quae ad communionem inter gentes spectant" (*ibid.*, p. 27).

[23] Johann Jakob Moser, *Versuch des neuesten europäischen Völkerrechts in Friedens- und Kriegszeiten*, Part I (1777) (Verdross, p. 28).

INTERNATIONAL LAW AND THE LAW OF THE STATE

As Verdross demonstrates, the scholastic doctrine visioned a conceptual unity of mankind which was supposed to have gradually grouped itself into states. The medieval idea of the *Unitas Christiana,* or the universal empire, under Roman, Greek, and German emperors was merely an attempt to establish a practical working order of this unity. The tie which was supposed to effectuate the conceptual unity of the scholastic world-order was therefore not the temporal authority of pope and emperor, but the *jus gentium,* or, as Zouch, the first analyst of international law, termed it, the *jus inter gentes.*[24] Hence the relation of the law of the state to international law was, as Verdross concludes, the relation of the law of the part to the universal law, i.e., the law of nations.

The scholastic concept of the unity of the world-order by virtue of a moral principle was adopted by the non-scholastic writers who accept the law of nature as the supreme law for individual and state alike. But while the scholastic writers were content to assert the efficacy of natural law as the compelling moral force within the universal world-order, Grotius, Zouch, Rachel, Wolff, and others proceeded to analyze the character of the moral principle with a view to ascertaining the reason for its effectiveness. Grotius held that it was the greater utility which constituted the superiority of the universal order over the law of the state.[25] Examining the different meanings of the term *international law,* Zouch came to distinguish between what Verdross calls an anterior and a posterior law of nations. The anterior international law is the law "which intercedes between the princes and peoples of different nations, for it is in accordance with this law [*ex hoc jure*] that nations are established, kingdoms [*regna*] founded, commercial relations instituted, and finally, wars waged."[26] What Verdross calls the posterior law of nations is what Zouch defines as the law "upon which the individual nations among themselves agree, as for instance by way of pacts, conventions, and treaties."[27] According to Rachel, this so-called primary international law is identical with the general concept of law as the moral principle uniting all the nations into a universal order ruled by law.

Starting with Rachel's concept of the law as an a priori moral principle that unites all political entities into a universal legal order, Verdross

[24] Verdross, p. 42.

[25] *De jure belli ac pacis,* Prol., sec. 23 (Verdross, p. 42).

[26] Zouch, *Juris et judicii fecialis, sive juris inter gentes et quaestionum de eodem explicatio,* Part I (1650), sec. 1 (Verdross, p. 42).

[27] *Ibid.*

proceeds to develop his system of the unity of the legal order and to assign
to international law a predominant place in that order. There is, he says,
a true and an artificial system of the legal order. The Linnéan system
of the botanical order was mechanical and artificial. It has been replaced
by a hierarchical structure based on the concept of the unity of the
botanical order. It has been suggested that the legal system, conceiving
law as a topical grouping of constitutional, administrative, criminal,
civil, procedural, ecclesiastical, and international law, should also be
superseded by an order which conceives of at least all state law, not as
separate spheres existing side by side on an even plane, but as a unity constituting a hierarchical structure. According to this suggestion, the law
of the state should be viewed and classified functionally rather than
topically, i.e., as constitutional, statutory, and ordinance law, on the one
hand, and as law embodied or manifested in decisions of the courts and
in executive rules and decrees, on the other hand.[28] But Verdross holds
that there is still a third dimension heretofore not recognized, namely,
that of depth and height. Introducing this third dimension, he constructs
the unity of the law as a hierarchical structure in the progressive order
of private, constitutional, and international law.[29]

This concept of the unity of the legal order, Verdross points out, is not
identical with the so-called monistic doctrine of the positivists. For the
positivist adherents of the monistic doctrine, such as Bergbohm, Jellinek,
and others, still consider the individual state or states collectively as the
authors and source of international law. They attempt to establish its
binding character by way of the concept of the self-limitation of the state,
thus positing the will of the state as the factor determining what shall be
considered international law. Verdross, on the contrary, conceives law
as an a priori existing idea superior to the will of the state, as a moral
order by virtue of which the state comes into being and remains what it is,
namely, a manifestation of a certain aspect of that legal order.[30] As the
positivists of the old school still left room for conflicts of law within their
monistic order, Krabbe, Duguit, Salvioli, Stammler, Sander, Wenzel, and
Kelsen started out to eliminate these conflicts by the construction of a
monistic order in which international law takes the place of the superior
or ruling law.

THE UNITY OF THE LEGAL ORDER

So far, Verdross has simply asserted the supremacy of international
law within the universal legal order. But he proposes to prove his asser-

[28] Verdross, p. 50.   [29] *Ibid.*, pp. 50 ff.   [30] *Ibid.*, pp. 53–54.

tion on the basis of the experience of law *(Rechtserfahrung)*, beginning with a quotation from Moser, the first to recognize the unity of the legal order in his (Verdross') own meaning. Moser writes:

I do not only not doubt that there is an international law, but I venture to prove its existence in a fashion which heretofore has not been undertaken by any one, but which is incontrovertible, namely by the admission of many entire nations or their rulers. . . . . By such an admission even the strongest doubt entertained against the existence and the binding force of international law is eliminated. . . . .[31]

Moser then offers pages of citations from official documents, such as declarations of monarchs and other state organs, which, as Verdross affirms, refer to international law as a superior and objective sphere, towering above the state. But since not all states can be proved to have thus referred to international law, Moser concludes that there is no general law of nations, but only one *quo saltem moratiores Gentes utuntur*,[32] one which is adhered to by the more moral nations. In a later work Moser writes:

It must at first appear somewhat contradictory that a state be independent and still—as a matter of legal necessity and responsibility [*Schuldigkeit*]— must be guided by what is customary not among all but only among some European states. Nevertheless, I have proven from the very official documents of many individual European states . . . . that the sovereigns concerned frequently refer to international law, that they understand under international law nothing but what is customary among those independent European states, and that they attach to these customs true and real binding force. And since they do so voluntarily, who will question with any substance the existence of international law?[33]

From these statements Verdross concludes that Moser, on the one hand, "shows the empirical relation of international law to the official documents, i.e., to the realities of the law of the state," and that, on the other hand, he "recognizes the superior legal rank of the objective order of international law."[34] This, however, can mean only one thing, namely, that "international law, or at least part of it, is comprised within the

[31] *Moseriana* (Leipzig, 1739), Part I, sec. 3, p. 72 (Verdross, p. 99).

[32] *Ibid.*, p. 88 (Verdross, p. 99).

[33] *Versuch des neuesten europäischen Völkerrechts in Friedens- und Kriegszeiten* . . . . , Part I (1777), p. 27 (Verdross, p. 99).

[34] Verdross, p. 99.

hierarchy of law," and that within that hierarchy "it rises above the legal order of the state."[35]

Verdross then points to Blackstone as proclaiming that international law in its entirety is part of the common law, that the legislature cannot enact any law incompatible with international law, but that it must secure the enforcement of the universal rules of international law.[36] Verdross accepts the interpretation of Blackstone's teaching on the subject of international and state law as the prevailing Anglo-American doctrine. He claims that the new German and Austrian constitutions have adopted the same doctrine in their respective provisions stating that the generally recognized principles of international law form part of the law of the land, and that as such they are binding upon the state, its functionaries, and its citizens. He admits, however, that in the opinion of the authors of the respective provisions, a particular principle partakes of the character of generally accepted principles of international law in the meaning of the constitutional provisions referred to, only when it is accepted as such by the state of whose law it is declared to be a part.[37]

SOURCES OF INTERNATIONAL LAW

In his argument to prove the existence of a conceptual or a priori international law, Verdross has so far cited only references from the supposedly inferior law of the state to the superior law of nations. He concedes that in order to prove the existence of the superior law, references from the superior to the inferior law may be demanded. The possible request for such references he meets by an analogy from constitutional jurisprudence. Great Britain, he points out, has no written constitution. The existence of the general fundamental principles which we call her unwritten constitution can be established by an analytical probe into the general principles by which the organs of the British government are guided. Though he does not expressly say so, Verdross apparently considers the guiding principles of such an unwritten constitution as a kind of a priori constitutional law, while the positivist sees in them nothing but precedents and conventions established at a time when it was not customary to have written constitutions.

Applying the same reasoning to the sphere of international law, Verdross affirms that the absence of a written international constitution is no

---

[35] *Ibid.*

[36] *Commentaries* (15th ed.; London, 1809), IV, 66 (Verdross, pp. 100–101).

[37] Verdross, pp. 111 ff.

proof of its nonexistence. In order to establish its existence we shall have to examine whether there are legal acts which refer to or are based upon general guiding legal norms. We shall have to resort to an analysis of the meaning *(Sinnanalyse)* of those legal acts. Assuming that the idea of "the will of the state" has been definitely displaced by the concept of law as the center of all problems concerning the state and international law, Verdross affirms that such an analysis proves state constitutions to be limited by a legal order higher than they themselves. He thinks that the concept of the collective will of the state as the basis of international law implies a recognition of the superiority of international over state law, and that the doctrine of world-sovereignty *(Weltmachttheorie)* of Somlo and Lansing as well as the theories of Krabbe, Duguit, and Salvioli constitute a step farther in the same direction.

But insomuch as the authors of these theories failed to prove from legal experience the legal connection between this law superior to the state *(zwischen diesem überstaatlichen Recht)* and the "positive" sources of that law, they failed to meet the objection of the positivists that the so-called law superior to the state lacked all positive foundation.[38] Verdross undertakes to offer proof where the authorities cited did not. The positivists, he says, are the ones who are the real non-positivists in positing as sources only treaties and common law. The state documents cited by Moser are based not only upon these, but also upon international justice. Hence, international justice is a third source of international law.

Verdross then cites a number of instances of recent date in which treaties, agreements, and arbitration decisions refer to the concept of international justice as such a source. In the documents cited there occur such phrases as "the concepts of justice" and "good faith";[39] "res judicata" and "equity" as applied in state law;[40] "the laws of humanity and exigencies of the public conscience."[41] Verdross next quotes from article 38 of the statute of the International Court of Justice, which gives four sources of international law as the basis for its decisions: (1) international conventions; (2) international custom; (3) the general principles of law recognized by the civilized nations; (4) the judicial

---

[38] *Ibid.*, p. 120.

[39] Decision of Permanent Court of Arbitration of February 22, 1904 (Schücking, *Die Judikatur des ständigen Schiedshofes von 1899–1913*, Part I, [1917], p. 303) (Verdross, p. 120).

[40] Decisions of October 14, 1902, and of November 11, 1912 (Schücking, p. 246; Verdross, p. 121).

[41] Hague agreement concerning rules of warfare of 1907 (Schücking, p. 299; Verdross, p. 122).

decisions and the teaching of the most qualified publicists of the different nations as auxiliary means for the determination of the rules of law.[42] The third source here referred to was defined by Baron Descamps, president of the committee of jurists appointed to prepare the draft of the statute, as "conscience juridique des peuples civilisés."[43] To Mr. Root's objection that this judicial conscience varies in different peoples, Baron Descamps replied that this was true only in secondary matters, in principle it was the same in all civilized nations.[44] Verdross continues with references to publicists who speak of "certain principles of law beyond all controversy";[45] of "certain general rules of justice which enter into the consideration of each case."[46] Finally, he cites the preamble of the Covenant of the League of Nations, which speaks of the necessity "d'entretenir au grand jour des relations internationales fondées sur la justice et l'honneur," and "de faire régner la justice,"[47] which, as Verdross comments, means that the Covenant of the League posits "justice and honor" as one of the sources of international law.

THE INTERNATIONAL CONSTITUTION

Verdross now proceeds to examine what he calls the international constitution (Völkerrechtsverfassung). He considers as proved the existence of international legal norms based upon a sphere of law higher than the law of the state. He considers as proved also that "justice" is a source of international law in addition to treaty and customary law, and to judicial decisions. It is this higher sphere of law which he calls the *international constitution*.

The international constitution, he says,[48] calls for two primary but co-ordinated methods of procedure for the establishment of generally valid international legal norms: the procedure of treaties among states and that of international customary law. In principle, then, it is left to these two methods to establish what is international law. There is posited before

[42] Verdross, p. 123. Verdross refers here also to art. 7 of the agreement of October 18, 1907, concerning an international prize court.

[43] *Procès-verbaux des séances du comité, 16 juin–24 juillet, 1920,* I, 318 (Verdross, p. 123).

[44] *Ibid.,* pp. 310 ff. (Verdross, p. 123).

[45] Fernandes, *ibid.,* p. 345 ff. (Verdross, p. 123).

[46] Ricci-Busatti, *ibid.,* p. 314 (Verdross, p. 123).

[47] The official English text of the phrases reads: . . . . "by the prescription of open, just, and honorable relations between nations . . . . " and " . . . . by the maintenance of justice. . . . . "

[48] Verdross, pp. 126 ff. The following description is given partly in quotation, partly in brief paraphrase, with an effort to keep to the text as closely as possible.

the two, as a subsidiary method, international justice as a source to be drawn upon when the other two methods have not yet provided an international rule. However, the international constitution does not regulate these methods of procedure exhaustively. It is left to the constitutions of the states to designate the organs which apply the methods. Thus the international constitution enfolds within itself the constitutions of the states, and it declares its willingness to function only through them. The states are thus enfolded as organs of international law.[49]

But the existing international constitution is not only the constitution of international law, it is at the same time directly and indirectly also the constitution of the legal systems [*Staatsrechtsordnungen*] of those states which adhere to international law. As such it is the constitution of the uniform [*einheitlichen*] legal order itself. For in the international procedures [*Verfahren*] referred to we find a mutual delimitation of local and material spheres of competence of the state, within which the prevailing international law distinguishes two fields: the one concerning those topics which are under the exclusive competence of the individual states, the other those which are regulated "mutually" [*einvernehmlich*], i.e., only by international agreement between two or more states. Thus also the internal competence of the states is based upon the international constitution.[50]

To the objection that the states existed before international law and that they can therefore not be dependent upon such law, Verdross replies in effect as follows:

This objection is untenable because it confuses an historical and a legal relation. . . . . Prussia and Bavaria, for instance, have existed historically before the Reich. Nevertheless, they are legally subordinate to the Reich and its constitution. So, also, are the states in general subordinate to the international constitution from the time of its existence. This follows from the fact that they can legally act and develop only within the competences established by international law, though their competence of action has taken on so wide a scope that it is called "sovereignty."

Verdross even questions the fact that the states existed before international law. He holds that the existing states, at least the Christian cultural communities, did not originate before but as members of "universal Christendom [*der einheitlichen Christenheit*], i.e., under the dominance of its constitution." The question of "whether the existing international consti-

[49] *Ibid.*, pp. 126–27.

[50] In proof of this assertion Verdross refers here to the fact that art. 15, sec. 8, of the League Covenant excludes from settlement by the Council those matters "que le droit international laisse à la compétence exclusive de cette Partie," and to a number of opinions of the Permanent Court of International Justice, in which the court acknowledges this distinction (*ibid.*, p. 127).

tution is the result of an evolutionary development from the former or a revolutionary product" he leaves purposely unanswered.

ORGANS FOR THE APPLICATION OF INTERNATIONAL LAW

Concerning its relative position in the universal legal order, Verdross holds that international law is not an entity separable from other legal norms. It is not as a separate unit that it is related to other juridical spheres. Only those legal norms constitute international law which regulate the relations of states as *Hoheitssubjekte*. The concept is therefore formed in the same manner as the concepts of private, criminal, or constitutional law are formed, according to the object and purpose of the legal norms in question.[51] Hence, international law belongs somewhere in the hierarchy of the legal divisions of state law. In fact, it is to a large extent developed and applied by the same state organs which apply state law, i.e., by organs established for that purpose by the constitutional law of the state. This proves the connection between state law and international law. For the latter, by leaving to the state the appointment of the organs for its own applications, makes these organs serviceable to itself. In turn, the state law subordinates itself by the appointment of organs for the conduct of international relations. But this does not permit the conclusion that international law is completely absorbed in the law of the state, for there are international legal norms which originate not through treaties of state.[52] It therefore does not stand as a unit above or below constitutional law. The primacy of neither the one nor the other can be accepted. What stands above constitutional law are those international legal norms which form the international constitution. The other legal norms originate in practices or acts dependent upon the constitutions of the states. Hence the constitutions of the states fit in between the international constitution and the other international legal norms established by treaties and conventions.[53]

Disagreeing with Krabbe, Verdross holds that the organs of the state, when acting in the service of international law, do so not as international organs but as organs proper of the state. Only in an indirect sense are they organs of the international constitution upon which all legal acts are dependent. Even such so-called international organs as the League of Nations and courts of arbitration are created not directly by the international constitution, but through the medium of the state constitutions by way of agreement of the nations concerned.[54]

[51] *Ibid.*, pp. 129–30.
[52] *Ibid.*, pp. 129–34.
[53] *Ibid.*
[54] *Ibid.*, pp. 134–35.

But though the international constitution can manifest itself only through the medium of the constitutions of the states, it would, in the opinion of Verdross, be erroneous to hold that international law created by the co-operation of the state constitutions could be abrogated in the same fashion in which it was created. This would be true only if the state constitutions represented the higher legal order and as such the supreme authority for all law created by and through them. The constitutions of the states are subordinate to the international constitution which accords to them an exclusive competence only in internal affairs.[55]

UNIVERSAL APPLICATION OF THE INTERNATIONAL CONSTITUTION

As to the extent of the international constitution, Verdross believes that it is universal. Since such countries as Siam, China, and Liberia have become members of the League of Nations, since Russia and the United States were members of the society of nations before the League existed, since practically all nomadic and uncivilized units have of late come under the legal influence of the colonizing nations, and since some kind of legal obligation attaches even to the traffic on the sea, the universality of the international constitution is not a postulate but a reality.[56]

From this conclusion, Verdross admits, it does not follow that all law has always constituted such a unit, nor that it will always do so, in the future. In this connection he calls attention to the question of the sovereignty of the pope, of the Knights of Malta, to the question of rebellion, and of Soviet Russia as examples of the *jus inter potestates*. But he rejects the idea that the papacy and the Knights of Malta have, with the loss of their territorial possession, also lost their position as subjects of international law. The pope, he says, still concludes treaties with other states; he exchanges envoys; in short, he is a *Rechtssubjekt* in the same sense in which the states are *Rechtssubjekte* of international law. The same holds true of the Knights of Malta, who, since the loss of their territory in 1798, still enjoy the right of diplomatic representation. International law specifically recognizes the status of rebellion and, under certain conditions, of those waging a war of rebellion, as that of a faction waging war in the international legal sense.[57] Verdross shows that the failure of some states to recognize the Soviet government does not, as some authorities hold, place the Russian state beyond the pale of interna-

---

[55] *Ibid.*, p. 135.

[56] ". . . . kann heute von einer universellen Geltung der Völkerrechtsverfassung gesprochen werden" (*ibid.*, p. 136).

[57] *Ibid.*, pp. 139–41.

tional organization and law.[58] In the first place, the failure to recognize the government is not identical with the failure to recognize the state. In the second place, some states have recognized the Soviet government and are thus living under agreements which derive their sanction from the international constitution. In the third place, even the states which have not recognized the Soviet government nevertheless insist upon the recognition by that government of the financial obligation of the tsarist empire, thereby holding Soviet Russia to the execution of obligations receiving whatever validity they may possess from international law.[59]

CONFLICTS OF LAW

Verdoss finally shows that the existence of conflicts between international and state law is no proof that international law is not part of the universal legal order, nor that the international constitution does not form a sphere of law higher than that of the state. He argues that as there are rules and methods for the elimination of conflicts of law within the law of the constitution and other statutory law, so are there rules and methods for the settlement of conflict between international and state law. He points to the concrete case of such a conflict between Germany and the Allied and Associated Powers concerning article 61, section 2, and the corresponding provision of the Treaty of Versailles. Article 61, section 2, stipulated that after the creation of the Reichsrat the representatives of Austria could join that body. The Treaty of Versailles inhibited the political union of Germany and Austria. Germany was held by the treaty not to enact any law incompatible with the provisions of that treaty. By article 178 of her own constitution she was held to the same limitation. By article 4 of the constitution the treaty had become part of the law of the land in no less binding a fashion than by its later formal enactment as national law. It is certainly true, then, that Germany was bound by international law as well as by her own state law to observe the provisions of the treaty.

Verdross finally points to the conflict of German and French law in the occupied Ruhr district. Only by the application and enforcement of a higher international law could such a chaos of conflicting state law be cleared.[60] He concludes that such conflicts, be they between the law of different states or between state law and international law, are not really legal conflicts. Each of the conflicting laws is willed by the legal order

[58] A. Rapisardi-Mirabelli, *I limiti d'obligatorietà delle norme giuridiche internazionali* (Catania, 1922), pp. 80 ff. (cited, Verdross, p. 157).

[59] Verdross, pp. 157–58.   [60] *Ibid.*, p. 138.

from which it emanates, each is valid within the sphere of competence for which it was established. Both are and remain valid until one is eliminated by whatever formal process is legally possible. In other words, they are both "willed by law." Many legal norms may thus become practically illusory, but this state of affairs can be altered and improved only by law. It is not the object of legal science to disprove the existence of such conflicts by interpretation, but to examine whether it shatters the unity of the legal order. This, Verdross affirms, it does not. The fact that "there are legal methods and means for the straightening of such conflicts proves that all such apparently conflicting legal norms can be woven into a non-conflicting unity on the basis of a universal fundamental law, i.e., by reference to one and the same central co-ordinated system."[61]

THE CONSTITUTION OF THE INTERNATIONAL COMMUNITY

The present analysis requires the brief mention of what may be termed a sequel to the work here discussed. In the *Einheit des rechtlichen Weltbildes auf Grundlage der Völkerrechtsverfassung* Verdross aimed to prove the existence of a universal legal order in which international law, conceived as an a priori unwritten international constitution, holds a position of supremacy over the law of the state. On the assumption that he has succeeded in attaining his aim, Verdross published three years later another book, *Die Verfassung der Völkerrechtsgemeinschaft* ("The Constitution of the International Community").[62] As the title suggests, Verdross elaborates in this later work in considerable detail the international constitution whose existence he set out to establish in *The Unity of the Legal Order.* In this later work he thus gives special attention to the doctrine of the sources of international law, to the problems of general and particular international law, to the concept of subjects of international law *(Völkerrechtssubjekte),* to the system of competences *(Zuständigkeitsordnung),* to the nature of the state's territory, etc. Consistent with his views of *The Unity of the Legal Order,* he maintains the a priori character of fundamental legal norms, such as *pacta sunt servanda,* from which all international law emanates. It is on the basis of this postulate of fundamental legal principles, which are not the creation but the source of international and state law, that Verdross finally reaches the point where he posits the doctrine that "international law supersedes state law [*Völkerrecht bricht staatliches Recht*]" much in the same fashion in which in German republican jurisprudence "*Reichsrecht bricht Landrecht.*" Under this doctrine the state appears even more than in *The Unity of the Legal*

[61] *Ibid.,* pp. 168–69.   [62] *Op. cit.*

Order the creature and ward of the *Völkerrechtsgemeinschaft.* The state's territory assumes the position of *domaine réservé,* and the term *sovereignty* is replaced by that of *Völkerrechtsunmittelbarkeit,* which translated into English means something like "a status of direct relation or subjection to international law."[63]

RECAPITULATION AND CRITICISM

As an imaginative work *The Unity of the Legal Order on the Basis of the International Constitution* is fascinating. It is a brilliant vision. If we accept the premises, it is even logical. But the admission of the grandeur of its conception implies at the same time its rejection as an expression of what constitutional and international jurists consider the realities of present-day state and interstate life and relations.

The affirmation of a priori international legal norms *(des primären Völkerrechts),* viewed as an unwritten international constitution, can, according to present-day accepted scientific methodology, he made only on a purely conceptual basis. Nevertheless, Verdross asserts the intention of constructing his system of the unity of the legal order with the international constitution as the superior law on the empirical basis of the experience of law *(Rechtserfahrung).* It is this conflict between the conceptual aspect or thought content of the premises and the alleged adherence to the empirical method which makes itself felt throughout the work. The documentary evidence upon which Verdross relies as being experiences of law are the official documents of rulers and states, international treaties, conventions, and agreements, decisions of courts of arbitration, and the opinions of publicists. In these documents, etc., he finds references to and professions of recognition of international law as a system of legal norms binding the states and rulers concerned to the observation of the terms of these documents. He finds in them references to international justice and fair play, suggesting the existence of a morally binding force, which insomuch as it cannot definitely be proved the creation of the state or of the law of the state, must be conceived as an a priori moral law, the progenitor of all state and international law. These a priori principles of international justice and fair play Verdross considers to be fundamentally the same in all peoples, differing only in matters of detail. To the positivist, too, these documents and acts of state are experience of law. But to him they signify references to and an admission of the existence of international law whose binding force is derived from an honorable belief in the desirability of applying justice and fairness in

[63] See Karl Strupp's review of *Die Verfassung der Völkerrechtsgemeinschaft* in *Zeitschrift für Völkerrecht,* XIV (1928), 449–53.

international relations. They signify also that the international law to which they refer is not an a priori metaphysical unwritten international constitution, but practices and conventions which appeared just and fair to the rulers and states of the periods concerned. They further signify that these principles of justice and fair play differed among the different peoples not only in matters of detail but also in fundamentals, unless the differences in the treatment of the prisoners of war in ancient and in modern times are to be considered a matter of detail. Finally, these documents signify above all and as a matter of political reality that up to the present time their very existence is the result of compulsion or self-interest and that the professions contained in them are realized only under the persuasion of the same forces.

It is not surprising, then, that the interpretation which Verdross places upon these documentary references as premises leads him to conclusions which are not in accord with the realities of state and interstate life and relations. But this does not mean that the positivist denies the existence of moral principles of justice, honor, and fair play. These principles are recognized by all statesmen and jurists. Some hold that they are the essence of the human conscience implanted in man by his divine creator; others say they are the result of inheritance and environment. Be that as it may. The positivist admits their existence, to be sure, not as an a priori metaphysical international constitution, but as persuasive formative sources of international law in the same sense in which he admits their existence as persuasive formative sources of the law of the state. Nor need the positivist experience any difficulty in accepting the doctrine of the unity of the legal order even if that order is to assume the form of a hierarchy with international law as the *lex prima inter pares*. For more than one sovereign state has declared in its constitution that the generally recognized principles of international law are part of the law of the land. There is no apparent reason why these and other sovereign states should not by the same process declare that the principles thus recognized as international law and as law of the land shall be the superior or ruling law. It all depends upon the will of the state, the same will which Verdross denies and which the state, and with it the positivist, affirms. So finally, the idea of an international constitution may become more than a vision, provided again that it does not remain a phantom of a priori metaphysical principles, but that it assumes the form of an international code ratified by the states in the way international agreements or treaties are ratified. Whether the states concerned shall under the terms of such a code assign the execution of the obligations assumed to their own state organs, or whether they shall delegate such execution to a League of Nations, is of no concern to the positivist. It is quite patent, then, that with the method of logical deduction of *The Unity of the Legal Order on the Basis of the International Constitution* no fault is to be found. The difference between Verdross and the positivist is fundamental. It is a basic disagreement in the interpretation of the realities of life in the form of what Verdross calls the experience of law. In the last analysis it resolves itself into a failure to agree on a mutually acceptable definition of law.[64]

[64] [This analysis was first written in November, 1928, and was given final revision by the analyst in May, 1929.—EDITOR.]

SECTION II
THE DEFINITION OF OBJECTS OF INVESTIGATION

ANALYSIS 7

THE SOCIOLOGICAL METHODS OF VILFREDO PARETO[1]

By MAX SYLVIUS HANDMAN

University of Minnesota

Pareto's sociology is an attempt to apply to the general study of society the notion of equilibrium developed by Walras in economics and further enlarged and improved by Pareto himself.[2] The everlasting conflict between human desires and the obstacles opposed to the satisfaction of these desires give rise to a series of efforts at adjustment, the result of which is the economic system as we find it. Taking society as a whole, there is a similar process of adjustment taking place, which ultimately gives us the social equilibrium of a given collectivity at a given time and place. The forces at work in society which are comparable to the desires of the person for economic goods are the tendencies of human beings to engage in non-logical actions; to these tendencies are opposed equal tendencies to hide this same non-logical character by making it appear reasonable and logical. "Man has such a strong tendency to add logical development to non-logical actions, all of which serves him as pretext to abandon himself to this delightful occupation" of non-logical activity (180).[3] On analysis it is found that all these non-logical activities, even though they may vary from time to time and from collectivity to collectivity, still possess a central core which is common to all of them. The problem in understanding human society is to disentangle this common core from the accidental appearances with which it is covered up. Logical actions need no such explanation, since the relation between the individual and his action is apparent; it is only the non-logical actions which need explanation. A system of sociology should have as its primary purpose the disclosing of the mechanism which will make intelligible to us the system of non-logical human actions.

[1] *Traité de sociologie générale* (2 vols.; Paris: Librairie Payot & Cie, 1919). (Rev. trans.)

[2] G. H. Bousquet, *Vilfredo Pareto: Sa vie et son Œuvre* (Paris: Payot, 1928), p. 129.

[3] The Arabic numerals in parentheses refer to the paragraphs in the *Sociologie générale*. All quotations from that work will be indicated by reference to the paragraph, this being Pareto's own way of reference.

These non-logical human actions generally remain unintelligible to us, because they seem to be so closely tied up with the individual performer, until we realize that they are parts of a general scheme of human behavior common to all men in all places and at all times. The *Sociologie* is filled with a tremendous mass of evidence, collected from the life-history of Western European society, showing the everlasting repetition of non-logical actions in the fields of religion, politics, the social codes, and economic activity.

Once we realize the presence of these non-logical actions and the great desire of human beings to mask their non-logical character, we are on the way to the discovery of an explanation both of their existence and of their tendency to hide themselves. This explanation runs in terms of certain inherent forces of human nature which drive human beings to perform these actions, and of an equally powerful drive to hide them. Both drives have in common a set of deep-rooted sentiments inclosing an organized system of impulses, instincts, appetites, dispositions, and interests. These forces are not to be understood in the biopsychological sense in which they are generally accepted in modern psychology. They are not instincts in the McDougall sense nor sentiments in the Shand sense. Neither are they instincts in the sense of the common heritage of the race; but individual endowments, varying with every person, and more akin to the psychological description of temperament. They are in the nature of sociological irreducibles. They are the expression of what is most fundamental in human beings (850). Pareto never explains the meaning of the word "sentiment" because to him it is a datum, the explanation of which lies in the field of psychology (161). He accepts it as final; it is a something which causes action and he cares to go no farther. Critics of Pareto would have a right to ask of him, who is so pitiless in his criticism of metaphysics, whether he is not here postulating a metaphysical noumenon of the old-fashioned kind and whether it is quite fair to postulate the existence of something and ask someone else to explain it.

Granting, however, that there is within human beings this bundle of motivating forces, we come to the further step in Pareto's analysis which consists in classifying the manner in which these motivating forces are found manifested in the behavior of human beings. These manifestations he calls *residues*, as being the mechanical forces springing from the sentiments which will be found to organize non-logical human actions. They are themselves indifferent to what they organize or to the materials on which and with which they work, just as the laws of motion are indifferent to the materials on which and with which they work. This strictly organizing character of the residues will appear more clearly when we have seen them in the classification presented by Pareto.

This classification embraces six categories, as follows:

The first class comprises the residues of the *instinct of combinations;* that is, the tendency of the human being to indulge in putting together all sorts of things, partly for the pleasure it gives him, and partly because he cannot help it. People wish " 'to do something,' combine certain things and certain actions" (864).

It is this instinct of combinations which makes human beings put together things and operations, without any pre-established plan, without knowing exactly whither they are going, like a person who walks through a forest for the simple pleasure of walking [899].

This instinct manifests itself in special actions which result in putting together things which are similar or opposite; rare objects are linked with exceptional events, terrible objects with terrible events, good objects are united with happy events, and bad objects with unhappy events. Human blood is united with terrible occasions; a black sheep is somehow connected with tempest, and a white sheep with pleasant winds; certain numbers are good, others are bad; heroes must have a divine origin, criminals a diabolical origin, etc., etc. This same instinct of combinations will also affect the residues themselves, forcing them into certain combinations; and logic itself is at bottom a part of this same tendency to combine things into reasonable patterns (972).

- The second class comprises the residues of an instinct to refrain from tearing asunder what the instinct of combinations has put together. This Pareto calls the *persistence of aggregates.* The various forms taken by this residue include the tendency to persist of connections once formed between man and man, and man and place; e.g., family and class connections, relations between the living and the dead, between the dead and the things belonging to him, the persistence of an abstraction once formed and of uniformities once established, of sentiments which are transposed into objective realities, of personifications, etc. It is according to this instinct that pagan gods turn into Christian saints, and that trials for witchcraft turn into trials for "sexual *lèse*-religion" and "sexual heresy," other illustrations may be found in the cult of the ancient city; the feudal group, patriotism, and the caste system; sectarianism, racial consciousness, and ancestor worship; anthropomorphism; the belief in progress and democracy.

The third class of residues consists of the inner necessity felt by human beings to manifest their sentiments by external acts, so that one finds anti-religious sentiments making use of religious forms of expression and anti-militaristic socialists engaging in military parades and other forms of military discipline.

In the fourth class belong the residues bearing on man's social life. Man's social experience has endowed him with a set of fundamental sentiments which are grouped around the desire to get together with others in some form of collectivity as a fundamental group. Connected with this is the sentiment of uniformity, of a desire for likeness among the members of that collectivity. Imitation comes in as the mechanism reinforcing this uniformity, and neophobia as the force keeping away innovations and maintaining uniformity and the collectivity. In this connection appear the so-called social feelings, e.g., altruism, pity and cruelty, repugnance to suffering in general, suffering for others and its curious modifications in asceticism. Finally, there is to be mentioned the notion of "social distance" which appears here in the hierarchical organization of any collectivity, together with the compulsory force of social approval or disapproval issuing again in the desire of approval of the deity as manifested in asceticism.

Closely associated with the residues bearing on man's relations to his fellows is the fifth class, composed of residues tending to keep these relations intact. Any disturbance of these relations is regarded as a disturbance of the social and individual equilibrium. To counteract such disturbances man engages in actions of atonement, reconciliation, and retribution or expiation, remorse, and purification. It is this residue which lies behind such human actions as baptism, or such actions as the raising of a statue to Servetus by the Protestants at Geneva. Pareto might have added also that capital punishment, or the punishment of any criminal, is similarly an effort to re-establish the equilibrium disturbed by commission of the crime which is punished. The mechanism involved in this class of residues might be said to be similar to that involved in the persistence of aggregates. The last class of residues is that connected with the sexual instinct.

Human beings are not capable of finding any justification for their actions except in logical explanations. It is obvious that they cannot see, nor admit to themselves when they do see, that their actions are the expression of these fundamental residues. Any plausible explanation which will bear even the least resemblance to logic will be welcome. The result is a series of explanations which rest upon elements of a comfortable nature, because they are substitutes for logic or because they do not raise the logical issue at all. These explanations Pareto calls *derivations* (1400). The derivations are grouped in four classes.

The first includes various forms of simple affirmation. One escapes the need of explaining his actions by simply affirming his faith in the thing that he is doing or urging others to do. This form is common in the person who thinks that he has proved his point when he explains that "I believe" so and so. This seems sufficient proof to him. A brilliant example of this sort of derivation in high places is the manifesto of the German intellectuals at the outbreak of the war with its reiterated affirmation, "It is not true, etc."

The second class includes all explanations which rest on authority: the authority of persons (in which connection Pareto takes occasion to say some unnecessarily harsh things about Theodore Roosevelt); the authority of tradition, of usages, of customs; the authority of Homer among the Greeks; the authority of the Bible among the Christians, and of other so-called sacred books; the authority of a divine being or of a personification, personifications being particularly plentiful in our day and generation which is deprived of so many divine beings. Appeals to the latter have been replaced in our day with solemn appeals to progress, democracy, etc., in order to prove the necessity of a certain form of action, with as much failure to explain what one means by these terms and with as much luxury of assumption as any theologian might desire.

The third class includes all those derivations used in connection with the social character of man. By appealing to what is generally accepted or to a consensus of opinion, the justification for behavior is taken out of the domain of explanations and given the status of a self-evident proposition. The appeal to "common sense" by those who find no justification for what they want is an instance in point. Another derivation of a social nature appears when the individual's desire is made by him to seem to be for the good of the collectivity. This derivation is too obvious to need any further explanation. Almost the same can be said for those derivations which go about masked as juridical entities. Thus legal notions that are abstracted from one set of circumstances are applied to another set of circumstances. For example, notions that are only applicable to individuals are applied to collectivities, as when preparedness for purposes of war is urged because one should be prepared for purposes of personal protection in a robber-infested country. Again, the notion of individual contract is applied to group relations. How metaphysical entities serve the purpose of hiding the residues is familiar enough to anyone who has watched the use made of such concepts as humanity, reason, nature, the good, justice, science, progress, law of nature, the people, etc. From these to entities bearing a supernatural character it is only a step, and Pareto takes delight in showing how Auguste Comte took that step.

The fourth class includes those derivations which exercise control over human actions in virtue of purely verbal manipulations. All the derivations have in them a large element of playing with words, but this class includes those whose primary quality is that of mere verbal proof (1543). Enumerating the various subclasses, we find the following: (a) An indefinite term applied to a definite thing and an indefinite thing made to correspond to an indefinite term. That is seen in the use of such expressions as "much," "little," "small," "great," "heavy," "light," and, in economics, the notion of value. (b) The use of terms carrying with them certain sentimental connotations according to the desire of the user to awaken these sentiments in the listener. Persistence in one's own faith is called perseverance, but persistence by someone else in his faith is called obstinacy. (c) The use in only one of their meanings of words which can have more than one meaning without stating which meaning is intended; as, "prosperity," "good," "truth," "nature," the "end of man," the "real truth," etc. (d) The use of metaphors, allegories, and analogies, which in the nature of the case have a shifting and subjective meaning. The meaning is primarily that given by the first object of the analogy or the metaphor and then carried over to something else with which it has nothing but a superficial similarity. This type of derivation is illustrated by a wealth of detailed examples from Plato and the Gnostics to Fourier and the solidarism of Leon Bourgeois. (e) Doubtful and indefinite words corresponding to nothing concrete. Instances are again very easy to obtain. Pareto mentions the use of the words "static" and "dynamic," "mechanization," "living," "spiritual," etc.

When one wishes to understand the forces which move a collectivity and bring it through various oscillations to a state of equilibrium, one needs to keep his attention on the residues, not on the derivations. Similarly, when one wishes to modify the actions of individuals in a collectivity one should work on the former, not on the latter. The derivations may change and they do change from time to time, but the residues behind them remain the same.

The reason why individuals oscillate between sentiments and derivations is the necessity of the state of equilibrium. That state is deduced from mechanics as well as from economics. Economic life is understood in terms of man's efforts to adjust himself in the world by compromising between his desires and the obstacles which prevent him from satisfying his desires. When the adjustment is reached the individual is in a state of equilibrium. A collectivity, on the other hand, finds the state of equilibrium when it has achieved a certain adjustment which is generally spoken of as utility or prosperity. The similarity between the individual's efforts to attain equilibrium and the collectivity's efforts to attain the same is made possible by considering the collectivity as a unity (2133).

Proceeding from the analysis that a collectivity finds itself exposed to the stress of the individuals working within it under the influence of their residues, Pareto selects two residue-series to illustrate the notion of social equilibrium: the instinct of combinations, and the instinct of the persistence of aggregates. The collectivity in order to be in a state of equilibrium must obtain what it has decided upon as its maximum utility. Consideration of this utility reveals a two-fold aspect according to whether one sees it in terms of the collectivity as a whole in relation to other collectivities, or in terms of the individuals making up this collectivity as such. In the first instance, we can have a maximum of utilities *of* that collectivity. In the second case, we have a maximum of utility *for* that collectivity. An example: A large population may be a means of great utility for military purposes, viewing the interests of the collectivity as a whole. But that same size of population or the same rate of population increase may be far less useful to the interests of the individuals making up that collectivity. A different rate of increase may be desirable for that purpose. The important thing is to know beforehand the type of utility one is speaking of and to keep that consistently in mind throughout the entire discussion. "Good," "bad," "right," "wrong," "useful," "useless," "legitimate," "illegitimate," and all other forms of expressing a state of equilibrium must be viewed in the light of the equilibrium which is agreed upon as the aim to be obtained.

Pareto assumes that the equilibrium agreed upon is the maintenance of a collectivity in the conditions of existence acceptable to Western Europe from the time of the Greeks. These conditions of existence require a certain amount of economic prosperity within the collectivity; ability to defend itself against other collectivities which might wish to take from it what it possesses and to rob it of its freedom and sovereignty; and, lastly, ability to adjust itself rapidly to any new situation which would give it these essentials. Any other equilibrium would be equally acceptable to Pareto, provided one states explicitly what it is and the conditions essential to its maintenance.

In the maintenance of such equilibrium the two residue-systems most in operation are the *instinct of combination* and the *persistence of aggregates*. Since those intrusted with the maintenance of the equilibrium are the ruling class, the manner in which these two residue-systems operate in it becomes of greatest importance for the whole collectivity. But since this ruling class must exercise its power over a ruled majority, the problem becomes complicated by the resistance offered by that ruled majority, in virtue of these same two residue-systems. The problem of the maintenance of the social equilibrium is therefore seen as the problem of the adjustment of the functioning of these two residue-systems in the two groups of a collectivity.

It is obvious that a ruling class made up of individuals in whom the instinct of combinations predominates will be primarily concerned with innovations and experimentations, either because these activities give it more pleasure or because it is not enough interested in the process of government to keep the organization intact and under its control. The stock example is the ruling class of the ancient régime of France. It was far more interested in playing with ideas, new notions of government, and new social ideals than it was in its own maintenance in power. Hence it encouraged all manner of combinations, economic, political, intellectual, religious, which tended to undermine the stability of the collectivity, until the final break came when the whole collectivity became completely disequilibrated and chaos followed. Instead of being dominated by the instinct of the persistence of aggregates and sternly putting down any attempt at breaking the existing equilibrium, the ruling group itself helped in that break-up. Animated by humanitarian sentimentalities, it refused to use force in order to destroy a too-wide use of the instinct of combinations and itself became a victim of this instinct. In the ruled majority, on the other hand, there predominated the instinct of the persistence of aggregates so that it was ready to take advantage for itself of the loose control exercised by the ruling class and to take over the economic goods as well as the political control of the latter.

On the other hand, it is equally plain that a ruling class which is completely dominated by the instinct of the persistence of aggregates, and which does not permit any play to the instinct of combinations, finds itself soon outstripped by another collectivity which has kept up with new discoveries and new inventions. When a conflict ensues, this ruling class is overthrown because even though it is willing to use force to maintain itself it has only an antiquated system at its disposal. Venice is the classical example of this form of social equilibrium. The opposition, which is made up of those in whom the instinct of combination predominates, is more alert intellectually and more nimble in the use of the latest devices.

The best system for the maintenance of the social equilibrium is a proper mixture of residues I and II (2255). The ruling class must by no means be averse to using force if it looks as though the instinct of combinations is gaining so much strength that it threatens the collectivity with dissolution. But it must also be ready to use cunning when the use of force will endanger its own position. In conflict between capital and labor, the use of cunning is often more productive of good results for the capitalistic group and the social equilibrium than an open show of force. The history of Graeco-Roman antiquity, as well as that of France and Italy, is shown to be explicable on the basis of the struggle between these two residue-systems. Athens, as representing the instinct of combination, and Sparta, as representing the persistence of aggregates, are made to prove conclusively the failure of the exclusive use of the one or the other residue-system. Thebes under Epaminondas and Pelopidas is made to prove how a proper mixture of both can result in lifting a comparatively small and obscure collectivity to the front rank of political greatness.

The mechanism of this shift of power from one group to the other is further illuminated by viewing the predominance of the one or the other residue-system in terms of the control of the individuals in whom these residue-systems work. At any one given time within a collectivity these two residue-systems are found operative with greater or less force within certain individuals. The type in whom the residue of combinations dominates Pareto calls the *speculator;* the one in whom the persistence of aggregates dominates he calls the *rentier.*[4] The speculator is the fearless type with nothing to lose and everything to gain who rejoices in daring combinations, who is not held back by scruples of any kind, and who will take his success wherever he finds it and at no matter what cost. The rentier is the timid investor who is afraid to make any move lest his capital be impaired and he suffer a loss. The economic behavior of speculator and rentier exemplify two fundamentally different psychological types.

In a situation in which the political control is in the hands of the rentiers, they will be too timid to take any decisive step and will let emergencies control them rather than use strong measures to control the emergencies and to continue at the helm. The speculators gradually acquire power on account of their unscrupulous behavior, and then at the appropriate moment they displace the rentiers and take over the

---

[4] *Rentier,* the French term applied to those who live on a fixed income derived from the interest on loans, primarily government loans.

management of affairs. The process Pareto calls the *circulation of the élites*. Yet the two types do not need to come to blows. Often the process of circulation takes place peacefully by the gradual absorption into the rank of the rentiers of the most likely, the most fortunate, or the most pliable of the speculators. This rejuvenation of the élite, noticeable particularly in countries like the United States and Great Britain, results in giving the ruling class the necessary combination of residues; the social equilibrium remains intact and the collectivity is able to face the necessary changes without violence and chaos.

Many of the concepts utilized in constructing this theory of residues will be familiar to readers of sociological and anthropological literature, although Pareto does not mention them. The instinct of combination bears a striking similarity to Veblen's instinct of workmanship and Taussig's instinct of contrivance. Perhaps the whole discussion of these sentiments and instincts bears too much of a vague and formalistic character, growing out of Pareto's logical rather than his psychological approach. He marshals an amazingly wide array of facts to discover that behind their apparent dissimilarity there is to be found at work a common factor. Yet this common factor is perceived in a classificatory fashion, the similarities between two situations being similarities which would appear on the outside. He never analyzes the psychological mechanism with which the individual operates when he manifests behavior having behind it the residue of the persistence of aggregates. In a sense Pareto is a most thoroughgoing behaviorist. He deals with nothing but the outside manifestations of individuals. What goes on within the individual's consciousness does not concern him, although he would not deny the right of a psychologist to study such phenomena. Yet one has a suspicion that he would consider such a study as "metaphysical." Hence, also, his utter neglect of the entire field of psychopathology. Phenomena studied by Freud in the processes of "rationalization," which would throw so much light on Pareto's whole theory of derivations, are utterly neglected. There is no evidence that Pareto has ever heard of Freud.

An example will illustrate Pareto's method of approach. Speaking of those who wish to force their own moral ideas upon others, he says:

The state of mind of these seems to be as follows. They have within them certain persistences of aggregates, so alive and powerful that they completely dominate their minds. It is this phenomenon which is called faith. The object of this faith may vary; let us indicate it in a general way by *A*. The person who has that faith attributes to *A* an absolute value, puts away from his mind all doubt, every consideration of opportunity, every intrusion of other facts which might enter into calculation. To constrain others to have the same faith in *A*, or at least to act as if they had it, amounts in the end to compulsion. People are compelled to follow their own good and that of others. It is simply a way of giving concrete shape to the absolute *good; Compelle intrare.* So far as concerns the substance of the phenomenon, it matters little whether *A* is the faith of Anytos and Melitos, or that of Saint Augustin, or that of Torquemada, or that of Mr. Béranger, of educated people, of imbeciles, of statesmen, of litterateurs, of a large number of people or a small number: there is nothing variable in this except the derivations by which it is made to appear that the conclusions of faith are the demonstrations of a "science," which is nothing but pure ignorance. It is to be noticed that the oscillatory movement takes place today around a line which indicates that on an average, in our own day, the phenomenon has decreased in intensity. We are no longer in the days when the dissenters were condemned to drink the hemlock or to burn at the stake. Our "moralists" and our *dominicans of virtue* must content themselves with inflicting lesser punishments [1715].

The purely logical character of Pareto's analysis comes out here very clearly. He states a psychological phenomenon in mechanical terms, thereby simplifying it. In so far as a mechanical process is clearer to us than psychological process, the phenomenon is also clarified. Taking psychological processes for granted, Pareto shows how a certain form of human behavior springs from a certain inherent mechanism, noted but not explained, which is dependent upon a set of psychomechanical traits also noted without explanation. Pareto might argue that it is no more his province to explain the things that happen behind the mechanism than it is for the physicist to go behind the power of gravity or to indulge in speculations as to the ultimate nature of matter. They are legitimate speculations but not necessary to an explanation or a description of how certain phenomena of matter and motion take place.

Given the residues and their derivations, the problem remains to ascertain what residues will select what derivations as expressions of themselves. That problem is insoluble because it depends upon too many accidental factors. At one time a certain residue will express itself in certain derivations, at another time in others. Pareto says that certain derivations will appear when they can be used effectively to influence the sentiments of others (1716). But he does not tell us how those derivations originate which start by convincing the individual first, or those which are used to convince anyone else.

There is the further fact that derivations once expressed have a reinforcing effect upon the residues which they express, since the relationship between residues and derivations is not that of cause and effect but that of mutual influence. Hence there appears great difficulty in separating the influence and the motivation of residues and derivations within the human being. A proper derivation coming at the appropriate time may serve to give expression to a set of inarticulate and confused residues so that we often stand in utter amazement before a perfectly indifferent or frivolous "cause" of very weighty and far-reaching events. It is also possible that a derivation manifesting a certain residue is similar to the derivation of another residue; by suppressing one derivation, the result will be to reinforce the one left free, which will then carry the burden of two residues, much to the damage of the effort to differentiate clearly. Derivations of the same residue, which are so important in the eyes of the vulgar, often find support in the eyes of the statesman who pays little or no attention to the different derivations, because he is more interested in maintaining the residue behind them. A statesman might encourage all religious forms (derivations) because he believes in the stabilizing influence of religion.

Pareto may feel that it is enough, for the time being, to have pointed out that derivations vary while the residues remain constant, without pointing out in detail what forms of derivations represent the appropriate residues at specific times and places. As it is, we are left quite in the dark as to the connection. In the main we have to take Pareto's word that a certain derivation represents a certain residue, contenting ourselves with the more or less reasonable and more or less probable explanation that it may be so. Someone else might contend that a certain derivation represents a certain other residue, and the argument will have to go on without any solution. It is the same problem which confronts those who try to bring some order into the language of the symbolism of the Freudians. The same symbol may stand for so many different repressions that it is difficult to establish any connection until the analysis develops the connection which is disclosed by the patient. Pareto has not this check on his derivations, hence the whole theory of derivations is nothing but a very first approximation to something that may prove useful after a great deal more is discovered about the various shadings and differences within the derivations themselves.

Pareto's classification is after all very rough, but he would contend that this is the way to proceed. He intimates that under certain differences of economic political conditions, which may be multiplied indefinitely when we have sufficient information to distinguish social and economic phenomena quantitatively, there is noticeable a difference in the manner in which the derivations express themselves. He even attempts to give each of them a certain index, but in view of our ignorance of the details of these conditions, the indices are bound to remain abstract, leaving us nothing but the suggestion of a method of procedure.

It is possible to state Pareto's theory as follows: If we had a quantitative measurement of the whole set of conditions correlated with a certain given set of derivations, and if we had quantitative measures of the differences between two or more forms of the same derivation and of the extent to which certain derivations are the functions of a certain residue, we could then group the derivations in an ascending or a descending scale. By referring the minutely described derivation to its scale of influencing conditions, we would then be in a position to ascertain the intensity of the residue, as well as the character of the mutually influencing conditions which give us the particular derivation. At any given time and place any social expression could at once be classified as a derivation of a certain intensity, and, because of this intensity, of a certain set of conditions. Finally, it could be classified as a derivation of the residue which the intensity of this derivation and its conditions disclose.

For Pareto, the whole phenomenon of social life becomes a series of equations in which ineluctable sentiments mask their inescapable push by a series of accidental manifestations frantically trying to conform their non-logical character to an equally ineluctable necessity to appear logical to themselves as well as to others. The same inevitable tendency to be non-logical also compels them to appear logical. The history of mankind is therefore a succession of efforts to appear logical. The situation may change, but underneath it all there remain the sentiments as forces seeking manifestation, and the successive stages of human history are simply a series of derivations varying in form from age to age and from people to people. The substance remains the same while the form changes, and even the changes obey certain laws so that they can be organized and classified, giving us a veritable alphabet and key to the things that lie behind.

It is difficult to escape the feeling that Pareto has proceeded in his *Traité* very much after the manner of Spencer and Frazer. From reading and observation he has conceived the notions of residues and derivations. With these notions so conceived, he has gone over the vast field of Western European life and selected instances and illustrations on which his notions could be used as instruments. It is questionable whether any other method of obtaining social categories is possible at present.

In spite of his violent assertions that he is only seeking experimental uniformities, it is plain enough that in the field of social behavior uniformities are made and not found. This is particularly true in the field of historical phenomena. He finds "inductively" that the history of Greece, Rome, and the Middle Ages, the history of the church, and a large portion of the history of modern and contemporary Europe, America, and Asia, contain the uniformities demanded by his "logico-experimental" method. Yet he seems to have no conception that in finding uniformities he is *selecting* them; that inside an enormous storehouse of facts such as the history of Western Europe, of which certain periods are known to us only scantily and where the interpretations of the recording historian saturate the facts which he records, it is very easy to find just what one is looking for. He does not seem to realize that another scientist equally devoted to the "logico-experimental" method might find things precisely the opposite.

Pareto's "scientific method" proves to him conclusively that it is absurd and foolish[5] ever to expect anything but war and conflict among nations and social groups. Yet it is conceivable that his own method of multiple equations might be used to show that, as new combinations emerge, it will be impossible under the circumstances to resort to force. This could result, not necessarily because human beings are better, but because in a certain epoch a certain people belonging to a certain social class will find themselves so situated that a recourse to force will be impossible. Peace as a "virtual movement" contrasted with war as a "real movement" may, when certain "conditions" occur, become reversed; peace then being the real movement and war the virtual movement. Certainly peace and war, according to his own method, are movements observed at all times and places; because of this it is not difficult to believe that peace is as reasonable and as "uniform" as war. Such a situation may be less "desirable," but that is another question.

Although Pareto disclaims any bias in favor of any social system, such as democracy or aristocracy, pretending that both are odious to him in the way in which they are operating or have operated, yet one could more easily find a defense of aristocracy than of democracy in the pages of the *Traité.* Even though he is very uncomplimentary about the people characterized by the *persistence of aggregates,* one has a feeling that in the main they are more to his taste than the nimble-witted and shrewd "speculators" in whom predominates the *instinct of combinations.* Ob-

---

[5] For an "objective" person Pareto's pages are liberally strewn with expressions such as "cowardly," "useless," "harmful," "stupid," "foolish," "absurd," "ridiculous," "pedantry," and others.

jectivity that protests its objectivity so much perhaps "protests too much." The saving clauses thrown in here and there as sops to mathematical-logical conscience fail to stay with the reader who has waded through 1,761 pages with objectivity at the boiling-point.

Still the *Sociologie Générale* is a monumental work, monumental because of that very passion for a scientific approach which it does not reach and for the terrific blows it gives to the numerous preconceptions different from its own. It is a pity that so many hard blows should have been wasted in fighting the "demagogic plutocracy" of European parliamentarism. This will make the book more or less unintelligible to an English or an American reader. Pareto is speaking primarily to an Italo-French audience. His occasional references to England and America are rather insignificant and sometimes grotesque (2267). The combination of politics and economics which has given rise to "Panamas"—graft on heroic scale—is unfamiliar to English-speaking readers, except perhaps during the period of the late war. This unfamiliarity is due to the fact that the speculators and combinators in English-speaking countries resort to the technique of legitimate business in order to get rich. In comparison with the profits of legitimate business the benefits of political graft pale into insignificance. Pareto's study provides a most searching and penetrating analysis of the period of European parliamentarism from 1870 to 1914. An enormous literary and historical erudition in the life-history of Europe, particularly of the Mediterranean culture and its fringes, serves as a background.

For an adventure in the realm of human folly the *Traité* is a certain, if at times a too voluble, guide. But the immense mass of material presented will be culled differently by persons who approach it with different conceptions. A fascist will consider it as his Bible: so also can a liberal free-trader, an anticlerical, or a free-thinker; but the fascist will get the best of the bargain. For scientific purposes the greatest service performed by Pareto is in fashioning new tools,[6] through the notion of residues and derivations; even though it may appear that these tools came too late, and that the field is already pre-empted by the similar and probably more effective schools of modern psycho-pathology.[7]

[6] Something may be gained in precision—if not in clarity—by Pareto's method of mathematical symbolism.

[7] [This analysis was first written and revised by the analyst in the year 1929.— EDITOR.]

ANALYSIS 8

THE SOCIOLOGICAL METHODS OF WILLIAM GRAHAM SUMNER,[1] AND OF WILLIAM I. THOMAS AND FLORIAN ZNANIECKI[2]

By ROBERT E. PARK
University of Chicago

I. SUMNER

Folkways, published in 1906, is undoubtedly Sumner's most important work. It is one of the two or three most important books in the field of sociology by American authors. It is not, however, a systematic treatise. On the contrary, it is a rather loosely organized collection of observations and notes, in which there is much repetition and some inconsistency. The very form in which the matter is presented reveals lack of co-ordination and structure. There is likely to be something about everything in every chapter, and not even the very full Index reveals the wealth of materials and of suggestion which the volume contains on any one of the many topics discussed. In fact, the book, which resembles an encyclopedia in its organization as well as in the multitude of special topics with which it deals, has the character of a traveler's notebook rather than of a systematic treatise, although most of Sumner's travels were made vicariously, through the medium of other writings.

In spite of the unsystematic manner in which its materials are presented, *Folkways* reveals a fundamental point of view and contains implicitly a system of sociological categories or, to use the language of E. W. Hobson, "a frame of reference."[3] It is because points of view and frames of reference are elementary necessities of anything that seeks to call itself scientific, in the strict sense of that term, that Sumner's work is important with regard to method as well as content.

In view of the nature of his interest and of the task that he set himself,

[1] William Graham Sumner, *Folkways: A Study of the Sociological Importance of Usages, Manners, Customs, Mores, and Morals* (New York: Ginn & Co., 1906; pp. vii + 692). [Cf. comments in the Introduction, p. 4.—EDITOR.]

[2] W. I. Thomas and Florian Znaniecki, *The Polish Peasant in Europe and America.* First published, Boston: Richard Badger, 1918 (5 vols.); republished, New York: Alfred A. Knopf, Inc., 1927 (2 vols.; pp. xv+vi+2250). All citations are to the original publication.

[3] E. W. Hobson, *The Domain of Natural Science* (Cambridge: At the University Press, 1926; pp. xvi + 510).

it is not easy to describe or define, in formal terms, the methods by which Sumner carried on his researches. They were, on the whole, the methods of an explorer and a naturalist rather than of a technician. Actually, he seems to have undertaken to survey the whole realm of human nature and human behavior, so far as it is crystallized and exhibited objectively in custom and in habit. So far as the *folkways* are concerned custom in the group and habit in the individual are simply two different ways of looking at the same thing. It is important to note that Sumner started his investigations with an interest rather than a problem. It is, however, only after problems have been formulated that we ordinarily speak of method in reference to their investigation. In this sense it might be said that Sumner had no methods at all. He was an ardent and widely read student of history, but his methods and point of view were not historical. He was profoundly impressed by Herbert Spencer and the evolutionary point of view, and he regarded culture, along with physical nature, as one of the incidental products of the cosmic process. But the processes of cultural life and change were not, as he described them, evolutionary processes.

"There is," he says, "no development of the mores along any lines of logical or other sequence. The mores shift in an endless readjustment of the modes of behavior, effort, and thinking, so as to reach the greatest advantage under the conditions."[4] There is, to be sure, growth and decay, but evolution in the sense of a continuous advance to better and better is an illusion. "Progress," he concludes, "is an object of faith."

Sumner's knowledge of anthropological literature was profound, but he was not concerned with the historical and geographical aspects of culture; it was not the fact that certain customs exist at a time and a place that seemed to him important, but rather that they are not now what they once were; that they change in response to conditions. Manners, customs, usages, and the mores were for him not events to be recorded merely, but they were things; things which grow up and decay, and, in general, behave in ways which can be described and explained. Folkways, as Sumner described them, are cultural traits, viewed from the point of view of action rather than artifact. They are action patterns, artifacts being merely the instruments with which the action is effected. He says:

The processes and the artifacts which are connected with the food supply offer us the purest and simplest illustration of the development of the folk-

[4] *Op. cit.,* p. 476.

ways.[5] The processes are folkways. The artifacts are tools and weapons which, by their utility modify the folkways.[6]

It is in his conception of the folkways that Sumner most nearly approaches the point of view of anthropology. Folkways are habits and customs, that is to say, forms of human behavior. Tools, artifacts, arts and crafts, language, science, political organization, and institutions are merely extensions of structures and of functions, of which the habits of the individual and the customs of the group are the most elementary expressions. Folkways cover all the ways in which men habitually act. They are the "products of use and wont."

The operation by which folkways are produced consists in the frequent repetition of petty acts, often by great numbers acting in concert or, at least, acting in the same way when face to face with the same need. The immediate motive is interest. It produces habit in the individual and custom in the group.[7] . . . . Every act of each man fixes an atom in a structure. The structure thus built up is not physical, but societal and institutional, that is to say, it belongs to a category which must be defined and studied by itself.[8]

It is when we look at customs, institutions, and cultural traits as an aspect of action, individual and collective, that the transition from anthropology to sociology and social psychology is effected. Social anthropology becomes sociology as soon as it ceases to be description of something that exists and becomes a description and explanation of the processes by which that something changes and assumes a new and different character.

If in his conception of the folkways Sumner seems to include within his point of view almost all that ordinarily falls within the field of cultural anthropology, in his conception of the mores he trenches on the field of political science and ethics. The mores are those folkways, which, at a given time and place, define and prescribe what is right and proper.

All notions of propriety, decency, chastity, politeness, order, duty, right, rights, discipline, respect, reverence, co-operation, and fellowship, especially all things in regard to which good and ill depend entirely on the point at which the line is drawn, are in the mores. The mores can make things seem right and good to one group or one age which to another seem antagonistic to every instinct of human nature.[9] . . . . The notion of right and ought is the same in regard to all the folkways, but the degree of it varies with the importance of the interest at stake.[10] . . . . Out of the unconscious experiment

[5] *Ibid.*, p. 119.
[6] *Ibid.*, p. 137.
[7] *Ibid.*, p. 3.
[8] *Ibid.*, p. 35.
[9] *Ibid.*, p. 231.
[10] *Ibid.*, p. 28.

which every repetition of the ways includes, there issues pleasure or pain, and then, so far as men are capable of reflection, convictions that the ways are conducive to societal welfare. . . . . When this conviction as to the relation to welfare is added to the folkways, they are converted into mores.[11]

Political philosophy and ethics are implicit in the mores. They are never original and creative, but secondary and derived. Changes in history are due to changes in life-conditions. Then the folkways (mores) change. Then the new philosophies and ethical rules are invented to try to justify the new ways.

All forms of what we call social control, including religious beliefs and political dogma, are in the mores. . . . . The folkways dominate the societal life. Then they seem true and right, and arise into mores as the norm of welfare. Thence are produced faiths, ideas, doctrines, religions, and philosophies, according to the stage of civilization and the fashions of reflection and generalization."[12]

"The word 'moral' means what belongs or appertains to the mores." It is only when the word is used in this sense that it corresponds to anything real. "The modern peoples have made morals and morality a separate domain, by the side of religion, philosophy, and politics. In that sense, morals is an impossible and unreal category. It has no existence and can have none."[13] Modern peoples have attempted to establish the status of morals on principles of general application, "so that it shall be universal, absolute, and everlasting." But such attempts are "disastrous to a sound study of facts."[14]

Every class or group in society has its own mores. This is true of ranks, professions, industrial classes, religious and philosophical sects, and all other divisions of society. These mores are facts; they are the only morals there are. Principles that have no foundation in the habits of any group are mere abstractions.

This defines the relation of mores to morals, and the relation of sociology to ethics. Sociology treats the moral codes as facts; describes them, but does not seek to criticize or correct them. To criticize and correct morals is a problem, as Thomas and Znaniecke say, for the technician.[15] The situation is the same with reference to the state and its laws.

Acts of legislation come out of the mores. In low civilization all societal regulations are customs and taboos, the origin of which is unknown. Positive laws are impossible until the stage of verification, reflection, and criti-

---

[11] *Ibid.*, p. 3.
[12] *Ibid.*, p. 38.
[13] *Ibid.*, p. 37.
[14] *Ibid.*
[15] Cf. *The Polish Peasant*, I, 67–73, in reference to the task of the social technician.

cism is reached. . . . . Legislation to be strong must be consistent with the mores.[16]

The mores are a phenomenon of society and not of the state. There is, strictly speaking, no such thing as "administration of the mores." "The state administration fails if it tries to deal with the mores, because it goes out of its province." This does not mean "that reform and correction are hopeless." "Observation and consideration of cases which occur affect opinion and form convictions. The statesman and social philosopher can act with such influences, sum up the forces which make them, and greatly help the result." But politics is, like medicine, an art rather than a science. "Intelligent art can be introduced here as elsewhere, but it is necessary to understand the facts of nature with which it will have to deal."[17]

Here again it is important to emphasize the fact that the folkways and the mores, as Sumner understands them, are "not creations of human purpose and wit."

They are like products of natural forces which men unconsciously set in operation, or they are like the instinctive ways of animals, which are developed out of experience, which reach a final form of maximum adaptation to an interest, which are handed down by tradition, and admit of no exception or variation, yet change to meet new conditions, still within the same limited methods, and without rational reflection or purpose.[18]

It is clear, then, that the sphere of the folkways lies between those inherited capacities and instinctive forms of behavior that E. L. Thorndyke calls "original nature" and those rational constructions of human wit and forethought, erected upon a foundation of custom and habit, that we call "institutions." The distinction between mores, on the one hand, and law and institutions, on the other, is that laws and institutions are subjects for discussion, and, so far as that is true, they are rational. The mores are not matters for discussion; they are simply facts. "They have nothing to do with what ought to be, will be, may be, or once was, if it is not now."[19]

It is within the limits of the region thus defined that Sumner's investigations and researches lie, so far as they are recorded in *Folkways*. It would be interesting, if it were possible with the information which his biographer has given us, to outline a little more precisely than anyone has yet done the manner in which he arrived at his point of view and deliminated the field of his study. Sumner started life as a clergy-

---

[16] Sumner, *op. cit.*, p. 55.   [18] *Ibid.*, p. 4.

[17] *Ibid.*, p. 117.   [19] *Ibid.*, p. 77.

man. He became an economist. He had, as an officeholder, some political experience. He sought, through his numerous essays and papers, to impress himself and his ideas—but without much success—upon the course of current events. His conviction, reached by a wide survey of manners and customs, convinced him that political doctrine and moral code did not, and could not, have the absolute and universal validity that had ordinarily been attributed to them. He learned, perhaps from his own experience, the futility and the mischievous character of much that passes under the name of idealism and reform. All this led him to seek, in a broad, disinterested, and empirical study of human nature, a sound basis for all practical efforts to direct the course of current events, to control political action, and to improve social life generally.

Sometime early in the nineties economic problems and public questions had begun to lose for him the interest which they formerly held. He began at this time to devote himself more exclusively to the fundamental questions of sociology. As early as 1881, however, he stated:

It is to the pursuit of sociology and the study of the industrial organization in combination with the other organizations of society that we must look for the more fruitful development of political economy. We are already in such a position with sociology that a person who has gained what we now possess of that science will bring to bear upon economic problems a sounder judgment and a more correct conception of all social relations than a person who may have read a library of the existing treatises on political economy. The essential elements of political economy are only corollaries or special cases of sociological principles.[20]

In 1899 Sumner began to write out a textbook on sociology, based upon materials which he had been selecting and using in his lectures for ten or fifteen years. From the four volumes recently published by A. G. Keller we may see what these materials were like, and what, in all probability, the textbook would have been if it had been completed in the form in which he then conceived it.[21]

The method—if it can be called a method—which he used in collecting this material is described by his biographer in this way:

He made and classified thousands of notes containing information derived from an almost incredible number of sources, many of them difficult of access. No task the performance of which promised to make him better fitted for the work seemed too exacting. After he was forty-five years old,

[20] Sumner, "Sociology," in the volume *War and Other Essays.* Quoted by Harris E. Starr, *William Graham Sumner* (New York: H. Holt & Co., 1925), p. 388.

[21] W. G. Sumner and A. G. Keller, *The Science of Society* (4 vols.; New Haven: Yale University Press, 1927).

on evidence of dates in his dictionaries and grammars, he acquired a good working knowledge of the two Scandinavian tongues, Dutch, Spanish, Portuguese, Italian, Russian, and Polish. In 1899, he began to write out the results of all this study in the form of a textbook.[22]

The word *classified* should be especially noted, because it was presumably out of his classifications that the concepts of *Folkways* grew up.

The result of these studies was: (1) a collection of materials illustrating the wide diversities of ways in which human beings customarily act, and the characteristic forms of belief and sentiment that have arisen in the efforts of men to live together; (2) a description, neither complete nor wholly systematic, of the characteristic types and classes of human behavior, which take form in use and wont and are transmitted in the form of tradition; (3) a description—rather inadequate, to be sure—of the way in which custom and the mores when they become objects of reflection and discussion, assume the rational character of social institutions.

One of the most important of Sumner's contributions to social science was the set of categories and concepts which he worked out as an incident of his researches, and as a means of carrying them on. The concepts and the frames of reference with which scientific work, as soon as it becomes systematic, is invariably carried on, are the most important parts of scientific method. But these are usually, as Charles H. Cooley has suggested, the by-products of research and not antecedent to it. This is inevitably so when, as in the case of Sumner, the work is creative and original rather than routine and technical.

In the course of collecting and presenting the materials on which *Folkways* is based, Sumner formulated, as a mere incident of his task, a very large number of concepts. Later, in recording his observations and reflections upon these materials, he employed these concepts as a means of description and interpretation; and he defined them in such general and conceptual terms as to make them useful for other students in this field. Among the most important concepts to which Sumner gave an original and more precise definition in addition to those of the folkways and mores, are: (1) social groups, that is, the family, the "we-group" and the "other group," sects, parties, and social classes; (2) ethos, or group character, a term which is comparable to the anthropological concept of the culture complex, but with the emphasis on action and function rather than on form and structure; (3) ethnocentrism, patriotism, chauvinism—characteristics peculiar to nationalist and racial groups; (4) asceti-

---

[22] *William Graham Sumner*, pp. 388–89.

cism, a characteristic, primarily, of sects and religious groups, as ethno-centrism is of political and ethnic groups; (5) the masses and the classes, particularly with reference to the rôle that each plays in the formation of custom; (6) taboo, convention, etiquette, and social ritual—the specific forms in which the mores come to be defined and exist in society; (7) fashion, poses, fads, and cant—forms in which the mores change; (8) ceremonial, literature, and the drama—all of them characteristic expressions of the mores; (9) institutions—the forms which language, law, and customs generally assume when they become objects of reflection and subject to revision, correction, and reconstruction, in accordance with rational principles.

This list of terms by no means does justice to the wealth of ideas which are found scattered through the six hundred and fifty pages of *Folkways*. It does suggest, however, that there is implicit in this volume a body of concepts that could have been given a form that would give *Folkways* a systematic character which it does not possess. These concepts are at once Sumner's contribution to the methodology of the social sciences and at the same time the method he actually employed in organizing, classifying, and interpreting the material with which his wide-ranging excursions into the literature of all the languages of Europe had made him acquainted.

There seems to be no reason why Sumner should not have sorted out the fruits of his reading and observations in a more systematic way had he chosen to do so. Perhaps he believed that, in the state of sociological science then existing, his work would be more interesting and give a truer picture of his field of research and investigation if he presented the materials about as he found and recorded them. If so, his faith was justified by the results. *Folkways* is still one of the most useful, stimulating, and widely read books in the whole field of social science. Sumner was an explorer. His task was to survey the general features of the region in which future studies of sociologists lay. The effect of his researches was to lay a foundation for more realistic, more objective, and more systematic studies in the field of human nature and society than had existed up to that time.

It seems to me futile to attempt to characterize more precisely Sumner's methods of research. There are in *Folkways* what might be described as case studies of institutions, notably his chapters on slavery and marriage. But these have been as well or better done by other writers. What Sumner achieved in the *Folkways* was a point of view. The methodological tools with which he worked were his concepts and his manner of formulating them on the basis of a wide knowledge, not of cases merely, or of individual instances, but of cases in their whole cultural context. This is, it seems to me, an essential step in the progress of a science, which, having been merely descriptive and impressionistic, is seeking to be systematic and explanatory.

One may, perhaps, best define Sumner's position and point of view if one compares his work with such studies as those of Westermarck or Hobhouse—Westermarck, in *The Origin and Development of the Moral Ideas,* and Hobhouse, in his volume *Morals in Evolution.* Both Hobhouse and Westermarck were, after all, historians. They were trying to make clear just how the existing moral ideas and conceptions of the modern civilized peoples came into existence. What they achieved was a natural history of morals. Sumner, on the contrary, was trying, by analysis of existing cultures, to describe and classify their different and typical forms in such a way as to make these the objects of systematic investigation and explanation. What he did was to revive an interest in the study of human nature based, not upon instincts, physiology, and the lower animals, but upon the study of man and society.

II.   THOMAS AND ZNANIECKI

The only other work of an American sociologist involving research that is comparable to Sumner's *Folkways* in point of view, method, and importance is *The Polish Peasant,* which is the joint product of William I. Thomas and Florian Znaniecki. The work as originally published consisted of five volumes. These are described in the Preface as follows:

Volumes I and II comprise a study of the organization of the peasant primary groups (family and community), and of the partial evolution of this system of organization under the influence of the new industrial system and of immigration to America and Germany. Volume III is the autobiography (with critical treatment) of an immigrant of peasant origin but belonging by occupation to the lower city class, and illustrates the tendency to disorganization of the individual under the conditions involved in a rapid transition from one type of social organization to another. Volume IV treats the dissolution of the primary group and the social and political reorganization and unification of peasant communities in Poland on the new ground of rational co-operation. Volume V is based on studies of the Polish immigrant in America and shows the degrees and forms of disorganization associated with a too-rapid and inadequately mediated individualization, with a sketch of the beginnings of reorganization.[23]

Stated in terms of the problems involved, *The Polish Peasant* is concerned with such matters as immigration; racial prejudice; cultural as-

---

[23] *The Polish Peasant,* I, viii.

similation; the comparative mental and moral worth of races and nationalities; crime, alcoholism, vagabondage, and other forms of anti-social behavior; nationalism and internationalism; democracy and class-hierarchization; efficiency and happiness, particularly as functions of the relation of the individual to the social framework containing his activities; the rate of individualization possible without disorganization; the difference between unreflective social cohesion brought about by tradition, and reflective social co-operation brought about by rational selection of common ends and means; the introduction of new and desirable attitudes and values without recourse to the way of revolution; and, more generally, the determination of the most general and particular laws of social reality, preliminary to the introduction of a social control comparable to that of the material world, resulting from the study of the laws of physical reality.

What one actually finds, upon reviewing these five volumes, is a study of the changes that are taking place in the cultural life of the Polish peasant in Poland and in America. To state it more succinctly, and in the language of Sumner, it is a study of the mores of a peasant community, but of a community which, owing to the breakdown of the historic isolation and to its "contact with the more complex and fluid world," is in process of evolution. It is, one may add, migration which is mainly responsible for the changes here studied; migration to the expanding industrial centers of Poland and Germany, and to the United States. All the specific and practical problems with which these several volumes are concerned are viewed in relation to, and as a consequence of, the breakdown of tradition and custom, and the changes in habit and attitude which this migration has initiated.

It appears, then, that the authors of *The Polish Peasant* and the author of *Folkways* are interested in substantially the same phenomenon, the difference being that they have approached the subject from different points of view and have investigated it by different methods.

Thomas and Znaniecki are not interested, as Sumner is, in a conceptual description of the mores. They do not, as a matter of fact, use the term *mores* at all. They have other concepts—social attitudes and social values —which seem to suit better the purposes of their analysis and better to describe for them the aspects of culture in which they are mainly interested. One may say, in a manner of speaking, that Sumner discovered the mores, and that his task, as he conceived it, was to work out a scheme and a classification on the basis of a wide comparison, for materials which history and ethnology put into his hands. Thomas and Znaniecki, on the other hand, are interested primarily in changes in the mores and folkways; the conditions under which these changes take place, and the character of the processes by which they are effected.

The Polish Peasant is a case study, and the plan, as originally conceived, assumed that other studies of other peasant communities and other peasant cultures would follow, making possible a wider comparison and a more general and accurate deduction. The distinction in point of view from which the authors of *The Polish Peasant* and the author of *Folkways* attack their several problems will appear in a clearer light if we recall Sumner's statement that what is "custom in the group is habit in the individual." The customs of the group impose themselves upon the individual, and his habits are consciously and unconsciously formed in conformity with them. On the other hand, the habits of individuals support group custom. Changes in habits undermine custom, and eventually destroy its influence and authority. It is evident, therefore, that one may study custom, as the ethnologist studies it, descriptively; or one may distinguish and describe general types of culture, as Sumner does, under such general categories as convention, social ritual, fashion, etc. On the other hand, one may study cultural forms from the point of view of change—change not merely in form but in content. But changes in the content of custom are brought about by changes in the experience of individuals—changes in attitude and in habit.

Things at home look different to the man who has enjoyed a sojourn abroad. Customs that once seemed as much a part of the natural order as the changing seasons look strange and quaint to the returned traveler. Things at home have not actually changed much, perhaps, but the returning traveler sees them in a different light. It is not the old home or its people and their customs but the traveler himself who has changed.

It is when things which have, or should have, the same meaning for everyone concerned turn out to have different meanings for different individuals that the concept of attitude arises. A social attitude is the subjective or individual aspect of a habit which has an accepted and conventional definition by the group of which the individual is a member. This is implied in the more or less familiar statement that a fact is a fact only in a universe of discourse. Every group has, or tends to have, its own universe of discourse; that is to say, its own language as well as its own conventions. The Polish peasant brings to America a body of tradition and custom in which, as Thomas would say, the situation has a definition different from that of the native population. Gradually he accommodates himself to the customs of the country. He acquires new habits and new points of view. In the language of *The Polish Peasant,* he acquires new attitudes and new values.

Society everywhere presents these dual aspects, the individual and the group, habit and custom, attitude and value. In practice, the social problem is, as the authors of *The Polish Peasant* state it: "How shall we produce with the help of the existing social organization and culture the desirable mental and moral characteristics in the individuals constituting the social group?" And, "How shall we produce, with the help of the existing mental and moral characteristics of the individual members of the group, the desirable type of social organization and culture?" The solutions of these problems require two kinds of data, namely, "the objective cultural elements of social life, and the subjective characteristics of the members of the social group."

To these two kinds of data—(1) "objective cultural elements" and (2) "subjective characteristics of the members of the group"—Thomas and Znaniecki give the names "social values" (or simply "values") and "attitudes." It is evident that these two terms correspond, in a general way, to "custom in the group and habit in the individual," as Sumner uses that expression. I say this in spite of the fact that the authors of *The Polish Peasant* have expressly stated that neither attitudes nor values were "a psychological phenomenon," and that attitude could not be identified with habit.

The distinction is important, but I shall not undertake to make it here. I am mainly concerned in pointing out the differences in the point of view of, and the intimate relation between, *Folkways* and *The Polish Peasant.* Sumner is concerned with the objective, Thomas and Znaniecki with the subjective, aspects of culture. As the fundamental concept of *Folkways* is the mores, so *The Polish Peasant* is mainly concerned with attitudes. *Folkways* is sociology; *The Polish Peasant* is social psychology.

It amounts in substance to this: Social attitudes are the individual and subjective aspects of the mores. The methodological problems with which the authors of *The Polish Peasant* were confronted were: (1) how to obtain a body of documentary materials in which the characteristic attitudes of *The Polish Peasant* were adequately expressed; (2) to find language and concepts in which to describe the attitudes which these materials disclose.

The first problem was solved (1) by the discovery of a large body of intimate family letters which had been exchanged between Polish immigrants in America and members of their families in Poland; and (2) by a collection of life-histories of Polish immigrants, one of which is published in full in Volume III of the series.

Since the publication of *The Polish Peasant*, the life-history, employed as a means for exploration of the attitudes and the cultural backgrounds of immigrants, has proved useful in the study of the behavior of delinquents, and in the investigation of personality types generally. The life-history has been used, also, as a device for exploring the inner life and content of institutions like the family and the church, and in discovering the cultural patterns of local communities. The life-history may have a character varying all the way from a mere record of obvious and external events to that of a confession, depending, finally, upon the extent to which the individual has been able to participate freely and without conflict in the social life about him, and, in doing so, has found a free expression of his attitudes and wishes or has been inhibited and introverted. It is the introverted individual who ordinarily writes a confession.

There is, as the authors of *The Polish Peasant* say,

no pre-existing harmony whatever between the individual and the social factors of personal evolution, and the fundamental tendencies of the individual are always in some disaccordance with the fundamental tendencies of social control. Personal evolution is always a struggle between the individual and society—a struggle for self-expression on the part of the individual, for his subjection, on the part of society—and it is in the total course of this struggle that the personality—not as a static "essence" but as a dynamic, continually evolving set of activities—manifests and constructs itself.[24]

As self-consciousness and subjectivity are themselves an effect of this conflict of the individual with the society of which he is a member, so the extent of this subjectivity and the character of the life-history will correspond to the nature and extent of this conflict. If the individual is by temperament and by character a social individual, what we call a "good mixer"; if he is able, in other words, to express himself easily and naturally in every situation he encounters, the story of his life will tend to assume the character of a mere record of events; events in which he participated. If, on the contrary, he is one who finds it difficult to express himself and is habitually frustrated in his efforts to act effectively in the social milieu, his life-history will be a record of his frustrations, of his feelings, of his incompleted acts, of his dreams, of his fantasies. A life-history will then have for him the effect of a catharsis.

[24] *Ibid.*, III, 35–36.

In the case of human beings, it is the wide range, of this subjective life, of mental and imaginative behavior, which intervenes between stimulus and response, which makes human behavior fundamentally different from that of the lower animals. It is this, too, which makes human behavior, particularly in the case of certain persons, so problematic and so difficult to understand. It is the purpose of the life-history to get a record of this inner life.

Life-history materials may be said to include any sort of record or document, including the case histories of the social agencies, which tend to throw light on the subjective behavior of individuals or of groups. The fifth volume of the series on the Polish peasant is largely based, for example, upon records of social agencies. Case records of this sort, however, are in themselves quite inadequate for the understanding of what is problematic in the behavior of the Polish immigrant. But they assume a new value when they are studied in connection with the earlier and more intimate life-history documents in the series.

It is assumed that the behavior and the attitudes reflected in these materials are representative of the Polish community itself and of the different types of personality of which that community is composed. But in order to analyze and describe these different personality types, accurately and conceptually, so that their representative character is manifest, it is necessary for the authors to formulate a conception of personality and to find language in which personality traits can be adequately described. This constituted the second methodological problem which the authors of *The Polish Peasant* were called upon to solve. In the methodological note, published as a sort of Preface to the whole series, and more particularly to the Introduction to Volume III, "The Life Record of an Immigrant," the authors have undertaken to formulate and set forth in rather a systematic way the terms and concepts in which life-history materials, and particularly the autobiography of an anonymous peasant, can be described and interpreted in such a way as to do two things: (1) make that life intelligible by reference to the organization and customs of the Polish community, and (2) throw light upon the nature of personality in general, and particularly upon the relation of personality and culture, and upon the relation of the individual and the group.

These conceptions constitute a frame of reference for the analysis and interpretation of documents and life-history materials in general. More than that, they may be said to constitute, even in the scattered and fragmentary way in which they are presented, a treatise on the fundamental concepts of social psychology.

The most important of these concepts are: (1) temperament, character, life-organization; (2) the three personality types represented by the philistine, the bohemian, and the creative personality; (3) the four fundamental "wishes," so called: curiosity and the desire for new experience, fear and the desire for security, desire for recognition, and the desire for response—that is to say, for love and affection; (4) social organization, including the mores and folkways; (5) the elementary units in which all these dissolve themselves, namely, attitudes.

Attitudes, as the authors conceive them, are of two sorts—temperamental and character attitudes.

We may call temperament the fundamental original group of attitudes of the individual as existing independently of any social influences; we may call character the set of organized and fixed groups of attitudes developed by social influence operating upon the temperamental basis. The temperamental attitudes are essentially instinctive, that is, they express themselves in biological action but not in reflective consciousness; the attitudes of the character are intellectual, that is, they are given by conscious reflection. This does not mean that the temperamental attitude cannot be experienced; it usually is experienced when for some reason the activity is inhibited. But with the temperamental attitude there is no conscious connection between the separate actions in which it expresses itself; every single feeling and satisfaction (e.g. hunger) is for the individual a separate entity; the living being does not generalize these feelings as forming one series, one permanent attitude. On the contrary, every manifestation of a character-attitude is given to the subject as a single expression of a more or less general tendency; a helpful or harmful action is accompanied by a consciousness of sympathy or hate, that is, by a conscious tendency to the repetition (or remembrance) of actions with an analogous meaning; the attitude accompanying the actual production of some piece of work is given as one element of a series that may be willingness or unwillingness to do such work, desire to realize a plan, to earn money, etc. This consciousness need not be always explicit, but it must be implicitly present and become explicit from time to time if the attitude is to be defined as a character-attitude.[25]

Temperament, character, and life-organization are intimately related but not identical. The individual man lives in the world which is limited by his experience. What he finds in nature and makes part of his world depends on what he is interested in, what occupies his attention, and what objects have significance for him. Thus different individuals, even when

[25] *Ibid.*, pp. 18–19.

they live in the same physical surroundings, may be said to live in different worlds because the objects they encounter have for them a different significance. This is what the authors mean when they say that individuals define the situation differently. The way the individual, within the limits of his experience, defines the situation determines his life-organization. This is the way the matter is stated in *The Polish Peasant:*

We must remember, first of all, that the environment by which he [the individual] is influenced and to which he adapts himself, is *his* world, not the objective world of science—is nature and society as he sees them, not as the scientist sees them. The individual subject reacts only to his experience, and his experience is not everything that an absolutely objective observer might find in the portion of the world within the individual's reach, but only what the individual himself finds. And what he finds depends upon his practical attitudes toward his environment, the demands he makes upon it and his control over it, the wishes he seeks to satisfy and the way in which he tries to satisfy them. His world thus widens with the development of his demands and his means of control, and the process of this widening involves two essential phases—the introduction of new complexities of data into the sphere of his experience and the definition of new situations within those complexities.[26]

The authors make a great deal of the distinction between the individual as an example of the human species, a "biological formation," as they call it, and the individual as a member of a society, "a social personality," or what we ordinarily describe as a person.

An individual with nothing but his biological formation, or—in social terms—with nothing but his temperamental attitudes, is not yet a social personality, but is able to become one. In the face of the world of social meanings he stands powerless; he is not even conscious of the existence of this reality, and when the latter manifests itself to him in changes of the material reality upon which his instincts bear, he is quite lost and either passively submits to the unexpected, or aimlessly revolts. Such is the position of the animal or the infant in human society; and a similar phenomenon repeats itself on a smaller scale whenever an individual on a low level of civilization gets in touch with a higher civilized environment, a worldling with a body of specialists, a foreigner with an autochthonic society, etc. In fact, human beings for the most part never suspect the existence of innumerable meanings—scientific, artistic, moral, political, economic—and a field of social reality whose meanings the individual does not know, even if he can observe its sensual contents, is as much out of the reach of his practical experience as the other side of the moon.[27]

[26] *Ibid.*, p. 21.   [27] *Ibid.*, p. 24.

Just as there is in the mores a rational element, an implicit philosophy, according to Sumner, so in the personality, as Thomas and Znaniecki conceive it, there is something more than character; there is an intellectual element, and it is this intellectual element that is represented specifically in the life-organization. One might perhaps express the notion by saying that the individual has a conception of himself, and that this conception of himself and his rôle in society is an integral part of his personality. It is, in fact, through this conception of himself that the individual gets and maintains control over his original nature, his impulsive life.

In order to become a social personality in any domain the individual must therefore not only realize the existence of the social meanings which objects possess in this domain, but also learn how to adapt himself to the demands which society puts upon him from the standpoint of these meanings and how to control these meanings for his personal purposes; and since meanings imply conscious thought, he must do this by conscious reflection, not by mere instinctive adaptations of reflexes. In order to satisfy the social demands put upon his personality he must reflectively organize his temperamental attitudes; in order to obtain the satisfaction of his own demands, he must develop intellectual methods for the control of social reality in place of the instinctive ways which are sufficient to control natural reality. And this effective reorganization of temperamental attitudes leads, as we have seen, to character, while the parallel development of intellectual methods of controlling social reality leads to a life-organization, which is nothing but the totality of these methods at work in the individual's social career.[28]

This means that the world in which men live is not merely a physical, but a moral, world; a world defined in terms of the attitudes and wishes of other men; a world which, so far as it has any stability at all, is defined in terms of the mores. It is in this moral world, the world of attitudes and wishes, that the individual with his heritage of instincts becomes a person, i.e., an individual with a status.

As Thomas and Znaniecki conceive personality, it is not something that can be described in static terms. It is not an action pattern or a system of habits merely. Personality is in constant evolution. It evolves, however, not merely under the influences of an environment which exists external to it, but more especially under the influence of an environment which it selects and defines and in a sense creates. In short, a man—and this distinguishes him from the lower animals—may be said to have a career.

A child comes into the world not merely without a character, but without personality. It is at the outset a mere bundle of reflexes. Its instincts,

[28] *Ibid.*, pp. 24–25.

whatever they may be, are, in the language of Thomas and Znaniecki, temperament attitudes. Gradually, by a process that has been described elsewhere as conditioning, the child's impulses are integrated, and instincts are converted into habits. In the natural course, and under the influence of associations with other individuals, the child develops self-consciousness and a conception of himself. At the same time, and in the same natural way, he defines his rôle in a social group; he may define it in several social groups. In so doing, however, he gains a control over himself which he did not possess so long as his life was a mere series of more or less automatic responses to stimuli. In becoming self-conscious the child makes himself not merely an object, but he makes his life, as he projects it ahead of him in imagination, a project. Eventually he formulates principles of action and organizes his life in ways which seem likely to further his life aim. This conception of himself, and the codes and rules by which the individual seeks to maintain this conception and this project in a changing world, is what the authors mean by a life-organization.

With this conception of personality as growing up in response to the changing social situations, the authors have described three different types of personality with reference to their ability to adjust themselves to a changing moral world: the philistine, the bohemian, and the creative personality.

The philistine is the individual who conceives himself in the conventional social pattern; whose life-organization is taken over from, and stabilized in, the patterns which he finds in the society about him. The philistine achieves a consistent life and a stable character, but on such terms as "practically [to] exclude development of any new attitude in the given conditions of life."

Opposed to the philistine is the bohemian, "whose possibilities are not closed simply because his character remains unformed." The philistine is always a conformist, always "accepting social tradition in its most stable elements." The bohemian, on the other hand, is likely to be a radical, responding to every new program or project as it presents itself, but never able to achieve a stable character or make a career. In any case, "Inconsistency is the essential feature of his activity."

In contrast with the philistine and the bohemian is the creative personality. He is one who is able to maintain a consistent life-organization in a changing world; a man who, in order to widen his control over his environment and himself, learns "to adopt his purpose to the continually increasing sphere of social reality."

The Philistine, the Bohemian and the creative man are the three funda-mental forms of personal determination toward which social personalities tend in their evolution. . . . . These three general types—limits of personal evolu-tion—include, of course, an indefinite number of variations, depending on the nature of the attitudes by which characters are constituted and on the schemes composing the life-organization of social individuals.[29]

Personalities, in short, may be distinguished with reference to their tendencies to grow. The philistine, with his tendency to develop a stark, fixed character, constitutes the solid structure of society. The more mobile bohemian, disposed as he is to reflect the changing aspects of social life, becomes a medium for communicating them. The creative personality makes the original contribution to culture.

Personalities may be further characterized by the degree to which they are predisposed by temperament or experience to respond to (1) the desire for new experience, (2) the need for security, (3) the desire for recognition, and (4) the desire for response.[30]

In general, it may be assumed that these wishes represent in one form or another the things that men want; these are the values which they will seek and find in society. It may be said, perhaps, that young men want new experience, and that old men want security. That men want fame (recognition), that women want love (response). But individuals will differ in respect to these matters. At any rate, these terms serve in a general way to characterize personality types, and by so doing explain human behavior as we find it.

From what has been said, it is not difficult to foresee that the social organization and the life-organization of the individual are, like custom and habit, different aspects of the same thing. The community imposes its rules, codes, and "definitions of the situation" upon its individual members, and as these are accepted and become established in the habits of individuals, they give support and strength to the social organization of which they are a part. The more firmly the social organization is fixed in tradition, the more completely will the individual's life-organiza-tions be integrated in an existing social order, and the less he will be able, in consequence, to accommodate himself to a new and a looser social order, such, for example, as the Polish peasant finds in America.

It is upon the basis of considerations of this sort that the authors are able to explain much of the demoralization which Polish peasants ex-hibit in America. The disorganization of the second generation, which is even greater than that of the first, is explained in a somewhat different

[29] *Ibid.*, pp. 30–31.   [30] See appendix at end of this paper.

way, but upon principles which are substantially like those already referred to.

There is much other material in these five volumes of *The Polish Peasant* that is important, to which, however, no reference has been made, since it seemed best to focus attention upon the concepts, and the methodological problems, which are relatively novel and characteristic of this particular study. For example, the authors have written, by way of introduction to Volumes I and II, interesting and important papers upon (1) "The Polish Family," (2) "The System of Polish Society," and (3) "The Religious and Magical Attitudes of the Polish Peasant." As these offer no methodological problems that are in any way peculiar to the type of research charactistic of these volumes, I leave them with this bare reference.

In conclusion, as defining the scientific character of this work, I can do no better than quote this statement from the fifth volume:

Our work does not pretend to give any definitive and universally valid sociological truths, nor to constitute a permanent model of sociological research; it merely claims to be a monograph, as nearly complete as possible under the circumstances, of a limited social group at a certain period of its evolution, which may suggest studies of other groups, more detailed and more perfect methodically, thus helping the investigation of modern living societies to rise above its present stage of journalistic impressionism, and preparing the ground for the determination of really exact general laws of human behavior. The analogies which we have mentioned are in this respect encouraging, for they allow us to presume that such laws are possible and that their determination will not meet any exceptional difficulties.

On the other hand, our study makes it very clear that a search for similarities in human behavior can lead to valuable and secure results only if it takes fully into account the important differences that exist between various societies, differences due chiefly to the widely varying lines of their past cultural evolution rather than to divergent biological tendencies and unequal natural abilities of their members. . . . . The Polish peasant is not and cannot be exactly the same kind of man as the native American, for his character has been moulded by his social milieu, and his social milieu has a set of traditions, an organization, a form and standard of living very different in their concrete complexity from those which are familiar to the American reader.[31]

The Polish Peasant, like the *Folkways,* must be regarded as a work of pioneers. It was necessary, first, to discover new sorts of materials; and, second, to find language in which to describe them. Quite aside from

[31] *The Polish Peasant,* V, 340–41.

any practical value which Thomas and Znaniecki's studies have because of the light they throw upon the problem of the immigrant, *The Polish Peasant* is chiefly significant as representing a point of view, a new approach to social problems. Its chief contribution, therefore, is not a body of fact, but a system of concepts.[32]

APPENDIX: THE "FOUR WISHES"

1. The desire for new experience is seen in simple form in the prowling and meddling activities of the child, and the love of adventure and travel in the boy and the man. It ranges in moral quality from the pursuit of game and the pursuit of pleasure to the pursuit of knowledge and the pursuit of ideals. It is found equally in the vagabond and in the scientific explorer. Novels, theaters, motion pictures, etc., are means of satisfying this desire vicariously, and their popularity is a sign of the elemental force of this desire.

   In its pure form the desire for new experience implies motion, change, danger, instability, social irresponsibility. The individual dominated by it shows a tendency to disregard prevailing standards and group interests. He may be a complete failure, on account of his instability; or a conspicuous success, if he converts his experience into social values—puts them in the form of a poem, makes of them a contribution to science, etc.

2. The desire for security is opposed to the desire for new experience. It implies avoidance of danger and death, caution, conservatism. Incorporation in an organization (family, community, state) provides the greatest security. In certain animal societies (e.g., the ants) the organization and co-operation are very rigid. Similarly, among the peasants of Europe, represented by our immigrant groups, all lines of behavior are predetermined for the individual by tradition. In such a group the individual is secure so long as the group organization is secure, but evidently he shows little originality or creativeness.

3. The desire for recognition expresses itself in devices for securing distinction in the eyes of the public. A list of the different modes of seeking recognition would be very long. It would include courageous behavior, showing off through ornament and dress, the pomp of kings, the display of opinions and knowledge, the possession of special attainments—in the arts, for example. It is expressed alike in arrogance and in humility, even in martyrdom. Certain modes of seeking recognition we define as "vanity," others as "ambition." The "will to

[32] [This analysis was first written in December, 1928, and revised by the analyst in March, 1929.—EDITOR.]

power" belongs here. Perhaps there has been no spur to human activity so keen and no motive so naïvely avowed as the desire for "undying fame," and it would be difficult to estimate the rôle the desire for recognition has played in the creation of social values.

4. The desire for response is a craving, not for the recognition of the public at large, but for the more intimate appreciation of individuals. It is exemplified in mother-love (touch plays an important rôle in this connection), in romantic love, in family affection, and in other personal attachments. Homesickness and loneliness are expressions of it. Many of the devices for securing recognition are used also in securing response.

Apparently these four classes comprehend all the positive wishes. Such attitudes as anger, fear, hate, and prejudice are attitudes toward these objects which may frustrate a wish.[33]

[33] See W. I. Thomas, "The Persistence of Primary-Group Norms in Present-Day Society," in Jennings, Watson, Meyer, and Thomas, *Suggestions of Modern Science Concerning Education* (New York: Macmillan Co., 1917).

ANALYSIS 9

TYPOLOGICAL METHOD: E. KRETSCHMER'S STUDY OF PHYSIQUE AND CHARACTER[1]

By HEINRICH KLÜVER

Institute for Juvenile Research, Chicago

A great number of investigators in the different fields of psychology, in psychopathology and psychiatry, in sociology and criminology, take it as a matter of course that their material necessitates the introduction of the concept of "types." We shall illustrate the use of this concept by considering the way in which Kretschmer is led to the formulation of types in his work *Physique and Character*. This analysis will lead us to the more important question as to what constitutes the typological "method." Kretschmer's work is only the point of departure for this inquiry. Kretschmer starts from special psychiatric problems. He is interested in certain constitutional factors, i.e., in the relations between physique, psychological dispositions, psychiatric and internal morbidity. His investigation results in two "general biotypes," the cyclothymic and the schizothymic, which are said to differ with regard to psychesthesia and mood, psychic tempo, psychomotility, and affined body types. These differences are more clearly presented in Table I. Cases of manic-depressive insanity are chiefly found in the cyclothymic group; the schizophrenic psychotics are scattered among the individuals of the schizothymic group. In both groups there are personalities fluctuating between normality and psychosis. In the schizothymic group we find "schizoid" individuals, and in the cyclothymic group we have "cycloid" individuals.

The question arises: How did Kretschmer, starting from Kraepelin's distinction between manic-depressive or "circular" insanity and schizophrenia (*dementia praecox*), arrive at this fundamental dichotomy?

Kretschmer answers:

The types . . . . are no "ideal types" which have emerged, consciously created in accordance with any given guiding principle or collection of preestablished values. They are, on the contrary, obtained from empirical sources in the following way: when a fairly large number of morphological similar-

---

[1] E. Kretschmer, *Körperbau und Charakter: Untersuchungen zum Konstitutionsproblem und zur Lehre von den Temperamenten* (Berlin: Springer, 1922; pp. xii + 195). Cf. also E. Kretschmer, *Physique and Character* (New York: Harcourt, Brace & Co., 1925; pp. xiv + 266). (Translated from the second edition.)

ities can be followed through a correspondingly large number of individuals, then we begin measuring. When we compute averages the outstanding common characteristics come out clearly, while those peculiar marks which only occur in isolated cases, disappear in the average value. In exactly the same way we treat the remainder of the characteristics which can only be described from mere optical observation. So we proceed as if we were copying at the same time the picture of one hundred individuals of a type on the same picture-surface, one on top of the other, in such a way that those characteristics which cover one another become sharply outlined, while those which do not fit over one another disappear. Only those characteristics which become

TABLE I

	Cyclothymic Type	Schizothymic Type
Psychesthesia and mood...	Diathetic proportion: between raised (gay) and depressed (sad)	Psychesthetic proportion: between hyperesthetic (sensitive) and anesthetic (cold)
Psychic tempo	Wavy, temperamental curve: between mobile and comfortable	Jerky temperamental curve: between unstable and tenacious, mode of thought and feeling alternating
Psychomotility	Adequate to stimulus, rounded, natural, smooth	Often inadequate to stimulus: reserved, awkward, inhibited, stiff, etc.
Affined body type.........	Pyknic*	Asthenic,* athletic,* dysplastic,* and their mixtures

*[Consult the glossary appended to this analysis.—EDITOR.]

strongly marked in the average values are described as "typical." We must not believe that it only requires careful observation to discover such a type clearly delineated and that we can do without wearisome practice of our eyes on our material; we find, on the contrary, in concrete cases, the typical elements always veiled by heterogeneous "individual" characteristics, and, in many respects, blurred. . . . . From this it follows, that our description of types, such as will be found in what follows, refers not to the most frequent cases, but to ideal cases, to such cases as bring most clearly to view common characteristics which in the majority of instances appear only blurred, but which, all the same, can be empirically demonstrated.[2]

The special technique employed by Kretschmer with hundreds of psychotics in collecting data—"solid data, which satisfy all the demands of physical science"—is of no interest to us in this connection. It may suffice

[2] *Physique and Character*, pp. 18–19.

to state that Kretschmer uses a combination of diagrammatic description, measurement, and registration by drawing and photography. It is clear that by using such a procedure with manic-depressive and schizophrenic patients one may be able "empirically" to demonstrate that there is a biological affinity between the psychic disposition of the manic-depressives and the pyknic body type, and a biological affinity between the psychic disposition of the schizophrenics and the body types of the asthenics, athletics, and certain dysplastics. It is clear, furthermore, that the same procedure may be applied to prepsychotic and normal individuals. This is essentially Kretschmer's procedure.

We see that body build and psychosis are considered here the two "guiding paths" in the investigation of constitution. Body build *and* psychosis are viewed, so to speak, as partial symptoms of the one fundamental constitutional organization of the individual. Thus, the conclusion is reached that the endogenous psychoses are nothing but pronounced, exaggerated temperamental types. The statistical findings constitute the trustworthy and provable basis for this conclusion; the individual case "may be typical or atypical."

There is no doubt that Kretschmer's "empirical" procedure in deducing two fundamental biotypes is open to various criticisms. But this is of secondary importance since, at present, we are not interested in constitutional factors per se. It may be that, in employing a certain method, the investigator neglects certain facts or is not clear about the nature of some facts. But the incorrect or the inadequate use of a method is not a defect of the method itself. We see clearly how the material obtained by Kretschmer may reasonably shape itself into types. But we are not clear yet about the nature of the typological method.

We may start from the assumption that light will be thrown on this method by considering the *verification* of types. But this is no doubt a wrong assumption. One may use the methods of statistics, of biochemistry, of sensory physiology, etc., with the view of verifying a monotypic, antitypic, or polytypic scheme. This leads us to the following points: (1) the means of verification change with the nature of the type or the types proposed, i.e., an inquiry into the ways of verifying types would leave us in the dark concerning the typological procedure itself; (2) it would take us too far afield even to touch upon the problem of verification in science in general.

Another and more promising procedure is available. We have to find an answer to the following two questions: (1) *What* is done by means of the typological method? (2) *How* is it done?

In regard to the first question, we may point to an analogy. We know that when using stains in microscopic studies, certain fibers become visible while others do not. We may not even know the exact chemical composition of the stain, and we may have no precise idea as to how the result is brought about. In other words, referring again to typology, all that we need to know is that by the use of this method certain phenomena we want to study become visible; i.e., that method A "works" in studying phenomenon B. *How* it works may be a difficult question to settle.

The foregoing questions, then, may be stated as follows: (1) What kind of phenomena become "visible" by means of the typological method? (2) How is this result brought about?

To answer the first question we have to turn to the "typologies" of different investigators. They present us various definitions of "type" and various type classifications. But if we abstract the difference in the nature of the data used and the differences in the fields explored, we are able to see remaining the general *form* of the phenomena arrived at by using the typological method.

Let us take Jung's types: the introverted and the extraverted.[3] For Jung, the relation of the individual to his environment, the subject-object relation, plays the decisive rôle. It is a relation of adaptation. The different modes of adaptation present themselves psychologically in two ways: in introversion and extraversion. Thus, two general attitude types arise: the introverted and the extraverted type. The general attitude, the special mode of adaptation, implies in both cases the presence of certain psychological mechanisms. It presupposes that the ways in which the psychological functions interact are different in these two types. Two different systems of functioning, so to speak, are assumed.

Or let us consider the T- and the B-type of W. Jaensch.[4] Here again we are dealing with biotypes with certain psychophysical characteristics. The "typical" characteristics are supposed to be present in after-images, eidetic images, and memory-images, in affective and intellectual life. At the same time these types imply differences in somatic respect. It is assumed that the T- and the B-complex represent two "psychophysical vege-

[3] C. G. Jung, *Psychological Types* (New York: Harcourt, Brace & Co., 1923; pp. xxii + 654). Cf. also H. Klüver, "An Analysis of Recent Work on the Problem of Psychological Types," *Journal of Nervous and Mental Disease,* LXII (1925), 561–96.

[4] W. Jaensch, *Grundzüge einer Physiologie und Klinik der psychophysischen Persönlichkeit* (Berlin: Springer, 1926; pp. x + 483). Cf. also H. Klüver, "Studies on the Eidetic Type and on Eidetic Imagery," *Psychological Bulletin,* XXV (1928), 69–104.

tative systems": the first of which seems to be chiefly dependent on the subcortex; the second, on the cortex.

Let us turn to the field of "cultural science psychology." Spranger[5] starts from the personality as a whole as we find it in intimate contact with a historically developed cultural environment. The acts of the individual are viewed in their relations to "art," "science," and other manifestations of cultural life. Around these relations, Spranger develops six "ideal" types: "the theoretical type," "the economic type," "the æsthetic type," etc. Let us imagine an individual for whom *one* "meaning-tendency," as Spranger calls it, *one* value, appears as dominant—for instance, the value of science. Here we have the *Lebensform* of the "theoretical" man, the theoretical type. The fact that empirically "the fundamental principle of science," objectivity, cannot dominate a *Lebensform* entirely does not matter here. We need the "ideal" theoretical type as a construction for understanding the complexities of historical life. The assumption is made that one "meaning-tendency" is dominant in the individual although it is assumed that the other five are also present to a certain extent.

If we consider Jaspers' work[6] we note that the person—*Weltanschauung* —relation is the starting-point in developing a typology. For Stern,[7] it is a "dominant disposition of a psychic or a psychophysically-neutral kind" in the individual.

Instead of adding more examples let us recall our question: what is the general form of those phenomena which become visible by means of the typological method? The answers given by different investigators point to phenomena such as "psychophysical vegetative system"; "interaction of psychological functions constituting a special mode of adaptation to the world"; "*the* fundamental psychological function"; "dominance of one value"; dominance of a psychic or a psychophysically-neutral disposition," etc. Neglecting the differences in material handled, it becomes apparent that the different investigators point to "essential characteristics" or "one fundamental characteristic," to the general denominator for a set of phenomena, or to a "system." Even a superficial analysis shows that the entity conceived of as type is never an *unitas simplex,* but always an *unitas multiplex.* In short, the typological method in psy-

---

[5] E. Spranger, *Types of Men* (Halle: Niemeyer, 1928; pp. xii + 402).

[6] K. Jaspers, *Psychologie der Weltanschauungen* (Berlin: Springer, 1922; pp. xii + 486). Cf. also H. Klüver, "M. Weber's 'Ideal Type' in Psychology," *Journal of Philosophy,* XXIII (1926), 29–35.

[7] W. Stern, *Die differentielle Psychologie in ihren methodischen Grundlagen* (3d ed.; Leipzig: Barth, 1921; pp. ix + 545).

chology and related fields seeks to uncover dynamic systems of some kind.
This statement is general enough to include the various applications of
this method although it seems to be specific enough to exclude many type
classifications as having nothing to do with the typological method.

In answering our first question we have two warnings: *First,* one has
to steer clear of the ambiguities arising from the question concerning the
existence of types. *Beer as well as e^{-x} exist;* the objects of predication
reveal differences in existential status. But why consider this philosophical problem in this connection? If somebody should raise objections to the typological method on the ground that types "do not exist,"
it would mean just as little as the assertion that e^{-x} does not exist. It may
suffice to say that the range of existence in the case of types is about as
great as that between beer and e^{-x}. The distinction between "empirical"
and "ideal" types ("ideal" to be taken, for instance, in Spranger's sense)
is rather superficial.

This leads us to the *second* warning. There is some danger that the
description of types may delude us about the nature of the typological
method. The mere description, the morphology of the type, may lead us
astray in our attempt at clarifying the method. If the description refers
to nothing but relations among static elements, it does not refer at all
to a multiple unit, to a dynamic system, to an action-system called type.
The typological method seeks to uncover certain specific modes of interaction in this system. The *conditio sine qua non* is that such modes of
interacting are at least *hypothetically* assumed. Through the use of the
typological method, it is true, *units* of some kind become visible, but
these units are *dynamic* units.

If we consider this point well established, it follows that any additive
account, no matter how complete it may be, cannot lead to establishing
a type. This information about the coexistence of one hundred traits does
not refer to a system. We may finally have an addition of "traits," "functions," "attitudes," "reactions," "performances," "excitations," etc. Even
adding "general" traits to "specific" traits does not do away with the
additive nature of such an account. In such a way we do not arrive at
one system, at a *Wirkungssystem,* the interrelations of which are scientifically intelligible. In the T- and the B-system of W. Jaensch the interplay
of endocrine, vegetative, central, and peripheral factors is made intelligible. The question whether or not these systems, these types, are established or the question as to how far they are established is of no concern in this connection.

At this point of our analysis we may be fairly clear about what can be done with the typological method. We may clarify our results by stating the case negatively in considering what cannot be done by means of this method.

It is not a tool for the exploration of the *individual*. The typological method does not want to reach and never reaches the empirical individual. Jung informs us that "introversion" and "extraversion" are "mechanisms" which can be "inserted or disconnected at will." In his "types" the "typical characters are stressed disproportionally." W. Jaensch tells us that in every organism the T- as well as the B-complex is present. Spranger writes that in the theoretical type, for instance, *all* "meaning-tendencies" are present.

This logically implies that when we examine, as often as possible, as many individuals as we please, a subsequent comparison can *never* lead to "types." Types cannot be reached in such a way; only the point may be reached where we can assign the individual a place in a filing system constructed *more geometrico*. The investigator interested in such assignments will not discover types since he does not want to discover them. Starting from the individual with his traits, he is able to inform us where the individual stands in the various distribution-curves of these traits. He will tell us finally, as Giese[8] does, that "the structure of the individual reveals itself to us only in the correlation" and that the individual always fits into the one or the other "complex group of mathematically related psychic factors." But in such a way we shall not arrive at a dynamic system the interrelations of which are causally intelligible. We shall never be led to Kretschmer's result—that there are "two types of human nature," nor to W. Jaensch's assumption—that the T- and the B-type hold for human personality in general. If we start out investigating the relation between "reading-ability" and "memory" and continue examining relations of this kind, we may arrive at a result which is of no psychological or biological significance. This is not meant to be an objection to this method, but it is apparent that the phenomena made "visible"—to employ the foregoing term—through the use of the typological method are different from those made visible, e.g., by the psychometric method. Even Giese, for whom the structure of the individual is revealed in the correlation, points out that to obtain worth-while results in psychology the examination of *significant* traits is necessary. In the case of the typological method there is not only no doubt about the significance, but we have from the very beginning different *degrees*

---

[8] F. Giese, "Das Ich als Komplex in der Psychologie," *Archiv für die gesamte Psychologie*, XXXII (1914), 120–65.

of significance. The typological method *isolates* systems, the interrelations of which are or must be established. Again we have to point out that the way a certain relation is established is of no consequence in this connection. We may put a pharmacologist to work to find out whether Jaensch's types can be distinguished on pharmacological grounds. As regards our analysis it is neither the use of *pharmacological* methods in this case nor the fact that we want to establish the absence or the presence of a *difference* which is of any importance. What is important is that the typological method in this case has already isolated certain facts and their relations, certain action systems the behavior of which is expressible in a general formula.

It is not easy to demarcate the *limits* of the typological method. We want to investigate a certain set of phenomena and isolate certain dynamic systems or types. Suppose we want to study the relation of the individual to his "optical," "legal," or "scientific" environment. Since there is an overwhelmingly large number of factors which have bearing, e.g., on the *relations* between "individual" and "legal forms," we cannot expect that a proper use of the typological method will reveal units such as "individuals" or "legal forms."

The objection may be stated that the action systems isolated by the typological method are nothing but *preliminary* formulations. To begin with, they are more than formulations, at least they should be; second, they are no more of a "preliminary" nature than a large number of phenomena established by other scientific methods. To discard types does not mean, in general, "destroying them," but "saving" them by replacing them by more general systems.

Some writings on "types" and "typification" emphasize the fact that the typological method blurs or effaces concrete and individual features. But, as a matter of fact, this defocalization implies that another group of phenomena is brought into focus by this method.

This leads to another point. If in the study of the relation, e.g., of the individual to the legal factors in his social environment, one or several types have been isolated for the study of this relation, it becomes apparent that in the extreme case questions concerning the *frequency* of these types are, roughly speaking, about as nonsensical as questions concerning the frequency of the general relativity theory. The general relativity theory will be proved or disproved by experiments of some kind; a "type," to be sure, will be "proved" or "disproved" by observation and experimentation on empirical individuals or by reference to facts of some sort.

But we may ask, Is it not strange that only in the biological and the social sciences, and especially in psychology, has a typological method been developed? Why is it that just in the field of psychology is such an ill-defined method advocated? Is not the final word in all scientific work a complex group of mathematically related factors? No doubt, we can go on working in psychology without ever using the typological method, although one difficulty arises: the difficulty that without recourse to the typological method certain phenomena and their relations never become visible. "Scientifically" they have no existence, and they will never exist unless one abandons the idea that phenomena which cannot be investigated by one of the available "scientific" methods do not exist.

We must adopt a different line of reasoning. We must start from the facts and somehow find the tools adequate for their investigation. If we find in psychology that certain dynamic systems, certain behavior units, exist to which we cannot do justice by pointing out the few mathematical relations known at present; if, at the same time, there seems to be no hope whatsoever for rapidly increasing our knowledge of these relations or of relations found by other "exact" methods; then, even the *description* of these behavior units by means of these "exact" methods (not to mention a thorough scientific treatment) is *inexact* since the tools are totally inadequate. *In such a case a "type" may be far more "exact" than an equation.* Only one who thinks about method as something divorced from the facts and from the material at hand will doubt this statement. The general point we wish to make is this: The main reason that psychology and related fields are in need of the typological method is that in these fields there *exist* phenomena which cannot be adequately treated by other methods.

In answering the question as to *what* phenomena are revealed through the use of the typological method, we think we have also thrown light on the question as to *how* the typological method proceeds.

It seems that the investigators who have used the typological method as conceived of in this analysis have either reached significant results or, at least, have stimulated experimentation along various lines. "Types," as Stern points out, "can never be gained by a mere collecting of data, but by working them up logically."[9] It is this logical function of the concept "type" which we have emphasized. At the same time we have tried to show that a type is more than a working hypothesis, and that the typological method evolves empirical *Funktionszusammenhänge* as we find them in certain action systems in the field of psychology. If we

[9] *Op. cit.*, p. 196.

have such a system as $F(A,B,C,D, \ldots)$, where A is $f(a_1, a_2, a_3, a_4, \ldots)$, and where again $a_1, a_2, \ldots$ are very complex, we have in terms of our analysis something which is both empirical *and* non-empirical.

In closing we should like to call attention to the fact that physicists inform us that there are scientific procedures which enable us to test the validity of a proposition by reference to a *single* observation. We may express here the hope that our analysis has clarified the nature of the typological method to such an extent that the implications of this statement for our problem will be readily seen.[10]

GLOSSARY

Asthenic type.—Persons whose thickness is deficient compared with their length.

Athletic type.—Persons with a strong development of skeleton, musculature, and skin.

Circular insanity.—Form of manic-depressive psychosis in which periods of depression and excitement follow each other without interruption.

Diathetic proportion.—"The relation, in which the hypomanic and melancholic elements in the individual cycloid personality come together, we call its diathetic or mood proportion."—KRETSCHMER.

Dysplastic types.—"We should naturally always be on the right side if we describe as dysplastic a high degree of profile angularity, asthenic emaciation, or athletic sturdiness, in so far as we understand under "dysplastic" such forms of growth as vary very markedly from the average and commonest form of the type in question. With regard to the groups which we are about to describe, not only the extremes, but also the majority of the cases fall well outside the typical form; they even impress the laity as rare, surprising, and ugly."—KRETSCHMER.

Eidetic imagery.—A person with eidetic imagery is able to see (in the literal sense of the word) an object again after it has been removed from sight. Eidetic images differ from hallucinations in that the subject does not believe in the objective reality of his images; from memory-images in that the phenomena are really seen.

Psychesthetic proportion.—"The mixture relations, in which, in any given schizoid, the hyperesthetic and the anesthetic elements fit in with one another, we call his 'psychesthetic proportion.' "—KRETSCHMER.

Pyknic type.—Persons "characterized by the pronounced peripheral development of the body cavities (head, breast, and stomach), with a more graceful construction of the motor apparatus (shoulders and extremities). The figure tends to appear squat (even when the person is fairly tall) and there is a decided tendency towards fat."—KRETSCHMER.

[10] [This analysis was first written in September, 1928, and given final revision by the analyst in December, 1929.—EDITOR.]

ANALYSIS 10

WILLIAM McDOUGALL'S METHODOLOGICAL CONCEPT OF INSTINCT[1]

By CALVIN P. STONE

Institute for Juvenile Research, Chicago

PRIMARY SUBDIVISIONS

For the purpose of this analysis one may consider McDougall's *Social Psychology* as consisting of two primary divisions. The first, together with certain supplementary chapters, deals with (1) definition, elucidation, and estimation of the fundamental importance of the human instincts in the light of concepts from comparative psychology; (2) a general account of the manner in which instinctive dispositions become organized into systems of increasing complexity and dynamic significance through the individual's reactions to his social environment; (3) an intelligible correlation of the lower, purely instinctive modes of action, with the higher forms, which, in man, find their finest exemplification in volitional activities. The second division gives a suggestive sketch of the various ways in which the principal instincts and the primary emotions play their respective rôles in society. For the present purpose, the first division is regarded as important because in it are stated and exemplified the more fundamental postulates underlying the author's system of social philosophy.

NATURE OF THE INNATE BASES OF BEHAVIOR

A survey of the evolution of animal behavior and a common-sense, analytical study of human psychology led McDougall, following William James and other influential writers of the day, to postulate, as the underlying basis of all individual development, a group of native dispositions of which certain relatively stable and unchanging central elements forever remain the fountain source of all bodily and mental activity. These are the instincts and their accompanying emotions. He lists them under two subdivisions:

(1) The specific tendencies or instincts.

(2) The general or non-specific tendencies arising out of the constitution of mind and the nature of mental process in general, when mind and mental process attain a certain degree of complexity in the course of evolution [p. 21].

[1] [References are appended at the end of the analysis.—EDITOR.]

According to McDougall, evidence for the existence of these innate human dispositions is real and in a measure can be marshaled by any thinker who is willing and competent to employ the comparative method of scrutinizing and interpreting human and animal behavior. Strictly speaking, however, one cannot prove their existence in quite the same objective way one proves the existence of a pineal gland, a "blind spot," the circulation of the blood, etc. Hence, final evidence for their existence is admittedly hypothetical and *one ultimately accepts or rejects them on rational grounds* (McDougall [1922], p. 286). Their use in psychology is justifiable only if they correspond to and effectively co-ordinate the verifiable facts of human and animal behavior.

In the original edition, and in all succeeding editions, a specific tendency or *instinct* is defined as "an inherited or innate psycho-physical disposition which determines its possessor to perceive, and to pay attention to, objects of a certain class, to experience an emotional excitement of a particular quality upon perceiving such an object, and to act in regard to it in a particular manner, or, at least, to experience an impulse to such action" (p. 30). Recently McDougall has repudiated the physical element of this so-called *psycho-physical* disposition. This change of thought was first made clear in an article of 1922 on the use and misuse of the concept of instinct. In this he makes the following statement (p. 311):

Either instinctive action is purely and wholly reflex action, more or less compound (as Herbert Spencer said), and the mechanists are right in asking us to reject the conception of Instinct (as McDougall conceives it— analyst's note) from psychology; or instinctive action is distinct from mechanical reflex action, and an instinct is not, and does not essentially comprise in its organization, any motor mechanism. If we take the latter view, we must recognize that an instinct, or a given instinctive impulse, may make use at need of a large array of motor mechanisms, different instincts expressing themselves on different occasions through the same motor mechanisms; although it may be true that any one instinct most readily finds expression through some one such mechanism, or through some one co-ordinated system of such mechanisms. This is the alternative which, I believe, we must accept. This is the novel contribution to the theory of Instinct which I herewith propound. I have needed nearly twenty years of observation and reflection to reach this conclusion—so strongly was I influenced by the reflex-arc concept and the mechanistic dogma.

In a supplementary chapter to the 1926 edition of the *Social Psychology* this point was elaborated, but numerous inconsistencies of exposition to which it gives rise in the early chapters of the book were not removed. This fault is probably graver than the author foresaw, or he would have taken the necessary steps to harmonize all chapters of the revised edition.

The word "disposition" as herein used would seem to have no wholly satisfactory and reliable equivalent in psychological terminology because of the prevalent acceptance of what McDougall calls the "mechanistic dogma" [1922], p. 295. The innate disposition was formerly regarded as always having *psychical* as well as physical components; hence, from McDougall's point of view, any formulation based on purely mechanical principles is probably misleading, inadequate, and a failure for general or social psychology. To most students, excepting possibly lay readers, the terms "tendency," "determining adjustment," "set," "impulse," or "predisposition," too strongly imply the mechanical or the physiological aspect of the concept "disposition," and almost invariably fail to convey convincingly the implicit idea of persistent striving toward a goal. It appears that no psychologist who accepts the mechanistic theory as opposed to McDougall's *hormic* theory of the innate dispositions will find his views quite acceptable to McDougall. In fact, indorsement of this mechanistic doctrine marks the parting of the ways for McDougall and his followers, on the one hand, and such other influential writers as Herbert Spencer, Carpenter, Lloyd Morgan, James, and Thorndike, on the other.

Like every mental process, the instinctive disposition is said to have a cognitive, an affective, and a conative aspect which, in a rough way, parallel the three components of the reflex arc; namely, the afferent, the central, and the efferent limbs. That is to say, an instinctive disposition causes its possessor to perceive a thing or object of a class, to have a feeling aroused by or directed toward it, and finally to strive for or against this object or thing. Although no claim is made in all instances for direct observability of the threefold aspect, the author affirms that ample grounds for the assumption of its universal presence are in evidence if one reviews and interprets all grades of behavior in the lower animals and man. To illustrate his line of reasoning: the potency of a particular stimulus to initiate an instinctive act, while many others are simultaneously received, suggests the presence of a cognitive aspect which in nature is a perceptive process of one or another grade of complexity. In the higher animals, whose psychical development most nearly corresponds to that of man, one may observe in many instances a specific emotional accompaniment of the instinctive act (such as fear, anger, elation, etc.), which in similar instances invariably accompanies this kind of behavior. The emotional accompaniment is associated physiologically with the central component of the instinctive disposition and, irrespective of the many changes undergone by the cognitive and the conative elements in the lifetime of the individual, forever remains its most permanent and unchanged aspect. However faint it may be manifested in certain instances, he assumes that the emotional excitement is never absent. By analogy with human experience, it is deduced from the persistency with which an individual seeks to attain the ends toward which instinctive acts are directed, that a conative element of the innate disposition likewise is always present, and that this, in its higher ideational form, is akin to what man calls desire or aversion and in its blind form is recognized as impulse, craving, or ill-defined want.

McDougall's hypothesis as to the internal connection of the principal instincts and the primary emotions has not been found acceptable to the majority of leading psychologists whose opinion might fairly be said to deserve equal weight. Concerning this point McDougall writes as follows:

. . . . It is not accepted by Ward, Thorndike, Warren, Shand, Watson, Titchener, Stout, Woodworth, Lloyd Morgan or Drever, all of whom have discussed the emotions or instincts in authoritative books published or revised since my formulation was proposed; and it is, of course, rejected explicitly or implicitly by all the recent deniers of the instincts of man. And it has not, so far as I am aware, been accepted by any continental psychologist (1922, p. 325).

Without analyzing the individual objections to McDougall's formulation of the emotions, it is pertinent to say that one of the chief objections, and one most vigorously stated, is that the alleged connection is purely hypothetical and does not correspond to the facts of observation or the facts of experience. Another objection specifically states that the emotions and the instincts are distinct in origin and function. A third objection is based on the belief that emotions arise only by virtue of checking or thwarting potential instinctive acts and are not part and parcel of the original innate disposition. For the present it is hardly worth while hazarding a guess as to which, if any, of the foregoing views is substantiated by the small body of unequivocal data on the subject of the emotions. *All are hypothetical; all may be partially substantiated by special examples; all have a definite but limited value for social theory.*

INHERITANCE OF THE INNATE DISPOSITION

With regard to the inheritability of an instinctive disposition, Mc-Dougall is quite specific concerning its material side. On this point he writes as follows: "The instinctive action implies some enduring nervous basis whose organization is inherited, an innate or inherited psychophysical disposition, which anatomically regarded, probably has the form of a compound system of sensorimotor arcs." Concerning the mental aspects, however, no view as to the mode of transmission from parents to offspring is explicitly stated, but the reader naturally (perhaps erroneously) infers that its transmission is intimately related to that of the central nervous structures. In the later article (1922) McDougall definitely avows an attitude of open-mindedness toward a theory of the inheritance of acquired characters. This no doubt would pertain equally to the mental and the physical aspects of the disposition.

MODIFICATION OF THE INNATE DISPOSITIONS IN THE HISTORY OF THE RACE

It is his opinion that the instinctive dispositions of the race have undergone very little change in the known period of cultural history. Indeed, the changes have probably been so minute that for social theory they are wholly negligible. Hence it follows that theories of social changes, cultural epoch, etc., founded upon alleged changes in the nature of the instinctive dispositions of the human race, are probably starting from erroneous assumptions and working along unfruitful hypotheses.

MODIFIABILITY OF INSTINCTS IN THE INDIVIDUAL

McDougall has never stressed as essential the absence of previous experience in the instinctive act or the lack or awareness of the end to be attained. Indeed, he stresses the opposite fact that in man and the higher animals the instinctive processes become greatly complicated as a result of the modifying influence of experience. Four principal modes of modification are apparent: (1) new objects, *ideas* of the original exciting objects, or *ideas* of the new exciting objects become capable of initiating instinctive acts; (2) the overt, physiological process in which an instinct finds expression may be modified as to the variety and the arrangement of its constituent elements; (3) a complex series of stimuli may simultaneously arouse several instinctive acts, in which case the instinctive processes fuse and blend; and (4) instinctive acts become more or less organized about specific things or ideas. For the most part, in fact almost exclusively, the cognitive and the conative elements of the instincts undergo the changes outlined above. The only unchanging element is the central core or the affective component. To the habitual responses of the adult it gives whatever dynamic quality they possess. Its perpetuation in the face of incessant change of the physiological outlets of the innate disposition gives stability and permanence to these innate fundaments from which all activities of the adult are derived. Its omnipresence and dynamic quality prompt the author to make the following sweeping generalizations:

Take away these instinctive dispositions with their powerful impulses, and the organism would become incapable of activity of any kind; it would lie inert and motionless like a wonderful clockwork whose mainspring had been removed or a steam-engine whose fires had been drawn [p. 45].

Vigorous criticisms have been launched by contemporary psychologists against McDougall's retention of the word "instinctive" for the complex acts of the adult which no longer issue from a single purely instinctive disposition (Dunlap, 1919; Bernard, 1921; Kuo, 1922). Conventional usage today reserves the name "habitual" or "learned" for such reponses. This is particularly true of American psychologists whose thinking on this subject during the past three decades has been greatly influenced by comparative psychology and by numerous objective studies of the acquisitions of skills in typical vocational and school subjects. They have taken the alternative view, *not adopted by McDougall,* of reserving the term "instinctive" for original responses in their *initial, unmodified form* and giving the name "learned" or "habitual" to all types of psychomotor activities which result from the splitting and the compounding of original responses, or the directing of innate tendencies or capacities into intellectual pursuits or specific trends of character formation. When this fact is recognized by the student, it becomes obvious at once that McDougall and his critic will quite generally use different class names for one and the same animal or human response. Likewise, it will be equally obvious that they are basing their distinctions on quite arbitrary, academic, and preferential bases. To follow either whole-heartedly in his criticism of the other is only to step from the frying pan into the fire, since *both assume that the mobilization of all energy for action is somehow accomplished by what was originally or still is the innate psychomotor disposition of the individual.*

THE PRINCIPAL INSTINCTS AND PRIMARY EMOTIONS

Seven principal instincts and seven primary emotions specific for and peculiar to these instincts were listed by McDougall in the original and in the subsequent editions of this book: namely, (1) the instinct of flight and the emotion of fear; (2) repulsion and disgust; (3) curiosity and wonder; (4) pugnacity and anger, (5) self-abasement and subjection; (6) self-assertion and elation; and (7) the parental instinct and the tender emotion. In addition to the seven principal instincts, there are four important human instincts without well-defined specific emotional attachments, namely, the instinct of reproduction; the gregarious instinct, the instinct of acquisition, and the instinct of construction. Other minor instincts there may be, such as laughter, those underlying the locomotor responses, etc., but the foregoing constitute the most important revealed so far by human and animal psychology. Instincts of play, rivalry, emulation, imitation, etc., may be accounted for as derivatives of the principal instinctive dispositions.

Each of the principal instincts and the primary emotions is thought to have a considerable degree of independence and may at any time become pathologically strengthened or weakened, thereby giving rise to a mental disorder of one or another characteristic variety. Indeed, it is this capacity of a primary emotion to become pathologically accentuated or reduced, coupled with the facts that it is associated with one of the principal instincts and appears in the higher animals as well as man, which guides McDougall in his separation of the primary emotions from the derived emotions. By way of evaluating his threefold method of selecting the primary emotions, the reader should not overlook the fact that this concept of relative independence or autonomy of the instincts and the emotions is a logical offspring of the old faculty psychology which makes its strongest appeal to those who adopt a "personal experience," "case study," "anecdotal" method of analyzing human nature. Likewise, he should not overlook a truth which McDougall's frequent appeal to the field of animal psychology inadvertently dissimulates, namely, the fact that *those who deal with the emotions of animals are sailing a relatively uncharted sea.* This field of comparative psychology is little understood as yet, and can hardly be said to have emerged from the level of unsystematic, casual, and sporadic observation. To base a superstructure of social theory upon such unstable foundations is no safer than to erect a dwelling upon a mound of shifting sand.

NATURE OF THE SENTIMENTS AND COMPOUND EMOTIONS

When in the course of an individual's development his emotions become crystallized about an object, the name "sentiment" is used by McDougall, following the lead of Shand, to indicate this constellation and to differentiate it from those compounds of the primary emotions which are not organized about an object. Of these, love and hate are familiar examples.

Likewise, the sentiment of self-regard is one with which we are all more or less familiar. For McDougall, it is especially important because of its intimate relation to his theory of volition.

An emotion is to be regarded as compound when it is not found to be the inner core of a principal instinct or when careful analysis does not reveal it to be composed of two or more primary emotions. Thus, admiration, which is not associated with any instinctive disposition, is said to be composed of two primary emotions, namely, wonder and negative self-feeling; while reverence is compounded of wonder, fear, gratitude, tender emotion, and negative self-feeling. Some of the primary emotions are said to be compounded only by virtue of existing sentiments. Thus, reproach, which results from a fusion of anger and tender emotions, arises within the sentiment of love. Other emotions that owe their existence primarily to well-developed sentiments are jealousy, shame, sorrow, and remorse.

As has already been intimated McDougall does not conceive of a sentiment or a compound emotion as being an innate disposition. All are organized in the developing mind as a result of the modifying influence of environmental agencies playing upon the original instinctive dispositions. Nevertheless their importance is great.

THE NATURE OF VOLITION

McDougall accounts for volitional acts without going beyond or outside of the realm of the innate or the acquired dispositions. Speaking of volition, he says: " . . . . It involves no new principles of activity and energy, but only a more subtle and complex interplay of those impulses which actuate all animal behavior and in which the ultimate mystery of mind and life resides" (p. 237). Thus the doctrine of free will is rejected.

His first step toward demonstrating that volitions are only special cases or classes of conations is the step showing that in the animal series or in the individual man all conations may be arranged on a graduated scale of complexity and that in no instance will the distribution be found to be discontinuous. Volitional acts fit into the upper end of the scale and require a special class name only for convenience of discussion. Close analysis shows that this class of acts is manifested when a desire or an ideal motive is reinforced by another impulse arising within the system of the *self-regarding sentiment*. Accordingly, volition may be defined as "the supporting or reinforcing of a desire or conation by the co-operation of an impulse excited within the system of the self-regarding sentiment" (p. 255).

INSTINCT AND CHARACTER

In the light of what has already been said concerning instinctive dispositions, sentiments, and volition, what can be said as to the essence of human character? Is it fundamentally innate or is it derived? The latter is the point of view taken by McDougall. Essentially it consists of the organization of the individual sentiments into a harmonious system or a *hierarchy* with a dominant sentiment at the helm. Strong character in the fullest sense of the word is attained in the individual when his sentiment of self-regard, organized about an ideal of conduct, surmounts the hierarchy of sentiments. Thus, it is argued, the essential foundation of all individual and social conduct ultimately rests upon the fundaments of the innate dispositions.

The account of volition and character formation is regarded by McDougall as the most original and the most praiseworthy element of his contribution to social theory. For it, his account of the principal instincts and the primary emotions is only a necessary background. [2]

REFERENCES

BERNARD, L. L. "The Misuse of Instinct in the Social Sciences," *Psychological Review*, XXVIII (1921), 96–119.

DUNLAP, KNIGHT. "Are There Any Instincts?" *Journal of Abnormal Psychology and Social Psychology*, XIV (1919–20), 307–11.

KUO, Z. Y. "How Are Our Instincts Acquired?" *Psychological Review*, XXIX (1922), 344–65.

McDOUGALL, WILLIAM. "The Use and Abuse of Instinct in Social Psychology," *Journal of Abnormal Psychology and Social Psychology*, XVI (1921–22), 285–333.

———. *An Introduction to Social Psychology*. Rev. ed., 1926.

[2] [This analysis was first written in September, 1928, and revised by the analyst in 1929.—EDITOR.]

SECTION III
THE ESTABLISHMENT OF UNITS AND SCALES

ANALYSIS 11[1]

METHODS INVOLVED IN THE FEDERAL CENSUS OF POPULATION

By LEON E. TRUESDELL
Chief Statistician for Population, United States Bureau of the Census

THE PROCESS OF TAKING THE CENSUS

The method which has been employed in taking the more recent decennial censuses is as follows:

The country is first divided into supervisors' districts, the number of such districts established in 1920 being 372. Each of these districts is placed in charge of a supervisor who reports to the central office in Washington. This supervisor conducts the enumeration of population and agriculture in his district and is responsible for the selection of the enumerators, the prompt completion of the enumeration, and the completeness and accuracy of the returns. Each supervisor's district is subdivided into enumeration districts, or enumerators' assignments. These are made small enough so that they may be canvassed within the time allotted, which is two weeks for a city district and thirty days for a rural district. The enumerator visits each dwelling or home in his territory and obtains the information required for each person in the family from some competent member of the family.[2]

The population schedules are printed on large sheets (23 by 16 inches in 1920), each side of the sheet containing 50 lines, designed to accommodate 50 names. Columns are provided in which to enter on each line

---

[1] [The editor and his associates desire to express their indebtedness to Mr. W. M. Steuart, director of the census, and to members of the Advisory Committee on the Census, for their co-operation in devising the project for the present analysis and for the arrangements with Dr. Truesdell for its preparation. The analysis as first prepared was dated October 30, 1928. It is sent to the press while the tabulations of the 1930 census are in progress, and no extensive reference to the latter, in consequence, has been possible.—EDITOR.]

[2] Employed as these enumerators are for a brief period only and working mainly on the basis of printed instructions furnished by the Census Bureau, supplemented by such hurried oral instructions as the supervisor can find time to give, it cannot be assumed that they are qualified to make any very fine distinctions in classification, or to use any very high degree of diplomacy in obtaining information. Because of the method of enumeration, therefore, it is essential that the census schedules be made as simple as possible, omitting inquiries that are likely to be answered unwillingly, and that the printed instructions for enumerators be made plain and specific and complete.

the 15 or 20 items of information called for. After the tabulation is completed, the schedules are bound and filed away for permanent future reference.

Upon the completion of the enumeration, the schedules are sent to Washington, where they are compared with the records of the previous census and subjected to other checking processes, to make sure that no bit of territory has been overlooked. Then a hand count of the population represented by the schedules is made, which provides the data for the first series of census reports, showing the total population of all the various geographic areas.

The schedules are next turned over to a force of clerks who inspect them for completeness and consistency in the information returned, make sure that all entries are clearly legible, and otherwise prepare them for tabulation.

The first stage in the tabulation is the punching of a card for each individual, on which are recorded the various descriptive items shown on the schedule. These cards are next run through electrical sorting machines which sort them in accordance with certain fundamental characteristics, such as sex, race, and nativity. Then they are tabulated on specially constructed machines, which print the results of the count, in whatever detail may be required. These machines are, in effect, very complex counting machines, designed to count individual units in a large number of classifications or combinations of classifications, rather than to add quantities (which is the function of the more familiar commercial tabulating machine).

The result sheets, as they come from the machines, contain information in much greater detail than it is practicable to publish, since it is necessary to plan the tabulation in such a way that many different statistical tables may be obtained from one "run" of the cards.[3] A large clerical force is therefore required to make the necessary consolidations, to inspect the figures for consistency and accuracy, and to rearrange the material and put it into the form required for publication.

CONCEPTS INVOLVED IN COUNTING THE POPULATION

Primarily the census is a count of the population; and so far as concerns the constitutional requirements[4] it need be nothing more. Actually,

[3] The machine sheets and intermediate computation sheets on file in the Census Bureau always contain a vast amount of unpublished information, which is available to the public under special arrangement, the main requirement being that the person requesting the information shall pay the cost of the clerical labor of compiling it from the machine sheets.

[4] The decennial census of population enjoys the unique distinction of being the only statistical inquiry which is provided for by the Constitution of the United States. The constitutional provisions with regard to apportionment and the decennial census,

however, in response to a growing demand for more and more information about the population, various classifications have been added to the count until in 1920 there were at least eighteen distinct classifications on the basis of personal characteristics recorded on the schedule.

Any count of objects presupposes a definition whereby the objects to be counted may be positively distinguished from other objects which are not to be included in the count. It would seem at first thought that, aside from a possible reminder that infants and children were to be counted, as well as adults, little in the way of a formal definition of a "person" would be required as a basis for counting the inhabitants of a given state or city.

But the census must count persons who belong in or to a given geographic area on a given date. There's the rub. The census of the United States cannot be taken instantaneously, nor even within the space of a single day. The period of enumeration spreads out over two, three, or four weeks, during which time persons come and go, are born, and die, in appreciable numbers.

Further, there must be some criterion by which to settle the question as to who belongs in a given area which is being enumerated. In the English census a person is counted as a part of the population of the place where he is found at midnight of the census date, giving what has been termed the *de facto* population. In the United States a person is counted as a part of the population of the area within which he has his "usual place of abode," giving the *de jure* population. In the early days, when most persons were to be found for 365 days in the year at or near their "usual place of abode," the problem of counting the population was far simpler than it is now and the American census plan presented few of its present difficulties. With the increase of travel, the loose ties which bind people to their living places, and the facility with which whole families now move from one locality to another, following seasonal occupations or actuated by other motives, it seems likely that eventually the census of the United States also will have to be taken on the *de facto* basis, counting the people where they are found, even though the results have to be tabulated in such fashion as to assign each person to that

---

as given in art. 1, sec. 2, par. 3, modified by Amendment XIV, par. 2, are as follows: "Representatives shall be apportioned among the several states according to their respective numbers, counting the whole number of persons in each state, excluding Indians not taxed. The actual enumeration shall be made within three years after the first meeting of the Congress of the United States and within every subsequent term of ten years, in such manner as they shall by law direct."

area in which he has his customary residence (or perhaps his legal residence).

Theoretically, the census enumeration is made "as of" the census date. The enumerator is instructed to record on the census schedule for each family all those persons who were living with the family on the census date (plus members of the family temporarily absent), even though the actual enumeration may be made on a date three weeks or more subsequent to that census date. He ought therefore to include a person who had died between the census date and the enumeration date, and to exclude an infant born during the same interval. There is reason to believe, however, that a large proportion of the enumerators record the situation as it is at the time of their call, returning information for those persons in the family on that date and not for the family as it was on the official census date.

In the mere counting of the population, then, we can discern two distinct theoretical concepts; that of enumerating "as of" a single day, the census date; and that of including in the population of a given geographic area all persons having their usual place of abode in that area, even though some of them may be elsewhere (away at school, on business trips, absent for temporary employment, or traveling for pleasure), and excluding persons who may be present in the area on the census date, but whose "usual residence" is elsewhere.

Roughly, it may be assumed that usual place of abode (the basis of the census enumeration) will correspond with legal residence, though this is not always the case. The most extensive group of exceptions is found in the city of Washington, D. C., where literally thousands of the normal, permanent inhabitants of the city maintain legal residence in some one of the forty-eight states, usually the state in which they had legal residence when they entered the government service. Government employees living in Washington maintain their legal residence elsewhere in order that they may enjoy the rights and privileges accruing to citizens of the various states (such as the right to vote) and the advantages of apportionment in the federal service. Other persons, however, for other reasons, such as more favorable tax rates, maintain a legal residence in some state other than the one where they reside for the major part of each year and carry on their regular occupations.

There are, therefore, three different concepts under which a geographic location might be assigned to a person for census purposes; namely, (1) where the person is found on the census date (or on the date of actual enumeration); (2) where his usual home or place of residence is located; and (3) where he has his legal or voting residence. Of these three the English census, as already noted, chooses the first. The census of the United States is now taken in accordance with the second, and conceivably some future census, seeking a strictly logical basis for apportionment of representation, may choose the third.

GEOGRAPHIC AREAS

The entire area of Continental United States is divided into forty-eight states plus the federal District of Columbia, which for statistical purposes forms a somewhat troublesome appendix to the list of states.

Each state is divided into counties, and for the most part the counties taken together (including occasionally certain "unorganized" counties) comprise or cover the entire area of the state. In a few states, however, there are independent cities, in some cases entirely surrounded by the territory of a county but politically not forming a part of the county. These independent cities must be added to the list of counties in order to make a list of primary subdivisions which will account for the entire state area.

The typical county is divided into townships or other corresponding areas (variously designated townships, precincts, election districts, towns, etc.) which cover the whole area of the county. Cities and other incorporated places usually occupy a part of the territory of a township, so that their area and population are included in the total for the township. There are two exceptions to this relation, however. In rather numerous instances, occurring in many different states, the incorporated place is coextensive with the township; and even more often the incorporated places are entirely independent of the townships and co-ordinate with them as primary divisions of the county. This is uniformly the case in a considerable number of states, including Massachusetts, Pennsylvania, and Wisconsin.

The most irregular of the geographic areas, in their plan of formation and in their relation to the larger areas concerned, are the cities and other incorporated places (towns, villages, and boroughs). Many of these incorporated places are located on the boundary line between two townships or perhaps even at the point where four townships come together. In a case like this it is necessary to handle throughout the census processes each one of the four parts of this incorporated place (that is, the part which is in each one of the four townships) as a separate unit. Conversely, in a state where the townships or corresponding units are very small, it frequently happens that one incorporated place will include all of certain of these units, together with parts of certain others.

The concepts involved in the two major classifications, the state and county, are relatively simple and consistently applied, aside from the exceptions already noted. The concepts of the township and of the city or other incorporated place, however, are not as definitely established and are subject to rather numerous and perplexing variations and interlocking relations.

The typical township is a territorial subdivision of the county. The typical incorporated place is a thickly settled area specially incorporated, which may be an independent subdivision of the county or may occupy all or part of the territory of one or more townships. While the term "city" is usually reserved for the larger incorporated places in a state, this is not always the case. In Kansas, for example, there are numerous cities with less than three hundred inhabitants. The smaller incorporated places are usually called "towns" or "villages" (or in a few states, "boroughs"); while in some states, like Massachusetts, there are no small incorporated places.

As if there were not enough complications to be found with these definite political subdivisions, there is a constantly growing demand that the census give figures for every thickly settled area, including many that are not incorporated as a city, town, or village. So far, the Census Bureau has declined to give the population of such areas, for the reason that they have no definite boundaries. The lack of data for such places seriously affects the urban-rural classification in some states, however; and consideration has been given to a plan for establishing boundaries and tabulating separately the population of the larger unincorporated places in connection with the tabulation of the census of 1930.

CLASSIFICATION OF POPULATION

The principal classifications under which the population data for the United States are published are as follows:[5]

1. Color or race
2. Nativity
   a) General classification—native or foreign born
   b) State of birth of the native population
   c) Country of birth of the foreign born
3. Parentage (of the native population only)
   a) General classification—native parentage, foreign parentage, mixed parentage
   b) Country of birth of parents of persons of foreign parentage

[5] Items omitted which appear in the 1920 census reports include dwellings, families. and tenure of home, which are not strictly classifications of the population.

4. Sex
5. Age
6. Marital condition
7. Educational status
   a) Illiteracy
   b) School attendance
8. Special items on status of foreign born
   a) Citizenship
   b) Year of immigration
   c) Ability to speak English
   d) Mother tongue
9. Occupational status
   a) General classification—gainfully employed or not
   b) Specific occupation
10. Urban-rural classification
   a) Urban or rural residence
   b) Farm or non-farm—subdivision for rural only

Underneath and back of the classifications and definitions which have found a place in the census reports lie a long series of concepts, explicit and implicit, gradually becoming more definite in their use by the Census Bureau and slowly gaining recognition on the part of the general public which uses the census statistics.

Nearly a generation ago Professor A. L. Bowley, discussing the schedule used in the English census of 1891, stated that the only question on the schedule about which there did not arise some difficulty as to what the answer should be was the question relating to sex. The same statement might now be made with regard to the schedule used in the census of population for the United States. Even the geographic allocation of the persons enumerated, which is perhaps the first problem of the census, requires arbitrary definition, as indicated above; and even when the definition is formulated its application involves difficulty for the enumerator and at least occasional failure to conform to it.

The fundamental classification in the statistics of population is that based on color or race. This distinction is probably, next to sex, the most definite and specific of all the classifications. Yet its application requires at the outset certain arbitrary definitions: one, to the effect that all persons having any Negro blood whatsoever shall be returned as Negroes; and another, somewhat inconsistent, that persons of mixed white and Indian blood shall be returned as Indians only when they are so regarded in the locality where they are found.

Supplemental to the racial classification, in a way, and of importance mainly for the white population, are the classifications by nativity and parentage. The classification according to nativity is just as specific in the matter of definition as the question with regard to sex; for, excepting occasional cases of persons born at sea or of American citizens born abroad, a person is certainly either of native or of foreign birth. The concept of "nativeness" is complicated somewhat by the inclusion of persons born in the outlying possessions in the native class; but the principal added factor in this classification is the frequent difficulty in obtaining the needed information.

The classification according to marital condition[6] is likewise easy to formulate, but the doubtful or borderline cases are more numerous— cases where a marriage has been annulled, for example; the information necessary to make the classification is more difficult to obtain in these and other doubtful cases; and there is a definite bias in the tendency of persons reporting to give purposely wrong information—in particular to report themselves as married or widowed when they really are divorced.

The question as to the country of birth of the foreign-born is apparently very simple in its concept, and one might judge that the only difficulty met with in connection with this question would be the difficulty of getting the information. Another problem has arisen, however, which might be considered the result of a change in the underlying concept. Between the time when the major part of the foreign-born persons now in the United States left their native lands and the present time, extensive changes have been made in the map of Europe. What is wanted for the classification of the foreign-born by country of birth is a report, in terms of the present political subdivisions of Europe, of the place from which each person came. What these foreign-born persons have in mind, however, in very many cases, is the name of the country in which their birthplace was located in what we now term pre-war days. The problem of translating pre-war geography into post-war terms has therefore been added to the task of handling a question which was already one of the most troublesome on the schedule.

Age is defined for census purposes as the age of the person on his last birthday; that is, his age in completed years. This element is definite and

---

[6] The underlying concept in this classification—the status of the individual as single, married, etc., at the time of the census—is closely related to another statistical concept having its tangible representation in the annual statistics of marriages and divorces. Newspaper feature writers and others often try to deduce one of these concepts from the other, or to use them interchangeably in support of an argument or in the presentation of a situation. (A thorough study of the relations—casual and otherwise—between these two sets of statistical data would furnish material for an interesting article.)

positive, representing the passage of time since birth; but people do not keep track of it and are not able to report it accurately. Old people, especially, fail to remember their ages exactly; and there is a marked tendency for ages to be reported in multiples of five.[7] Further (though this is really a factor of the enumeration rather than of the classification), the number of children under one year of age is never completely reported, the number in the first year of age being always less than the number in the second year. This is not peculiar to the United States, but occurs generally in the statistics of other countries.

The illiteracy classification is less definite and more dependent on what might be termed an artificial definition. An illiterate person is defined as one who, being ten years of age or over, is not able to read and write either in English or in any other language. The enumerator is not provided with any specific test of this ability, however, but simply accepts the statement of his informant. Hence there is likely to be considerable variation in the actual standard represented by the literacy classification. In the official explanation of the classification, stress is put upon ability to write; and the statement is often made that the census requirement for classification as literate is the ability to write one's name. No such test has ever been prescribed, however; in fact, as indicated above, there has been no prescribed test.

A more significant classification, applied also to the population ten years of age and over, is that of gainful employment. Gainfully employed persons are distinguished from those not gainfully employed; and the gainfully employed are classified in considerable detail according to occupation.

The gainful-employment classification is dependent in considerable measure on another artificial or "manufactured" definition. The borderline along the edge of gainful employment is rather indefinite, and even the definition given to the enumerators is not as specific as one might wish. They are asked to return as gainfully employed all those persons who are at work, or who would be at work if it were not for temporary unemployment, except "women doing housework in their own homes and having no other employment," and "children who work for their parents at home merely on general household work, on chores, or at odd times on

---

[7] The age classification provides one of the very best examples of the expansion, census by census, in the detail in which a classification is presented—expansion both in the detail of the classification itself, ranging from two groups (under sixteen, and sixteen years of age and over, shown for white males only) in 1790 to single years of age in recent censuses, and in the number of population classes and of geographic areas for which the data are presented. See *Fourteenth Census Reports*, Vol. II, chap. iii, pp. 143–380.

other work." Especially with respect to rural women and children working on the "home farm" is the classification indistinct; and the figures indicate that such persons were much more extensively returned as gainfully employed in 1910 than in 1920.

The occupation classification has been criticized because women doing housework in their own homes were not included with the gainfully employed, though this criticism seems to be based largely upon a confusion of ideas—upon the assumption that because these women are counted as without *gainful* employment they are being classified as without *any* employment. The underlying idea in this classification is to include all persons who are producing anything of market value, either services for which they receive payment, or tangible products, including products for which they do not receive payment and even products which may not be placed on the market, as where a farmer is producing for home consumption. Perhaps it is only a short way farther to include the services of the housewife, which are in the same way "consumed" in her own family; but the Census Bureau has so far hesitated to go this additional distance, and sees the way filled with difficulties growing out of the uncertainty as to who should be counted as a housewife, and the certainty that the introduction of this new "occupation" would seriously affect the comparability of the data for the regular gainful employments.[8]

The classification of the gainfully employed by occupation presents many difficulties, because the number of distinct occupations, especially if both process and industry be taken account of, far exceeds any practicable number of classification groups.[9] It is necessary, therefore, to combine many specific occupations into one group, so that a large part of the occupation classification is made up of such groups rather than of specific occupations. This is true, in large measure, even when the designation used is that of a specific occupation. "Semi-skilled operatives in cotton mills" bears evidence of including a considerable variety of specific occupations; but the designation "carpenter," with all its outward appearance of unity and homogeneity, includes a wide variety of occupations having little in common except that they involve the use of tools or machinery to cut and manipulate wood or lumber, ranging from light cabinet work at a bench in a shop to the erection of bridges and trestles in the primeval wilderness; and from cutting and fitting standard parts

[8] In response to urgent demand, it is proposed to indicate on the 1930 census schedule, the woman in each family who is responsible for the care of the home and to tabulate the returns for these women under the designation "Home-makers."

[9] The number of occupations or occupation groups shown in the census reports for 1920 was 572.

under close supervision to planning and supervising original construction.

ESSENTIAL COMBINATIONS OF CLASSIFICATION

Certain rather extensive combinations of the classifications listed above are essential to the significant interpretation of the data. Illiteracy, for example, must be shown separately for white and colored, and for native and foreign-born; and the presentation of illiteracy by age, showing uniformly a lower percentage of illiteracy in the younger age groups, affords an element of encouragement for the future which would be wanting without this cross-classification. In general, however, the data for illiteracy among males and females run along parallel lines, so that the sex classification appears less essential.

The marital-condition classification, to be significant, must be shown in combination with both sex and age. The percentage married increases very rapidly from age fifteen to age thirty or thereabouts; and the increase starts at a decidedly earlier age among females than among males.

School-attendance data depend for their value absolutely upon a rather detailed age classification. Occupation data must be shown separately for males and females, with emphasis upon different sets of occupations; and there is special interest in the occupations of children, presented in detail by age, and in the occupations of women classified as married and single.

As a matter of fact, practically all the classified data in the census reports are presented by color and nativity and by sex, and a large part of them also by age—and for the urban and the rural population. In fact, it is the presentation of these cross-classifications, in detail for many geographic areas, that is responsible for the characteristic bulk of the census reports.

THE EVOLUTION OF THE URBAN-RURAL CONCEPT

As an example of the gradual development of one of the important concepts now embodied in the census reports, we may consider in some detail the growth of the distinction between urban and rural population, which is in large measure an artificial or arbitrary distinction—devised and adopted, however, to meet a real need.

The urban classification was first officially presented in a *Statistical Atlas of the United States*, prepared under the direction of Dr. Francis A. Walker and published in 1874. In this volume the population living in cities of 8,000 inhabitants or more made up the urban population, and figures were presented for all of the decennial censuses, beginning with 1790. This classification has been maintained and published for its historical interest in the reports of all subsequent decennial censuses. The census of 1880, however, contained, in addition, a new classification in which the inhabitants of all cities having 4,000 inhabitants or more were included in the urban population.

So far, the emphasis had been on the urban group. In the 1890 census, while the urban classification on the 8,000 basis was maintained, emphasis was placed on a new group at the other end of the scale, the rural population, which was defined as the population outside all closely settled places having 1,000 inhabitants or more.

In the 1900 census the 4,000 limit for urban population, which had been used in 1880, was revived and in addition the population living outside cities of 4,000 or over was divided into two parts, the semi-urban, which was that living in incorporated places having less than 4,000 inhabitants, and the rural, which was that living outside any incorporated place whatever. This last classification (that is, the population living outside any incorporated place) has been maintained, it might be noted incidentally, as a subdivision of the rural population in subsequent censuses. It is designated in the tables "population living in unincorporated territory" and is sometimes referred to as the "country" population.

In 1910 was established the current definition of urban and rural population, urban population being that living in incorporated places having 2,500 inhabitants or more and rural population that living outside such places.[10] This classification was carried back through three earlier censuses, so that comparative figures on this basis are available beginning with 1880. While it is based on an arbitrary limit and is affected somewhat by the variation among the states in the practice of incorporating thickly settled areas, this definition appears to be very satisfactory. In any case, it is widely used and is perhaps more generally understood than any other specific definition which has been formulated by the Census Bureau. Certainly it is far better understood than the census definition of illiteracy.

The urban-rural concept stands entirely on a geographic basis. A person is included in the urban population if he lives in an incorporated place of the specified size. The classification is made in the census office on the basis of the tabulated returns as to population and does not depend on any question carried on the schedule.

[10] A forecast of this definition appears in the 1890 census report, in the form of a suggestion that a place of 2,500 inhabitants might reasonably be assumed to be urban in its characteristics. The first official presentation of data on the 2,500 basis is found in *Supplementary Analysis and Derivative Tables* of the 1900 census figures, prepared by Professor Walter F. Willcox and published by the Government Printing Office in Washington (1906).

In 1920 a further refinement was added to the classification of the population according to nature of place of residence, by the introduction of a new concept, that of the farm population. The new group, made up primarily of persons living on farms, was tabulated for both urban and rural areas, though only a small fraction of the farm population (less than 1 per cent) was found in urban territory. It is proposed in the further application of this classification to regard it as a basis for subdividing the rural population and to neglect the very small number of farm residents who are found in urban areas, except possibly to record their total number. The result of this will be to substitute for the urban-rural classification a threefold classification made up of the following groups: (1) the urban population; (2) the rural farm population; (3) the rural non-farm population.

This threefold classification gives promise of serving the needs of those who use the population statistics better than the urban-rural classification has done. From a logical point of view, however, it is a mixed classification, based partly on one set of factors—the size of the place of residence and its status as incorporated or not incorporated; and partly on another—the question as to whether or not the family lives on a farm. The latter factor, in turn, is dependent on the definition of a farm, which is becoming increasingly complicated and difficult to establish, with the use of many one-time farm areas as places of residence, often without any "farming" being done, even so much as the raising of a garden. The underlying concept of the new threefold classification is not, therefore, and can never be made so simple as the concepts which underlie most of the other census classifications.

ANALYSIS 12

A DEVICE FOR MEASURING THE SIZE OF FAMILIES, INVENTED BY EDGAR SYDENSTRICKER AND W. I. KING[1]

By WILLIAM F. OGBURN

University of Chicago

In the research studies of King and Sydenstricker we have the report of what is very rare in social-science literature, namely, of an invention and how it was made. It will be interesting therefore to examine so far as we may the method whereby this tool was invented.

This invention is a device for measuring the size of families. There is, of course, a measure of the size of families in the numbers of individuals composing them. For instance, a mother and a father with three children aged five, three, and one are a family of five. But this is not sufficiently accurate if we are measuring food costs, for obviously a family of five adults is larger than a family of two adults and three young children, if the size of the family is to be measured in food requirements.

Hitherto this need has been met by considering children as fractions of adults and a woman as a fraction of a man. Thus the above-mentioned family would be 1.0+0.9+0.4+0.15+0.15, or 2.6 adult males. The family is thus measured in equivalent adult males rather than in number of persons. In comparing family expenditures, the former is obviously a better measure than the latter, for children are not so costly to maintain as are adults.

But how do we know what fractions to use for the children? There are a number of these scales of fractions for measuring the family in percentages of adult males developed by physiologists in determining the calorie values of food consumed at different ages. Their device was then discovered by food experts and borrowed or adapted by economists and sociologists. The next step in the evolution of this instrument of family measurement was to pass from calorie needs to food costs. Since the food of women and children was not essentially different from that of men, it was assumed that scales of food costs would be the same as the scales for calorie requirements. So far as comparison of the food costs

---

[1] Edgar Sydenstricker and Willford I. King, "The Measurement of the Relative Economic Status of Families," *Quarterly Publication of the American Statistical Association*, N.S., XVII, No. 135 (September, 1921), 842–57. Cf. comments on this analysis in the Introduction, p. 7, n. 5.

of men and of women was concerned, it was found by several investigators[2] to be about the same as the comparison of their calorie requirements.

Then followed the step of passing from the scales of food cost to the scales of total expenditure costs. The question was whether the total expenses of women and children of different ages bear the same relation to the total expense of an adult male as the food expenses of women and children do to the food expense of the adult male. It has been assumed that they do roughly but without test of this assumption,[3] and these scales have been so used as indexes of total expenditures for different members of the family, for there were no better ones known. The reason for the use of these food-expense ratios for family-expense ratios was also due to the fact that food costs are often between 40 and 50 per cent of the total family expenses in the cases of workingmen's families.

Such was the state of development of the method of measurement at the time King and Sydenstricker took up the question. They were engaged in studying the budgets of cotton-mill families for the purpose of measuring the relation of food and income to sickness. One of the authors appears to have used for a time the scale of equivalent adult male units based on calorie requirement. He recognized the inaccuracies of these scales as most others did. But after a time the authors began to try to make a better scale. Just why the authors began these improvements they do not say in their account, for they were not writing an introspective autobiography but an objective record of a research. They were confronted with a problem, the sort of problem which John Dewey has so frequently spoken of as precipitating reflective thinking. It was the problem of measuring accurately the size of families in making comparisons of costs. But other investigators had been confronted with this same problem at different times without solving it.

Just why did King and Sydenstricker make the solution and not the others? Inventions are to be explained on three grounds: (1) inherited mental ability; (2) the presence of the basic and necessary cultural elements that go into the making of the invention; (3) the social situation which directs the attention, trains the individual, and creates the need. Of course, in regard to the first point it may be that King and Sydenstricker have exceptional hereditary mental equipment. There are, how-

[2] Horace Secrist in particular.

[3] In 1919 W. F. Ogburn showed that the ratios of clothing expenses of children to adults was very nearly the same as the ratios of food expenses (W. F. Ogburn, "Analysis of the Standard of Living in the District of Columbia in 1916," *Quarterly Publication of the American Statistical Association*, N.S., XVI, No. 126 [June, 1919], 374–89).

ever, others at the same point on the frequency distribution of inherited mental ability. As to the second point, it seems that this invention might have been made many years earlier so far as the underlying technological knowledge necessary is concerned, but perhaps with less probability than at that time. The equivalent adult male scale had been used somewhat earlier but not very extensively. Its use was increasing about this time. In regard to the third factor in inventions, the social situation was rather favorable. These investigations came at a time when there were many studies being made of budgets and costs of living, for this was a period of rising prices. There was great interest in costs of living, although this study, strictly speaking, began before this movement reached its peak. Still, budgets were in the air, and the history of the interest of one of the authors in the matter can be traced to particular persons greatly interested in furthering cost-of-living studies.

The question remains, Why were these two authors rather than others the inventors? For one thing, the problem may have been more acute with them than with other students of family budgets. Although the authors do not state it, it seems highly probable that their work on disease and food may have required more accuracy than was demanded by the general work of budget studies. Another reason, perhaps, is that the particular process of their solution, which turned on a series of approximations obtained by holding a factor constant in a certain way while varying the other factors, is somewhat suggestive of the economic analysis involved in the study of diminishing returns and value, with which at least one of the authors was familiar. Further both are trained statisticians.

If these speculations are correct, there was thus a combination of events which came to a focus at this time; namely, an evolving measurement of families, a great and growing social interest in budgets, a problem that called for relatively greater accuracy than usual, men trained in statistics with a special familiarity with the technique of economic analysis. The probability that these five events would happen at the same time (if they are independent) is equal to the product of their probabilities. Such a conception explains the rarity of the solution.

Can further light be thrown on the origin of this invention? It is evident that it did not come suddenly, for one of the authors had been thinking about the problem for several years. They worked it out gradually, for there is evidence of some trial and error in the write-up. The method was tried on 1916 data and then on 1917 data. There was much refining of the device, once they had the main idea, for they used several different methods in their successive approximations, i.e., fluctuating percentages, medians, graphs, smoothing processes, and trend lines. Perhaps it is fair to say that their accounts give one the impression of much exploration before and during the development of these scales of measurement. Their description does not, indeed, make a smooth-running, perfected account. The exposition itself suggests that the exploration habit was still on.

It is also apparent that there was much hard work involved. The authors do not say how much technical assistance they had. After the family budgets were collected there was long tedious figuring of these various percentages in the different classifications of the several large samples. The work involved might have deterred others. It is not known to the analyst what the exactions of their time schedules were. Many investigators now work on time schedules to which they hold rather rigidly. Other students of family budgets, accustomed to work on a rigid schedule or hurrying their work to a finish through ambition or outside pressure, would never have taken the necessary time for the exploration which seems to have been essential for this discovery. It is known that the authors put several years' work on the budget studies out of which this discovery came.

Perhaps it is time that we should cease talking about the discovery and tell what it is. The discovery is that of *fammains* and *ammains*. (Fammain is a condensation of the phrase "food for adult male maintenance" while ammain is the abbreviation for "adult male maintenance"). Formerly we had a short scale of equivalent adult males such as the following, based on food requirements and used by the United States Bureau of Labor Statistics:

	Adult Male
1 adult male	= 1
1 adult female	= .9
1 child 11–14 years	= .9
1 child 7–10 years	= .75
1 child 4– 6 years	= .4
1 child 3 years and under	= .15

King and Sydenstricker developed a scale of ammains of 80 places (for each year of age) for each sex, based on actual expenditures for approximately all items of the budget, as is shown in the table below.

The decimal fractions show the relationships between the expenditures for the males and females of all ages and expenditure of the male at his age of maximum expense. Their significance lies not so much in their detail as in the fact that they are based on actual expenditures for all items of the budget and not on calorie requirements which are supposed to be the same as food costs.

Person 1 year old = .241 male adults of 25 years and .241 if female
Person 2 years old = .281 male adults of 25 years and .281 if female
Person 10 years old = .442 male adults of 25 years and .429 if female
Person 19 years old = .960 male adults of 25 years and .776 if female
Person 25 years old = 1.000 male adults of 25 years and .788 if female
Person 40 years old = .931 male adults of 25 years and .739 if female
Person 80 years old = .731 male adults of 25 years and .616 if female

How could these proportions be obtained when food and rent and light are consumed by all members of the family collectively and not measured for each individual separately? This was the nut to crack. And this is the way they did it. They worked out the scales for food alone first, which was done as follows:

There were the following factors to deal with: size of family as made up of a number of individuals of two sexes, of varying ages and with different food costs and different incomes. The Atwater Scale, based on calorie needs for men and women and children, was used to compute the size of the family as an approximation to be tested. The problem was to test whether expenditures for food conformed to this scale, and, if not, to correct the scale. The first point investigated was the comparison of males and females as to food costs. That is, were the relative food needs of females as compared with males by the Atwater Scale the same as, more than, or less than the relative food costs of females as compared with males? Incomes were held constant by dealing only with families of the same incomes. Size of family was roughly held constant by working only with the food costs per adult male determined by dividing total food costs by total equivalent adult males. The age was not held constant, but it is almost certain that it was proportionately divided according to sexes and income groups. These three factors being eliminated, the sex composition of the families was varied and compared with the food costs. This was done by ranking the families according to percentages of females in the family. If the food expenses of females were the same fraction of the food expenses of males as are the calorie requirements of females to those of males on the Atwater Scale (here used), then the food costs should be the same among the families classified by percentages of females in the families. But in reality the food costs were slightly greater as the femaleness of the family increased. This meant that in the Atwater Scale the proportion which females were of males was not quite as large as it should be for comparisons on the basis of food expenses. The authors then found that by dividing the Atwater Scale by 0.964 the best correction was obtained.

Such was the chief idea in the solution of the problem. The idea of holding factors constant and varying only the two concerned is not new. Such is the familiar technique in the laboratories. In statistics there are various devices, such as partial correlation, the method of standard population, and the method of minute subdivisions. But in this particular problem the situation was complicated by the fact that these factors, at least sex and age, were not readily isolated, because the food was purchased for the whole family and allocations of the parts consumed were not easily made. The first idea, then, was to assign a proportion of the food expenses to each sex more or less arbitrarily (the proportions of the Atwater Scale were assigned). The next step was to apply the technique of holding constant certain factors and varying the two factors concerned, to see if the assigned fractions were too high or too low, and as a result to make the corrections, if any, in the directions indicated. The procedure was not quite so simple as appears for the reason that assigned fractions for ages had to be used instead of true ones in the testing of the assigned factors for the sexes. Consequently, the corrections on the fractions for the sexes were approximations which had to be revised again after the age fractions had been revised.

We see, therefore, that a guessed or assigned scale for family size, namely, the Atwater Scale, was corrected as a measure of food expense for sexes by varying the sex proportions of families and comparing with food costs per equivalent adult male while keeping other factors constant. In the same way this corrected scale for sexes was assigned for further correcting fractions of the Atwater Scale for ages as indices of relative food expenditures by ages. Thus the families were classified according to age and compared with food costs per equivalent adult male, while the other factors were kept constant. The costs for food as measured by the Atwater Scale were thus found to be too high for older people and too low for the younger children. A series of adjustments were therefore made, yielding an Atwater Scale corrected and adjusted for age and sex. This was virtually a new scale, though somewhat similar to the Atwater Scale. This new scale was worked out on 1916 data. It was then applied and in similar manner recorrected on some new 1917 data. The result is the scale of fammains.

The next step was to derive scales not for food expenses but for total expense. Food expense was perhaps between 40 and 50 per cent of the

total family expense of these southern cotton-mill families. The remainder
of expenditures—other than for food—was divided into two classes: those
expenses that could be assigned to particular individuals, such as clothing, personal objects, etc.; and those expenses that were common to all,
such as fuel, rent, and light. The authors dealt first with those expenses
that could be assigned to particular individuals. From the budgets of
140 families of 672 individuals the total expenses for assignable items
were determined for males of each age and for females of each age. These
totals were then expressed as percentages of the similar total expenses
of the adult male at the year of his maximum expense. These percentages
were added to the scale of food costs. The result gave a scale based on
the total budget except for those expenses such as light, fuel, and rent
that could not be separated. The non-separable expenses constituted for
these families only about 11 per cent of their total budgets. This fractional remainder is small and it is quite probable that it should be allocated among the different age and sex groups in the same ratios as
those determined for the 89 per cent of the budget made up of assignable
items. Hence, the resulting scales, found by adding the food-expense
scales and the allocable-expense scales, show the fraction or per cent
which the expenses of individuals of different ages and sexes bear to the
expenses of the adult male at his most expensive year. That year is rated
as 1.0, and the other years for both sexes are therefore rated as fractions
of 1.0. This is the scale of ammains. The size of the families can be
computed from this scale in such a way as to make them comparable
when comparing income or expenses. Thus a family of the following
composition has the size indicated here.

$$
\begin{array}{lll}
\text{Father} & 25 \text{ years} = & 1.000 \\
\text{Mother} & 25 \text{ years} = & .786 \\
\text{Boy} & 5 \text{ years} = & .352 \\
\text{Girl} & 3 \text{ years} = & .306 \\
\text{Girl} & 1 \text{ year} = & .241 \\
\hline
& & 2.685
\end{array}
$$

The scale of ammains which the authors have invented is thus seen to
be another step in the evolution of measures of family size to be used in
budget studies and elsewhere. The authors themselves state in the closing
paragraph of their article that they expect other improvements to be
made later. Other inventions similarly analyzed show very much the
same origin and development. They are not the creation of something
wholly new. They are rather steps in a process, and always built upon

bases that have previously been built up. The addition of an invention to the base means often a new base on which still other inventions will be built.

What will be the next invention, the next step in this evolution of family measurement? It may not be that the next step can be predicted. But that prediction which grows out of criticisms of the invention under discussion will be the soundest. The validity of the new scale depends on how successful the approximations or adjustments are in modifying the Atwater Scale. A future improvement may be a more careful division among sex and age groups of the items of the budget other than food and the items assignable to individuals of a known age and sex. Perhaps better approximations can be made than the inventors worked out. This could be done with a very large sample so that the age factor could be held constant in much the same manner as income in making comparisons of the sexes. With a very large sample, the age differentials in expenditure might be worked out better. In working out the scales for individual expenditures the size of the sample, 140 families, seems perhaps rather small. The authors tried to overcome this inadequacy of the sample by methods of smoothing out the variations, but throughout the article the reader feels the need of knowing more about the error of these estimates.

This point brings up the question of the adequacy of the authors' presentation. This is important for two reasons. First, the material should be in sufficient detail to enable the critical reader to form a judgment as to its accuracy. Second, it should be presented in sufficient fulness to permit other investigators to understand readily the new tool and to construct a similar one from their own data.

The article is not well presented. The journal in which it appeared demanded no sacrifices of accuracy in the interest of literary or emotional appeal to readers.[4] All that was demanded was clarity. However, this journal does make exactions in space allotments, and to have given the necessary fulness and illustration it would have been necessary to write a much longer article. The article is very hard reading, and must be read several times with great care in order to understand it or to make adaptations to other problems. Even then, some points might not be wholly clear. New scales should be drawn up for different income classes at different times and places by investigators using them if very great

[4] [The analyst was editor of the journal referred to at the time of the publication. —EDITOR.]

exactness is demanded. The greatest weakness in the presentation is the insufficient account of error.

Is the invention a significant one? Will it have wide use? The significance of an invention is, of course, apart from the methodology of the process. It needs to be discussed, however, because it concerns the very important point of accuracy. The writer is under the impression that this invention has had little adoption by research workers. Why is this? It may be due to the difficulty in understanding it and in adapting it to other economic classes as a result of the unsatisfactory presentation or of the labor in making the adaptation. The old Atwater Scale and others similar to it are still in use. Also it may be that the improvement in accuracy over the Atwater Scale is not sufficient to warrant the trouble in constructing a new set of ammains for each study. The published scale of King and Sydenstricker, however, may be more accurate than the Atwater Scale. But here again the relative accuracies should be demonstrated.

In the family used as an illustration in this essay the size of the family in fammains was 2.685, and in equivalent adult male units of the scale used by the United States Bureau of Labor Statistics it was 2.6. According to the Atwater Scale it was 2.9. There is not much difference. Other families might have been chosen where there was greater difference. But the scales are based on averages and their statistical use largely concerns averages.

In order to compare the scale of ammains with other scales for averages of whole groups rather than for individual families, I have taken a sample of 151 families with incomes ranging from $1,890 a year to $1,015 and varying in size from husband and wife without children to husband and wife with 8 children. The average size of the 103 families having incomes under $1,400 a year was 2.52 according to the Adult Male Unit Scale of the Bureau of Labor Statistics (called here the B.L.S. Scale), 2.44 according to the Atwater Scale, and 2.26 according to the King and Sydenstricker scale of ammains constructed on cotton-mill families. On the B.L.S. Scale the average size of the families is 11.5 per cent larger than the average size on the ammain scale, while on the Atwater Scale the average size is 8 per cent larger. The uses of the scale are often comparative, as, for instance, in comparing the average sizes of families in different places or in different income groups. For instance, in the case of the foregoing families the B.L.S. Scale shows the average size of families with incomes under $1,400 to be 71 per cent of the average size of families having incomes over $1,400. The same comparison on the Atwater Scale shows 74 per cent, and on the ammain scale 77 per cent. Perhaps these illustrations give a fair comparison of the different scales for measuring the size of the families, and if the ammain scale be assumed to be correct, then the foregoing comparisons give the errors involved in using the other scales as indices of family size in budget studies. The probable improvement of the ammain scale over the other scales seems to be around 10 per cent, the B.L.S. Scale being somewhat greater in error than the Atwater. This estimate is based on averages for a group. For smaller samples the difference might be greater. The value of the ammains lies not only in their greater accuracy, but also in the fact that they provide a standard by which the error in the other scales may be measured.

The analysis of the researches of Sydenstricker and King has thrown considerable light on the nature of invention and the process by which it is attained. The invention was not so wholly new as the strange word "ammain" indicates; it was rather an improvement by 10 per cent more or less in a measurement already in existence, which had itself been in process of evolution. The invention, then, was a step in a process. We are able to single out the new idea in the invention, and to make some speculations as to where the new idea came from. A combination, arousing out of the factors of inherited mental ability, existing equipment and knowledge, and necessity, led to the invention. There were also concrete practical situations involved, such as opportunity and urge for exploration, hard work, time schedules, and absence of accident. It seems understandable that the invention occurred at the time it did and that it was made by the particular inventors.[5]

[5][This analysis was first written in December, 1928, and revised by the analyst in the following spring.—EDITOR.]

ANALYSIS 13

TESTING AND SCALING METHODS: E. L. THORNDIKE'S MEASUREMENTS OF HANDWRITING[1]

By JOSEPH PETERSON

Jesup Psychological Laboratory, George Peabody College

The progress from qualitative to quantitative methods in psychology has been a gradual one, advancing now in this field of the subject and now in that. In the particular branch of testing there have been gradations from the mere *rating* of persons or of educational products on the basis of three or more groupings, such as "good," "medium," or "poor," up to actual measurement by an approximately objective scale. The contributions of outstanding individuals, however, mark certain easily recognizable steps in this progress. The rating methods served several immediately practical purposes when applied carefully to definable and isolable qualities or traits, or to general accomplishments of individuals in particular lines; and they are still in use. But accurate definition of "good" or "poor" was impossible, and the fixing of boundary lines to mark off the different classes led to inconsistencies, especially when applied to groups and situations other than those immediately present and familiar alike to all the judges. Webb (1915) used the method of rating into seven classes (—3, —2, —1, 0, 1, 2, 3,) in an important study of character and intelligence, but the more recent use of ratings on a large scale in the United States Army was found to be unsatisfactory from a scientific point of view (Rugg, 1921).

The *order-of-merit*, or *rank*, method used by Binet and his collaborators in the nineties, by Cattell (1903, 1903A), Spearman (1904), Burt (1909), and others, requires more direct comparison of individuals and samples, but is otherwise only a refinement of the rough classifications by the rating method. When applied to very small groups or to relatively few samples to be evaluated comparatively, the well-known modification called the *method of paired comparisons* is a great improvement, because of its simplification of the conditions under which each judgment is made. By this method each individual or sample is severally compared with every other one and simply judged superior or inferior, or greater or smaller, etc., as the case may be, and scores are systematically recorded

[1] [References are appended at the end of the analysis.—Editor.]

so as to show the number of times each individual or sample was judged superior. But in cases of large numbers, paired comparisons are very laborious and time consuming. The order-of-merit method is subject to grave errors if all the individuals to be ranked are not well known to each judge, since misplacement of any individual through lack of acquaintance with him results, as a rule, in wrong ranks being assigned to many others. Thorndike (1916) showed that fairly accurate ranking is possible even when all the judges do not know all the individuals to be compared, if each judge ranks only those whom he knows well. His method is too complicated to consider here, but it has been shown that a much simpler method of handling the judgments in such cases—that of simply averaging all the ranks assigned to each individual—is as good (Garrett, 1924; Wood, 1928) and requires very much less time. Wood's demonstration of this consisted in applying the two methods to the ranking of objects as to weight, and checking by means of an objective criterion.

Ranks come to have more general application and more objectivity if made on a percentile basis, that is, if stated in terms of position in an order-of-merit arrangement of one hundred cases (percentile scores), especially if each individual is ranked either by several judges or on the basis of measurable performance of some definite task under uniform conditions as to time allowance, equalization of practice, etc. The percentile ranks are then numbers which may be treated by ordinary statistical methods; norms for each age, grade, or otherwise homogeneous group can be given in very condensed and easily understood tables and graphs. Certain authorities prefer this method of treating mental measurements to any other yet available, as having possibly the fewest objectionable aspects, despite its inaccuracy (common to all methods of ranking) of equalizing all difference between successive individuals in the serial order.

Cattell early used the order-of-merit method in his studies of eminent men (1903) and of American men of science (1903A). In the second of these he secured the rank of each scientist by averaging the ranks assigned him by the most competent judges in his own line of work. Cattell showed that differences in merit between any two scientists in a rank-order series who are not extremely far apart vary directly with the distances between their average ranks and inversely as the probable errors of these averages. In England, Galton (1869) early assumed that abilities followed the so-called normal probability curve, and Pearson (1909), on this same assumption, which he supported on the basis of measurements of various physical structures, worked out a system for rating persons as to mentality by classification under one of seven heads, each of which was defined in terms of standard deviation units measured from the central tendency. Cattell had been a close student of Galton and was also active in early mental measurement methods (particularly in reaction times) in Wundt's laboratory at Leipzig (Cattell, 1885). He has exerted a strong influence toward the use of quantitative measurement in the social sciences. His gifted student, Thorndike, has emphasized the use of objective scales which measure abilities and educational products in terms of equal units numbered from an established zero-point. We shall examine in some detail his first scale—that for measuring the handwriting of children (1910).

This scale was not designed for analyzing the *behavior* of handwriting, but only for measuring the *product* of such behavior in so far as "goodness," "quality," or "merit" is concerned. The successful measurement of handwriting reacted back, of course, and increased the precision in analysis of handwriting behavior itself, as any scale is sure to do with respect to the behavior, or the traits, or the capacities which it measures. Rough empirical trials had convinced Thorndike that the handwriting of children in grades V–VIII, inclusive, could be classified by competent judges into only ten or eleven groups, ranging from the poorest to the very best; that finer groupings would be indistinguishable. He, therefore, had a considerable number (" 23 to 55") of competent judges select from the samples of the formal writing at natural rate of 1,000 children of the grades indicated those samples which would represent equally spaced points in a continuous scale of merit ranging from 1 (the lowest) to 11, inclusive. It is evident that a given sample might, for instance, be assigned quality 3 by one or two judges, 4 by several others, 5 by a considerable number, 6 by a smaller number, and 7 by two or three only; and that, therefore, the average merit assigned might be anywhere from, say, 4.6–5.5. From the large number of samples used, Thorndike found it possible to get one or more specimens lying very near—all but two within .1 step—the exact points 1, 2, 3, 4, 5, 6, 7, 8, 9, 10, and 11. It was desirable to have several samples of different styles for each of these qualities of merit, but in some cases only one was obtained. A complete scale would have each style represented at every exact quality-point in the scale. To get the extreme samples in the scale properly placed, Thorndike found it necessary to have some artificial samples that were lower and one that was higher in quality than any included in the original 1,000. Otherwise the extremes, not having gradations on both sides for comparison, would have to be placed by mere inference and

not by measurement; because the average of the estimates of 1, for instance, would be too high, being based on no estimates below 1 but on
some above 1; and that of 11, for similar reasons, but applied in the
other direction, would be too low. Zero quality of writing was defined
by Thorndike as handwriting that was "recognizable as such but of
absolutely no merit as handwriting" (p. 7).

The next step was to arrange the other quality-points in the scale with
respect to the zero-point. This Thorndike freely admits was done largely
by a subjective estimate. He says that he judged as best he could the
distance that the approximately best sample was from zero in terms of the
distance from this point of about the worst sample, and that "a ratio
somewhere between 3 to 1 and 3½ to 1 seems the most reasonable." But
he admits that he "could argue plausibly for a ratio as low as 2½ to 1
or for one as high as 5 to 1" (p. 44). This certainly shows that there is
nothing physically determinative or objective about the zero-point of his
scale. Moreover, the real scale (Scale A) itself actually has a ratio of
2-3/7 (17/7) to 1, so far as the fifth-to-eight-grade children's writing is
concerned, having samples for the equidistant quality-points as follows:

$$(0) \ldots (4) \ (5) \ (6) \ 7 \ 8 \ 9 \ 10 \ 11 \ 12 \ 13 \ 14 \ 15 \ 16 \ 17 \ (18)$$

Samples for the points in the scale which I have inclosed in parentheses
came from outside his group of children of Grades V–VIII. The samples
for qualities 0 and 4 are artificial, as is also that for quality 18 (a copy-
book model), and those for qualities 5 and 6 are poor samples from fourth
grade children. Thorndike says explicitly of the scale that "it is not a
scale of merit of the writings of children of grades 1 to 4 or of the writings of boys and girls of high-school age. It can, however, be more or
less well used for such cases until we get more appropriate scales" (p. 7).
He also says that quality 17 is "nearly the best writing of eighth-grade children" as quality 5 is "nearly the worst writing of fourth-grade children"
(ibid.).

Despite some ambiguity and contradiction, then, in the various statements by the author, the scale as given above (including steps from 7 to
17, inclusive) seems to be the scale derived from the 1,000 samples by the
children of Grades V through VIII. Thorndike recognizes that it would be
desirable to have the children's scale also include samples for quality-
points 1, 2, and 3, but it is obvious that he regards this first scale and
Scales B and C as mere demonstrations of the possibility of scale-making
rather than as complete and final scales. The amount of work necessary
to get a complete scale with all styles for each quality-point and all sam-

ples at exactly these equidistant points would be very great—much greater than the inexperienced reader will suspect. The establishment of a reliable zero-point in a psychological scale is a very difficult task—one, indeed, which has never yet been satisfactorily accomplished, although attempts from many angles have been made and we have already several kinds of "zero-points." Thorndike was aware of the practical impossibility of establishing a true or absolute zero-point, and the consequent absolute values of the other points of the scale, but held that those who use the scale in the way that we use money values would "commit no error of much consequence or, at least, no error so great as they would be likely to commit by measuring it [handwriting] in any other one way" (p. 44).

In the same article Thorndike prints also another scale for children's handwriting, Scale C, to illustrate a different method of scaling, based on *equally noticed differences* in ranking according to quality. This scale extends from quality 7 through quality 17 (and it includes also the artificial sample of quality 18). It contains only one sample of each quality. In his own words:

> Suppose competent judges to compare each sample with every other,[2] stating in each case which was better. If then we picked out samples *a, b, c, d,* etc., such that *a* was judged better than *b,* just as often as *b* was judged better than *c,* and just as often as *c* was judged better than *d,* and so on, we could have, in samples *a, b, c, d,* etc., a scale by equal steps, if two other conditions were fulfilled by them. The first of these conditions would be that *a* should not be judged better than *b* and worse than *b equally* often. For if it were, *a* would be equal to *b,* *b* to *c,* *c* to *d,* and so on, and we would have no extent to our scale. The second of these conditions would be that *a* should not *always* be judged better than *b.* For, if it were, it might be just enough better to barely be so judged, or it might be very, very much better. Only if differences are not always noticed can we say that differences equally often noticed are equal [p. 56].

This method (an adaptation of the "method of right and wrong cases"), it will be noted, is that of *comparing each sample directly with every other one,* with a view to judging only which one in each case is of superior merit.[3] The method used in the construction of Scale A, on the contrary, was that of *rating each sample by an* (imaginary) *ideal scale.* The two methods, Thorndike found, do not give results that correspond

---

[2] This was certainly not done with the 1,000 samples, but apparently only with a selected few which had been roughly ranked in preliminary work.

[3] It is obvious that the greater the difference between any two samples x and y, the more often the difference will be noticed, i.e., the greater will be the percentage of judgments that "x is better than y," or that "y is better than x."

exactly, the differences appearing chiefly in the lower parts of the scale where the samples represent poor writing. His results showed that judges will notice differences between pairs and samples low in the scale more readily (and that they will detect smaller differences) by the *direct-comparison* method than by the *rating* method. That is, the lower steps in Scale C are smaller than those in Scale A. It was, of course, practically impossible to get samples for the different quality-points which would make the steps exactly equal. Each sample in Scale C was, however, judged superior to the one next below it by a per cent of the forty-two judges varying only as follows: 81, 80, 79, 79, 79, 77, 83.5, 79, 78, 80, and 74. That is, 81 per cent of the judges estimated the highest sample (in the order finally arranged in the scale) as better than the next highest, 80 per cent the next highest as better than the third, 79 the third as better than the fourth, and so on.

The use of the scale, say Scale A, may be illustrated as follows: One takes a specimen of writing to be measured and moves it up and down slowly beside the samples of increasing merit on the scale until a sample is found which equals, or most nearly equals, the specimen. The quality value of this sample is then recorded, e.g., 9 or 10, or even a fractional value, e.g., 9.3, if the match is not perfect and one wishes to note finer points than whole steps. Greater accuracy can be obtained if the average of the measurements by several judges (or of several independent ratings some days apart by the same judge) is recorded as the "score." Experience with such scales has shown that greater objectivity results when several judges measure the specimens. This is because the various personal biases as to peculiar styles and other such irrelevant qualities are then balanced against, and cancel, one another.

Thorndike's handwriting scale was not the first standardized test-scale to be used in psychology and education. As early as 1905 Alfred Binet, after some fifteen years of experimental work with tests, published his first (tentative) scale for the measurement of intelligence (Peterson, 1925). This so-called scale was really only an arrangement of tests in increasing order of difficulty as determined by the reactions to them of about fifty normal children and a considerable number of feeble-minded children. The scale consisted of thirty test-exercises (or in some cases groups of exercises). No attempt was made to place them equally distant in difficulty; but the limits of ability of normal children of certain ages, and of idiots, imbeciles, and morons, were indicated as only approximate limits. This first scale, which was only experimental—to try out the possibility of making a scale—had clear implications of *mental age* as a unit of measure. The later scales of 1908 and 1911 developed this concept more explicitly and carried definite age-levels, but these units were not assumed to be equal throughout the range of ages in the scale. That is, Binet did not imply that a year's growth for the normal child is equal at any growing age to that at any other. The contrary is known to be true. What *is* implied in the Binet Scale is simply that any individual may consistently be rated in terms of the accomplishment of normal children in the growing periods (to about sixteen years). A child's mental age is the age of normal children whose score his equals. The simplicity and the practical usefulness of this method, despite its several limitations, especially at higher levels, make its contribution by Binet one of capital importance. Mental acceleration or retardation of a child is measured in terms of difference between his own age and that of normal children whose score equals his. There had to be specific rules, of course, for the determination of the exact mental age of any individual, but we cannot consider them now. Binet also standardized roughly certain year-level scales of educational achievement in arithmetic, reading, and spelling, the first of these being published as early as 1905, or five years before Thorndike's writing scale appeared; and he suggested the making of graded "exercises in composition" (Binet, 1909).[4] Thorndike's works do not indicate the degree of his indebtedness to Binet.

Thorndike, and his students especially, gave impetus to the scale-making movement as applied to the measurement of educational products or achievements, and various scales followed that of handwriting. Extensive observations and measurements convinced him that most mental traits, as is true of many physical traits, conform roughly to the so-called normal curve of distribution; that is, that there are relatively very many cases near the central tendency or average, and a constantly decreasing number with divergence from this point, both up and down the scale, giving the familiar bell-shaped curve. Stated differently, individuals, items, or test-exercises, arranged in a rank order of merit with respect to any trait or ability, are much nearer together near the average than when far above or below it. The size of any variation has an inverse relation to the frequency of its occurrence. Assuming normality of distribution, we can readily determine, in the case of any individual whose rank in a definite number of cases is known, how far he is below or above the average—i.e., his exact position—on a scale of equal (sigma or P.E.) units on the base line of the curve of distribution. In making

---

[4] This statement probably appears also in the first edition, 1905, which is not at hand.

tests and scales for measuring educational products, Thorndike's students have determined the position of samples or test-units of children on the P.E. base line of the distributions of several groups of different ages or school grades, by finding the percentages in every group that pass each item or test. From these data the distances of the several items from the point on the base line just passed by practically 100 per cent of each group are found. These are not the same for different ages and grades. Then, by means of a number of assumptions and calculations, weightings, etc., to establish a sort of consistency and to eliminate contradictions, an "absolute zero-point" of merit, difficulty, or ability, as the case may be, is finally obtained.

The main difficulty with this so-called absolute scale is that its zero-point, as we have seen, is not absolute and has never been consistently and indisputably established. Even in a recent important investigation by Thorndike and his collaborators on the measurement of intelligence (1927), the zero-point is located by a method which will certainly not secure universal acceptance, and it would probably have a considerably different value if similarly but independently worked out by other workers using different tasks and different judges. To establish his zero-point of intellectual ability Thorndike had forty psychologists, "especially such as were expert in animal and infant psychology, or the psychology of the very dull," rank fifty-six tasks (mostly verbal in one respect or another) "according to their difficulty, that is, according to the degree of intellect required for a man to perform each, supposing the man to have lived twenty years with the average opportunities of a person born and bred in an average English-speaking home," etc. (p. 342). From these rankings of *judged* (not actually attested) difficulty, Thorndike established by various measurements and inferences, which space will not permit us to consider, the "absolute zero-point." We must note that while the ratings by the psychologists were "in entire independence," their training and points of view were not so independent. Moreover, experiments have shown that persons may agree rather well on the description and the relative evaluation of certain named traits and yet in their reaction to these "traits" themselves they may show no significant agreement. It certainly would have been better to have had the various tasks tried out extensively on individuals of different ages and abilities. Of this Thorndike was well aware, but circumstances limited him to the less valuable procedure.

The best that has been attained in scale-making in psychology is the establishment of scales of approximately equal units (if "normality" of distribution be granted) but with no thoroughly satisfactory zero-point. The limitations of such scales are therefore considerable. Despite this difficulty, the use of scales has enormously extended our knowledge and, especially, our technique in certain fields of the social and biological sciences. Of by no means the least importance is the naturalistic attitude toward behavior that results from the application of quantitative methods to a large realm of experiences which were once supposed to be under the influence of spirits, demons, supernatural charms, faculties, and special "gifts." When we apply definite measurement methods, even though imperfect ones, tangible results are obtained which present problems for further study and explanation, requiring the setting-up and the testing of scientific hypotheses.[5]

REFERENCES

BINET, ALFRED. *Les idées modernes sur les enfants.* Paris: E. Flammarion, 1909.

BURT, CYRIL. "Experimental Tests of General Intelligence," *Brit. Jour. Psychol.,* III (1909), 94–177.

CATTELL, J. McKEEN. Articles in *Philosophische Studien,* Vol. II ff. (1885).

———. "A Statistical Study of Eminent Men," *Pop. Sci. Mo.,* LXII (1903), 359–77.

———. "Statistics of American Psychologists," *Amer. Jour. Psychol.,* XIV (1903A), 310–28.

GALTON, FRANCIS. *Hereditary Genius.* London: Macmillan & Co., 1869.

GARRETT, H. E. "An Empirical Study of the Various Methods of Combining the Incomplete Order of Merit Ratings," *Jour. Educ. Psychol.,* XV (1924), 157–71.

PEARSON, KARL. "On the Relationship of Intelligence to Size and Shape of Head," *Biometrika,* V (1906), pp. 105–46.

PETERSON, JOSEPH. *Early Conceptions and Tests of Intelligence.* (Includes a detailed treatment of the work of Binet and of his scales, with complete references.) New York: World Book Co., 1925.

RUGG, HAROLD. "Is the Rating of Human Character Practicable?" *Jour. Educ. Psychol.,* XII (1921), 425–501.

SPEARMAN, C. " 'General Intelligence' Objectively Determined and Measured," *Amer. Jour. Psychol.,* XV (1904), 201–92.

THORNDIKE, E. L. "Handwriting," *Teachers Coll. Rec.,* II, No. 2 (1910).

———. "The Technique of Combining Incomplete Judgments of the Relative Positions of N Facts Made by N Judges," *Jour. Phil., Psychol. and Sci. Methods,* XIII (1916), 197–204.

[5] [This analysis was first written in September, 1928, and revised by the analyst in 1929.—EDITOR.]

————. *The Measurement of Intelligence.* New York: Bureau of Publications, Teachers College, Columbia University, 1927.

WEBB, E. "Character and Intelligence," *Brit. Jour. Psychol. Mon. Suppl.,* I, No. 3 (1915).

WOOD, C. R. "Does 'Personality' Have a Definite and Consistent Use in Education?" *Cont. to Educ.,* George Peabody College for Teachers, No. 56 (1929).

SECTION IV
ATTEMPTS TO DISCOVER SPATIAL DISTRIBUTIONS AND TEMPORAL SEQUENCES

ANALYSIS 14

A DETAIL OF REGIONAL GEOGRAPHY: OBJECTIVES AND METHODS IN ROBERT S. PLATT'S STUDY OF THE ELLISON BAY COMMUNITY[1]

By K. C. McMURRY
University of Michigan

Objectives and methods in geographic field study have been given much more attention during the past few years than any other phase of the general subject. Development has been so rapid, and present attitudes are so different from those of a few years ago, that the analysis of almost any modern field investigation requires an appreciation of this recent background. This is especially true in the case of Mr. Platt's study, for he has been in the midst of a most active group concerned with experimentation in this type of work.

As in the case of other social sciences, it is difficult to get complete agreement as to definition, objectives, and methods in geography at any period in the development of the subject. The broad field or fields commonly included, together with the newness of the subject as a realm of scientific research, have made the situation more incoherent than in most of the other social disciplines. However, as a starting-point for the discussion of geographic field methods and objectives, there is a definite basis of general agreement. For many years interest has centered largely about the study of regions. The "geographic region" has become dominant in discussion and in classification, and has formed the basis of study. It has commonly been defined as an area in which the conditions of physical environment are essentially similar throughout, as are also the human adaptations to these conditions, while both environment and human activity are different from adjoining areas. Whatever may be the individual attitude toward the regional concept in detail, it certainly has had a dominant influence on the greater part of geographic study in recent years.

Guided by the idea of the geographic region, emanating from various centers, students began work in the field. There was little precedent in method of procedure, especially in gathering data, and objectives were

---

[1] "A Detail of Regional Geography," *Annals of the Association of American Geographers*, XVIII, No. 2 (1928), 81–126.

obscure. Many of the earlier regional studies were the results of efforts to determine and catalogue the geographic relationships and the geographic influences within the area. If sufficient "relationships" and "influences" could be catalogued, a satisfactory report might be prepared.

Relations and influences, in themselves abstractions, were found to be difficult to observe in the field. Different individuals, at different times and under varying conditions, found that their observations and interpretations of these abstractions varied widely for the same area. It became clear that while relationships might remain the final objective in geographic study, better methods of determination, truly scientific in character, must be developed.

The outcome of experimentation in field methods during the past five or six years is evidenced clearly in the study of the Ellison Bay community. (As noted by the author, the article should be taken in connection with other published reports on the same area.) In both the description of the area and in the interpretation of the life of the area a very extensive body of data has been used. The "survey" or "inventory" method was used in collecting these data. The facts of the physical environment, soil, surface, natural vegetation, etc., were mapped in detail. Facts of land utilization, cultivated land, crops, pastures, idle or unused land, orchards, farmsteads, etc., were similarly mapped. Transportation facilities were mapped, and detailed information as to economic and social activities of the people was procured by means of definite and carefully prepared questionnaires. After study extending through several seasons, by several field parties, the available detail concerning this area is probably not surpassed anywhere.

A number of generalizations have been worked out. Relationships have been established between environment and human activity in many cases, and they meet the objective of regional study as described above. The determination of such relationships from definite data, and in many cases by means of quantitative correlations between different maps, is a very different procedure from the more or less casual observation of relationships noted in earlier regional field studies. The survey method has brought scientific accuracy into field study, and is the great accomplishment of recent field activity.

The survey method, as used in this study, does not differ materially from the method of several other studies. While there must be some variation from place to place, and while each worker must adapt his methods to peculiar conditions, there is essential agreement as to the value and the necessity of the method in all field work. However, it has certain weaknesses when applied to the study of large areas. Obviously, it is impossible to cover completely any area of large size. Time and cost preclude the extension of the detailed inventory beyond small areas of a few square miles in extent. How is the necessity of such detailed information to be reconciled with the idea of the geographic region, perhaps thousands of square miles in extent? How is the idea of economic unity to be given areal representation, and what are the relationships of the economic organism to the physical environment? Attention has been focused so closely upon the technique of the survey method that little question has been raised as to its practicability in solving the larger problem.

The unique contribution of Platt's study is the demonstration of the Ellison Bay community. On the basis of data derived by the survey method, carried out in unusual detail, the boundaries of a community are given definite areal representation. Economic phenomena are used almost exclusively in this determination. The focusing of all economic activities upon the village of Ellison is worked out carefully, and boundary lines for the community are drawn accordingly. The work is done with such care, and the data are so clearly correct, that little question can arise as to the scientific value of the project. An area is depicted upon the map which owes its unity essentially to economic focus upon this particular village. A new idea has been the basis of an experiment, and has been demonstrated satisfactorily.

In attempting to determine the value of this method it becomes necessary to project the idea, presumably toward the solution of the problem of regional study. How does the community organization fit into the study of the geographic region? That the idea should develop in this direction is made clear by the author. "The study of Ellison Bay is a primary case, an elementary unit in the science of geography." And again, "It is a geographic unit, and regional geography in its lowest terms is the objective of the study." This is the gist of the experiment; the community, defined areally on economic grounds, becomes the basic unit in regional study.

If the community is the basic unit, it should be possible to build from the simple to the complex. Presumably, the Ellison Bay community may be considered as one of a number of small or unit communities which combine to form some larger community. This larger community, in turn, taken with other similar units of magnitude, doubtless helps to form a still larger community unit. And so on to communities of the largest magnitude. It should be possible to apply the idea to large areas by means of the type-study method. A few typical communities are studied in detail by the survey method. Generalizations are made from the type studies for the other presumably similar communities of the same order. The survey method is applicable under the community organization, as well as under any other organization. If, however, the small community is the basic unit of regional geography, it follows that the community next in magnitude is the next larger unit of regional study, and that the community of largest magnitude is the major geographic region.

If the projection of the idea to the larger problem is correct, the basis of all regional geography becomes entirely economic. It is quite conceivable, for instance, that the unit community may include areas of great diversity in physical environment. It is certain that this is the case in many communities. The community of larger magnitude should tend more and more to include such diversity. If, however, the economic organization is essential to the geographic region, such diversity of physical environment becomes of no consequence. The economic organism is basic.

Reference to the commonly accepted definition of the geographic region indicates an entirely different conception. Unity in physical environment has been an essential part of that conception. Community organization has not been a necessary part of the older idea. Community boundaries, arrived at on a purely economic basis, might or might not coincide with the physical basis of regional determination. The community idea, therefore, as worked out by Platt, seems to present an entirely different method of attack, which, if carried out to its logical conclusion, may result in an entire redrawing of regional boundaries. As an experiment in determination of the unit community, the study has been a definite success. The underlying community idea must be worked out to its logical conclusion, and the effectiveness of its application to regional geography must be demonstrated, before it can find general acceptance by geographers.[2]

[2] [This analysis was first written in November, 1928, and revised by the analyst during the following spring.—EDITOR.]

ANALYSIS 15

THE INFLUENCE OF GEOLOGY AND PHYSIOGRAPHY UPON THE INDUSTRY, COMMERCE, AND LIFE OF A PEOPLE, AS DESCRIBED BY CARL ORTWIN SAUER AND OTHERS[1]

By V. C. FINCH

University of Wisconsin

The *Geography of the Pennyroyal* serves as a recent and interesting example of a regional method in geography. It is the purpose of the authors of this study to portray the regional characteristics of a large portion of south-central Kentucky, a portion called, from the popular appellation for its nuclear area, "the Pennyroyal." Professor Sauer states his view of the task in the Preface to the work in question:

The field of regional geography is not concerned with an encyclopaedic compendium of facts that are bound together simply by their occurrence in a particular region. . . . . The dominant theme, as conceived in this report, is the expression of the individuality of the region, as the site of a particular group of people and their works. To begin with, there is the physical fact of the area, characterized by a distinctive location, by a climate, and by a particular body of land. The natural region consists of an area which, in the sum of its physical characteristic, is set off from adjacent regions. This physical site has been occupied by a group of people or by successive groups. The occupation has led to a series of characteristic contacts with the area, or "cultural" forms. Man's areal activities are expressed by the kind and the distribution of his homes, storerooms, workshops, highways, fields and other marks of his tenure. These marks which man has inscribed in the landscape are the cultural forms with which we are concerned.

Many of man's activities vary from place to place. . . . . This areal differentiation of cultural impress is the main body of material with which regional geography is concerned. These facts it attempts so to order that they may be grasped in their essential relations. That we may understand the culture of an area it is necessary to consider first its physical characteristics. Climate, soil, and surface are materials out of which or by means of which the cul-

---

[1]["Geography of the Pennyroyal," *Kentucky Geological Survey*, 6th ser., Vol. XXIII (Frankfort, Ky., 1927). Professor Sauer was assisted in this study by John B. Leighly, Kenneth McMurry, and Clarence W. Newman. Release from copyright to permit quotation in the present analysis has been kindly given by Mr. Willard R. Jillson, director of the Kentucky Geological Survey.—EDITOR.]

tural forms of an area have been made. What men do in a country is, however, determined in the end primarily by man. The physical equipment of
the area sets limits within which there is wider or narrower choice of
activity, as the case may be. Physical resource, stock of people, and time are
the elements out of which results the full geographic expression of a region.
The region is not simply a mass of ridges and valleys, of rich soils and poor
soils. In it are farms and forests, towns and highways, manifold cultural
forms. The changeful combination of these features, the areal pattern of the
natural landscape as overlaid by a cultural landscape, the how and why
thereof are the object which this volume attempts in some measure to answer
for one of the regions of Kentucky.[2]

This quotation states in brief the outstanding tenets of a philosophy
of regional geography to which, with minor amendment, most geographers
would subscribe. It will be observed that the concept involves two fundamental assumptions. The first of these is that there exists such an entity
as a geographic region, i.e., a district of more than local order of magnitude for which statements respecting forms in the natural or cultural
landscapes apply throughout. That this assumption applies to the Pennyroyal the authors are at considerable pains to develop in the first two
chapters of the report. Although it is comprised of districts which are
recognized and later described as "natural subdivisions," it is demonstrated in these chapters that the Pennyroyal, on both physical and cultural bases, exhibits, when compared with surrounding territories, contrasts greater than those existing between its subdivisions. The region
stands, therefore, as justification of the first assumption.

The second assumption is fundamental to geographical philosophy. It
is assumed that a definite and sometimes measurable interrelationship
exists between certain features of natural environment, on the one hand,
and, on the other, some of those landscape forms that are the expression
of human activity. The development of such interrelationships involves
the interpretative function of geography. Obviously, features in the natural and cultural landscapes must be adequately described before the
presence or the absence of these essentially geographic interrelationships
can be established. It is at this point that much geographical writing,
and to a degree the report in question, departs from the ideal. Some
geographers consider their geographic function fulfilled by adequate
description of the phenomena of an area. With this viewpoint the analyst
must completely disagree. In the portrayal of interrelationships between
the natural and cultural forms of an area the geographer makes his
unique contribuition to the field of learning.

[2] *Ibid.*, pp. ix–x.

The factual basis for the study is adequate. The picture of the Penny-royal is built upon observations by the authors, made and recorded in note and map form during several seasons of field study in the region. These facts are supplemented by others gleaned from meteorological, geological, economic, and historical literature and several types of official publications. The degree of success with which these facts are ordered so "that they may be grasped in their essential relations" is less complete. It is the opinion of the analyst that the wide array of facts assembled for this extensive region would have been endowed with added geographi-cal quality and significance had they been ordered more nearly after the following plan:

1. A consideration of the Pennyroyal landscape in a broad way and as a composite unit with evidences for or against its physical and cultural unity.

2. The recognition and delimitation, upon the basis of composite charac-teristics, of local units of geographical entity within the Pennyroyal.

3. A description of the natural and cultural landscape forms and an inter-pretation of their interrelationships in each of the local units recognized un-der 2.

4. A synthesis, involving an interpretation of the significant types of inter-relationship in terms of the composite unit.

To a degree this order was followed, but only in part.

1. Chapter ii, "Bases of Regional Unity," does indeed mark the unity of the Pennyroyal, but the unity portrayed is of a dual sort. The region is a unit physically because it involves "an open, broadly rolling upland, the extensive development of solution features, a distinctive valley pattern, and a soil series not developed elsewhere in Kentucky." It is a unit cul-turally because it has functioned consistently as a corridor and "because its people belong together rather than elsewhere." Here are two general sets of phenomena described with an apparent assumption of interrela-tionship but without sufficient interpretation to show even broadly its nature and extent.

2. The suggested order seems to reappear in chapter iv, "Natural Sub-divisions: The Central Pennyroyal," and chapters v, vi, and vii, "Mar-ginal Areas," "The Cumberland Enclave," and "The Barrens." It may be added that the first two of these subdivisions are still further parti-tioned for purposes of convenient description. Here apparently are the desired local units of geographical entity. But again disappointment looms, for the subdivisions are not determined by their composite char-acteristics but upon a basis which is almost wholly physical. The central Pennyroyal and any one of its subdivisions, such as "the Greensburg

Area," are almost purely physiographic and soil regions. To be sure, the text is accompanied by excellent illustrations of physical features, from which the careful observer can scarcely fail to glean some facts about the cultural landscape and its relation to the physical forms. It is also accompanied by two field maps, one showing physical features and one cultural forms, but not for the same area. In the text geomorphological processes are discussed at length—discussions that frequently seem unrelated either to the purpose of natural form portrayal or to any of the cultural forms later described. Though these chapters picture in great detail the forms of the natural landscape they do not include the cultural landscape or any hint of an areal interrelationship between the two.

3. Two fairly extensive chapters (ix and xiii), "Rural Cultural Patterns" and "The Cultural Landscape of Town and Village," are reserved for the description and interpretation of the cultural landscape as such. Other chapters, "Problems in Conserving the Land Resources," "Farm Crops and Systems," "Forms of Transportation," and "Louisville," add to the concept but in a somewhat informal manner. In these chapters is the available material for the completion of the geographical picture. We come again upon "the Greensburg area." The cultural landscape is described, essentials of natural landscape are reviewed, and interrelationships between elements of the two are indicated. Here also are maps, the cultural and physical counterparts of those previously noted. The nature of the textual description and interpretation may be briefly indicated:

The wooded valleys break the area into communities, chiefly of four types, in so far as types can be isolated: (1) smooth districts on compact uplands beyond the limits of dissection; (2) ridgetop communities on ridge spurs; (3) cross-roads communities at the place of junction of several ridges, and (4) valley bottom communities. . . . . The wooded valleys are for the most part the back lots of the farms which front toward the ridge-crests.

The continuity of the ridges determines in major part their significance. The big roads are on the big ridges. Here frontage is most in demand. Large old farm houses along such roads have between them numbers of smaller, newer houses, indications of the subdivision of holdings that has been going on. The newer places are especially numerous on the ridge spurs, near the valley margins. Here "deadenings" and stump fields are familiar sights, many of them descending perilously far down into the valley breaks. Log cabins and clapboard dwellings, rail fences and wire fences, forms of different agricultural periods are largely intermingled in this area.[3]

This is excellent geographical description. It includes good geographical interpretation. Yet it would have been much more effective had it

[3] *Ibid.*, pp. 162–63.

been combined and interlarded with the essential details relating to the natural environment. Much more significance would have attached to the carefully made field maps had the physical and cultural maps of the same district faced one another; or, better still, had the two sets of data been combined in one map.

4. Finally, what is the broader significance of the many natural features and the many cultural forms of the Pennyroyal? What importance may be attached to the changeful combination of the areal pattern of the natural landscape *as overlaid* by the cultural landscape of farm and road and village? To this question the report gives no clear answer, for it contains no synthesis where the significant types of interrelationship may be viewed briefly in terms of one another and of the whole.[4]

[4] [This analysis was first written in November, 1928, and revised by the analyst in the following year.—EDITOR.]

ANALYSIS 16

THE CALIFORNIA RAISIN INDUSTRY: C. C. COLBY'S STUDY IN GEOGRAPHIC INTERPRETATION[1]

By RAOUL BLANCHARD
Université de Grenoble and Harvard University

This is an excellent study. It is built upon an abundant bibliography and a thorough knowledge of the place and the people; it indicates the factors of the geographical environment without neglecting the historical and the economic phenomena. In this analysis I wish to indicate how the author utilized and presented the data. I wish also to indicate how I should have presented them according to my concept of geography, and what I should have added and omitted, in order to explain my own method in the light of his study.

Following some pages of introduction, the study includes four parts: an account of the development of the cultivation in California; a study of the localization of the industry in the Fresno region and its causes; the practices and the natural conditions of the cultivation; and, last, the marketing problem.

In the Introduction the author indicates briefly, using a very expressive map, where the production of raisins is established, the contrast between this production and wine-growing in the other parts of California, the "human" aspect of the producing region, and the rapid growth of the cultivation. Next comes the historical sketch. At this point, I think two observations can be made.

The first observation is that the author's very useful data concerning the distribution of the houses, the value of the holdings, the return per acre, and questions concerning operation by the owners, should have been developed. Information should have been given showing the influences exerted by this special cultivation upon the architecture of the buildings and upon the farm; upon the site of the farmsteads in relation to the fields; upon the size of the fields in relation to the type of cultivation; upon the modes of landholding; upon the density of the population and the characteristics of this population. All of these geographic consequences seem to me of highest interest, and I am inclined to regard as in-

[1] "The California Raisin Industry—a Study in Geographic Interpretation," *Annals of the Association of American Geographers*, XIV (1924), 49–108. Figs. 13.

complete a study which touches upon them very slightly or not at all. There exist some useful references to these questions scattered throughout the study, but it would have been better to have expanded them and to have presented them *en bloc,* at the end of the article, since they are geographical consequences of the raisin cultivation. Geography must bring to light reciprocal actions and reactions. If the climatic, edaphic, and human phenomena act on the raisin cultivation and explain it, the latter in turn reacts on the phenomena of habitat, population, and soil management, the explanation of which is integral with the cultivation itself.

For the same reason I should have presented a complete picture of the physical phenomena which explain the presence and the distribution of the raisin cultivation in California. Without them, whatever might have been the human phenomena, this type of agriculture would not have existed. I realize that Mr. Colby shares my opinion, and throughout Parts I, II, and III he discusses these physical phenomena and emphasizes their importance. In my opinion, from the point of view of what I believe to be the true geographical method, that does not suffice. Since these phenomena are basic, they must be placed first. I should have preferred to have Mr. Colby give first a clear picture of the normal climate of California, especially of the southern San Joaquin Valley, with graphs, to bring out in a few lines its effects upon agriculture. Then should have followed a discussion of the conditions of the soil. I should have preferred then to have him explain how, on the large fans spread out at the foot of the Sierras, the northern rivers, linked to the sea base-level, have deepened their beds clear to the mountains. Those of the south, flowing into a basin without outlet, hardly begin to cut downstream, whereas upstream they flow at the surface of the fans, thus facilitating irrigation. Last, I should have placed here the interesting considerations regarding the flow of the streams, which the author has treated in the second part. To sum up, I should have set at the beginning of the work a coherent chapter on physical geography, supplying a presentation and an explanation of all the physical phenomena which act upon the cultivation studied; because, to repeat, the action of these physical phenomena is ineluctable, whatever may be the human conditions. For I am convinced that human geography cannot do without a solid prop of physical geography, and that a statement of physical geography must be placed at the head of every study of human and economic geography.

Mr. Colby begins by presenting the first stages of the vine cultivation in California, under the influence of the Spanish missions; then of the needs for wine and fruit in the mining centers; the attempts at introducing European stocks, the success of the Malaga muscate, the earlier localization in the Sacramento Valley, the first appearance of the vineyards in Fresno in 1873. Nothing among these facts seems to me superfluous, for these historical phenomena sometimes exert on the geographical facts influences which take a very long time to obliterate. In Europe we face a considerable number of facts of human geography incapable of being explained today except by history.

The second part of the study, "Localization of Raisin Production," is, to my mind, an illustration of the ideal method of human geography. The author explains first why the cultivation can be located only on the alluvial fans of the upper San Joaquin plain. The bottom of the depression is too moist and the water table is too near the surface to supply other kinds of cultivation than meadows and forage crops. But on the fans there are very different possibilities. Thanks to the late melting of the high mountain snow, the major rivers which head far back in the Sierras run high in May, June, and July, when the vine needs to be watered. But this irrigation is difficult to practice on the northern fans, because the rivers here are already deeply trenched in the piedmont plain. On the contrary, in the upper part of the plain the rivers hardly begin to bite into the lower part of their fans, and on the upper slopes they flow close to the surface of the fan, the gradient of the stream being only slightly greater than the general slope of the alluvial piedmont. Here, very simple brush dams, and channels easy to trace, make irrigation cheap and convenient. Therefore, one can understand why the irrigated raisin cultivation is located on the piedmont fan of the Kings River, a powerful stream of the south. The Kern River fan, another main southern stream, could have served the same purpose had it not been appropriated at an early date by large owners whose principal interests were live stock and grain. One sees that in these considerations an accurate balance is reached between physical and human factors.

There are still other applications of this principle. Irrigation does not only depend upon climatic, physiographic, and hydrologic conditions, but the law has something to do with it, and Mr. Colby discusses the curious conflict between the English common law of riparian rights, adopted by California, and the Mediterranean environment of the region which imperiously calls for a different regulation. The presence of large estates might be another obstacle; fortunately, the light soils of the piedmont fans did not attract the grain farmers who established themselves elsewhere on huge landholdings throughout the plain. Another aspect to consider is the question of irrigation from ground water, since an increasing number of farms in Fresno county are being irrigated from wells. There is also to be considered the danger of a serious shortage of water if the snowfall should be too light in the Sierras—a danger which will cause the construction of dams and reservoirs in the high valleys in the near future.

The third part of the author's work is called "Vineyard Problems and Practices as Related to the Natural Environment"; in short, the geographical conditions of the cultivation. He here presents the adaptations to the soil, his treatment being rather brief. His analysis of the adaptations to climate is really compelling. The climate of the upper San Joaquin Valley is perfectly suited to raisin production; nevertheless, some hazards are to be feared. Frosts, excessive heat, and high winds may cause some ravages. The critical season is that of the ripening and of the curing in the open air. At this point the author describes the phases of the agricultural job according to the seasons, thus making this part of the study still more vivid. There are the biological hazards to be feared—insects, and diseases. The most dangerous pest is the phylloxera, which came from Europe to America with the imported stock; nevertheless, on the rich virgin soils of California, the regeneration of the well-cared-for vines is quickly effected. Thanks to the atmospheric dryness, the other diseases of the vine are easy to control by sprinkling the vines with sulphur. Finally, regulatory measures of the government prove to be very efficient.

It is to be regretted that among the conditions of cultivation the author has not given special place to a factor so decisive as *man*. Who are the raisin-growers? What is their race, and whence do they come? Where do they find workers at the time of the critical phases and who are these workers? Allusions to Portuguese and to Japanese do nothing but stimulate our curiosity. Just as a complete analysis of the physical factors should have been placed at the beginning of the study, so specific data about the human factors should have been placed here—data concerning the density of population in the districts studied and, by contrast, in the neighboring districts; data concerning the racial qualities of the men; and the possibilities of recruiting workers. These are considerable problems. Again, it would have been valuable to set forth in detail the phases of agricultural activity, to show the laborers at work, to indicate the periods of rest and of maximum effort; in short, to make a kind of agricultural calendar of the raisin cultivation. This would have allowed us to see better the grape-growers' life, to perceive them acting under the influence of the geographical factors. For, as a matter of fact, in a study of human geography *man* must be placed in the foreground, and not be an invisible factor—the effects of which we perceive without seeing it in action.

After these criticisms it is very pleasant to express complete approval of the fourth part of the author's work, on "Marketing Problems of the Industry." Some geographers think that trade problems have no place in a geographical study; that only physical conditions, and perhaps the distribution of population, are worthy of consideration. This is not my opinion, and Colby's study strengthens my belief. The relations among the raisin-growers, the packers, the dealers, and the consumers, and the means of conquering the distance which separate growers and consumers, have had as much influence upon the progress of cultivation as have irrigation facilities or the vagaries of climate. Advertising has exerted as much influence on the development of the vineyards during the past fifteen years as has agricultural progress. In studying problems of human or economic geography, too many geographers, at least in Europe, have disregarded these questions as mere contingencies. In reality they are technical factors, more important in human geography than is the decomposition of the feldspars. Therefore, I am in total accord with the author when he studies the marketing problems, follows their evolution, indicates vividly the influence of the seasonal nature of the crop, describes the earlier attempts at co-operation, and enumerates the markets reached by the California raisin. He ends with a statement of the problems caused by the type of growers' association that seemed to fall under the Sherman Anti-Trust Act; problems which finally were resolved in favor of the California Association Raisin Company.

In my opinion, Mr. Colby's study should not have ended at this point. In order to be complete, and to be fully worthy of the title of "geographic," it should have entered upon the geographical consequences of the raisin cultivation on the regions considered. There is no doubt that this very special agriculture has transformed the geographical characteristics of the region where it exists. I presume, for instance, that vegetation has been much modified. It is certain that raisin production on a large scale has affected the density and the nature of the population, the extent of the ranches, and the type of landholding; and that the site of the farms, their form, and the location of the communication routes have adapted themselves to this type of cultivation. All these phenomena, thoroughly geographical, are in close relation to the raisin cultivation; they are derived from it; and, therefore, they should be analyzed. The author refers to some of them very briefly in the beginning; but these references seem to me insufficient, and, since they are consequences, wrongly placed. From the viewpoint of method there is here a wide gap.

All of the criticisms I have expressed seem to come to this: The study is more economic than geographical. It is faultless in its economic documentation, but it sins, from the geographical point of view, by the lack of classification of the phenomena, and by ignoring some of them. It omits to place first the indispensable physical basis; it does not give to the human factor, next, the importance it merits; it neglects, at the end, to show the geographical consequences of the problem studied. Thus, we are not in accord as to method. I persist in thinking that human geography cannot do without the indispensable prop of the physical factors, under pain of remaining "in thin air"; that, in this kind of study, the factor "man" must be the object of the most careful attention; and that, although the purely economic facts have their interest, for geographers the knowledge of the geographical reactions of the phenomena studied is more attractive and more essential.[2]

[2] [This analysis was first written (in English) in November, 1928, and revised by the analyst in 1929.—EDITOR.]

ANALYSIS 17

THE CULTURE-AREA AND AGE-AREA CONCEPTS OF CLARK WISSLER

By A. L. KROEBER

University of California

The concepts of the culture-area and of the age-area ("age and area") method as applicable to culture have been developed by Clark Wissler in three books: *The American Indian* (1917); *Man and Culture* (1923); *The Relation of Nature to Man* (1926).[1] The two concepts have this in common, that they deal with the space distribution of culture phenomena. They differ in that the culture area refers to culture traits as they occur aggregated in nature, whereas the age-area method is applicable to separate traits or isolable clusters of elements. They differ further in that the culture area, as such, is not concerned with time factors, whereas the age-area concept is a device for inferring time sequences from space distributions. Both ideas have long been in use in the biological sciences. An areally characterized fauna or flora, such as the Neo-tropical or Indo-Malaysian, obviously corresponds to the culture aggregation within a culture area. The term *age-area* was coined in the field of natural history, and the method of inferring areas of origin from concentration of distribution, and antiquity of dispersal from marginal survivals, has long been in use in so-called systematic biology. Perhaps because the comparable method applied to culture developed independently, the term *age area* has not gained currency in that field. Anthropologists have not been wholly happy in their terminology. They speak consistently of *culture areas*, whereas it is the content of these areas, certain culture growths or aggregations, that they are really concerned with, the areal limitation being only one aspect of such an aggregation.

ANTICIPATION

Both concepts are not new in anthropology, although for long they were employed implicitly, or without methodological formulation. Ratzel, who spoke of marginal peoples and backward cultures as long ago as

[1] *The American Indian* (1st ed., New York: McMurtrie, 1917; 2d ed., New York: Oxford University Press, 1922); *Man and Culture* (New York: Thomas Y. Crowell Co., 1923); *The Relation of Nature to Man in Aboriginal America* (New York: Oxford University Press, 1926).

1891,[2] was close to thinking in age-area terms. Sophus Müller's main thesis was that prehistoric Europe is to be conceived as culturally belated, marginal to, and dependent on, the higher centers of the Orient.[3] His notable five principles and three extensions not only embody the cardinal age-area idea, but state some of its chief qualifications as they are generally accepted today. Had Müller's prime interest been theoretic instead of concretely historical, he would no doubt have formulated his principles in terms of abstract methodology. In 1916 Sapir, in his "Time Perspective,"[4] discussed "the concept of culture area from an historical standpoint."

The germ of the culture-area idea is still older. It is implied in such concepts as Orient and Occident, vague though these be. The idea has had its most active development among Americanists. Among the reasons for this is the far greater length of the documentary historic record in much of the Old World. This tended to set a pattern of narrative approach which Americanists could not follow. Further, culture phenomena were on the whole more varied and their currents more complex in the Eastern than in the Western Hemisphere. This is a consequence of the fact that the Americas are smaller and were more sparsely populated (probably later) by what was essentially a single race, containing no extremely advanced civilizations. They were more isolated from the totality of the larger land masses of the Eastern Hemisphere than almost all parts of this were from one another. This comparatively uniform and undocumented mass of native New World culture almost necessitated a static, descriptive approach. The result was that Americanists grew more and more to think in terms of naturally given culture aggregates or types of the order of the Southwestern United States, Mexico, the North Pacific Coast, the Plains; whereas students of the Old World tended to pass more rapidly to direct historical interpretations of the mass of non-historic culture. It is probably no accident that the diffusionist historical explanations of both the Graebner-Foy-Schmidt school and the Rivers-Smith-Perry school, which make almost no use of culture areas as such[5] but attempt to account for most of prehistoric culture, originated

[2] *Anthropogeographie* (Stuttgart: J. Engelhorn, 1891), Vol. II.

[3] *Urgeschichte Europas* (1905). Abstract in Kroeber, *Anthropology* (New York: Harcourt, Brace & Co., 1923).

[4] "Time Perspective in Aboriginal American Culture, A Study in Method," *Canada, Geological Survey, Memoir 90* (1916) (Anthropological Series, No. 13) ; see esp. pp. on p. 260.—EDITOR.]

[5] [Cf. Herskovits (see n. 7): "The 'culture-area' and the 'kulturkreis' are not the same thing, and must be differentiated." Cf. also the distinction drawn by the analyst on p. 260.—EDITOR.]

in Europe; that they have had almost no following in America; and that they have not even been countered by rival theories here. In the same way, within the Americanistic field Europeans like Rivet and Uhle have advanced views as to the sequence of interrelations of North and South America that are both more ambitious and more specific than any which Americans have ventured to express. In Africa, Frobenius, a German, long ago formulated a Congo-West Coast culture[6] but it was Herskovits, an American, who first attempted to lay out the whole continent in areas.[7]

So far back as the nineties, culture areas were not only "in the air" but actually being used in American ethnology. Eskimo, North Pacific Coast, Plateau, California, Southwest, Plains or Prairies, Eastern Woodland, and Mexican areas had indeed scarcely been defined as to content or delimited on the map, but they were generally accepted as obvious empirical findings, and referred to in placing tribal cultures or culture traits. The evolutionistic display of museum materials had given way to a geographical arrangement, and in this the culture areas were implicit in the names of sections or halls. In 1900 the California Academy of Sciences exhibited a sketch map of North American Indian culture areas. In 1907 Otis Mason, in the article on "Environment" in the *Handbook of American Indians North of Mexico*,[8] listed twelve "ethnic environments" north of Mexico, which, although ecologically conceived, at the same time anticipated the culture areas that later became generally accepted. They were: Arctic, Yukon-Mackenzie, St. Lawrence–Great Lakes, Atlantic Slope, Gulf Coast, Mississippi Valley, Plains, North Pacific Coast, Columbia-Fraser, Interior Basin, California-Oregon, Pueblo Country. In 1912 Wissler used in the American Museum a map label of American archaeological areas; and in 1914 Holmes published[9] an article defining a set of fairly coincident areas.

THE CULTURE AREA

These details are adduced here to make clear that the culture-area concept is in origin a growth, a community product of nearly the whole school of American anthropologists, although largely unconscious or implicit. In 1917 appeared Wissler's *The American Indian*, which has ac-

[6] *Der Ursprung der Kultur: I, Afrika* (Berlin: Gebrüder Bornträger, 1898).

[7] "A Preliminary Consideration of the Culture Areas of Africa," *American Anthropologist*, XXVI (1924), 50–63. *The Cattle Complex in East Africa* (reprinted from the *American Anthropologist*, 1926), 137 pp.

[8] *Handbook of American Indians North of Mexico*, ed. F. W. Hodge (published by the Smithsonian Institution, *Bureau of American Ethnology Bull. 30*), Part I.

[9] "Areas of American Culture Characterization Tentatively Outlined as an Aid in the Study of the Antiquities," *American Anthropologist*, N.S., XVI (1914), 413–16.

quired some repute as having originated the concept. Wissler himself never made such a claim. He says (p. 218):[10] "A perusal of the literature of our subject shows it to be customary to divide the two continents into fifteen culture areas, each conceived to be the home of a distinct type of culture." This is an overmodest statement; custom before 1917 was still too chaotic to agree on specified areas. Yet it does justice to the essential situation. What Wissler did in his *American Indian* was to name and delimit areas for the whole hemisphere; to list the principal traits characterizing each; to discuss internal subtypes and define the one most characteristic, thereby throwing the ultimate emphasis on culture *centers* instead of culture areas; to examine the relations of these culture aggregates to classifications of earlier culture, of language, and of physical type, as well as to individual culture-trait distributions and to environment. In short, the culture area was both formulated concretely and examined as to its meaning. The standardization, although by no means hard and fast, appealed as so sound that it has been generally accepted by anthropologists, modified or supplemented only in details,[11] and the theoretical findings have never been seriously attacked. At the same time it is historically significant that so important a piece of work was not issued as a contribution to theory but as part of a concrete review and an interpretation of the culture of one native race.

Wissler begins (chap. i) by setting up eight areas of characteristic food: Caribou, Bison, Salmon, Wild Seed, Eastern Maize, Intensive Agriculture, Manioc, Guanaco. These are later (chap. xiv) elaborated into fifteen culture areas, essentially though not formally through subdivision.

Food Areas	Culture Areas
Caribou	Eskimo, Mackenzie (and north part of Eastern Woodland)
Bison	Plains
Salmon	North Pacific Coast, Plateau
Wild Seed	California
Eastern Maize	Southeast, Eastern Woodland (except north non-agricultural portion)
Intensive Agriculture	Southwest, Nahua-Mexico, Chibcha, Inca-Peru
Manioc	Amazon, Antilles
Guanaco	Guanaco

[10] Page reference is to the second edition (1922).

[11] The only other hemispheric map and list of areas, by Kroeber, *op. cit.*, p. 337, is based on Wissler and differs chiefly in attempting to follow natural boundaries instead of representing the areas diagrammatically.

In the Plains, for example, eleven named tribes, centrally situated, possess the typical culture of the area as defined by some twenty enumerated traits (bison, tepee, dog-traction, camp circle, round shield, sun dance, no pottery, no agriculture, etc.). To the east were fourteen tribes "having most of the positive traits" of the former group, plus some that these lacked (agriculture, pottery); to the west three or four tribes substituting new traits for certain of those possessed by the group in the heart of the area; and similarly on the northeast two or three tribes.

The rather "difficult" Eastern Woodland is treated as follows: There are four subdivisions: (1) Northern (Cree, Naskapi), non-agricultural, similar in material culture to the adjoining Mackenzie area; (2) Eastern Algonkian (Abnaki, Delaware), similar to the last but with feeble cultivation of maize; (3) Iroquoian (Huron, Iroquois), with most intensive cultivation of maize, and culture largely of southern origin; (4) Central Algonkian (Menomini, Fox, Winnebago). This last group is taken as typical of the whole area and defined by forty or fifty traits. The three less typical divisions are more briefly defined.

The summary of the chapter emphasizes intergradation between areas, but disposes of this as an obstacle to classification because the "condition arises from the existence of culture centers, from which culture influences seem to radiate." While a culture area on the map "is in the main an arbitrary division," it contains a culture center which coincides with the habitat of the most typical tribes. Hence the areas "serve to differentiate culture centers." Their mapped "boundaries, in fact, are merely diagrammatic." (The "centers," it must be remembered, are not points, but rather extensive nuclei.) "Social units" (tribes) are a different kind of phenomenon from "culture complexes" (aggregations of culture material).

Subsequent chapters (xv, xvii, xviii) give an analogous classification into twenty-four archaeological, an indefinite number of linguistic, and twelve somatic areas. Chapter xix correlates the classifications. Archaeological cultures are found to tend to coincide with recent cultures, except that in the regions of eastern and intensive maize culture the ancient areas or centers are more numerous, owing to a fundamental change having taken place with the introduction of agriculture (pp. 364, 374). Language and physical type show "a kind of agreement" with culture. The three are "independent groups of human phenomena, each of which tends toward the same geographical centers" (p. 366). Each "culture area tends to have distinctive characters in language and somatology. However, the reversal of this formula does not hold," owing to causes not yet perceived (p. 367). Migration has not been a normally important factor in America, else the centers would have been less stable. In general, populational "shifting was by successive small units" (p. 369); "migratory groups seem unable to resist complete cultural assimilation" (*ibid.*).

A number of environmental correlations are noted. The southeastern culture lies below an altitude of 500 feet; the Eastern Woodland, between 500 and 2,000; the Nahua, above 5,000; the eastern and western divisions of the Plains are separated by the 2,000-foot contour (pp. 368, 369). These altitudes are recognized as only rough indices of areas of climate, flora, and fauna. Wissler is not an environmentalist. Human phenomena, he says,

manifest a strong tendency to expand to the limits of the geographical area in which they arise, and no farther. Language and blood seem to spill over the edges far more readily than culture [p. 369]. . . . . [Although] the location of food areas laid down the general lines of culture grouping . . . . , yet not even all of the more material traits can be considered dependent upon the fauna and flora; for example, pottery [p. 371]. . . . . While the environment does not produce the culture, it furnishes the medium in which it grows, and . . . . when once rooted in a geographical area, culture tends to hold fast [p. 373]. . . . . The origin of a culture center seems due to ethnic factors more than to geographical ones. The location of these centers is largely a matter of historic accident, but once located and the adjustments made, the stability of the environment doubtless tends to hold each particular type of culture to its initial locality, even in the face of many changes in blood and language [p. 372].

In *Man and Culture* (1923) Wissler comes back to review the culture complex, type, area, and center (pp. 51–63), without adding anything new except a greater emphasis on zonal distribution as indicative of age. This inferring of time relations from culture-trait distributions had already been touched upon in *The American Indian* (p. 296). *Man and Culture* further presents time charts of New World culture and Old World prehistory suggested by Spinden and Nelson, and one of Old World culture by Wissler (pp. 216, 218, 220), in which cultural areas (roughly defined in geographical terms) are expressed as abscissae of a time scale. Farther on in this chapter on "The Genesis of Culture," in answer to the question as to where and how the universal culture pattern (chap. v) first arose, the "fundamental lines of cleavage at the dawn of cultures" are defined as arising in a setting of partly arboreal Tundra, warm dry Mesa, and humid tropical Jungle (pp. 227–32); and in the following pages, Euro-American (map, p. 346), Oriental, and Middle

American culture are examined as to their rooting in these three type areas. With reference to the historical functioning of culture centers, an analogy is drawn (pp. 156–57)

to volcanic activity, these different centers appearing as so many crater cones of varying diameter, all belching forth the molten lava of culture, their respective lava fields meeting and overlapping, but, as in true volcanoes, the lavas differ one from the other and from time to time, and each crater contributes something new to the growing terrain. Again craters become extinct and new ones break forth in between.

AGE AREA

The age-area concept or method of inferring at least the relative time sequences of stages of culture-trait or culture-complex developments from the more or less concentrically zonal distribution of phases of such developments is briefly approached by Wissler in *The American Indian* (pp. 296–99, with references to use of the method of Sapir, Boas, Spinden, Lowie, and Hatt); it is enlarged upon in *Man and Culture* (pp. 57–63, 110–57); and it is made the theme of a book in *The Relation of Nature to Man in Aboriginal American* (1926). In this last work, the concept is systematically developed by Wissler, analogous to its use in the biological sciences, but, as in the case of his forerunners, apparently as the result of independent empirical findings. Essentially, this concept implies that of the culture center as a locus of superior productivity. This center, normally maintaining itself for some time, tends inevitably to radiate culture content or forms to a surrounding zone, which in turn imparts the contribution to a more peripheral belt, while the center, in the interim, is likely to have advanced to subsequent phases of development which normally obliterate more or less the earlier ones. These earlier phases, however, are likely to survive, with greater or less modification, in the marginal zone which they have only recently reached. In principle, a distinction must be made between cases in which the time sequence is independently known through history, inscriptions, or cultural stratigraphy (in biology through paleontological evidence resting ultimately on stratigraphy), and is in agreement with the observed recent space distribution; and cases in which the time sequence is unknown and becomes the goal of investigation, being in that case merely deduced from the space distribution. In anthropology, at least a number of seemingly clear-cut instances of the first type were established[12] before Wissler's venture to set up the principle as a generally valid one and employ it for the finding of the time factor in

[12] As by Sophus Müller, cited above, and Nelson, reproduced in Kroeber, *op. cit.*, p. 191. [Cf. analysis 19, esp. p. 280.—EDITOR.]

cases lacking time data. A still further logical step, though apparently an inevitable one, is the inference that the present center of culmination is also the presumptive locus of origin. In short, there are three elements involved: related phases of a culture trait or complex or culture whole; the spatial or geographical distribution of these; and the time consumed in the accomplishment of the distribution of the phases. When all three elements are known and correlate approximately, there can be no reasonable doubt as to the story of what happened. When the time factor is sought instead of given, the result is no more than an inference; and since the known factors are usually either complex or variable, and difficult of exact measurement, judgments are likely to differ as to the degree of validity of the findings.

In *The Relation of Nature to Man*, Wissler reviews seven traits of material culture (chap. i: tipi, stone collars, hoop and ball games, etc.), nine of social culture (chap. iii: age societies, sun dance, vision-seeking, etc.), and four cases of segregated distributions (chap ii: monolithic ax, feather mosaics, lip plug and the nose stick, ring-neck vase). He concludes that an approach without preconceptions justifies the principle. Segregated distributions of typologically related but differentiable traits warrant the inference of independent invention in each area on the basis of an antecedent "plateau" of continuously distributed culture from which these inventions rise like peaks. Chapter iv applies the same method to somatic traits, with similar results. These have been vigorously assailed by Boas;[13] but as the involvements are biological and not cultural, neither set of arguments need be considered here.

In the fifth and final chapter, on "The Distribution Form and Its Meaning," Wissler first sets up a law of diffusion, "that anthropological traits tend to diffuse in all directions from their centers of origin" (p. 183). Several "dated distributions" (peyote cult, introduction of the horse, grass dance) are next examined and found to support "the assumption that when the distribution of a culture trait-complex takes the concentric zoned form, the zones can be safely interpreted as superpositions, and from these, time relations can be inferred" (p. 197). From this follows a generalized "New World chronology," or sequence of culture stages (p. 203). The concluding section on "The Ecological Basis" (pp. 211–22) inquires into the mechanism which has brought about a form of distribution that is universal, and finds it in ecological factors. However, only a few examples of partial correspondence between ecological and culture areas are suggested; no systematic review of data is attempted; and the conclusion

[13] *American Journal of Physical Anthropology*, IX (1926), 503–6.

is the essentially reasoned one that the American Indian in an ecological area is the end result of a sequence of factors such as climate, flora, fauna, culture.

Of the three books, *The American Indian* presents, organizes, and interprets the largest mass of concrete data; *Man and Culture* is the broadest and most philosophical; *Nature and Man,* the most concisely diagrammatic.

CRITICISMS

The Wissler points of view as to culture area and age area have apparently been used extensively in only one other general work, Kroeber's *Anthropology* (1923) (esp. chaps. vii–viii, x–xiv). There are indications of some growing readiness to apply the method in special cases, as in a recent monograph by Davidson.[14] In Europe, Wissler's works, while commended, appear to have made relatively little impression. This is the more surprising in that *The American Indian,* apart from everything else, provides a most useful outline organization of American data. The reasons apparently are: the current European preoccupation for or against diffusionist theories of single or few origins, and the habit of many students of dealing with actually or essentially historic data.

The first general criticism, of points of view rather than of Wissler's particular works, came from Wallis in 1925.[15] He argues that actual historical data do not bear out the age-area principle. In 3000 B.C. mudbrick dwellings had a wider distribution than bronze; in 100 B.C. bronze extended more widely. Also, the center of distribution or intensive development of a trait shifts within the area with the passage of time. Inference of age from distribution is impossible except at given moments, and these can be determined only from historical data. Wallis' first objection is valid largely when intrinsically unrelated elements of culture are compared, much less so for traits of the same complex. As Wissler points out (*Man and Culture,* p. 146), side-blown trumpets used within an area of end-blown trumpets are almost certainly the later development, whereas comparison with the distribution of rubber balls means very much less. Wallis' counter-examples are of the latter class. His second objection, as to shifting centers, does not seem to strike at the root of the age-area principle, which is not committed to permanent centers, although it may tend to assume them. On his third point Wallis offers no substitute

[14] *The Chronological Aspects of Certain Australian Social Institutions as Inferred from Geographical Distribution* (Ph.D. Thesis; Philadelphia: University of Pennsylvania, 1928).

[15] "Diffusion as a Criterion of Age," *American Anthropologist,* N.S., XXVII (1925), 91–99.

suggestions, and his attitude seems negativistic toward a historical attitude or the recognition of diffusion except within the field of conventional history.

Kroeber, in two papers,[16] has touched on Wissler's ring-neck-vase and arrow-release interpretations. In the first case, additional data lead him to modify certain of Wissler's special findings. In the second case, the same evidence is gone over with partly different construals. The age-area method is accepted in principle by Kroeber, but employed more cautiously. The different conclusions are due partly to a somewhat different rating of the relationship of the five forms or phases of release examined—a point on which agreement is obviously necessary before identical results are even possible; partly to a greater readiness of Wissler to assume probable continuities of distribution across geographical gaps in knowledge; and partly to his not hesitating to relate all the world-wide data in one grand scheme. Kroeber considers this last attempt as of possible but unproved validity.

Dixon's *The Building of Cultures* (1928), which aims to balance diffusion with independent origins, migration, and environmental influences, takes issue with the age-area method on general grounds (pp. 65–75, 179–85) and specifically attacks a number of Wissler's applications: the outrigger (pp. 75–104), the moccasin (pp. 124–28), the grass dance, and the peyote cult (pp. 176–79). Dixon concludes that specialization and modification of traits arise not only at the center of origin, but independently near the margin of diffusions (p. 74); that "the most striking specializations take place as a rule at the very end of the diffusion stream" (p. 140); and that trait complexes disintegrate as they pass into neighboring culture, incorporating as well as losing elements, until they may become quite unrecognizable (p. 180).

Dixon's contention that specializations occur mostly at the peripheries of diffusions seems to be based on the history of the alphabet, which is in its nature an essentially closed system, like a dogma, an established religion, or an art style, which can alter, wear down, split into varieties, disintegrate, or be absorbed, but hardly develop into something else with which it stands in "organic" or intrinsic relation. Its "specializations" are essentially distortions and of a different order from the "specialization" of a three-piece or hard-soled moccasin as against a one-piece moccasin, or of the string-pull Mediterranean release or the ring-engaging

[16] "Ancient Pottery from Trujillo," *Field Museum of Natural History, Anthrop., Memoirs*, II, No. 1 (1926), 1–43 (see pp. 20–21); "Arrow Release Distributions." *University of California Publication in American Archaeological Ethnology*, XXIII, No. 4 (1927), 283–96.

Mongolian release compared with the Primary arrow-hold which a novice with the weapon almost invariably resorts to. Dixon's specializations are, in fact, the Ogham writing with new signs and values, the essentially syllabic Indian systems, Manchu and Korean written vertically in imitation of Chinese, Ethiopic with consonant characters altered for vocalic context. The only fundamental specialization in the alphabet comparable to most of Wissler's cases would be the addition of vowel signs to the original pure consonantal Semitic system; and the historically earliest case of this, by the Greeks, occurred near the hearth of the invention soon after it, and did not spread nearly so far. On the other hand, a highly complex, accreted, presumably recent phenomenon like the sun dance, many of whose parts demonstrably have no intrinsic interrelation but only a secondarily historical and functional interrelation, is also different from elements like moccasins and arrow releases. When Wissler, therefore, subjects the sun dance to the same distribution treatment as moccasins and releases, even though he gets analogous results, the meaning of these results must be different. There is likely to be further argument at cross-purposes in these matters until the various kinds of culture phenomena are more sharply conceptualized.[17]

Dixon's criticisms of Wissler's specific interpretations are based on the grounds that the latter's classification of traits or complex forms is at times arbitrary; that carefully plotted maps show a far less regular distribution than the diagrams or schematic maps used; that data are sometimes loosely employed; and that considerations favorable to the method are weighted at the expense of contrary considerations. When accuracy of scholarship is involved, Dixon's strictures are probably true. Yet, if Wissler suggests or forces interpretations on incomplete or discordant evidence, Dixon evidently combats the age-area method in general, since he concerns himself with it only to refute it. He disinclines as consistently as Wissler inclines.

The sun dance is a case in point. Dixon reproduces Wissler's schematic

---

[17] Even Sapir, usually extremely exact, speaks of a culture phenomenon appearing "in its most typical or [sic] historically oldest form at the cultural centre" (op. cit., p. 26) and of "the centre of distribution" (in time or space?) of American agriculture as probably assignable to the valley of Mexico (ibid.). Again, he holds that the simple plank house of the marginal Hupa, as compared with the more elaborate one of the Kwakiutl who are central in the North Pacific Coast area, "undoubtedly represents a later period of diffusion, though not necessarily a later type of house" (p. 27). To the contrary, it seems reasonable that the simple house is the earlier in the area, but there is no evidence one way or the other whether the arrival of the simple house at the margin or the development of the elaborate one at the center is the earlier. Apparently all thinking along these lines of distribution and age is so recent that the categories involved in processes like "diffusion" or phenomena like "complexes" have not yet become sharply defined.

arrangement of Plains tribes (on a basis both of geography and degree of participation in this dance complex) and contrasts it with precise distribution maps, which are far less regular (pp. 168–73). Actually, the case is rather weak both ways: first, because the movements of the tribes in question render a map not very much more significant than a geometric diagram, in this particular instance; second, because both authors leave out of consideration the known historic affiliations of tribes. Both maps (pp. 171, 175) show the Arapaho and Gros Ventre as the tribes possessing most primary traits of the complex. These two tribes spoke closely related languages, associated frequently, and considered each other offshoots of one stock. Next in order come the Blackfoot, with whom the Gros Ventre were in intimate alliance during most of the nineteenth century; the Cheyenne and Wind River Shoshone, who have actually been on reservations with the Arapaho; and the Crow, who were situated between Gros Ventre and Arapaho. Then follow the Teton Dakota, also more or less intermediate geographically; the Kiowa, allies of Arapaho and Cheyenne, who although now marginal on the south were originally farther north; and the Plains Cree and the Assiniboine, for whom no cogent explanation is obvious. The other Plains tribes participate less extensively. Spier's original data on *all* traits in the complex show clearly the influence of the same historic associations. The Arapaho show 54 traits, Cheyenne 46, Blackfoot 37, Gros Ventre 36, Teton 30, Crow 29, Kiowa 28, all others below 25. Only the Wind River fall out here, as might be expected from what is known of their general culture as well as associations; evidently the selection of "primary" traits has happened to read them in. Both proof and disproof are, therefore, largely not pertinent, because the historic facts have been disregarded for a formal distributional approach, which in this case touches accidentals chiefly. What no doubt is significant is that all the highly participating tribes inhabited a continuous territory in the western Plains and were non-agricultural as well as in close relation of some sort with one another; and that the agricultural tribes to the east, and those west of the Rockies, possessed the complex in an attenuated form.

While the other instances examined by Dixon are not wholly parallel to this, they tend also to be technically correct refutations of essentially technical misapplications of the method in question.

REVIEW

If now we attempt to place and appraise the culture-area and age-area principles, it becomes clear that, first of all, they are essentially historical concepts. Wissler says expressly: "In so far, then, as anthropology deals with culture, which is, after all, the only distinctly human phenomenon in the objective sense, it conceives of it as historical phenomena and this conception is in so far the soul of its method."[18] Whether cultural anthropology is necessarily historical may be and has been questioned; but there is no doubt that the development of the two principles by Wissler is in accord with his enunciation. At the same time, cultural data are being treated from other approaches than the historical. There is the method of examining the functional relations of the parts of one culture at a time, in the hope of finding more or less fixed relations—presumably psychological—that hold good universally or prevalently. This is the "functional" method of Radcliffe Brown and Malinowski, in a measure and less avowedly of Lowie and Goldenweiser, to a greater or less extent of Fraser and other earlier students, and by implication perhaps of Bastian. Another attack recognizes the historic aspects of culture phenomena so far as these aspects are actually demonstrated, but dissects the phenomena in order to isolate their processes as such. This is the aim of Boas and his school, which has sometimes been called, not wholly appropriately, "historical," but might be characterized as "dynamic." In the main the functional, dynamic, and actually historical methods are of course not in conflict, but they differ in objective and weighting of interest. Each is presumably equally legitimate, and its results in its own field should be equally valid. The three approaches have however not often been clearly differentiated and formulated; perhaps because no student has consistently followed one alone.

The difference between Wissler and the English diffusionist and the German *Kulturkreis* schools, which also aim to supply history for historically undocumented periods and areas, lies in the fact that these make their explanations in terms of a single or few origins, respectively, in place of an indefinite number of variable centers. The limitation of factors yields a simplified scheme, but almost inevitably involves an arbitrary or subjective choosing of the original centers. It is characteristic that discussion of the views of these two schools has revolved not so much about the validity of determination of the asserted centers as to whether the facts of culture can be made to fit the schemes of derivation from them. By comparison, Wissler is inductive. The culture areas dealt with are in their nature empirical, and the age-area method, provided it is critically used, is an inductive device.

Turning now specifically to the culture area, we may fairly say that it represents normally a synthesis useful in the organization of knowledge, tinged with a subjective element, and yet evidently resting on something

[18] *The American Indian*, pp. 387–88.

objective because empirical opinion tends to be in essential concord in specific cases. In all these points the culture area is analogous to the faunal or the floral area. In other words, it aims at determining and defining a natural area. Adjacent areas normally intergrade, and progressive dissection can therefore always analyze them out of existence. When analytic interests predominate, this dissecting away happens through the stressing of the intergradations, though even then current culture-area concepts are likely to be retained as lowly, useful tools. The core of the concept, in particular instances, is likely to be the culture center, as Wissler has recognized. This, however, is likely to be not only a "crater" of diffusing productivity, as Wissler has in the main treated it, but also a "focus" or gathering-point. The prevalence of fraying-out margins and intergradations is no warrant for merely diagrammatic representation, except in a preliminary and tentative stage of investigation. A classificatory areal study that cannot be mapped has not found its permanent basis. The same holds true of the center, whether this be conceived as a nuclear area or drawn to a point. If it is worth determining and using, it is worth delimiting. In fact, its utility value in further penetration into history is bound to depend on the accuracy with which it has been determined. Centers shift; they may be multiple for one area; or the centers for different aspects of culture within an area may be more or less distinct. All this is likely to be slurred over if there is no sharp definition. Wissler has done a broad piece of organization where chaos or indecision prevailed before, and perhaps should not be held too heavily responsible for failing to carry his pioneer work into finer detail. The danger is in stopping with his often sketchy and diagrammatic formulations, when they ought to serve as a stimulus for revision and surer knowledge.

For instance, Wissler[19] gives a diagram map of the Plains area with "the most typical tribes" underlined. This "center" however includes a full third of the tribes in the area, and the basis for its determination is only summarily stated. However, an approximation toward a more intensive center can be made from Wissler's own data.[20] The tribes possessing the greatest number of traits of the sun-dance complex are (as above): Arapaho, Cheyenne, Blackfoot, Gros Ventre, Teton, Crow, Kiowa. Of tepee foundations, the three-pole form is probably the most specialized, and is central in distribution. These same tribes use this, except the Blackfoot and the Crow. Age-grading, a specialization on men's societies and also central to the distribution of these, does not occur among Cheyenne,

[19] *Ibid.*, p. 221.

[20] *The Relation of Nature to Man in Aboriginal America*, pp. 2, 81, 85, 233; *The American Indian*, p. 383.

Teton, Crow, or Kiowa. This gives a total of participation in the most intensive forms of these three traits as follows: Arapaho, Gros Ventre, 3; Cheyenne, Blackfoot, Teton, Kiowa, Mandan, 2; other Plains tribes, 1 or 0. This result tallies well with the geographical position and historic affiliations of the tribes. Of course three traits are not enough for final judgment; but twelve or fifteen would begin to furnish a fairly representative sample of the various tribes' status. In this way there might be segregable a nucleolus as well as a nucleus, a median, a submarginal, and a truly marginal series of tribes; and significant subcenters might become apparent. The relations of these in turn to the various intensification stages of adjacent culture areas could then be examined. With enough exact data, precise findings of fairly high probability should result. Of course the point in this example is not the specific conclusion but the method of attaining greater refinement.[21]

Another point at which the Wissler scheme can probably be elaborated with advantage is in the recognition that the culture areas are not equivalent in culture-historical significance but are of different orders. Sapir long ago dwelt on this fact in his *Time Perspective*. In North America, Mexico is obviously unique in being of the first order of intensity of culture. Of second order are the Southwest, the Southeast, and the North Pacific Coast. Of these, the first two are about equally similar to Mexico and therefore presumably partly derived from it, though in different ways. The North Pacific Coast is much less dependent on Mexico, and represents either a largely independent intensification or considerable derivation from Asia. The remaining areas in North America would have to be rated as of the third or even of the fourth order. The Northeast, for instance, is obviously dependent on the Southeast. It differs less in sum total of its culture content from this than the Southeast differs from Mexico, and is more immediately derived. The eastern Plains or Prairies (Pawnee, etc.) are also clearly dependent at many points on the Southeast. It is very doubtful if their total culture is less rich than that of the tribes of the western or true Plains (Arapaho, etc.). The question therefore arises whether a "Plains culture area" as formulated by Wissler and accepted by American anthropologists has full historic validity. What has been considered the "Plains center" may be only a quaternary and late specialization developed on the tertiary culture of the Prairies, which

[21] In an earlier paper, "Material Cultures of the North American Indians," *American Anthropologist*, N.S., XVI (1914), 447–505, 472–73, Wissler actually uses the method suggested above, though with different traits as material to operate on, and comes to the conclusion that "we have good grounds for localizing the center of Plains culture between the Teton, Arapaho, Cheyenne, and Crow, with the odds in favor of the first." The point, however, has not been developed further by him.

in turn is a marginal form of the culture of the Southeastern center, which is secondary to the primary South Mexican growth. Views of this kind cannot be vindicated by evidence here, hardly even fairly developed, but the suggestions cited may suffice to indicate the point of view.[22]

In short, the culture areas codified by Wissler are unduly uniformized as to size, number of included tribes, and implied level. They remain essentially descriptive; their historical potentialities have only begun to be exploited. Wissler recognizes this, but scarcely attempts to use his culture areas for larger historical interpretations. These interpretations[23] are chiefly built up on his reviews of culture traits, complexes, and aspects;[24] the review of culture areas[25] stands apart as a promising but largely unutilized block of organized knowledge.

As regards the environmental basis, Wissler has clearly discerned the primary relation of this to the culture area as a stabilizer and a binder, and has given some apt illustrations of ecological-cultural correlation. These relations, however, in spite of some striking cases, promise on the whole to be highly complex and to yield satisfactorily only to accurate analysis. This aspect of the subject has scarcely been opened as yet.

As to the age-area principle, the analogy to recognized biological method gives support to the essential soundness and the utility of this concept, the more so as its anthropological use was empirically and independently arrived at, not borrowed from the life-sciences. Interest in this method will vary directly with the ultimate objective of study; and when historical interest is slight, distrust of the method will be pronounced. It is in its nature merely a method of inference, supplementary to the direct evidence of documentary history and archaeological superposition; but, as such, it is warranted when it is desired to push beyond the confined limits of this sort of evidence. The age-area principle may never be applied mechanically; culture is too complexly irregular, the resultant of too many factors, to be approached without care, accuracy, and discrimination.

---

[22] Somewhat analogously, Sapir (*op. cit.*, p. 45), suggests three "fundamental" areas in North America: Mexican, Northwest Coast, and a large "Central" area with Pueblo and Eskimo as its "most specialized developments." The Plains culture he is inclined to see either as a specialization of a more general Eastern Woodland (Northeast) or as a "culture blend" by tribes with original Woodland, Southeastern, Plateau, and probably Southwestern affiliations. In the latter case, the specific Plains features would be construable as "superimposed" or historically late, but as strong enough to have broken up and reassembled the older culture within the Plains area. As regards the fundamental areas, it is interesting that Ratzel (*op. cit.*, Vol. II, map) is not so far from Sapir's suggestion with four North American areas: Mexican, Northwest Coast, "Northeastern," and Eskimo.

[23] *The American Indian*, chap. xix–xxi.

[24] *Ibid.*, chaps. i–xiii.   [25] *Ibid.*, chap. xiv.

The relations of distributional facts assembled by Wissler do seem on the whole to substantiate his claim that migration was culturally a rather unimportant factor in pre-Columbian America. But it did occur; and his own Euro-American area shows that it may at times be of fundamental importance. This is true, similarly, with respect to all other factors that may cut across the operation of normal diffusion and the age-area principle. The danger lies in utilizing the latter too exclusively.

In general, Wissler is circumspect. He is constantly qualifying with terms like "seem" and "suggest," and issuing his findings as merely preliminary indications subject to revision. Their cumulative effect on the reader, however, is likely to be much stronger, and one-sided; and occasionally, in summarizing or in framing broader syntheses, Wissler slips and speaks as if his inferences were proved. Also, Wissler has attempted something rather unique. Two of his books, and much of the third, are historical in objective and yet emphasize process more than result. The historically minded, therefore, complain of looseness and inexactness of facts; those who are interested in processes take alarm at the historical reconstructions as too speculative. Basically, however, this means that Wissler's approach has been broad but lacking in intensiveness and reliably sharp edges. He has done enough with the age-area concept to show that it is not a mere instrument of speculation but a legitimate means of inferential reconstruction when other data fail. That it must be critically handled goes without saying. The age-area principle cannot be applied as between diverse and unrelated elements of culture. Wissler has made this clear. Much of the criticism leveled at the method rests on failure to understand this fact; which also holds in biology. No one would infer respective age of birds and snails from their distribution; but within the limits of a group such as an order, and especially within the genus, the method is constantly being used and apparently with fair reliability.

The culture-area and age-area concepts both rest on the idea of a normal, permanent tendency of culture to diffuse. This principle seems well established. It is accepted even by those who find satisfaction in pointing out cases where other factors have produced contrary results. The two concepts, however, have been brought into little relation so far. The one aims at a static description of large natural aggregations of culture; the other, at discovering sequential developments within isolable items or parts of culture. The concept of the culture center seems to hold the potentiality of co-ordinating these two approaches. It can give the culture area historic depth, and can synthesize discrete age-area findings so as to be interpretable in generalized areal as well as in temporal terms.

To summarize Wissler's contribution: First, he has formulated and made useful two important concepts which had previously been ill defined and hesitatingly employed; but his results have suffered at times from sketchy, loose-edged handling of data. In consequence, his work has perhaps had most sympathetic appreciation in sciences outside of anthropology, most criticism within. Second, he has laid some foundation for an understanding of the culture-center concept and of the relation of culture to environment; but these two lines remain to be developed.[26]

[26] [This analysis was first written in August, 1928, and received the analyst's final revision in June, 1929.—EDITOR.]

ANALYSIS 18

HUGO OBERMAIER'S RECONSTRUCTION OF SEQUENCES AMONG PREHISTORIC CULTURES IN THE OLD WORLD[1]

By ROBERT H. LOWIE

University of California

I. SYNOPSIS

Ostensibly, this paper purports to give a survey of the present state of knowledge concerning the pre-Neolithic culture of Spain. Obermaier, however, does not confine himself to this descriptive task, but attempts to fix the relations of the prehistoric Spanish cultures to those of Europe as a whole, of Western Asia, and of North Africa. The significance of the paper lies in these comparative considerations.

The essay is divided into four main parts: (A) "The Paleolithic of Spain"; (B) "The Epipaleolithic"; (C) "The Protoneolithic"; (D) "Geological Chronology"; (D) will be considered only so far as its points are relevant to social science.

A. Following the conventional subdivisions of prehistory, Obermaier argues that the Chellean and the Acheulean culture reached Europe from the south and were lacking in Central and Eastern Europe, where their place is taken by a synchronous pre-Mousterian.

The Upper Paleolithic of Spain has origins similar to that of North Africa, its Aurignacian being derived from the North African Capsian. The latter was not followed by the Solutrean and the Magdalenian of France. These cultures were also absent from all but northernmost Spain.

B. The Terminal Capsian of Southern Spain and Northern Africa is ancestral to the Tardenoisian of France and influenced the Azilian. For all three Obermaier suggests the term "Epipaläolithikum."

C. The Protoneolithic is represented by the French Campignian because of its live stock, cereals, stonework, and pottery; and by the Asturian of Spain because of its stratigraphic position—before the Neolithic and after the Azilian.

D. The several Paleolithic industries were of quite different duration in different areas, e.g., the Solutrean occupied a greater span, temporally as well as spatially, in the East than in the West. The chronology of

---

[1] "Das Paläolithikum und Epipaläolithikum Spaniens," *Anthropos*, XIV–XV (1919–20), 143–79. [Cf. glossary appended at end of the analysis.—EDITOR.]

Pleistocene Europe is accordingly far more intricate than has often been assumed.

II. FACTUAL CONTRIBUTION

A. Dealing with an area hitherto imperfectly known, the author systematically lists the most important stations that correspond to the recognized prehistoric cultures. He thus finds evidence in Spain of Chellean, Acheulean, Mousterian, Aurignacian, Solutrean, and Magdalenian cultures. The last three, however, constituting the Upper Paleolithic, are not uniformly distributed over the peninsula. Southern and Central Spain exhibit that fusion of early and late Aurignacian implements characteristic of the Lower Capsian of North Africa; the Middle Aurignacian is lacking except in Cantabria. The Lower Capsian of South Spain is followed by an Upper Capsian horizon with a gradual reduction in size of stone tools and preference for the representation of human figures absent farther north. In this South Spanish zone, then, the Solutrean and the Magdalenian are lacking; they are restricted to Northern Spain, i.e., Cantabria and Catalonia.

B. The Epipaleolithic of Spain as a whole corresponds to the Terminal Capsian of North Africa and coincides essentially with the Tardenoisian of France. In the Northwest, i.e., in Cantabria, a blend of Terminal Capsian and Azilian forms occurs.

C. There has been no evidence of a Campignian horizon in Spain; instead, a new Protoneolithic culture appears in shell-heaps of the province of Asturias, where it overlies Azilian layers. The stone tools are wholly unlike the delicate Epipaleolithic microliths. Most typical are unifacially fractured pickaxes unworked at the butt. Pottery is lacking in the typical Asturian sites.

More recent heaps reveal quartzite pebbles with small pecked pits and crudely sharpened, unpolished bone awls. In still later sites occur the first signs of rude pottery sherds.

These two latter cultures were as yet imperfectly known at the time of Obermaier's paper.

III. CLASSIFICATORY CONCEPTS

Obermaier adopts the accepted concepts of prehistory in the definition of cultural layers. Since these concepts are, of course, not directly observable but only convenient summaries of observations, a subjective factor here enters the description. This is in part recognized by the author in the discussion of Acheulean stations in Spain (p. 149). Two difficulties are mentioned by him: (a) continuous settlement in open sites led to a mingling of Chellean and Acheulean remains; (b) the frequent use of quartzite renders a separation of Acheulean from Chellean difficult, owing to the crudity imposed by the refractory material.

In general, two criteria seem to be considered by Obermaier: a stratigraphic and a typological. That is to say, when types corresponding to the accepted "Acheulean" form underlie "Mousterian" or overlie "Chellean" forms, their "Acheulean" character is established. This is, of course, an unexceptionable procedure.

The new concept of an "Epipaleolithic" is to be welcomed since it is based on the sound notion that cultures displaying no trace of the Neolithic can only be characterized as epigonal to the Paleolithic proper. On the other hand, in the discussion of the Protoneolithic a strange inconsistency is manifested. The Campignian (including the South Scandinavian Kitchen Midden culture) and the newly disclosed Asturian are both grouped under the head of "proto-Neolithic" (p. 167), but on two avowedly distinct grounds—the former because it corresponds to the modern conception of the Neolithic, the latter because stratigraphically it is intermediate between the Azilian and the Neolithic.

This mixture of chronological and typological considerations can only lead to confusion. Obermaier himself rightly rejects the term "Mesolithic" for the cultures intervening between the Paleolithic and the Neolithic (p. 161) because it would imply "the organic evolution, the progressive development and transformation of the Paleolithic into the Neolithic," which is contrary to the facts. By the same token Protoneolithic can be applied only where the characteristics of the true Neolithic are somehow prefigured. Since the Asturians lacked all traces of stock-breeding and tillage, as well as of pottery, they are not proto-Neolithic but pre-Neolithic, i.e., Paleolithic, by virtue of both their lithic industry and their economic existence.

In this context it should be noted that M. C. Burkitt[2] has recently reasserted the validity of a Mesolithic period, to include Azilian, Tardenoisian, Asturian, Maglemosean, Kitchen Midden, and Campignian cultures—in short, Obermaier's Epipaleolithic and Protoneolithic. In the analyst's opinion this is a serious error. Burkitt contends that the Maglemosean and the Kitchen Midden culture, though distinct, show too close an affinity to be separated simply because of the crude pottery occurring in the Danish shell mounds: "For anyone who has studied the two on the spot it is impossible to separate them as belonging to two totally different civilizations" (p. 45). But what is meant by "two totally different

[2] *Our Early Ancestors* (Cambridge: University Press, 1926), pp. 8–47.

civilizations"? No absolute break with the Paleolithic is to be assumed *in the place of origin of the Neolithic*. People did not overnight begin to domesticate sheep, goats, cattle, and pigs, to raise cereals, and to fire clay vessels. It becomes a matter of classificatory convenience, then, as to where the line is drawn. The earlier division on the basis of stone-grinding having long ago proved impracticable, prehistorians have generally used pottery as the most useful criterion. In consonance with their practice (often unformulated), the terms pre-Ceramic and Ceramic might well be substituted for the traditional Paleolithic and Neolithic. But wherever the line of demarcation may be traced, a breach of continuity is not to be expected and does not occur where ample evidence is extant for a relatively undisturbed area. Thus, even in the full Neolithic the earlier art of stone-chipping persists. The continuity noted by Burkitt in Denmark is no greater than might be expected within the narrow spatial and temporal limits in question; and there can be no more objection to classifying the Kitchen Midden folk as Neolithic in culture than to so classifying the majority of American Indians, even though they lacked live stock and often husbandry as well.

But whatever warrant might exist for uniting the Kitchen Midden and the Maglemosean culture, there is none whatsoever for including under the same head the Asturian, the Azilian, and the Tardenoisean. To apply to all six the term "Mesolithic" is to deprive that concept of any *cultural* meaning. What, for example, is common to the Asturian and the Tardenoisean? The typical Tardenoisean pigmy flints are absent in Asturias, whose lithic products, according to Obermaier, display "nicht die geringste Reminiszenz an die Klein- und Feintypen des Epipaläolithikums" (p. 169). On the other hand, the Asturian "type fossil"—the quartzite pick unifacially fractured into a point—is peculiar to this region. Lumping together such diverse cultures under a "Mesolithic" category is a far more serious matter than separating Ceramic and pre-Ceramic cultures. Chronology is important, but contemporaneity is not equivalence.

IV. REGIONAL DIFFERENTIATION

Perhaps the most convincing point in Obermaier's discussion is the importance of regional differentiation in the earlier portions of culture history. This may be traced backward step by step from the latest to the earliest of the periods considered. The Asturian, roughly contemporaneous with the Campignian and the Danish shell mounds, presents altogether peculiar characteristics in its lithic products (p. 169). In approximately the same period the pure Tardenoisean differs from the Azilian proper; the former lacks the painted pebbles and, more important, every trace of bone implements, while the flat harpoon of stag's antler is the Azilian type-fossil. Only where the two cultures clashed, as in Cantabria, a fusion of types resulted (pp. 161–67). Still more suggestive are the phenomena of the Upper Paleolithic, for, except in the North, Spain (like North Africa) lacks the Solutrean and Magdalenian cultures, for which an Upper Capsian is substituted. This difference is marked also in the art style of the "Franco-Catabrian" and the "Levantine" areas, as they have since been designated (pp. 152–61). Finally, the Lower Paleolithic reveals an even more striking diversity: The Chellean fist-hatchet is absent in the whole of Central and Eastern Europe, where a synchronous pre-Mousterian is noted (pp. 145–52).

These data have an obvious bearing upon theory. If an identical initial Capsian is followed in one region by the Solutrean and the Magdalenian, and in another by an Upper Capsian; if the Mousterian of Central Europe is not preceded, after the French pattern, by fist-hatchet cultures, but by the wholly distinct pre-Mousterian, then, evidently, the theory of unilinear evolution is untenable. Instead we have proof of *culture areas* at a very early period indeed; of a constant tendency to subsequent cultural differentiation; and of resemblances due to the accidental contact of peoples.

This result is all the more remarkable because Obermaier, writing as he does in the chief organ of German diffusionism, somewhat naïvely combines with his diffusionist conclusions a faith in parallelism—naïvely because he feels no need of justifying it. Thus, beyond the realm of Europe and neighboring Mediterranean zones he accepts independent evolution as a matter of course; resemblances are due to innate *Elementargedanken,* "welche während des Quartärs an verschiedenen Zentren und völlig unabhängig zur Auslösung und Verwirklichung gelangten" (p. 145). Again, he is willing to admit two independent centers for the Solutrean: one in Hungary (p. 155), the other in Central Africa. "Diese afrikanische Stufe hätte sich in vollständiger Unabhängigkeit von der europäischen entwickelt und scheint nach Norden bis in die südliche Sahara vorgedrungen zu sein" (p. 157).

By characterizing Obermaier's position as naïve, it is not meant to discredit. On the contrary, as his work has provided proof of regional diversity, so it also demonstrates the occasional reality of independent evolution. With reference to this very Solutrean he has since shown[3] that the Sbaikian laurel-leaf form of North Africa presents a genetically unrelated counterpart of the Hungarian equivalent. In Hungary, the technique is

[3] "Nördliches Afrika," in Max Ebert's *Reallexikon der Vorgeschichte,* IX (1927), 110–21.

pressure; in Tunisia, it is delicate fracturing; but the gross result is strikingly similar. Resemblances thus *can* result from a different point of departure. Characteristically, this important conclusion is not formulated in terms of the convergence concept.

To revert to Obermaier's culture areas, his results have not always been fully assimilated by prehistorians. For instance, the epoch-making discoveries of E. Licent and P. Teilhard de Chardin[4] establish a Pleistocene culture in China of partly Mousterian character. Now, if Obermaier is right in his segregation of a West and an East European sphere, it follows that we need not expect the Chinese Mousterian to be preceded by a Chellean-Acheulean, but that here, too, a *faustkeilfreies Primitivpaläolithikum* in the form of a pre-Mousterian may have paved the way for the true Mousterian. It is even possible to envisage a dualism—scraper versus *coup de poing*, unifacialism versus bifacialism—over far vaster areas than those conceived by Obermaier, with China, Siberia, Eastern and Central Europe pitted against India, the Near Orient, North Africa, and Western Europe.

V. CHRONOLOGICAL PRIORITY

Whenever resemblances are explained by dissemination, the *direction* of the flow of elements constitutes a further problem. How does Obermaier cope with it? As we have seen, he assumes that the Aurignacian of France is a derivation of the Capsian, etc. What warrants this against the alternative conclusion of a contrary movement?

It must be admitted that Obermaier is not always clear on this point. He is perhaps most explicit as to the Solutrean (p. 155). Arranged in logical sequence, the reasoning may be represented as follows: An advanced technique, like the Solutrean, requires preliminary stages. Such have never been found in the West, but they do occur in Hungary. Here a hitherto-unknown proto-Solutrean has been discovered by E. Hillebrand, revealing indifferent forerunners of the laurel-leaf point. The demonstration is perfect when, as happens in several sites, it is linked with stratigraphic observations—the proto-Solutrean resting on an Aurignacian and supporting a typical Solutrean horizon. Hence, Hungary is the center of origin, whence Poland, Moravia, Lower Austria, Southern Germany, Central and Southern France successively received the new industry.

In this case the proof is of course quite satisfactory. It will be noted that it rests on evolutionary assumptions: Stage B presupposes Stage A. Such assumptions have indeed become suspect, but are inevitable in the reconstruction of history and not in themselves objectionable. No one

[4] "Le paléolithique de la Chine," in *L'anthropologie*, XXXV (1925), 201–34.

denies that calculus presupposes geometry. It is in each case a question of fact whether a given step really is or is not a prerequisite.

As regards the Tardenoisian, Obermaier's logic is similar to that of the Solutrean argument but less lucid. The French Tardenoisian and the Terminal Capsian of Spain coincide in their geometrical microliths; hence, they are genetically connected. The Tardenoisian could not develop out of the preceding Magdalenian; hence, it is rooted in the Iberian Capsian, whose development can be traced step by step (p. 162). The stringency of this demonstration evidently rests on the correctness of the view that the sequence Magdalenian-Tardenoisian is technologically excluded.

Parenthetically, we may note that the outsider can rarely judge the cogency of technological considerations. Obermaier cites the frequent assertion that Magdalenian harpoons are cylindrical because reindeer antler is specially adapted for that shape, while the Azilian equivalents are necessarily flat, owing to the spongy nature of stag's antler. This, Obermaier explains, is refuted by the fact that in Spain round and flat harpoons are all invariably carved out of stag's antler (p. 160).

Obermaier is very hypothetical, overconcise, and hence far from clear in his treatment of the Lower Paleolithic. Because the Chellean is absent in Central and Eastern Europe, it must have come from the South (p. 145). This evidently presupposes that the Chellean could not have evolved on European soil. This assumption is quite probably correct, but its grounds are not stated. The Acheulean is at first defined as occupying virtually the same area as its predecessor, except for rare isolated finds. Later a Western Acheulean is distinguished from an essentially identical South Acheulean, which is supposed to have migrated from Anatolia into Hungary and Poland via the Balkan Peninsula. No reason is given for this hypothesis. Again, an *independent* Eastern Acheulean is assumed to have developed in West Siberia and to have reached Central Europe in its younger phases. Once more, the reason for such an idea remains obscure. We naturally ask: From what did this Eastern Acheulean evolve? The Acheulean is generally regarded as the logical successor of the Chellean, but *ex hypothesi* this prerequisite stage was lacking in the East.

As for the Mousterian, the presence of a pre-Mousterian and the absence of a Chellean in the East do not suffice to prove that the French Mousterian came from there, as Obermaier suggests. A priori, it is conceivable that a Mousterian might also naturally evolve out of the French Acheulean. Indeed, quite recently Obermaier[5] recognized two Mousterian cultures that are supposed to have evolved independently of each other: the Eastern *(Kleinmoustérien)*; and the Acheuleanoid Mousterian *(Mous-*

<hr>

[5] "Moustérien," in Ebert, *op. cit.*, VIII (1927), 314–20.

térien von Acheuléenmorphologie), which developed out of the Later Acheulean. The former is still believed to have invaded the West in successive waves, ultimately fusing with it. Whether the concept "Mousterian" is applicable to cultures varying as much as its two representatives are supposed to do remains to be seen.

VI. EVALUATION

Regardless of the obscurities mentioned, Obermaier's paper must be highly valued as a pioneer attempt to determine prehistoric culture areas and to trace their historical interrelations. It indicates the intricacy of Paleolithic developments due to contacts of various kinds. At the same time, it suggests the possibility of independent evolution. In short, it provides noteworthy data for culture-historical theory, all the more to be prized because they relate to a dim past.

Implicitly, it also suggests that a fuller comprehension of prehistory can come only from an extension of research to embrace the entire world, and from a deeper understanding of technical processes.[6]

GLOSSARY

NOTE:—The sequence of the archaeological periods generally accepted by prehistorians is as follows: Chellean, Acheulean, Mousterian (together forming the Lower Paleolithic); Aurignacian, Solutrean, Magdalenian (forming the Upper Paleolithic); the Azilian-Tardenoisian (= Transitional); early Neolithic; full Neolithic; Copper Age (often not to be separated from the Bronze Age); Bronze Age; Iron Age.

Acheulean.—The division of the Lower Paleolithic following the Chellean *(q.v.)*, characterized by greater delicacy in the manufacture of the *coup de poing* typical of both. The technique remains essentially similar.

Aurignacian.—The first division of the Upper Paleolithic. The characteristic stone tool is the blade. Bone implements, including awls, painting, etching, and carving, make their first appearance in this period, as do objects of personal decoration, such as shells, teeth as pendants, etc.

Azilian.—A "transitional" period, geologically between the Pleistocene and the Recent, culturally between the Paleolithic and the Neolithic, hence also classed by some authors as "Mesolithic." The stone implements are characterized by their smallness; harpoons are of stag's antler (contrast to preceding Magdalenian). There is no trace of pottery.

Capsian.—A North African culture period coinciding temporally with the Upper Paleolithic of Western Europe. The Aurignacian is genetically connected with it.

Campignian.—Sometimes classed as Mesolithic on a chronological basis, this culture is characterized by crude pottery, hence is better treated as proto-Neolithic or early Ceramic.

[6] [This analysis was first written in February, 1928, and revised by the analyst in February, 1929.—EDITOR.]

Chellean.—The earliest universally accepted division of the Lower Paleolithic. The typical tool is the *coup de poing,* i.e., fist-hatchet, made by fracture from a core of flint, quartzite, etc., not from the splinters struck off, and
worked on both sides.

Kitchen Midden.—A mass of shellfish and kitchen refuse generally. The
Kitchen Midden culture is sometimes classed as Mesolithic, but the presence
of pottery connects it with the Campignian and warrants placing it in the
Neolithic.

Magdalenian.—The last period of the Upper Paleolithic. Flint tools cease
to be of importance, while work in bone and antler is perfected. Paleolithic
art reaches its acme in the Magdalenian cave paintings of Northern Spain
and Southern France.

Maglemose.—This Danish site is characterized by a small, narrow, unilater-
ally barbed harpoon and pierced antler tools. It belongs to approximately
the same "transitional" period as the Azilian.

Mesolithic.—This term is applied by some authors to all the "transitional"
cultures intermediate in time between the true Paleolithic and the unques-
tionable Neolithic.

Mousterian.—By contrast with the two cultures that precede it in Western
Europe, the Mousterian has, as a rule, not a core but a flake industry, the
slivers struck off being made into tools such as scrapers, which are naturally
smaller than the *coup de poing.*

Neolithic.—"Neolithic," originally applied to the age of ground stone tools,
is now extended to the ceramic cultures. These fall wholly within the geologically Recent. In the full Neolithic, pottery is linked with tillage and stock-
breeding.

Paleolithic.—Negatively, the Paleolithic is defined by lack of pottery,
tillage, stock-breeding, and ground stone tools; positively, by hunting and
gathering as food-getting activities, and the shaping of stone tools by fracture
and pressure. Geologically, the European Paleolithic falls wholly within the
Pleistocene.

Pleistocene.—The geological period preceding the Recent and following the
Tertiary.

Solutrean.—The Solutrean belongs to the Upper Paleolithic, following the
Aurignacian and preceding the Magdalenian *in Western Europe.* It is interpreted as an intrusion from the East that originated in Hungary. The distinctive technique is the removal of delicate scales by pressure applied to
both sides of the flint blade.

Tardenoisian.—A "transitional" or "Mesolithic" culture characterized by
tiny tools of geometrical shape. It lacks the stag-antler harpoon typical of
the Azilian.

N. C. NELSON'S STRATIGRAPHIC TECHNIQUE IN THE RECON-STRUCTION OF PREHISTORIC SEQUENCES IN SOUTHWESTERN AMERICA[1]

By LESLIE SPIER

University of Washington

The significance of this paper lies in its being the first exposition of a refined method for determining exactly the time sequence of archaeological materials in a primitive area. On its foundation, the edifice of south-western chronology has been subsequently reared, constituting today the fullest set of cultural observations for any primitive prehistoric area.

SYNOPSIS

The data under consideration were obtained from a single locality within the "glazed-ware area" in the northeastern sector of the Southwest occupied in historic times by the Tanoan peublos. This is one of several areas in the region characterized by definite local styles of pottery and more or less clearly defined in their limits. Three hundred ruins, many of them large, had been discovered in this inhospitable area. "The implied population mounts to figures out of proportion on the one hand, to the productivity of the country and, on the other, to the historically known facts. We may, therefore, reasonably suspect a lengthy occupation by either a shifting or a changing population; in other words, that the ruins in question are not of the same age" (p. 161). On this assumption, the ultimate aim of the study was to establish the time relations of these ruins; the immediate aim was to establish the sequence of ceramic types associated with them and by which they were identifiable.

Excavation revealed small ruins with black-on-white painted pottery, large ruins with glazed wares, and a historic painted ware. Hypothetically, small ruins should be of earlier date than the large. Of the three types of glazed wares, one was placed chronologically as of the historic period by its association with domestic animal bones, etc. Superpositions in various ruins showed historic glazed pottery in contact with an earlier glaze, and

[1] "Chronology of the Tano Ruins," *American Anthropologist*, N.S., XVIII (1916), 159-80.

again the second early glaze with the preceding black-on-white painted ware. The relations of the two earlier glazed types were still unknown.

The answer was found in a large refuse heap of Pueblo San Cristobal. Black-on-white and the two early glazes (designated Types I, II, and III) were there found in as many successive strata, in a manner demonstrating that each had been substituted for its predecessor. The chronological position of the two remaining wares (historic glaze [Type IV] and modern painted ware [V]) had already been fixed by documentary evidence.

The method of analysis of the stratified material in the refuse heap was as follows: "A visibly stratified section of the refuse exposure showing no evidence of disturbance was selected" (p. 165) and a block of this was carefully excavated in foot levels. The potsherds from each level were kept segregated. They were then classified into seven types, i.e., the five noted above and two cooking wares. These types had become familiar from general digging in this ruin and over the whole glazed-ware area. The number of each type at each interval of depth was noted.

A tabular statement of these results showed, according to Nelson, that the cooking wares (corrugated and biscuit ware) had no chronological significance, being found in all layers in much the same frequency. Type I, however, appeared in large quantity at the base of the heap, becoming negligible halfway to the top. Type II made its appearance (in three varieties) as Type I was diminishing, attained a maximum halfway up, and diminished to the top (a normal frequency distribution with truncated upper end). Type III appeared well toward the top coincident with the diminution in Type II. "It now seems probable . . . . that the successive styles of ceramics arose one from the other."

The following section of the paper contains a description of the pottery types. This does not concern us here. Incidentally, the descriptive nomenclature for these wares devised by Nelson in this connection, thus avoiding local geographical names for types, has been generally followed.

Having established the sequence of pottery types, Nelson next established the sequence of forty-five ruins of the Tano district by checking for each the presence of pottery Types I–V. "Substituting for the five successive pottery types a corresponding number of time periods" (p. 180) and adding earlier pre-Pueblo periods, not previously mentioned here, he found the ruins had been occupied in one or more of these six periods. The number of ruins was successively 4 (pre-Pueblo and little known), 29, 21, 19, 6, and 3.

Of particular interest is the steadily decreasing number of ruins marking the successive Pueblo periods, but until the capacities of the various ruined villages have been estimated it is useless to put definite constructions upon the figures. The offhand impression is, however, that the housing facilities during the first three periods of Pueblo history in the Tano district remained very nearly uniform because as the villages decreased in number they increased in size. This might mean among other things that the population remained fairly stable [*ibid.*].

CONCEPTS AND ASSUMPTIONS

Conceptually the paper is very simple. Nelson operates primarily with the following: the local culture area, stylistic pulsations in a single art (ceramics), typological discrimination of the wares, and simple stratigraphy.

1. The stratigraphic possibilities rest on an observation of present-day Pueblo Indian habits. Each day the hearth is swept out and the broken sherds and ashes cast on the refuse heap. It may be assumed that the sherds bear constant proportions to the several types of ware currently fashionable. The heap thus contains from bottom to top a ceramic record of the pueblo's existence.

The sample obtained in excavating the heap involves the assumptions implicit in all sampling processes (questions of size, homogeneity, how far it is random and representative, etc.). It is in keeping here to point out only these special considerations affecting this kind of sampling.

Nelson chose a visibly stratified block free from disturbance, a cut having been made across the entire heap. Freedom from disturbance was indicated by continuous cross-bedding. His block was small, three by six feet on the horizontal; had it been larger or even included the entire heap, it would doubtless have included areas disturbed by burials, slumping, oblique depositing, etc. Chosen at random, it may be assumed representative.

A minor factor involved in preserving the homogeneity of the sample is the simple expedient of preventing extraneous ware from falling into it. The point seems childishly obvious, but it is a matter of experience that this accident has happened to the confusion of results.

Most important is the assumption that the wares in the refuse heap are representative of those in use at any given time. F. W. Hodge has challenged this, at least verbally, maintaining that the modern Indians make a practice of retrieving sherds from the heaps to grind for tempering in pottery they make. If they exercised selection, the relative proportions of the wares in the heap would be seriously affected. It may be pointed out that even if this were so it would not affect the *sequence* of the wares (Nelson's immediate concern). Kroeber and Spier observed, however, that at modern Zuñi, for example, no selection was made and the number taken was insignificant.[2]

The intervals of depth chosen for comparative units are necessarily arbitrary and convenient. The only assumption of concern here is that equal intervals give significant results. This will not hold if the heap is building more rapidly at one time than another, or if natural agencies (wind and water) are depositing or removing the matrix (sand and ashes) at varying rates. This would not militate against interpretations of the *sequence* of wares, but might invalidate other interpretations; such as the rapidity of fluctuations in ceramic fashion, the relative extent of manufacture of pottery at various periods, fluctuations in population, and even the continuity of the art.

There is also an obvious limit to the utility of the method in that shallow heaps are all too frequent in this area. Nelson, for instance, was limited by the fact that his heap began with Type I in full flower and terminated with Type III just beginning. Types IV and V were not contained at all. (Our present knowledge of southwestern prehistory indicates that his heap begins well along in the career of the whole.)

2. The typological discrimination of the wares depends on the classification chosen and the identification of the sherds (fragments) in the heap.

The validity of the classification rests on the objective distinctness of the criteria. In this case, the differences lay, primarily, in technique of ornamentation (paint, glaze paint, and a combination of the two); secondarily, in body color, form, size, surface finish, and paste composition. Implicitly, the types chosen were each sufficiently homogeneous and numerically large to dwarf the inevitable minor variations and overlapping. The classification was made on the basis of a large number of vessels found in the ruins of the Tano area, not on the fragments in the refuse heap; hence, it was made prior to an analysis of the sample from the heap. That is, this was truly a typological grouping uninfluenced by chronological factors. The chronological sequence did subsequently prove the validity of the classification.

The identification of the sherds presumes that the fragments, many of them minute, can be segregated into these classes, and that the types can be identified equally well. The answer is to be found in the distinctness of the styles and the observer's familiarity with the wares. (Of Nelson's competency there can be no doubt.) It is the analyst's experience that

[2] The best answer to Hodge is that he found the same sequence in both refuse heap and ruin at Hawikuh, near Zuñi (F. W Hodge, "Pottery of Hawikuh," *Indian Notes*, I, No. 1 (January, 1924), 8–15.

some of the fragments cannot be readily classified, but that these are a minor fraction. It may also be assumed that, with respect to the comparative ease in recognizing the several types, there is no appreciable difference among them.

3. Nelson interprets the observed frequencies as indicating stylistic pulsations in the ceramic art, that is, a series of substitutions of favored styles. Such an interpretation is not necessary for establishing the sequence of types, as Nelson was fully aware, but it is supplementary. There are alternative explanations.

Criticism may be directed at the presentation of the results in absolute numbers alone. This may, and in fact does, obscure even the matter of sequence. Thus Nelson observes: "Examining the table as it stands, we see at once that column I has no chronological significance, corrugated cooking pottery of essentially the same style having been in use throughout the period represented by the ten-foot accumulation of débris." If, however, the absolute values are reduced to percentages of each type present in each level, corrugated ware shows (from bottom to top) 55, 46, 25, 23, 19, 17, 21, 15, 31, and 37 per cent. That is, the ware was going out of style during the period represented by the lower two-thirds of the heap and had a recrudescence later.

A percentage distribution also shows more adequately the extent to which each type was favored in comparison with its fellows.

The data show a growing predominance of a particular type followed by a decline in use, the decline being more or less coincident at its onset with the appearance of a new type which follows in plan the same life-curve. Nelson interprets this as a series of stylistic pulsations.[3] Alternatively, the new type might indicate the presence of another population. This does not wholly change the view that the pulsation was one of fashion. A complete alternative is that the rise and the fall of a type may be indicative of the growth and the decline of the population[4] or of the ceramic art. This is clearly so if one type (or several coincidently) shows such a fluctuation, in absolute numbers. As the total number of sherds in each level is in this case randomly distributed, this interpretation is precluded. There is, however, still another interpretation for such a normal frequency

[3] Departing from this general interpretation, Nelson proposes a special explanation in the case of Type I. "The few fragments of this ware found in the upper four feet indicate probably heirloom vessels held over from early days or else specimens dug out of the ruins and not at all that this type of ware continued to be manufactured." There is no necessity for this special assumption nor is it substantiated in the paper.

[4] Gamio so interprets a similar sequence at Teotihuacan. (M. Gamio, "Investigaciones arqueológicas en México, 1914–1915," *Proceedings, 19th Internat. Cong. of Americanists* [Washington, 1917], pp. 125–33).

distribution. The whole sample may be derived from a single source, all parts being of contemporaneous origin, but laid down in a rapidly accumulating matrix (as a body of artifacts moved bodily by a stream and redeposited in a growing sand bar).[5]

4. The concept of the local culture area is involved at two points. In defining the pottery types it is assumed that the ceramics of the several ruins of the Tano area were historically connected and culturally homogeneous. Again, in ranking the ruins on the basis of the types they contain, the same assumptions were made.

The local culture area is objectively determined. A culture trait (as a pottery type) is found distributed over a larger or smaller territory. At any given time we find this territory characterized by a predominant type of the trait, adjacent areas by dissimilar types, with marginal zones common to them containing either the dissimilar forms mingled or types presenting the characters of the several wares in combination. We *infer* that the trait has been imitated throughout the area of its distribution, there adopted without change or modified in novel form or amalgamated with a second derived (imitated) form.

The condition for cultural homogeneity of the trait, then, is that the local area be defined well within the marginal zones. It is the analyst's opinion that Nelson has observed this condition by restricting comparison to the quite limited Tanoan area. (Subsequently it was demonstrated that his types and their sequence hold for a wider area in the Southwest.)

The ranking of the ruins on the basis of the types they contain is founded on the assumptions: first, that the sequence of types represents a series of periods, or that a type is characteristic of a period; and, second, that identical wares were in use throughout the Tano region at one time. The verification of the first is found in the fact that a sequence was established in the refuse heap and that each vertical segment was characterized by a predominant type. The second assumption is justified in the preceding paragraph.

DEVELOPMENTS FROM THIS METHOD

The general limitations to this method are the obvious ones; it cannot be applied to a non-material trait, it is confined primarily to traits of highly variable form like pottery, and it does not establish a true chronology. While Nelson styles his paper "Chronology of the Tano

---

[5] Spier has demonstrated such a case for the Trenton sand deposits (L. Spier, "The Trenton Argillite Culture," *Anthrop. Papers, Amer. Mus. Nat. Hist.*, XXII, Part IV [1918], 167–226).

Ruins," he has established only the relative time relations, not the duration of their occupation or their antiquity in terms of years.

The best evaluation of his contribution can be given by indicating that all subsequent developments in unraveling the prehistory of this area hinged on it. It is well to repeat that, as a result of Nelson's work, our conception of the culture history of the prehistoric Southwest, is more nearly complete than for any other primitive area.

Simultaneously with Nelson's exposition, Kroeber proposed another suggestive method.[6] Using random collections of potsherds from the surface of ruins and heaps in the Zuñi area, i.e., samples giving terminal data ("dates") for each ruin, he isolated a series of wares, first, in historic ruins, in ruins of reputed late date, and clearly prehistoric ruins. The wares of historic ruins overlapped with those of the second class; the latter, with the third. This suggested a time sequence. A more refined discrimination showed the ruins could be ranked according to the proportions of the several wares present.

A combination of Kroeber's method with Nelson's, which resulted in a verification of Kroeber's procedure, was made by Spier among Zuñi ruins.[7] Applied to historic ruins, Nelson's method yielded a sequence of types; applied to proto-historic ruins, it yielded a sequence reaching back in time. In default of other deep refuse heaps, he was thrown back on Kroeber's method. The samples from the surface of other ruins were ranked according to the percentage of one particular ware which they contained. The suggestion for the order (an increasing percentage) was derived from the sequences in the refuse heaps. The sequence being arranged for the type ware, it was found that the other types presented a relatively smooth sequence of percentage ranking. (This is obviously a valid test only when three or more wares are present to show concurrent variations.)

Nelson followed his detailed analysis of Tano chronology with an outline for the chronology of the whole southwestern area.[8] Sequences obtained in the Tano region, Zuñi, and elsewhere in the heart of the area showed a single common sequence of ceramic types, from those associated with earliest pueblo life upward to the historic forms. A superficial examination of the whole area showed a geographic sequence of types from the periphery, where forms analogous to the earliest wares alone

[6] A. L. Kroeber, "Zuñi Potsherds," *ibid.*, XVIII, Part I (1916), 1–38.

[7] L. Spier, "An Outline for a Chronology of Zuñi Ruins," *ibid.*, Part III (1917), 207–33.

[8] N. C. Nelson, "The Archaeology of the Southwest: A Preliminary Report," *Proc. Nat. Acad. Sci.*, V (1919), 114–20.

were to be found, to the center where the Pueblo Indians still reside. The areal sequence coincides with the stratigraphic, a result analogous to the biologists' "age and area" hypothesis. On this basis Nelson postulated a concentration of population coincident with the spread of the successive cultural forms (e.g., pottery types) over successively narrower zones.

A full exposition never having appeared from Nelson's hand, Kidder set himself to the task.[9] His detailed presentation of the cultural development of the area does not differ conceptually from Nelson's outline. It marshals all known evidence from superposition, stratification, and seriation into a consistent whole. It goes beyond Nelson's outline especially in establishing, by superposition, the time relations of the earliest (Basket-Maker) cultures for which there is no ceramic evidence. He also demonstrates that the center of Pueblo development had shifted.

A development in the direction of an absolute chronology was afforded by Douglass' investigation of beams taken from ruins.[10] Having found that trees in this area show definite sequences of annular growth and having established a growth series for a thousand years or more, he discovered that sections of the beams were identifiable in his growth series by reason of their rings. By this method it was possible to date precisely the time at which a particular beam was cut and, hence, the age of the ruin.

It is hoped that this brief presentation of the developments flowing from Nelson's paper does not minimize the fact that the gross product was the result of the labor of many men.[11]

APPENDIX: ARCHAEOLOGICAL METHODS OF ESTABLISHING CHRONOLOGY

Since the methods of achieving chronology in archaeology may not be generally known to the readers of this analysis, a summary of seven methods in current use is appended. These methods are not logically exclusive and in practice are usually combined.

1. *Documentary method.*—A dated inscription (or one dateable) indicates the exact maximum age of the associated finds. A trade piece of

[9] A. V. Kidder, *An Introduction to the Study of Southwestern Archaeology* (New Haven: Yale University Press, 1924).

[10] A. E. Douglass, "Dating Our Prehistoric Ruins," *Natural History*, XXI (1921), 727-30.

[11] A summary of our present knowledge, representing the consensus of opinion of most southwestern archaeologists, will be found in A. V. Kidder, "Report: Southwestern Archeological Conference," *Science*, N.S., LXVI (1927), 489-91. [This analysis should be compared especially with analysis 17. It was first written in September, 1928, and revised by the analyst in February, 1929.—EDITOR.]

definite and datable type (as an early dynastic Egyptian vessel in Crete) gives evidence of the same nature. The evidence may not be strictly documentary, but merely oral tradition defining the relative age of several deposits.

2. *Typological method.*—Types of artifacts are distinguished and their relative antiquity (and relations) *asserted* on the basis of some such criterion as relative crudity, elaborateness, disintegration, etc. (e.g., "palaeoliths" versus polished stone tools in Australia). The validity of the classification may be checked by an investigation of its statistical probability (e.g., Strong's investigation of pottery at Ancon, Peru).

3. *Distributional method.*—On the familiar assumption that of two culture traits (types) occupying the same area that having the wider distribution is inferred the older. The inference is better founded when the two compared are directly related forms (e.g., small house versus large ruins in the Southwest).

4. *Geological method.*—A bald application of geological history (including faunal and floral associations) to determine the relative position of an artifact bearing stratum (e.g., Chellean tools in third interglacial terraces, reindeer remains in Magdalenian caverns).

5. *Annual-deposit method.*—A count of the rings of a tree growing on a deposit fixes a minimum date for the abandonment of the site; the rings in a beam from a ruin fix a date for its occupation; the rings of a stalactite *may* indicate when a cavern was occupied; clay varves (deposited by recurrent waters) may indicate approximate age; the rate of deposit of débris (e.g., in shell mounds) may be calculated. This is the only true *chronological* method other than the documentary; others establish relative time relations only.

6. *Stratigraphic methods.*—(*a*) Direct superposition (e.g., the superposed cities of Troy); (*b*) stylistic variation (the method of Nelson's ashheap analysis); (*c*) concomitant distributions (e.g., the identical distribution of artifacts and pebbles in the Trenton sands).

7. *Seriation method.*—Remains of a stylistic variable (such as pottery) occurring in varying proportions in a series of sites are ranged, by some auxiliary suggestion, according to the seriation of one element (one pottery type). Its validity is established if the other elements (two or more other pottery types) fall in smooth sequences (e.g., the Zuñi ruin series obtained by Kroeber and Spier).

SECTION V
INTERPRETATIONS OF CHANGE AS A DEVELOPMENTAL STAGE

THE CONCEPT OF PROGRESS AND ITS INFLUENCE ON HISTORY AS DEVELOPED BY J. B. BURY[1]

By SIDNEY B. FAY

Harvard University

With the exception of evolution, probably no concept of the past hundred years has so profoundly influenced writers in the social sciences as the idea of progress. It has come to be taken for granted as axiomatic. It is assumed as the animating and controlling idea of Western civilization. It is the general test to which social aims and theories are submitted as a matter of course. The frequency with which one meets at every turn such stereotyped phrases as "liberty and progress," "democracy and progress," "civilization and progress," indicates the popular acceptance of progress as an unquestioned fact.

From the idea of progress is derived the ethical corollary that we can and ought to provide a progressively improving world for posterity. As Professor Carver has said:

The study of sociology . . . . can hardly justify its existence unless it furnishes us a theory of progress which will enable us to shape the policies of society with a view to future improvement. In other words, the fundamental task of the sociologist is to furnish a theory of social progress.[2]

Progress, however, is a relatively modern and novel conception. It is not stamped with the authority and the approval of centuries like many other fundamental philosophical ideas. It was unknown to the Hebrew prophets; in fact, the word "progress" nowhere occurs in the Bible. It was incompatible with the Greek and the Roman notion of "cycles" and "decadence" no less than with the medieval notion of Providence. It was not until the sixteenth century that Bodin began speculations which ripened through Bacon, Descartes, Fontenelle, Turgot, Comte, and others into the present-day idea of progress which is accepted so axiomatically.

Is progress really a sound doctrine? Has there really been a steady advance in civilization during the past (even by oscillations or cycles), and will it continue to take place in the future?

[1] J. B. Bury, *The Idea of Progress: An Inquiry into Its Origin and Growth* (London: Macmillan & Co., 1920).

[2] T. N. Carver, *Sociology and Social Progress* (Boston, 1905), p. 7.

Progress in the realm of scientific knowledge and of man's control over nature is hardly to be doubted as one surveys the ages from the first use of fire, pottery, and iron down to our own days of television, flights over oceans, and modern surgery. But in the realm of art and creative imagination—in architecture, sculpture, painting, oratory, literature, or philosophy—does our age produce greater geniuses or show a striking advance over that of Pericles and Plato or even over that of the Italian Renaissance? Or again, in the art of living together, does the much-vaunted liberty and democracy of our modern industrial society and the infrequency of wars clearly prove that there has been social progress? These are difficult questions which Professor Bury does not attempt to answer. Nor can they be dealt with in any brief essay. They involve the measurement of factors like genius and taste which are difficult to commensurate. But at least it would probably be true to say that in recent years, with the World War and its train of consequences, the idea of progress receives a less confident, optimistic, and universal affirmation than it did a generation ago. Spengler and the pessimists have more of a hearing, and cautious sociological leaders today are less optimistic than the immediate disciples of Comte.

Though contributions to the history of the idea of progress had been made by several French writers,[3] Professor Bury's admirable volume, published in 1920, is the first extended, discriminating, and thoroughly satisfactory inquiry into the subject in English. With his wide erudition as historian of ancient Greece and of the Byzantine Empire, as annotator of Gibbon, as biographer of St. Patrick, and with his philosophic bent of mind, Professor Bury traces in fascinating fashion the interplay of new ideas and scientific discoveries which have gradually combined to form the modern idea of progress. Though no brief summary can more than hint at his breadth of treatment and wealth of knowledge, it may at least indicate a few of the leading points in his stimulating account.

At first sight, says Professor Bury, it may seem surprising that the Greeks, who were so fertile in their speculations on human life, did not hit upon an idea which appears so simple and obvious to us as the idea of progress. But on second thought, the reasons are evident. The recorded history of the Greeks did not go back far, and so far as it did go there had been no impressive series of new discoveries suggesting

[3] Notably by Javary, *De l'idée de progrès* (1850); Rigault, *Histoire de la querelle des Anciens et des Modernes* (Paris: L. Hachette et cie, 1856); Brunetière, "La formation de l'idée de progrès," *Etudes critiques* (5e sér.; Paris: Hachette et cie, 1893); and more fully by Jules Delaville, *Essai sur l'histoire de l'idée de progrès* (Paris: F. Alcan, 1910).

either an indefinite increase of knowledge or such a growing mastery over nature as to transform the conditions of life and to open up great vistas into the future. On the contrary, there was a widely spread belief in an earlier "golden age" of simplicity, which had been followed by a degeneration and decay of the human race. Plato's theory of degradation set forth a gradual deterioration through the successive stages of timocracy, oligarchy, democracy, and despotism. The Greek theory of "cycles," with its endless monotonous iteration, excluded the possibility of permanent advance or "progress." Moreover, even if the idea of progress had occurred to the Greeks, it would have struck them as perilously audacious and impious. Man should not try to rival the gods. Daedalus was properly punished for trying to be the precursor of Lindbergh. According to the Greek idea of Moira, there is a fixed order in the universe, which men must respect and not attempt to conquer and change. Human progress toward perfection—toward an ideal of omniscience or of happiness—seemed too proud and perilous a breaking-down of the bars which divide the human from the divine.

The Romans were dominated by Greek thought. Though Seneca recognized the progress of knowledge, he did not expect from it any improvement in the world. He too, like the Greeks, accepted the theory of degeneration and the hopeless tendency of mankind to corruption. Progress in arts and inventions merely promote deterioration by ministering to luxury and vice. Time is the enemy of man.

Nor were the Middle Ages any more congenial than the classical period to the idea of progress. According to Augustine, who was the dominant influence for a thousand years, original sin and "otherworldliness" were all pervasive. In the later version of the *New England Primer,*

> In Adam's fall
> We sinnéd all.

In Augustine's philosophy the whole movement of history aimed to secure the happiness of a select few in another world. It did not postulate a further and indefinite development of the human race on this earth. The Day of Judgment may come at any moment. The Christian Era introduced the last period of history, the old age of humanity, which would endure only so long as to enable the Deity to gather in the fortunate ones predestined to salvation. Furthermore, medieval doctrine did not regard history as a natural development in accordance with regular laws—the sun could be made to stand still in its course—but rather as a series of arbitrary events ordered by divine intervention and revelation, that is, by an active Providence. Providence might prevent the complete deterioration of mankind which would otherwise result from original sin, but it was incompatible with the growth of a doctrine of progress and of the moral amelioration of mankind by any gradual process of development.

Even in the Italian Renaissance, which was generally so fruitful in its "discovery of man and of the world," but which was accompanied by the Revival of Learning, there was such a veneration for the classical writers that ancient notions smothered the birth of a conception of progress. The Renaissance exaltation of Greek and Roman antiquity to a position of unattainable superiority led easily and naturally to the inference of a degeneration of humanity during the intervening fifteen hundred years. Machiavelli, who was the most brilliant political thinker of this age, the first "political scientist," did not rise above the ancient theory of recurring cycles. For him, human nature remained always the same and was dominated by passion, weakness, and vice.

In the course of the sixteenth century, however, men began, here and there, somewhat timidly and tentatively, to rebel against the tyranny of antiquity. Copernicus undermined the authority of Ptolemy; Vesalius injured the prestige of Galen; and Aristotle was attacked on many sides by men like Telesio, Cardan, Ramus, and Bruno. The exploitation of the discoveries of printing, the compass, and the navigation of new worlds opened fresh prospects and stimulated a new intellectual atmosphere which was congenial to new philosophies of history.

Nearly forty years after the death of Machiavelli, a French historian, Jean Bodin, published an essay on the easy understanding of history, and ten years later a book on political theory.[4] While seeking to prove that monarchy is the best form of government, Bodin incidentally set forth a new view of universal history. Rejecting the current medieval view, based on the prophecies of Daniel, which divided the course of history into four periods corresponding to the Babylonian, Persian, Macedonian, and Roman monarchies, Bodin suggested a division into three great periods: (1) some two thousand years in which the southeastern peoples were predominant, that is, what Hegel and his followers were to call Oriental history; (2) another two thousand years of Mediterranean, i.e., Greek and Roman, history; and (3) the period of the northern or Germanic civilization since the downfall of Rome. Each period is stamped by the psychological character of its racial groups, being respectively in each of the three periods: (1) religion, (2) practical sagacity, and (3)

[4] *Methodus ad facilem historiarun cognitionem* (1566); *Les six livres de la République* (1576).

warfare and inventive skill. In addition to these anthropological considerations, Bodin showed his modernity by taking climate and geography into account.

Bodin also made a step toward the idea of progress by rejecting the classical doctrine of degeneration, with its tradition of an antecedent age of virtue and felicity. His reason for this rejection is significant: the powers of nature have always remained the same; it would be illegitimate to suppose that nature could at one time produce the men and the conditions postulated by a theory of the golden age and not produce them at another. History depends largely on the will of men, which is always changing; every day new customs, new laws, new institutions, come into being, and also new errors, resulting in a series of oscillations. Rise is followed by fall, and fall by rise. But on the whole, through the series of oscillations there has been a gradual ascent from the period in which men lived like wild beasts to the social order of sixteenth-century Europe. Thus Bodin recognized a general progress in civilization in the past, but he gave little consideration to the future. Moreover, his style was dull, and his thoughtful contributions were overlaid with theological and astrological theories, including a curious mystic doctrine of numbers— 7, 9, 12, 496—which he sought to use as a key to historical change.

The idea of progress involves optimism and contemplates a more ideal form of society. This found expression, in the course of the hundred years in which Bodin stands midway, in three famous utopian pictures of a new and more perfected ideal society: More's *Utopia* (1516), Campanella's *City of the Sun* (1620), and Bacon's *New Atlantis* (composed about 1623 and published in 1627 after his death). Plato and Aristotle had conceived their utopian constructions within the geographical limits of Hellas; unlike them, More and his followers placed their imaginary commonwealths in distant seas, and this remoteness in space helped to create a certain illusion of reality; the device was suggested by the maritime explorations of the fifteenth and the sixteenth century. The more modern method, which was the result of the later rise of the idea of progress, is to project the perfect society into a period of future time.

Francis Bacon also divided history into three periods somewhat like the divisions of Bodin. But his great contribution was his insistence on scientific experimentation as the key for discovering the secrets of nature, and on the utility of these discoveries in furthering "the happiness of mankind."

Though Bodin and Bacon had adumbrated the idea of progress by recognizing an augmentation of knowledge through the past, they were both much bound by respect for the classics and by the doctrine of an active, interfering Providence. This was not true of Descartes. In affirming absolutely the immutability of the laws of nature and the supremacy of reason, Descartes dealt a devastating blow to the doctrine of Providence, and to the respect for authority and tradition which had hitherto tyrannized the minds of men. He was proud of having forgotten the Greek which he had learned as a boy. He gloried in breaking sharply and completely with the past and in constructing a system which borrowed nothing from the dead. With a magnificent confidence in his own analytical method, he looked forward to an advancement of knowledge in the future, on the basis of his own method and his own discoveries. He conceived that this intellectual advance would bring far-reaching benefits to mankind. The first title he had proposed to give to his *Discourse on Method,* published in 1637, had been *The Project of a Universal Science Which Can Elevate Our Nature to Its Highest Degree of Perfection.* But precisely because he was pleased to ignore or make light of what had been achieved in the past, he failed to develop a doctrine of progress of knowledge, as he might otherwise have done. For any such doctrine must take into account the past as well as the present. Though he did not develop a theory of progress, his Declaration of the Independence of Man had prepared the free intellectual atmosphere in which it was to be developed by men imbued with the Cartesian spirit.

It was Fontenelle, according to Professor Bury, who formulated brilliantly and popularized effectively the essential points of the theory of progress. He did this with paradoxical wit and with no little felicity in his *Dialogues of the Dead* (1683) in his *Digression on the Ancients and Moderns* (1688), and in the numerous obituary discourses in which he illuminated for the general public the scientific views of the members of the French Academy of Sciences, of which he was the perpetual secretary for the extraordinarily long period of forty-two years. In the two essays just mentioned he entered the controversy between the Ancients and Moderns, which had already been opened by Perrault and others, and which was to be so delightfully satirized a generation later by Swift in the *Battle of the Books.* Fontenelle took the side of the Moderns. He offered what he regarded as a formal Cartesian proof that man had not degenerated and that the forces of Nature are permanent. If today the lions are as fierce, and the oaks and beeches are as large, as in the days of Pericles, must it not be assumed that Nature is as vigorous today as formerly? And if as vigorous, can and will she not produce today men of equal brains and ability? To be sure, he recognized that differences of climate might make a difference; but he concluded that the climates of Greece and Italy are too similar to that of France to cause any sensible differences between the Greeks or Romans and the French.

Having established the natural equality of mental capacity as between the Ancients and the Moderns, Fontenelle went on to argue that the Moderns enjoy a certain advantage owing to "time." The Ancients were prior in time to us, therefore they were the authors of the first inventions. For that, they cannot be regarded as our superiors. If we had been in their place, we should have been the inventors, like them; if they were in ours, they would add to those inventions, like us. With time comes accumulation of knowledge, the elimination of false theories, and improvements in the methods of reasoning. Therefore we excel the Ancients, and in the same way we must expect that posterity will excel us. Thus Fontenelle looked clearly to the future as well as to the past, both of which are essential to a complete idea of progress.

On the other hand, said Fontanelle, "external conditions" may affect certain periods of civilization disadvantageously. Even though the forces of nature are permanent, such disasters as the inundations of barbarians, long wars, or the existence of governments which discourage or do not favor science may impose long periods of ignorance or bad taste. There may therefore be "breaches of continuity" in progress, but they are not permanent. Such are the considerations which apply to scientific knowledge and man's control over nature. But they do not necessarily apply to art and creative imagination. For poetry and eloquence do not depend as much as science on the accumulation of knowledge and on correct reasoning. They depend on vivacity of imagination. If the Ancients did achieve perfection in imaginative literature, it follows that they cannot be surpassed; but we have no right to say, as their admirers are fond of pretending, that they cannot be equaled.

Fontenelle lived to be a hundred (1657–1757); during his century great advance was made in the physical sciences by men like Boyle, Newton, Leibnitz, and others. New recognition was being given to the importance of science, as compared with theology, by the founding of Royal Academies of Science. The achievements of science, then as ever, did more than anything else to convert the popular imagination to the general doctrine of progress, and Fontenelle was one of its most lucid and charming exponents. He did not, however, pay great attention to another aspect of progress—the art of living together. This problem of social progress was left to the Abbé de Saint-Pierre and the Encyclopedists of the eighteenth century.

In the last years of Louis XIV, which were filled with almost continuous wars, and under the wretched misgovernment of his successor, the contrast between the mental enlightenment of the Cartesian philosophers and the dark background—wars, oppressive taxation, obscurantism, and the social evils and miseries of the kingdom—began to insinuate itself into the minds of men. What was the value of the achievements of science, and the improvement of the arts of life, if life itself could not be ameliorated? So men began to concentrate their attention on the problems of social science, and to turn the light of reason on the nature of man and the roots of society.

In this new effort at social amelioration the Abbé de Saint-Pierre took an indefatigable part. He was a born reformer and would have been called a humanitarian had he lived in the nineteenth century. He devoted his life to the construction of schemes for increasing human happiness. With much ingenuity he worked out projects of all sorts for reforms in government, finance, economics, and education. But he lacked the practical sense necessary to get his projects put into operation, and the insight to understand their full consequences. Most notable was his project for establishing perpetual peace, which, as Professor Bury believes, might have caused more suffering than all the wars from that day to this, because it was based on a perpetuation of the political *status quo* in Europe and all the evils of autocratic government. The Abbé de Saint-Pierre's special contribution to the idea of progress was his emphasis upon the immense improvement possible in the future. He resorted to the analogy, already used by Bacon and others, between the life of the individual man and race of mankind. But whereas Bacon thought of mankind as having reached its "old age," the Abbé de Saint-Pierre believed it to be still only in its infancy. He contemplated the glorious prospect and remote destinies awaiting posterity. There had been progress since the days of the Greeks in spite of obstacles, such as wars, superstitions, and the jealousy of rulers who feared that progress in the science of politics would be dangerous to themselves. But with the removal of these obstacles in the future the rate of progress would be accelerated.

Turgot is chiefly remembered as an economist and an administrator. However, at the age of twenty-three he had designed "discourses on Universal History." Though the work was never written, some of its conceptions are embodied in two lectures which he delivered at the Sorbonne in 1750. They contain the fundamental conception that the course of history is determined by general necessary causes—by the nature of man, his passions, and his reason, and by his environment, i.e., by climate and geography. He conceived universal history as the progress of the human race advancing as an immense whole steadily, though slowly, through alternating periods of calm and disturbance toward greater perfection. He even anticipated Comte's famous "law" of the three stages of intellectual evolution: (1) the theological stage, when men suppose that they were produced by intelligent beings, invisible but resembling ourselves; (2) the metaphysical stage, when philosophers recognize the absurdity of fables about gods, but have not yet gained an insight into natural history; and (3) the positive stage, when later, by observing the reciprocal mechanical action of bodies, hypotheses are formed which can be developed by mathematics and verified by experience. Turgot, of course, did not give to this idea the fundamental and wide-reaching importance which Comte claimed for it, but he deserves the credit of having been the first to suggest it.

Though the idea of progress received a rude buffet from Rousseau's Arcadian doctrine that civilization had been a gigantic mistake, it gained a new impetus from the optimism inspired by the triumph of liberty in America and in the French Revolution. Condorcet, the friend and biographer of Turgot, took up his ideas and developed them. He believed that the study of the history of civilization enables us to establish the fact of progress, to determine its direction in the future, and thereby to accelerate the rate of progression. He maintained that it is possible to foresee events, if the general laws of social phenomena are known, and that these laws can be inferred from the history of the past. He announced the idea which in the next generation was to be worked out by Comte.

In the nineteenth century came the search for a law of progress. The time had come for systematic attempts to probe its meaning and definitely to establish the direction in which humanity is moving or ought to move. Fourier, St. Simon, and Comte all claimed to have discovered the secret of social development and had in view the practical object of remolding society on general scientific principles. From them came the new science of sociology; and the idea of progress, which presided at its birth, has been one of its principal problems ever since.

Since the middle of the nineteenth century two things have greatly strengthened the general acceptance of the idea of progress. One of these is the doctrine of evolution. Evolution, however, says Professor Bury, "does not necessarily mean, applied to society, the movement of man to a desirable goal. It is a neutral scientific conception, compatible either with optimism or pessimism. According to different estimates, it may appear to be a cruel sentence or a guarantee of steady amelioration. And it has been actually interpreted in both ways." The other influence is the unparalled progress in the natural sciences, which has taken place with such accelerated speed, and which has been made familiar to millions both by the popularization of knowledge through education, books, and lectures, and by such obvious mechanical conveniences as telephones, automobiles, radios, and aircraft.

Professor Bury closes with a paradoxical interrogation. In achieving its ascendancy, the idea of progress had to overcome a psychological obstacle which he describes as *the illusion of finality*. This is strongly rooted in man. The men of the Middle Ages would have found it hard to imagine that a time was not far off in which the last Judgment would have ceased to arouse any emotional interest. Hegel and even Comte did not recognize that their own systems could not be final any more than the system of Aristotle or of Descartes. But if we accept the dogma of progress, must we not carry it to its full conclusion? In escaping from the illusion of finality, is it legitimate to exempt that dogma of progress itself? Will not a day come when a new idea will usurp its place as the directing idea of humanity—as the criterion by which progress and all other beliefs will be judged?[5]

[5] [This analysis was first written in December, 1928, and revised by the analyst in February, 1929.—EDITOR.]

ANALYSIS 21

THE CONCEPT OF PHONETIC LAW AS TESTED IN PRIMITIVE LANGUAGES BY LEONARD BLOOMFIELD[1]

By EDWARD SAPIR[2]

University of Chicago

A large part of the scientific study of language consists in the formulation and application of phonetic laws. These phonetic laws are by no means comparable to the laws of physics or chemistry or any other of the natural sciences. They are merely general statements of series of changes characteristic of a given language at a particular time. Thus, a phonetic law applying to a particular sound in the history of English applies only to that sound within a given period of time and by no means commits itself to the development of the same sound at another period in the history of English, nor has it anything to say about the treatment of the same sound in other languages. Experience has shown that the sound system of any language tends to vary slightly from time to time. These shifts in pronunciation, however, have been found to work according to regular laws or formulas. Thus, the *f* of the English word *father* can be shown by comparison with such related languages as Latin, Greek, and Sanskrit to go back to an original *p*. The change of *p* in the original Indo-European word for "father," reflected in the Latin *pater* and the Greek *patēr*, is not, however, an isolated phenomenon but is paralleled by a great many other examples of the same process. Thus, *foot* corresponds to Greek *pous*, genitive *podos*; *five* corresponds to Greek *pente*; *full* corresponds to Latin *plēnus*; and *for* is closely related to Latin *prō*. A comparison of English with certain other languages, such as German, Swedish, Danish, Old Icelandic, and Gothic, proves that these languages share with English the use of the consonant *f* where other languages of the same family which are less closely related to English than these have a *p*.

Inasmuch as such languages as Latin, Greek, Sanskrit, and Slavic differ

---

[1] "A Set of Postulates for the Science of Language," *Language: Journal of the Linguistic Society of America*, II (1926), 153–64; "On the Sound-System of Central Algonquian," *ibid.*, I (1925), 130–56; "A Note on Sound-Change," *ibid.*, IV (1928), 99–100; also E. Sapir, MS materials on Athabaskan languages.

[2] [In preparing this analysis, Professor Sapir was invited to discuss his own work at length because of its similarity to the work of Bloomfield.—EDITOR.]

among themselves about as much as any one of them differs from the Germanic group to which English belongs, it is a fair assumption that their concordance is an archaic feature and not a parallel development, and that the *f* of English and its more closely related languages is a secondary sound derived from an original *p*. This inference is put in the form of a phonetic law, which reads: "Indo-European *p* becomes Germanic *f*." The change cannot be dated, but obviously belongs to at least the period immediately preceding the earliest contact of the Germanic tribes with the Romans, for in all the Germanic words and names that have come down to us from the classic authors this change is already manifest. It is important to realize that two distinct historic facts may be inferred from such evidence as we have given, which is naturally but a small part of the total evidence available. In the first place, the change of *p* to *f* is regular. In other words, we do not find that in one correspondence *f* is related to *p* while in another correspondence *f* seems to parallel *w* or *b* or some other sound. In the second place, the general consensus of the Indo-European languages indicates that the change has been from *p* to *f* and not from *f* to *p*. Incidentally, this is in accord with general linguistic experience, for stopped consonants more often become spirants (continuous "rubbed" consonants) than the reverse.

Such phonetic laws have been worked out in great number for many Indo-European and Semitic languages. There are obviously many other historical factors that contribute their share to the phenomena of change in language, but phonetic law is justly considered by the linguist by far the most important single factor that he has to deal with. Inasmuch as all sound change in language tends to be regular, the linguist is not satisfied with random resemblances in languages that are suspected of being related but insists on working out as best he can the phonetic formulas which tie up related words. Until such formulas are discovered, there may be some evidence for considering distinct languages related— for example, the general form of their grammar may seem to provide such evidence—but the final demonstration can never be said to be given until comparable words can be shown to be but reflexes of one and the same prototype by the operation of dialectic phonetic laws.

Is there any reason to believe that the process of regular phonetic change is any less applicable to the languages of primitive peoples than to the languages of the more civilized nations? This question must be answered in the negative. Rapidly accumulating evidence shows that this process is just as easily and abundantly illustrated in the languages of the American Indian or of the Negro tribes as in Latin or Greek or

English. If these laws are more difficult to discover in primitive languages, this is not due to any special characteristic which these languages possess but merely to the inadequate technique of some who have tried to study them.

An excellent test case of phonetic law in a group of primitive languages is afforded by the Algonkian linguistic stock of North America. This stock includes a large number of distinct languages which are, however, obviously related in both grammar and vocabulary. Bloomfield has taken four of the more important of the languages that belong to the central division of the stock and has worked out a complete system of vocalic and consonantal phonetic laws. We have selected in Table I five of these phonetic laws in order to give an idea of the nature of the correspondences.

TABLE I

PCA	Fox	Ojibwa	Plains Cree	Menomini
1. tck	hk	ck	sk	tsk
2. ck	ck	ck	sk	sk
3. xk	hk	hk	sk	hk
4. hk	hk	hk	hk	hk
5. nk	g	ng	hk	hk

Table I shows how five different consonantal combinations in which the second element is *k* were respectively developed in Fox, Ojibwa, Plains Cree, and Menomini. The Primitive Central Algonkian prototype (PCA) is, of course, a theoretical reconstruction on the basis of the actual dialectic forms.

Observe that this table does not say that a particular *k* combination of one dialect corresponds uniquely to a particular *k* combination of another dialect, but merely that certain definite dialectic correspondences are found which lead to such reconstructive inferences as are symbolized in the first column of the table. Thus, the Plains Cree *sk* does not always correspond to the Fox *hk* but may just as well correspond to the Fox *ck*.[3] The Cree *sk* that corresponds to the Fox *hk*, however, is obviously not the same original sound as the Cree *sk* which corresponds to the Fox *ck*, as is indicated by the fact that in Menomini the former corresponds partly to *tsk*, partly to *hk*, while the latter regularly corresponds to *sk*. None of the four dialects exactly reflects the old phonetic pattern, which must be constructed from series of dialectic correspondences.

[3] *C* indicates the sound of *sh* in *ship*; *tc* indicates the sound of *ch* in *chip*; *x* indicates the sound of German *ch* in *ach*.

The methodology of this table is precisely the same as the methodology which is used in Indo-European linguistics. The modern German *ei* of *mein* corresponds to the diphthong *i* of English *mine*, but it does not follow that every modern German *ei* corresponds to the English diphthong. As a matter of fact, a large number of German words with *ei* have English correspondents in *o*, as in *home*. Thus, while *mine* corresponds to German *mein*, *thine* to German *dein*, and *wine* to German *Wein*, the English *home* corresponds to German *Heim, soap* to German *Seife*, and

TABLE II

PCA	Fox	Ojibwa	Plains Cree	Menomini
1. *-alakatckw-* . "palate"	....	-inagacku-	-ayakask	-inākatsku-
ketckyäwa .. "he is old"	kehkyäwa	....	....	kotskīw
2. *ickutäwi* ... "fire"	ackutäwi	ickudä	iskutäw	iskōtäw
3. *maxkesini* ... "moccasin"	mahkasähi (dim. form)	mahkizin	maskisin	mahkäsin
4. *nōhkuma* ...	nohkuma "my mother-in-law"	nōhkumis	nōhkum	nōhkumeh
nohkumehsa "my grandmother"	nohkumesa "my grandmother"			
5. *tankeckawäwa* "he kicks him"	tageckawäwa	tangickawād	tahkiskawäw	tahkäskawew

loaf (of bread) to German *Laib*. We have to conclude that the modern German *ei* represents two historically distinct sounds. In this particular case we have the documentary evidence with which to check up a necessary or, at least, a highly plausible inference. The type illustrated by English *mine* :: German *mein* corresponds to Old High German *ī* and Anglo-Saxon *ī*, while the type illustrated by English *home* :: German *Heim* corresponds to Old High German *ei* and Anglo-Saxon *ā*. We can briefly summarize all the relevant facts by saying that Early Germanic *ī* has become a diphthong in Modern English and a practically identical diphthong in modern German, while an Early Germanic sound which we may reconstruct as *ai* (cf. Gothic *ai* in such words as *haims*, "home") has developed to *ā* in Anglo-Saxon, whence modern English *ō*, and *ei* in Old High German, whence the diphthong in modern German. The important thing to observe about the English and the German examples is that even in the absence of historical evidence it would have been possible

TABLE III

PCA	Fox	Ojibwa	Plains Cree	Menomini
1. tcp	?	hp	?	tsp
2. cp	hp	cp	sp	sp
3. xp	hp	hp	sp	hp
4. hp	hp	hp	hp	hp
5. mp	p	mb	hp	hp

to infer the existence in Early Germanic of two distinct sounds from the nature of the correspondences in English and German.

Table II gives examples of actual words illustrating the five phonetic laws in question. The examples given are not isolated examples but are,

TABLE IV

PCA	Fox	Ojibwa	Plains Cree	Menomini
5. *meçkusiwa* . "he is red"	*meckusiwa*	*mickuzi*	*mihkusiw*	*(mehkōn)* ·

for the most part, representative of whole classes. The true generality of the phonetic laws illustrated in Table I goes even farther than there indicated, as is shown by the set of correspondences in Table III.

TABLE V

PCA	Fox	Ojibwa	Plains Cree	Menomini
6. çk	ck	ck	hk	hk

It will be observed that in this table *p* takes the place, for the most part, of *k* of Table II.

Bloomfield found, however, that there was one Algonkian stem evidently involving a *k* combination which did not correspond to any of the five series given above. This is the stem for "red" illustrated in Table IV.

For this series of correspondences Bloomfield has constructed a sixth phonetic law, which is expressed in Table V. It should be understood that the symbol ç is not a phonetic symbol in the ordinary sense of the word. It is merely a formula or tag which is intended to hold down a place, as it were, in a pattern. It may represent a sound similar to the *ch* of the German *ich*, or it may represent some other sound or combination of sounds. Its chief purpose is to warn us that the *ck* or *hk* of the Central Algonkian dialects is not to be historically equated with other examples of *ck* or *hk* in these dialects.

The justification for setting up a special phonetic law on the basis of one set of correspondences is given by Bloomfield himself. He says, "Since there appeared to be no point of contact for analogic substitution of *hk* for *ck*, or vice versa, in any of the languages, and since borrowing of the stem for *red* seemed unlikely, it was necessary to suppose that the parent speech had in this stem for *red* a different phonetic unit."

Sometimes one is in a position to check up a phonetic reconstruction such as is implied in the use of the symbol *çk*. A related dialect may turn up in which the theoretical phonetic prototype is represented by a distinctive sound or sound combination. As a matter of fact, exactly this proved to be the case for Central Algonkian. Some time after Bloomfield set up the sixth phonetic law, he had the opportunity to study the Swampy Cree dialect of Manitoba. Interestingly enough, this Cree dialect had the consonant combination *htk* in forms based on the stem for "red," e.g., *mihtkusiw*, "he is red"; and in no other stem did this combination of sounds occur. In other words, the added evidence obtained from this dialect entirely justified the isolation for Primitive Central Algonkian of a particular phonetic-sound group, symbolized by *çk*. The setting-up of phonetic law No. 6 was, by implication, a theoretically possible prediction of a distinct and discoverable phonetic pattern. The prediction was based essentially on the assumption of the regularity of sound changes in language.

Bloomfield's experience with the Central Algonkian dialects is entirely parallel to my own with the Athabaskan languages. These constitute an important linguistic stock which is irregularly distributed in North America. The northern group occupies a vast territory stretching all the way from near the west coast of Hudson Bay west into the interior of Alaska. To it belong such languages as Anvik (in Alaska), Carrier (in British Columbia), Chipewyan, Hare, Loucheux, Kutchin, Beaver, and Sarcee. We shall take Chipewyan and Sarcee as representatives of this group. The geographically isolated Pacific division of Athabaskan consists of a number of languages in southwestern Oregon and northwestern California. We shall take Hupa as representative. The southern division of Athabaskan is in New Mexico and Arizona and adjoining regions, and is represented by Navaho, Apache, and Lipan. We shall take Navaho as representative of the group. In spite of the tremendous geographical distances that separate the Athabaskan languages from each other, it is perfectly possible to set up definite phonetic laws which connect them according to consistent phonetic patterns. Navaho, Hupa, and Chipewyan are spoken by Indians who belong to entirely distinct culture horizons, yet the languages themselves are as easily derivable from a common source on the basis of regular phonetic law as are German, Dutch, and Swedish.

TABLE VI

Ath.	Hupa	Chipewyan	Navaho	Sarcee
I. 1. s	s	θ	s	s
2. z	s	δ	z	z
3. dz	dz	dδ	dz	dz
4. ts	ts	tθ	ts	ts
5. ts	ts'	tθ'	ts'	ts'
II. 1. c	W	s	c	s
2. j	W	z	j	z
3. dj	dj	dz	dj	dz
4. tc	tcw	ts	tc	ts
5. tc'	tc'	ts'	tc'	ts'
III. 1. x	W	c	s	c
2. y	y	y	y	y
3. gy	gy	dj	dz	dj
4. ky	ky	tc	ts	tc
5. ky'	ky'	tc'	ts'	tc'

Table VI shows the distribution in Hupa, Chipewyan, Navaho, and Sarcee of three initial consonantal sets, each of which consists of five consonants. In other words, the table summarizes the developments of fifteen originally distinct Athabaskan initial consonants in four selected dialects. Each of the entries must be considered as a summary statement applying to a whole class of examples.[4]

The table merits study because of its many implications. It will be observed that no one dialect exactly reproduces the reconstructed Athabaskan forms given in the first column. Series I is preserved intact in Navaho and Sarcee and very nearly so in Hupa, but has been shifted to

[4] The apostrophe symbolizes a peculiar type of consonantal articulation, characterized by simultaneous closure of the glottis and point of contact in the mouth, with glottal release preceding oral release. *J* is the French *j* of *jour*; *dj* is the *j* of English *just*; *x* is the *ch* of German *ich*; *W* is approximately the *wh* of English *what*; θ is the *th* of English *thick*; δ is the *th* of English *then*.

another series in Chipewyan. Series II is preserved intact in Navaho, but has been shifted in Sarcee to identity with the series that corresponds to original I, while Hupa has introduced several peculiar dialectic developments and Chipewyan has shifted it to the original form of I. Series III is nowhere kept entirely intact but nearly so in Hupa, while in Chipewyan and in Sarcee it has moved to the original form of Series II, in Navaho to a form which is identical with the original and the Navaho form of Series I. It is clear from the table that a Sarcee *s* is ambiguous as to origin, for it may go back either to Athabaskan *s* or Athabaskan *c*. On the other hand, a Sarcee *s* which is supported by either Navaho or Hupa *s* must be the representative of an original Athabaskan *s*. Sarcee *tc* is, in the main, unambiguous as to origin, for it corresponds to the original Athabaskan *ky*. It is curious and instructive to note that, of the four

TABLE VII

Ath.	Hupa	Chipewyan†	Navaho†	Sarcee†
*kyan .... "rain"	....	*tcq*	*n-l-tsq* "there's a rainfall"	*tcq*

† *q* represents nasalized *a*, as in French *an*. Sarcee *q* is a peculiar *a* with velar resonance, regularly developed from Athabaskan *a*.

languages given in the table, Hupa and Chipewyan are the two that most nearly correspond as to *pattern* but never as to actual *sound* except in the one instance of *y* (III, 2).

Let us take a practical example of prediction on the basis of the table. If we have a Sarcee form with *tc*, a corresponding Navaho form with *ts*, and a Chipewyan form with *tc*, what ought to be the Hupa correspondent? According to the table it ought to be *ky*.

Table VII shows the distribution in three dialects of the Athabaskan sound *ky* (III, 4) in the word for "rain." When I first constructed the Athabaskan prototype, I assumed an initial *ky*, in spite of the absence of the test form in Hupa, on the basis of the dialectic correspondences. Neither an original *ts* nor *tc* could be assumed in spite of the fact that these sounds were actually illustrated in known dialects, whereas *ky* was not. The Hupa column had to remain empty because the cognate word, if still preserved, was not available in the material that had been recorded by P. E. Goddard.

In the summer of 1927, however, I carried on independent researches on Hupa and secured the form *kyaŋ-kyoh*,[5] meaning "hailstorm." The sec-

⁵ *ŋ* is the *ng* of English *sing*.

ond element of the compound means "big" and the first is obviously the missing Hupa term corresponding to the old Athabaskan word for "rain." In other words, an old compound meaning "rain-big" has taken on the special meaning of "hailstorm" in Hupa. The Hupa form of the old word for "rain" is exactly what it should be according to the correspondences that had been worked out, and the reconstruction of the primitive Athabaskan form on the basis of the existing forms was therefore justified by the event.

Table VIII gives the chief dialectic forms that were available for the reconstruction of the Athabaskan word for "rain." Observe that not one of these has the original sound *ky* which must be assumed as the initial of the word. This is due to the fact that the old Athabaskan *ky* and related sounds shifted in most dialects to sibilants but were preserved in

TABLE VIII
DIALECTIC FORMS FOR "RAIN"

Anvik (Alaska)	*tcɔN**
Carrier (B.C.)	*tcan*
Chipewyan	*tcą*
Hare	*tcǫ*
Loucheux	*tcien*
Kutchin	*tscin*
Beaver	*tcǫ*
Sarcee	*tcą*
Navaho	*n-ł-tsą*

* ɔ represents open *o*, as in German *voll;* ǫ is nasalized *o*. *N* is voiceless *n*.

Hupa and a small number of other dialects, some of which are spoken at a great remove from Hupa. In other words, in working out linguistic reconstructions we must be guided not merely by the overt statistical evidence but by the way in which the available material is patterned.

For those interested in a summary statement of the concepts and assumptions involved in the foregoing, the following quotations from Bloomfield's "A Set of Postulates for the Science of Language " may prove of interest:

Def.—A minimum same of vocal feature is a *phoneme* or *distinctive sound.*

Assumption.—The number of different phonemes in a language is a small sub-multiple of the number of forms.

Assumption.—Every form is made up wholly of phonemes. . . . . Such a thing as a "small difference of sound" does not exist in a language.

Assumption.—The number of orders of phonemes in the morphemes (i.e., "minimum forms") and words of a language is a sub-multiple of the number of possible orders.

Assumption.—Every language changes at a rate which leaves contemporary persons free to communicate without disturbance.

Assumption.—Among persons, linguistic change is uniform in ratio with the amount of communication between them.

Assumption.—Phonemes or classes of phonemes may gradually change.

Def.—Such change is *sound-change.*

Assumption.—Sound-change may affect phonemes or classes of phonemes in the environment of certain other phonemes or classes of phonemes.

Def.—This change is *conditioned sound-change.*

At the end of "A Note on Sound-Change," in which the Swampy Cree forms in *htk* are discussed, Bloomfield remarks:

The postulate of sound-change without exceptions will probably always remain a mere assumption, since the other types of linguistic change (analogic change, borrowing) are bound to affect all our data. As an assumption, however, this postulate yields, as a matter of mere routine, predictions which otherwise would be impossible. In other words, the statement that *phonemes change* (sound-changes have no exceptions) is a tested hypothesis: in so far as one may speak of such a thing, it is a proved truth.

It may be pointed out in conclusion that the value to social science of such comparative study of languages as is illustrated in the present paper is that it emphasizes the extraordinary persistence in certain cases of complex *patterns* of cultural behavior regardless of the extreme variability of the content of such patterns. It is in virtue of pattern conservatism that it is often possible to foretell the exact form of a specific cultural phenomenon.[6]

[6] [This analysis was first written in December, 1928, and revised by the analyst in February, 1929.—EDITOR.]

ANALYSIS 22

THE PREDICTION OF CULTURAL CHANGE: A PROBLEM ILLUS-
TRATED IN STUDIES BY F. STUART CHAPIN
AND A. L. KROEBER[1]

By FLOYD H. ALLPORT and DALE A. HARTMAN

Syracuse University[2]

I. INTRODUCTORY METHODOLOGICAL STATEMENT

One of the most interesting developments of the recent anthropological school in sociology has been the consideration of culture as an independent object of scientific investigation. To the anthropologist the culture of a human tribe or nation seems to be an intrinsically interesting phenomenon. In both its material and immaterial aspects it has been studied as more or less independent of the biological nature of man, and even of his innate psychological equipment. Material inventions, fashions, and institutions appear to some to follow an order of development or recurrence so definite as to give rise to the belief in natural laws on the purely cultural or superorganic level. Closely following this conclusion comes the corollary that prediction of the rate, levels of development, and rhythmic changes in culture is a possibility. The curve of culture phenomena being known, it may be possible to predict changes in invention, fashion, and institutions with some degree of reliability.

It is the purpose of this paper to examine the general merits of this cultural argument, and in particular to analyze the claims which have been made for cultural prediction in the two recent and interesting investigations by Professors Chapin and Kroeber, cited in footnote 1. Though differing in their conceptions of cultural units and types of index, these two researches are alike in their hypothesis of an orderly and predictable sequence in culture. In its essentials this represents an attempt to import into the somewhat intangible field of culture, material and immaterial, the concepts, techniques, and principles employed in the natural sciences. It will make our task easier if we begin not with a direct analysis of the

[1] F. Stuart Chapin, *Cultural Change* (New York: Century Co., 1928); A. L. Kroeber, "On the Principle of Order in Civilization as Exemplified by Changes of Fashion," *American Anthropologist*, N.S., XXI, No. 3 (July–September, 1919), 235–63. Acknowledgments are made in a footnote at the end of this analysis.

[2] [Mr. Hartman was at Syracuse University when the present analysis was written.—EDITOR.]

researches cited, but with a formulation of the various possible methodological approaches to cultural phenomena.

There are four principal ways in which objects of common experience (including cultural objects) may be approached. These ways of approach represent not so much the ultimate character of the objects as our attitudes toward them. Indeed, the foundation of any method of investigation, it seems to the analysts, lies in the way in which the investigator looks at his world. The four ways of approaching experience here referred to are as follows: (*a*) *the natural-science approach,* (*b*) *the genetic-explanatory approach,* (*c*) *the telic approach, and* (*d*) *the stylistic approach.* Our first task is the description of these various approaches and the consideration of their logical interrelations, limitations, and possibities.

a) THE NATURAL-SCIENCE APPROACH

By this we refer only to a specific kind of attitude and procedure which seems to have been present in the making of significant scientific discoveries. That is, the attitude of looking at, or into, phenomena in such a way as to see *what is there* and to discover *invariable sequences* between one identifiable happening and another. Such sequences as are found always to occur under uniform conditions are known as natural-science generalizations, or "laws."[3]

The examination of material in order to discover its composition and laws involves two corollaries as requisites of method. The first is that of an *analytical attitude,* with the reduction of the material into simpler levels; the second is the criterion of *explicit denotation.* We shall describe these in order.

If one follows strictly the approach just described, the environmental objects one confronts will be found to have more than one level of complexity. A behavior psychologist, for example, looks at the human organism at first as a whole. He is interested in what people do and say, in other words, in behavior at the integrated, "human" level. If he looks

---

[3] Such laws are merely statements of a high degree of probability that a given phenomenon will recur under the stated conditions. More careful observations usually disclose exceptions; and these exceptions lead to further analysis and the making of altered and more widely applicable generalizations. Scientific laws are in no way forces or agents *causing* the particular phenomena which are said to illustrate or embody them. They are merely summaries of the experience of careful observers. We mean by the "natural-science approach" the *taking of an attitude toward the material studied such as to yield these new generalizations.* The moment such a generalization is secured, if one dwells upon it, or applies it to human purposes, the natural-science attitude, as we have defined it, at once disappears and a different attitude takes its place.

more closely, however, with the purpose of discovering certain general-izations as a basis of understanding or prediction, he begins to see the parts of which the organism is composed, or at least to think in terms of these parts. He begins to interpret behavior through the generaliza-tions which can be given him by the neurologist and the general physi-ologist. The physiologist, in his turn, describes the action of nerve and muscle fibers and then analyzes the cells of which they are composed, either actually or conceptually, into their organic, and finally into their inorganic, components. By the aid of generalizations in the fields of organic chemistry and physics the nerve impulse and the muscle con-traction are interpreted in the simpler and more general terms of chemi-cal dissociation, electrical polarization, and the like. The physical chem-ist, in his turn, peers into such phenomena as electromagnetism and "ether conduction," seeking to identify a still more elementary plane upon which even broader generalizations can be discovered.

Our second corollary, the criterion of *explicit denotation*, is here offered as a condition which must be fulfilled by all objects which are to be approached by the natural-science method. In order to understand this criterion let us recall a distinction made by psychologists between ex-plicit and implicit behavior. Explicit responses consist, for our purpose, of skeletal movements which are capable of manipulating or modifying things in our environment. Implicit responses, on the other hand, consist of abridged skeletal movements, verbal reactions, and postures which we substitute in our thinking process for explicit contacts with objects. The phenomena studied by the natural-science method are characteristically things toward which one can make some sort of explicit reaction. They are stimuli for our responses of denoting, manipulating, measuring, weigh-ing and other discriminatory and graded reactions. There occurs the pos-sibility of some explicit response to a natural object *as a beginning of every natural-science investigation.* Such investigations never begin from purely implicit responses. Something, in other words, always obtrudes itself upon our experience and presents to us a problem for study. Nat-ural-science material is thus more than that which we can see, hear, taste, touch, or smell. There is also the possibility of altering and refining our impressions from it. This means, in the last analysis, that we can obtain from the situation a *kinaesthetic* (or motor) experience arising from our manipulation of the object of study. Connected with explicit denotation is the important factor of verification of our experience by others—a check which guards against hallucination in the sense fields already named and which is made possible only by our capacity for explicitly denoting the phenomena concerned. It is our thesis that entities which can be "encountered" only in a *metaphysical* sense or *by definition,* for example, "immaterial culture," do not satisfy the criterion of explicit denotation, and therefore cannot be approached by analytic reduction to simpler levels and discovery of laws at these various levels.[4]

The significance of the natural-science approach as a possible avenue of prediction deserves special comment. All statements of natural laws are essentially statements not of effective or causal agencies, but of probabilities that, given the same conditions, certain explicitly identifiable changes in the phenomena will follow. Laws, are, in other words, merely statements of the likelihood that an event will happen. They are, therefore, the bases of prediction. Laws are relative in degree. Probably no law as stated by natural scientists is infallible. Those laws which express the higher degrees of probability that an event will occur have the higher predictive value. Predictability, being based upon laws of varying reliability, is therefore also a relative matter. On the whole the laws formulated in such sciences as physics, chemistry, and biology express a fairly high degree of probability and have therefore relatively high predictive value.

b) THE APPROACH OF GENETIC EXPLANATION

The second approach, which is often confused with that of natural-science procedure, is concerned not with experimental analysis and observation, but with tracing the history or genetic development of the phenomenon in question. Take, for example, the mineralogical findings in a given region. The natural-science approach would take a sample of the material and analyze it into its constituents, discovering laws of crystal formation, molecular combination, cohesion, etc., at the various levels. It would make no difference from the standpoint of this approach what had been the history of the specimen or how long a time had been required for its formation. The geneticist would look backward in time, attempting to explain by the use of laws at the various levels the course of events by which the particular mineralogical compositions of the region had come into existence. A large part of historical theory follows this method. Another example, from the field of human behavior, will show that much which passes under the name of psychology belongs to this approach rather than to the natural-science method. From the natural-science view in the study of habits, for example, we should seek

---

[4] For a fuller discussion of the natural-science approach and its various criteria consult an article by Floyd H. Allport entitled " 'Group' and 'Institution' as Concepts in a Natural Science of Social Phenomena," *Papers and Proceedings of the American Sociological Society,* XXII (1927), 83–99.

for laws as mere descriptions of processes which are always found in the changes of neural resistances involved in the learning process. From the genetic approach one would be interested not in the laws of neurological changes involved in all habit formation, but in *what particular habits had been formed*. The interest would be, not in discovering the laws of neurological change, but in applying these laws intellectually to a study of the individual's past so as to account, through a knowledge of environmental stimuli, for the formation of particular traits. We thus see that the entire case-history method in the study of personality, as well as the more academic accounts of the modification of native responses through learning, belong in the field of genetic explanation rather than that of natural-science investigation. The process is essentially one of explanation. It gives us a body of knowledge which is satisfying not because it represents a discovery of laws, but because it seems to combine all known laws into a coherent explanation of the origin and the development of the phenomenon.

Another fact is especially significant here. In the natural-science approach we find continual necessity for caution against accepting scientific laws as statements of efficient causes. In the approach of genetic explanation, however, this caution is forgotten and laws are assumed to involve an inner condition or a necessity in the universe, by virtue of which sequences *are compelled* to occur in a certain way. Since, however, we are forsaking explicit contact with nature in making this assumption, we must remember that the only authority for our interpretation in the genetic approach is its satisfying character, and not its infallible one-to-one correspondence with data that may be explicitly encountered. It therefore follows that we must expect far less reliability in prediction than from the natural-science approach. Furthermore, both historical explanations and predictions must be altered whenever further discoveries reveal more generally valid laws in the natural-science sense.

Turning now to the main question, that of prediction, there can be claimed for the genetic approach in comparison with the natural-science method only an inferior degree of reliability. Suppose that, as explanatory geologists, we are facing a cut of soft material recently made by a running stream. We might predict that this sharp cliff will eventually be eroded to a low bank, and estimate the approximate length of time required for this erosion. The estimate will hold good only providing that a vast array of attendant conditions remain unchanged, and is based upon a knowledge of "how natural laws work." But it may be that through some unforeseen chance some other natural law than the one counted on will be "brought into operation." The continual shifting of conditions, even in a field so stable as that of geology, makes the alteration of phenomena, from the human standpoint at least, an almost fortuitous matter.

If one gives up the goal of tracing the history and foretelling the future of such a complex pattern of phenomena, and takes the natural-science approach, prediction becomes fairly certain. The natural scientist in the narrow sense, would not attempt to predict the fate of a cliff or river valley, but would say, with respect to any specimen of the region, that when erosion or other changes *were* taking place one would always find certain definite molar or molecular processes at work capable of being formulated as precise laws. We have thus quite a reliable prediction with regard to the composition of the substance, as found upon analyses, and the behavior of its parts, but a very limited and unreliable prediction of the future pattern of the whole phenomenon which we have tried to explain by the genetic approach. We may summarize this matter by saying that prediction from the standpoint of the past of a given phenomenon, while not impossible, is relatively unreliable, because of (*a*) the impossibility of counting upon a repetition of the same conditions in the future, and (*b*) the impossibility of predicting the unusual without penetrating, through the natural-science approach, to the more elementary levels.

c) THE TELIC APPROACH

Our third approach to experience is not concerned so much with the phenomenon in itself as with the significance of the phenomenon to the observer. This significance, moreover, does not consist merely in an interest in explaining the phenomenon to our satisfaction, but in its use for some *other purpose* in our life-adjustment. For what are the objects about us useful? Conversely, which objects are useful in fulfilling certain of our needs? These questions express our attitudes. In the telic approach, it is the *implicit* rather than the explicit significance of objects which is important. A knife and a fork have meaning not from the standpoint of an analysis of their substance into its components, with laws at various levels (the natural-science approach), nor yet from the standpoint of explaining the human activities and events through which they were manufactured (genetic approach), but from the standpoint of what one can do with them; in other words, what they imply in human life. For this reason it will be seen that the problem of reduction to simpler levels is wholly irrelevant. Our behavior is upon a single level, if indeed the notion of levels can be applied at all. There is, however, a certain similarity of this approach to that of genetic explanation. Both fulfill some sort of purpose and both are prone to employ natural-science laws as effective causes in the task of prediction. In the telic field one predicts no less than in the natural-science and genetic fields, but the prediction in this case is not made for the purpose of confirming some hypothesis or establishing a law; it is made rather for the purpose of getting some practical basis of decision or action in human affairs. There is no interest in the law or its validity in itself, but only in the use of the law in helping us to choose a course of action which will be most likely to yield us profitable results. It goes without saying, therefore, that the telic approach must rest for its predictive ability upon the formulations made by the natural scientists and can only follow these formulations more or less blindly without itself contributing to the problem of predicting either similarity or change.

From another standpoint, however, there is a peculiar type of prediction inherent in the telic approach. One's purpose may for the time being be regarded as a causal agent in itself. Thus Mussolini on the day before taking over the local governments *(podestàs)* of Italy might have predicted, because it was his will, that by the following evening he would be the dictator of citizens in their community relationships through local governmental machinery. That there is some value in this type of prediction no one will deny. But its limitations are equally clear. An untold number of occurrences may thwart our purpose. It will be noted also that the prediction of what will take place in the future can only be couched in telic (not explicit) terms. It might have been possible fifty years ago, for example, to predict that people in 1930 would travel through the air. This prediction would be based mainly upon the telic approach. For example, we have the desire to be able to fly and we know that modern human ingenuity and determination have overcome an increasing number of obstacles in the past. Our prediction thus is entirely in terms of fulfilling our purpose. It has no relation, however, to the explicit manner in which the purpose may be fulfilled. Thus, while we might have predicted with a certain assurance that we would fly, no one fifty years ago could have predicted just what the modern flying machines would be like. The prediction of an invention in anything more than a bare telic sense is practically impossible. The explicit prediction would be the invention itself and hence its own fulfilment.

It will be noted that as we have passed through three types of approach, we have been getting nearer to that definition of experience connoted by the term *culture*. The natural-science approach, which is mainly explicit and divorces the phenomenon from significance in human life other than an understanding of itself, can have little meaning in the cultural field. It will not do to argue, as some might, that science itself is a part of culture; for this is to shift one's ground so as to destroy the meaning of the natural-science approach, which is a psychological and not an objective cultural phenomenon. A scientific treatise embodying natural-science laws as principles of explanation and utility has, of course, large cultural implications. But the actual taking of an attitude to approach a phenomenon explicitly and analytically, while it may be fostered by custom and practice in various places, does not depend upon a telic or a cultural attitude toward experience. Many persons seem to have a natural-science interest in and for itself.

It is the thesis of the present writers that the telic approach is necessary in order to speak in the same universe of discourse with the cultural anthropologists and sociologists. Without *implicit* denotation and the significance of culture objects or patterns for human life there would be no such thing as culture. But this consideration is equal to an admission that, as one leaves the natural-science approach and enters the field of cultural phenomena, prediction becomes more and more limited and unreliable. One loses that constancy of surrounding conditions which renders the prediction of repetition of similar occurrences a reliable one, and qualitative prediction, or the foretelling of unexpected configurations, becomes extremely difficult (as indeed it is from any approach).

AN ILLUSTRATION OF APPROACHES *a*, *b*, AND *c*

Before proceeding to our fourth approach let us consider a simple illustration which will help to fix in mind the relationships discussed up to this point—the development of the automobile. An automobile may be studied purely as a natural-science object. The physicist, for example, would first study its larger parts under such formulations as the laws of motion and mechanics. He could then descend to the more elementary levels and study the molecular phenomena of cohesion, the laws of gaseous expansion, or the subatomic phenomena of electrical conduction. In this approach it will be observed that the automobile as such disappears. Any other specimens of the same materials in the physicist's laboratory would do as well. On the other hand, the knowledge of the natural-science laws at these various levels is an indispensable aid in inventing automobiles as telic, or cultural, objects. It will be further observed that, whereas the elementary natural-science laws are statements having a high reliability for prediction of the events with which they deal, these events have nothing to do with the automobile as a final product of human ingenuity. They do not enable one to foretell how human beings might adopt and combine these laws in automobile construction. The particular combination of parts making up a modern automobile was in other words, unpredictable before it was actually achieved.

Taking the same automobile from the genetic-explanatory approach, we may study historically the modifications of human behavior which have been involved in producing it. In such a study we should deal with prepotent or instinctive responses as modified by the development of more effective methods of transportation. The automobile becomes an extension of our locomotor behavior. We would deal also with conditioning of various manual responses to different types of materials in construction, and the mechanisms of implicit response used in thinking. We should also find the stimulation of one person by another through language; and one person working with the problem where another left off. There would be expressed, perhaps, habits of a more complex order, such as desire for aesthetic qualities. Our natural-science approach could here be applied to the human organism, and we could descend again to the biochemical processes of the organisms which are involved in learning, thinking, and constructing. Thus at any point, in dealing with the automobile or the human being himself, we may take either the natural-science or the genetic approach. We should be compelled, however, to bear in mind the limitations of the latter approach in the matter of prediction. That is to say, we could never hope to predict accurately just what kind of object would be constructed or what lines its future development would take.

Starting again from the automobile, at any point in its development we may adopt the *telic* approach. Here we proceed not in the backward direction (genetic explanation) but in the forward manner, putting ourselves in place of the man who is trying to invent or perfect the object. As soon as we think in terms of a human purpose to be fulfilled and reflect on how we are to accomplish it, we take an attitude very different from that of the natural scientist or the geneticist. Invention is to be understood only through the telic approach. Without such an approach there would be no invention. This fact marks the difference between invention and scientific discovery. Our sole basis of prediction upon the telic ground is our desire and determination to perfect the invention and our confidence in our ability to do so. Since we have entered the field of objects culturally conceived, we must lose much of the support of prediction of repetition or change which is possible within the natural-science and to some extent within the genetic approach.

d) THE STYLISTIC APPROACH

We have, finally, a fourth approach to experience. It is possible to derive significance from such an object as an automobile without taking either the natural-science or the genetic approach, and still without having as our main interest a utilitarian motive. We may look at the object as something which is aesthetically satisfying, as something which harmonizes with our habits in perceptions of form, proportion, and balance. Our approach to the phenomenon is thus *stylistic*. We may examine the size or proportions of the hood of the automobile, the color, the form of the decorative devices, etc. Such considerations are treated by the anthropologist as a part of culture. They are also related to the telic approach, since our enjoyment of proportion and balance are probably dependent upon the empathic responses of keeping our balance and the like. These phenomena, moreover, may be studied by the method of genetic explanation, since we may try to understand the origin and the development of aesthetic attitudes in human beings in terms of natural-science laws.

It is, however, possible to observe these stylistic phenomena in and for themselves. And this is essentially the approach taken by Professor Kroeber in the study to be considered. His problem is that of measuring and determining the laws (if any exist) of progressive changes in the pattern of stylistic units. For material he has taken the dimension of women's garments as shown in the files of fashion magazines. The central question of Professor Kroeber's research concerns the possibility of prediction from this linear stylistic approach. Let us assume with Professor Kroeber that we can detach the stylistically conceived units from all other human purposes, and from all approach by way of natural-science levels —in short, that we can regard them upon a plane of their own, which he calls the "superorganic." We have to remember here that prediction means simply reliance upon a fixed trend of events learned from past experience. If, therefore, fixed trends can be established in a given stylistic measurement over a long-enough period of time, we might rely upon a continuance of that trend, or upon a reoccurrence if it is cyclical. The proof of this lies entirely in the evidence produced. It should be mentioned, however, that there are some drastic handicaps. Since we have isolated the stylistic measurement from all contact with the rest of nature, it is impossible to use the natural-science laws which are serviceable both to the inventor and to the geneticist. The case must rest entirely upon its own merits. Removing the stylistic sphere from the natural-science levels renders impossible that universal type of prediction based upon discoveries at more elementary levels. Each case must therefore be dealt with by itself. Thus the establishment of a trend or a cycle in the proportions of an automobile-hood design would not prove a similar trend or cycle in the proportions of other decorative features, to say nothing of proving trends in stylistic units derived from other culture objects. If the measurement of a great many of such stylistic units should establish similar trends almost without exception, we might predict with fair probability that the next stylistic unit measured would show the same trend. But the proof of this must lie entirely in the data themselves. We cannot assume it from the existence of universal laws derived from the explicit and analytical methods of the natural-science approach; for that approach is in a different world from the superorganic reality of stylistic units.

In summary, we may say that any object may be viewed from the standpoint of (a) natural science, (b) genetic explanation, (c) telesis, and (d) style. Only in the last three approaches, however, can it be understood as a culture object. It must be remembered that the preceding analysis is a priori, and wholly tentative. From a purely logical standpoint, however, we are led to wonder whether we may really attain in cultural phenomena an order of prediction similar to that in the natural-science approach. We are justified in at least questioning the assumption that the grounds of scientific prediction must exist in the world of cultural phenomena. Let us pass on, however, to our analysis of the investigations of Professor Chapin and Professor Kroeber.

II.   CHAPIN'S INVESTIGATION OF THE NATURE OF CULTURAL CHANGE

A.   SUMMARY OF CHAPIN'S RESEARCH

The author deals with the origin, the development, and the modification of human culture, in a treatise, descriptive in character, which contains formulations concerning societal patterns, institutions, and the background of inventions.[5] With the aid of such documents as legislative records, university catalogues, minutes, municipal records, and patent-office registers, the author seeks to plot temporal or spatial successions in the development or spread of inventions, and thereby establish, if possible, laws describing the growth of cultural phenomena. For instance (chap. viii), curricular changes in a college and poor-relief legislation go through three phases, according to the author's qualitative analysis. There is first the formal and inelastic enforcement of existing mores which begin to come into conflict with requirements of a changing order.

[5] F. Stuart Chapin, *op. cit.*

This leads to the second phase, which consists of a mass of special and unco-ordinated legislation based upon trial and error. There finally evolves the third stage, one of consolidation, in which the problem is solved for the time being and successful group practices are achieved. In time, however, general social conditions again change, and the cycle begins anew. This three-stage "societal reaction pattern" is evidently put forth as a tentative hypothesis, with the implication that it may be found to exist as a general pattern throughout all phases of cultural change. The cycle is regarded as dependent upon a learning process, having its analogue in habit formation in an animal organism.

Invention is viewed as the process of putting together certain previously existing elements of culture, involving known scientific laws, for the production of a new complex or cultural integration to satisfy some human purpose. It therefore depends upon the previous development of the necessary parts. In other words, all inventions have a cultural threshold which may be analyzed into the state of readiness of each of the parts to be brought into the complex. This principle is well illustrated by the dates of development of different parts of the automobile. The same analysis applies to institutional inventions, such as the commission plan of government, in which the various parts were developed at different times and places previous to their final integration.

For our purpose the most important part of Chapin's research is contained in chapter xii, "The Growth of Social Institutions by the Accumulation of Culture Traits." Here the treatment is quantitative and definite, and tentative laws with predictive possibilities are stated. In general, the plan is to trace the development of a given invention, noting year by year the number of improvements or subsidiary inventions added until it reaches a point of stability where no further additions or changes are made. Thus, S. Simon Kuznet's data upon the number of patents issued in successive four-year periods between 1855 and 1923 in connection with the plow sulky are plotted in a "frequency cycle curve." It resembles the curve of normal or probable distribution, starting at a low point and increasing in number of inventions up to the year 1884 when the number begins to decline gradually, coming to a minimum in 1923. Chapin prefers, in the case of such data, to plot the *cumulative frequency* of the subsidiary inventions. "When we have done this," he says, "we have a curve showing changes in the rate of growth of the *fundamental invention* during its life cycle" (italics by analyst). He conceives of the fundamental invention growing slowly at first, then taking a spurt and ascending rapidly until it begins to taper off and reach a point of stability. A purely generalized diagram of the types of curves revealed is shown in Figure 1.

Passing now to the field of social institutions, Chapin analyzes Upson's data on the growth of the varied activities and functions of the government of the city of Detroit since its organization in 1824. After taking account of various criticisms and taking necessary precautions, hinging upon the identification and definition of the units employed, the author concludes that "in any event, the structure of the institution grew." The growth curve, when plotted, is similar in the first and the middle portion

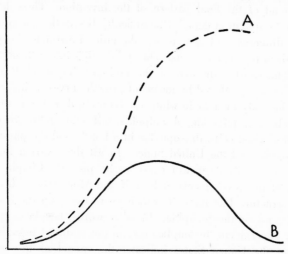

Fig. 1.—Generalized types of curves illustrating Professor Chapin's conception of the growth of a fundamental invention. A = Cumulative, B = Frequency.

to that which represents inventions in connection with the plow sulky. It does not show an analogous decrease at the upper end, however, which may or may not indicate that the institution has not yet reached the corresponding period of development. The functions of administrative units of the state government of Minnesota from the period 1858 to 1923 provided further illustrations. It was found that if subgroups, or administrative units of government, were studied separately, each taken by itself would follow the first phase of the growth curve representing all items added together.

Turning his attention to the growth of the commission form of government, the author adopts a radically different method of treating temporal change. Instead of plotting the accretions of subsidiary inventions, he derives a curve based upon the number of towns or cities adopting the commission form of government each year between 1901 and 1923; in other words, upon the rapidity with which, year by year, the idea was adopted. A similar study was made of the number of cities adopting the city-manager plan. The frequency cycle and growth curves of both these inventions, with respect to their spread by number of cities adopting them per year, were strikingly similar to those of the purely mechanical invention, the plow sulky.

Chapin is careful to point out that we are dealing in one case with the number of supplemental inventions, and, in the other, with the geographic spread of the final pattern of the invention. These latter data, he says, are "population data." One difficulty lies in the question whether or not the differences of size among the cities invalidate the procedure of adding them together as units. The author goes into a theoretical comparison of his work with that of the biologist Raymond Pearl. Pearl has described and predicted by means of growth curves such varied populations as the body of a male white rat (conceived as the multiplication of body cells), a pumpkin, a tadpole's tail undergoing regeneration, a collection of yeast cells, drosophylae in a bottle, and the populations of France, Sweden, and the United States. In all these varied forms Pearl found the same sort of growth curve to be present. Chapin compares the growth of the governments of Detroit and Minnesota with that of an integrated structure like the cells which go to make up the body weight of the white rat or the pumpkin. In other words, he places the institution of city government, by implication, in the realm of organisms.

A map of the United States indicates the spread of the commission plan from Galveston over the entire country from 1900 by intervals of six years. The year of greatest numerical gain in adopting the plan (1913) is also the year of greatest geographical spread of the institution.

Our three graphic methods of description, the frequency cycle curve, the growth curve, and the plot of diffusion, merely express in quantitative form the conclusion to which political scientists have come into respect to these new political institutions, namely, that they have both passed the crest of their popularity and are on the wane.[6]

The author's tables also show a number of cities abandoning the two plans year by year; and he observes that the experience of abandonment goes through a frequency cycle.

In drawing conclusions from the data just described, Chapin seeks to discover whether such fragmentary results conform to any principle. With commendable caution he refuses to claim a basis of prediction in the curves derived from the meager data so far collected. Moreover:

[6] *Ibid.*, p. 374.

Our quantitative analysis has not disposed of certain difficult problems connected with the homogeneity of the units involved. These problems can only be solved by many studies similar to the present one. If independent verification of our results comes from such future studies, then the trends and laws of growth suggested by this study may be found to be universal principles.[7]

For purpose of "concise description of the phenomena" the author considers the possibility of fitting the curves of his data to mathematical formulas.

Chapin explains the dynamic aspect of the growth of an invention or an institution as follows:

To the original fundamental invention . . . . the attention of many persons with original minds is attracted. The result is that many efforts are made to improve upon the original pattern. These efforts bring about an increasing flood of supplemental inventions and modifications in the fundamental pattern. . . . . But since the fundamental invention was designed to serve a specific function, it is clear that in time the original pattern will by increment and modification attain a point of relatively perfect adaptation in meeting the situation for which it was designed. Thereafter the number of increments or supplemental inventions will diminish.[8]

Recalling his previous description of the societal reaction pattern, Chapin points out that the cumulative growth curve of the institution or invention is closely similar in principle. The period of slow growth at the beginning of the invention corresponds to the first phase of the societal reaction pattern in which the existing mores were enforced and few innovations attempted. The middle period of the reaction pattern, with rapid increase in special legislation, corresponds to the period of rapid rise in number of inventions in the cumulative growth curve. Finally, the period of general laws and consolidated and simplified structure of the reaction pattern corresponds to the period of diminished growth in the cumulative curve of inventions. Both these cycles begin again when social conditions change and new requirements produce a strain upon the existing mores or the existing level of the invention. Thus the "growth of institutions is not steady, but occurs in waves or pulsations."

The author has an interest in the apparent cyclical occurrence of cultural phenomena which are broader in character than the special examples hitherto cited. He describes alleged cycles of social change belonging to a number of different orders of time and distribution. Cycles of the first order relate to material culture. They may be illustrated by the business cycle, the displacement of one machine in industry by another,

[7] *Ibid.*, p. 376. [8] *Ibid.*, p. 382.

or the invention of a process of manufacturing. They include also larger phenomena, such as the rise and the fall of the slave system in Rome, or the rise of industrial capitalism in Europe. Cycles of the second order relate to non-material culture. They are illustrated by the rise and the fall of religious sects, the adoption of a commission form of city government, the patriarchal family, or the monarchical form of government. Cycles of the third order relate to larger cultural composites such as national cultures of civilizations. Within the span of the larger cultures of the third order, there occur numerous overlapping cycles of the first and the second order. These separate minor cycles may be spread over the various phases of the greater cycle or may be entirely completed within a single phase of the greater cycle.

The author suggests certain a priori assumptions in order to pass to a working hypothesis.

(1) It may be postulated that every cultural form (whether it be a manufacturing machine, a tool, a paleolithic implement, the commission form of government, a Family Welfare Association, a cultural nation, a fraternal order, a social club, hobble skirts, and so on) has its own law of change, with the qualification that for certain classes of social phenomena there may be some basic and common law of change. (2) The law of each cultural form is probably cyclical and may be periodic. (3) It is possible to discover and express quantitatively (perhaps in mathematical formula) the law of its life cycle or periodic function. (4) When the cycles or periods of a number (majority?) of cultural forms of the first and second order are synchronous, we have the era of maturity of the cultural nation or group in which these cultural traits are found.[9]

In his speculations upon a law of cyclical recurrence which may be characteristic of cultural forms as such, Chapin's work is similar to that of Kroeber, who likewise prefaces his factual research by allusions to a wide variety of cycles of a more general sort. Both authors would probably recognize upon analysis certain fundamental differences between these various types of cycle, but neither has taken special pains to discover the nature of these differences. It may be said that throughout his study Chapin has advanced his formulations not as established laws, but merely as tentative statements which may prove serviceable in guiding future research.

B.   DISCUSSION OF CHAPIN'S INVESTIGATION

I.   CULTURAL UNITS IN RELATION TO METHODOLOGICAL CONSIDERATIONS

We may ask whether the cultural data used by Chapin satisfy the criteria for a natural-science approach. It will be observed at once that

[9] *Ibid.*, pp. 210–11.

material inventions and institutions are very different, in that the former can be approached as natural-science objects while institutions cannot. But even material inventions, when approached from the natural-science standpoint, lose their significance as culture objects. A natural-science view of these objects would reveal only the laws at the different levels which are operating in the perfected and working invention. It would not show the significance of the reciprocal action of the various parts for human uses, nor would it explain genetically how the given complex of mechanical features came to be assembled. One could not, in the natural-science view, react to the invention telically, or understand it as an object of culture. There would be, as we have seen, no satisfactory ground for prediction as to what the next modification or the final form of the invention might be. Such prediction, or prediction of new natural-science laws discovered and applied to the invention, would be equivalent to the discovery itself.

The concept of institutions as an entity to be studied empirically further violates a criterion of the natural-science method. We cannot measure that to which we cannot react, and we are not able to react to an institution explicitly. An enumeration of practices of individuals in city government which by definition comprise parts of an "institution" is really a type of measurement very different from that familiar in natural science. Such enumeration does not consist in counting similar units in the magnitude of something which we encounter. It consists, rather, in counting *implicit* and *differing* elements which seem to belong together in that they work together to serve some ulterior human purpose. The result is the measurement (if it can be called measurement) of something established rather by logical definition than by explicit denotation. It seems, therefore, that the notion of establishing laws dealing with such subjective elements of culture as city governments is quite foreign to the discovery of laws by the natural-science approach, where the attitude is one of explicit analysis rather than telic adaptation of groups of elements to human needs. This fact, of course, does not prove that such cultural laws do not exist. It only means that our confidence in them should not be based upon the prestige and past successes of natural-science methods.

It is to be noted, however, that when Chapin comes to his factual investigation he makes no attempt to predict from his curves the nature of institutions or inventions (i.e., he does not invent in advance), but merely suggests the prediction of certain quantitative features such as the enumeration of subsidiary inventions. He does not attempt to tell what these subsidiary inventions will be, only how many there will be and the ratios of their numbers in the succeeding **years.**

The more general type of alleged cycle is that of a civilization or national culture. One of the main problems is that of definition or identification of the phenomena. When we speak of the rise, the culmination, and the fall of the Roman Empire, what is it that is really rising, culminating, and declining? Suppose that we say it is the power of Roman consuls or emperor; that is, the number of people subject to such power and the extent to which they allow the command of the ruler to dominate their lives through institutional channels. In this case we are not measuring the power of any explicitly denotable continuing thing, but only the number of people who year by year are subservient to a man who is addressed as *imperator,* and the degree of their subservience in successive years. The *imperator* himself, of course, may change. Historians and sociologists have read into the situation a continuing entity known as the "Roman Empire" proceeding in a cycle form, through rise, culmination, and fall, from nonexistence to nonexistence. Translated, therefore, into explicit language, it will be seen that we are measuring the number and intensity of attitudes in response to symbolic stimuli rather than an institution per se. Though we have dealt here with only one phase of the Empire, namely, allegiance to the emperor, it would be possible to pursue the same method with respect to any element of the "pattern" sufficiently explicit to be measured. We should thus have countings of pluralistic behaviors rather than "measurements" of the "height of a civilization."

When we deal with the pattern of culture rather than with the political dynasty we see the subjective character of the culture object from a new standpoint. We may ask, for example, what we mean by the rise, the culmination, and the decline of the Elizabethan drama or the Hellenic culture. A number of questions arise here which demand empirical investigation. Is there a pattern of traits making up such a period which shows a certain cohesion gradually diminishing as we go outward toward the extremes of the curve, that is, toward the period just preceding and the period just following the era in question? Some objective type of definition and access to data which can be identified and tabulated is obviously required. It may be found, for example, that there is no particular modal point at which all the phenomena of the age of Pericles tend to culminate. They may instead spread themselves over a longer period of Greek history, and yet be identified *in our minds* with the age of Pericles through association with two or three prominent figures who attract our attention. The whole matter needs to be investigated in explicit terms before we postulate a law of universal culture cycles.

There is also a large valuational element present in the identification of culture eras, which makes quantitative treatment difficult. We are especially interested in the writings of Edmund Spenser and William Shakespeare because of their outstanding merit. Around them, at least around Shakespeare, we have, therefore, built up the concept of a literature and drama with its rise and decline. If we took instead some obscure writer halfway between Shakespeare and Spenser, we might perhaps find that he also was the center of a certain pattern, the cohesion of whose elements diminished as we proceeded forward or backward in time. In any event we are dealing in these great civilizational complexes with a vast array of factors whose correlations we only assume and which lend themselves to actual investigation much less readily than a single mechanical invention, a governmental charter, or the width of the skirt. It would seem wise, therefore, to omit speculation upon cycles of this character, which involves elements that are so subjective in nature, as a preface to the study of phenomena affording some measure of explicit denotation. By omitting these references we shall tend to keep our approach inductive rather than deductive.

III. OF WHAT KIND OF DATA ARE CHAPIN'S CURVES CONSTRUCTED?

Perhaps the chief difficulty in the interpretation arises from regarding a mechanical invention or an institution as a unitary thing. It is true that it is a single thing from the standpoint of name and juxtaposition of parts. That is, all the parts are said to be *in* the plow sulky and all the functions of city government adhere in a group of officers working in proximity. More strictly conceived, however, we have from the telic standpoint not *one* thing but a number of things.

In the case of the automobile, for example, the bare purpose of transportation was achieved in the first crude productions. As time went on other needs were felt. Danger to human life and increased traffic demanded improvement in safety devices such as brakes, steering gear, and horns. Thus was added to the purpose of transportation the further purposes of safety for driver and others. The purpose of thrift entered the situation and devices were created to increase economy in the consumption of fuel, oil, and electric current. The demand for physical comfort while driving led to improvements of the body and springs. Eventually there emerged the purpose of aesthetic expression giving rise to improvement of design, shape, and ornament. Finally, there is the purpose of display for raising social status. It is to be noted that these various purposes did not play rôles of equivalent importance, and that they appeared in the guise of subsidiary inventions during the course of time.

From this standpoint we would change Chapin's formulation. For the concept of a single basic invention growing to the highest degree of perfection we would substitute the concept of a finite number of purposes gradually being realized in connection with a complex culture object. An automobile from a purely telic standpoint is not a single thing, but a *number of things* which, however, can all be propelled, directed, and stopped at the same time and at the will of a single driver. Moreover, it is by the telic approach that the automobile can be understood as an automobile. Hence it seems preferable to accept the telic view rather than the natural-science view, for from the latter we have merely a pile of steel, wood, and leather.

We believe that the multiple-purpose view that we have been developing would help us to interpret the upper portion of the author's cumulative growth curve. Since the number of purposes which can be satisfied in connection with any one telic object is limited, we find a gradual diminution of these purposes as they are satisfied one by one. Finally, none is left which is possible of satisfaction in connection with the integration of that object. In other words, the pattern of elements in the object would have to be changed radically in order to admit of the satisfaction of any further purposes. An example of such change would be the transition from automobile to aeroplane. At this point we would naturally expect the cumulative curve to flatten out.[10]

These considerations throw important light upon the problem of prediction and show why prediction of the content of inventions is such a doubtful matter. We can never tell beforehand just how many values or purposes will be brought to bear upon an invention, or what its possibilities for human satisfaction may be. One stage of the invention complex may reveal the potential satisfaction of an entirely different set of purposes from the preceding stage. An example of this is the variety of uses to which radio may now be put and the devices both mechanical and institutional for securing the maximum enjoyment of these satisfactions. The reason for the appearance of prediction which accompanied the construc-

[10] In comparison with the automobile we might mention a pair of scissors as an example of a culture object showing little possibility of satisfaction of other purposes than the one for which the object was originally invented. Aside from the aesthetic purpose of embellishment it seems that there are few other purposes capable of satisfaction through this object. Hence we find relatively little change or subsidiary invention with regard to scissors in the course of many generations.

tion of the Liberty motor lies perhaps in the fact that all the purposes for which it was to be used were known and stated in advance. It was built, in other words, according to strict specifications. It was also built in a period when the perfection of motors was probably reaching the culmination of the curve.

IV. THE NATURE OF UNITS IN CHAPIN'S CURVES

The addition of successive subsidiary inventions involved in the growth of mechanical inventions or institutions raises one of the most debatable questions in Chapin's study. In referring to his analysis of the growth of a political institution, the author himself says: "We have added together such varied functions and administrative units as garbage collection, zoo, band concerts, wire inspector, forestry, ferries, continuation schools, and so on."[11] While conscious of the questionable nature of such additions, Chapin attempts to show that the procedure is justifiable. First, the number of increments added together is relatively large (549 in the case of the plow sulky) and in the aggregate the errors will cancel one another; second, the total is broken up (in the case of the city government of Detroit) into subgroups of relatively homogeneous units which follow the same law of growth.

It is also contended that the functions of new administrative units are woven into the texture of the old structure; for example, "Electrical inspectors help diminish fire hazard and indirectly affect the functioning of the fire department." Thus, "The concept of homogeneous units, equal and interchangeable, is seen to be over-mechanical and unsuited to the analysis of such a psycho-cultural organism as a political institution."[12] It is inferred further that the difficulty growing out of the heterogeneity of the units added together in the growth curves is partly more apparent than real. These units are to be thought of as extensions and elaborations of functions already potential in the expanding structure. The institutional situation is compared with growth in a living organism, since the latter is composed of different types of cells growing at different rates, but nevertheless expands and elaborates as an organism in accordance with the growth curve.

Chapin's contention concerning the large number of cases and the possible cancellation of errors does not meet the essential difficulty. The real problem lies in the impossibility of adding together heterogeneous units. One may *count* successive additions to the manufactured plow sulky of theless expands and elaborates as an organism in accordance with the blade, the character of the seat, etc., but one can hardly add these units

[11] *Cultural Change*, p. 364.   [12] *Ibid.*, p. 380.

in a quantitative sense unless one can find a common denominator to which they can all be reduced. Chapin seems to imply that the common denominator is the fact that they somehow participate in the entity known as the plow sulky. It would be very difficult, however, to point out what the essence of the plow sulky is, aside from the integration of its various mechanical parts. Likewise, if one abstracted from a city government the functions of mayor, aldermen, and all the bureaus, one might ask what would be left as a common denominator or as the essence of the government itself in which each of the bureaus participated.

It would seem that the common denominator really exists only in the verbal habit of speaking of all of the parts as making up the complex known as the "plow sulky" and all of the bureaus as making up what is known as "city government." Moreover, by the continued use of these parts or bureaus certain human purposes can be satisfied at the same time. It is impossible to state a telic concept of this type in quantitative terms. The chief difficulty, therefore, is that the notion of increments of growth appears to be a figurative concept which cannot be explicitly denoted. It is not the discrepancy in size which prevents the additive relation among these increments so much as the impossibility of reducing them to a homogeneous character. If one were "measuring" a complex group of apples and pears, it would not do to use apples and pears as units; nor could we say that the variations were such that in the long run large apples would correct for small pears and vice versa. One might, however, reduce them to a common denominator in terms of weight and add the units of weight contributed by each piece of fruit regardless of its species.

This is what Pearl did in plotting his growth curves of body weights. He ignored all differences between cells except their weight, since this was a function which could be determined in quantitative terms. Following this reasoning, Chapin has ignored all distinctive features of the subsidiary inventions, basing his conception of their totality on the consideration that they are all parts of, or partake of the nature of, the invention or the institution. It is not possible, however, to measure this "partaking" factor by itself as one would measure the weight of cells, because both the institution and the mechanical invention, telically understood, are incapable of explicit denotation. Recourse is thus had to definition. The units are defined as part of a given whole, but the whole itself cannot be explicitly encountered or measured.

It has been pointed out that growing inventions are really multiple rather than single objects. The reason why the units are not homogeneous lies partly in the fact that they are satisfactions of distinct and qualitatively different purposes, which since they are subjective cannot be added. It would have seemed more logical, therefore, had Chapin employed column diagrams rather than continuous curves—particularly curves in cumulative form. Column diagrams would show, in discontinuous form, the number of purposes satisfied at each of the dates given on the horizontal axis. It is true that without a continuous curve it would be less easy to illustrate the growth of a continuous thing—the institution or invention —but the existence of this single thing in any explicit or measurable sense is just what we have been questioning.[13]

In order to reduce units of invention to a common denominator, we might employ the economist's device of reducing them to some set of exchange values. Thus the cost of plowing in successive years might be taken as a fair index of the satisfaction of all purposes except the aesthetic involved in the development and use of the plow sulky. For example, we might calculate the total cost of plowing per acre in the successive years of plow-improvement. We could infer that, other things being equal, the lower this cost, the more fully each purpose (i.e., each aspect of successful plowing) was being satisfied by the use of the plow as perfected in any particular year. A curve constructed from such data would describe directly the

[13] The existence of the institution or invention seems to depend upon our giving it a name or, in short, reacting to the institution or plow as though it *were* a unitary thing. Reacting to it in this manner, however, does not prove its unity in a natural-science sense but only the convenient co-ordination of our behavior. Thus a general issues orders to and commands the "army." From a strictly explicit and measurable standpoint he is issuing orders only to so many thousands of men. It is far more convenient, however, for him to reach them through certain key persons or officers and to call this whole system an army. In this way he needs to issue only one command instead of thousands of commands. The illusion is thus readily established when one takes a telic viewpoint that the army is a single thing. As soon as one approaches from the natural-science standpoint and wishes to find something which is explicit and therefore measurable, the army of course resolves itself into so many discrete units. That which is a unit from a telic approach is therefore a plurality from a natural-science approach.

The same consideration applies to the analogy with Pearl's curves of growth in a country or in a cake of yeast in explaining the spread of the city-manager form of government. In order to make the comparison exact, it would be necessary for us to imagine that Pearl personifies the population with which he deals; or that he considers it as an entity whose measurement consists of the count of the separate individuals. Furthermore, Pearl's conception of population included *all* of *each* of the individuals enumerated. Chapin's notion of the special growth of the institution involves only the particular habits of the city officials and citizens which are directly concerned with government and civic duties.

This last criticism is based upon a criterion of natural-science objects which has been given the name "total inclusion." This concept is more fully explained in an article, " 'Group' and 'Institution,' etc.," *Publications of the American Sociological Society*, XXII (1927), 83–99.

integration of such purposes in the behavior of the individuals using a plow.

Chapin might object to such treatment as purely economic and contend that it leaves out of account the institutions or the cultural problem as such. On the other hand, we might reply that it is a truer measurement of the growth of the cultural object in its telic significance than is the counting of its parts. And it is by means of the telic approach, as we have seen, that culture can be more clearly understood. Material culture, in other words, is as fully implicit as explicit, and a curve representing use and satisfactions would seem to be at least as significant as the adding-up of mechanical details shown in patent-office records.

V. INTERPRETATION OF CHAPIN'S CULTURAL GROWTH CURVES

Two general lines of interpretation of his curves are employed by the author. First, inventions, at least institutional inventions, represent a "process of organic growth and not of mechanical increase."[14] That is, the growth of culture objects, by implication, is considered to be analogous to the growth of organisms studied by Pearl.[15] Second, the "process of cultural change gives body and content to the claim that the cultural process is a learning process."[16] This statement is made directly only in regard to the cycle of the societal-reaction pattern; but the author considers this cycle to be of the same general type as other movements represented by his cumulative growth curves.[17]

In discussing the organic analogy let us consider, first, the manner in which organisms and inventions grow. In organisms all the component organs, with such minor exceptions as the sex gonads, are laid down in their characteristic form and function at birth. Growth subsequent to birth seems to consist mainly of further cell division within the respective organs. This analogy, if strictly applied, would mean that in the plow sulky or the city government *all the component structures* were present and functioning when the original invention appeared, although on a smaller scale or with fewer personnel. It would have been a closer analogy had Chapin compared the growth of the culture product with the development of an embryo in the uterus, *provided* embryonic development follows Pearl's curve of growth. The essential difference between organisms and inventions lies in the fact that organs of the body develop according to known laws, discoverable at the various levels in the natural-science approach, whereas the invention of the parts of an institution or tool depend upon human conditioning, and upon so complex a set of circumstances

[14] *Cultural Change*, pp. 423–24.   [16] *Ibid.*, p. 422.
[15] *Ibid.*, pp. 373–78.   [17] *Ibid.*, pp. 383–84.

(see above, pp. 325–26) that their occurrence is sporadic and very difficult to predict. All natural events take place in accordance with law, but we cannot predict what laws will be "called into play" at particular moments in the process of future human adaptation. Then, too, the parts of an invention do not have the same telic relation to the entire invention which organs have to the organism as a whole. The unity of the invention does not consist of the integration of its parts through the purpose of the invention itself, but through the purpose of a *different being, man;* whereas the reciprocal action of parts in an organism seems, with respect to purpose or function, to be directed solely from the standpoint of the organism itself.

But the organic analogy may be criticized on more general grounds. Either Chapin means that institutions and inventions are on the same natural-science level as biological organisms, that is, they are organisms among other organisms; or he means that they are of a different order of existence, that is, they are *not* organisms but somehow exhibit and are explained by the laws of organic phenomena.

Let us take the latter assumption first. If Chapin is dealing with the approach of natural science, we must suppose that the level with which he works can be resolved by analysis, like all natural-science levels, into units of a more general and simpler order. Thus we would have the invention, the institution, or the societal-reaction pattern standing as a superorganic level with formulations and laws of its own, which by natural-science analysis could be broken up into its constituent parts, human beings or their common forms of behavior. If this is the case, we then have a right to inquire what *are* the formulations and laws stated for the level of the superorganic itself. And these formulations, to be in keeping with the standard of uniqueness shown at each of the other natural-science levels, must be drawn in novel terms and not borrowed from the biological, the chemical, or the physical realm. What we find, however, is that the author has borrowed the terminology of the biologist or the behavior psychologist, and has stated his superorganic in terms of "organisms" and their laws of growth. Clearly then, if the superorganic fails to have a describable content of its own, we are not entitled both to describe it in terms of a simpler level and yet to insist that it comprises an independent class of phenomena within the natural-science approach.[18]

[18] It may be objected that we are here omitting the telic approach which is so necessary to an understanding of culture objects, and treating all the data from the analytic or natural-science standpoint. Our only reply is that these two approaches cannot be confused or else each of them will become unintelligible, and since Chapin

Suppose we now adopt the alternative hypothesis, namely, that institutions *are biological organisms*. We are then confronted by the anomaly that their parts (individuals) could *live*, in a biological sense, when the institution as such had disappeared; that is, when the individuals, no longer functioning together for certain purposes, were forced into isolation. This independent viability of the parts of the "social" or "cultural organism" is in marked contrast to our knowledge of all other organisms of a highly integrated type. Parts of the human body, or of vertebrates, quickly die and disintegrate upon removal from the organism, unless they are preserved in media in which the essential materials upon which they normally depend in the individual's body have been provided. The only organisms in which the parts have true independent viability are those of a very low order, such as sponges and coelenterate colonies. These could scarcely be used as analogies or prototypes of "societal organisms"; for they lack the necessary integration and reciprocal action of parts. Thus it is fair to raise the question whether more confusion than light has not been thrown upon the curves of cultural change by referring to them as processes of organic growth.

The author's second interpretation of his curves involves the claim that the cultural-change process is a learning process. With this thesis we agree. But the learning is by individuals and not *societal*, as Chapin implies. The curve derived from the study of societal change during adaptation to a crisis is not a learning curve, though the learning of contemporary and succeeding individuals has probably helped to produce it. It is rather the accumulated resultant of these individual learnings as reflected by changes in the invention over a long period of time. If we were to assume that the curve represented the learning *of the group*, we would attribute to a supposed complex level of phenomena (societal pattern) the characteristics and laws of its units at a simpler level (human beings). This, as shown above, would amount to tautology.

Another objection to the "group-learning" hypothesis is that the curve does not represent the inventive activity of a single person, but of a number of persons of succeeding generations; and learning has no meaning as a psychological process when spread over a succession of separate individuals. To this objection Chapin replies by the ingenious argument that within a *biological organism* there occurs, over a period of time, a

---

has entered the field of natural science in his organic analogy, we can only follow him and consider his argument upon its own ground.

For a fuller discussion of the "criterion of uniqueness" consult the article cited above, n. 14, " 'Group' and 'Institution,' etc.," pp. 92 ff.

change of the materials (units) of which the organism is composed; yet the organism as a whole continues the process of learning in accordance with the usual curve of such processes.

But upon closer examination the analogy will be found unsatisfactory. Stated more explicitly, the argument is as follows: Group learning may be a *continuous process* although the individual learning is in separate persons who may disappear and be replaced from time to time. That this view is not unreasonable is shown by the fact that an individual's learning also is a continuous process, although the elementary or ultimate learning is carried on by the separate neurones which disappear and are replaced by others. When thus formulated as an exact analogy the comparison is seen to be untrue to fact, since it requires that single nerve cells learn. Learning, as understood by psychologists, does not apply to the activity of a single nerve fiber, but to the functional linkage of two or more neural elements so as to combine a stimulation process with a response. It is a neural-arc, not a nerve-trunk, modification—a phenomenon of t' · entire organism (i.e., afferent in connection with efferent portions), a̤   not of separate cells. Nerve fibers conduct impulses, but human being> *lea*)

To be true to neurological fact the analogy would have to be re. lted thus: Individual learning consists of the joining-together of nerve cells (which do not individually learn) into patterns of stimulation and response which constitute the true learning and which remain constant, though the separate nerve cells may change. In the same manner the group learns, and this learning persists, although the individuals, who *do not* learn, and who function together in such a way as to comprise the pattern of group learning, may disappear and be replaced by others. But this statement, though probably correct in its psychological reference, is untrue regarding the *cultural* level. In order that an individual may retain his habits over a long period it is not necessary for the *separate nerve cells,* as they are renewed, to learn these habits; it is enough that they are there. But in order that *culture* shall be continuous it *is* necessary that, in each replacement of human personnel, the individuals shall learn the current cultural habits (institutions and use of inventions). Otherwise culture will not develop or even persist, but will disappear. Group learning, therefore, is either individual learning, or else it is a metaphysical abstraction. Whenever we try to interpret group or cultural phenomena in organic terms the old tautology reappears.[19]

[19] The reader should note that if we were to change the analogy to the following form it would be quite acceptable: Just as the individual *continues to exist* even though his component cells may completely change, so the group continues to exist even though its personnel may have been completely replaced. We have no quarrel

VI. SUGGESTED CHANGES OF HYPOTHESIS FOR FURTHER RESEARCH

Professor Chapin has opened up a new and fascinating field. His cultural growth curves, if confirmed through later investigations, offer an interesting problem for further study and interpretation. The analysts, however, would seek for working hypotheses along a somewhat different line. The difficulties which arise in trying to assign cultural phenomena to some level of the natural-science series have been pointed out. Because of the telic factor in all culture and the impossibility of denoting this factor explicitly, culture objects cannot be made the objects of a natural-science approach without violating criteria which are definitive of that approach itself. The desire to predict with something like the certainty of natural-science generalizations is of course a worthy one. But it seems better to think of cultural phenomena as "indices" of human achievement in the use of natural laws for progressive adaptation rather than as objects through which one endeavors to derive laws of universal predictive value.

Cultural objects may be regarded as tools which individuals, working singly or together, construct or perfect, and which they teach individuals of succeeding generations how to use. The cultural process is the learning processes of individuals as they invent, adopt, and learn the use of cultural objects. Culture, therefore, is not an organism, or indeed anything which can be handled explicitly for the discovery of natural laws regarding its component parts or their behavior. It is simply the ways and methods which human beings use to adjust themselves to their surroundings. The forward viewpoint in this adjustment process is, as stated in Part I, the purposive, or *telic*, approach. The backward view is that of *genetic explanation*, an approach which *uses* the natural-science laws as conceptual explanations, helping us to understand the way cultural phenomena have come about, but which does not attempt to *establish* such laws. Taking this point of view, the cultural process becomes a complicated series of modifications of human behavior, involving the construction and the use of tools for an increasing number of purposes and the stimulation of one individual by another or by objects or records made by another. Principles of general and social psychology may here be of help.

---

with regard to the *existence* of the group, which seems to be a metaphysical question. We object only to endowing it, or its cultural continuity, with the capacity to learn—a function understood solely from our experience with individual organisms.

It is interesting that the shape of Chapin's cumulative growth curve for the group is really not that of the curve of human learning at all. Whereas the rise of the cultural curve is at first slow and gradually acquires momentum, the psychological learning curve is one whose most rapid rise is at the very start. Barring plateaus probably introduced through spurious factors, the latter remains throughout a curve of negative acceleration.

In our hypotheses for further research we would recognize two general groups of factors: first, the pluralistic aspect of the mass of inventors and users of the object or institution; second, those special manufacturers or officials having a vested interest in its progress. Let us take these in order.

So far as the initial portion of the cumulative growth curve is concerned, we would accept Chapin's own working hypothesis, namely, that the interest of many is attracted by some new possibility opened by a scientific discovery or some basal invention. Thus, an enormous set of possibilities was opened up by the invention of the electric motor and the internal-combustion engine. At the beginning improvements are slow and based on fortuitous adaptations without special realization of the "principles" involved. The sudden rise in the curve may be due to the fact that people are "getting the idea." The case may be similar with institutions. People probably "got the idea" that just as a few functions had been efficiently administered by mayor and council so other functions might be handled through municipal departments and bureaus. This sudden realization of a principle is a factor which might have been given more emphasis by the author. Other factors which may help to explain the sudden rise of the curve belong in the field of social psychology. Suggestion, social facilitation, and rivalry must be added to the usual economic motive and to the professional curiosity of the inventor. When new ideas about a mechanical invention or a political institution are heralded they become a part of the lively news of the day. Impetus is given to the efforts of individuals, not only by the crowd, but also by the face-to-face interstimulation between inventors and other interested persons. It is not outside the realm of possibility to devise techniques for studying processes of this sort.

Next we note that the special interests of those most concerned are chiefly in the direction of increasing, rather than decreasing, the number of structures and functions to be added to the invention. High officials may desire to extend their power by increasing the number of bureaus and personnel. Certain countertendencies may, of course, be present in the motives of some of the lower officials. In the mechanical field, the vested-interest factor involves the desire to increase business. Competition induces industrial plants and commercial organizations to employ experts and to add new features which may serve new purposes. Automobile salesmen know well the value of particular and exclusive "talking points." Sometimes rather irrelevant interests of the prospective user are brought into play to induce him to purchase, as when dash-clocks and cigar-lighters are added to automobiles. These factors of motivation are perhaps difficult to measure or estimate in their contribution to the rise of the curve, but patient investigation might in time yield a promising technique.

The declining growth in the upper segment of the cumulative curve is less obvious in its suggestion of working hypotheses. The fact that there is a limit to the number of purposes that can be fulfilled in connection with a single inventional complex has been suggested. But we have to explain why this limit is gradually rather than suddenly reached. A partial explanation might be found in the diminishing returns to manufacturers of money spent upon invention and promotion beyond a certain point. The factors of social facilitation and rivalry also decline as the limit of inventive possibilities is approached. Finally, there is the distracting influence of new mechanical or institutional possibilities, suggesting inventions in other directions. Some of these factors may perhaps be susceptible of investigation by the study of individuals actually engaged in manufacture and invention.

Because it points the way to inductive and explicit studies of this character, Professor Chapin's *Cultural Change* is a valuable contribution. Our present criticism is directed not against the author's technique or findings, but deals only with the question whether the attempt to measure and interpret cultural growth as one would handle the explicit objects of natural science will, in practice, justify the methodological assumptions upon which it is based. But before summarizing our conclusions on this point, let us examine the second investigation we have chosen with respect to the measurement and the prediction of cultural change.

III.   KROEBER'S INVESTIGATION OF CULTURE CYCLES

In his study entitled "On the Principle of Order in Civilization as Exemplified by Change of Fashion" Professor Kroeber has selected for measurement certain style traits appearing in women's full evening toilette for the period 1844–1919. The actual data were taken from style-journal illustrations. Measurements were taken of the following eight traits.[20]   (1) total length of figure from the center of the mouth to the tip of the toe; (2) distance from the mouth to the bottom of the skirt; (3) distance from the mouth to the minimum diameter across the waist; (4) length of décolletage, measured from the mouth to the middle of the corsage edge in front; (5) diameter of skirt at its hem or base; (6) maximum diameter of the skirt at any point above the base; (7) minimum diameter in the region of the waist; (8) width of décolletage across the shoulders. All these measurements were recorded in millimeters.

[20] An exact description of these measurements may be found in Kroeber, *op. cit.,* pp. 239–40.

As a general rule the first ten figures suitable for measurement in the style journal were taken for each year. Occasionally, however, it was necessary to take a few from the last months of the previous year. The author notes that there was scarcely a year for which ten illustrations could be found in each of which all eight measurements were recordable. In some cases estimates had to be made: "The majority of the eight features observed are represented, year by year, by less then ten measurements, sometimes only by four or five." The series of data are fullest for measurement items 1, 2, and 5. The author does not print his raw measurement data in full, but gives those of three years (1859, 1886, and 1910) as samples, the first of which is reproduced in our Table I. The absolute

TABLE I*

THE RAW DATA (INDIVIDUAL MEASUREMENTS) FOR 1859

1	120	125	113	125	133	125	125	129	125	123
2	120	125	113	125	133	125	125	129	125	123
3	(30)	31	29	31	34	30	32	33	32	29
4	16	17	16	18	24	14	16	17	22	13
5	(115)	147	142	140	153	150	140	146	142	135
6	.....	145	136	142	.....	.....	145	.....	.....	.....
7	(9)	9	10	.....	.....	.....	10	.....	.....	9
8	(19)	24	20	23	24	23	21	23	(22)	25
10	14	14	13	18	17	7	10	.....	15	.....

* Lines 1–8 refer to measured traits as defined above, p. 336; line 9 refers to distance from mouth to middle of maximum diameter of skirt (not given in Kroeber's table for 1859); line 10 refers to distance from minimum diameter at waist to waist line or point of corsage (all in millimeters). Figures in parentheses are estimates.

numbers in this table, representing millimeters, were then converted throughout into percentage ratios to the length of the entire figure. That is, each item in lines 2–10 inclusive was converted into a percentage of the corresponding item in the same column in line 1. The percentages for each measurement were averaged for each year. The figures used on charts, tabulations, and in discussion are these "year-percentage averages." These are exhibited in our Table II for the selected ten-year period 1850–59 from the entire series 1844–1919. Table II gives data for the period named on six measurements in terms of year-percentage averages. No measures of reliability for the averages are furnished, nor can the reliability be estimated by the reader since the number of cases on which the individual averages are based does not appear, except for the three samples of raw data for the years 1859, 1886, and 1910. The author has plotted his data for measurement items 2, 3, 4, 5, 7, and 8 and reproduced them in the article cited.

Kroeber considers the curve of trait 5 (width of skirts) as his best case[21] Upon the basis of these data, and of general impressions of the width of the skirt before 1844, he believes that "they do seem to suggest a certain regularity of curve, a tendency toward recurrence." He finds here "a swing of about sixty years in each direction; a period for the whole wave or cycle of a hundred or a hundred and twenty years, in this particular trait."[22] The following prediction is made:

By 1912 the tide has once more turned—no doubt to continue now for another two or three score years unless the periodicity of the rhythm is accelerated by some unknown new cause or is totally broken off by an alteration of fundamental fashion, such as the substitution of trousers for skirts.[23]

TABLE II

RATIO OF DRESS DIAMETERS TO HEIGHT OF FIGURE
(Selected Period, 1850–59)

YEAR	2	3	4	5	7	8
	Length of Dress	Length of Waist	Décolletage	Width Skirt	Width Waist	Width Shoulders
1850	97.8	28.6	12.7	64.2	8.2	20.7
1851	98.7	29.4	13.9	61.3	8.4	21.2
1852	97.6	27	14.1	70.3	8.3	21.4
1853	98.1	27.7	12.8	70.2	7.7	21.2
1854	97.9	27	14.1	79.3	8.4	20.6
1855	98.2	27.9	13.3	83	9	21
1856	98.3	27.7	13.4	89.2	8.6	19.1
1857	98.4	26.7	13.9	86.2	9	19.6
1858	99.6	26.8	15.2	100.3	7.9	18.8
1859	100	25.3	14.4	115.6	7.8	18.2
Average (1844–1919) .	97.7	26.4	13.8	65.3	9.4	15.6

Kroeber reaches the conclusion that "the rhythmic period for skirt length is only a third that for width; about thirty-five years as against a century."[24] It is pointed out that the possible length of a dress is automatically cut off when it reaches the ground, but that it can shorten indefinitely.

[21] "The Study of Cultural Phenomena," *Proceedings of the Hanover Conference of the Social Science Research Council* (1927), pp. 220–40. [This reference is to the mimeographed copy of the stenotyped records of the evening discussions at the Conference. It is not published.—EDITOR.]

[22] *Ibid.*, p. 228.

[23] "On the Principle of Order in Civilization, etc.," *op. cit.*, p. 250. [Full reference in n. 1.—EDITOR.]

[24] *Ibid.*, p. 253.

This brings it about that when skirt length attains its maximum, it remains apparently stationary for a time, whereas at its minimum it reaches a climax and quickly descends again. It might be said that fashion clearly tries, and is prevented only by physical impossibility, to draw the bottom of the dress several inches into the ground.[25]

It is predicted:

The child whose braids hang down her back may be reasonably sure that in the years when her daughters are being born she will wear longer dresses than her mother now goes about in; and that her skirts promise to be wider each successive decade until she is a grandmother.

On the more important of the other traits there is

some indication that the position of the waist line may completely alter, also following a "normal" curve, in a seventy-year period; and a possibility that the width of shoulder exposure varies in the same manner, but with the longest rhythm of all, since the continuity of tendency in one direction for seventy years establishes a periodicity of about a century and a half, if the change in this feature of dress follows a symmetrically recurrent plan.[26]

Kroeber considers that he has given "reasonable evidence of an underlying pulsation in the width of civilized women's skirts, which is symmetrical and extends in its up and down beat over a full century; and of an analogous rhythm in skirt length, but with a period of only about a third the duration" and possibilities of orderliness in some of the other traits, as we have mentioned in the paragraph above. He states that "there is something in these phenomena, for all their reputed arbitrariness, that resembles what we call law: a scheme, an order on a scale not without a certain grandeur." While he does not hold that the fashion of a future date can be written now, he at the same time maintains that

it does seem that some forecast can be made for any one basic element whose history has been sufficiently investigated; and that, when the event arrives, if the anticipation proved to have been more or less erroneous, the source of the aberration may be clear, and the disturbingly injected forces stand revealed as subject to an order of their own.[27]

Professor Kroeber draws conclusions of still broader significance. He states that "the fact of regularity in social change is the primary inference from our phenomena." The amplitude of the periodicities is of al-

[25] *Ibid.*, p. 252. The statement is somewhat qualified in a later statement where it is mentioned merely as a suggestion. See "The Study of Cultural Phenomena," *op. cit.*, pp. 229–30. [Cf. n. 21.—EDITOR.]

[26] *Ibid.*, p. 258.

[27] The full statement of these detailed conclusions will be found in *ibid.*, pp. 256–62.

most equal importance since their magnitude dwarfs the influence any individual can possibly have exerted in any alteration of costume. Rejecting the gifted individual or innovator as the source of these trends, he offers as the other alternative the operation of "superindividual principles which determine the course of social events."[28]

These alternatives, in the opinion of the analysts, do not exhaust the possibilities. One might employ a psychological explanation. Underlying these stylistic phenomena we might, for example, point to *emulation* as a motive within the individuals who are fashioning, advertising, and wearing the various gowns. If this factor were shown to be strong, we might have a possible explanation for trends and even cycles. It is assumed for the moment that the existence of these fashions could not stay constant, for to do so would prevent outdoing other people. If a trend in fashions had started in a given direction, it would be more likely to continue than to return, since to go back would be to repeat a fashion quite recently current. This would be contrary to the nature of the motive of emulation. Somewhere, however, there is a limit to such a trend. It may, perhaps, be physical, such as the ground in the case of the skirt; or it may be a conflict with some moral habit or notion of decency; or it may, perhaps, be mere inconvenience, as in the case of a skirt too wide. Here the trend would stop, turn, and begin its long swing in the other direction. Traced over a period of years the general effect would be cyclical.

Underlying such long trends as the decrease in the length of the skirt, we might find such factors as changes in the economic and social position of women, their greater participation in sports, and changes in the mode of dancing. Economic factors, such as the relative cost of certain materials, are possibly present. Explanations of this nature would avoid acceptance of the interpretation in terms of gifted personalities, which Kroeber dislikes, and at the same time make it unnecessary to postulate the operation of superindividual principles which determine the course of human events.

It is difficult to accept Kroeber's conclusion that "the fact of regularity of social change is the primary inference from these phenomena." Granting for the moment that regularity in certain fashion changes has been demonstrated, it must be remembered that the phenomena have been noted within narrow limits of time and source. Only certain features or traits of evening gowns have been dealt with. The data offer far too narrow a basis for the inference that regularity in social change is a fact. The

[28] *Ibid.*, pp. 260–61.

phenomena dealt with are not to be considered as representative of social change in general, but rather as a group of selected cases.

The author himself states this criticism at the beginning of his study.[29] He tells us that he observed that some fashion traits "don't change enough, others too much."[30] Data concerning such traits he rejected along with cases where sudden and radical change was followed by a new era of comparative stability.[31] It is apparent that the material for the study was subjected to a highly selective process. While this in no way invalidates the results found in the separate traits investigated, it does decidedly lower their value as the basis for an inference as to the regularity of social change in general. Nor can we even go so far as to accept Kroeber's dictum that if any principle could be found in the narrow limits of his study of evening gowns, "it would apply *a fortiori* to the more changeable kinds of clothing."[32] If a general law of social change is to be formulated, the materials investigated should be determined by some random method and should be sufficiently large in number to afford adequate measures of reliability.

The analysts cannot help but feel that the whole notion of determinism in relation to a natural law is employed by Kroeber in a sense foreign to that of natural-science prediction. A confusion has arisen here between the philosophical viewpoint, or what might be called "rational" or "intelligent determination," and the natural-science approach of empirical observation and experiment. Determinism of any sort is, strictly speaking, not a natural-science concept. When the scientist observes a concomitance between two variables he does not maintain that one determines the other, but merely that they are present together in his observation. He may from the appearance of one of them predict the occurrence or behavior of the other. By observing one of the variables whose concomitance with the other is expressed as a scientific law, he may adjust himself telically (i.e., in practical life) to the whole situation. In a sense, then, the sequence is for him *practically* determined. He can, moreover, appreciate it intelligently; and it seems to make his world more coherent and dependable.

A subtle illusion of determinism thus results from shifting our sphere of discourse from the practical or telic to the philosophical mode, without realizing that in making such a change a critical inspection of our concepts is necessary. The curve of temperature in the different seasons coincides fairly well with the other criteria by which we identify winter, sum-

[29] *Ibid.*, p. 242.
[30] "The Study of Cultural Phenomena," *op. cit.*, p. 227.
[31] "On the Principle of Order in Civilization, etc.," *op. cit.*, p. 238.
[32] *Ibid.*, p. 239.

mer, spring, and fall. To the man, therefore, interested only in giving an intelligent verbal expression it is sufficient to say that temperature is determined by the season of the year. In his treatment of cultural change, Kroeber, in fact, goes farther in that he implies that the height of one part of the curve is determined by the part just preceding, since the whole curve is to be understood as obeying some necessary law. Upon this view winter temperature determines the warmer temperatures of the spring to follow. It is, of course, only our *prediction* or *understanding* of what is to come next, and our corresponding practical adjustment, that is determined by the so-called law of the curve together with our present location upon it. We have no evidence that either seasonal or cultural phenomena are in themselves, and, apart from our interpretation, determined by one another in this way.

Notions of cultural determinism such as Kroeber's must be taken in the sense of philosophy of human interpretation rather than facts revealed by a natural-science approach. As a system of metaphysics or a religion they may have value in certain phases of life. They should not, however, be represented as emerging inductively from data of an empirical sort which are capable of analysis and explicit denotation.

In the foregoing discussion we have granted temporarily the reliability of the data tabulated and plotted by Kroeber, and of the trends and cycles thus produced. Upon inspection of the raw data, however, it becomes apparent that little assurance can be attached to the year-percentage averages upon which he bases his conclusions. The reliability of his average is of necessity low, since in no instance is it based on more than ten cases, and in some instances upon so few as four. This lack of reliability in the year-percentage average is a vital defect. In many instances very high variability appears in the data within a given year. Consider, for example, the figures on the length of the waist for the year 1859 (items in line 3 of Table I). There are nine actual measurements and one estimate, which, for convenience, we shall consider as ten cases in all. Reducing the raw data to ratios based on the length of the entire figure (i.e., to percentages of items in line 1 of Table I) we find a total range of 2.41. This range within the individual measurements for the year 1859 is greater than that within the yearly averages which the author assigns for the years 1859–64. The range within the year 1886 in the width of the skirt (which is the trait Kroeber considers the best) is greater than the range of year-percentage averages between the years 1870 and 1908. There is a greater range in the length of the skirt in 1886 than there is in the averages from 1881 to 1912. Considering the small number of cases and the wide variability within a

given year, we question whether the reliability of the averages, and consequently of the plotted curves, is adequate.

IV. SUMMARY AND CONCLUSIONS

The analysts have suggested as useful for the approach to culture a number of methodological concepts, which also represent approaches to the
phenomena of experience in general. The first is that which we have called,
in a narrow sense, the *natural-science approach*. It requires material
toward which one can react in an *explicit* manner. By reactions toward
the material either by manipulating it under control or by changing the
viewpoint in the process of observation, the scientist is able to derive generalizations or laws. These laws refer not only to the action of the object
which is initially studied, but also to the analysis of this object into simpler components and to the discovery of generalizations which hold at
various levels or stages of analysis. The second approach is that of *genetic
explanation*. The attitude here taken is to trace the history of the phenomenon in question, showing phenomena which are its usual antecedents,
or so-called "causes," and attempting to explain through natural-science
laws seen in perspective how the event or the object came into existence.
The third approach, which may be called the *telic* view, is one in which
we do not attempt to analyze, to discover laws, or to explain the object
before us, but merely attempt to use it for other purposes, and to make
such adjustments in it or in ourselves with relation to it as to serve
more purposes and to serve them more effectively. The fourth approach
is like the telic in that it is not interested in the object for itself, but
only in human feelings or purposes toward it. It is the *stylistic* view.
From this aspect we are interested only in measuring or predicting the
formal or incidental changes (usually of an aesthetic character) in the
man-made objects which are the materials of investigation. We have seen
that culture, as understood by ethnologists, cannot be viewed or investigated from the first of these approaches, the natural-science view; but
retains its identity as culture only in the latter three. Culture is fundamentally telic in character. When we approach an object with a view to
manipulating it for the sake merely of analysis, it is no longer a cultural
object.[33]

[33] The objection might be raised that the dilemma of the cultural sociologist is no
different from that of the biologist or any other natural scientist; for we find that
as soon as the biologist analyzes his material into chemical or physical components he
loses the unique character of his field and is no longer studying life as such. And
the same may be true of other natural-science levels. Hence it might be alleged that
there is really no difference between the cultural level and any of the natural-science

Implied in the writings of Professors Chapin and Kroeber is the assumption that, since culture is a part of the natural world, its development must follow certain definite laws. In discovering these laws we can proceed as we would in dealing with the materials of the natural sciences. The problem, they assume, is one merely of devising accurate units of measurement and obtaining adequate samples of the data. The fact that prediction in social science lags so far behind prediction in "physical science" is due, in Chapin's opinion, merely to the fact that, whereas in physical sciences we have reached the level of "projected invention" through symbolic trial and error (use of principles), we have not yet passed in social science beyond the level of "empirical invention" through overt trial and error.[34] Kroeber thinks that there is a "principle of order" governing cultural phenomena, which we may find inductively by a study of cultural changes, and which both describes such change and furnishes us a basis for prediction. Acting upon these hypotheses, the authors have set out to select their units and their data, and to measure cultural changes as a natural scientist measures the changes in objects within *his* realm of observation.

Against such experiments, when carried out with consideration for statistical accuracy, no valid objection could be raised. In the last analysis

levels, strictly speaking. This objection however cannot be sustained, since it ignores other aspects in which these planes of experience sharply differ. These may be stated briefly as follows: (1) An unfamiliar culture object, e.g., an implement of primitive culture unknown to ourselves, can have no significance to us except as a natural-science object; whereas a natural-science object, e.g., a non-useful stone, can be broken up and analyzed by a person of any culture whatsoever. (We are speaking, of course, of what *can* be done; not of that which it is customary to do.) Natural-science levels are universal and require no special training for their explicit denotation. (2) The laws discovered by analysis in the natural-science approach give us knowledge of changes which are concomitants of (hence means of describing) changes at a more complex level. E.g., the growth of plants may be partially understood in terms of osmosis, which is a physical rather than a biological principle. Such laws of simpler components, however, are related *in no constant fashion* to changes of culture (which require instead a telic interpretation and human invention). Hence in natural science certain levels are always bound up conceptually with other levels, while in the cultural plane objects must stand alone so far as the laws respecting natural-science levels are concerned. If culture were merely a complex (superorganic) level in the natural-science series this would not be true. (3) The natural scientist, having "lost" his original phenomenon by reducing it to a simpler level, can, however, in many cases readily restore it by a synthesis, simply by following the laws of combination of the parts themselves. Synthesis of a dissociated culture object, e.g., a clock, cannot readily be effected without a knowledge of the ulterior relation of the whole to human purposes. (4) Certain portions of culture, e.g. institutions, are, as such, not capable of explicit denotation at all, and hence fail in regard to the primary criterion of a natural-science level.

[34] *Cultural Change*, pp. 349–50.

their success and vindication must rest upon the findings themselves. It is, therefore, not the empirical procedure which we are here criticizing, but only the hypotheses upon which the authors have proceeded. The problem is probably not so simple as they imagine. The opinion that the only difference between our ability to measure and predict culture and our ability to measure and predict other phenomena is one of degree and is due to backwardness in our techniques is an assumption which leaves out of account some fundamental methodological problems. We have shown, for example, that one cannot explicitly handle, or react to, cultural phenomena in such a manner as to reveal the way they behave independently of human beings; and one cannot analyze them into parts and describe the laws of action of those parts. As soon as such an attitude is taken the object loses its cultural significance and we find we are investigating a different phenomenon, and one which tells us nothing about the behavior of the "cultural" phenomenon. This is, perhaps, the same as saying that in the natural-science approach we deal with the object and its changes, so far as possible, as *independent* of ourselves. It is external; our behavior toward it is *explicit*. In the cultural approach, on the other hand, we understand or define the object in terms of *our own response toward it*. Its meaning is carried in our own implicit responses. It is, therefore, largely *internal* or *implicit* in character. Experiences of this sort must be regarded as upon a plane of their own; one cannot treat them by the method of explicit denotation and analysis. They are uni-level rather than multi-level phenomena, and their level, indeed, is not one with which one might *begin* a multi-level analysis.

The consequences of this fact are important both for prediction and for the possibility of social laws. When one asks, for example, what sort of phenomena the cultural sociologists are measuring, we must conclude that their measurements are more largely of implicit than of explicit phenomena. What Chapin is really predicting in his cultural growth curves is the number of purpose-fulfilling objects which may be found in a given year as parts of a complex cultural object to which we assign a certain name. He is, in other words, predicting our own *counting behavior* at some stated future time when we shall take an attitude of enumerating these telically conceived parts. He is not predicting the growth of a specific object as one would predict the growth of an organism. The more highly perfected automobile does not grow out of the primitive automobile, except by a ludicrous stretch of the metaphor. It is not the *same* automobile whose parts we are counting after a period of inventive development; it is a different and complex object which we now denote by the name of "automobile," just as we formerly denoted its crude predecessor by that name. Or to put it in another way, we are here predicting the number of details in the pattern of implicit, or thought, reactions which will be exhibited in the behavior of a future manufacturer as he sets up a factory to produce the objects which we shall call by the old name, "automobile." The "culture object," therefore, whose "growth" Professor Chapin is measuring, is more within ourselves (in our naming and thinking reactions) than it is outside. The *measuring behavior* which he uses in plotting its growth is also implicit rather than explicit. It does not consist of running an eye or a finger along a meter stick laid against some explicit object (e.g., as in measuring the stature of an organism); but in counting the things we conceive to be parts of a "culture object" which *is* an object not by virtue of its own continued existence, but *because things of its class arouse in us the same name continuously*. Certainly, therefore, the difficulty inherent in measuring cultural change by the counting method, with resulting inequalities in the things counted, is not merely one of degree, to be overcome by the refining of our technique; but it is inherent in the very nature of the problem. It is the inevitable result of trying to apply to the telic, or cultural, approach the natural-science concept of measurement.[35]

The discrepancy between the telic and the natural-science approach is most marked with regard to the universality of social laws and the resulting capacity for prediction. Let us suppose that the methods of Chapin and Kroeber were carefully employed in studying thousands of different inventions and institutions, and that in these measurements the same cultural growth curves and periodic cyclical changes were demonstrated without exception. Since scientific laws are merely statements of probability, we should then feel fairly confident that the next cultural phenomenon would conform to the same law. In other words, we could conclude that the author's hypothesis was verified with extreme scientific precision. Let us suppose, however (and this supposition seems more in accord with the facts), that in the measurement of a certain cultural complex the growth curve of its parts is found to be distorted, or that there is

---

[35] Chapin does not attempt to predict with his curves the motions we shall make in handling the future appliances added to the basic invention; for to do this would be to describe what the appliance will be and how it will work. He simply says that our count of these appliances (really our own implicit responses or purposes) will be "so many." As we have said above, prediction of the quality or nature of an invention (prediction of our *explicit* behavior in using it) is not really prediction, but invention itself. The *nature* or *content* of inventions is extremely difficult (perhaps impossible) to predict; and this is quite as true from the standpoint of the natural scientist as it is from the cultural approach.

no change at all; or let us suppose that the stylistic measurements of certain objects, or of certain dimensions of those objects, fail to conform to the law of periodic cyclical change. Or again, let us merely focus our attention on the fact that periodic cyclical changes, even if their existence be proved, vary greatly in span between different elements. Now, under all of these conditions there emerge special limits to the universality of cultural laws. It seems that many cultural phenomena are obeying laws of their own, thus limiting the very notion of scientific generalization. A plurality of laws of cultural change, with apparently no explanation beyond these laws themselves, is an unsatisfactory condition. We know nothing of cultural change as such, but only the laws of change of this or that invention or organization. There are no universal principles which explain the discrepancies between cultural elements; and there is no way of predicting whether a certain element, not yet measured, will differ in growth from the hypothetical pattern, or what the direction of that difference will be. Clearly this condition calls for further investigation. We must reduce these differing phenomena to their essential components and discover laws at simpler levels, which will account for their varying appearance and will give us a wider basis of prediction.

Natural scientists are continually faced by the same problem. And this dilemma is in fact one of the most familiar and important incentives for the advancement of research. Certain unpredictable changes of appearance or position of the stars call for deeper astronomical study. The unexpected behavior of bacteria in a culture, violating the laws *usually* holding for such organisms, leads to a minuter analysis. It was found, some years ago, that epidemics of puerperal fever in a hospital usually attended unsanitary conditions. This relationship, however, was not a universal law, since the incidence of this disease under unsanitary conditions was not 100 per cent. Searching for some generalization to explain both the usual incurring of the disease and the cases which escaped from it, it was necessary to find a technique for breaking the present factors (human tissues, dirt, etc.) into their components, and revealing the laws of action of those parts at their own level. As soon as the microscope revealed the bacillus and its behavior in the human organism that particular problem was solved. It was easy to explain through a knowledge of the conditions of microbe communication, not only the law of connection between puerperal fever and unsanitary conditions, but its exceptions. Moreover, such exceptions could be, in some measure, successfully predicted.

A more recent example is to be found in attempts to explain the exceptions to the law of gravitation which occur in certain electromagnetic phenomena. Gravitation and electromagnetism have long been regarded as two separate and ultimate forces. The genius of an Einstein, however, was not content to leave them so; and he has been seeking, perhaps successfully, to conceive them under a more nearly general law which will enable us to predict and to account for exceptions to either principle. When the objects of nature can be approached in an explicit manner it is thus possible to analyze them into simpler components and arrive, through a study of those components, at wider and more valid generalizations which enable us both to understand and, to some extent, to predict the unusual within our experience.

Returning now to the problem of the exceptions to cultural laws, we meet with a sudden *impasse*. It is impossible to deal with objects explicitly and analytically and have them retain at the same time their cultural significance. And without explicit behavior and analysis, no wider underlying generalizations can be discovered. If the plow sulky is analyzed into its components, giving more general laws at simpler levels, we can never come back to it as the plow sulky again. The natural laws derived are the same as would be gained by an analysis of any piece of wood or iron in the chemist's laboratory. Such laws tell us only about the action of wood or metal; they reveal nothing concerning plow sulkies. Hence we are unable to explain irregularities or exceptions to the norm of the growth of inventions which the history of this article might reveal, or to pass below these differences to some more general law through which they might be understood. We can arrive at fundamental laws enabling us to predict different kinds of change within *physical* materials; but we can find no such elementary principles through which we can predict variations of *cultural* change. The methodology which is at the very heart of the natural-science approach is entirely foreign and irrelevant to the field of cultural phenomena. We must realize, therefore, that the gap between our capacity to generalize and predict regarding culture and our capacity for generalization and prediction in the "physical" sciences is not a matter merely of the degree to which we have refined our technique. It is a fundamental difference of kind. This fact, to be sure, does not reduce the possibility that there may exist laws upon a societal or cultural plane; nor does it argue against our capacity to discover such laws upon their own level. But it does suggest that deeper penetration to secure *wider* generalizations, that the explanation of any variations in cultural development, that the prediction of the unusual, and that the organization of inductive principles into a coherent body of knowledge are at the present time unlikely within the field of cultural change.

The failure to grasp the fundamental difference between natural-science and cultural material has led students of culture to advance certain hypotheses of doubtful value. Chapin, assuming cultural phenomena to belong in the world of natural science, looks about for natural-science principles through which to interpret them. Since no explicit analysis of his phenomena is possible, he resorts to describing them in terms of analogy. He borrows laws from a natural-science level, the biological, and interprets his cultural changes in such terms as organic growth and the learning process. Against this procedure we have found two fundamental objections: first, when the analogy is stated in exact form it requires a distortion of the biological facts; second, it obscures the requirement for uniqueness of formulation at different natural-science levels. It either assumes that culture is an organism, a comparison which cannot be maintained, or that we have a superorganic world which behaves in terms of the laws of organisms. This conclusion amounts to tautology.

Kroeber has attempted to meet the difficulty in another way. He boldly asserts that we should cut loose from our moorings to the levels of natural science, and seek our interpretations of the superorganic in terms of that level itself.[36] He sets up superorganic forces, such as the sweep of fashion or the determinism of culture-cycle curves, as explanations of his phenomena. He speculates upon the operation of some extra-human power which alters the length or the width of women's skirts, and which even attempts to push the hem of the garment into the ground. We thus arrive at a mystical notion of determinism which is quite as hopeless for directing future research as the organic analogies of Chapin.

Such unworkable hypotheses not only lead to far-fetched interpretations, but detract attention from more promising investigations within the cultural field. The analysts believe that the approach best fitted to give us knowledge concerning the cultural changes under discussion is that of *genetic explanation*. Remembering that the phenomena which distinguish objects as *cultural* are implicit rather than explicit, we shall expect to find them in the behavior of the human beings who invent and perfect such objects. Though not to be found by natural-science research into culture objects, a conceptual linkage of cultural phenomena with the realm where natural laws are revealed may still be achieved through the study of the culture-producing behavior of human beings. In this way we should use psychological and biological laws not as descriptions of cultural change upon its own abstract level, but as principles in the historic explanation of cultural development. The changes in culture from this view are iden-

[36] Cf. "The Possibility of a Social Psychology," *American Journal of Sociology*, XXIII (1918), 633–50; also "The Superorganic," *American Anthropologist*, XIX (April–June, 1917), 163–213. The latter has been reprinted by the Sociological Press, Hanover, N.H.

tical with the history of human thinking and learning; and these in turn are conceptually dependent upon known natural-science laws working amid a complexity of conditions. This statement of the problem opens a field of investigation, in terms of human behavior, which would have been ignored by postulating cultural phenomena as a level within the natural-science series. We have attempted above to suggest a few hypotheses useful in such a study. It is to be regretted that the approach of genetic explanation has been so little stressed by Chapin and has been deliberately rejected by Kroeber.

Notwithstanding their methodological difficulties, these two investigators have made a genuine contribution in that they have opened the cultural problem for scientific investigation. The student of human behavior, in particular, should be grateful for their attempt. Certainly the average laboratory psychologist or case-worker would not have thought of surveying these wide fields of cultural traits or of attempting to describe them in clear and simple terms. And until such a description was given, and tentative laws formulated, the psychologist could not have seen the implications of his principles and methods for the study of human nature. The historic trend of cultural behavior, and its sweep in geographical areas, are discoveries which cannot fail to stimulate fresh thought and imagination in human research. Only commendation can be given these investigators for their boldness in asking of nature the questions: Are there laws of cultural change? And is the prediction of culture a possibility? Their techniques also are of much interest, and although not fully relevant to the purpose intended, are illuminating for purposes perhaps still more important. The sole object of this article is to question certain assumptions regarding the nature of culture and the meaning of cultural investigations. In using their culture-measuring techniques, however ingenious and revealing such techniques may be, are these investigators really doing what they think they are doing? This challenge is merely a suggestion that their methodological postulates be examined afresh; it is in no way a detraction from the contribution they have made.[37]

[37] The writers wish to acknowledge the kind co-operation of Professor Chapin and Professor Kroeber in the preparation of the preceding study. Both of these authors not only expressed their willingness and interest in having their works critically reviewed, but supplied the writers with copies of their writings which at the time were difficult, if not impossible, to obtain. Appreciation is also expressed to the Century Company for permission to quote selections from Chapin's *Cultural Change*, and to Professor R. H. Lowie, editor of the *American Anthropologist*, for permission to reprint portions of Kroeber's article in that publication. [This analysis was first written in April, 1928. It was given final revision by the analysts in February, 1929.— EDITOR.]

SECTION VI

INTERPRETATIONS OF TEMPORAL SEQUENCES WITH
CONSIDERATION OF SPECIAL TYPES OF "CAUSATION"

307
R 36 m

THE SECTION AND THE FRONTIER IN AMERICAN HISTORY: THE METHODOLOGICAL CONCEPTS OF FREDERICK JACKSON TURNER[1]

By MERLE E. CURTI

Smith College

Frederick Jackson Turner has never definitely formulated a philosophy of history, nor set forth in organized form his conception of historical method. In his published work, however, and even more clearly perhaps in his productive seminars, he has developed indirectly a consistent view of American history and its methodology. This view is now very widespread if not dominant, yet when it was first presented it was strikingly new. At that time American historians were much influenced by the school of Ranke, who aimed to determine the past "exactly as it was." Interpretations were exceptional, and constitutional and political interests overshadowed all others. The need for understanding the economic and social basis of politics, which some of the early Federalists had appreciated, and which Hildreth made use of, seemed to have been largely forgotten. When a McMaster or a Henry Adams used economic and social data, he made little effort to relate them to political, diplomatic, and institutional facts. Regional history, and especially the history of the West, was treated in an antiquarian or romantic fashion. Under the influence of Herbert B. Adams at Johns Hopkins University, historians were inclined to emphasize the continuity of American institutions with those of Europe. When Turner in 1888 went to Baltimore, at that time the Mecca of historical students, he heard Adams remark that American institutions had been "well done," and that for a further understanding of their origin one must turn to their germs in the Old World. This point of view largely overlooked the differences between America and Europe, for differences, unlike similarities, could scarcely be inherited.

It was Turner who made the historiographical declaration of independence against these canons, and his work in so doing is unique and significant in the history of historical writing in America. Professor Carl Becker, one of Turner's most distinguished students, has described in a

---

[1] The writer is deeply indebted to certain scholars who have made valuable suggestions in connection with the writing of this paper.

charming essay the influences which in part explain his revolt from the accepted usages in American history.[2] Becker has also spoken for all of Turner's students in emphasizing the difficulty of divorcing his methods of research and pedagogy from the charm and inspiration of his personality. It is this difficulty which makes students of Turner, who attempt to write of him, feel incapable of comparing his work in a critically objective way with that of his contemporaries who have also made outstanding contributions. His students can, however, try to give to others, who know him only through his relatively few publications, a more accurate idea of what he has done and stood for.

For Turner the chief purpose of history is to aid in understanding the process by which interacting forces have made society. Both in his writing and in his teaching he gives meaning, by what a distinguished student calls "a new and strangely sudden illumination," to the familiar theory that the history of human society is more than a sequence of changes. History has a pattern, one which can be discovered through unwearying industry and imagination. Yet this does not mean that history can be reduced to a formula, that historical laws are to be postulated. Even the concepts of the frontier and of the interplay of sectional forces, the two contributions with which Turner is most often associated, are not for him ultimate explanations; they are rather keys to the understanding of the process by which man and his environment in America have reacted on each other. This process is an evolutionary one. Like the natural scientists whose point of view influenced him, he assumed the development, through a process of change, of complex social, economic, and political forms from simpler species.

The United States, Turner believes, affords an unusual laboratory for studying the problems involved in the evolution of society. To America came Europeans, bringing their ideals and institutions from the Old World, and they were compelled to adapt these to their needs in the new environment; and

to create new institutions to meet the new conditions; to evolve new ideas of life and new ethnic and social types by contact under these conditions; to rise steadily through successive stages of economic, political and social development to a highly organized civilization; to become themselves colonists in new wildernesses beyond the first spheres of settlement; to deal again with the primitive peoples at their borders; in short, continuously to develop, almost

---

[2] Carl Becker, "Frederick Jackson Turner," in H. W. Odum, *American Masters of Social Science* (New York: H. Holt & Co., 1927), chap. ix. This article should be read by everyone wishing to understand the character and significance of Turner's work. It contains a bibliography of his writings.

under the actual observation of the present day, those social and industrial stages which, in the Old World, lie remote from the historian and can only be faintly understood by scanty records.[3]

In these words Turner emphasized his fundamental interest in the social evolution of America, an evolution which the concepts of the frontier and the section help greatly in understanding. Such an interest might be called sociological as well as historical. "Without so describing himself," Giddings has said, Turner is "a sound sociologist, and a ground-breaking one of first-rate importance." In reality the name matters little, so long as progress is made toward ascertaining the truth.

In interpreting the facts of this evolutionary development of society in America, Turner has not entirely overlooked the problem of control, nor the applications of the generalizations made. It cannot be too strongly urged, however, that this consideration is entirely secondary to his main object of ascertaining the truth regarding social evolution. None the less, he has felt that if there is to be a just public opinion and a statesmanlike treatment of present problems, they must be understood and appreciated in their historical relations, in order that "history may hold the lamp for conservative reform."[4] All American experience had gone to "the making of the spirit of innovation," and historical study should result in appropriating out of the past "something which may serve the ideal of social progress which is the sum and substance of our modern faith."[5] History, in other words, has a practical as well as a theoretical value—its aim is not *merely* to understand, but also to aid in control.

If one turns from this conception of the aims of historical study to methodology, one again finds that the natural sciences have greatly influenced Turner's work. He early concluded that if history was to enable a people to understand itself by understanding how it had come to be what it was, then it must call into co-operation many sciences and methods hitherto little used by the historian. Data must be drawn from "studies of literature and art, politics, economics, sociology, psychology, biology, and physiography." Moreover, "the method of the statistician as well as that of the critic of evidence" was "absolutely essential." In 1904 Turner said:

[3] "Problems in American History," *Congress of Arts and Sciences: The Universal Exposition, St. Louis,* II (1904), 184–85.

[4] Quoted by Carl Becker, "Some Aspects of the Influence of Social Problems and Ideas upon the Study and Writing of History," *American Journal of Sociology,* XVIII (1912–13), 667.

[5] *Ibid.,* p. 675.

There has been too little co-operation of these sciences, and the result is that great fields have been neglected. There are too many overlapping grounds left uncultivated owing to this independence of the scientists, too many problems that have been studied with inadequate apparatus and without due regard to their complexity.[6]

Six years later, in giving his presidential address before the American Historical Association, Turner still further insisted that the historian must "so equip himself with the training of his sister subjects that he can at least avail himself of their results, and in some reasonable degree master the essential tools of their trade."[7] At this same meeting James Harvey Robinson made a similar plea for the use of the sciences as the indispensable tools of the historian, and in 1912 published his essays, *The New History*, which urged the social and practical values of history, rightly studied. Although Turner has not been generally thought of as one of the founders of "the new history," and although he would probably not think of himself as one, it might be said that little can be found in "the new history" that he had not emphasized from the beginning of his work.

Before illustrating the use which Turner has made of the relation of historical research to other sciences, it should be pointed out that in still other ways the natural sciences have affected his methodology. Like the scientist, he believes in the necessity of data, and then more data, and his influence in the work of collecting and classifying materials for the study of American society has been far reaching. His interest in heuristics, for example, has led him to contribute as much, probably, as any other contemporary scholar to the illumination of our diplomatic history from the material of foreign archives. But living and surviving institutions as well as documents have also furnished him with data.[8]

While making use of all the accepted principles of historical criticism, Turner's attitude toward his facts resembles that of the natural scientist in two distinct ways. For him any conclusion is always extremely tentative, and it is the essence of his method that he works as though his wiser successors would correct, reconstruct, and be reconstructed.[9] Besides this

[6] "Problems in American History," *op. cit.*, p. 193.

[7] F. J. Turner, *The Frontier in American History* (New York: H. Holt & Co., 1921), p. 334.

[8] "It is important," Turner said in his 1910 address before the American Historical Association, "to study the present and recent past, not only for themselves but also as the source of new hypotheses, new lines of inquiry, new criteria of the perspective of the remoter past" (*ibid.*, p. 323).

[9] See, e.g., the Preface to *The Frontier in American History*, in which Turner insists that only the future can measure the truthfulness of his interpretations.

ideal and achievement of tentativeness, conditioned by a consideration of the personal equation in selecting and eliminating facts, he has been impressed by still another safeguard used by scientists. It is what T. C. Chamberlin calls the method of multiple hypotheses, and Turner, who read and digested the paper of this geologist, has applied the conception to his own research. This is, in brief, the attempt to postulate the largest conceivable family of explanations for a given historical problem, to regard these hypotheses with an unbiased eye, to test them successively by all the available evidence, and finally to allow the hypotheses to fight out their battle. This method of attack, Turner felt, would avoid "the warping influence of partiality for a simple theory." It also recognizes the varied and complex character of the factors involved, and guards against the tendency of the historian to make judgments according to the point of view "to which his special training or interest inclines him."[10] Causation, in other words, is highly complex, and no one type of explanation, geographical, economic, or any other, is adequate.

The criticism has been made that Turner's method tends to exalt the influence of environmental factors while neglecting the individual. This, however, is hardly true. He has not subscribed to the "great man" theory of history, yet he by no means excludes the ideas and the acts of individuals as factors in the historical process. Even a single outstanding personality, itself the product of a complexity of conditions, may color the events of a particular period. Many historians and biographers have probably tended, however, to exaggerate the influence of unusual leaders. Turner has not gone deeply into the philosophy of the relation between the individual and his larger environment—he has concentrated on the work of arriving at proximate explanations of particular historical processes, using all the data available. The working out of speculative theory, an important task to be sure, he has left to others.

It would be easy to carry too far the analogy of Turner's method to that of the natural sciences. His work implies a belief that it is too soon to determine exactly, though exactness is the aim, the conditions of the historical process. He has not assumed that history can actually establish any large body of principles, or be more than one among many disciplines to aid in social control. The present task of the historian, as he has conceived it, is to make a preliminary recognition and study of the "forces that operate and interplay in the making of society," rather than to determine the ultimate laws of history. He has thus contented himself with the attempt to establish tendencies and to understand mass movements and processes in America.

[10] *Ibid.,* p. 333.

In this task he proceeds very carefully. As Woodrow Wilson observed in 1896, he has peculiar power in combining the large view with the small one, the general plan and conception with the minute examination of particulars. His method of synthesis, which is based on far-reaching, acute analysis, takes cognizance of certain pitfalls in the task of generalizing from the data of the social sciences. It is necessary, he feels, to give attention to the relativity of facts and to the transiency of conditions. For the fact

is not planted on the solid ground of fixed conditions; it is in the midst and is itself a part of the changing currents, the complex and interacting influences of the time, deriving its significance as a fact from its relations to the deeper-seated movements of the age, movements so gradual that often only the passing years can reveal the truth about the fact and its right to a place on the historian's page.[11]

Turner has thus pointed out, for example, that environment includes both physical and social factors, and that the physical environment itself is constantly being changed by economic processes and interests. The fur-trading area of Lake Superior was the same area in part as the later lumber area and the present-day mining area; tomorrow, the water power of the region may be utilized to create still another type of environment. The social environment changes still more, and physical and social factors react on each other. Environment, in other words, is a relative, not an absolute, factor. The problem of generalization in the social sciences thus becomes quite a different matter from the task of generalizing in the more exact natural sciences. In practice the writing of history becomes an art as well as a science. The emphasis on the need of considering and correlating diverse factors in understanding causation and historical process can be illustrated, very briefly, by suggesting how this point of view compelled the rewriting of American history. In 1894 Turner called attention to the need of an economic interpretation of American history,[12] and, according to Professor A. M. Schlesinger, was "the first historian who perceived the importance of economic influences in American history."[13] It was he who pointed out the significance of group conflicts, particularly

[11] *Ibid.*, p. 332.

[12] O. G. Libby, Editor's Note, *The Geographical Distribution of the Vote of the Thirteen States on the Federal Constitution, Bulletin of the University of Wisconsin,* "Economics, Political Science and History Series" I, No. 1 (1894), 1–116.

[13] A. M. Schlesinger, *New Viewpoints in American History* (New York: Macmillan Co., 1922), p. 69. See also the valuable discussion of N. S. B. Gras, "The Rise and Development of Economic History," *Economic History Review,* I, No. 1 (January, 1927), 27–28.

the conflicts between the debtor and the creditor class, which generally synchronized with the newer and developing regions on the one hand, and the older, more developed areas on the other. In this treatment of economic conflict there is a complete absence of the cynicism shown by some writers who emphasize the conflicts of group interests. This is to be accounted for by a combined human and scientific interest, and by the lack of any desire to strike down historical illusions or to create new dogmas.

It is these group conflicts that have illuminated financial history and currency legislation, public-land policies, and political behavior. In a series of remarkable papers, pioneer consideration was given to the economic background of the diplomatic intrigues of European powers for the control of the Mississippi Valley.[14] Students of Turner, such as Frederick Merk, Samuel Flagg Bemis, I. J. Cox, Joseph Schafer, W. S. Robertson, A. P. Whitaker, and others, came under his influence in this respect, and have made notable contributions to diplomatic history, contributions in which the economic background has been emphasized.

By employing statistics in the study of wheat prices between 1840 and 1850, it was found that agricultural hardship in the wheat areas explains in part the migration from these regions to Oregon and Texas in that period. By minute tabulations of statistics in the census reports this versatile scholar traced the westward migration of sheep production, and correlated this migration with the increasing interest of the West in tariff on raw wools. In still other studies he has charted the relation between surplus produce areas and demands for internal improvements.

Some have felt that Turner has not paid adequate attention to industrial capitalism as a factor in explaining American development.[15] His address before the American Historical Association in 1910 shows, however, what his students have always known, that he has long recognized the importance and significance of industrial capitalism, and that this recognition has deeply influenced his researches and his historical thinking. He has recognized that as the West became settled cities and developing in-

---

[14] "Diplomatic Contest for the Mississippi Valley," *Atlantic Monthly*, XCIII (1898), 676–91, 807–17; "English Policy towards America in 1790–1791," *American Historical Review*, VII (October, 1901–July, 1902), 704–6; "Policy of France toward the Mississippi Valley in the Period of Washington and Adams," *ibid.*, X (1905), 249–79; the "Correspondence of Clark and Genet," *Annual Report of the American Historical Association*, I (1896), 930–1107; the "Mangourit Correspondence," *ibid.* (1897), pp. 569–79; and "Correspondence of the French Ministers to the United States, 1791–1797," *ibid.*, Vol. II (1903).

[15] Charles A. Beard, review of *The Frontier in American History*, in the *New Republic*, XXV (February 16, 1921), 349–50.

dustrialism complicated its economic interests, and that it often spoke in federal councils with a divided voice. It must also be remembered that he has concerned himself, not with a particular region, but with the country as a whole, and that industrial capitalism has only recently invaded large areas of the country.

In the field of economic history Turner's students have worked ably with their master. H. B. Hibbard, G. M. Stephenson, Miss A. C. Ford, and R. G. Wellington have studied the influence of public lands, an influence to which Turner called attention in his first notable paper on "The Significance of the Frontier in American History."[16] L. B. Schmidt, H. C. Taylor, J. L. Coulter, Solon J. Buck, A. O. Craven, Nils Olsen, and Oscar Stein have done outstanding work in agrarian history. In the field of transportation history L. H. Haney, H. B. Meyer of the Interstate Commerce Commission, E. R. Johnson, and James B. Hedges are outstanding authorities. Allyn A. Young, another of Turner's students, was a distinguished economist and statistician. Although Turner and his students have avoided the terminology of the economic interpretation of history, it is not too much to say, as Charles A. Beard has said, that Turner was the leader in restoring the consideration of economic facts to historical writing in America.[17]

Turner was also a pioneer in bringing to the study of our history the data and point of view of the physical and human geographer. While he recognized that physiography, with which he thoroughly familiarized himself, was "far from dictating the precise way in which a region acted," he explained in what ways it does influence political and cultural phenomena. He developed a technique which showed how certain types of physiographic areas attracted certain types of societies; how geographic resources conditioned economic and social interests; and, especially, how all these environmental factors affected political behavior. He showed, for example, how the river systems of the trans-Alleghany region influenced the process of state-making during the Revolutionary period, and how salt springs and limestone pathways conditioned the selection of sites for settlement and the development of transportation arteries.[18]

[16] Schlesinger (*op. cit.*, p. 70) has made the point that as early as 1865 E. L. Godkin called attention to the influence of the frontier in explaining the differences between America and Europe. Turner later, and independently, applied the conception to our history so thoroughly and effectively that it has come to be generally accepted.

[17] Letter to the writer, August 9, 1928.

[18] "Western State-making in the Revolutionary Era," *American Historical Review*, October–January, 1895–96, p. 265; Archer B. Hulbert, "The Increasing Debt of History to Science," *American Antiquarian Society Proceedings*, N.S., XXIX (1919), 35. For an interesting discussion of the relation between geographic and human factors as

In such investigations maps were used extensively in the study of correlations between geographic conditions and political, social, and economic tendencies. The technique is illustrated in a study in which, correlating geological maps with census reports and statistics of voting in presidential elections, Turner discovered certain interesting relationships. One map series[19] indicated that certain kinds of terrain attracted the types of people familiar, in the homes from which they migrated, with similar terrain. Thus in migrating to Ohio, Indiana, and Illinois, the southern upland people, habituated to a wooded country, sought the forested, non-glaciated areas, while for the later New England–New York group was left the open prairie country. These maps also show that over a long period of time the forested counties of southern Illinois, Indiana, and Ohio, which had attracted southern upland groups, returned Democratic majorities; while the New England–New York prairie counties favored the Republicans. By a great many maps showing political voting Turner demonstrated that, in general, the rough country with the least valuable lands tended to be, over a long period of time, Democratic; while the favored soil regions, the most highly capitalized and industrialized districts, tended to be anti-Democratic, Federal, Whig, or Republican.[20] Equally significant were the cultural-physiographic correlations which Turner studied with the aid of a similar map technique. By comparing physiographic areas with census reports of illiteracy, Turner showed that, in general, the inhabitants of glaciated, more fertile regions were more literate than those of the less favored soils of the non-glaciated regions.

This method of correlating political and cultural behavior with the physiographic map, a method which grew out of Turner's seminary, and which was used as early as 1894 by one of his students, O. G. Libby, was a notable contribution to the technique of historical research. Turner has used this method extensively but with great caution. In interpreting the maps he has been especially careful to apply the principle of the multiple hypothesis. Thus he has pointed out that sometimes, as in the case of the

---

historical causes see the "Report of the Conference of Geography and History," over which conference Turner presided (*Annual Report of the American Historical Association*, I [1907], 47 ff.). See also Harry Elmer Barnes, *The New History and the Social Studies* (New York: Century Co., 1925), pp. 66–67.

[19] Maps showing influence of sectional groupings on voting in "Presidential Elections in Ohio, Indiana and Illinois, 1856, 1868, 1888, and 1900," *American Journal of Sociology*, XIII (March, 1908), 664, Plate I.

[20] "The Significance of the Section in American History," *Wisconsin Magazine of History*, VIII, No. 3 (March, 1925), 277. For a stimulating discussion of some of the problems involved in map methodology see O. G. Libby, "The Study of Votes in Congress," *American Historical Association Report*, I (1896), 333 ff.

maps referred to above, it is not a question of direct influence of physical environment on sectional or political alignment. People voted as they did largely because they followed old political habits; but indirectly the physical conditions affected sectional alignment, since they helped to determine the location of migrating stocks. In other instances, however, the influence of physiography, as revealed by the map technique, is more direct. In map studies of congressional votes on tariffs and other public questions, Turner showed how the economic resources and potentialities of physiographic regions often, though not always, directly affected their political reactions to such questions. In all cases he has insisted on emphasizing the exceptions to the general patterns or correlations. Eschewing a simple explanation of a historical phenomenon, he has pointed out how often human and psychological factors rather than geographic determinism furnish an explanation. No one has been more alert than Turner to show how, in given cases, electoral majorities might be due to a powerful political machine. No one has been more acute in recognizing that a majority coloration often obscures a very large minority in a given district. It was to avoid this pitfall that he insisted on the use of small units, such as the county, in mapping elections or literacy, and emphasized the necessity of a multiplicity of maps and the repeated checking of findings. In the use of map methodology he aimed merely to establish general tendencies, which could be postulated when the same pattern of voting, for example, persisted over a long period of time. This methodology, which has been widely and sometimes less carefully used by his imitators, contributed materially to a realistic understanding of the relationships between physiography and the colonizations of people, and of the relationships between these factors and political and cultural phenomena.

The concept of the section, closely associated with this method of correlating political and cultural behavior with physical environment and economic units, has perhaps been as significant as that of the frontier process in leading to a reinterpretation of American history. "The vast spaces into which the American people moved were themselves a complex of physiographic regions," which with the type of peoples moving into them conditioned the development of sectionalism.[21] The artificial boundaries of state lines had obscured to the historian the existence of these natural physiographic regions, but Turner showed that "natural, economic, and

[21] "Is Sectionalism in America Dying Away?" *American Journal of Sociology,* XIII (1908), 661–75; "Sections and Nation," *Yale Review,* XII (October, 1922), 1–21; "Geographic Sectionalism in American History," *Annals of the Association of American Geographers,* XVI, 85–93; "The Significance of the Section in American History," *Wisconsin Magazine of History,* VIII, No. 3 (March, 1925).

social sections" were fundamental in explaining American development. Comparable to the nations and empires of Europe, they produced their typical leaders, attitudes, and cultures. "Interacting with each other and in combination they formed the United States," to understand the development of which was the task of the American historian. Turner has traced the colonization of these areas, and the makeup, contributions, and influence of their colonizers, particularly in the physiographic regions called "the Old West" and in the North Central states. In detailed researches he has also studied in this way New England and her colonies in the Old Northwest,[22] pointing out why the migrations took place and how they affected the parent- and daughter-regions as well as the nation as a whole. His investigations showed, among other things, that if the new environment in many ways made the transplanted New Englanders "westerners," at the same time the influence of the squire, the school, and other New England institutions and ideals persisted.

Without indicating the significance of these sectional studies for the political and social history of the country as a whole, mention must be made of the importance for politics of Turner's studies of interprovincial relations. In large measure he interpreted American political history in terms of "a contest between the economic and social sections." Below the surface of politics sectional groupings disclosed the lines on which new party issues were forming. Rival sections made alliances, ententes, for no section could by itself determine the national policy to suit its needs, whether in regard to tariff, currency, public lands, internal improvements, or foreign policy. The existence of subsections within the larger sections complicated these interprovincial relations, often restrained sectional leaders, and sometimes accounted for political "straddling." National parties had their sectional wings, and party organization also tended to diminish sectional antagonisms.

It has been an important contribution to demonstrate that, despite the development of intercommunication and standardization, sectional differences tend to persist. The fact that certain areas of the country must continue agricultural and rural in order to supply the urbanized areas with food promises to check the advance of eastern industrial capitalism over the whole country, although it has made inroads into the South and West. A striking example of the significance of recent sectional rivalry is found in the conflicting attitudes of different areas on the project for a

[22] "Greater New England in the Middle of the Nineteenth Century," *Proceedings of the American Antiquarian Society*, N.S., XXIX (April 9, 1919–October 15, 1919), 222–41.

Great Lakes–St. Lawrence deep-water route. "The triumph of Bolshevism or capitalism," Turner has observed, "would still leave a contest of sections." Thus his interest in physiography and demography led to a fertile re-examination of our history, with the conclusion that "the significance of the section is that it is the faint image of the European nation." Many of his students have illustrated, in their researches, this point of view. Such names as those of O. G. Libby, L. K. Mathews, Louis Pelzer, J. A. James, U. B. Phillips, C. H. Ambler, W. A. Schafer, H. C. Hockett, Clarence E. Carter, Arthur Darling, and Frederick Merk are representative, while William E. Dodd and others have also been deeply influenced by the new interpretation of sectionalism. Marcus Hansen and G. M. Stephenson have concerned themselves with the history of immigration and some of its far-reaching effects.

Turner not only made use of data from economics, physical geography, and demography, or the statistical composition of peoples, but he also studied the development of the national mind, its fundamental assumptions and attitudes. If the frontier made us expansionists in diplomacy and democratic and nationalistic in politics,[23] it no less strikingly, he believed, conditioned national ideals. Out of the frontier process came our peculiar ideal of self-determination, which expressed itself in the philosophy of our Revolution and of the trans-Alleghany state-builders, in the Northwest Ordinance, in squatter's sovereignty, and finally in the ideals of many of those who supported our participation in the World War. "For what was theory in Europe was history in America." Here men went out into new regions and made social compacts. They insisted on and won the right to control their own destiny. Out of the frontier experience came habits of neighborly co-operation, the spontaneously formed associations to meet common problems—the husking bee, the raisings, the squatter associations, the vigilance committees. It was frontier experience which gave America the ideal of religious equality and the demand for the freedom and equality of the individual.

Out of the frontier process came also, it has been maintained, the typical American characteristics of buoyancy, optimism, "a forceful recklessness in the presence of vast opportunities," indifference to the lessons of the Old World, a capacity to see things in the large, in terms of future

[23] The far-reaching extent of the influence of the frontier on national legislation, party alignments, and such fundamental problems as the causes of the Civil War cannot be suggested even in outline. Turner's emphasis on the frontier is so well known that it has obscured his significance for American history as a whole. This is due to the fact that only his students have understood how broadly Turner conceived the frontier; its history was the history of the country.

development, and an ability to dream dreams and to work them out in a practical way. A respect for the self-made man, a readiness to live and to let live, to give and to take, to compromise, to make adjustments—these also came from the frontier experience and from interprovincial relations. Thus the origin of American ideals is found in our historical processes. In these investigations Turner used literary documents, and pointed out the effect of the frontier process on the minds of men like Emerson and even on Old World thought and aspirations, as, for example, on German romanticism.[24] The social psychologist might object to this method of analyzing cases, and might insist that before Turner's conclusions can be accepted as more than probabilities extensive measurement and the testing of alternative hypotheses would be necessary. No one would welcome such a procedure more than Turner himself.

The problem of the relation of ability to heredity and environment has been considered in two papers.[25] The upshot of these investigations is to show that many of the children of pioneers have achieved distinction in every walk of life, and particularly in spheres demanding initiative, organization, and utilitarian idealism. Allowance is made for complex conditions, and methodological errors of predecessors in the field are corrected. Turner's methodology is not final, nor does he claim that it is. Further research should consider more exhaustively other hypotheses, and his generalizations should be further tested by data not used in his studies of *Who's Who* and lists of distinguished men. The questions as to whether the famous cases cited might not have been more famous in the East, whether there were not relatively more eminent ones left in the East, whether the frontier did not cramp the success of the talented children to some extent— these are questions which cannot be answered by his method. The problem of weighing eminence in order to evaluate how favorable or unfavorable the frontier was would have to be attacked, and the problem of why the southern frontier did not produce more distinguished men would have to be considered. Turner does not claim to have given a complete treatment of this problem, and in no sense goes beyond his data. He merely

[24] The ideals conditioned by the frontier experience and by sectional adjustments are a precious heritage, and Turner, as an idealist, hopes that this heritage may help in the solution of such current problems as the conflicts between labor and capital, city and town, region and region. Yet he is very tentative, even in his hopes, for the frontier environment, which he believes conditioned these ideals, has largely passed, and only the future can determine to what extent attitudes conditioned by one type of experience can persist in a very different environment (see Becker, "Frederick Jackson Turner," *op. cit.*, p. 309).

[25] "Greater New England" (cf. n. 22), and "Children of the Pioneers," *Yale Review*, XV (1926), 645–70.

indicates the probable effect of the pioneer environment upon natural ability.

In the field of cultural history Turner has had great influence. While the studies of Dorothy Anne Dondore, Lucy Hazard, and R. L. Rusk have obviously been inspired by him, many other literary and social critics have leaned heavily on the frontier and sectional interpretations of American life.

Although Turner modestly maintains that at most he has guided and encouraged his students, he has done far more than that in setting forth his illuminating concepts. "Out of his seminar at Madison," writes Clarence W. Alvord, not a student but an authority in western history, "have come almost all the men who are today reinterpreting American history from the new viewpoint first established by this pioneer scholar." Even those who did not enjoy his teaching, continues Alvord, were "drawn into the circle of his influence by his personal magnetism and scholarly attainments."[26] Thus men like Alvord, Milo M. Quaife, Frederic Paxson, Reuben Gold Thwaites, Archibald Henderson, and many others owe much to Turner, though they were not products of his seminary. Professor J. W. Thompson applied his conception of the frontier process to the history of medieval Germany, and concluded that "the significance of the frontier in conditioning the history of Germany in the Middle Ages was little less than the significance of the frontier in shaping American history."[27] Victor A. Belaunde demonstrated that in Hispanic-American history the frontier had not shown the same results as in our country, since the geography was such as to favor large possessions rather than "the gradual, agricultural occupation of large contiguous areas by masses of settlers."[28] On the other hand, Herbert E. Bolton, an early student of Turner, has with significant results applied the concept of the frontier to the study of the conflicts of European powers for predominance in the New World, and Carl Russell Fish has likewise considered the frontier process as an international problem. Economists, sociologists, political scientists, and geographers have found the ideas and methods of Turner fertile for their purposes.

It was Turner's custom in his seminary to study each year a relatively small portion of American history. In this study his function was that of the porter at the gates or of the Socratic questioner rather than that of

[26] Clarence W. Alvord, review of Turner's *The Frontier in American History*, in *Mississippi Valley Historical Review*, VII, No. 4 (March, 1921), 404.

[27] "Profitable Fields of Investigation in Medieval History," *American Historical Review*, XVIII (April, 1913), 494.

[28] *Ibid.*, XXVIII (1922–23), 428.

a drill sergeant. Each student took, for the given period, some field in which he was interested, such as agriculture, transportation, immigration, internal improvements, banking, finance, tariff, land policy, literature, labor, or religion; or perhaps he studied the activity of some sectional leader. He was required not only to find and work out a problem in his own field, but also to correlate his problem and to some extent his field with those his colleagues were studying. Out of these studies came many fruitful researches in the fields mentioned, as well as a more realistic type of political history, representative of which are the studies of W. J. Trimble, Charles McCarthy, and Arthur Darling. This catholicity, resulting from Turner's belief that all the social sciences were essentially one, explains in part the significance of his work and that of his school.

No mere list of Turner's students can suggest the almost immeasurable influence which he has exercised by his writing, his teaching, and his personality—an influence so great that American history has been reinterpreted and re-written because of him. It has moreover been re-written in such a way as to integrate it with the other social sciences, and through a methodology no less catholic than critical, to contribute to a significant understanding of the complex forces that have made American society.[29]

[29] [This analysis was first written in October, 1928. It was given final revision by the analyst in August, 1930.—EDITOR.]

ANALYSIS 24

THE WORK OF HENRI PIRENNE AND GEORG VON BELOW WITH RESPECT TO THE ORIGIN OF THE MEDIEVAL TOWN[1]

By CARL STEPHENSON

Cornell University

A hundred years ago historians still glibly asserted the persistence of Roman municipal institutions. By 1880, it is true, better scholars had abandoned that assumption, but their substitute theories, though grand in sweep, were flimsy of structure. To say this is not to sneer at the honest efforts of men who were doing what they could; it is only to state the recognized fact that today standards of criticism are more exacting than they were then, that historical scholarship is sounder than it was. And so far as the medieval town is concerned, this result is due primarily to the work of two eminent medievalists, the late Professor Georg von Below of Freiburg-im-Breisgau and Professor Henri Pirenne of Ghent.

The earlier attempts to elucidate municipal origins in Western Europe have been so often and so well described that detailed repetition here will not be necessary. By 1880 four rival doctrines, originally propounded by Arnold, Nitzsch, Wilda, and Maurer, still claimed their devoted followers. The first derived the town from a group of freemen, who as subjects of the bishop shared the privileges of immunity that he had secured from the emperor; the second from a servile community under the manorial jurisdiction (*Hofrecht*) of a great landlord; the third from

[1] [The original purpose of the present analysis, as it was proposed to Professor Stephenson, was to illustrate the process by which "entities," or objects of investigation in a broad sense, might be identified and defined. The "entity" in this instance was "the medieval town," and it was suggested that the divergent terms in which this object of investigation had been conceived by Henri Pirenne and Max Weber might be compared. After devoting considerable attention to the topic, Professor Stephenson felt that a much sharper comparison could be made between the work of Pirenne and Georg von Below. Moreover, he felt that, since these writers represent the two foremost schools of interpretation, a review of their contributions would serve to introduce the whole controversial subject of town development in the Middle Ages. In proceeding according to the revised plan, the original purpose has not been lost from view. The analysis, to quote the chairman of the Advisory Committee from the American Historical Association, provides "an admirable example of the way historians attack an elusive problem, face all the facts, develop hypotheses, and then revise them in the light of new evidence, especially economic evidence. . . . . " —EDITOR.]

a private association, the gild.[2] These theories need detain us no longer, but the fourth, one of the most captivating theses of the nineteenth century, demands more particular attention. According to Maurer, the town was nothing else than a variant of the *Mark,* the self-governing village, the primeval unit of Teutonic society, the germ from which the free institutions of Europe later developed.[3]

It was thus a bewildering conflict into which' Georg von Below flung himself with the straightforward and not unviolent ardor that always characterized him. Hitherto, his primary interest had been the public authority of the *Landesherr,* the Carolingian count or other holder of regalian right.[4] From *öffentliches Recht* he had been led to taxation and the burgher estate, and so to the town, which, he was convinced, must have begun as a free community. Going then forth to do battle against the disciples of Nitzsch, but not aligning with those of Arnold, he soon found himself in a general mêlée. The outcome was the establishment of a new epoch for historical research in municipal institutions.

Two articles, published in 1887 and 1888, decisively proved the inadequacy both of the *Hofrecht* theory and of the immunity theory.[5] The medieval town, said Below, had risen as an essentially free community, but it did so by assuring liberty to the immigrants who came there, many of whom were of servile origin. Such a settlement differed from the contemporary village in four respects: it had a market; it was walled; it constituted a jurisdictional unit; and it enjoyed special dispensation with regard to fiscal, military, and other political responsibilities. All four of these characteristics were matters of public law, for they came

[2] W. Arnold, *Verfassungsgeschichte der deutschen Freistädte* (Hamburg, 1854); K. W. Nitzsch, *Ministerialität und Bürgertum* (Leipzig, 1859); W. E. Wilda, *Das Gildenwesen im Mittelalter* (Halle, 1831). For the modification and extension of these arguments by other writers see the general criticisms of literature on the towns by Below, Pirenne, Ashley, and Bourgin cited below.

[3] The well-known books of G. L. von Maurer began with the *Einleitung zur Geschichte der Mark-, Hof-, Dorf-, und Städteverfassung und der öffentlichen Gewalt* (Munich, 1854) and ended with the *Geschichte der Stadtverfassung in Deutschland* (Erlangen, 1869–71).

[4] G. von Below, *Die landständische Verfassung in Jülich und Berg bis zum Jahre 1511* (Düsseldorf, 1885–91). For Below's own account of how he came to deal with the town and a general criticism of pertinent writings see *Der deutsche Staat des Mittelalters* (Leipzig, 1914), pp. 45 ff., 91 ff.

[5] "Zur Enstehung der deutschen Stadtverfassung," *Historische Zeitschrift*, LVIII, 193–244; LIX, 193–247. The first of these articles Below in large part reprinted in his *Territorium und Stadt* (Munich, 1900), pp. 303–20.

by virtue of state endowment. All four also were necessitated by the new economic life developed through trade and industry.[6]

Nevertheless, contended Below, these four elements did not make up the town in its entirety; they were accretions which, making a village into a town, still left the village at the heart of the new agglomeration. The urban community had at first been a village community, and to the *Landgemeinde* the *Stadtgemeinde* owed the germ of its constitution. Its self-government was not a matter of *öffentliches Recht*, not the consequence of a jurisdictional delegation from the monarchy, but merely the logical evolution of the primitive *Markgenossenschaft*. The thesis of Maurer was fundamentally sound.

These ideas, briefly stated in his earlier articles, Below developed in a third study, and this in turn was followed by a fourth, especially devoted to the refutation of attacks upon his former publications.[7] Little more needed to be said on the exploded arguments of Nitzsch and Arnold, but the popular gild theory called forth the combined efforts of Hegel, Gross, and Below before it succumbed.[8] Meanwhile, another doctrine, which, emphasizing the mercantile character of the town, derived it from the market, had been given great prominence by the brilliant Sohm. Below, as we have seen, had himself attributed all the characteristic features of town life to an economic revolution, but had insisted that, none the less, the town at heart remained a village. In the promulgation of this doctrine he had considered himself as much a disciple of Sohm as of Maurer, for it was the former who had proved that the *Landgemeinde* had never been a *Gerichtsbezirk*, had never been made a political unit within the Carolingian state.[9]

To Below, the *Marktrecht* theory seemed a desertion of first principles, and he forthwith turned to attack his old master.[10] At the same time,

[6] "Das Stadtrecht is das Recht eines freieren Verkehrs: es ist die Weiterentwickelung des überkommenen Rechts auf einer wirtschaftlich vorgerückteren Stufe," *Hist. Zjt.*, LIX, 207.

[7] *Die Enstehung der deutschen Stadtgemeinde* (Düsseldorf, 1889); *Der Ursprung der deutschen Stadtverfassung* (Düsseldorf, 1892).

[8] K. Hegel, *Städte und Gilden der germanischen Völker im Mittelalter* (Leipzig, 1891); C. Gross, *The Gild Merchant* (Oxford, 1890); G. von Below, "Die Bedeutung der Gilden für die Entstehung der deutschen Stadtverfassung," *Jahrbücher für Nationalökonomie*, LVIII (1892), 56–68.

[9] On the *Mark*, etc., see R. Sohm, *Die altdeutsche Reichs- und Gerichtsverfassung* (Weimar, 1871); on the market theory see *Die Entstehung des deutschen Städtewesens* (Leipzig, 1890).

[10] For Below's attitude toward Sohm and Maurer see particularly "Zur Entstehung der deutschen Stadtverfassung," *Hist. Zjt.*, LIX, 204; *Stadtgemeinde*, pp. 1 ff.; *Stadtverfassung*, pp. 4 ff.; *Der deutsche Staat*, pp. 48 ff., 95 ff., "Ich musste den Schmerz

defending his own thesis, he reasserted his confidence in the *Landgemeinde* as the source of urban self-government. Maurer's *Stadtverfassung* had been sharply assailed for undue reliance upon late documents, for depicting eleventh-century conditions according to fifteenth-century evidence,[11] and that criticism was obviously as valid against the revised version as against the original. Nevertheless, Below insisted that the use of late records was necessary to supplement the fragmentary sources of an earlier age, and was justifiable, provided only that the younger be interpreted in the light of the older. So far as the town was concerned, he said, its development from the village was clearly demonstrated by the many agricultural features that it preserved all through the Middle Ages. It was only when historians wrongly limited their research to a few large and rapidly growing centers that they failed to discover this elemental connection between the urban and the rural community.[12]

At this point in the discussion a young Belgian scholar made a name for himself by contributing two remarkable essays to the *Revue historique*.[13] Having from the outset concentrated his study on the medieval town, Henri Pirenne was already professor at the University of Ghent. His first book, a dissertation on the early history of Dinant,[14] was published in 1889, and in the years immediately following various critical reviews proved his thorough familiarity with the works of Below, Hegel, and other scholars.[15] For fifteen centuries Belgium had been the meeting-point of Latin and Teutonic influences. It was eminently fitting that a Belgian should undertake the elucidation of a problem that concerned France as well as Germany.

Pirenne's essay of 1893 set out first of all to explain for French readers the tangled controversy that had grown up round the beginnings of urban life in medieval Europe. With precision and clarity the con-

---

erleben dass eben auch Sohm, dem ich gerade bei der Schilderung des Verhältnisses von Staat und Gemeinde gefolgt war . . . . , sich jenem Kreis anschloss und die Gemeinde, welcher er früher eine so stolze Stellung neben dem Staat zugewiesen und Bedeutung gerade für die Bildung der Stadtverfassung beigemessen hatte, ganz hinter den Staat zurücktreten liess."

[11] See particularly A. Heusler, *Der Ursprung der deutschen Stadtverfassung* (Weimar, 1872), pp. 157 ff.

[12] Below, *Stadtverfassung*, pp. 4 ff.

[13] H. Pirenne, "L'origine des constitutions urbaines au Moyen Âge," *Revue historique*, LIII (1893), 52–83; LVII (1895), 57–98, 293–327.

[14] *Histoire de la constitution de la ville de Dinant au Moyen Âge* (Ghent, 1889).

[15] A complete list of these reviews will be found in *Mélanges d'histoire offerts à Henri Pirenne* (Brussels, 1926), I, xxxi ff.

flicting views mentioned above were in turn analyzed, appraised, and—in so far as each laid claim to finality—rejected. Pirenne accepted the restatement of the problem that Below had effected, but disagreed with the particular answer that he had given it. In an autonomous village of the early Middle Ages, whether called *Markgenossenschaft* or *Landgemeinde,* Pirenne refused, so long as it was attested only by late medieval evidence, to place confidence. The derivation of municipal institutions as a matter of juristic logic from such an imaginative reconstruction to him lacked historic reality. On the contrary, he believed that the medieval town was pre-eminently the product of social and economic forces which, in spite of all ethnic and political variation, had been fundamentally the same in both halves of the Carolingian Empire. To interpret European phenomena in terms of nationalism was wrong. Only by ignoring such artificial lines as those drawn at the partition of Verdun could the historian hope to arrive at the truth.

The sequel, embodying Pirenne's own ideas on the town, appeared in 1895. Starting with the *civitas* of the late Roman Empire, he showed how, with the advent of the Dark Age, it ceased to be either an economic or a political entity. Important still as a fortress, an administrative center, and a residence for bishop or other prince, it had lost all but an insignificant number of its original inhabitants and all but a few vestiges of its ancient industrial activity. Economically the city became dependent on the agrarian countryside; politically it became a patchwork of rival jurisdictions and immunities.[16] True urban life no longer existed, and before it could be reborn there had to be a revival of commerce.

Meanwhile, Western Europe had come to be dotted with abbeys and castles, round which towns occasionally grew. However, such developments were the exception rather than the rule and were in no instance due to the magnetism of the earlier institution, ecclesiastic or lay. No more could fairs and markets in themselves create towns. In all such cases the true cause for the urban concentration was a geographic situation favorable to trade. Towns grew up in medieval Europe as naturally as they have in modern America. And since the old Roman cities had originally been evolved in response to similar demands, it was to be expected that when trade revived they would revive. This was what happened throughout the larger part of Gaul, but in regions where ancient colonization had been slight, as in Flanders and in most of Germany, new towns arose to meet new needs.

[16] In this connection Pirenne cited particularly J. Flach, *Les origines de l'ancienne France,* Vol. II (Paris, 1893), and Rietschel's work referred to immediately below.

Thus, no matter what the site or whose the soil, the nucleus of the medieval town was a settlement of traders, generally a stockaded quarter outside older fortifications. There, by virtue of the mercantile calling, personal freedom became the rule; seignorial obligations tended to disappear; a new land tenure, a new peace, a new law, a new status developed. And with the rapid expansion of these new elements, what had been the dominant features of the older establishment—agrarian, military, and official—were entirely submerged. It was not from them that the medieval town sprang, but from the exigencies of bourgeois society. Self-government was as new as the middle class itself.

While Pirenne was thus sketching a more comprehensive theory of municipal origins than had as yet appeared, the work of Below was being followed up in Germany by two younger historians, Friedrich Keutgen and Siegfried Rietschel—one in remarkable agreement with Pirenne's ideas, the other in almost diametrical opposition. To Keutgen, the town was not primarily a phenomenon of economic history, but a legal concept. The Anglo-Saxon borough might be treated as homogeneous with the German *Stadt*, because they had a common Teutonic base, but not the Roman *civitas* or the French *ville*. Below had rightly emphasized the distinction between *Gemeindeverfassung* and *Gerichtsverfassung;* whatever the origin of the town as a community, as a jurisdictional unit it began by formal act of the state. And in that respect the cities of the Rhine were copied from the older creations of Henry the Fowler. The primitive German name for town was *Burg; Stadtfriede* was originally not *Marktfriede* but *Burgfriede*. The town as a legal entity was primarily military rather than commercial, for it evolved out of the king's *Burgbann*, which afforded the protection eventually sought by traders. Thus, without denying the primitive communal element in the town, Keutgen made it quite subordinate. The *Dorf* was no *Stadt* until it was made a *Burg*.[17]

While Keutgen was making a particular study of the *Burgen* of Saxony, Rietschel was re-examining the cities of the Rhine Valley, and his conclusions—so far as they went—were quite the same as those shortly afterward published by Pirenne. Until the revival of commerce in the eleventh century, the medieval *civitas* utterly lacked political autonomy, legal unity, and economic self-sufficiency. Socially its inhabitants were

---

[17] F. Keutgen, *Untersuchungen über den Ursprung der deutschen Stadtverfassung* (Leipzig, 1894) ; see also his article, "Commune," in the fourteenth edition of the *Encyclopaedia Britannica*, reprinted from the eleventh. The value of this article for present-day students may be judged from the fact that Pirenne's name does not appear in the bibliography.

indistinguishable from those of the countryside. Nor did the Germans imply that the city was a town when they called it *Burg*, for that was merely their name for any fortified enclosure. Neither dense population, nor mercantile life, nor municipal organization occasioned the usage, but solely the wall. In fact, the early Germans, whose society was thoroughly agrarian, could have had no conception of a town as an urban center; that meaning of the word *Burg* was the product of later centuries.[18]

These ideas Rietschel further elaborated in a second book published three years later.[19] Still a believer in the *Mark*, and in many respects a disciple of Below, he found little evidence for the derivation of the *Stadtgemeinde* from the *Landgemeinde*. On the other hand, he held with Pirenne that the medieval town regularly grew from an independent source, from a mercantile settlement alongside a previously existing castle, church, village, or episcopal city. From the older institution the new one got nothing but its name. Below had overestimated the importance of the primitive rustic element in urban evolution. The possession of forest and pasture rights by burghers did not imply that they lived by agriculture; merchants had to have horses, and artisans regularly kept cows, goats, and pigs. Moreover, villages that in later ages secured rights copied after towns were of no importance for explaining municipal origins. Both *Marktrecht* and *Burgrecht* had their influence in *Stadtrecht*, but the significance of market and wall must not be exaggerated. "Die Stadt ist ein Markt der zugleich Burg ist. Alle Städte sind Märkte, aber nicht alle Märkte sind Städte; alle Städte sind Burgen, aber nicht alle Burgen sind Städte."[20]

With the close of the century it thus became apparent that such narrow and arbitrary interpretations of the sources as had once prevailed were forever discredited. To that extent the joint efforts of Below and Pirenne had proved decisive. Though on the constructive side there was no complete agreement, it could soon be seen that the really controversial matters were rapidly shrinking. The debate still continued; old slogans were still repeated; but little by little viewpoints were shifted and the antagonists made notable concessions to each other's opinions.

Keutgen, as we have seen, had greatly emphasized the importance of fortification for municipal history, and his thesis, while rendering the factor of the *Landgemeinde* relatively insignificant, by no means denied

[18] S. Rietschel, *Die Civitas auf deutschem Boden bis zum Ausgange der Karolingerzeit* (Leipzig, 1894), esp. pp. 1 ff., 124 ff., 142 ff., 162 ff.
[19] Rietschel, *Markt und Stadt* (Leipzig, 1897). See below, notes 23, 27.
[20] *Ibid.*, p. 150.

it. Indeed, in later publications Keutgen posed as the great champion of Below's doctrine against the onslaught of Rietschel and Pirenne. Their fundamental contention had been that places called *civitates, castella, urbes,* or *burgi* in the ninth and the tenth century were not necessarily towns; that the real origin of the latter lay in mercantile settlements attached to the old centers. Keutgen, however, could not see the point. In an article of 1900 he insisted that *Burgrecht* could mean nothing but *Stadtrecht,* and accused Rietschel of exaggerating the significance of artificial *Marktansiedelungen.*[21] Even if, he added in 1903, most towns had been thus founded, the truth neither of his own nor of Below's theory was in the least impaired.[22] In his last book Rietschel entered into no long controversy, but did produce new evidence to support his original thesis. He found that even as late as the twelfth century walled towns were rare in Germany. By 1200 not more than a dozen had appeared, of which nine were old Roman cities. And although, as shown by Gerlach, Rietschel's figures were too small, it became more absurd than ever to describe Henry the Fowler as a great founder of towns.[23]

The proof of Rietschel's victory lay in the acceptance of his doctrine by Below. In an article of 1915 the latter scholar frankly accredited Rietschel with having accomplished a great simplification of the problem and unreservedly adopted his reclassification of the German towns.[24] Furthermore, said Below, his own *Landgemeinde* theory had in no way denied the decisive influence of trade; it had sought to explain, not why the town grew, but out of what it grew. And with that amicable outcome the case has since rested.[25]

[21] Keutgen, "Der Ursprung der deutschen Stadtverfassung," *Neue Jahrbücher für das klassische Altertum, Geschichte und deutsche Litteratur, und für Pädagogik,* V (1900), 275–99. Specific criticism of Pirenne and his school is slight. Keutgen's defense of his earlier insistence on nationalism constitutes a strategic retreat.

[22] Keutgen, *Aemter und Zünfte* (Jena: Gustav Fischer, 1903), pp. 110 ff.

[23] Rietschel, *Das Burggrafenamt und die hohe Gerichtsbarkeit* (Leipzig, 1905), pp. 323 ff.; W. Gerlach, *Die Entstehungszeit der Städtebefestigungen in Deutschland* (Leipzig, 1913), esp. pp. 21, 36, 74. Cf. Pirenne's comment in *Rev. hist.,* LVII, 65. A more recent article by Carl Koehne, *Hist. Zft.,* CXXXIII, 1 ff., accepts Rietschel's conclusions and seeks only, by a rather doubtful garrison theory, to explain the growth of trade in the old military foundations. See below, n. 27.

[24] Below, "Zur Geschichte der deutschen Stadtverfassung," *Jahrbücher für Nationalökonomie and Statistik,* CV (1915), 651–62. On the notion that his thesis contradicted Rietschel's see p. 654: "Wer so argumentiert, übersieht, dass die Landgemeindetheorie ja nur erklären will, in und aus welchem Rahmen die Stadtgemeinde sich entwickelt habe: Handel und Gewerbe haben rein faktisch aus der Landgemeinde die Stadtgemeinde erhoben."

[25] For Below's final word on the subject see his *Probleme der Wirtschaftsgeschichte* (Tübingen, 1920), p. 474, n. 4: "Ich habe früher die Zahl der Städte, die unmittelbar aus Landgemeinden hervorgegangen sind, erheblich höher angeschlagen,

Meanwhile Pirenne greatly developed and strengthened the arguments that he had tentatively offered in 1895. In a brief article of 1898 he joined Keutgen and Rietschel in writing finis to the *Marktrecht* theory. Disagreeing with Rietschel only in his explanation of the *Stadtfriede,* wherein the latter followed Keutgen, Pirenne gave further support to the theory of the town as a mercantile colony. In Flanders, he pointed out, the great communes all began as *portus,* or trading settlements, beside the count's castles.[26] This important fact, it should be remarked, was no recent discovery of Pirenne's. Though very briefly touched in his article of 1895, it had earlier been noted in his edition of Galbert de Bruges and had been learned from him by many pupils.[27] But from now on the fortress as a great factor in helping to produce the Flemish towns was more and more to be emphasized. Briefly sketched in the *History of Belgium,*[28] Pirenne's idea did not receive definitive treatment until 1905.[29] Since then it has been made very familiar, even in English-speaking countries, by many popular presentations.[30]

Today it is well known that the old Flemish *burg* was a castle; that the new *burg* or *port* was a colony of traders; that by the twelfth century the new *burg* had entirely engulfed the old and had become a town where recently no town had been. And with this knowledge we are not only in-

---

als ich es heute, namentlich durch die Forschungen Rietschels eines Besseren belehrt, tue." It should be noted also that, while he often disagreed with Keutgen, Below cited with virtually unmixed approval various works of Pirenne and his pupils (see his Index of Authors).

[26] Pirenne, "Villes, marchés et marchands au Moyen Age," *Rev. hist.,* LXVII (1898), 59–70.

[27] See *Rev. hist.,* LVII, No. 1 (1895), 74; Galbert de Bruges, *Histoire du meurtre de Charles le Bon,* ed. Pirenne (Paris, 1891), p. 15, n. 2 (on *suburbium*), p. 49, n. 1 (on *burgus = castellum*); H. van Houtte, *Essai sur la civilisation flamande au commencement du XIIe siècle d'après Galbert de Bruges* (Louvain, 1898), pp. 74 ff.; G. des Marez, *Etude sur la propriété foncière dans les villes du Moyen Âge et spécialement en Flandre* (Ghent, 1898); G. Espinas, *Les finances de la commune de Douai* (Paris, 1902).

[28] First published as *Die Geschichte Belgiens* (Gotha, 1899); but see the second edition of the *Histoire de Belgique* (Brussels, 1902), I, 169 ff.

[29] Pirenne, "Les villes flamandes avant le XIIe siècle," *Annales de l'Est et du Nord,* I (1905), 9–32.

[30] Pirenne, *Les anciennes démocraties des Pays-Bas* (Paris, 1910), translated as *Belgian Democracy* (Manchester, 1915); *Medieval Cities* (Princeton, 1925), published in French as *Les villes du Moyen Âge* (Brussels, 1927). The latter is much to be preferred to the American edition, having fuller notes and not suffering from obscurities and inaccuracies of translation. The title should be *Medieval Towns,* for in the text "city" is used to mean the Roman *civitas.* See also Pirenne's chapter on the northern towns in the *Cambridge Medieval History,* VI, 505 ff.

spired with greater confidence in Rietschel's explanation of the primitive German *Burg*, but we are also predisposed to favor a similar explanation for the revival of the Roman *civitas*. We may even imagine a reconciliation of Pirenne's theory of the town peace with Keutgen's.[31] However that may be, his thesis concerning the Flemish towns has far-reaching consequences. The decided skepticism concerning Pirenne's theory expressed by Ashley in 1896[32] is no longer possible, for much of the specific information that he then called for has since been supplied.[33]

For a long time, of course, it will be foolish to indulge in positive assertions concerning the beginnings of all Western European towns, each of which has its individual history to be worked out. It is altogether probable that wide scope must always be allowed to local variations. There is no reason, for example, to believe that traders never settled within ancient fortifications, that every merchant was migratory and hibernating, or that purely agricultural colonies might not be given special law and privileged status. But enough evidence in favor of Pirenne's general contention has been produced to throw the burden of proof squarely on those who deny its validity.

Old ideas, nevertheless, are hard to down, especially the romantic convictions of one's youth. Below's last work voiced a confidence in the primitive *Landgemeinde* still unshaken—and adduced no new evidence.[34] Vanderkindere, after the lapse of thirty years, went back to the *Mark* to demonstrate an ancient pedigree for medieval munipical institutions.[35]

[31] In proportion as the trading class sought the protection of the fortress, *Burgfriede* would tend to become *Stadtfriede*. This was Rietschel's idea for Germany (see above, n. 19) and Maitland's for England (see below, n. 39).

[32] W. J. Ashley, "The Beginnings of Town Life in the Middle Ages," *Quarterly Journal of Economics*, X (1896), 359–406; reprinted in *Surveys Historic and Economic* (London, 1900), pp. 167 ff. It should be noted that in his review of Pirenne's *Geschichte Belgiens* Ashley in 1899 somewhat revised his judgment (*ibid.*, pp. 238–41).

[33] For example, the subject of burgage tenure has been greatly clarified by applying the mercantile theory of Pirenne and Rietschel. See des Marez, *op. cit.*, above, n. 27; R. Génestal, *La tenure en bourgage* (Paris, 1900); *Eng. Hist. Rev.*, Apr., 1930, pp. 185 ff.

[34] Below, *Probleme der Wirtschaftsgeschichte*, pp. 62 ff. For the very considerable revision of his previous doctrine on the competence of the *Landgemeinde* see the references in n. 4, p. 474. An excellent summary of the real evidence on the *Mark* will be found in A. Dopsch, *Die Wirtschaftsentwickelung der Karolingerzeit* (Weimar, 1921), I, 361 ff. See also Ashley, *Surveys*, 161 f.; and J. W. Thompson, *Economic and Social History of the Middle Ages* (New York, 1928), chap. iii, pp. 87–109.

[35] *Bulletin de l'Académie Royale de Belgique*, XXXVIII (2e sér., 1874), 236 ff.; *ibid.*, Classe des lettres, XLIII (3e sér., 1905), pp. 749–89; *Annales de l'Est et du Nord*, I (1905), 321–67. For a criticism of these articles see Pirenne, "La question

In England, where Maurer's doctrine was consecrated through adoption
by Stubbs,[36] and where Below's work was well advertised by Keutgen's
contributions to the *English Historical Review*,[37] the conviction seems to
be general that the town must have developed from a village. Even the
distinguished Vinogradoff, relying on nothing better than fourteenth-cen-
tury sources, continued to insist on the self-governing Anglo-Saxon township,[38] although Maitland had refused to accredit the village with more
than a rudimentary system of co-operative husbandry.[39]

To the great historian of the English law, the original borough was
not a variant of the rural township, but a royal fortress, used as an administrative center and endowed with a special peace which, with the
economic changes of the eleventh century, made it a favorable place for
trading. Maitland, it will be noted, was quick to follow Keutgen, but
saw no necessity of accepting the *Landgemeinde*. And if Maitland had
lived to know the later work of Pirenne, would he not immediately have
seen how the history of the Flemish *burg* helped to explain that of the
English borough? At any rate, until British scholars agree as to what
they mean when they say *town*, the problem of municipal origins in their
country will remain obscure.[40]

---

des jurées dans les villes flamandes," *Revue belge de philologie et d'histoire*, V
(1926), 401–21; also F. L. Ganshof, in *Le Moyen Âge*, XXVI (1926), 349–68.

[36] *Constitutional History* (6th ed.; Oxford, 1903), I, 53 f., 88 ff., 99: "The 'burh'
of the Anglo-Saxon period was simply a more strictly organized form of township."

[37] *Eng. Hist. Rev.*, VIII (1893), 550–51.

[38] P. Vinogradoff, *The Growth of the Manor* (London, 1905), pp. 185 ff.: his argument to justify the use of late evidence is much the same as Below's (see above,
n. 12). For Vinogradoff's idea of the borough as a variety of township see *ibid.*,
p. 261, n. 27; also *English Society in the Eleventh Century* (Oxford, 1908), pp. 398 ff.

[39] F. W. Maitland, *Domesday Book and Beyond* (Cambridge, 1897), pp. 340–56,
and on the borough, pp. 172–219. Maitland had already published a summary of
these ideas in connection with a review of Keutgen: "The Origin of the Borough,"
Eng. Hist. Rev., XI (1896), 13–19, Tait's review of Maitland's book (*ibid.*, XII
[1897], 768–77) upheld the orthodox doctrine of Maurer, Below, and Stubbs.
On the other hand, Keutgen devoted a large section of his article (see above, n. 21)
to an enthusiastic but inaccurate résumé of Maitland's conclusions.

[40] Up to the date of its publication an admirable guide to the literature on the
English borough is furnished by C. Petit-Dutaillis, *Studies and Notes Supplementary.
to Stubbs' Constitutional History* (Manchester, 1908), pp. 67–90. For a good comment on books that appeared in the next ten years see J. Tait, "The Study of Early
Municipal History in England, *Proceedings of the British Academy*, X (1921–23),
201–17. Since the accompanying text was written, I have discussed the literature on
the English towns much more thoroughly in "The Anglo-Saxon Borough," *Eng. Hist.
Rev.*, April, 1930; see esp. pp. 190 ff., 202 ff.

As to France, one would not expect the native land of Fustel de Coulanges to be a hotbed of enthusiasm for the Teutonic *Mark*. However, as late as 1903, Bourgin, in a general review of literature on the towns, expressed a decided leaning toward the Maurer-Below doctrine.[41] The reason, of course, was the prominence of agriculture in the Soissons group of communes to which Bourgin was devoting his special attention.[42] But just how Soissons differed from Noyon, or Liège, or Strasbourg, or how the communal development of France can be explained as the natural product of a purely feudal society, remains a mystery. Luchaire, indeed, who popularized the misleading doctrine of the commune as a *seigneurie collective*, declared the problem of origins insoluble.[43] Flach, after a brilliant description of the Roman city in Frankish Gaul, left the revival of town life rather more obscure than when he started to elucidate it.[44] The classic sketch of the emancipation movement by Giry and Réville, to be sure, gave as its real cause the economic and social transformation of the eleventh century, but being written before Pirenne's articles had appeared, stopped with a vague generalization.[45] This, it is safe to say, will no longer be done by French historians. Halphen, in re-editing

[41] G. Bourgin, "Les études sur les origines urbaines du Moyen Âge," *Revue de synthèse historique*, VII (1903), 317: "Néanmoins la théorie Maurer-Below nous paraît avoir eu cet avantage de nous rappeler que le caractère essentiel de l'économie médiévale est agricole: dissocier cette économie et la révolution communale est une erreur fondamentale de ceux-là même qui ont vu dans l'état économique de la société aux XIe XIIe siècles la cause profonde de cette révolution."

[42] Bourgin, *La commune de Soissons et le groupe communale soissonais* (Paris, 1908). See the penetrating criticism of this book by Espinas in *Le Moyen Âge*, XIII (2e sér., 1909), 309–46.

[43] A. Luchaire, *Les communes françaises* (Paris, 1890), pp. 11–25. On the commune as a *seigneurie collective* see my articles in *Le Moyen Âge*, XXIV (2e sér., 1922), 332 ff., and *Anniversary Essays in Medieval History by Students of C. H. Haskins* (Boston, 1929), pp. 296 ff., 305. More detailed consideration will be given the subject in a forthcoming article, "Communes and Other Towns."

[44] J. Flach, *op. cit.*, Vol. II. On Flach and other French writers see Ashley, *Surveys*, pp. 122 ff., 178 ff.; Bourgin, as cited above, n. 41; and Pirenne's first article. Flach replied to Pirenne in A. Foville. *Enquête sur les conditions de l'habitation en France* (Paris, 1894), II, 53, but misunderstood Pirenne's argument—see Espinas, *Les finances de la commune de Douai* (Paris, 1902), p. 12. More recently F. Funck-Brentano, in his popular history, *Le Moyen Âge* (Paris, 1922), chap. II, has gone beyond Flach in identifying *château* and *ville*, but his patriarchal-feudal theory is not to be taken seriously.

[45] In Lavisse and Rambaud, *Histoire générale* (Paris, 1893), II, 418 ff. The chapter by Eleanor Constance Lodge in the *Cambridge Medieval History*, V (Cambridge, 1926), in the matter of origins, hardly goes beyond the essay of Giry and Réville. A recent summary of the entire problem by J. W. Thompson (*op. cit.*, chap. xxviii) agrees whole-heartedly with Pirenne.

Luchaire's book, frankly threw the prestige of his support to Pirenne's doctrines.[46] And more recently another leading scholar of France has given approbation as enthusiastic as it is authoritative to the central theme of the *Villes du Moyen Âge*.[47]

To summarize the foregoing materials and assess their value for historical method would at first glance seem difficult enough. However, by clearing away irrelevant obstructions, the problem may be resolved to reasonably simple terms. In the first place, all particularist theories of municipal origins—*Hofrecht, Marktrecht,* etc.—can at once be ignored. And so far as it cannot be combined with Pirenne's general thesis, Keutgen's doctrine is beside the point; for it obviously deals primarily with the *Burg,* not with the town. In the second place, all controversies over local peculiarities of *Stadtrecht,* exceptional features of Carolingian trade, technical definitions of *mercator,* and the like, can be passed over as quite secondary to the main issue.

Below, while allowing the commercial revival decisive influence toward increasing the town's population and delimiting its political responsibilities, held that as an autonomous community the town could only be what the village already was in miniature. For how could either economic revolution or state intervention create something that antedated both? And so today any one who accepts the *Mark* theory—whether under that name or another—as an established fact will have no difficulty in explaining the beginnings of self-government in Europe apart from economic phenomena. It will not be hard for him to believe that what we call liberty is *uralt;* that it has survived the feudalism and manorialism of the Dark Age. He may even talk of it as a racial heritage.

On the other hand, one who does not start with confidence in the *Mark* system will have difficulty in avoiding Pirenne's major contentions. To follow Below, he must believe that all of the medieval town except the communal germ at the heart of it was the product of economic revolution. Leaving Below there, will he not then attribute that germ also— if he must have one—to the creative force of commerce? The net result of a hundred years of research has been to prove the newness of town life in medieval Europe. Pirenne's theory has the advantage of meeting the issue squarely and offering an explanation of how towns grew up. Whether or not the argument is correctly stated in all of its parts only further research can tell. It has certainly received striking confirmation

---

[46] Luchaire, *op. cit.* (Paris, 1911), Introduction.

[47] A. Coville, "Les villes du Moyen Âge," *Journal des savants,* XVI (January-February, 1928), 15–22, 72–80.

in many regions outside Flanders, and there the justice of its application seems beyond question. In any case, it is offered, not as a proposition in logic, but as a working hypothesis subject to verification.[48]

That is the nub of the matter. If anyone accepts Pirenne's theory, he should do so because it best fits the data of our sources. And so with the *Mark* theory; he should not hold it as true just because an Indo-Germanic ancestry for the New England town meeting appeals to his fancy. As I see it, the problem of the medieval town, like other historical problems, is one of fact-finding. I do not believe that there is one set of facts for legal history and a contradictory set for economic history. Before the historian can study the origin of the town, he must decide whether a town is primarily a juristic idea or a human settlement. To Pirenne, obviously, it is the latter. He belongs to the more modern school that emphasizes social and economic factors in history as, if not paramount, at least of more fundamental significance than legal theory. He believes that law can at best only define certain aspects of life; that to create or to kill a living social organism it is and always has been powerless.

This viewpoint, undoubtedly, is part of the age in which we chance to live; we have no assurance that it will outlast our century. But as historians, the best we can ever do is to use the knowledge of today and through it hope to explain the past. Some years ago Carl Becker wrote some very true words about the futility of the historian's trying to detach himself from the present.[49] Must we on that account despair of scientific history? I cannot think so. I do not see that the methods of the historian differ essentially from those of the geologist or other natural scientist who deals with past phenomena that cannot be reduplicated. His peculiar difficulties arise from the nature of his sources and the instability of the premises with which he must begin. Comparable to those of the geologist, he has no fundamental sciences from which to draw his postulates. For most of his work he has nothing on which to build but the unformulated observations of the man in the street.[50]

Nevertheless, to the extent that the study of economics has been able to prove its basic importance for modern life, history may be subjected to economic interpretation. And so far as we are now able to judge, historical research has thereby become infinitely richer and truer. To take the specific case of the medieval town, can any amount of juristic analy-

---

[48] See Pirenne's preface to his *Villes du Moyen Âge*.

[49] "Detachment and the Writing of History," *Atlantic Monthly*, CVI (1910), 524–36.

[50] My own ideas on this much-debated question will be found in "Facts in History," *Historical Outlook*, November, 1928, 313–17.

sis ever tell us what it was like? On the other hand, can any inquiry on the subject afford to dispense with our present conviction as to the mercantile basis of town life?

That many urban communities of the Middle Ages long continued to show agricultural features is certain, but that urban communities were ever predominantly agricultural we cannot believe. For, knowing the character of medieval husbandry, how can we suppose any settlement of men larger than a village to have supported themselves by it? Or if we add together a religious congregation, a military garrison, and a household of officials, we do not make a town; we still have only a monastery and a castle and an administrative bureau. The fact is that our experience does not teach us of a town without trade. Because Pirenne's reconstruction of the past is founded on that certainty of everyday observation, it bids fair to stand.[51]

[51] The substance of the foregoing essay, with fuller treatment of the literature on French and English towns, will form the introductory chapter of a book, *Borough and Town*, now in preparation. [This analysis was first written in September, 1928. His citations were checked and revised by the analyst in September, 1930.—EDITOR.]

ANALYSIS 25

HISTORY AND NATIONALISM AS PORTRAYED
BY SIDNEY B. FAY[1]

By WILLIAM L. LANGER

Harvard University

In undertaking a study of the origins of the World War, Professor Fay was obliged to face many of the problems of the modern historian in their most acute form. Taken in the broadest sense, the war was a general cataclysm resulting from the peculiar conditions of our civilization and striking at the very foundations of the social structure. This is hardly the place to draw a comparison between the latest and greatest of international conflicts and other general European struggles. Suffice it to say that the basis of earlier conflagrations was a different social system. Even the Napoleonic wars were fought before ideas of democracy had widened the basis of political life, before such ideas as universal military service had transformed the old professional armies and created the modern nation in arms, before the shibboleth of nationalism had aroused popular passions, and before the economic transformations of the nineteenth century had welded the nations of the world together, making contact and conflict almost inescapable.

Fay recognizes the almost insurmountable difficulty of discussing adequately these underlying causes of the conflict.

These are so complex and reach so far back into the past that any attempt to describe them adequately would involve nothing less than the writing of the whole diplomatic history of Europe since 1870, or rather from 1789; some questions go back to the age of Louis XIV, and even to that of Charlemagne. It would also involve the difficult technical study of the military and naval forces of the various countries, their plans of campaign, the relation of the military to the civilian authorities in each country, the psychology of fear, and all the other factors which go to make up the somewhat vague conceptions of "militarism" and "navalism" as causes of war. No less important would be the analysis of that complex force which first began to be a powerful, disruptive agency during the French Revolution, and which steadily gathered strength for a century and a quarter, which we call "nationalism." This in turn is

[1] Sidney B. Fay, *The Origins of the World War* (2 vols.; New York: Macmillan Co., 1929. 2d ed., revised, 1 vol.; New York: Macmillan Co., 1930). References are to the first edition.

closely bound up with psychological and political questions of race, religion, democracy, education, and popular prejudice. Still more important, in many minds, as underlying causes of the War are the intricate political and economic problems which have arisen from the transformation of society during the past hundred years by the modern industrial system which began in England and subsequently penetrated more or less all the great countries of the world—problems of excess population, food supply, foreign markets and raw materials, colonial possessions, and the accumulation of capital seeking investment abroad. Finally, the influence of the newspaper press is a factor much greater than commonly supposed in causing the World War. . . . . Obviously, no single volume can hope to deal thoroughly with all these complex and interrelated factors which constitute the underlying causes of the World War.[2]

It may, in fact, be doubted whether any one person could ever master all these different aspects of the problem, even in a lifetime of study. The task would, indeed, involve a complete critique of modern society in its racial, economic, religious, intellectual, and psychological expressions.

Fay's book is primarily a study of European diplomacy and international relations from 1870 to 1914. He makes no defense or explanation of his choice of viewpoint or line of approach. It is clear from the foregoing quotation that he is not blind to the non-political aspects of his problem or to the ultimate implications of the subject. He has, in fact, briefly summarized the more intangible factors in the situation and has never left them out of account in his narrative of events. They are inextricably bound up in his whole account of the diplomatic negotiations. But he does not consider them decisive, singly or jointly: "It is very doubtful whether all these dangerous tendencies would have actually led to war, had it not been for the assassination of Franz Ferdinand." The conclusion is one based on a careful examination of the evidence pertaining to this particular problem. "It is not so much questions of economic rivalry as those of prestige, boundaries, armies and navies, the Balance of Power and possible shiftings in the system of alliances, which provoke reams of diplomatic correspondence and raise the temperature in Foreign Offices to the danger point."[3] But there is more involved than this. The whole school of so-called "diplomatic historians" has been under fire from the advocates of the "new history" for some time past. Fay belongs unreservedly to neither school, but represents a modified view which has been widely accepted by writers of modern history. He regards diplomacy not as the profession of the trained intriguer maneuvering for the benefit

[2] *Ibid.*, I, 32–33.   [3] *Ibid.*, p. 46.

of his sovereign or government without consideration for larger human interests. Diplomacy for him is merely the machinery through which the country's needs and aspirations find expression. The subject matter of diplomatic negotiation may change from age to age, but at any given time it will be the reflection of the interests of the powers it represents. In our own day it mirrors not only the striving for power in the political or military sense, but the surge of nationalism, imperialism, and public opinion as well. And in this broad sense the study of diplomatic history or the study of history from the diplomatic angle needs no justification or defense.

The question has often been raised as to whether or not recent events can be satisfactorily treated by the historian at all. The difficulty does not arise so much from dearth of material. For the study of recent economic, intellectual, or social history there is usually more than enough material at hand. In the case of political or diplomatic history this is less likely to be true, because, as a rule, the state archives are not opened for fifty or seventy-five years. The World War is a noteworthy exception, for various reasons have combined to bring about the publication of large masses of official papers, to say nothing of diaries, memoirs, and private correspondence. This taken together with material on economic, social, and other aspects makes the amount of source data so impressive that no one man could conceivably master the whole of it. There are still gaps, as there are likely to be in the sources for any historical study, but it is probably safe to say that we have more available information on the origins of the World War than on the cause of any other great conflict in history. More important yet, we have a larger relative amount of authentic and official material than we could normally expect to possess for several generations.

The question of the abundance of sources does not, then, enter into this problem. The real difficulty is in getting the proper perspective. Few historians today would subscribe to the viewpoint of a Droysen or a Treitschke or identify their mission with that of the apostles of nationalism. But the problem is not solved by saying that the historian must be impartial. His attitude may be conditioned by the very nature of the material at his disposal. Fay himself has outlined the various phases through which the study of the origins of the war has passed in the last decade, and has indicated the objections that might be raised to most previous treatments of the subject.

One finds one's self here first in the bewildering maze of official war propaganda, then in the deluge of post-war apologias and justificatory writings. Accounts written during the war are worthless, for they were of necessity based upon insufficient and one-sided material and were written to serve a political end. Many of the post-war productions are equally valueless, because very few of them were written *sine ira ac studio* by competent historians. You have men like Kautsky and Pokrovsky writing from the socialist or bolshevik viewpoint, aiming primarily to discredit the old régime in Germany or Russia. You have men, especially in France and England, who may be classed as idealists, humanitarians, pacifists, and radicals whose attack is directed either against the representatives of the existing régime in 1914 or against the "international anarchy" as such. Others, like Heinrich Kanner and Senator Owen, appear to be possessed by a fixed idea and strive to reduce everything to a formula which will prove the validity of their thesis. On the other hand, there are the nationalist historians, particularly in Germany, who devote their efforts to the exoneration of their governments. Some of the work done by these men is of high value and has paved the way for sounder conclusions, especially in regard to the immediate origins of the war. But, after all, even the trained historians of this group are likely to be descendants of the earlier nationalist writers. It would be unreasonable to expect them to write against their country. Convinced as they are of the justice of their viewpoint, they quite naturally adduce all evidence which tends to support their thesis. Renouvin in France may be taken as an example of a well-trained and conscientious historian who, in spite of everything, ends up more or less as the official historiographer of his country. So long as historians remain human they will be unable to free themselves from innate or subconscious prejudices, social, national, religious, or what you will. It should be clear that the ideal historian is really an ideal. But in dealing with recent events it is obvious that the historian should be so far removed as possible from active interest in all or any parties to the dispute, and that he should have no preconceived notions of any kind, either political or social.

No writer on the subject to date has so nearly fulfilled the requirements as Fay. His early training as a historian was of the highest grade, and he has had wide experience in historical work on other periods. During the war he was one of the few members of the profession, even in the United States, who resisted the rising tide of propaganda and maintained a critical attitude. After the war he appeared as one of the first writers of sound history based on authentic material. He has taken the necessary time to study the immense volume of data carefully. As an American, he stands outside the dispute. No one has ever seriously questioned his impartiality or accused him of serving any cause but that of the truth. If men of his type are not to write on recent history, then the writing of such history must be renounced entirely.

Reference has already been made to the difficulties presented by the immense amount of material. Other problems arise from the nature of the material itself. In the first place there is the language question, which is certainly not insuperable, but which, nevertheless, is a great obstacle to the student. The growth of nationalist sentiment led, even before the war, to the abandonment of the French language as the language of correspondence between ambassadors and their governments. This means that diplomatic documents and other state papers are written in the various national tongues, including Russian. In the same way, the memoirs written by participants in the events are not necessarily published in western languages. The recollections of Bilinski, a high Austrian official of Polish nationality, appeared in Polish and have not been translated. The revelations from Serbia appeared in Serbian and have been translated only in part. In some instances, the translations must be used as the originals have never been published, but it is clear that the use of translations is dangerous and is to be avoided whenever possible. The nuances of the original are frequently hard to render, and much may depend upon them. In the case of the Benckendorff correspondence, the originals have never been published and the revised translation of the second edition (in German) shows that the first edition was in many respects regrettably loose. The fact is that the student of modern diplomatic history must be able to read many of the European languages and that, like Fay, he must rely upon the originals when possible in order to avoid dangerous pitfalls.

The material itself is, of course, of different types. First and foremost come the official documents, beginning with the very deficient and frequently unreliable "colored books" of 1914 and 1915, and ending with the great government publications, some of which are not yet complete. The German collection *(Die Grosse Politik der Europäischen Kabinette, 1871-1914)* is by far the most extensive and voluminous and fills forty volumes. Unlike other collections it covers the entire period since the Peace of Frankfurt in systematic fashion. The British collection is complete for the crisis of July, 1914, but goes back only to the year 1898 and still lacks the volumes covering the period from 1910 to 1914. The Russian documents have never been systematically published, but we have papers dealing with certain subjects from 1870 on, and the correspondence between St. Petersburg and London and Paris is fairly complete for the period from 1910 to 1914. The Austrian government has published all the documents bearing on the July crisis, and Pribram's *The Secret Treaties of Austria-Hungary* contain the text of all agreements made by the government between 1879 and 1914, as well as a complete narrative of the negotiations dealing with the Triple Alliance. The French and the Italian governments have promised collections of correspondence, but these have not yet seen the light. It may be thought that the lacunae in this branch of the material are so serious as to make definitive treatment of the subject impossible, but experience has shown that the new material that has appeared recently adds comparatively little to what has been known from sources published earlier. Some points will undoubtedly remain forever obscure, but the historian can never hope for exhaustive material. There comes a point beyond which further waiting or further search becomes unprofitable. By some historians it was felt that Fay waited longer than necessary, but it is clear that he would have made a mistake in not waiting for the British documents on the July crisis, for example. Now, however, most of the important material is at our disposal, especially so far as the events of July are concerned. It is very doubtful whether the French documents would alter Fay's fundamental conclusions, though they may affect the shading and emphasis.

Official documents have sometimes been described as dead records of past events. They have, however, the great advantage of being contemporary records which were not intended for publication, and they frequently throw light not only upon the actual events but upon the mentality and motives of the writer or the participants. An appreciation of Napoleon or Bismarck written without reference to their state papers would be a sorry performance at best. The official records of the governments must always remain the most important source material for the history of international relations. On the other hand, supplementary material in the form of diaries and memoirs may be of the greatest significance. As between the two, contemporary diaries, written informally and usually without the thought of publication, are likely to have high value as the records of the ideas and motives which conditioned the action of statesmen. Fay carefully distinguishes between these sources and the memoirs which were written with the advantage of hindsight. Unfortunately, records of this kind are very few so far as the crisis of July is concerned. There are not very many dealing even with the earlier period, and their absence is bound to be felt keenly by the historian.

The volumes of recollections and memoirs, however, are exceedingly numerous. As might have been expected, the first ones appeared in the

defeated countries and were intended to serve as apologies. But the publication of these defensive writings on the one side was bound to call
forth rejoinders from the other side, and we are now well supplied with
contributions of statesmen and diplomats in almost all the leading and
decisive positions. Material of this sort must be used with the greatest
caution, due consideration being given to the writer's object and to the
question whether the writer was relying solely upon his memory or upon
correspondence or notes. Much of this material has been analyzed by
Gooch in the various editions of his *Recent Revelations of European Diplomacy,* and some excellent critical work has been done in the analysis
of such memoirs as those of Bismarck, Eckardstein, Grey, Poincaré, and
Sazonov. Fay himself reviews the material in an introductory chapter
and gives a succinct estimate of the value he attaches to the different
contributions.

Writing within the first decade after the end of the war, it might have
been possible for Fay to consult some of the surviving statesmen of the
1914 period. Some writers on the subject have, in fact, sought and obtained interviews with men like William II, Grey, Berchtold, Jagow, and
others. It may well be doubted, however, whether information secured
in this way can have high value, coming, as it does, so long after the
events and being offered in reply to questions and criticisms. At best,
this information would have the value of written memoirs. Still it cannot be denied that personal interviews with the actual participants in the
events may lead to more accurate estimates of character and juster understanding of motives, provided always that the interviewer is a sound
judge of men and is not led astray by his interlocutor's personal charm
or suavity.

A particularly knotty problem is that presented by the newspaper and
the periodical as source material for historical writing of this type. Is
the press an important source of information or an accurate index of
public opinion? Fay refers to newspapers only in isolated instances.
He discusses the influence of the press in poisoning public opinion and
preventing the development of good relations between governments. His
view is evidently that the press makes opinion rather than expresses
it, and he points out that the attitude of the press in many countries
was influenced by the governments. It was a "reptile" press in Bismarck's
sense. The whole question of the relation of the governments to the press
and the influence of public opinion as made by the press or expressed in
the newspapers requires careful study. The material is, of course, so
voluminous that the problem can be approached only in the way of

careful monographic study. Meanwhile, the historian is forced to rely in this matter upon second-hand information. The diplomatic documents frequently discuss public opinion in the various countries, and diplomats frequently inclose with their reports such newspaper excerpts as appear to them of significance. This in itself gives the historian an excellent clue as to what expressions of opinion in foreign countries were likely to affect the decisions of foreign offices. Further information can be gleaned from the memoirs of journalists like Blowitz, Steed, Chirol, Spender, Wolff, etc. Finally, a start has been made on the scientific study of the press, the most recent and perhaps the best example of this type of work being W. Zimmermann's *Die englische Presse zum Ausbruch des Weltkrieges* (1928), which is based upon an analysis of the stand of fifty English papers, including all the important London dailies. Little need be said of the value of the newspaper as a source of information as to actual facts. The great journalists frequently had excellent connections and were able to send their newspapers information which we now know to have been correct. But most of this information we now have in official documents, so that the newspapers can be safely left aside excepting in questions inadequately dealt with in the official papers.

With such a wealth of material the question may be raised whether or not the application of the canons of historical criticism to individual documents is at all possible. The reply is that in the great majority of cases such criticism is unnecessary. The problem of authenticity arises but rarely. Documents seldom have to be dated or placed. The very abundance of material makes comparison and confirmation relatively simple, for, as Fay says in speaking of publications from the German, Austrian, and Russian archives, "the new material fits together like a mosaic, and one part confirms the other." The canons of documentary criticism come into play only in isolated instances, but then they are employed with the same rigor and conscientiousness which is generally attributed to medievalists. Some of the critical work done on the colored books of 1914, and Fay's own fascinating analysis of the sources on the Sarajevo plot or on the so-called Potsdam Conference will serve as excellent examples.

The starting-point of Fay's study is the year 1870. He realizes fully that many of the conditions and causes underlying the war go back much farther, as, for example, the Alsace-Lorraine problem, the Russian advance in the south, or the factors controlling British policy, to mention only a few political questions. But obviously some point must be taken for a beginning, and 1870 is the logical starting-point, because, as Fay points out, "the Franco-Prussian War reversed a situation which had existed for two hundred years."[4] It marks not only the readjustment of the European balance, but also the rise of militarism, the victory of nationalism in Italy and Germany, the beginning of the spread of nationalism to the countries of Eastern Europe and the Near East, and above all the beginning of the great changes wrought on the continent by the industrial revolution, which transformed the very bases of international relations. Quite rightly Fay lays special stress on the period following 1900, which is the turning-point in Anglo-German relations and marks the beginning of the Entente Cordiale.

The historian is always confronted by the problems of the topical as against the chronological approach. Whatever may be the advantages of the former in dealing with non-political questions, it has been generally felt by historians of diplomacy that the chronological method is for them the only safe one. The action and interaction of events in time is so close that any other approach is likely to end in confusion. Fay has, in general, adhered to the chronological arrangement, but here again he has avoided dogmatism and has frequently modified his procedure to meet special requirements. For example, there is a special section dealing with Franco-German relations from 1870 to 1890, a period during which France played a minor rôle in general international relations, while her relations with her neighbor were particularly critical. In dealing with the crisis of July, 1914, Fay more frequently turns to a modified topical arrangement within the general chronological scheme.

Writing on an extremely controversial subject, Fay was obliged to take a definite stand toward the mass of literature which has grown up about the question. The value of such writings for the historian is likely to be rather slight. He cannot expect to get new information in this way, for he will himself use the same material as preceding authors, and will probably use it more extensively and judiciously. The controversial writer, "by centering attention on the acts of any one man or country, and by picking out passages in the documents to support his contention, can easily make a seemingly convincing argument for the uninitiated, that this or that man or country was altogether angelic or devilish in motives and methods." The historian, on the other hand, "may conscientiously try to look fairly at both sides of the question, explain acts from the point of view of the actors themselves instead of from that of their champions or enemies, and try to reach an unbiased judgment."[5] Fay has, of course, read the great bulk of this controversial material, but

[4] *Ibid.*, p. 50.   [5] *Ibid.*, pp. vi–vii.

this was primarily a precautionary measure. At best, the historian may get from such writings a lead to material which has hitherto escaped him, or may save himself from blindness to some point of view or some particular emphasis. He may, from the polemics of others, gain some idea of the outlook of different national or political groups. Beyond this his indebtedness would hardly go. Fay has, therefore, refrained from references to this type of literature, "because he wishes to avoid controversy and reach his conclusions as far as possible from documentary evidence."[6] Secondary authorities are usually cited only where special monographs deal at length with matters which the author is unable to take up in detail. Disagreement with other writers is mentioned only where the point is crucial or where the writer's views are at variance with generally accepted interpretations. On the other hand, direct quotations from original documents are frequent and extensive, because the author, as he points out, "wishes to avoid as far as possible picking out phrases or sentences which might give a *suggestio falsi* or *suppressio veri*."[7] The use made of the Wiesner report by the Commission set up by the Peace Conference to establish responsibility for the war is a striking example of this danger.

Much has been written in recent years on the question of style in historical literature of the present day, and there has been a general feeling that literary quality and scientific accuracy are not incompatible in historical work. There is undoubtedly some truth in this, for history, unlike mathematics, is a form of literature no matter how scientific the procedure. At the same time it should be remembered that the historian is always confronted with the dilemma of choosing to some extent. Highly technical investigations do not appeal to the general public and are not intended to do so, and modern monographic work, based upon careful weighing of great masses of conflicting evidence, can hardly be composed in the eloquent and sometimes vehement style of the great classics. All that can be demanded of the author in cases like this is that he should present his material and results in clear and concise language made as attractive as possible. Fay's book may be taken as a good specimen of careful and moderate, yet attractive and convincing, writing.

The success of the synthesis is likely to be the mark of the great historian. Fay states that his purpose is "simply to carry out what a great master has defined as the proper task of the historian—to tell how it really came about." It may be assumed that neither Ranke nor his follower understood by this that the task of the historian is simply to

[6] *Ibid.*, p. vi.   [7] *Ibid.*, p. vii.

establish the facts. A historical work without synthesis would be hardly more than a chronicle and would certainly have no greater value than a chronicle. In a subject of the magnitude and complexity of this, only the specialist can be left to form his own conclusions. There is a "feel" about the sources, a certain flavor, which cannot be easily conveyed at second hand. The historian's viewpoint is, then, of prime importance. It is woven into the very fabric of the narrative and bound up with his whole line of attack upon the problem. Above all it comes out in his conclusions.

But in this particular instance the conclusions are the more important because the question of the origins of the war can hardly be divorced from the question of responsibility for the war. Fay wisely shuns the expression "war guilt," but since the assertion of Germany's sole responsibility is laid own in article 231 of the Versailles Treaty much of the value of his book depends upon the amount of light it throws upon the justice or the injustice of this dictum. The author himself "has no political motive, either to justify the Treaty of Versailles or to demand its revision,"[8] but he cannot evade the historian's own responsibility and refuse to take a stand. In writing of the origins of the war he must of necessity have had constantly in mind the question of responsibility. The rôle of the historian can never be wholly divorced from that of the teacher, unless the historian is prepared to admit that he serves no useful purpose in human society.

The question of responsibility in this instance is of particular interest because it raises in an acute form the old problem whether history is made by persons or groups, by intellectual or religious movements, or by economic and other forces. A better test case than the great world-cataclysm could hardly be found. Fay recalls in his Preface that in the years immediately following the war, when attention was focused on the immediate causes and the actual outbreak, the simpler "scapegoat" or "personal devil" theory went almost unchallenged. Only the publication of more material and the new emphasis on the more remote causes led to a realization of the fact that all the powers were more or less responsible, and the responsibility was then attributed to the international anarchy, to the system of secret alliances, to armaments, or to secret diplomacy.

The second explanation satisfied Fay no more than the first. Here again he seeks the truth between two extremes.

After all, the "system" was worked by individuals; their personal acts built it up and caused it to explode in 1914. In the discussion of the future, it will be the work of the historian to explain the political, economic, and psycho-

[8] *Ibid.*, p. vi.

logical motives which caused these individuals to act as they did. He will also cease to talk about "war guilt," since no person in authority was guilty of deliberately working to bring about a general European War. But he will still continue to discuss the "responsibility" which each statesman must bear for acts which ultimately contributed to the catastrophe.[9]

In his concluding chapter Fay reiterates this view emphatically and strives for a just apportionment of blame.

One cannot judge the motives which actuated men before the War by what they did in an absolutely new situation which arose as soon as they were overtaken by a conflagration they had sought to avert. . . . . It is a curious psychological phenomenon that as soon as a country engages in war, there develops or is created among the masses a frenzy of patriotic excitement which is no index of their pre-war desires.

These notes of warning and caution are oft repeated. Speaking of the efforts of some writers to "fix positively in precise mathematical fashion the exact responsibility for the war," Fay says that he "deprecates such efforts to assess by a precise formula a very complicated question, which is after all more a matter of delicate shading than of definite white and black."[10] Even if a general consensus of opinion could be reached with reference to the responsibility for the immediate causes of the July crisis, the same relative responsibility would not necessarily hold for the underlying causes.

Throughout, there is a conscious effort made to strike a just balance between the underlying factors in the international situation and the specific actions of certain men or groups of men. The world has already grown away from the exaggerated materialistic interpretation of history, as the deluge of biographies of recent years clearly indicates. Fay's viewpoint, and that of most serious historians in this field, is a compromise between extremes. Indeed, it may be said that this whole work is an admirable example of detached and dispassionate historical writing based upon exhaustive use of an immense amount of material, careful critical examination of the evidence, and unusually sound judgment in the synthesis.[11]

[9] *Ibid.*, pp. 2–3.   [10] *Ibid.*, II, 548–49.

[11] [This analysis was first written in December, 1928, and revised by the analyst in March, 1929.--EDITOR.]

ANALYSIS 26

THE HISTORICAL METHOD OF JULES MICHELET[1]

By HENRY E. BOURNE

Western Reserve University

The method of Jules Michelet as a historian was influenced (*a*) by his deep interest in philosophy, (*b*) by his appointment in 1827 as professor of history and philosophy at the Ecole Préparatoire (later Ecole Normale), especially as after two years he was assigned to history alone, and (*c*) by his appointment in 1831 as chief of the historical section of the National Archives, a position which he held for twenty-one years. The first of these influences affected his conception of the organization of historical phenomena as well as his notion of what should be included within the scope of historical treatment. The second concentrated his interest. The third "placed him at the source even of the documents, still in large part unexplored."[2] It is commonly supposed that the Romantic movement also had an important influence upon his work. He did not belong to the inner circle of adepts of that school. Gabriel Monod, the most authoritative interpreter of his work, says that he was a romanticist by his love for the Middle Ages, by his lyrical style, by his love for color and life, but that he rejected much that the Romantic school taught, and persisted in

---

[1] [It was first suggested to Professor Bourne that he contrast in a single analysis the historical methods of Michelet and of Ernest Lavisse, who edited the *Histoire de France*, the most successful history on the co-operative plan. It was thought that the work of the first might display the influence upon historical method of the Romantic movement, while the work of the second would exhibit modern "scientific" methodology. However, actual work upon the assignment convinced Professor Bourne of the need of alteration in the original plan. He called attention to the fact that in the work mentioned Lavisse's own contribution was limited to the period of Louis XIV, and that this was the weakest part of Michelet's work. A "warm admirer" of Lavisse ever since he "used to hear him lecture at the Sorbonne in 1901–2," moreover, he felt that the latter's methods as a scientific historian "are those which characterize scientific work in the historical field everywhere today, and so do not stand in need of description by contrast with the methods of Michelet which were in process of transition and development." Lavisse was therefore dropped. In handling his subject, Professor Bourne says, he took as guides "the authoritative pronouncements of the ablest Frenchmen who have studied Michelet, and especially Gabriel Monod." The extent to which, as first suggested, Michelet may be regarded as a representative of the Romantic movement is indicated in the analyst's opening paragraph.—EDITOR.]

[2] Gabriel Monod, "La vie et la pensée de Jules Michelet, 1798–1852," *Bibliothèque de l'Ecole pratique des Hautes Etudes*, I, 182–83.

regarding himself as a classicist, a son of Virgil, and a disciple of Voltaire.[3]

During the period of his more intense interest in philosophy he gained from Cousin the conception that behind facts lie ideas, and that the task of the historian is to find generalizations in which great masses of facts become simplified. Here he was moving from philosophy toward history through sociology. But Cousin's influence soon paled before that of Vico, whom Michelet throughout the rest of his life called his sole master, and whose *Scienza nuova* he translated. Vico's theory of the self-creative power of humanity, acting upon itself, and director of its own fate, Michelet adopted and developed in conversations with his friend Quinet. From Vico also he learned to look to language, laws, and literature as the source in which may be discovered the general characteristics of mankind at any period. He was so sure that his philosophy of history enabled him to discern the general processes which facts signified or symbolized that he supposed he could restore an epoch as Viollet-le-Duc would restore the plan of a *château* with a few characteristic fragments at hand.[4] Thus he proposed as his aim the *résurrection de la vie intégrale*.[5] Fortunately his daily responsibilities as an archivist sobered his imagination and ordinarily saved him from extravagances. In preparing to write his early volumes Michelet was preoccupied with five phases of the development of France, "the origin of the people, law, ethnography, religion, and geography."[6] He carefully analyzed material upon all phases of ecclesiastical life, including canon law, the writings of churchmen, and administration. When he came to deal with a particular period, however, his theory led him to select certain bodies of fact and to fasten attention upon them, often to the neglect of other and equally important aspects of national life. For example, in dealing with the age of the early Capetians, he omitted much that did not contribute to his main thesis, for instance, the fact that the church was the principal stay of the monarchy. The impression left upon even friendly critics was of a lack of proportion, especially because he often described what he regarded as symbolic facts or incidents in great detail. He had done the same thing in his famous schoolbook entitled *Précis d'histoire moderne*, portraying the facts which for the ma-

[3] *Ibid.*, p. 214. Cf. G. Lanson, "La formation de la méthode historique de Michelet," *Revue d'histoire moderne et contemporaine*, VII, 11.

[4] Lanson, *op. cit.*, p. 12.

[5] Jules Michelet, *Histoire de France* (ed. 1871; Preface of 1869), I, 3.

[6] Monod, *op. cit.*, p. 264. Monod also calls attention to the fact that most of the auxiliary sciences upon which Michelet desired to draw for aid were still in their beginnings.

ture mind were to be symbols in such fashion that they served as vivid images to the young. Similarly when he came to treat the French Revolution he was so deeply interested in the struggle for liberty that he consciously belittled the importance of social and economic facts. What he did say is often incomplete and incorrect.

To the question of how much emphasis the historian of the Revolution should place upon economic or social facts Michelet gave an answer in his sharp criticism of Buchez et Roux, *Histoire parlementaire*.[7] He says that they, and those who have followed them, made the mistake of putting in the forefront of the Revolution "questions which we term *social*, eternal questions of proprietors and non-proprietors, between the rich and the poor, questions which are formulated today, but which appear in the Revolution under other forms, still vague and obscure, and so in a secondary position." In his Preface of 1868, after the interest in economic facts had become greater, he says that all have now (since 1848) returned

à la tradition nationale. Nul de nous aujourd'hui qui ne voie dans la Liberté la question souveraine. *La question économique* qui lui fit ombre, est une conséquence, un approfondissement essentiel de la Liberté. Mais celle-ci precède tout, doit couvrir et protéger tout.[8]

He rightly points out in the earlier statement that there was not at the time of the Revolution a working class in the sense in which the term was used even in 1847, and that it is unhistorical to attribute to the masses a consciousness of antagonisms which they had not yet begun to feel. But although social and economic interests and class antagonisms may not have entered largely into the political vocabulary of parties, economic and social facts deeply influenced the course of events. Even he remarks, apropos of the sale of church property, "La Révolution était donc fondée, très bien fondée, et dans les intérêts et dans l'opinion."[9]

It was not to be expected that before the economic point of view was fully discerned Michelet should include the economic and financial history of the Revolution within the scope of his treatment. He deals with such subjects incidentally, in some cases with scarcely more than an allusion. One illustration is the wholly fanciful treatment he gives of the early sales of public lands at the close of his second volume. He misconceives entirely the report of the *Comité d'aliénation* on August 26, 1791, treating it as naïvely counter-revolutionary because it proposed to abandon its task to the executive, that is, to an "inactive and paralytic ministry." He suspects the committee of being frightened by the very success

[7] Michelet, *Histoire de la Révolution française* (ed. 1868), II, 421 ff., in his essay, "De la méthode et de l'esprit de ce livre."

[8] Preface, *ibid.*, I, iii.   [9] *Ibid.*, IV, 167.

of its labors and of desiring to slow down the sales.[10] The fact was that the task of the care of such vast properties had proved too great for a legislative committee, and the work was turned over to the *Caisse de l'extraordinaire*, which, under its director A. L. A. Amelot, managed it with great success.

Michelet's references to financial matters are often equally superficial. He says that in the spring of 1790 taxes were "regularly and religiously paid." Of the first assignats he says, "A chaque papier un lot était assigné, affecté; ces billets furent dits *assignats*. Chaque papier était du bien, de la terre mobilisée."[11]

In the scope of Michelet's conception of what is germane to history special emphasis must be given to his use of geography. Nearly a quarter of his second volume, immediately before his description of feudal society, is devoted to his famous *Tableau de la France*. He placed it there because feudalism was in a sense localism triumphant, and he had before him the task of tracing the long process by which this was to give way before the growth of a national consciousness of unity. In his *Tableau* he attempted to describe France, province by province, pointing out the relation of geographical facts to the characteristics of the people. The idea was a suggestion of genius, but the execution suffered from the fact that when it was written geographical science was in its first stages of development.[12]

The descriptions are full of charm, but often what is said is of greater interest to the tourist than to the historian. If we compare it with the masterly work of Vidal de la Blache in the first volume of Ernest Lavisse's monumental *Histoire de France*, we note the defects of Michelet's method. Provinces are not geographical entities. Vidal de la Blache deals with regions and their characteristics which have had a proved influence upon the history developed within them. The basis of his work is the geological structure of the country.

Moreover, the order of presentation with Michelet is arbitrary. He begins with a long passage on Brittany, perhaps because he had recently visited Brittany and his interest was vivid.[13] He then proceeds through the circuit of outlying provinces and finally reaches the Ile de France, the heart of the Paris basin. While he gives eleven pages to Brittany, he gives two to Normandy, a much more important province, and none to

---

[10] *Ibid.*, II, 406–7.   [11] *Ibid.*, I, 415.

[12] Monod remarks that "il était nécessaire de connaître la composition géologique du sol, son relief exact, le régime des pluies, des eaux, et des vents; les habitations des hommes et les conditions de l'industrie" (*op. cit.*, I, 289).

[13] *Ibid.*, p. 290.

Champagne. In the wealth of his fancy he not infrequently discovers geographical influences where they do not exist. He ascribes to Descartes the hardy boldness of the Bretons, not knowing that Descartes was actually born in languorous Touraine.

We may next consider the extent to which Michelet's philosophical theories or vast generalization affected his historical work. It is obvious that they did less harm to his treatment of medieval France than to that of the Revolution. While he was writing his earlier volumes his attitude was that of sympathetic comprehension of the work of the church and of intense interest in the architectural triumphs of the Middle Ages. His attitude appeared to change after 1841, three years after his appointment to the chair of history and *la morale* at the Collège de France. During these three years his teaching, remarks Monod, was founded upon a direct study of the facts. After that he began to emphasize the second part of his title, and to feel that it was his duty to act upon the young generations, to form their soul. He developed a tendency, which he later recognized as an error, to "abandon the tone of research and instruction for that of preaching, and even that of prophecy." In this period of his work "trop souvent, dans sa hâte d'exercer une action morale, Michelet a manqué aux devoirs du savant, de l'érudit et du critique."[14]

This tendency was naturally accentuated by his controversy with reactionary churchmen, especially the Jesuits, who were attacking the university monopoly in their struggle to capture the education of youth. Echoes of the controversy appear in his lectures on the *Jésuites*, which were published in 1843, and on the *Prêtre, la femme et la famille*, which came two years later. His moral ardor became so intense that he looked upon the Revolution as the embodiment of justice upon earth, the emancipation of a people from the shackles of Christianity with its doctrine of hereditary sin. He believed that it restored to France the spiritual leadership of the world. The first two volumes of his *Histoire de la Révolution française* appeared in 1847, and they can fairly be called a trumpet call to a new revolution. Professor Aulard[15] would limit their controversial character to the Preface and the Introduction and thought that as soon as Michelet reached the pages of the history he became a scholar and a historian. His tirade against Christianity and the French monarchy in the Introduction is certainly far removed from the calm atmosphere of historical thought.

[14] *Ibid.*, Vol. II, Book III, chap. i, p. 9.

[15] Alphonse A. Aulard, "Michelet, historien de la Révolution française," *Révolution française*, LXXXI, 136–50, 193–213.

It would seem that the same remark might be applied without undue exaggeration to certain passages of the history of the Revolution. For example, in chapter ii, to prepare the way for what he esteems the right attitude toward the seizure of church property, he draws an almost hysterical picture of the iniquities, the avarice, and the oppressions of the higher clergy. From these introductory paragraphs the reader would also be led to infer that it was to save the starving and the destitute that church property, which was essentially a fund for the poor, was to be taken over by the state.

In similar fashion the reader cannot avoid the feeling that his enthusiastic belief in the impeccability of the people has guided his selection of facts in the description of the first year of the Revolution. On the night before the assault on the Bastille he fancies the people examining their consciousness of the past and condemning it without qualification. "L'histoire revint cette nuit-là, une longue histoire de souffrances, dans l'instinct vengeur du peuple. L'âme des pères qui, tant de siècles, souffrirent, moururent en silence, revint dans les fils, et parla." The people of Paris also looked into the future and contemplated the liberty they were making possible for future generations. "L'avenir et le passé faisaient tous deux même réponse; tous deux, ils dirent: Va! ... Et ce qui est hors du temps, hors de l'avenir et hors du passé, l'immuable Droit le disait aussi." It was as a united people the next day that Paris forced the surrender of the Bastille. To one who reads the essential documents of the period this seems more exaggerated and fantastic than Taine's description of "spontaneous anarchy."

Before dealing with Michelet's technique in the more exact sense of the term it is necessary to say a word about his use of oral tradition in the history of the Revolution. By this he did not mean reliance upon the testimony of witnesses still living. He occasionally made use of such testimony. Referring to the reason why the peasants hoarded their grain, he said, "A peasant said to me, what good times there were in my father's day! He hid his sacks well. . . . . What good times! One could buy a whole field with one sack of wheat." This is an interesting illustration of a well-understood situation. Another bit of such testimony, cited in the Preface of 1847, is not so good. To prove that an "infinitely small" number of men took part in sanguinary acts of violence like the massacres of September he gives the testimony of old men whom he had questioned, especially that of a man of the *faubourg* Saint-Antoine: "We were all at the tenth of August, and not one at the second of September." This is only true in the sense that relatively few took part in the actual kill-ing, but his own account of the murders at the Abbaye and Carmelites indicates that the murderers were men of the same type as his witness from Saint-Antoine, petty shopkeepers and artisans of the neighborhood.

By oral tradition Michelet meant the *national* tradition, shared alike by people in town and countryside, even by children. If, says he, one enters a village inn at nightfall, or finds a man resting by the wayside and begins the conversation by talking about the rain or the fine weather, then the dearness of food, and turns to the times of the emperor and finally the Revolution, the judgments of his interlocutor may be embodied in the following catechism: "Qui a amené la Révolution? Voltaire et Rousseau.—Qui a perdu le roi? La reine.—Qui a commencé la Révolution? Mirabeau.—Quel a été l'ennemi de la Révolution? Pitt et Coburg, les Chouans et Coblentz.—Et encore? Les Godden et les Calotins.—Qui a gaté la Révolution? Marat et Robespierre."[16] Nobody regards this as other than a fantasy.

If now we examine Michelet's method in the narrower sense, his technique as an investigator who embodies his results in his historical writings, we find that he was in advance of his contemporaries. In his Preface of 1869 for the *History of France* he says he was the first to go to the Archives for much of his material. If he referred to writers of general history, the statement is substantially true, and so his work marks a stage in the development of historical method. But the question remains, How comprehensive and critical was his use of these documents? In the similar Preface to the *History of the French Revolution* he makes even greater claims. He declares that for essential facts his account is "identical with the documents themselves" and "as liable to change as they." He adds that his reader can find each fact "at its proper place in the register or carton from which I have taken it." Fortunately, enough of his notes, manuscripts, and proof-sheets remain to facilitate the task of determining his proceedings with considerable exactness.

For his *French Revolution*, for example, neither Monod nor Aulard, who have examined the notes upon which his manuscript is based, accept his statement as correct, although Aulard calls his history "well documented." The first two volumes, with the exception of the account of the federations, are based chiefly upon Buchez et Roux, *Histoire parlementaire*, as we know from the references given on Michelet's manuscript. Beginning with the third volume, he draws more material from the Archives, some also from the Archives of the Seine and the Archives of the Prefecture of the Police which were later destroyed in the fires of the Com-

[16] *Histoire de la Révolution française*, II, 413–15.

mune. As an illustration of his lack of knowledge of the scope of material on some phases of the Revolution, he supposed that the registers
of the Committee of Public Safety which he discovered contained all its
acts, although they did not contain one-hundredth part of those Professor
Aulard has included in his twenty-six volumes of the *Actes du Comité de
Salut Public.* He also takes texts of laws from newspapers instead of from
the *Collections* or *Bulletins des lois.* It seems also that he makes no use
of the *procès-verbaux* of the several assemblies, which, Professor Aulard
has remarked, furnishes the only thread through this "Daedalus" of discussion. Such criticisms are in point because of Michelet's own claims,
for students now realize that a general history can only to a limited
extent be based upon the personal researches of the writer, and must
find its principal source of information in the monographs of specialists.

The most exact critical determination of Michelet's method for any part
of the *History of France* we owe to M. Gustave Rudler, author of *Michelet:
historien de Jeanne d'Arc.*[17] He conjectures that Michelet first read the
documentary record[18] of the two trials, the *Procès de condamnation* and
the *Procès de revision,* but that in the presence of the enormous task of
disentangling the facts he yielded to the temptation to take as guides the
two writers Lebrun[19] and L'Averdy,[20] who had apparently accomplished
the work in authoritative fashion. M. Rudler's investigations have led to
the conclusion that when Michelet gives references to manuscript sources
he has borrowed the references for the most part from L'Averdy,[21] while
to Lebrun he owes his material, his order of treatment, except differences
in rhetorical arrangement, as well as many of his opinions and critical
appreciations. Turns of thought hitherto attributed to the suggestions
of his genius appear to be borrowed in many cases from Lebrun or
L'Averdy. In the account of the trial he follows L'Averdy directly or
across Lebrun. Unhappily L'Averdy, although a penetrating student
of the case, did not understand the procedure of the medieval inquisition,
and so attributed to Cauchon's evil intent acts which were purely con-

[17] 2 vols.; Paris: Les Presses Universitaires de France, 1925, 1926.

[18] M. Rudler has identified these manuscripts as U 820 and U 821, belonging to the
Archives, which are late copies of no value, but convenient and in a clear handwriting. Michelet made indexes of each, but made no use of them except in preparing a
few notes.

[19] Lebrun de Charmettes, *Histoire de Jeanne d'Arc, Surnommée la Pucelle d'Orléans*
(4 vols.; Paris, 1817).

[20] L'Averdy, *Notices et extraits des manuscrits* (Paris, 1790).

[21] This appears from the fact that for references to Lebrun on the margins of the
manuscript are substituted in the proof-sheets references to sources indicated in
L'Averdy.

ventional. This was the current attitude until the publication of Quiche-rat's *Aperçus nouveaux* in 1850. For the language of the interrogatories Michelet relied upon Buchon's translation,[22] which, explains M. Rudler, was a defective rendering of an imperfect manuscript. This Michelet should have known through his study of Lebrun, but the version was con-venient and so he utilized it. He seems to have felt that he should go to the originals, but this feeling did not send him to the real original but to a convenient translation. This M. Rudler calls a scruple *de demi-mé-thode mal entendu.*

In his work M. Rudler also examines Michelet's principles of criticism in dealing with the character of testimony and the credibility of witnesses. He finds that he made no effort to examine the materials and study the conditions under which, for example, the records of the trial were made, in order to determine whether there were distortions or omissions due to Cauchon. In the same way the trial for revision requires minute criti-cism, because in the lapse of time opportunity had existed for the growth of a doctrine which would necessarily influence the testimony. He seems to have proceeded upon the rough-and-ready principle that the testimony of Jeanne herself was of more value than that of witnesses who spoke at the trial of revision many years later. But her testimony should be subject to the usual cautions that she might have forgotten, or been mis-led, or been influenced by bias.

M. Rudler sums up his conclusions by explaining that Michelet was obliged to acquire his method as he proceeded, because he had not learned the trade of an investigator. "Ni son tour d'esprit philosophique et imaginatif, ni sa vive sensibilité, ni ses études antérieures ne l'avaient préparé au nettoyage et au collationnement des manuscrits, à la critique si difficile des témoignages, à la comparaison et à la réduction des textes."

Upon Michelet's methods of research as a whole M. Ch. V. Langlois, late director of the National Archives, has said:

Il a grapillé dans des archives nationales dont il avait la garde conscien-cieusement et avec ardeur, mais vite, et un peu au hasard: entreprendre des recherches à la façon des érudits, dépenser son temps à résoudre les petits problèmes préalables que soulève l'interprétation de la plupart des documents anciens, de pareils soins étaient pour lui hors de question.[23]

Langlois also says that the men of Michelet's generation believed that his-tory could be written from *les sources brutes,* and did not realize that the

[22] Buchon, *Collection des chroniques nationales françaises,* etc., Vol. XXXIV.

[23] Langlois, "Michelet," *Questions d'histoire et d'enseignement* (Paris: Hachette et Cie, 1906), p. 89. This is taken from a lecture on Michelet, pp. 33–95, delivered at the University of Pennsylvania in 1905.

historian cannot work with security until after the collections and monographs of the *érudits* have been completed.

In this brief analysis an attempt has been made to touch the main features of Michelet's general method and of his technique as an investigator rather than to assign to him a place in the literature of history. His work upon France, as M. Monod remarks, made of the history of his country for the first time a living thing.[24]

[24] [This analysis was first written in December, 1928, and was revised by the analyst in February, 1929.—EDITOR.]

ANALYSIS 27

THE HISTORICAL METHOD OF ERNEST RENAN[1]

By JEAN POMMIER

Université de Strasbourg

I

In reaction against scholasticism, and under the influence of Scottish philosophy, Renan found his method at the seminary of St. Sulpice, where he studied for the priesthood. V. Cousin had already applied the procedures of this school of thought to psychology; Renan transferred them to history. The study of the human past appeared to him to be ruled, like that of nature, by two principal factors: (1) the collection of facts, (2) their elaboration into laws by the methods of induction, analogy, etc. During his whole life he remained faithful to these principles, never sacrificing one of the two processes to the other. He was persuaded that without preliminary documentation generalizations are mere hollow abstractions; and that without ulterior interpretation the investigation of facts is worthy, at the most, of the useless and ridiculous erudition which La Bruyère stigmatized under the *sobriquet* Hermagoras.

While in St. Sulpice he also became aware of what must be his specialty. Although his work contains numerous pages devoted to the Middle Ages, and even to contemporaneous French history, Renan is primarily the historian of Christianity and Judaism. In this field he worked while at the seminary, especially on Judaism; for although he was nominally pursuing Pauline studies, he actually studied rather the Pentateuch and the Psalms. It is remarkable that afterward, whether by his *Histoire générale et système comparé des langues sémitiques*,[2] to which the Académie des Inscriptions gave a prize in 1847, or by his translations of Job, of the

---

[1] [The responsibility of securing an analysis of Renan's historical method was assumed for the Committee by Professor Solomon Reinach. Its indebtedness to him in this respect is here gratefully expressed. In sending us Professor Pommier's manuscript Professor Reinach said: "Here is the article you want about Renan, by the most competent hand." The manuscript was written in French and was translated into English by Miss Martha Anderson, of the Council on Foreign Relations, Inc., New York. The translation was read and revised in English by the author in February, 1929. It was finally reviewed with particular reference to questions of idiom by Dr. Howard P. Becker of the University of Pennsylvania.—EDITOR.]

[2] Paris: 1863 (3d ed.).

Song of Songs, and Ecclesiastes, or finally in the teaching which devolved upon him in the Collège de France after 1870 (he had not had time in 1862 to be a professor), Renan established himself as a Hebraist, an interpreter of the Old Testament. Less than ten years before his death he began to write the *Histoire du peuple d'Israël*.[3] He did not start this until he had finished the seven volumes of his *Histoire des origines du christianisme*,[4] in which, strictly speaking, he was not in his own field. On this, to some degree, depend the relative values of these works. The sources of the Pentateuch, for example, are seen better in the *Histoire du peuple d'Israël* than are those of the gospels in the *Vie de Jésus*.[5]

Be that as it may, the fact that he devoted himself to religious history, and especially to the history of Christianity, implied a condition within himself and an importance in the subject, both of which Renan perceived and characterized. The condition is not given to all: it is necessary to have believed and to believe no longer. If one still has faith he is incapable of being scientifically disinterested; if one never has been a believer, the essence of religious phenomena remains impenetrable, and one does not rise above the point of view of the eighteenth century, of which Renan certainly had an exaggerated mistrust. The importance of the subject is apparent to one who is interested in the question of origins and transitions. According to Renan, only the first of these is of philosophical significance in history. The future is hidden from us or is perceived only in the deceptive light of hope. What would we not give to know the origin of the earth and of humanity, the origin of language, etc.? At least let us try to study Christianity in embryo. (I use the term "embryogeny" advisedly because Renan has not brought his *Histoire des origines* beyond 180 A.D.—the beginning of ecclesiastical history, for which material is easily enough interpreted.) And as in natural history one organism is always the product of another, this historian sets himself to show how Christianity arose in Judaism, how it was held by Peter and John, how it was detached little by little by Paul, etc.

But a work is not determined by its method and its object alone; it is no less essential to know in what spirit it was written. No historian can assign this or that direction to the evolution of history on more or less a priori grounds. If any one sort of speculation characterizes the nineteenth century, it is probably the philosophy of history, formerly represented by Bossuet and Montesquieu, which gained a particular ascendancy among the contemporaries of Renan. Vico, Herder, and V. Cousin, who adapted Hegel for the use of the frequenters of the Sorbonne,

---

[3] Paris: 1887–93.   [4] Paris: 1863–83.   [5] Paris: 1867.

exercised the greatest influence in this matter. It was impossible that these principles should not govern to a certain degree Renan's historical research; the more so because, self-imposed, they so profoundly impressed themselves upon him in his youth.

For the Hegelians of this period, the history of facts was only that of ideas. Without going so far, Renan tried to discover the succession of ideas. He believed that he found their law to be one of action and reaction. A system wins its way into favor, engenders other systems which carry its principles to an extreme, and thereby predisposes the mind to abandon it for a directly contradictory theory. It is like the oscillations of a pendulum—when it swings too far to the right, it promptly swings too far to the left. Little by little, however, the oscillations lose their amplitude; in the same way the mind deviates less and less from the truth which is the central point. Thus Renan believes in intellectual progress. In all fields, moreover, humanity advances, but not in a spiral as Vico believed, nor in a straight line. Renan adopted rather, like Goethe, the analogy of an angular bend. Let us suppose a point B which is farther from point C, absolutely, than the point A. However, if one must pass via B in order to go from A to C, at B the traveler will be nearer his goal than when he was at A. Thus there are apparent setbacks which in reality constitute progress.

If such is the general direction of historical change, what are the factors which contribute most to it? At the epoch in which Renan began to think, the nineteenth century oscillated between two contradictory conceptions. On the one hand, the teaching of V. Cousin and the recent experience of Napoleon favored the theory of great providential men. On the other, literary research into epic poems tended to the conclusion that they were the spontaneous product of a school or a people; Michelet, on his side, wanted to make the French people the real heroes of the Revolution. Should the chief rôle be given to powerful individuals or to the crowd? The most important development in Renan's method consists in the two successive responses which he made to this question in so far as Christian origins are concerned.

II

We said above that the first stage of investigation is the collection of facts. This task was especially delicate for Renan, because the religious history with which he was occupied was not like secular history. In fact, it is in large part on the margin, so to speak, of the latter. It is banal to recall the silence of secular historians upon the first origins of Christianity. Only a few details, such as the census of which Luke speaks (2:2), or the edict of Claudius which exiled Aquila or Prisca, or the government of Felex, establish points of contact.

The principal materials which Renan used are manuscripts, coins, and inscriptions. He neglected none of these sources of information; moreover, his European reputation put him in a position to have excellent correspondents in all countries. As we might say, his eye traveled from the Syrian manuscripts in the British Museum, where Cureton had found a collection of Ignatian epistles, to the study of Jewish inscriptions in Rome made by P. Garucci, etc. In France he made great use of his colleagues' learning, and as a member of the Académie des Inscriptions he could consult a numismatist, such as Longperier, or an archaeologist, such as Waddington. On the other hand, he himself was occupied in 1860 with excavations in Phoenicia. The care which he bestowed upon documentations of this kind is indicated by the importance which the *Corpus Inscriptionum Semiticarum*, which he planned in 1867, assumed in his life. Let me recall that, in the dream which he had one day of the ideal Collège de France (which was, according to his idea, "like a monastery of St. Bernard's time, lost in the midst of woods, with long avenues of poplars and oaks, with streams, rocks, and a cloister where one might walk in rainy weather"), he imagined "rows of unused rooms in which, on long tables new inscriptions, molds, *estampages*,[6] etc., would be laid to view."

From this it is easy to understand that he often visited the Louvre. He would go there, for example, to see the vase of Amathonte, in order to visualize what the brass basin of the Jewish temple could have been like. Or perhaps he would examine there (as also in the Bibliothèque Impériale) the Greek papyri, in order to gain an idea of the appearance of Paul's letters. If he perhaps did not draw all the critical conclusions possible from this examination, he at least neglected nothing that would help him to familiarize himself with ancient epistolography.

These documents and others made him familiar with secular history, the knowledge of which gave him reliable frames of reference. It has been shown, apropos of Adrian, that in a single page Renan alluded to the neo-Egyptian style, which he knew from the ruins of Adrian's villa at Tivoli, to the neo-Phoenician style, remembered from his own visit to Phoenicia; to urban life in the Hellenic world, known by the inscriptions of the *Corpus Inscriptionum Graecarum*. And of course nothing of ancient literature was neglected from the archaeologists to the moralists, as

---

[6] [Professor Pommier suggests "impressions" or "prints" (of inscriptions) as the translation of *estampages*.—EDITOR.]

Juvenal. This is perhaps the reason for Renan's success in his history of Christian origins: so fine was the "net"—to use Taine's expression—which served him to mass facts of all kinds capable of restoring this Greek-Roman civilization, in the midst of which that of Christianity developed.

With these tools of information, Renan, like other nineteenth century historians—for example, Michelet—combined another: the inspection of places where historical events must have taken place. In two thousand years the surface of the earth has of course changed in all that regards politics, especially in a country which, like Asia Minor, has been the theater of so many conflicts. But the landscape in general remains the same. It is said that Renan sought in Galilee and Jerusalem a "fifth gospel" mutilated but still recognizable, and that he wished, but was prevented by advancing age, to visit Sinai, which played such an important rôle in the early days of Israel. Although entailing certain questionable consequences, his trips gave Renan more than one advantage, enabling him to describe precisely such towns as Antioch, the true cradle of Christianity, or Smyrna. Moreover, inasmuch as the customs and mentality of the countries he visited were much less mutable than those of our Occident, Renan was able to believe that the human past lived again before his eyes, and he took good care not to neglect this vivid documentation.

III

Now we come to the second stage of investigation. Here especially must the historian bring all his sagacity to bear. If one wishes to have a model of Renanian critique, one must consult the monographs, either those which appear at the beginning or in the appendixes of the principal volumes of the *Histoire des origines,* or those which their author gave to the Académie des Inscriptions. Do we need to state that the great principles—for example, the preference shown for the oldest documents—are always respected in it? But just here one of the special difficulties enters: Nothing is more uncertain than the date and the original text of the majority of pre-Christian writings, nothing less known than their authors—anonymity or a pseudonym being almost always the rule. And to this must be added the miraculous tales of which they are full, and toward which the historian must take some position.

In order to decide upon the date and the authenticity of a given writing, Renan studied carefully the series of extrinsic indexes, that is to say, the citations or allusions to it elsewhere; and the intrinsic indexes, that is, the relation between its contents and the character, the style, and the epoch of the hypothetical author. Although he leaned too much toward a conservative criticism, especially at the beginning, he ended by perceiving and pointing out the ordinary features of the apocrypha: absence of precise circumstances, abundance of commonplaces, plagiarisms (so obvious in the Epistle to the Ephesians), tendency to establish such or such a thesis. The difficulty, moreover, is more or less great according to whether all the writings attributed to one author are suspect (as in the case of Ignatius) or only certain ones (as those of Paul). For in the latter case one can gain an idea of the doubtful texts by comparing them with the authentic.

As for the accounts of the miracles, Renan took many pages to explain and justify the method which he intended to follow in regard to them. The negation of the supernatural is for him a philosophical principle prior to the exegesis—a part of his conception of the world which is governed by laws made once for all and which do not suffer (as present experience shows) the least abrogation. Having learned from Malebranche that God did not proceed by a "particular will," he always affirmed that no free will, save that of man, intervened in historical change. Every text mentioning a miracle shows by the mere fact of such mention that it must be interpreted with a view to ascertaining how much reality, imposture, credulity, or enthusiasm it incloses.

The precise caution to which the historian of religions is thus committed will render necessary in him what Pascal called the *spirit of finesse*. Renan always insisted upon the necessity for tact, for a feeling for what he called "general color" without which truth vanishes. Truth does not stand revealed but is discovered—indirectly—out of the corner of one's eye. One must catch and fix the fleeting glimpses. Among several possible conceptions, the most coherent and plausible must be chosen. This choice is justified because the fact or the character to be represented has certainly "conformed to the necessity of things, naturally, harmoniously. Let us suppose that in restoring Phidias' Minerva according to the texts, a dry, rough, artificial ensemble was produced; what would be the conclusion? That texts must be interpreted with taste, gently probed until they furnish an ensemble in which all the data are harmoniously merged." The essential is, as the painters say, that your subject "stands up." Renan thus defended, curiously enough, the method followed in the *Vie de Jésus* with arguments similar to those used by Flaubert to justify his reconstitution of the past in *Salammbô*.

To achieve this result, Renan preferred to use the process of analogy. One may say that he had the advantage of illuminating the distant past with the light of the present, or at least of a better-known past. He considered that he was right because the identity of human nature persists, he thought, through a variety of circumstances. Let us take, for example, the figure and the life of Jesus. In order to understand them, he is guided by what is known of St. Francis of Assisi, and of the evolution of Mahomet, as well as by the phases which Michelet introduced into the biography of his Jeanne d'Arc. He did not hesitate to put the program for arriving at the essential truth of the Gospels in the following terms:

Suppose that fifteen or twenty years ago, three or four old soldiers of the Empire each set to writing the life of Napoleon from his recollections. It is clear that their essays would contain numerous errors, striking discrepancies. One would put Wagram before Marengo, another would write that Napoleon drove Robespierre's government out of the Tuileries . . . . but one thing would result from these naïve recitals, that is, the character of the hero, the impression which he made upon others.

Renan had such great confidence in this method that he used it more and more, perhaps even to excess, as has been the charge in regard to his *Histoire du peuple d'Israël*. In it do we not find David compared with Charlemagne, then with Augustus, and Israel with Geneva, that rallying-point of the righteous, etc.? In any event, one sees that the terms of comparison are not always individual. In this respect Renan derived great profit from his Breton origin. In the Bas-Bretons, he claimed to find a naïve faith, a superstition clothed in myths, a mentality similar to that of the early Christians.

The impelling forces of the method having been thus analyzed, the method itself must be characterized. We shall limit ourselves to two remarks. In the first place, Renan took the adage *In medio stat veritas* too seriously. He had great confidence in the natural balance of his mind, and the spectacle of two excesses led him to take the mean: on the one hand, Catholic exegesis appeared to him much too conservative; on the other, the radical negations of the Tübingen school seemed to him measureless and without discernment. Even here he was faithful to the eclecticism of his youth. In the second place, as if he were reminded of a project for a treatise on history that Fénelon had hinted at in his *Lettre à l'académie*, Renan constantly took care to distinguish, by the most scrupulous forms of language, what is certain (and he knew how narrow this field is in history), what is probable, what is plausible, what is possible. This accounts for the abundance of "perhaps's" and "it-seems-to-me's" with which his scientific probity obliged him, he thought, to sprinkle his prose.

IV

As it is, his work had certain important results which can be grouped about three questions: What is the part respectively played by individuals, races, and classes in historical change?

We have seen above the reservations on the first point. Today we know of an *Essai psychologique sur Jésus Christ*[7] which Renan wrote while at the seminary (he was then twenty years old), from which I have made the following excerpt:

The critique which I undertake of Jesus Christ is not historical but psychological. I do not set out to criticize the facts of his history, to reduce it to its most exact expression. I take Jesus Christ . . . . as the manifestation of an idea . . . . , of which the most remarkable monuments are the four gospels. . . . . Suppose, if you will, that he is a fabulous hero of whom the authors of these writings have given their conceptions, what does it matter to me? How these conceptions arose always remains to be explained. The only change which we would meet in the problem would be in the individual person who would be the object. In one case, he would be called Jesus, son of Mary; in the other, he would be multiple and would be called Matthew, Mark, Luke and John.

Eighteen years afterward Renan wrote, in the Introduction to his *Vie de Jésus:*

When I conceived for the first time a history of the origins of Christianity, I wanted to do . . . . a history of the doctrines in which men have played almost no part. Jesus would scarcely have been mentioned; attention would have been centered upon showing how the ideas which were produced in his name took root and spread throughout the world. But I have since learned that history is not a simple play of abstraction, that men are of more account in it than doctrines. A certain theory did not bring about the Reformation, it was Luther, Calvin. Likewise Christianity is the work of Jesus, of St. Paul. . . . . Previous movements belong to our subject only as they serve to explain these extraordinary men who naturally could not have existed without some connection with what preceded them.

The *Histoire des Origines* took a strictly biographical course. The anonymous crowd was given second place; even in politics Renan affirmed more and more the superiority of a man, mediocre though he might be, to a group, and he almost reduced French history to a succession of conquests by the Capet family.

It would take too long to indicate here the defects of this second conception applied to the problem of Jesus; too long even to explain this

[7] Paris, 1921, pp. 14–15.

penchant for the "portrait," to which Michelet and Taine, like Renan, offered sacrifice—this penchant which makes them more attractive, if not more true, than the severe Fustel de Coulanges in his *La cité antique*. It would be better simply to mention the fact that the works cited above represent the trends from which the historians of Christianity have to choose, and which serve to separate the partisans of historical fact from those preferring myths. Thus the duality of the systems which Renan envisaged has the value of a symbol.

But Jesus, if it is to him that we owe Christianity, was a Jew. And this race, in Renan's eyes, had a particular avocation—that of imposing its religion upon the world. The historian of Israel was confirmed in the opinion that races, and even nations, all have their missions to fulfil. Sometimes these lead to suffering, sometimes to death. Thus the Jews have spent all their spiritual energy in conceiving the universal religion: they have also been the victims of military power from the Babylonians to the Romans. But in the end their part is none the less glorious. To Renan, monotheism was an invention of the Semitic race and related to their nomadic life. The criticisms which this theory received after its appearance did not induce him to abandon it. Before Jesus, the crowning moment in the religious history of Israel, and consequently of humanity, was the prophetical movement of the eighth century B.C., out of which Christianity developed. But in assimilating it, our Occident has modified this religious teaching. "Christianity has doubtless made us, but we have also made Christianity." In the depths of his romantic forests, the Celt transformed the conceptions which the sunburnt land of Judea had of old brought forth, imparting to them a certain mysterious, sweet poetry inspired by his sense of the infinite. With a somewhat clumsy sort of credulity he took the Gospels seriously, with all of their oriental metaphor. On the other hand, is not socialism the heritage of Jewish Messianism? Finally, religion, if an indispensable element in our civilization, is not as such unique. Science and art are no less necessary to the complete development of man, and they come to us from Greece. Harmonious collaboration of the races!

Again, Renan noted carefully in what classes of the population the first Christians had been recruited. He observed accurately the social rôle of those brotherhoods, those "associations" in which the disinherited had found companions, pecuniary assistance, all sorts of "aid." He showed the importance which the nuclei constituted by the synagogues had had for the development of Christianity. He followed the progressive formation of the Christian clergy as it separated from the lay world. He might have occupied himself advantageously with the sacerdotal caste. Not that he neglected it; all that concerned the material organization of the Israelite cult, for example, was pointed out in detail. But the rôle of the interested impostor, from the Urim and Thummim of the high priest to Esdras and the pastorals, could have been more clearly brought to light not only after Voltaire but especially after the *De la réligion*,[8] etc., of Benjamin Constant.

In brief, the work of Renan was all it could be, given his object. His history is psychological, ethnic, and social—not military, diplomatic, or even economic. His training led him to neglect material factors, but on the other hand fitted him better than anyone else to sense the action of the spiritual principle. In fact, how can a historian of religions, if he is an idealist like Renan, fail to see, as he saw, the Spirit developing through the various cults, none of which can exhaust or satisfy it? In this lies the meaning of the reproach which he one day addressed to a skeptical historian, Sainte-Beuve, for not having perceived how near to God is the mind of man. Save for certain moments of discouragement and doubt, when he asked himself whether history were not a farce which an ironic demiurge plays, Renan saw in it a forward march toward a goal, mysterious indeed but worthy of pursuit; he read into it, in the absence of a God that is, a God in the making.

[8] Benjamin Constant de Rebecque, *De la religion considérée dans sa source, ses formes et ses développements* (5 vols.; 1824–30).

ANALYSIS 28
SPIRITUAL VALUES IN THE WORK OF ERNST TROELTSCH[1]
By FRANCIS A. CHRISTIE
Lowell, Mass.

I

The main contribution to history by Ernst Troeltsch is his massive and amazingly erudite volume on *Die Sozialehren der christlichen Kirchen und Gruppen.*[2] Presupposing the knowledge offered by narrative accounts of church history, he attempted a history of Christian ecclesiastical civilization viewing all that is religious and theological as the subsoil of social ethical results or as themselves mirroring the sociological environment. This he considered a truer picture of Christianity's historical reality than those that had been shaped by ecclesiastical interests. For an understanding of this profound and difficult work we are helped by a knowledge of the author's career.

The son of a physician who was occupied with scientific inquiries, Troeltsch was initiated precociously in his boyhood home into the methods and the current generalizations of natural science. On the other hand, his love of history, awakened by the instruction of the Gymnasium, made him aware of a sphere of reality contrasting in kind with the reality found in nature by the scientist's methods. This early divination of a great problem related to his youthful religious ardor led him on entering the university in 1884 to devote himself to *Religionswissenschaft,* to the search for critical, organized knowledge of historical religion. Theology in this form he found to be an absorbingly interesting and revolutionary science, dominated as it then was by historians like Wellhausen and Weizsäcker, and breeding a younger generation of scholars who were to investigate Christianity by the methods and points of view belonging to a general history of all religions. Even more acutely aware now of the problem raised by the all-devouring naturalism of modern science, he

---

[1] [The work of Troeltsch was independently suggested for analysis by Professors Charles H. Haskins, Sidney B. Fay, and the analyst. Professor Christie says of his paper: "In the first part I expound Troeltsch's conception of what the historian aims to do—and in the second I try to indicate by a highly condensed abstract how he actually surveys Christian history." This analysis was first written in September, 1928, and was revised by the analyst in February, 1929.—EDITOR.]

[2] Tübingen, 1912.

was driven also to the study of philosophy. In this he found himself most responsive to Lotze and Dilthey, who brought him nearer to the firm conviction that the life of the human spirit could not be understood by the methods of naturalism. Its difference of content from physical nature required a different process of apprehension, and that content was such as to provide immediate certainties to experience.

With this growing insight into method, Troeltsch as a student, and then as *Dozent* in Göttingen, was gnawing at a vast problem—the historical evolution of religion as rooted in the general life and the special significance of Christianity within this evolution. Using the methods of empirical history with a philosophic interest, he thought his way to a logic of history. For this, more than he formally recognizes, he was in debt to Wilhelm Dilthey. Dilthey's *Einleitung in die Geisteswissenschaften*, which at first was meant to have the significant title of *Kritik der historischen Vernunft*, was the starting-point for highly important thought concerning discriminated spheres of knowledge on the part of men with whom Troeltsch was closely associated, especially Windelband, Rickert, and Lask. These and others have elucidated the bifurcation of human knowledge which began when Descartes turned from the medieval preoccupation with ontology to an analysis of consciousness.

This analysis resulted in two directions of thought. One concerned itself with what is corporeal and resolvable into simple atomic elements whose action is seen in regularities of law, the reduction leaving us a world without quality. On the other hand, there has come a historicizing of all thought about man, the recognition of a mode of reality only intelligible as pervaded by values regnant over the human spirit. So have developed diverse rationalities of process dictated to the investigator by the character of the data studied. The actual instinctive practice of great historians, illuminated by such philosophical analysis, shows that the historian has a logic of his own, compelled by his materials. That material comes to us in structures of historical reality. We are compelled to use principles of selection, of formation, of connection. With only detailed differences our philosophical observers agree that these principles center around the notion of individuality. The historian depicts an individual configuration of historical movements, such as feudalism, Renaissance, Reformation, French Revolution. While the physicist must reduce his reality to simple elements and the abstract laws of their interaction, the historian starts with an individual totality, a compound unity not to be resolved causally as a mere product of compilation of simples. It is an individual structure, original, never repeated, to be accepted as offered, one of life's mysteries.

What, then, is "understanding" or "explanation" of such a complex? If we were using the procedure of pure natural science we should refuse to consider the French Revolution alone. We should view together all revolutions in Greece, Rome, China, Russia. We should reduce them to causally related steps and find a general law of revolutionary process. But such is not the historian's "understanding." He appropriates the significance of any great movement of historical life by *Einfühlung*, by intuitive sympathetic participation, by putting himself back into the situation and the flux, appreciating it as if he were in the same situation. Obviously the object viewed has in it the action of values that claim the historical observer. The general character of Greek civilization or the Renaissance movement cannot be found by mere addition of the single processes they include. The general character of the whole totality lurks in the single processes, and the unity is due to what thus lies hidden in the details.

We must therefore be content to accept as given any such peculiar life-formation that emerges from life's hidden background to employ for its own intention the processes of body and mind. Its individual essential character is a unity of value, meaning, tendency, which is immanent throughout the movement and can be apprehended only by the historical sense with which we are fortunately endowed—our capacity to recognize intuitively and to feel some value or meaning. We are always dealing with a unique, a *novum*. Obviously then, causality here rests not as in natural science on a quantitative equivalence of cause and effect. The purely causal processes within the movement are governed by the ever-present unity of tendency that is working itself out, the *Werde Einheit* that blends them all and gives them their continuity. They are used by the productive life that emerges from the hidden background but they do not account for that emergent special type. They act teleologically for its organic totality. The value that they serve is not to be formulated as an abstract general notion. It must be exhibited as in the concrete realities of the particular unfolding formation of life.

The significant historical idea that makes a movement of definite form cannot live by itself alone. It needs the causal nexus and, in that, social forces are always in one degree or another operative—eventually, then, economic factors. To understand such a historical complex as Christianity we must look deeper than its dogmatic expressions and note that its practical power in life is not intelligible until we reckon also the influence of economic structure on all group life. Such a consideration need not be distorted into economic materialism. Religion springs from a specific, distinctive, irreducible functioning of consciousness, and its expressions in ideas, myths, and cults have a relative independence. Nevertheless, religious life and economic life affect one another intimately. Religion creates large sociological organizations—churches, sects—which cut into the economic system, while shapings of life due to economic forces increase their power by absorbing religious ideas. By inculcating its virtues as a means to earthly prosperity Judaism had great economic importance. The Koran is an obstacle to European culture since it binds Islam to a primitive economic organization. The Christian church by its formative religious idea left economic work to itself unhindered as a purely worldly affair. Later, the economic standards natural to their time and place were made divine mandates by ascribing them to divine revelation and, in fact, economic practice was affected by an infiltration of Christian spirit. There is a relative dependence of religion on the social, of the social on the religious. The individual periods and episodes must always be separately studied. Love of generalization must not blind us to the complexity of this whole matter.

With such prepossessions, Troeltsch undertook a historical study which might answer an anxious question: How far were the origin, the development, the changes, and the modern slackening of Christianity sociologically conditioned, and how far is Christianity itself a direct formative sociological principle? What follows may, we trust, indicate the nature of his conclusions.

II

To know what the specific essence of Christianity is, we must see what actual history shows of the relation of its social organization to other elements of civilization. Like any other development that by the psychological appeal of worth controls the human spirit, Christianity developed sociological forms, but always in accord with the fundamental religious idea that was its organizing principle. By these creations it injected social ideals into the general historical movement.

Christianity began as a purely religious movement. Jesus founded no religious community. His gospel declared a relation of man and God in terms of a religion of pure transcendence. The soul's quest must be for the eternal good of the Kingdom of God, which transcended family, state, and the social economic structure. This meant the hallowing of the private heart and such conduct as issued from inner union with the divine love. This individualism ignored all natural differences and earthly hardships; simply proclaimed the infinite value of every soul; made no compromise with actual necessities of the world, and offered no program of reform of the existing social order. It had, to be sure, within itself the germ of a new community in its communism of voluntary sharing, but it did not debate its relation to the established forms of contemporary civilization.

The first step beyond this transcendency was the Paulinism that made the risen Jesus, the pneumatic Christ, the object of a cult. This necessitated a special organization. In this body of Christ all were equal in participation of the cult, but the equality began to have limitations through the idea of differences in the bestowals of divine grace and by inevitable distinctions of leader and led in this devotion of love. Only an external compromise was made with the world without. The state was accepted as divinely instituted for order and morality, but the spiritual life was unrelated to the existing social system.

All further developments are in Troeltsch's view the outcome primarily of the transcendent religious idea. Since it was relation to Christ that made a holy divine community apart from the world, there came thereby the doctrine of Christ's divinity and eventually the trinitarian dogma. Philosophical interests here were secondary and limited to the learned few. The grace that gave ethical renewal came by participation in sacred usages conducted by leaders who were ever more venerated as dispensers of a salvation won by Christ's death. So came sacrament, priest, and episcopates, an approximation to the pagan type, but yet strictly a natural development from the formative Christian idea. Doctrine became definite and fixed, churches were brought into one unity by common creed and sacraments. The church became an independent organism with its own code of right. It stood opposed to the world, the realm from which one was rescued by the grace provided by Christ. Still absent was any project of transforming the world. Either one must withdraw from it with rigorous asceticism or use its goods and its forms with moderation. Asceticism, however, was never the fundamental trait. The primary and generative principle was the transcendency of the religious conception. Only in the intellectual sphere was there more fusion with the world, through the prevalence of platonic and stoic thought. The stoic's law of nature was identified with Christ's law of absolute love, and to soften the conflict of love and the world's hard facts the Christian agreed with the stoic fiction of a Golden Age where alone the law of nature had full control. Like the stoic, the Christian accepted as of relative justification coercive power and war and struggle for possessions as consequences of and remedial discipline for sin.

The ancient Catholic church, the saving institution, source of grace and truth, controlled by consecrated officers, was on the scene. Latent tendencies divergent from this were subdued by the rejection of montanist sect and mystical gnosticism.

With the Middle Ages began the dream of a Christian civilization in which the organizations of the family, the state, the economic system, and the systems of law, science, and art should be under the sway of the transcendent principles of divine love and human brotherhood. It was the Christian form of Plato's ideal of a society governed by the expert wise, of the stoic ideal of humanity responsive to a universal moral law. New conditions allowed the idea to find entrance into the world's life. The world now was the crude barbarian life that must learn culture and efficiency from the Christian organization, turning to the clergy for law and administration, to the convent for culture and model agriculture. The church aided in the organization of the Frankish kingdom. Charlemagne was an emperor willing to enforce Christian doctrine and practice. The church, socially powerful by its wealth, served the royal power. There was a relative conciliation.

A check came with the Hildebrandine struggle for the church as an independent organism, divinely founded for human redemption through sacraments enacted by its priests, centralized in Rome, and claiming the obedience of princes. The church was asserting again the original Christian ideal of a community responsive to absolute eternal values. Priest and monk lived in this transcendency, and the inferior compromises of men of the world were rectified by the effective system of penance. The world indeed was no longer seen in the old sheer opposition. There was an infiltration of Christian ethics. Feudalism had something like the Christian's patriarchal care for the weak. Village life retained something of communism resembling the Christian principle. The simple life of agriculture with its scant use of money knew less of competition. The crude and violent instincts of warring knights could even be diverted to the crusades and knighthood made an ecclesiastical order. The new towns of free citizens depending on handicrafts displayed a more real approach to a Christianized order by their philanthropic institutions and their cathedrals. The Catholic church, now in fully developed form, earthly representative of the absolute, presided over a cosmos of social order viewed as natural and rational. Its ascending scale of callings had their relative justification as making a divinely instituted sphere of discipline and of preparation for grace. The world's order found Christian interpretation in the ethics of Aquinas, where the natural is a step to the enjoyment of supernatural good. *Gratia naturam non tollit sed perficit.*

In the medieval period we find in more distinct emergence, however, group expressions of Christianity separate from the church form. They too are generated from the original idea. They are the sects in which rigorous religionists, conscious of their regeneration and inspired by the revival of hope of a coming Kingdom of God, unite in free unions to live strictly by the law of the Sermon on the Mount, so stressing legalism rather than grace. Or they were more loosely related circles of mystics seeking inward and feeling realizations of the truth given objectively in doctrine and cult. For them dogma lost its rigor of definition and the cult was but occasion and stimulus for a personal direct experience.

According to Troeltsch, the great breach with this dominant medieval conception came only in the eighteenth century. Luther purified the Catholic church. He broke with the materialistic notion of sacramental grace. Grace became a psychological experience of forgiveness. Religion was made personal. Morality was the believer's free impulsive response to a gracious God. But, for Luther the church was still the institution of salvation into which man is born, an overindividual power independent of the ethical achievements of its members. In this historic institution the preacher's proclamation of the divinely given Bible was the agency of salvation, the Bible supplanting priest, tradition, and pope. When this idealism showed anarchic tendencies, Lutheranism gave the control to princes guided by theologians and became a coercive orthodoxy. There was no right of revolution. The believer must passively endure even the wicked will of the ruler, for magistrates have come by the divine order. The calling and the class into which one is born are by divine provision, and in them one must render the full obedience due to Christianity's absolute demand. The calling, not the convent, is the place for religious perfection. There is the discipline that God provides. The Christian is not a reformer of this stable order. He is a pilgrim in it. Lutheranism could house mystics but not aggressive sects.

With the same general scheme, Calvinism had more of the future in it. Here God was not an infinite compassion for the sinner but a majestic incalculable will acting by the sheer decree of untrammeled sovereignty. Man stood before him not by the mediating agency of the church, but alone, directly, through the certainty of his election, the recipient of a grace that could not be lost. Hence the Calvinist, with a certitude of security that intensified activity, undertook to show forth his election by doing his work for the glory of God and for the building of a Christian community. All callings are given as rational means to that end. While Luther left moral control to the magistrate, Calvin's church was a system of discipline applied through the office of elders divinely appointed for that end. The state must support this discipline and become a Christian state. Geneva learned that idleness was sin, that labor at crafts was service of God, and that wealth should be sought for the common good. The rich are God's treasurers. The ban on interest was lifted. Capital was seen to have productive value. Calvinist teaching helped the development of modern economic life.

The state must obey the church or Christians may resist it. When Calvinism spread to lands where the state power would not yield to its demands, the interest of discipline led ultimately to separation of church and state. Thus came out of Calvinism voluntary sect formations with a leaning to democracy, though democracy needed also to have recourse to stoic rationalist ideas.

Catholic, Lutheran, Calvinist—these are the church types that Christianity has produced for the spiritual housing of total populations. From the same original formative religious principle it had produced also limited sects of legalistic moralism and less defined companies of mystics who valued religion as an individual inner experience of communion with the divine life. The typical instances of the Reformation period are the Anabaptist sect and the spiritual circle of Franck, Denck, or Castellion, mystics who were also humanists. In faithful loyalty to the medieval ecclesiastical ideal, the older Protestantism rejected these supplementary and rival types. But sect, mystics, and humanists are the creators of the modernity in which we find ourselves.

The truly modern world must be dated only from the eighteenth century. Then most distinctly came the revolt against the notion of a world corrupt and sinful, subject to an authoritative church. Then began the faith in a divinity of value working itself into expression in the free development of the full human endowment and, therefore, in the civilization that had been viewed with such condescension. Infallibility and ascetic pessimism now yielded to tolerance and to the optimism due to faith in progress. The human good was now seen to outrun the redemption that the church had offered. It embraces all the rich exfoliations of the human endowment. *Im Ganzen, Guten, Schoenen, resolut zu leben.* The idea of humanity looms high—a humanity guided by science rather than by theology. A new religiosity that transforms the old. It substitutes for the old metaphysics a science of religions that studies all forms of religious consciousness, not merely those that rest on miracle. The state is now secularized. The church must live as a corporation. It is in Anglo-Saxon lands that this modernity finds fullest expression. To this modernism the future belongs. The Protestantism of the new Anglo-Saxon type must develop the church of the future that shall wrestle with the problems of this new age. Doubtless it is not destined to create the Kingdom of God, but it will dauntlessly take up life's combat and bring the world forward toward its goal even without hope of a perfect realization.

In our day, the driving urge of Christianity for a perfection of good beyond the given scene is perceptibly slackened by the movement of modern society, its utilitarianism, its optimism, its immanence, its natu-ralism. But that mundane optimism is ever inclined to hesitate and break down, and the Christian ethos always asserts itself anew. It is no simple denial of self and world. It asks at least an asceticism of rigorous disci-pline. The Christian principle needs, as supplement and restraint from one-sidedness, a theory of civilization with which it can join. By itself alone it cannot be adequate in an abiding world. We can no longer, as of old, find this supplement in an ethical law of nature. Here lies the task of a new Christian ethics.

May this meager outline suggest the wealth of thought with which Troeltsch depicts the struggle of an idea to mix itself with life.

This investigation of the Christian movement is significant when com-pared with those that find its essence in a simple doctrine proclaimed by Jesus, and that view later features, like the Greek metaphysical dogma, or the hierarchy and the papacy, as intrusions from without. Troeltsch conceives Christianity as an individual totality. How, then, can such great diversities as the preaching of Jesus, the theology of Origen, the fully de-veloped Catholic system of the medieval period, and Protestantism with its dispersive individualism be conceived as a unity of movement? What is the *continuum* that binds these diverse expressions together? The an-swer cannot be found by an abstraction of elements common to the suc-cessive periods. It is necessary to find a central spiritual dynamic tend-ency that can assume such contrasted expressions in the whole complex of European civilization. We do not arrive at a simple formula. We are shown not the simple development of a germ but an oscillation of dualistic tendency: optimism and pessimism, transcendence and immanence, con-flict and harmony between God and world. No single period, but only the whole history, can disclose this inner-life vibration. The disclosure comes to the penetrative intuition of the Christian soul that is sensitive to the full appeal of all the constraining values of life and will "see life steadily and see it whole."

ANALYSIS 29

VOLTAIRE, HISTORIAN OF CIVILIZATION AND EXPONENT OF RATIONALISM[1]

By FERDINAND SCHEVILL

University of Chicago

Whoever wishes to reach an understanding of Voltaire, the historian, will do well never to forget that, although he became a historian and one, moreover, who ranks with the relatively small group of great innovators, he began his career as a devotee of letters spurred by the consuming desire to win a place beside the *grands écrivains* of the splendid age of Louis XIV, which in his boyhood was slowly dropping to its setting. He had already made a notable advance toward this goal of his ambition when certain special circumstances of his life and times, coupled with a sturdy realism characteristic of his genius, carried him into the serious study of the institutions, religion, philosophy, science, and art obtaining in the Europe of his day; and his curiosity on this score, once aroused, proved so insatiable that he extended his inquiry to the Renaissance and Middle Age and, finally, to the equivalent manifestations among all the famous societies and civilizations of the past of which an account was obtainable. His ardent and persistent labors enabled him at the zenith of his life to enjoy a wider prospect of the diverse movements among our human species than was enjoyed by any contemporary or, in all probability, had ever been enjoyed by any individual before his time.

In this boundless ocean of data touching man and his destiny, Voltaire, like many another zealous scholar, might have gone under never to reappear, if a masterful and creative element in his nature had not obliged him to suppress, prune, and select his material with reference to a guiding principle or, as he would have preferred to say, with reference to a philosophy of life. As a result of studies, broad but carefully directed, he put

---

[1] [In a letter Professor Schevill explains his purpose in this analysis as follows: "I . . . . tried to summarize the contributions made by Voltaire to historiography. What is Voltaire trying to do as a historian? This question was ever before me; and in my answer I tried to consider both what he *said* he was doing and what he actually *did*. And of course I constantly had in mind also the troubled state of historiography in our day." Professor Sidney B. Fay adds this appreciative comment upon the paper: " . . . . He (the analyst) has caught a little of Voltaire's own literary flavor in the wording of his own critique." It was first completed in October, 1928, and was revised by the analyst in February, 1929.—EDITOR.]

forth many works, all of them alike illustrative of the view that history represents a judicious mixture of the three elements of literature, facts, and philosophy. If his earlier product in this field was excessively influenced by the literary tradition in which he grew up, his later work was frequently overcharged with philosophical emphasis; and in both instances we are likely to feel that his third element, the subject matter, has often been unduly slighted. However, Voltaire's theory, which on the whole he followed with notable consistency, was that the business of the historian was to present the carefully sifted facts, that is, the essential truth, in the most attractive form attainable and with an explanatory comment representative of the enlightened understanding which was the special boast of his age. No historical production of his own or of any past period met the great rationalist's critical approval if it was not brewed in about equal parts of these three ingredients. Whereby it will at once appear that the issue so passionately debated in our time as to whether history is an art or a science did not arise to disturb his equanimity. To him, as to all his predecessors back to the far days of Herodotus, it was one of the best-established and more authentic categories of the literary art.

Voltaire's first contribution to history was his *Histoire de Charles XII* (1731). An unsurpassed masterpiece of lively narrative, it is a most imperfect history, since it makes no effort whatever to relate Charles to his age and country. Still immersed in his literary preoccupations, the author saw the Swedish sovereign primarily as a tragic hero carried by a capricious fate to the highest pinnacle of success only to be hurled in the end to the lowest depths of defeat. He was remarkably conscientious about the facts which he recounted—they have been found to meet the acid test of our minute modern research—but his main concern was to shake his readers with that mingled pity and terror which, since Aristotle, was held to be the true hallmark of tragedy.

When he took up the preparatory labors for the next work, the *Siècle de Louis XIV*, he first adopted a plan hardly more attentive to the deeper historical values; but now gradually catching fire and burning with the desire to know the age under investigation in all its aspects, he steadily enlarged his studies until he had acquired a view of the march not only of European society from the reign of Charlemagne forward to that of Louis XIV but also, as already said, of our human kind in every important area of the globe. As a result, he labored on his *Louis XIV*, with prolonged interruptions, for almost two decades; and when he published it in 1751, he regarded it as but the concluding, though indeed the crowning, section of a universal history, which, under the name of *Essai sur l'histoire*

générale et sur les mœurs et l'esprit des nations, was already under way at
the time and which saw the light in 1756. As Voltaire grew older, he became more and more attached to historical studies. This is attested by his
putting out several other elaborate works, as well as by innumerable
sketches, letters, notes, and special articles. But his universal history,
that is, the rather infelicitously named *Essai* culminating in the *Siècle de
Louis XIV*, is without any question his ripest production. From it we may
hope to learn what profitable impulse Voltaire imparted to historiography
in this day, and, more particularly, what his answer may be to the question put to the famous wraiths summoned before the inquisition collectively
responsible for this book and exhorting them to tell what, in their view,
history is all about.

That Voltaire was moved to lift himself to a height from which he could
scan universal history was not as original an action on his part as might
appear at first blush, since histories claiming universality were at every
man's call in his day. In the first place it was still usual to write history
in the form of chronicles, which might go back to Adam and which in any
case tabulated the disconnected events of the past centuries. Voltaire
treated these dull compendia with scorn and, as products of medieval
ignorance, denied them shelf-space in the library of a cultivated gentleman.
But there existed another type of universal history which, equally medieval, rested on a basis of authoritative and unifying thought. Of this
class the ancient and unequaled model was Augustine's *City of God;* and
its immense merit was that it preserved and set down in chronological
order all the facts of man's earthly pilgrimage which from the orthodox
Christian viewpoint were worth knowing. Augustine accordingly unfolded
God's marvelous plan of salvation, starting out with the garden of Eden
and Adam's sin and continuing with the history of the Jews until he
reached the incarnation, crucifixion, and founding of the community of
the faithful represented by the Christian church. Such a scheme made
Jewish history the absolutely pivotal fact of the human record and, apart
from a contemptuous side-glance at Greek and Roman history, heartily
consigned every other people to oblivion. In short, in the name of divine
history the saintly Augustine superseded and completely sabotaged human
history, just as, not by his single strength indeed but with the aid of the
other Christian Fathers, he successfully sank, in the name of faith, the
precious intellectual cargo of antiquity. So long as the Christian church,
dedicated to its rejection of our earth, ruled society, there was no escape
from the Augustinian theory of history. It was therefore disclosed to be-
lievers in learned versions well into the seventeenth century. As late as

that brilliant Age of Louis XIV which moved our historian to raise his voice like a trumpet in its praise, Bishop Bossuet had composed a *Histoire universelle* which was nothing more than a variation in a post-Reformation key on the ancient theme of Augustine.

No sooner had Voltaire begun to wrestle with the issues of history than he encountered Bossuet's work, which was in everybody's hand and which, in accordance with the accepted Christian pattern, propounded a supernatural power directing human destiny from its distant beginning in Adam to a foreseen majestic conclusion in the Day of Judgment. But for Voltaire and an intellectual handful in France and elsewhere this view was no longer tenable. Under the inspiration of the natural sciences the evolution of European thought had recently produced that movement which we sweepingly call the Enlightenment and which, summarily eliminating God from the stream of events, attempted to explain nature and history alike in terms of comprehensible and measurable forces. In the struggle to popularize this attitude, felt by orthodox Christians to be shockingly irreligious, Voltaire aroused the wrath of the church; and, provoked by this antagonism to fight back, he became gradually as intolerant of Christian tradition as the church was of his heated exaltation of man's intellectual autonomy. Before long he spoke of the church habitually as *l'infâme*, the "infamous one," and constantly extending the dominion of his skepticism, came to regard all organized religion of whatever age and climate as due to the machinations of priests selfishly moved to keep man in ignorance and subjection.

There can be no doubt whatever that the point of departure for Voltaire, the historian, was the naturalism inherent in the scientific orientation of the Enlightenment, and further, that this position, leading to a ferocious conflict with the supernaturalists, accounts for the consistent misrepresentation in the *Essai sur les Mœurs* of the part played by the church and by religion in general in world-history. However, apart from this single passionate distortion, the new viewpoint brought an unmitigated gain to the survey of the past. With the Christian squint corrected, the Jews fell from their eminence and assumed their proper place as the relatively unimportant inhabitants of a barren corner of Syria almost constantly overrun by more powerful neighbors. Nor was that all. History had hitherto been Europa-centric. Now, as at a signal from a magic flute, mental walls fell away and the wide prospects of Asia, Africa, and America were disclosed to the delighted eye. With Voltaire's brilliant *Essai* the subject of history became man, man in all his earthly variations; and in the place of what in the Middle Age had been falsely called universal history, a history inclusive of all the great societies of which a record had survived became for the first time a possibility and a promise.

With history thus made coextensive with the two concepts, man and earth, the issue arose as to which of the numerous earthly activities of man the historian should regard as his special province. And here Voltaire made another revolutionary contribution. Already in his *Siècle de Louis XIV* he had declared that his eye was not directed primarily on a great king and his wars, but that he wished to paint *le génie et les mœurs des hommes*. Nor, resolved, as we have seen he was, to write history *en philosophe*, that is, with subjective purpose, does he conceal the fact that he plans also systematically to disseminate useful information and to inculcate the love of virtue, country, and the arts. When he wrote the *avant-propos* of the *Essai sur les Mœurs* he enumerated, with but slight variation, as his aim *l'esprit, les mœurs, les usages des nations principales;* and in the body of his text, as if aware that he was joining issue with an inveterate prejudice regarding the accepted content of history, he repeated again and again that conquerors and sovereigns, except when they have made *leurs peuples meilleurs et plus heureux*, constitute the useless baggage carried by his predecessors of which he intended, so far as possible, to lighten his pages. Closely scrutinized, does not this position mean that the man who rode into the lists against Christian historiography, dominant for over a thousand years, rejected also the only other kind of historiography known to his time and enjoying the veneration with which everything connected with the shining names of Greece and Rome was regarded? It admits of no doubt that for Thucydides, Livy, and the other pagan historians the theme supremely engaging their attention was the secular state and its rulers. Their writings were therefore essentially and, to all intents, exclusively political. When, in the Italian Renaissance, history in such leading representatives as Machiavelli and Guicciardini for the first time departed from the Augustinian formula, it adopted apparently as the only possible alternative the outlook and the procedure of the ancients. And as late as the beginning of the eighteenth century it was still generally held that history was exhausted with the two accredited forms, the Christian and the classical.

Under the circumstances, it produced no less than a sensation when Voltaire arose in his place to propound a third type of history based on a revised, up-to-date, and much more far-reaching conception of man than either the Middle Age or antiquity had attained. Admitting that man is properly concerned, as the Christians said, with God, and no less properly, as was contended by the ancients, with the state, are God and the state the sum of man's concern? Voltaire emphatically said no. Though religion and politics must not be overlooked, there are, besides, the materials from which intellectual history, social history, economic history, and the history of literature and the arts await construction. And of all these possible inquiries none may be neglected if we wish to arrive at a halfway adequate understanding of what man has already achieved in the past and what he may look forward to in the future. In short, the broad task of the historian is *to describe the various civilizations* which man, whether white, black, or yellow, has created; and he must unfold them, not with a view to the entertainment of idle readers, but to the inspired end, deduced from a philosophic survey of existence, that our human kind, by becoming more enlightened, may learn at last to overcome the stupidities, violences, and cruelties which have been its unbroken lot throughout the ages.

A book like the *Essai*, so destructive of authoritarian and limiting traditions, so clearly and persuasively tracing the line by which Europe emerged from a fancied "Gothic barbarism" into the light and progress of the eighteenth century, so vividly comparing European civilization with that of the Chinese, the Hindus, the Greeks, the Romans, and the Arabs, was bound to achieve an immediate vogue. Add that, although gravely composed, it was touched with the clarity and wit of one of the most sparkling geniuses of all time, and that, further, it was a reform pamphlet, every page of which reverberated with a passionate war-cry, and we can understand that the vogue rose almost to a frenzy. The *Essai* became a not neglible affluent of that tumultuous stream of opinion which, beginning with the revolutionary movement of 1789, leveled all the ancient landmarks of France and inaugurated the modern democratic era. And in this destructive and exaggerated triumph we encounter one of life's irrepressible ironies. For Voltaire, although an enraged rationalist and reformer, never thought for a moment of intrusting the elevation of humanity to the unchained and untutored masses. These were to him but *canaille*, incapable by themselves of achieving any good, even their own. In his eyes the great work of social uplift was reserved either to a benevolent despot or to an aristocracy of merit composed of men like himself and his comet-tail of intellectuals.

Under the circumstances, it was perhaps not so strange that the French Revolution, in sweeping aside the evil inheritance against which the *Essai* had declared war, swept the *Essai* too into oblivion. For the general public it had been essentially a revolutionary pamphlet and as such it had done its work. But if for the hundred and more years which have passed since the French Revolution, professional historians also have neglected a work, admittedly a main gateway to modern historiography, there must be reasons having to do with the development of historical studies since that time. And such is indeed the case. On the defeat of the Revolution a reaction against its tenets set in, which poured the ever fluid human mind into the molds prepared by the Romantic movement; and the school of historians shaped by the forces of Romanticism quarreled with all three of the characteristic elements of Voltaire's work, with his passionate rationalism, his skimpy facts, and even his too frail and transparent literary form. Most violently of course with his rationalism. Superficial, cocksure, and inclined to treat every inheritance from the past as a hoary iniquity, it had, the Romantics contended, been utterly discredited by the political and cultural cataclysm of which it was a leading cause. To check the danger arising from too blindly accepting an abstract reason as our guide the new group of thinkers evolved the great principle of historical continuity, and in instinctive opposition to Voltaire and the Enlightenment inculcated an almost holy respect for the past and, more particularly, for that section of it, the Middle Age, which the eighteenth century had represented as a hideous and unrelieved barbarism. Therewith, Voltaire's evaluation of the human past, the fiery portent of his own period, fell flat with the scholars who came to the front in the age bearing the label of the Congress of Vienna. It was not that they objected in principle to introducing a philosophical element into history; or, if they said they objected, they completely failed to practice what they preached, for in the course of the first half of the nineteenth century they completely re-wrote the story of Europe and even of mankind by visioning it from the dominant romantic angle. The only tolerable philosophy was their own.

But with hardly less vehemence the new nineteenth-century school objected also to Voltaire's facts. The great Frenchman had been a remarkably conscientious student, poring diligently over the available sources and dissecting them with notable critical acumen. This must always be insisted on against the ignorant body of his detractors who make light of his scholarship. However, the materials at his or any contemporary's disposal were simply inadequate. That the first requisite for better histories was a richer and better-accredited corpus of facts became the solemn conviction of the leading post-revolutionary students in all countries of Europe. Hence they devoted themselves with high ardor to the critical study, the classification, and the editing of documents; and these labors, continued throughout the nineteenth century, have prospered to such an extent that we are now in possession of a body of knowledge touching the past of our race, on the one hand, so immeasurable in scope and, on the other, so exact in detail, that poor Voltaire by comparison offers a mere nose bag of sawdust. Furthermore, under the new scholarly dispensation the pursuit of history requires a long apprenticeship in diplomatics, paleography, and other ancillary studies, and has come more and more to be cultivated by specialists content to work intensively in a narrowly staked-off field. The laboratory habits of these modern Benedictines prompted them to think of themselves as scientists and, as a natural corollary of their dryly factual outlook, they developed a scorn for literary composition or, at best, looked upon it as a work of supererogation. Therewith, the third and last element of Voltaire's formula, literature, went by the boards and history assumed that character of pure research which has overwhelmingly distinguished it from the time of Ranke to the present day.

But whoever scans the horizon closely may detect numerous symptoms of an approaching change of weather. In accordance with the pendulum movement characteristic of our human thought and illustrated by the swing, around 1800, from a rationalist to a romantic outlook, we are growing tired of the excessive atomization of history in recent decades and are demanding a new synthesis involving a new picture of the human whole. And this means unescapably a return to the theme of civilization and therewith to Voltaire. And, more, it means a return to Voltaire's practice of regarding history as a literary art concerned with presenting relevant human happenings in terms of the particular understanding of the mundane situation reached by the living generation of men. The extraordinary popularity attained by such recent works as those of H. G. Wells and Osward Spengler furnishes unmistakable evidence of this newest trend. Removed in method and philosophy as Wells is from Spengler and different as both are in every detail from Voltaire, they none the less mark a return to the historical type of which Voltaire is the distinguished originator. Further, the favor enjoyed, especially in the United States, by the so-called "new history" fathered by Professor Robinson should not be overlooked. Exactly as with Voltaire, the new history predicates a science-inspired "progress" as our human goal and urges an active and even passionate intervention on the part of the historian to effect its realization. Although the new history therefore hardly justifies its claim to being new, it may with entire propriety insist on its descent from him whom the eighteenth century hailed as the Apostle of Humanity.

If Voltaire, as seems to be the case, is in our day to experience a rehabilitation, a final issue with regard to him must be faced, and we must question him as to his views of historical causation. For, apart from their unflagging interest in critical method, no other matter has so engaged the attention of recent generations of historians as this. In fact, the leading groups contending for recognition within the profession at the present time may be set off from each other most incisively with respect to their view regarding the nature and the cause of historical change. This is fully borne out by the *Case Book* for which the present study is written. While undoubtedly offering an opportunity to its contributors to discuss problems of method and scope, its real *raison d'être*, so far at least as the field of history is concerned, is to analyze the various views regarding historical causation championed by eminent recent practitioners in the field.

Let us admit at once that Voltaire subjected this important matter to no systematic investigation and that he maintained with regard to it an attitude as inconsistent and uncertain as that of the overwhelming preponderance of historians since his time. For Bishop Bossuet and the Christian school, all events in heaven and earth had been referable to a supernatural agent carrying out a foreordained plan. Breaking away from this convenient doctrine, as we have seen, Voltaire did not hesitate to place the responsibility for our social order in man and, more particularly, in that precious spark of reason which distinguishes man from the other animals. It was this conviction which made him a rationalist, exalting reason or, as we would prefer to say, intelligence as the *causa movens* of the phenomena of civilization. Pursuant to this train of thought, he was able to entertain and champion the idea of human progress and envisage a society of the future more intelligently governed than had been the case in the past, and following as its highest end the alluring triad of universal peace, material well-being, and individual happiness. There can be no doubt that we here touch what, with qualifications, we may regard as the kernel of his historical theory.

But there *are* qualifications. To begin with, he was so deeply stirred by the misery and suffering of humanity through the ages that it frequently seemed to him that the situation was irremediable. The light of human reason should, of course, have helped; but the vast majority of men, far from accepting its guidance, stupidly remained the unresisting victims of their evil instincts. From the masses of men, in consequence, nothing at all was to be expected; and whenever mankind experienced a momentary respite from its woes, the happy interlude, according to this antidemocrat, was due to the action of a benevolent despot or of an enlightened intelligentsia, the only likely exercisers of a restraining and directive reason. In many sections of his writings, therefore, Voltaire spoke, not without an inner consistency it must be admitted, of the notable advances of civilization resulting, not from intelligence in general but from the activity of great and intelligent individuals, the heroes and demiurges of humanity. Nor does this item of "great men" exhaust his experimental list of "causes." Certain contemporaries had hit upon climate, legislation, and religion as the three essential forces accounting for all the significant differences noticeable among men and civilizations. To Montesquieu, for instance, climate and legislation (with religion hardly in the running) explained pretty much every human variation, including color and morality. Into this discussion Voltaire projected himself with his never failing vigor; and while he made much less than Montesquieu and the geographical school of the factor of climate, he made much more of the factor of religion and comported himself as if he believed, and at times he probably did, that whenever men acted like out-and-out devils it was due to the passion and intolerance excited by religious faith. For this religious diabolism there was no cure but a cold shower of restrictive laws, issued by a tolerant Confucius or some other philosophical legislator. Thus, coercion through enlightened legislation would seem at times to have figured in his mind as an efficient "cause" of historical change.

As profoundly influenced by the physics and the astronomy of his age, Voltaire played also with the theory of the control of human affairs by "natural law." The great name in the field of eighteenth-century science was Newton; and with Newton the new mechanistic cosmology had for the elect completely replaced the Christian world-picture. Like the leaders of opinion in general, Voltaire was not an atheist, as his opponents declared, but a deist holding to a purely mechanical god who, having created a world of inalterable law, was content to gaze at it from on high in rapt but strictly neutral admiration. No conceivable "overt act" on the part of his creatures could rouse this slumbering creator to a corrective participation in the drama he had set agoing. In this vast and majestically coherent system man appeared as a tiny agglomeration of matter-in-motion reeling through space under the same unescapable laws as the rest of the physical universe. Whenever the spacious Newtonian outlook ruled his mood, the French historian inclined to look upon man as the helpless victim of an iron necessity. Therewith progress and barbarism, good and evil, and all the other issues of life and history suddenly became pointless.

In such relatively rare moments he talked like a determinist, a mechanical determinist, let us note, in order to distinguish him from the economic determinists who, numerous in our day, had not yet raised their standard when Voltaire weighed in the balance these ultimate considerations. But in the matter of this "cause" too, as in all the others, he is erratic. Perhaps because our finite minds are incapable of grasping a mathematical order of infinite dimensions, he not infrequently fell into the opposite extreme and, in an access of childish triviality, accounted for historical events on the score of grotesque accidents such as a spilled glass of water, the possession of a Roman nose, or a dog's unexpected bark. In such moments he is literary, anecdotal, and frankly unfaithful to the serious purposes of history.

What can we say in conclusion but reaffirm that Voltaire had not thought this matter of causation through? Having broken with the Christian theory of a supernatural agent, he launched our historical craft upon a disturbed sea of speculation, on which, in spite of the occasional cry of "land" on the part of a passenger regularly found on investigation to be suffering from obstinate and confirmed astigmatism, it continues to toss irresolutely to this day.

ANALYSIS 30

WHAT ARE HISTORIANS TRYING TO DO?[1]

By HENRI PIRENNE

Commission Royale d'Histoire, Académie Royale de Belgique

I

The subject of historians' study is the development of human societies in space and time. This development is the result of billions of individual actions. But in so far as they are purely individual, these actions do not belong to the domain of history, which has to take account of them only as they are related to collective movements, or in the measure to which they have influenced the collectivity. History is thus allied to sociology and psychology and at the same time it differs from them.

Like sociology, it is interested in the phenomena of the masses which arise from physiological necessities or from moral tendencies which force themselves upon men, such, for example, as nourishment and family solidarity. Like psychology, it is concerned with discovering the internal forces which explain and determine the conduct of an individual. But the comparison stops there. While the sociologist seeks to formulate the laws inherent in its very nature which regulate social existence—or, if one wishes, in abstracto—the historian devotes himself to acquiring concrete knowledge of this existence during its span. What he desires is to understand it thoroughly: trace in it all vicissitudes, describe its particular characteristics, bring out all that has happened in the course of

[1] [This paper is not an analysis of individual inquiry. During an early discussion with Professors Dana C. Munro, H. I. Shipman, and R. G. Albion, of Princeton University, concerning the place of history and historians in the Case Book project, Professor Munro suggested that there be a statement introductory to the historical analyses which would set forth the historian's objectives in general terms. The proposal was later indorsed by the Advisory Committee of the American Historical Association, and further counsel and aid concerning it were given in particular by Professors James Westfall Thompson, James T. Shotwell, Charles H. Haskins, and J. F. Jameson. The present paper was the result. Professor Pirenne's manuscript was translated by Miss Martha Anderson, of the Council on Foreign Relations, Inc., New York, the translation being reviewed by Professor Sidney B. Fay and Dr. Howard P. Becker. Inasmuch as the structure of the Case Book has been altered since the analysis was prepared (the manuscript is dated October 18, 1928) Professor Pirenne's paper is placed at the end of the section in which the larger number of historical analyses appear. In this position it serves to sum up rather than to introduce these other papers, none of which was available to him at the time of his writing. A logical alternative would have been to place it in Section I.—EDITOR.]

the ages to make of it what it has in reality been. For him, chance and the deeds of prominent personalities, of which the sociologist cannot take account, constitute the essential data of his subject. In other words, the sociologist seeks to separate the typical and the general, while for the historian the typical and the general are only the canvas upon which life has painted perpetually changing scenes. The former uses facts only with a view to the elaboration of a theory; the latter considers them as the episodes of a great adventure about which he must tell.

The sociologist is not concerned with the perturbing rôles of those who have taken prominent parts in affairs and must therefore be considered by the historian. For the latter, Alexander the Great, Caesar, Cromwell, Washington, or Napoleon I are subjects for study of the same value as a system of institutions or an economic organism. Here his task is allied to that of the psychologist, for in order to explain the feats of these "heroes" a knowledge of their minds is imperative. But here also the same difference is perceived between the psychologist and the historian as between the historian and the sociologist. For the psychologist the study of a great man's soul is merely a contribution to the general knowledge of the human soul, while this study is necessary for the historian only by virtue of the influence exerted by this man upon his contemporaries. Great as the genius of an individual may be, the historian concerns himself with him only if he has influenced other men.

Although sociology and psychology are sciences allied to history, it is no less true that they are clearly distinguished from it as much by their fields as by their methods.

In the same way that sociology takes for its subject *all* social phenomena, and psychology *all* psychological phenomena, history has for its subject *all* historical phenomena. In its chosen sphere, it presents the same character of universality as do the other sciences, whether they be human or natural sciences. It is universal in the same way as is chemistry or physics—in the sense that, like physics and chemistry, it lays claim to a knowledge of the ensemble of phenomena which constitute its subject. The historical concept necessarily implies the universal historical concept. It does not matter that in the present state of our knowledge enormous portions of history are still totally unknown, just as innumerable natural phenomena take place of which we are ignorant. It matters still less that no historian consecrates himself to the study of universal history, just as no chemist or physicist devotes himself to the study of the entire field of chemistry or physics. What is important is to have for an ideal the unity of science; similarly, to bear clearly in mind that all historical work is only a contribution to the history of human societies conceived as a whole, and that the value of historical work consists in the degree to which it promotes the advancement of history as a whole. Specialization is here only a necessity resulting from the inferiority of man's capacities. Although no man can know everything, everyone ought nevertheless to work with a view to enriching the common treasury of knowledge, and in the degree to which he is conscious of this collaboration, the result of his effort will endure and be useful.

In pursuance of the goal he has chosen, the historian finds himself confronted with a double task. He must first of all establish the facts which constitute the materials of his study, then make use of them. His method consists essentially in these two processes; in following them out he answers the question which serves as title for this article. Both result from the nature of history. Since history has been written, both have been applied consciously or unconsciously. Fundamentally, history presents itself to us as it did to our predecessors. Our present progress is only the effect which general scientific progress has had upon the work of historians. We possess processes and methods of research of which Herodotus or chroniclers of the Middle Ages were ignorant, and in the explanation of events we use a quantity of ideas and a skill in criticism of which they had no idea. We find in history an amplitude and a depth which they did not suspect. But our method of working is only an improvement on theirs.

II

Historical facts are perceptible only by the vestiges which they have left. In this respect, the position of the historian vis-à-vis his subject is quite comparable to that of the geologist. The revolutions of men, like those of the earth, would be unknown if vestiges of their existence did not remain. But it is much easier to restore the picture of the latter than that of the former. The texture of the earth's surface is directly visible to the geologist; he can measure and analyze the material in it, and he knows that the elements of which it is composed act in conformity with the laws of mechanics, physics, and chemistry. The historian, on the contrary, only rarely finds himself face to face with an authentic fragment of the past. Almost always the monuments which have survived have been seriously altered either by the effect of time or by the hand of man which sought to demolish or restore. Nor can restoration reproduce an original state; too many factors due to individual genius, to need, to the circumstances of the moment—in short, to that imponderable which is human personality—have contributed to their construction for their genesis to be describable with the same accuracy as if they were the result of forces of nature. And how many difficulties are not raised in another way by the date, the origin, the nationality of an artifact which archaeologists' excavations or chance have revealed.

Thus even in the most favorable case the historian cannot deceive himself into thinking that he is observing the past directly. But the difficulties of his task are much greater when he works with written documents. Of all the sources of history, they are at once the most valuable and the most fallacious. The very way in which they have come down to us has almost always changed them more or less seriously. When we have the rare good fortune to possess the original text, its state of preservation generally makes its deciphering more or less difficult—torn, or disfigured as it usually is by words left out, smudges, or words written over others. But in most cases the original has disappeared. To reconstitute the text we have at our disposal mere copies, and often only copies of copies, all in some measure spoiled by negligence, ignorance, or the untrustworthiness of the copyist. But let us assume that this task is accomplished; other problems present themselves. It is important to know the origin of the document, to establish the exact date, to determine its degree of authenticity. Mistakes abound in all epochs, and individuals or governments have invented or modified texts to suit their interests.

Thus the materials to which the historian is reduced require singularly difficult and delicate treatment before they are ready for use. They are merely the vestiges of events and not even authentic vestiges. One might compare them with footprints in the sand which wind and rain have half-effaced. To reproduce even an approximation of the picture, arduous and minute work is indispensable.

This work involves different processes according to the special nature of the sources to which it is applied. These are the processes which, constantly being improved by use, have given rise to what are called the "auxiliary sciences of history." From the criticism of inscriptions is born epigraphy; from that of writings, paleography; from that of charters and deeds, diplomatics, or the art of deciphering documents; from that of monuments, archaeology; from that of money, numismatics; from that of seals, sigillography; from that of armorial bearings, heraldry. Each of these constitutes a particular application of historical criticism. And to each of these also are devoted, to the common advantage of science, specialized scholars. Of all historians, these specialists are the most favorably situated from the point of view of the results of their work. Thanks to the homogeneous character of the objects which they study, it is possible for them to establish methods of observation of such precision that conclusions often result in a probability so great as to border on certainty. But after all, perfected as the methods may be, it would be quite erroneous to believe that they do not leave a very large rôle to the tact, finesse, and intuition of the user. The most exact among them—epigraphy and diplomatics—are based in fact only upon empirical observations, and the regularity of the facts which they establish has nothing in common with the rigor of the laws which result from the natural sciences.

The complicated processes of source criticism which have been briefly indicated constitute only the prelude to the work of historians. After they furnish the evidence it must be evaluated. In other words, the criticism of authenticity must be followed by that of credibility. One sees at a glance that the second is infinitely more delicate and subjective than the first. In fact, it depends no longer upon the external character of the proofs but upon the personalities of their authors. It is no longer a question of identifying the document but of judging its value. And this judgment depends necessarily upon the training, the intelligence, and the honor of the witness, as well as upon the circumstances which surrounded the gathering of his evidence. Not only is it indispensable to understand thoroughly what he wanted to say but to extract from his words whatever of truth lies in them.

Let us admit at once that it is impossible to be entirely successful. Most often one cannot flatter himself that he has even understood perfectly what the author of the document wanted to say. For even when very familiar with the language used, one can never determine with sufficient exactitude the particular nuance which it has taken on under the author's pen. To discover the real meaning which lies behind his words, one would have to identify one's self completely with him and to relive his life. That is, his personality intervenes between us and the facts. And this interposition transforms them. They suffer a distortion analogous to that of the reflection of an object plunged in water. But easy as it is to reconstitute the real appearance of the submerged object, thanks to the laws of refraction of light, one can only guess very roughly at the changes which historical narratives have inflicted upon reality. One has to be content with examining the incomplete information at his disposal as to the author's biography, his individual or national prejudices, his environment, and the conditions under which he wrote. It goes without saying that all this can be obtained only very approximately and insufficiently.

For the majority of events we fortunately possess more than one proof. Although our evaluation of each proof is necessarily defective, from the comparison of these judgments it is possible to deduce some true semblance of the reality which otherwise disappears as each gives his own account of it. Historical criticism can thus arrive at an approximate representation of past facts. It perceives them in the wavering outline of objects which appear to us in mist.

Even of these inexact pictures of historical realities, we possess relatively few. Whatever in the way of monuments and writings has come down to us from preceding ages is almost nothing in comparison with what has disappeared. Historians are only too happy today to glean in the sands of the Fayum some miserable débris from the libraries and archives of the hellenized cities of Egypt. Of millions of documents drawn up by the bureaucracies of the Roman and the Byzantine empires only a few remain. What will be left to our successors from our books made of wood-pulp and our stenographic copies? Moreover, even if we had conserved all that had been written about an event, we could not pretend to complete information. No account, detailed as it may be, ever exhausts its subject. The fulness of reality can never be expressed either by speech or by pen.

In spite of all his efforts, therefore, the historian cannot gain an adequate knowledge of what has been. Realizing this limitation, he resigns himself to it. He accepts the limits which the very conditions of the knowledge of real history impose upon written history. To perceive the facts in the measure in which this is possible must suffice. Although in relation to the absolute this is not much, it is still a great deal from the viewpoint of man.

The account of perceivable historical facts is still infinitely far from being complete. Enormous gaps appear in it at first glance. Of many peoples and nations—China, for example—we are almost entirely ignorant. We are certain also that innumerable products of human art and industry remain buried in the ground and that in spite of archaeological expeditions actively and successfully conducted today it is impossible to exhume all. As for written documents, besides a large part of these which are contained in the archives and public libraries—not yet studied —how many are concealed by unknown possessors of which we do not even suspect the existence? It is also necessary to take into account all the evidence surrounding us that we cannot perceive. The vocabulary of dead or living languages, names of places, customs, popular traditions, costumes, superstitions, and religious beliefs contain treasures which philology, topical nomenclature, and folk lore are far from having exhausted. Let us note finally that the development of historical work has resulted in the establishment of facts, knowledge of which came only from reasoning. To take a very simple example—the historian can determine the unknown date of the birth of a person if he knows that it was contemporary with an event of whose chronology he is certain. Thus by hypothesis he adds a new fact to those already known and enriches by one simple intellectual process our knowledge of the past. This procedure is so frequent that its application can be noted on almost every page of historical works. One would not be mistaken in saying that a considerable portion of historical data has no other foundation than conjecture and is certified by no source; thus the mass of the materials of science increases in proportion to the progress of criticism.

It would be an error to conclude that it is necessary to postpone writing history until all the materials are assembled. They will never all be assembled insomuch as they will never all be known. Naturalists do not insist upon knowing *all* the phenomena of nature before formulating conclusions. No more can the historian abstain from making a synthesis on the pretext that he does not possess all the elements of his synthesis. We require nothing more or less of him than that he utilize all the data at his disposal at the moment.

III

Historical construction, the utilization of facts, is the inevitable result of all the processes of criticism that we have rapidly reviewed. They have meaning and value only through it; they are only the means to the end.

To construct history is to narrate it. From its first existence it has consisted in narratives, that is, the telling of a succession of related episodes. Indeed, the essential work of the historian is to bring these episodes to light, to show the relations existing between events, and in relating to explain them. Thus it appears that history is the expository narration of the course of human societies in the past.

All historical narrative is at once a synthesis and a hypothesis. It is a synthesis insomuch as it combines the mass of known facts in an account of the whole; it is a hypothesis insomuch as the relations that it establishes between these facts are neither evident nor verifiable by themselves. To unite the facts into an ensemble and relate them is in practice one and the same process. For it goes without saying that the grouping of facts will differ according to the idea one wants to give of their relation. Everything then depends upon this—as we are about to see—and upon the degree of creative imagination of the historian and upon his general conception of human affairs. This amounts to saying that in its highest and most essential expression history is a conjectural science, or, in other words, a subjective science.

This does not mean that it is at the mercy of fantasy and arbitrary procedures. It proceeds according to a method, but according to a method which its very subject obliges it to renew constantly. The historian is no less critical in making use of facts than in the study of sources, but the complexity of his task forces him here to have recourse in a much larger measure to conjecture.

All historical construction—which amounts to saying all historical narrative—rests upon a postulate: that of the eternal identity of human nature. One cannot comprehend men's actions at all unless one assumes in the beginning that their physical and moral beings have been at all periods what they are today. Past societies would remain unintelligible to us if the natural needs which they experienced and the psychical forces which stimulated them were qualitatively different from ours. How are the innumerable differences that humanity presents in time and space to be explained if one does not consider them as changing nuances of a reality which is in its essence always and everywhere the same?

The historian assumes, therefore, that he can treat the actions of the dead as he does those of the living who surround him. And this comparison suffices to make comprehensible the subjective element in his accounts. For to reason about men's actions is to trace them back to their motives and to attribute consequences to them. But where are these motives and consequences to be found if not in the mind of him who does the reasoning? Observers differ not only according to variations in intelligence but also in the depth and the variety of their knowledge. It is by intelligence that Thucydides is a greater historian than Xenophon, and Machiavelli than Froissart. But it is by the extent of knowledge that modern historians have the advantage over those of antiquity and the Middle Ages. They doubtless do not surpass their predecessors in point of vigor and penetration of mind; but by the variety of their knowledge they discover relationships between men's acts which have escaped the former.

For long centuries the destinies of societies were explained only by the intervention of some deity and the influence of great men. History appeared essentially as drama. Farsighted minds, Polybius, for example, perceived the importance of institutions in the activity of the state. But taken all in all, history, even in the case of the most eminent authors, was only the narration and the explanation of political events. The advance of the moral and social sciences has made the narrowness and insufficiency of this conception apparent. What these sciences teach us about all sorts of factors—religious, ethnic, geographic, economic—which have determined the development of societies at various epochs, has necessarily contributed to the understanding of a mass of phenomena which formerly passed unnoticed. The knowledge of social relations being inordinately augmented, historians are in a position to discover between the facts of the past a multitude of relations which were never before taken into account. They consider the history of much more remote periods than were formerly included, and from their vantage point they discover infinitely more variation, fulness, and life. One can say with strict accuracy that with much less material at our disposal than Roman and Greek historians had, we know Greek and Roman history better than they did. We know it better and yet we are not in agreement about it at all, any more than we are about any other part of history.

To achieve certainty about a subject as flowing, diverse, and complex as social behavior is impossible. Each kind of activity reacts upon all others. How, then, distinguish in the ensemble the part taken by each? How evaluate exactly the rôle which, for example, the economic or the religious factor has played in a given evolution? The conditions indispensable to all really scientific knowledge—calculation and measurement—are completely lacking in this field. And the interference of chance and individuals increases still more the difficulty of the historian's task by constantly confronting him with the unforeseen, by changing at every moment the direction which events seemed to take.

Not to historical method but to the subjects with which history is concerned must be imputed the historians' want of precision and the fact that their results seem uncertain and contradictory. The human actions which they study cannot appear the same to different historians. It needs only a moment of reflection to understand that two historians using the same material will not treat it in an identical fashion, primarily because the creative imagination which permits them to single the factors of movements out of chaos varies, but also because they do not have the same ideas as to the relative importance of the motives which determine men's conduct. They will inevitably write accounts which will contrast as do their personalities, depending upon the relative value they place on individual action or on the influence of collective phenomena; and, among these, on the emphasis they place on the economic, the religious, the ethnic, or the political factor. To this first cause of divergence we must add others. Historians are not conditioned in various ways solely by inherited qualities; their milieu is also important. Their religion, nationality, and social class influence them more or less profoundly.

And the same is true of the period in which they work. Each epoch has its needs and tendencies which demand the attention of students and lead them to concentrate on this or that problem.

Thus, historical syntheses depend to a very large degree not only upon the personality of their authors but upon all the social, religious, or national environments which surround them. It follows, therefore, that each historian will establish between the facts relationships determined by the convictions, the movements, and the prejudices that have molded his point of view. All historical narrative is, as we have said, a hypothesis. It is an attempt at explanation, a conjectural reconstitution of the past. Each author throws light on some part, brings certain features into relief, considers certain aspects. The more these accounts multiply, the more the infinite reality is freed from its veils. All these accounts are incomplete, all imperfect, but all contribute to the advancement of knowledge. Those whose results have passed out of date have served to elaborate others which are in their turn replaced. For, in order that history may progress, the parallel development of synthesis and source criticism is indispensable. Without criticism synthesis would be only a sterile play of the imagination, and criticism would be merely dead erudition if it did not continually enlarge the field of its investigation and open new roads by the problems which it raises and the conjectures to which it gives birth.

We must believe, moreover, that in the measure in which the field is enlarged the work of historians will be accomplished under more satisfactory conditions. Up to the present time it has touched only a very restricted part of the immense subject which concerns it. In the field of ancient history, Greece and Rome; and in more modern times, the various national histories have attracted the efforts of investigators almost exclusively. Only today have we begun to discover the Orient, and we know what a transformation has consequently taken place in our comprehension of ancient history. Hellenic and Roman genius, in the dim light of records coming from Crete, Syria, Babylon, and Egypt, appear today as results of contact and interpenetration among different civilizations.

The comparative method alone can diminish racial, political, and national prejudices among historians. These prejudices inevitably ensnare him who, confined within the narrow limits of national history, is condemned to understand it badly because he is incapable of comprehending the bonds attaching it to the histories of other nations. It is not due to *parti pris* but because of insufficient information that so many historians lack impartiality. One who is lost in admiration of his own people will inevitably exaggerate their originality and give them the honor for discoveries which are in reality only borrowed. He is unjust to others because he fails to understand them, and the exclusiveness of his knowledge lays him open to the deceptions of the idols set up by sentiment. The comparative method permits history to appear in its true perspective. What was believed to be a mountain is razed to the size of a molehill, and the thing for which national genius was honored is often revealed as a simple manifestation of the imitative spirit. But the point of view of comparative history is none other than that of universal history. Therefore to the degree in which history is viewed in the totality of its development, and in which one accustoms himself to study particular or national histories in the functioning of general evolution, will the weaknesses inherent in historical method be diminished. It will attain the maximum precision which its subject permits when the final goal is clearly perceived by its adepts to be the scientific elaboration of universal history.

SECTION VII
INTERPRETATIONS OF RELATIONSHIP AMONG UNMEASURED FACTORS

ANALYSIS 31

HISTORICAL INTERRELATION OF CULTURE TRAITS: FRANZ BOAS' STUDY OF TSIMSHIAN MYTHOLOGY[1]

By LESLIE SPIER

University of Washington

This work is to be taken as representative of a series of folk-tale studies by Boas and his students. It is chosen because it is the most voluminous and careful analysis of any primitive literature known to the analyst. It is marked, however, by a peculiarity of all Boas' writing; his interpretation is minimal and stringent.

Folk tales as material for analysis have certain advantages over other forms of cultural activity, in their quantity and by reason of the mani-fold combination into which their elements enter. This makes possible something of the objectivity and the rigor of comparison known in the exact sciences.

The importance of this work is to be found in the methods of analysis employed in the establishment of the growth of complex tales, and in the empirical study of the psychology of myths. The primary concepts illustrated are two: that culture traits are fashioned primarily as the result of historic factors, and that they receive secondary reinterpretations.

The subject of the study, the Tsimshian, is a typical tribe of coastal British Columbia. For comparison, all available materials on the neighboring peoples of this culture area were brought together. In large part, these were collected by the author.

The work presents (1) a brief description of Tsimshian material existence as a background for understanding the tales; (2) a huge bulk of Tsimshian tales and others; (3) a description of the overt and mental life of this people as it may be gleaned from the tales; (4) an analytic and comparative discussion of Tsimshian social organization; (5) an analysis of the structure of the myths in the light of their dis-

[1] *Thirty-first Annual Report of the Bureau of American Ethnology* (1916), pp. 29–1037.

[The title of the present analysis has been supplied by the Editor. Note, however, Kroeber's preference, in reference to the aims of Boas and his students, for the term "dynamic" rather than "historical"; see *supra*, p. 260. The analysis was first written in 1928, and given final revision by the analyst in February, 1929.—EDITOR.]

449

semination in the area; and (6) a discussion of the literary mechanisms employed.

We will confine our attention to those parts bearing primarily on the conceptual contribution (namely, items 3, 5, and 6).

MYTH STRUCTURE AND DISSEMINATION
I. THE DATA

It will not be possible, even with this limitation, to give attention here to the analyses of all of the seventy-five tales presented. We shall further confine ourselves to two typical examples. For this purpose I choose a brief tale and the complex raven cycles.

"The Prince Who Was Deserted" may be divided into five parts:

I. The story of the boy who, instead of catching salmon, feeds the eagles, is refused food in winter, and is finally deserted. II. The grateful eagles provide food for the boy. III. The boy sends a gull with food to a person who pitied him when he was deserted by the tribe. IV. The people send to ascertain the fate of the deserted boy. The messengers find that he is rich, and are given food. One of them hides some of the food and gives it to his or her child, who is starving. The child chokes, the chieftainess pulls out the morsel of fat, and thus it is found out that the deserted boy has become rich. V. The people return and seek the good will of the deserted boy.

Twenty versions of these tales are known among tribes of the area. Each of the five parts has the following variations:

Of I: (1) A boy, instead of catching salmon, feeds eagles. (2) He eats food sent home from a feast. (3) He is lazy. (4) A girl steals sea eggs. (5) A boy is greedy and begs for food. (6) A boy eats while training for supernatural power. (7) A girl marries a dog. (8) A girl has a child by an unknown father. (9) No details given.

Of II: (1) The eagles reciprocate. (2) He finds food. (3) He mends a heron's bill and the heron helps him. (4) The girl catches a sea-spirit in her fish basket. (5) The dog children help their mother. (6) A boy receives help in a vision. (7) The sun helps the children. (8) The father of the deserted girl's child helps her.

III has no variants.

Of IV: (1) A slave's child chokes as indicated above. (2) An old person who has visited the boy is discovered secretly eating the food.

Of V: (1) The people dress their daughters hoping the boy will marry them. He rejects them because they are greedy. (2) The youth marries a girl who has been kind to him. (3) The people are killed and transformed into stones. (4) A whale kills them. (5) All the people are fed except the youth's parents. (6) The food given them is inexhaustible.

Arranged in another manner, Boas shows the combinations in which the several variations in the five parts occur.[2] (I illustrate with only four versions; see Table I.) No two of the twenty versions are identical, presenting a kaleidoscopic combination of the incidents limited in their order only by the demands of the plot.

Many or all of these incidents occur in other plots both within and outside of this area. Thus, the dog-husband tale (I, 7) is known from Siberia to Baffin Land, from Oregon to Colorado, appearing sometimes as an independent tale, sometimes as an incorporated incident, with and without the implication of explaining origins, etc.

The tale of Raven's adventures is of enormous length, really a cycle, and is known in many versions from eastern Siberia to Puget Sound. Within its frame, Boas distinguishes two hundred and twenty-five individ-

TABLE I

Version	Combinations of Variants				
Tsimshian	I, 1	II, 1	III	IV, 1	V, 1
Masset	I, 9	II, 3	..	..	V, 2
Tlingit	I, 3	II, 1	..	IV, 1	V, 4
Cowichan	I, 6	II, 6	III	IV, 2	V, 4

ual incidents (brief tales), together with a number of complex tales which also occur apart from the cycle. The obviously related mink and transformer cycles add possibly two hundred more. Few of the incidents in the raven cycle have an extended inner connection, hence they follow a random sequence. The variety of them is so great that very few recur in any large number of versions. "The great variety of individual incidents . . . . suggest that there has been a tendency to incorporate in it any tale that would fit into the series of adventures" (p. 571).

Boas next characterizes the several directions which the tale takes locally. The northern versions turn on the raven's efforts to satisfy his voracious appetite. At the southern end of the range, the tales describe encounters between the ancestors of social units and the transformer, whose general occupation is rearranging the world after the manner of the raven. In the north the raven is a trickster as well as a hero; in the south, trickster tales occur only aside from this cycle. Comparison among the northern forms shows that they can be reduced to three types of plot: (1) a deluge on the subsidence of which the raven's adventures begin, (2) the deluge story remaining apart from the raven story, and (3) a mixed

[2] [Since this chart is removed from its original setting, slight alterations have been made.—EDITOR.]

form. These regimented forms are largely confined to the introductory portion of the myths, the miscellaneous adventures following at random.

II. THE INTERPRETATIONS

With this background of the nature of these tale complexes we may turn to Boas' interpretations (pp. 872 ff.).

I.   A historical inference: Since Tsimshian tales differ from the generality of coast tales in their strong resemblance to those of interior British Columbia, the Tsimshian are intrusive on the coast.

II.   Parallel forms of incident and plot are due to diffusion rather than independent invention. The incidents
are, on the whole, fantastic modifications of every-day experiences, and are not likely to develop independently with a frequency sufficient to explain their numerous occurrences over a large area [p. 874]. [The stories] show a unity of underlying idea. They are built up on some simple event that is characteristic of the social life of the people and that stirs the emotion of the hearers. . . . . Besides these, there are a large number of complex tales of fixed form, which are put together very loosely. There is no unity of plot, but the story consists of the adventures of a single person [p. 875].

III.   Disparate elements of the tale-complex from plot to detail have been diffused independently of one another. "In each area the connection between the component parts of the story is firm [but] the whole complex does not migrate over any considerable distance. On the contrary, the parts of the tale have a tendency to appear in different connections" (p. 875).

IV.   While the tale is the resultant of those historic circumstances that contributed each element, a secondary unity has been given by the prevailing literary structure. This is evidenced by the development of characteristic local peculiarities. There are a number of simple plots, which have a wide distribution, but which are elaborated by incidents peculiar to each area. For example, the introductory parts of the long tales are more dissimilar in the several local areas than the further adventures of the hero. A tendency toward unity that shows itself throughout the whole area is the tendency to integrate minor tales into the complex by assigning them to the hero. In some tales "the adventures conform to a certain definite character of the hero. . . . . This is the case in the Raven, Mink, and Coyote tales, in which greed, amorous propensities, and vaingloriousness are the chief characteristics of the three heroes" respectively (p. 876).

III. THE METHOD

Boas' method for determining the manner in which these myths were constructed is (a) to collect all comparable versions from a limited area, (b) to divide the myth into its several incidents and their details, and (c) to equate the comparable forms.

In interpreting the similarities, the guiding logic seems to be (1) that elements without analogues elsewhere are presumably of local origin or due to influence from outside the area inspected; (2) that the conceptual substitution of one incident for another argues historical substitution; (3) that historical priority cannot be credited to any one of several variants of a tale; (4) that the tale as recorded is the resultant of those historic circumstances which contributed each element; (5) that the unity of the tale as found is provided by its conformity to (a) the tribal literary style, (b) the common stock of incidents known to the tribe.

1. To examine this point further we must turn to an earlier schematic paper of Boas[3] of which the present study is logically only an enlargement. There it was stated that the tales show a gradual change from one end of the area to the other; that where an interruption occurs in the form of a tribe with many novel tales, the injection of this tribe into the area must be inferred. There are, however, two other alternatives; the novel tales may have been invented on the spot, or diffused to this tribe from outside the area under inspection. The Tsimshian anomalies have analogues in the interior. Because of other non-folk-loristic evidence Boas chooses the alternative that the Tsimshian have come to the coast rather than that the tales have diffused from there and displaced coast forms.

2. It is difficult to institute comparisons, for not all versions of a particular tale are known. On the other hand, this is the most systematically surveyed folk-lore area among primitive peoples.

The analogies cited are sometimes very tenuous. Whether two forms are considered similar will depend on what is considered essential. It also depends on the regularity with which transitional forms can be traced from one to the other. But, since every element of a tale is a variable, these end forms are likely to be transitional to still other tales quite remote from the initial forms. Hence, such transitional forms should logically do double duty as analogues to each of the disparate tales combined in them. Boas, recognizing this, does use them in this fashion.

Identical forms may not be historically identical; that is, they may not have appeared in two tribes by reason of diffusion. There is the possibility that they represent end forms of convergent development. Considering the manner in which tale elements are freely combined and the relatively small number of fundamentally diverse elements in this

---

[3] Boas, "The Growth of Indian Mythologies," *Journal of American Folk-Lore,* IX (1896), 1–11.

culturally homogeneous area, this possibility is far from remote. This is not a criticism of Boas' method, for he has long insisted on the convergent development of cultural traits as a fundamental principle, and does consider it in this case. Thus, the plots are of so general a character that identity by convergence is quite possible. On the other hand, the incidents are so artificial that such a possibility is much more remote in their case.

3 and 4. Boas' unwillingness to subscribe to any particular version as historically primary is methodologically of extreme importance. It sets him apart from the older mythologists. Some, like Ehrenreich, held that myths originated in explanations of natural phenomena and were subsequently transformed, hence versions containing references to these phenomena are the earliest extant. Others, e.g., Benfy, held that the most coherent form, with the greatest literary finish, represents the earliest version, all others being degenerative imitations.

Both of these views are deductive; Boas' view is empirical. Several of his students established the invalidity of assuming that a primary version can be discovered. They assailed the criteria by showing (a) that natural phenomena occupy a secondary place in tales, (b) that such explanations are accretions dictated by prevailing stylistic habits, (c) that the tendency to form coherent wholes is also a locally developed habit, and (d) that the components of tales are fluid and interchangeable. Hence, a given tale is the resultant of diverse historic forces and no primary version can be designated.[4]

5. Since complex tales do not normally diffuse as wholes (complexes), whatever unity they display must be historically secondary. The basis for the unity is found in the literary pattern of the tribe. New material acquired from foreign sources (and elements originated locally as well) are accreted to the previously existing literature and adapted to its style. Thus, incidents elsewhere told separately about the transformer and trickster-hero are combined among the Tsimshian as referring to a single hero.[5] That is, the historically diverse material is secondarily reinterpreted in terms of the cultural pattern or norm of the people.

[4] R. H. Lowie, "The Test Theme in North American Mythology," *ibid.*, XXI (1908), 97–148; T. T. Waterman, "The Explanatory Element in the Folk-Tales of the North-American Indians," *ibid.*, XXVII (1914), 1–54; G. A. Reichard, "Literary Types and Dissemination of Myths," *ibid.*, XXXIV (1921), 269–307; P. Radin, "Literary Aspects of North American Mythology," *Geological Survey of Canada Museum Bull. 16*, "Anthropological Series," No. 6.

[5] For a further discussion see Boas, *Primitive Art* (Oslo, 1927), pp. 329 ff.; "Stylistic Aspects of Primitive Literature," *Journal of American Folk-Lore*, XXXVIII (1925), 329–39.

This principle of secondary reinterpretation is one of far-reaching implication. By it one may understand why the majority of anthropologists have come to view every culture as a congeries of disconnected traits, associated only by reason of a series of historic accidents, the elements being functionally unrelated, but believed to be related by the bearers of that culture because of the interpretation the traits have undergone. One form which this takes is an individual's rationalization of his own culturally determined activities and attitudes, the rationalization as well being frequently provided by the culture, that is, being a cultural pattern for rationalization.

This view is conceptually related to Wundt's doctrine of the heterogeneity of origins and ends of developmental series. It strikes boldly at the proposition that there is any inherent sequence of cultural forms. The presence of the traits, the relations in which they stand, and the modifications they undergo are due only to specific historic determinism. Only from the point of view of the bearer of the culture have they any necessary relation, since he views them through the spectacles of rationalization. It will also be understood why the doctrine of the "functionalists" (Radcliffe-Brown, Malinowski) is invalid to the majority of anthropologists. No functionally primary relationship can be posited between a congeries of genetically unrelated traits. (If it means only that all parts of a culture are related because they are the body of habits of an individual, the doctrine is gratuitous.)

THE PSYCHOLOGY OF MYTHS

This broad subject is treated only in part and then largely by implication. The question of the nature of the content of tales is alone dealt with here.

It is advisable to note first some of the views expressed on this topic. It is agreed by all writers that folk-tales are fantasies. The psychoanalysts, e.g., Abraham, hold that the fantasy represents the fulfilment of a desire, in particular, that tales are for the most part transvaluations of one particular desire—that represented in the Oedipus complex. Here follows an interpretation in the familiar psychoanalytic manner asserting the latent content as against the manifest, that latent content being always in conformity with the rôles that the fundamental desires play in psychoanalytic ideology. This may all be true, but it does not explain the source of the specific form of the manifest content or the purely literary elements. Such a writer as Bartlett *(Psychology and Primitive Culture)* begins with a set of instincts of social behavior, etc., of the McDougall type, arrived at a priori. He then proceeds to illustrate them from the realm of folk tales. The same criticism may be leveled here. The older folklorists, e.g. Lang, Hartland, held that the only problem involved was to assign to the proper culture stage those "survivals" of custom found in a tale. These parallelists (evolutionists) held that cultures the world over developed independently in essentially the same stages with essentially the same forms. Hence, when an element is found which is at odds with the general culture of those who tell the tale, it is deemed a survival. A custom analogous to it may then be found among some historic people who represent one of the earlier stages in the development of mankind. This is indeed a historic explanation to account for the specific content of a tale, but it is pseudo-historic. The possibility of convergent developments or diffusion is not weighed. Here, too, no attempt is made to explain the literary form.

As against these Boas asks a simple question: What things are actually found expressed in a body of folk tales? A systematic analysis shows the great range of activities, social usages, sentiments, emotions, etc., etc., that are expressed in the tales. For an understanding of the thought and the feeling of a primitive people, at least so far as it finds expression in tales, this is one of the most valuable documents we have. Since the tales were recorded by a native they come as near to a valid record as is possible. Boas cautions, however, that because of Christian influences some "improper" elements may have been deleted.

The implication of this body of data is not directly discussed at any length by Boas.

There is no reason why we should not be satisfied to explain the origin of these tales as due to the play of imagination with the events of human life. It is somewhat different with the incidents of tales and myths, with the substance that gives to the tales and myths their highly imaginative character. It is true enough that these are not directly taken from every-day experience. that they are rather contradictory of it. Revival of the dead, disappearance of wounds, magical treasures, and plentiful food obtained without labor, are not every-day occurrences, but they are every-day wishes; and is it not one of the main characteristics of the imagination that it gives reality to wishes? Others are exaggerations of our experiences . . . . or they are the materialization of the objects of fear. . . . . Still other elements of folk-lore represent ideas contrary to daily experiences. . . . . So far as our knowledge of mythology and folk-lore of modern people goes, we are justified in the opinion that the power of imagination of man is rather limited, that people much rather operate with the old stock of imaginative happenings than invent new ones [p. 880].

The only criticism that can be leveled against this section is that the topic was not pursued. There is one step of procedure implied which the analyst is tempted to suggest. If other such systematic analyses were to be made of tales of peoples bearing wholly different cultures, we should be in a position to discriminate what elements of tale-content are based on the common psychic behavior of mankind, what elements determined by the specific culture.

EVALUATION

This study is a characteristic example of the empirical methods of the school of American anthropologists founded by Boas. It embodies *all* that could be learned of the folk literature of one people. The analysis to show the history of the tales and their psychic content is the most thorough and consequential yet known.

The conceptual contribution expresses some of the fundamental postulates of this school: that the form of a cultural trait is the resultant of historic determinism, in which diffusion of the elements of the trait independent of each other plays a large part; that a culture integrates its historically distinct traits by a process of secondary reinterpretation; that therefrom identities may arise by convergent development; in short, that the known history of culture traits establishes the fact of their diversity of origins and directions of development.

ANALYSIS 32

THE DEVELOPMENT OF RURAL ATTITUDES: A SEMI-INTUITIVE INQUIRY BY JAMES MICKEL WILLIAMS

By STUART A. RICE

University of Pennsylvania

SYNOPSIS

For more than a quarter-century Professor Williams has been intimately acquainted with an unnamed town on the southern slope of the Mohawk Valley in central New York, which he calls Blanktown. Three books have been published as a result of this acquaintance, the first being *An American Town*, which appeared in 1906. *Our Rural Heritage* is the second, and forms a continuous work with the third, *The Expansion of Rural Life*. The division between the latter two is chronological. The period covered by *Our Rural Heritage* is 1825–74. *The Expansion of Rural Life* deals with the two periods 1874–1900, and 1900 and following. This analysis is limited to the second of the three books.[1]

The author's object relates to patterns of attitudes within the single town referred to, and within the subperiod named. He seeks to describe characteristic attitudes and to find explanations of each by showing their relationships to the physical and social environment and to each other. In the broader aspect of his work (including both the second and the third book named above) there is the further object of showing the evolution of attitudes through the three successive periods, and of correlating changes with alterations in the social and economic environments. Since *Our Rural Heritage* is confined to a single "cross-section," the broader genetic or historical objective will receive no further attention in this analysis.

A still broader objective is visualized by the author. He conceives of his own work as a single contribution to a program of research into rural attitudes which would be carried on by many investigators who would give the same detailed scrutiny to selected communities that he has given to Blanktown. The need of such widespread inquiry arises from the local differences in attitudes which exist from community to community. In consequence, generalizations concerning the part played

---

[1] J. M. Williams, *Our Rural Heritage: The Social Psychology of Rural Development*. New York: Alfred A. Knopf, 1925. Pp. xvii + 246.

by rural attitudes in the characterization of American life can arise with safety only from such a series of studies. The author introduces some comparable evidences from other regions and indulges in some a priori generalizations based upon his own knowledge of other social phenomena. In part, these departures from his self-imposed limitations have the function of illuminating particular patterns of attitudes in Blanktown.

First, attention is given to the influence of the physical factors and the economic conditions which provided a setting for the community. These are described. The economic life was founded upon agriculture. The author then proceeds to describe in turn a number of "attitudes" which are expressed in relation to the following subjects: the weather and the moon; the family; the new conditions of pioneer life; the relations between the sexes; the relations of parents and children; the relations of kinship; economic activity; social intercourse; institutional religion; and public education. The list also includes attitudes of such defined types as humorous, intellectual, juristic, and political; also the attitudes of particular constituent parts of the population, such as those of business and professional men. It is apparent that this classification is not a logical one in the sense of being exhaustive or mutually exclusive in its parts. In a few final chapters the author introduces some generalizations concerning the importance of rural attitudes, pointing out that they have been carried over into the occupations and the activities of urban life.

THE METHODOLOGICAL PROBLEMS HERE EXAMINED

The development of methods for measuring attitudes is receiving much attention from American psychologists and sociologists. The work of the Allports, Thurstone, and others has been experimental. That is, it has been conducted with the co-operation and the presence of the individuals whose attitudes were being examined, and according to formalized procedures. The author here is confronted with the problem of ascertaining attitudes in a past period in which the great majority of the individuals concerned are no longer living.

The author refers to his inquiry as a "psychological" rather than as an "historical" study. That is, he attempts to distinguish his own inquiry from one which would be historical in the traditional sense. But it does parallel in objectives and procedure the work of the "new" or "social" historian. Perhaps it may be said to differ from the latter in its primary emphasis upon the psychological elements of attitude and belief. Williams' work might be called "psychological history."

The essential problems of procedure to which attention will here be given concern the types of source data which are employed, and the uses to which these are put for inference. Attention must first be paid, however, to some of the author's concepts as they have affected the organization of his work.

THE CONCEPT OF ATTITUDE

The author writes chiefly of "social attitudes" and "beliefs." The former (pp. 9–10) are

habits of thought and action that determine social relationships. [They] may be conscious and expressed as beliefs or they may be subliminal. [Again,] an attitude is a pronounced tendency to a certain way of reacting. . . . . Even in the case of attitudes expressed as beliefs it is hardly possible to state the different forms of the belief in individual minds. . . . . From the mere fact that individuals remain in a family or neighborhood or church, they implicitly unite on certain attitudes and beliefs which, therefore, explain, in the first instance, their behavior as a group.

Attitudes may be regarded either as patterns abstracted from individual minds and generalized as to common features or as socially sanctioned reactions which are learned by individuals, with minor variations of form or intensity. The author's work posits or assumes the second viewpoint.[2]

THE CONCEPTS OF NEIGHBORHOOD AND COMMUNITY

The author says (p. 21): "The rural population of the state was grouped in families, neighborhoods and villages."[3] The neighborhood is represented as a social group both geographic and psychological in character: It was "a group of families that were conscious of more or less intimate relations with one another."[4] The community was a functional group, likewise geographic:

[2] In a letter to the analyst Professor Williams says on this point: "A social attitude is a pronounced tendency toward a certain way of reacting that characterizes a number of individuals. . . . . They exist in individual behavior and nowhere else. But individuals differ in this behavior. Take for instance the attitude to tell the truth. . . . . People seemed to believe, quite generally, that one should 'tell it just as it was.' . . . . Some individuals maintained that a person should say frankly and fully just what he or she thought about anything under discussion and tended to do this, and they maintained that keeping silence when it would convey the impression that you believed what you did not believe would be untruthful; others maintained that a man can think what he wants to but is not under obligation to say it. So there was the social attitude to tell it 'just as it was' and there were these individual variations from it."

[3] This, it should be noted, is a generalization not limited to Blanktown.

[4] The author is a former student of Franklin H. Giddings. Giddings' concept, *the consciousness of kind*, may have influenced him at this point.

Neighborhoods were grouped around a village and this larger group formed the rural community. . . . . In the early days the centre of the community was the church. It was not only a place of worship, but also a centre of influence for fostering those family, economic, religious and other attitudes and beliefs that were essential in the character of the people in the community.

Changes are said to have occurred in the functional structure of these groups during the period of the author's general inquiry (p. 21):

The early New York neighborhood was not as strictly a farming community as rural neighborhoods are today. It was apt to include artisans and might boast of a local industry, a tavern, a store, a doctor. Today the artisans, the local industries, hotels, stores and doctors are located in the villages. Thus the community has increased and the neighborhood has diminished in importance as a rural unit.

In the earlier period the structure of the neighborhood and the community "was everywhere similar." Hence when he describes this structure for Blanktown, the author again assumes that his description will apply to an indeterminate number of other neighborhoods and communities in New York State. He thus falls back at this point, so far as the book which is being analyzed is concerned, upon a priori assertion, based upon his own wider knowledge or opinion. To this extent (and other similar examples could be found) the work ceases to be inductive.

Blanktown (a political unit) does not wholly coincide with the community involved, according to the author, in that the latter is larger than the former and includes a portion of the town immediately to the north. The town rather than the community forms the geographic unit of inquiry because of the employment as data of various town records.

DOCUMENTARY SOURCES

These are enumerated by the author as follows (pp. 15–16). In most cases they have been accessible only within Blanktown itself.

1. Town-meeting records, 1796–1923.
2. Assessment rolls for most of the years of the period 1825–1923.
3. The census returns for Blanktown of the state census of 1845.
4. Census records of Blankville for 1874, 1877–82, 1885–1923.
5. Records of district school meetings of seven school districts from 1850, and less complete records of other districts.
6. More or less complete records of the Baptist, Episcopal and Presbyterian churches during their entire history and of the Methodist Church since 1874.
7. File of the "Blanktown Intelligencer," a weekly paper published in Pleas-

ant Valley, for 1825–35, and of the "Blankville Times" for 1859, 1861–68, 1870–1923.

8. Records of the Board of Trustees of Blankville for 1873–1923.
9. An atlas published by D. G. Beers and Co., Philadelphia, 1874, containing a map of Blanktown that indicates the location of the homesteads of the town in 1874.

In addition, files of weekly papers circulating throughout the entire rural portion of the state have been employed. The most important of these are the *Rural New Yorker* and the *American Agriculturist*.

TESTIMONY AS A SOURCE

The author says (p. 16):

The testimony of old residents, used discriminately, proved to be an indispensable source of information. Among these old residents were several between eighty-two and ninety-two years of age. They had lived all their lives in the town and were in full possession of their faculties and had remarkably clear memories for people and events of their early life so that their recollections extended as far back as 1825. [The author's inquiries began before the year 1900].

The number of persons whose memories covered more recent years was, of course, larger.

The author says of the old residents (p. 17):

They thoroughly enjoy answering questions, for questions stir a flood of recollections. And it pleases old as well as younger people to find others who are interested in what so interests them. In all the communities studied there were sufficient documentary sources to serve as a point of departure for this exploration of the recollection of these living embodiments of the past history of the community.

It thus appears that the use of testimony and the use of documentary evidence were closely related. The latter frequently provided items of fact, not directly involving attitudes, which when injected into conversation with informants served to induce pertinent testimony by the latter.

Several problems are involved in the use of this testimony. The rules of evidence developed in legal procedure are not applicable in the circumstances under which it is procured. Hence, any criteria employed correspond more closely to those of the field anthropologist than to those of the lawyer or the jurist. Tendencies to distort and enlarge upon factual occurrences are present, for the events related have become mythical to a large degree.[5] Moreover, a highly selected portion of the population—the old—provides the testimony. On the other hand, the evidence really

[5] This assertion is challenged by the author. In the letter mentioned *supra*, n. 2, he says of the old residents: "They all had the rural attitude to tell the truth just

sought by the investigator does not concern overt factual occurrences except as these throw light upon psychological attitudes. From this stand-point the informants may be unaware of the testimony they are giving. Distortions or falsifications of fact may be even more important as evidence than truthful accounts, if they reflect the earlier attitudes. But have not the attitudes of the informants changed as attitudes in general have changed? Do they not relate past occurrences in the light of present-day patterns.[6]

Another problem involves the theory of sampling: The aged informants are samples of the earlier community, selected on the basis of survival. They uniformly represent, then, the younger generation of the earlier period. Assuming that their own attitudes have remained unchanged during intervening years, do they reflect the general attitudes prevailing in the days of their youth or do they reflect, perhaps, the attitudes of the youth of their day toward those general attitudes? For example (p. 53), the author refers to the austerity of parents in the rearing of children, and its origin in economic necessity:

A father told a son if he would do his stent of work in the forenoon he would let him off in the afternoon to go hunting. The boy did his work but was compelled to work all the afternoon. Under a generous impulse the father made the promise and then the old fear that a little leeway would unsettle the boy's habits impelled him to deny the half day of freedom that he had promised.

Is it so certain that this account of a grievance remembered since childhood presents a wholly unbiased datum for inference concerning one of the attitudes of the older generation of the earlier period?[7]

---

as it was. They recollected the occurrences they related with a clearness that made it evident that they remembered them well. . . . . I think our modern life of many newspapers, magazines and other stimuli has tended to weaken our memories for the events of our youth and that these old people had better memories and were more punctilious in truth-telling than we are today. Whenever it seemed to me that an old person was a little shady in recollection I threw out that testimony." The position of the analyst here is that a certain amount of distortion of memory is inevitable, one might say "normal." Selective processes are at work to determine the initial observations and perceptions, and they probably continue. Thus the tendency to "forget the unpleasant" may be presumed to counteract, in part, the rural attitude to "tell it as it was." Cf. n. 9.

[6] The author writes: "I would say that the attitudes of the old people I talked with had changed very little. Until they were very old they had lived in remote neighborhoods where life went on much as it had before." But the question remains, where is an unchanging standard of reference to be found by means of which one may determine the presence or absence of changed attitudes in these old people?

[7] The author comments: "The old people did not, as you say, uniformly represent the younger generation of the earlier period. I state that several were born be-

Still another problem concerns the distinction drawn by the author between social attitudes and individual variations therefrom. If the number of informants of a given individual age period is small (which must be true of those who are very old), it will at times be difficult to determine whether the attitudes expressed are typical or atypical. Where repeated interviews disclose similar attitudinal patterns among different individuals this difficulty disappears.

THE AUTHOR'S OWN OBSERVATIONS AND "INTUITIONS"

The author was unable to state precisely the manner in which documentary evidence, the testimony of old residents, and his own observations were fused together, in order to provide material for his descriptive analysis and interpretation of attitudes during the early period referred to. His inferences, while coherent, may therefore be regarded as in large measure "intuitive." That is, the precise logical processes which have gone on in his own mind with respect to this community over a period greater than a quarter-century would, in the aggregate, defy analysis. Any single element of his narrative or descriptions might be traced to its sources. In weaving these elements together the methodological process would consist of a large number of concealed logical inferences of both deductive and inductive character. The process becomes overt when two or more factors of attitude, or of the physical environment, have been identified by an explicit or implicit definition and are employed as terms in logical propositions. On the other hand, the manner in which these factors are identified within the author's mind is most difficult to follow, for it involves numerous conceptions and assumptions of which neither the author nor the reader may be aware. Some illustrations of overt logical procedure employed by the author are given below.

ILLUSTRATIONS OF THE METHOD OF INFERENCE: THE METHOD OF DIFFERENCES

The effect of topography in developing certain attitudes is inferred in the following (pp. 27–28):

The hill country tended to develop patience and resignation. A farmer could not hurry to town. He had to take half a day for it. He could not

---

tween 1808 and 1818. By the earlier period I suppose you mean the period of the cross section to which you refer, that is, 1845. In this period these old people were married and had families, so that they did not belong to the younger generation of that period. I think, therefore, that recollections of the younger generation, like that taken from page 53 which you quote, are justified when carefully selected in connection with the testimony of people of the older generation."

rush work on a steep hillside. He had to learn to go slow if he was inclined to the contrary. He had to resign himself to the hard work and poor crops of a hill farm. In winter the roads between the hills were impassable for weeks at a time because of the deep snow. "You have to take it in the hill country," they say. On the other hand this easy-going willingness to let things take their course tended to inefficiency on a rich valley farm where additional effort was well rewarded. The farmer who was of a "driving" temperament got out of the hill country as soon as he could. He had not the patience for it.

The method here starts with a series of observations concerning differences in the topographical aspects of certain portions of the town. There is the hill land and the valley land. Further observation (immediate or historical) discloses coincident differences in the attitudes of residents of the two regions. There seem to be no variable factors (such as two separate streams of immigration) to account for the differences in attitudes, except these which are topographical in origin. Assuming, then, a series of factors, $A, B, C \ldots . H,$ and a series of attitudes, $a, b, c \ldots .$ $h,$ it is found that when the series of factors is altered by the change of H (hill) to V (valley), the attitudes h likewise change to the attitudes $v.$ But topography might be responsible for the attitudinal differences in either of two ways: It might *select* those who came in accordance with their temperamental or attitudinal adjustment to the two modes of activity which the contrasted regions rendered most profitable. On the other hand, it might *change* the attitudes of those who remained in accordance with the same principle of adjustment. The author does not choose between these two explanations and allows the reader to infer that he believes both processes to have been operative.[8]

Again (p. 135), he compares attitudes with respect to Sabbath observance in two adjacent communities. In the first, the predominant crop was grain; in the second, peaches. Should peaches ripen suddenly in warm bright weather, "it was regarded as not only permissible but a duty to pick them on Sunday." In the grain region, on the other hand, the crop matured more slowly and it was regarded as incumbent upon the farmer so to plan his work that Sunday labor would be unnecessary; thus:

Old residents tell of a preacher who had a parish in the grain section and another in the neighboring fruit section, and preached in the morning in the grain section from the text, "Remember the Sabbath day to keep it holy," and in the afternoon in the fruit section from the text, "The Sabbath was made for man and not man for the Sabbath." For once he had to prepare two different sermons.

[8] He writes: "It was impossible to choose between the two explanations for the reason that the data did not permit me to know."

As in the first instance, we have here an identification and partial definition of two differing attitudes in two adjacent communities. Correspondingly, there is a differentiation between the predominating agricultural interests of the two communities. This is followed by an inference concerning the relationship between the economic interests and the attitudes. The logical process employed is again the method of difference.

ILLUSTRATIONS OF THE METHOD OF REASONING: THE USE OF COMPARATIVE RESULTS BY OTHER AUTHORS

There is a slight logical dissimilarity between the reasoning portrayed in the following illustration and in those of the preceding section. The dissimilarity consists in the sources from which the data are taken. In the one case the author has himself collected the observations employed by examining documents and taking evidence from original participants or observers. In the second case he utilizes comparatively the results obtained by other investigators of widely separated groups.

The author finds a relationship (p. 35) between the uncertainty of the weather and the attitude of the farmer in accordance with which he placed a higher evaluation upon industrious working than upon the results of labor. The results of work were regarded by the farmer as beyond control:

> Since the results were uncertain, because these depended on the seasons, if a man had worked industriously, he had done the best he could and could not be blamed if the results were poor. . . . . In the last analysis, the emphasis was on industrious working more than on the results. For, unless he worked industriously he would have no crops, and if he did work industriously, he might have none, in which case the comfortable frame of mind to cultivate was that, inasmuch as he had worked industriously he had done the best he could.

This inference is derived by implicit processes of inductive logic. It involves assumptions in particular as to human motivation (desire for a "comfortable frame of mind"). It is supported by a comparison with the results of Thomas and Znaniecki and other unnamed writers, who are quoted to support the following assertion (p. 36): "This attitude is pronounced and widely significant also in the behavior of the rural populations of Europe. Immigrants from Great Britain, Germany and other nations testify to it among their home people."

This resort to other authorities might be called the "comparative method" were it not for the ambiguity of this term, and its use for widely differing procedures. The present process involves the assumption that the attitudes discussed by the other writers referred to, and by the author, have sufficient similarity to be regarded as units of the same attitudinal type. It involves the further assumption that the conditions of economic dependence upon the weather in the American town discussed by the author and in the various European populations referred to are similar. To the extent that these assumptions are sound (or unsound) the comparative materials cited support (or fail to support) the inference.

METHODOLOGICAL CONTRIBUTION

By intimate acquaintance with a limited rural community and its residents, and by almost intuitive modes of inference, the author has described the character and the origins of a variety of attitudinal patterns which have played a large part in the *mores* and *folk ways* of the United States. The outstanding aspects of his method consist of the temporal duration and the limited area of the field of inquiry, together with the part played by oral testimony, local documents, and direct observation, woven together into coherent descriptive and explanatory patterns. The work may be regarded as a fragment of psychological history of a still unique type. In the growing area of social science such a study, employing so largely intuitive methods, serves a useful rôle in opening up hypotheses for more refined testing by other methods.[9]

[9] The analyst has attempted to apply critical standards comparable in exactitude to those which would be used in appraising work in physical or biological science. It is obvious that no work in the field chosen by the author could possibly satisfy such standards. The author's standpoint is the more pragmatic one of appraisal in the light of the practical possibilities. He says in his letter: "Such problems are difficult enough when problems of a contemporary population, to say nothing of one that is dead and gone. It may well be impossible to work out the patterns of a population of the past in the complete way that your criticisms have in mind. You must not, therefore, be dogmatic—no, that isn't the word—you must not be inflexible in your point of view and methods. I hold that it is a fine training to do what you can with a past population, as a preparation for the more complete work that can be done with a present one." The analyst would yield to the author's evaluation of testimony when made from this pragmatic standpoint. But he nevertheless has regarded the essential analytic task to be *appraisal as science with respect to methodology*. The author proposes in his letter "some frank recognition of the necessary limitations of such a study, and also of the importance, in group studies, of doing what can be done, however little, with the beginnings in the past." It is just such a recognition of necessary limitations that the present analysis should compel. [This was one of the first analyses prepared (winter of 1927–28). It was revised following the correspondence with Professor Williams cited in n. 2, p. 460.]

ANALYSIS 33

THE COMPARATIVE METHOD OF JAMES BRYCE[1]

By HAROLD D. LASSWELL

University of Chicago

BRYCE'S PROBLEM

Bryce writes that the aim of his book "is to present a general view of the phenomena hitherto observed in governments of a popular type, showing what are the principal forms that type has taken, the tendencies each form has developed, the progress achieved in creating institutional machinery, and above all—for this is the ultimate test of excellence— what democracy has accomplished or failed to accomplish, as compared with other kinds of government, for the well-being of each people" (pp. 5–6).

Bryce called his method the "comparative method," an exceedingly comprehensive term which included the procedures involved in gathering and in analyzing facts. He explicitly names two fact-gathering devices: participation in political life and the examination of documents. Strangely enough, he fails to mention the technique in which he so remarkably excelled, the technique of interrogation and of field observation. Certain other characteristics of his work habits are deserving of special emphasis, his caution in literary expression, and his scrutiny of his own preconceptions. The biography written by H. A. L. Fisher has supplemented the relevant information which appears on the face of Bryce's published writings.

BRYCE THE PARTICIPANT

At its best, the comparative method as Bryce understood it embraces some practical experience in politics. The give-and-take of a legislature is especially calculated to nurture that ample and delicate understanding of the realities of popular government which eludes the mere maker of books.

Bryce's first-hand sense of political realities is abundantly manifest in the manner and spirit of his entire output. More specifically, too, he is able to use himself as a source. Discussing the relation of personal views to collective political responsibility, he is able to add:

[1] The analysis is based on *Modern Democracies*. 2 vols. London and New York: Macmillan Co., 1921.

Cases of conscience do no doubt arise, and are sometimes perplexing, but twenty-seven years' experience in the British House of Commons have led me to believe that they are less frequent than one would, looking at the matter *a priori*, have expected them to be. Old members have often told me that they had more often regretted votes given against their party under what they thought a sense of duty than those which they had, though with some doubt, given to support it.

In connection with the instability of the executive in democracies, and its preoccupation with the exigencies of politics, he can write, "No one can sit in a British Cabinet without being struck by the amount of time it spends in discussing parliamentary tactics, and especially how best to counter a hostile motion in the House of Commons."

Participation in politics implies responsibility and responsibility implies reticence. The active politician invariably learns facts which are within the zone of privacy of his generation, and although this is an unmistakable advantage to the student who is in a position to test his own generalizations, it places the student who must rely upon the writings of another in a quandary. The latter, if he shows no alacrity in subscribing to a poorly supported proposition, seems to cast aspersion upon the integrity and the intelligence of the former. The disadvantages of undertaking to build up a sound body of knowledge under such conditions are partially mitigated by the oral tradition which is confidentially transmitted from one generation to the next.

Political responsibility not only entails reticence in reporting facts but in generalizing about them. The more important the part played by the "scholar in politics," the more serious the limitations imposed upon his freedom. Opponents are on the watch to take up his speculations, and to handle them in a spirit of destructive innuendo. Bryce, keenly sensitive to the reproaches of possible critics, refrained from analyzing the very democracy about which he knew the most and upon which his judgment would have been peculiarly valuable.

In the technique of active participation the social scientist has a unique method at his disposal. Neither the bacteriologist nor the geologist can possibly play the rôle of the micro-organism or the stalactite for the sake of adding to his stock of "ample and delicate realization of the realities" of his subject matter. But facts which are discovered in the course of a long process whose several phases are not quite capable of exact specification are facts which are notoriously difficult for an independent investigator to verify.

In a very real sense personal participation "savors of experimentation."

The active individual is confronted by situations which are roughly comparable, and as his experience grows he learns how to proceed successfully in coping with them. This type of "knowledge" is usually of unverbalized character, and for it such words as "flair" or "sixth sense" have been coined. But the student in politics who succeeds in retaining a certain power of detachment can frequently discover a great deal by putting his own adaptations into intelligible terms for others.

BRYCE THE JUDICIOUS USER OF DOCUMENTS

Bryce remarks that the student's direct contact with the hurly-burly of politics must be supplemented by the use of records of debates, pamphlets, and files of newspapers and magazines, "doing his best to feel through the words the form and pressure of the facts."

BRYCE THE INTERROGATOR AND FIELD OBSERVER

Above all, Bryce was the master-interrogator and field observer. H. A. L. Fisher remarks that the *American Commonwealth* differs in one important respect from most modern works on sociology.

It is written almost entirely from personal observation and from evidence collected orally or by letter from individuals, and only to a small extent from books. His own estimate given to Mr. James Ford Rhodes was that five-sixths of the three volumes was derived from conversations with Americans in London and only one-sixth from books. It may well be asked whether since the days of antiquity there has been any important historical work written so largely from the talk of living men. The historical material, out of which Herodotus composed his immortal history, was the same quality, less critically sifted indeed, but governed by the same views that everything in the world is interesting and many things entertaining.

This estimate is substantially true of the work of Bryce's old age, *Modern Democracies*.

Bryce levied contributions from everyone. The casual occupant of the smoking car, the waitress, the reporter, no less than the professional student and the official, found in Bryce an alert inquirer, and a respectful and appreciative listener. His travels and his studies familiarized him with the activities and interests of mankind everywhere, and he could quickly "find his feet" in any company. There was nothing of the frigid reticence so often associated by Americans with an Englishman. His unflagging and animated interest in human beings never left him. A. V. Dicey's characterization of Bryce during the visit of a group of Oxford men to Heidelberg is worth repeating:

His most agreeable, and I truly believe, his most valuable quality is his childlike "life" and "go." His kindness and friendship are beyond praise. He stirs us all up, rushes about like a shepherd's dog, collects his friends, makes us meet, leads us into plans and adventures, and keeps everything going. . . . . Most of the Oxford men are deficient in spirits. Bryce, who has talents and spirits, will go much further than many of his contemporaries, even though as able as himself. No one could do otherwise than rejoice should my prediction be verified.

Certain personal qualities are indispensable to the collection of many of the facts which are of special interest to the social scientist, and the personality of the investigator deserves more attention than it usually receives. Bryce's talent for striking up an acquaintance with a "random sample" should not obscure his ability to discover the best observers in a given society, and his exertions to keep on mutually valuable terms with them. He kept his connections open, when home in England, by strenuous exertions as a letter-writer. Among Americans, he corresponded regularly with Charles Eliot, president emeritus of Harvard; A. Lawrence Lowell, president of Harvard; James Ford Rhodes, historian; and many others. His *Modern Democracies* is dotted with references to the contents of his letter-bag. Jesse Macy is quoted on the American primary, "a Swiss friend whose great abilities and experiences entitle his opinion to high respect" has something to say about the referendum, and "a well-informed Australian friend, not belonging to the labor party, wrote to me in 1912" giving an opinion on the relation of Australian wage regulations to posterity. There is no evidence, however, that Bryce ever systematically classified various types of well-informed people, and exerted himself to discover the variations among them in opinion about a specific issue.

A fixed list of questions is often a convenient guide in the collection of material. This may be mailed out formally for answer, or openly used in a face-to-face interview. Again, it may be kept in the background and consulted from time to time by the field investigator for the purpose of discovering whether he is understressing some item. There is no evidence at hand that Bryce, in the preparation of *Modern Democracies*, indulged in any formal lists of points to be covered.[2] Certainly

---

[2] The Viscountess Bryce, in a gracious reply to an inquiry, has written: "I do not think that he ever made a formal list of specific points to work from in respect of comparisons. . . . . In planning his books he had always in his mind from the beginning a clear outline of their purpose and their form and the scale on which they were to be constructed, which he gradually filled in with the details, the illustrations, and the comparisons which occurred to him as he built up the picture."

he gave every appearance of informality in personal talk and in letters. It seems probable that he depended on his "flair" for the principal features of a political situation to guide him, until the material was in an advanced state of organization.

An interesting question which can be raised in Bryce's case is the relationship between training in the observation of physical phenomena and social phenomena. Early drill in natural history figured in his development. A geologizing father and a botanizing uncle influenced him profoundly, and his leisure time at school was spent on long rambles, for "sport had not yet arisen to monopolize the surplus energies of youth." Thanks to this apprenticeship in physical science, he never failed to bestow some attention upon the habitat of the peoples among whom he moved, and often his writing leaves the impression that he found the attractions of history and landscape more congenial than minute social observation. Certainly, as his biographer remarks, there was little of that supersensitive capacity for discerning delicate collective moods which one finds in the best realistic novelists.

In his big work on democracy, Bryce's knowledge of nature lent deftness to his descriptions of environments, and occasionally furnished him with a striking analogy, as when he remarks, "The Landesgemeinde thrives in Uri; the Referendum thrives in Zürich. But could saxifrages or soldanelles gemming a pasture in the High Alps thrive if planted in Egypt?"

BRYCE THE CAUTIOUS WRITER

There is an almost total absence of brilliant rhetoric in Bryce's book. An epigram is rare, though in referring to the republics of antiquity he was capable of saying, "These Republics did not live by Virtue. Rather might one say that they lived by disbelief in it." Imaginative figures are sparsely strewn through his pages, though of oligarchies he wrote that they "are drawn to selfish ways, and selfishness usually passes into injustice, and injustice breeds discontent, and discontent ends in the overthrow of those who have abused their power, and so the World-spirit that plies at the roaring loom of Time discards one pattern and weaves another to be in turn discarded." But peaks rarely thrust their heads above the plateau of uncolored fact and moderate statement.

His preference for "safety to sensation, platitude to paradox," to quote a felicitous phrase of his biographer, was a deliberate achievement. The lack of warmth in his style was not due to the frigidity of his spirit, for Bryce had a sensitive nature which was capable of quick, deep, and abiding sympathy and antipathy. His long devotion to the Boers and Armenians is a matter of public record; and that he was capable of saying sharp and even passionate things about public men and public issues is shown by his private correspondence from the very period when *Modern Democracies* was in active composition.

It does no violence to the truth to say that the perpetual pursuit of precise and moderate language was a cardinal feature of Bryce's method, and that as such his work serves as a model. The social scientist has a limited possibility of summing up the significant aspects of social life in mathematical symbolism. He must therefore lay capital stress upon the subtle integration of fragmentary data in some pattern of rather ordinary language. Bryce refined his sentences in the light of competent criticism and reflection until the dross of transitory sentiment and exaggeration was left aside. So methodical and laborious was his procedure that he quite excusably complained to Dr. Eliot that the *Modern Democracies* had been a most fatiguing task, "and you probably know how sick one may get of a book when you have been so long over it that the ideas which pleased you at first have come to seem commonplace, and you have even begun to doubt whether they are worth putting in print." It may be added that Bryce's achievement is especially noteworthy in a man whose first book was hailed as a literary as well as a scientific triumph. *The Holy Roman Empire* won universal praise for the pith of its generalizations and the warmth of its style.

BRYCE THE SELF-CRITICAL

Bryce deliberately sought to inventory his own preconceptions and keep clear of them. He sought to repress the pessimism of old age, and to dispense with the "jeremiads" of those who dwell in memory chiefly upon the things they used to enjoy in boyhood. He refrained from including Great Britain among his case studies of democracy for fear that he should be accused of partisanship in dealing with matters for which he was in a measure personally responsible.

How is the social scientist to wriggle free from the web of bias in which he is entangled? Bryce succeeded in his old age, with a great deal of self-scrutiny, in steering clear of several pitfalls, but he had succeeded when quite young in accomplishing a notable piece of pioneer work without apparently having given much thought to the matter of impartiality. As he once wrote:

I have been set to thinking how little love of enquiry for its own sake there seems to be in the world by the compliments paid me by the newspapers and by friends or acquaintances on the "impartiality" as they call it of my United States book . . . . in fact this detachment never cost me any trouble or even thought at all.

He was, in fact, worthy of J. R. Green's tribute, who wrote a letter to Bryce lamenting that politics robbed us of "the one writer who could do the work of Gibbon in a nobler and larger spirit than Gibbon's." These testimonials to the fact fail to show what there was in Bryce's early and later development which left him more judicious than other men.

BRYCE'S COMPARISONS

a) Definitions.—Bryce says that he uses "democracy" in its old and strict sense, as denoting a government in which the will of the majority of qualified citizens rules, taking the qualified citizens to constitute the great bulk of the inhabitants, say, roughly, at least three-fourths, so that the physical force of the citizens coincides (broadly speaking) with their voting power.

This definition is propounded after three or four pages of discussion in the course of which he disposes of several marginal cases which complicate the problem. But he avoids launching out upon a rigorous analysis of the more abstract difficulties at issue.

One searches in vain for a statement of the theoretical justification of the various criteria which he employs in comparing one democracy with another. Ambiguities often arise when he undertakes to use normative categories and to balance "merits" over against "faults." In one chapter he names three tests of democratic government, and presently confesses that the presidential scheme can be viewed as a "merit" or a "fault" depending upon the relative emphasis which one chooses to place upon the particular tests. This suggests the superfluity of his "valuational" comparisons, since composite judgments depend upon vaguely defined weighing factors.

Bryce's failure to set out more sharply his criteria of comparison is responsible, no doubt, for the failure to follow through several rather important items from one case to another. The data which he collects about the effect of democracy upon the economic life of various countries are especially fragmentary and non-comparable.

Perhaps more serious is the exaggerated impression of authoritativeness which is conveyed by a book which does not stop to criticize in detail the shortcomings of its own data. Bryce's moderation of statement cannot be denied, but the lack of discussion of the disparities between the possible and the desirable leaves an absolutistic impression on the unwary.

It is abundantly clear that Bryce did not strive very seriously for a symmetrical and logically articulated system of terms with which to distinguish "workings," "results," and "merits." An item which is called "workings" in one context reappears later as "results," and so on. It is probable that Bryce believed that the pursuit of clear-cut categories of comparison would do more to distort than to interpret his facts, for he was so reconciled to the multiple and interlocking character of political facts that he could rest peacefully when an arm or a leg protruded from a verbal tunic. Bryce, after all, was an Englishman, and one of his philosophical traditions was "common sense." There have been ruthless logicians like Hobbes, but Locke was far more congenial to successive generations of his countrymen.

b) Choice of cases.—Four of the six countries analyzed are English-speaking, and all of them share in the culture of Western Europe. No example is selected from the democracies of Northern Europe. Bryce did not feel bound to stay within the boundary of "induction" from six cases, for he introduced frequent comparisons with British experience, and gave a brief synoptic treatment to the democracies of antiquity, the republics of Spanish America, and the historical monarchies and oligarchies.

c) Types of comparisons.—Bryce hoped by the adroit use of comparisons to arrive at "what one may call democratic human nature, viz. the normal or permanent habits and tendencies of citizens in a democracy and of a democratic community as a whole." When he found differences in the working of democratic government in one country and in another he noted "the local or special conditions, physical or racial or economic," which might account for them. Thus he found municipal government in the United States to be notably corrupt, as compared with other democracies, but this he believed was due to foreign immigration, a special condition.

When Bryce cannot satisfactorily explain differences in the operation of democratic government by citing non-political factors, he seeks to discover some peculiar feature in the form of government. Several features of French democracy are thus held to be due, not to causes generally operating in democracies, but to the extreme over-centralization of the government.

Having arrived at his picture of the "normal or permanent habits and tendencies of citizens in a democracy," Bryce said that he wanted to compare it with the "ideally best," thus exposing the "aberrations . . . . to which popular government is by its very nature liable." Such a mode of treatment adds nothing to the common body of facts to which men and women of diverse normative preferences can agree, and is of no scientific interest. Bryce also hoped to make another series of comparisons which would show how the results of democratic government compared with the results of oligarchical and monarchical government.

He adopts the familiar types of comparison already used among democracies. Certain things are "plainly separable from democratic institutions," for they do not exist at all in certain democracies. Even though some facts are found in all democracies described, they are not inherent in democracy, for they "have been observed in all governments." The "power of money to pervert administration or legislation" is unaffected by the form of government.

The most significant comparisons are not those of absolute presence or absence, but of relative degrees of presence. Certain things, Bryce says, are more common in democracy than in other forms of government. Here again, his normative preoccupation creeps in, and he tries to class these items into the "undesirable" and the "desirable." An instance of the former is "the abuse of the doctrine of Equality and failure to appreciate the value of administrative skill"; of the latter, the tendency of democratic legislation to be "more generally directed to the welfare of the poorer classes than has been that of any other Governments."

Bryce takes occasion to remark that some social conditions are unaffected by the political organization, be it democracy, oligarchy, or monarchy. "The spirit of equality is alleged to have diminished the respect children owe to parents, and the young to the old. This was noted by Plato in Athens. But surely the family relations depend much more on the social structural and religious ideas of a race than on forms of government." ("Race" means "culture" or "civilization" in this passage.)

Bryce also points out that under certain conditions democracy cannot survive at all. He condemns as futile the effort to instal democratic institutions at one stroke in certain parts of the world, arguing that there are certain "virtues" which must be present if democracy is to thrive. These virtues would appear to be dependent upon a long series of non-political factors, as well as upon the slow development of traditions in an actual struggle for self-government.

An uncriticized assumption in this study is that, since democracy can be thought of as a distinct entity, it ought to have distinctive results. Beginning with such an assumption, an author is certain to find positive evidence when he deals with a small number of instances which are not subject to experimental control, and when he handles unmeasured categories. An equally valid starting-point would be the assumption that democracy is likely to exhibit a plurality of results. The ambiguity of the concept of democracy (a procedure supported by sentiments of a certain intensity) is at the root of the difficulty of valid comparisons from culture to culture and from time to time.

d) *Justification of the term "comparative method."*—It is obvious that Bryce's term for the various methods of procuring and comparing facts which he employed is in several ways objectionable. It is to be doubted whether the word "comparative" should legitimately be appropriated in the name of any single method, since it denotes a process which is a common aspect of all scientific thinking. And did Bryce use *a* method? His term is an omnibus category for several procedures which are commonly catalogued independently, and the loose terminology which he employs has often been criticized as more confusing than enlightening.

The expression "the comparative method," when seen in its historical setting, does have quite an intelligible meaning. It was coined for the purpose of contrasting a new tendency in scholarship with its immediate predecessors. This is clarified when Bryce's own language is remembered in which he justified the use of the comparative method in legal science, some twenty years before the publication of *Modern Democracies.* In the essay upon "The Methods of Legal Science," in his *Studies in History and Jurisprudence,* Bryce wrote that the comparative method was the youngest of the methods of legal science, its predecessors having been the metaphysical or a priori, the analytical, and the historical. It appears in two forms.

One of these must, like the science of comparative grammar, crave the aid of history, for the study of the differences between two systems becomes much more profitable when it is seen how the differences arose and this can be explained only by social and political history. This form may be deemed an extension of the historical method, which it resembles in helping us to disengage what is local or accidental or transient in legal doctrine from what is general, essential, and permanent, and in thereby affording some security against a narrow or superficial view. It is really an historical study of law in general; and, like history, it is not directed to practical ends.

The other form, though it cannot dispense with the aid of history, because the differences between the laws of different countries are not explicable without a knowledge of their sources in the past, has a narrower range in time, being directed to contemporary phenomena. It has moreover a palpably practical aim. It sets out by ascertaining and examining the rules actually in force in modern civilized countries, and proceeds to show by what means these rules deal with problems substantially the same in those countries.

Bryce's application of this method to politics retains the double aspect of which he speaks in relation to juristic science. It is affiliated with the first aspect when he compares the principal results of democracy; it is connected with the latter aspect when he discusses the technical advantages of certain detailed schemes of direct legislation or of constituting a second chamber.

e) Pessimism about politics as a science.—Bryce himself raised the question whether or not his work could be called scientific. This he did from no particular reverence for the scientific method as such, or for the sake of borrowing the prestige of the physical for the social sciences. He was quite willing to practice an art, and his general viewpoint is reflected in the answer he once gave to the question as to whether history is a science or an art. "You might as well ask whether the sea is blue or green," he replied. "It is sometimes the one and sometimes the other." His work on modern democracy he believed could be called scientific. "That which entitles it to be called scientific is that it reaches general conclusions by tracing similar results to similar causes, eliminating those disturbing influences which, present in one country and absent in another, make the results in the examined cases different in some points while similar in others."

But he hastens to declare that it is "impossible that politics should ever become a science in the sense in which mechanics or chemistry or botany is a science." During the dark days of 1919, he exclaimed in a letter to James Ford Rhodes, "How little can one talk of politics as a science when we see that at this moment no one can tell how things will work out in either Russia or Germany." This would seem to imply that a science ought to qualify one for forecasting, and not merely for prediction within circumscribed conditions. Such a criterion would rule out of the category of science several of the physical disciplines which are included by common consent. The difficulties of and restrictions on social science he stated in somewhat different terms in *Modern Democracies*. The facts of politics, he specifies, are not everywhere identical, while "oxygen and sulphur behave in the same way in Europe and in Australia and in Sirius." The facts of politics cannot be weighed and measured, because one cannot measure the "feelings and acts of men." Political experiments can never be repeated, because the environing facts never stay the same. Political facts and terms arouse emotions in the observer, but "nobody has either love or hatred for the hydro-carbons."

These dicta are not convincing as they stand. When Bryce complained that "the phenomena of an election are not the same in Bern and in Buenos Aires," while the phenomena of oxygen are the same, he ignored an important distinction. It should be remembered that the physical sciences began, not by studying oxygen, but by examining substances which, precisely because they did not remain the same under all observable conditions, needed the work of several generations to be resolved into relatively permanent components. That the student of politics finds such an object as an "election" too composite for comparative study suggests that he is still naïve in the analysis of his problems into significant relational categories. To compare an election to oxygen rather than to primitive objects of investigation such as "earth," "fire," or "water," and to use the results for pessimistic prediction about the future, reveals a curious confusion of thought.

The dogmatic, and even romantic, assertion that the "feelings and acts of men" are incapable of measurement does not appear to rest upon careful scrutiny of such achievements as have been credited to modern economists, to say nothing of the work of the professional psychologists. The capacity of their facts and theories to arouse emotion would scarcely appear to be an exclusive attribute of the social sciences, if the experiences of Galileo and Darwin are correctly reported.

It will be interesting to find whether the political scientists of the future envisage their problems in such wholesale terms as "democracy" versus "oligarchy" or "monarchy." The center of interest may, for instance, shift to the examination of the elementary situations in which "unrest" or "dissent" arises, and a loosely knit pattern of social action commonly named "democracy" or "oligarchy" may turn out to play a very subsidiary rôle in the matter. The vogue of such symbols of expression may itself be the problem which wants explaining.

In sum, Bryce's work is an admirable personal and practical achievement, which reveals the methodological state of political science A.D. 1921.[3]

[3] [This analysis was first written in the spring of 1928. It was revised by the analyst in the spring of 1929.—EDITOR.]

ANALYSIS 34

A HYPOTHESIS ROOTED IN THE PRECONCEPTIONS OF A SINGLE CIVILIZATION TESTED BY BRONISLAW MALINOWSKI[1]

By HAROLD D. LASSWELL

University of Chicago

SUMMARY

Briefly characterized, this book is an anthropologist's critique of a fundamental psychoanalytic theory. Malinowski first had his attention seriously drawn to the theories of Freud when he was engaged in field work among native Melanesian communities on a coral archipelago. The first part of his *Sex and Repression* handles one aspect of the problem: "Do the conflicts, passions and attachments within the family vary with its constitution, or do they remain the same thruout humanity?" He accepts the first alternative on the basis of the data drawn principally from the Trobriand Islands. Instead of repressed hatred of the father and repressed lust for the mother, he reports hatred of the maternal uncle and incestuous desire for the sister (who is rigorously taboo). He propounds the thesis that distinctive forms of family organization tend to bring into existence special constellations of family sentiment which he names the "nuclear family complex." Thus he regards the "Oedipus complex" as the nuclear family complex of our patrilineal society, and believes that he has described for the first time the nuclear complex of matrilineal society.

The second part of the book covers another aspect of the Freudian theory. Freud declared that the repressions which manifest themselves in the family produce fundamental effects upon social structure and tradition. Forms of government, myths and legends, obscenity, and a host of other manifestations are construed in terms of the basic Oedipus complex. Malinowski, having denied the universality of the Oedipus complex, but having discovered a complex peculiar to another type of family organization, now undertakes to decide whether the mother-right complex produces distinguishable results in the society where it prevails. He proceeds to interpret Trobriand myths and legends, obscenity, and similar

---

[1] *Sex and Repression in Savage Society*. New York: Harcourt, Brace & Co., Inc., 1925; London: Kegan Paul, Trench, Trubner & Co., Ltd., 1927. International Library of Psychology, Philosophy, and Scientific Method.

data in terms of this complex and reaffirms his principal conclusion that, while Freud was right in attaching profound importance to the basic family complex, he was wrong in universalizing one special form of it.

The first half of Malinowski's present work had been previously published. The second half devotes space to the discussion of the various criticisms leveled against this first part by psychoanalysts. He makes no concealment of the fact that his own views have undergone some modification. He says in a footnote to his own statement that "a young organism reacts sexually to close bodily contact with the mother," that this now appears "absurd."

The third part is devoted to detailed scrutiny of Freud's speculations about the origins of culture. Freud's theory is that culture began with the revolt of the band of brothers against the old man of the horde. This hypothesis is rejected by Malinowski, for reasons which will be examined later on.

The concluding part of the book contains the author's effort to propound a satisfactory theory of culture origins. He says that man could develop culture because he was endowed with plastic instincts, and that the medium for transmitting changed ways of satisfying instincts is culture and not a "mass psyche," conceived either as a biological or as a metaphysical entity.

ANTHROPOLOGY AND THE CRUCIAL INSTANCE

Perhaps enough of the substance of this volume has been given to render the discussion of its methodological significance intelligible. It is self-evident that it raises an usually wide variety of possible issues, since it brings into a single focus the facts and interpretations for which many classes of specialists are responsible, among whom are field naturalists, field anthropologists, comparative animal psychologists, clinical psychoanalysts, and students of heredity. Somewhat arbitrarily, a few points must be singled out for consideration, the first of which is the impression which the volume conveys of the extent to which an anthropologist can supply crucial instances for the testing of social-science hypotheses.

Systematic students of society are thinly scattered over a relatively restricted portion of the earth, and practically all share the presuppositions of Western European culture. Their data are usually taken where they can be found most readily, and linguistic and geographical barriers conspire to limit their range to Western European material. Lack of experience in thinking about cultural differentials leads to overgeneralization.

This appears to have been true of Freud. He was, of course, aware that mother-right exists. But his mind was saturated with clinical instances from one main culture, and the facts of culture difference were not his primary preoccupation. Malinowski was in quite a different position. From early years his center of inquiry concerned sociological (cultural) phenomena. When he encountered Freud's conjectures, he was among people who presented striking anomalies if one attempted a literal application of the Oedipus-complex theory. The frames of reference in Malinowski's mind were cultural to such a degree that he even undertook to reconcile differences between Moll and Freud on the basis of social differences in Western Europe. Freud appears to hold that children pass through a "latency" period in sexual interests, while Moll makes no mention of it. Malinowski suggests that the well-educated classes of Western Europe who consulted Freud were likely to show the latency phenomenon, while the less educated who consulted Moll were unlikely to show it. (The reasons need not detain us here.)

A principle of scientific thinking is to choose the most contrasting case for the purpose of testing a hypothesis. That the data collected by the anthropologist can call attention to the existence of such crucial cases is especially evident in the instance under discussion. That prolonged experience in reflecting upon the structure and the function of culture is necessary to create a vivid realization of its import seems to be illustrated affirmatively by Malinowski and negatively by Freud. Actual field work in anthropology may be expected to provide a corrective for overgeneralization.

THE DOUBLE-COMPETENCE PROBLEM

Anyone who possesses the temerity to test the hypotheses of a group of specialists with whom he is not professionally affiliated puts himself in an exposed position. What evidence did Malinowski have to offer the psychoanalysts that he was a capable judge of their theories? He made no statement about his own training in this respect. The inference is that his knowledge of psychoanalysis was gleaned from books when he was actually in the field, and from subsequent conversations with men of more or less competence. The professional analyst claims that no one can acquire a dependable sense of discrimination in dealing with psychoanalytic data unless he has himself submitted to psychoanalysis and has had some training in analyzing others under competent supervision. Dealing not with his credentials but with his results, rigorous specialists can find much to criticize. That Malinowski should so long continue under a misapprehension as to the meaning assigned to the term "complex" by the analysts is incriminating. And his profession of incompetence to understand the most recent elaborations of analytic theory sounds rather more defiant than judicious.

Obviously there are not many alternatives in procedure if the psychoanalytic hypotheses are to be tested in primitive communities. The job may be done, as in this case, by an anthropologist having more or less familiarity with the theory and the practice of some school of analysis as expounded by Freud, Adler, Stekel, Jung, or Rank. Or a practicing and accredited psychoanalyst ("accredited" referring to one of the principal schools which compete in the field) might study general anthropology and overcome the linguistic and allied difficulties in the way of field work. (We wave out of account the bibliographic psychoanalyst, for the moment, who is subject to the same objections by the anthropologists that can, in some measure, be leveled against Malinowski by the analysts.) A third possibility is that a technical psychoanalyst might accompany an anthropologist to a suitable field of investigation, where the two would presumably stimulate and correct each other. It is worth remarking that joint field work among specialists is woefully neglected. The Torres Straits expedition has had few successors.

THE TRANSFERABILITY OF TECHNIQUE

Another reason why Malinowski's statements are presumptive and not conclusive is that he did not use the psychoanalytic interview with individual natives. Thus he did not employ the psychoanalytic method to test psychoanalytic theories. The analyst is likely to believe that, if actual psychoanalyses had been skilfully conducted, the underlying Oedipus situation would have appeared.

This is not necessarily a criticism of Malinowski, for his own contention may be correct that psychoanalysis is so peculiarly a product of European civilization that it is wholly out of place in primitive cultures. In that case, cross-culture comparisons will always depend upon secondary means of collecting personality data, and we are thus far without standards for the evaluation of personal-history documents procured by diverse methods even within a single culture. There are documents which are written by the interviewer after the psychoanalytic interview, there are documents written during the interview in which the answers of the interviewed to a fixed list of questions are put down, there are documents which are privately prepared by an introspective individual, there are documents representing observations made by a participant observer in ordinary life situations; about the relative worth of all this material, no one can speak with finality.

The whole series of problems connected with the form and the dependability of records have received much less attention than they deserve. Original records gain in value when they contain full particulars of the circumstances attending the production of the information: the demeanor of the subject, the reputation of the subject, the attitude of the subject and the examiner toward each other, the evidence of those in a position to check specific statements. Tests of the characteristic form in which experience is elaborated and condensed by individual interviewers could profitably be devised.

Malinowski has not published his records, and one is unable to judge from his summaries in what measure he has faithfully applied such canons of method as those which he laid down in his *Argonauts of the Western Pacific.*[2]

Whatever exceptions may be taken to Malinowski's work, the fact remains that he has surmounted the tremendous difficulties involved with enough success to challenge the attention of psychoanalytic leaders. Dr. Ernest Jones gave Malinowski's early articles respectful and extended criticism. He accepted Malinowski's statement that there was evidence of repressed hatred of the maternal uncle and repressed lust for the sister in mother-right society. But he refused to concur in Malinowski's attempt to explain these facts as a function of the particular family system.

Malinowski says that the Trobriand father enters into the life of his children as a helper and not as an exponent of authority. The father is expected to tend the infant in many of its daily needs, and is a companion in play. Since he is not regarded as having a right to sexual gratification except as a favor from his wife, many sources of family disturbance are removed in which, as with us, the child takes sides against an aggressive father. The father is not the economic arbiter of the family destiny, for his obligations are to support his sister's household. The wife is supported economically by her own brother, who maintains a separate household. It is the maternal uncle, then, who interposes restrictions and positive directions in the name of custom, and not the father. These are among the particulars marshaled by Malinowski to explain why the sentiment organization in Trobriand mother-right society

[2] New York: E. P. Dutton & Co., 1922.

differs from that of Western European father-right society, where the father is expected to perform the double task of helper and disciplinarian.

The alternative explanations offered by Malinowski and the psychoanalysts may be reviewed in the light of the simplicity criterion. Jones (elaborating Freud) contends that uncle-hatred and sister-lust in mother-right culture are disguised manifestations of the Oedipus complex. Mother-right society was the earliest form of family organization. It arose when the racial memory of the original parricide was strong. The only way that society could hold together was to "split the Oedipus complex" by embodying authority in one who was not a member of the household and who was not the father (the keenly hated sexual rival). Gradually the racial memory became so dim that subterfuge was no longer necessary and patrilineal society became possible. Thus patrilineal society according to Jones "betokens acknowledging of the supremacy of the father and yet the ability to accept this even with affection, without having recourse to a system either of mother-right or of complicated taboos. It means the taming of men, the gradual assimilation of the Oedipus complex. At last man can face his real father and live with him. Well might Freud say that the recognition of the father's place in the family signified the most important progress in cultural development."[3]

Malinowski does not find it necessary to invoke a waning instinct of father-hatred to explain the greater prevalence of father-right in complex cultures. Neither mother-right nor father-right can ever be exclusive rules of counting kinship and descent, but all sorts of social advantages follow from the legal emphasis upon one or the other principle.

Under mother-right there is always a double authority over the child and the family itself is cleft. There develops that complex cross-system of relationship which in primitive societies increases the strength of social texture but which in higher societies would introduce innumerable complications. As culture advances, as the institutions of clan and classificatory kinship disappear, as the organization of the local community of tribe, city, and state has to become simpler, the principle of father-right naturally becomes dominant.[4]

Malinowski seems to have pushed the psychoanalysts into an extremely forced interpretation. The advantage of a hypothesis is, in part, that it prefers simple and easily verifiable elements. If this criterion be applied to these interpretations, Malinowski would seem to have the better of the argument.

[3] "Mother-Right and the Sexual Ignorance of Savages," *International Journal of Psycho-Analysis,* VI, Part II (April, 1925), 130.

[4] Malinowski, *Sex and Repression in Savage Society,* pp. 271–72.

THE CRITERIA OF A CULTURE-ORIGINS THEORY

When Malinowski considers Freud's theory of the "crime which began culture," he is not slow to point to inconsistencies which lie upon the surface. But Malinowski's principal point is his criticism of the whole style of thinking about the culture-origins problem which is represented in the Freud-Jones hypothesis. To observe the origin of culture is a manifest impossibility.

The factors of cultural development are intertwined and essentially dependent upon each other, and while we have no knowledge and no indications about sequences in development, while in all speculations about beginnings the element of time entirely escapes our intellectual control, we can yet study the correlations of the factors and thus gain a great deal of information. We have to study these correlations in full cultural development, but we can trace them back into more primitive forms. If we thus arrive at a fixed scheme of dependence, if certain lines of correlation appear in all cultural phenomena, we can say that any hypothesis which violates these laws must be considered void. More than this: if the laws of all cultural process disclose to us the paramount influence of certain factors, we must assume that these factors have also been controlling the origins of culture. In this sense the concept of origins does not imply priority in time or causal effectiveness, but merely indicates the universal presence of certain active factors at all states of development, hence also at the beginning.[5]

Malinowski shows that material culture could not have begun before man was able to use his implements in traditional technique, which implies knowledge, and knowledge and tradition imply language. "Language, thought, and material culture are thus correlated, and must have been so at any state of development, hence also at the beginnings of culture."[6] The same applies to material arrangements of living, kinship bonds, and morals. Culture changes slowly as we know it, and hence it becomes impossible to imagine a cataclysmic beginning.

Culture implies a plastic instinctive equipment. The behavior of individuals in accordance with cultural patterns molds culturally appropriate behavior. Culture may thus be identified as "the medium in which the experiences of each generation are deposited and stored up for successive generations. This medium is that body of material objects, traditions, and stereotyped mental processes which we call culture." He thus rejects the necessity for postulating a "mass psyche," a methodological assumption for which Freud, not comprehending the meaning of culture as a medium, had argued. He also rules out the assumption of a general "gregarious instinct" to explain collective behavior.

[5] *Ibid.*, pp. 180–81.   [6] *Ibid.*, p. 182.

THE FUNCTIONAL CONCEPT

Although the term "function" is often found in Malinowski's book, it is not defined. In certain contexts, the functions of an act are understood to be the consequences which flow from it, as they are described by observers who occupy particular places of vantage. The fact that this varies markedly with the imaginative agility of the observer causes no special confusion in non-experimental problems until an effort is made to classify a particular act as performing a needful or a needless function. When an act is supposed to be indispensable (i.e., irreplaceable) in the implementation of certain results which are held to be important (either as ends in themselves or as means to other ends), the act is needful. The classification of a particular act in this category, then, presupposes a consensus of opinion as to its irreplaceability, and its importance.

Malinowski speaks about the "need" of having a higher anthropoid remain with a woman who has brought an infant into the world "because of her helplessness." In non-human species this is accomplished by the appropriate instinct, but in man the undependability of instinct is such that cultural substitutes have been devised to hold the man to the protecting rôle. Malinowski accepts this as a "need," with the strong implication inherent in the term that substitutes are not thinkable. However, all anthropoid females do not become pregnant simultaneously, and are therefore available to protect one another. Institutional care in modern society provides frequent examples of the dispensability of the male.

The nature of this concept of function may be further explored by examining Malinowski's rejection of the idea that the relation of the infant to its mother is partly sexual in nature. The act which sets in motion the reproduction of the species (this being understood to begin with the contact of male and female cells) is, of course, thought of as ministering to a fundamental need. In man, the completed heterosexual act can be singled out as the apparently indispensable antecedent of this end-result. (A few years ago the word "indispensable" would have been taken in this context in a very absolute sense, but since the success achieved in initiating the act of reproduction in certain species by electrical or chemical stimulation, this is not so conclusive.) Now Malinowski, having identified the completed heterosexual act as the unambiguously "sexual" act, has the problem of deciding whether to regard other acts of the organism which look more or less like it as also sexual. He does not reject childish play with genital organs and in various postures as sexual, because this is interpreted as a direct preparation for finally integrated and biologically efficacious intercourse. However, he will not admit that the infantile-contact relation with the mother is any part of this prepara-tion. Apparently the critical determinant of his attitude is that another biological need (nutrition) can be postulated as an immediate goal or a function of this activity. By the same logic, it may be possible for someone to connect the genital play of children with another more im-mediate biological need, and expunge it from the category of the sexual.

Since the correlation of one set of tangible reactions with another is the aim of investigation, the controversy over the sexuality or the non-sexuality of infantile acts would appear to be idle unless it leads to the discovery of means by which it can be shown that certain childhood re-actions are of high predictive value in relation to the way in which later sexual situations are met. Malinowski's use of the concept of function is an instance of the style of thinking in terms of "tendency." He under-takes to interpret a given set of events as approximations or realizations of a set of events which are treated as terminal situations. The tendency pattern of thought is fruitful for science when it guides the attention of investigators to the selection of certain features of events which turn out to have high value for the prediction of other events.

CONCLUSION

Malinowski's work shows how the field anthropologist can put general-izations of a psychological sort which are formed under the influence of Western European culture to the test of contrasting conditions.

Freud stands for a single fundamental complex for all mankind; Mal-inowski stands for distinct sentiment clusters for father-right and for mother-right societies. Further investigation may show that the omnibus categories of "father-right" and "mother-right" society are inapplicable, and that it is necessary to distinguish a whole series of family environ-ments which produce characteristic sentiment organizations in the child.[7]

[7] [This analysis was first written in the spring of 1928. It was revised by the analyst in the spring of 1929.—EDITOR.]

ANALYSIS 35

THE PSYCHOLOGICAL APPROACH IN ECONOMICS REPRESENTED IN THE WORK OF J. A. HOBSON

By Z. CLARK DICKINSON

University of Michigan

Improvement of the scientific borderland between psychology and economics is like the weather, in that there has been more talk about it than corrective action. It is difficult to select a single thinker whose work shows forcibly what accomplishments may be expected within this field, although the sum of fragmentary offerings of value is perhaps considerable. The work of J. A. Hobson contains few explicit references to detailed psychological research, but it gives us some remarkably comprehensive views of psycho-economic problems, and some interesting modes of attack on them. The author definitely attempts to develop and improve social-economic science at its human foundations, which of course is a vastly different thing from that "economic psychology" which consists of commercial applications of psychological techniques. He tries to "deflate" the pretensions of marginal-utility analysis (formerly considered psychological economics par excellence). He deals extensively with questions of motives and welfare in work, management, saving, and consumption. Most of this treatment is found in his *Work and Wealth: a Human Valuation* (1914), which has stood the test of time remarkably well. Some practical elaborations are found in *Incentives in the New Industrial Order* (1922); and in *Free Thought in the Social Sciences* (1926) some McDougall-Wallas-Freud psychological concepts are employed with reference to possibilities of discounting and reducing prejudice or bias in social studies.

A summary of his psycho-economic system will first be presented. The task he sets himself is to indicate, somewhat in the manner of Ruskin, how economic phenomena may be best appraised in terms of human welfare. For such an undertaking one must determine, he says, not only the total of efforts and sacrifices, of benefits and enjoyments, but also the distribution of these "real" costs and utilities among persons, in relation to their capacities for bearing costs and utilizing benefits. The activities of production are easily shown to be not all "humanly costly." Creative work is enjoyable in itself and a source of welfare to its practitioner without regard to what he is paid. Routine labor and long-protracted and

489

subordinate work, especially when the worker's strength or the working conditions are unsuitable, are likely to be excessively costly in terms of social welfare. Saving, another type of production, is sometimes costly, but in ideal circumstances it would be as pleasant and wholesome as moderate fat-secretion in the animal body. Consumption, which might hastily be considered merely the realization of utility, contains also a number of social costs. Not only items like narcotics and ostentation, but many more reputable uses of income are opposed to social welfare. Thus, by a somewhat novel apparatus, the not unfamiliar conclusion is reached that the present economic order leaves much to be desired, in the nature and the distribution of both efforts and income.

Our author, moreover, is optimistic as to the possibilities of great improvements. He makes much of the idea that the "unproductive surplus," gained by many receivers of salaries, rent, interest, and profits, deprives well-to-do people of work and discipline which they need; and also deprives the rest of the community of capital, income, and especially leisure, which *it* needs. He assumes that redistribution of work and income are to be accomplished through socialist and trade-unionist measures. But will human nature stand the strain of such collectivist measures? Should we gain more from such reforms, in the long run, than from our more individualistic institutions, which do indeed tolerate some luxury, idleness, poverty, and waste, but which are thought by many to be indispensable as economic incentives? Mr. Hobson, in effect, defends collectivist reforms although within limits; he does not, for example, favor complete equality of incomes. One of his main buttresses (in 1914) was the notion that society is a controlling organism, with progressive ends of its own, we individuals being but shortsighted cells. His later little volume, *Incentives in the New Industrial Order* (1922), contains no explicit statement of philosophical-psychological premises, but its more practical and readable arguments amount to about the same temperate defense of socialist and trade-union pressures as did the earlier volume.

Out of Hobson's comprehensive dissertation I shall try now to extract a few leading issues of scope and method. A general question which may be briefly disposed of, is whether most of the matter is relevant to economics. Is it not rather sociology, social philosophy, social psychology, politics? The answer depends on whether we construe economics narrowly or broadly. The core of economic science, no doubt, is an abstract and hypothetical body of reasoning which gives birth to laws of supply and demand, stating determinants of the value of commodities and services under simplified assumptions as to production, markets, competition, and so on. This basic logic is not affected by psychological or other "fact-finding" (except by way of checking the almost universal tendency to deduce from it practical policies and prophecies, forgetting its limitations). Somewhat as geometry underlies engineering, so deductive economics is indispensable in dealing with infinitely complex economic facts. In a broader sense, however, economic theory includes numerous extensions and refinements of these general abstractions. Theories of money and prices, of international trade, of wages, of interest, etc., are constantly being overhauled—sometimes by means of economic-statistical techniques and sometimes, as in the work of Hobson, by means of observations on the psychological horizon.

As we begin to criticize Hobson's alleged contributions in the psychological quarter, we are at first baffled by the tangle of issues in positive science, aesthetics, ethics, and metaphysics which appears on almost every page. Our author's predilection for the social-organism theory, for example, frequently raises questions, not only of scientific "fact," but also of metaphysical or theological speculation, and of standards of the beautiful and the good.

Neither a metaphysical critique nor an inquiry into the merits of Hobson's ethical-aesthetic system can be included in the present analysis. It will suffice to note in passing that he does not consistently use the deterministic hypothesis of the uniformity of nature. In his concluding chapter on "Social Science and Social Art," he holds that social science can never be adequate to predict social events and so to provide for social policy; artistic intuitions must always supplement it. But the cautious skeptic who claims that present-day knowledge falls ridiculously short of explaining human action mechanically is not the logical opponent of determinism. This latter is rather the dogmatic vitalist who holds that the ways of nature, especially in human affairs, must always evade scientific formulation *substantially as much as they do now*. Despite the fact that vitalism is occasionally implied in his contentions, Hobson is rather to be classed with the skeptic than with the out-and-out vitalist. Moreover, his work makes sufficient use of the data, the methods, and the concepts of positive psychological science, with its emphasis on the development of laws of causation for mental and behavior phenomena, to provide ample ground for a critical analysis of his methods within that sphere.

Among Hobson's discussions of psycho-economic causation are some criticisms of the marginal utility picture of the spender (especially in chap. xxii),[1] which we may notice briefly. He says:

[1] Chapter and page references are to *Work and Wealth*, unless further citation is given.

In laying out my income I do not in fact compare all my several needs or tastes, and having assigned so much utility or desirability to each, plan my expenditure so as to spend on each just as much as it is worth, equalising all expenditure at the margins so as to maximise the aggregate. . . . . So far as I act like a free, rational being, not a creature of blind custom or routine, I employ my personal resources of knowledge, taste, affection . . . . in trying to realise my ideal of a good or desirable life [p. 333].

The process of apportioning resources, he thinks, is essentially artistic, like using materials for painting a picture. In an earlier chapter (xii) he assailed the common interpretations of "marginal productivity" as determining wages and other incomes.

Similar attacks have been made several times before and since on the marginal-utility psychology, although sensible theorists like Wicksteed and Pigou have made it quite plain that the marginal analysis gives only a general view of the way in which different wants compete for limited resources; that it does not necessarily imply a lot of hairsplitting calculations as the preliminary for each purchase; and that it tells us nothing whatever as to why the spender's wants for cigarettes, for instance, wax stronger with time, at the expense of his wants for popguns. Our author has simply opened up once more some of the problems in what we may call the psychology of want-development and of choice. Many discriminating readers, metaphysically or sociologically inclined, will consider that his qualitative discussion carries us forward to their solution. Those, however, who prefer a psychological method which is closer to the methods of the "natural" sciences will be less favorably impressed, by reason of the dogmatic vitalism sometimes involved, the looseness of the terms used, and the deprecation of quantitative inductions.[2]

More fully and freshly developed than these hints on value psychology are Mr. Hobson's theories on the motivation (actual and potential) of production, and the related problems of welfare of producers. We must pass by his treatment of saving and consumption, and concentrate attention on work, which is really his main interest. Notice that three logically distinct issues are involved, namely, (1) how a supply of work may be evoked and maintained; (2) how the supply may be economically distributed among alternative tasks; and (3) how the various methods of evoking it and performing it react on the feelings, the character, and the welfare in general of the workers. These threads are so interwoven, however, in Hobson's discussion, that we shall have to forbear keeping them sharply separated.

[2] Cf. M. A. Copeland, "Desire, Choice, and Purpose from a Natural-Evolutionary Standpoint," *Psychological Review*, XXXIII (July, 1926), 245–67.

Our author's analysis starts from the familiar proposition that payments to laborers, managers, artists, and so on for their services do not vary directly with the efforts and the sacrifices they make. As Mark Twain's Connecticut Yankee said, it almost seems the law of life that the easier and more interesting the work, the higher the pay in money also.[3] Observation of this situation has led Fourier, Ruskin, and countless others to raise the question: Is it possible by any sort of social reform to turn the bulk of the world's work into play? Can we obtain the consumptive benefits of equal or nearer-equal incomes, short hours, and wholesome working conditions without impairing too far the incentives to management and work? Our author is less optimistic than Ruskin or Morris; nevertheless, he argues that sufficient incentives will remain, after fairly drastic egalitarian reforms. Creative work, he thinks, whether in art, science, business management, or other activity, is so attractive in itself that in the long run most capable people would work at it just as vigorously in a collectivistic type of society as in an individualistic type. The real cost of such work, in other words, is only whatever is involved in supplying a plain living to the worker; whatever he gets above this is "unproductive surplus." The few persons of high ability who are incurably individualistic should be allowed (he maintains) to try for fortunes in new industries which are not ready for socialization. Routine work, on the other hand, and also varied work like that of a private secretary or a housemaid, which express the personality not of the worker but of the employer, Mr. Hobson considers "humanly costly" an repugnant, hence it offers the new society more difficulties; but he thinks these obstacles can be overcome in various ways. On this point, also, Mark Twain's Yankee agrees:

I know all about both [intellectual work and manual toil]; and so far as I am concerned, there isn't money enough in the universe to hire me to swing a pickaxe thirty days, but I will do the hardest kind of intellectual work for just as near nothing as you can cipher it down—and I will be satisfied, too.

Several suggestions are made toward a psychology of incentives and labor welfare. The first question which naturally arises is, How much does he lean on instinct theories? For a long time before 1914 various

---

[3] Hobson's favorite doctrine of "unproductive surplus" (that existing markets give many of the owners of the various factors of production payments in excess of the "necessary costs") surely owes much to the marginal value analysis of Hobson's predecessors. The whole idea was plainly suggested, for example, by two articles, "The Place of Abstinence in the Theory of Interest," pp. 40–61, and "The Theory of Wages Adjusted to Recent Theories of Value," from the pen of T. N. Carver in the *Quarterly Journal of Economics*, VIII (1893–94), 377–402.

writers had been deriving from biology and psychology the notion that we have instincts which tend to make us moral, and perhaps industrious, apart from expectations of material reward. Veblen, for example, started his line of publications in this vein by publishing a little essay in 1898 entitled "The Instinct of Workmanship and the Irksomeness of Labor,"[4] presenting the view that common labor is ordinarily distasteful, less by reason of its fatigues and pains (which are also encountered in many sports) than because of the social disesteem in which it is held. Mr. Hobson was somewhat influenced by these currents of thought. In his second chapter on "The Human Origins of Industry" especially he used these ideas as he started to prepare ground for the view that much work is not intrinsically unattractive to the workers:

To whatever source, then, we trace the origins of industry, to the use of weapons, snares and other male apparatus for the fight and hunt, to the instincts of play, imitation and adornment as modes of self-expression and of pride, or to the more distinctively utilitarian work of women and of slaves around the home, we find play or pleasure mingles with the work [p. 25].

Yet he rarely referred to alleged specific human instincts, such as workmanship or self-expression—that did not come until the publication of his *Free Thought in the Social Sciences* (1926). The supposed attraction of creative work and the repulsion of routine he did not feel called upon to prove or explain or analyze; he merely assumed these to be facts. When he tried to forecast the powers of various motives under socialism he used expressions such as the worker's sense of unfairness and exploitation in the existing arrangements, and his changed outlook when he sees that the burdens of necessary toil are equitably shared—expressions which clearly require justification. In 1925 some admirers would have congratulated him on having resisted the lures of the specific-instinct-sociology, which was in its prime when he was writing but has lately become rather unfashionable. These same readers, however, might not have accepted some of the marvels which Mr. Hobson attributed to the social organism. For example:

We perceive how this harmony between individual and social rights and interests is realized in the primary division of productive activities into Art and Routine. The impulses and desires which initiate, sustain and direct what we term art, including all the creative activities in industry, flow freely from the individual nature. We recognize that productive activities in which these elements are of paramount importance form an economic field which society, guided by its intelligent self-interest, will safely and profitably leave to in-

[4] *American Journal of Sociology,* IV, 187–201.

dividuals and private enterprise. Industries which are essentially of a routine character, affording little scope for creative activities of individuals, must pass under direct social administration. For free individual initiative and desires will not support them. . . . . The only volume of free-will and voluntary enterprise that can support those routine industries is the free-will and enterprise of Society. If we can bring ourselves to regard the great normal currents of routine industry, engaged in supplying the common daily needs, from the standpoint of a real live Society, we shall recognize that to that Society this individual activity and its achievements are full of interest and variety. What to the individual is dull routine is to Society creative art, ... Though the individual will soon flags before demands for work so irksome and repellent to its nature, the social will gladly responds to work in which that will finds its free natural expression [pp. 304–5].

Frequently he spoke of social phenomena as "half instinctive half rational." He realized how preposterous the notion would seem that the installation of government or trade-union administration into an industry like coal-mining would forthwith allow the social oversoul of the workmen to give zest to their work, while apparently in the more experimental industries which are still private, the routine workers would lack the coal-miners' enthusiasm. Yet he insisted that *esprit de corps* is something distinct from the spirits of individual members of the corps, and that something of the sort may lighten substantially the irksomeness of socialized labors.

The experimental psychologist might be expected to comment that these doctrines are doubtless important if true, but that objective evidence is so scanty that opposite opinions may be as confidently entertained. Two criticisms may be noticed—one primarily economic, the other psychological.

First, does our author adequately distinguish between the recruiting and the directing functions of industrial incentives? Taussig has shown, for example, that even if inventors would continue to invent when no profits could be made from such work, yet attention to prospective profits may direct their efforts into more useful channels than their talents would find in a more communistic state.[5] This point, of course, is not a great defense of capitalism; it merely suggests that a socialist state, even if it enforced equal ultimate incomes for everyone, might nevertheless find it useful to guide production in part by a price system rather than wholly by a political system.[6] Some radical readers will consider the problem

---

[5] *Inventors and Money-Makers* (New York: Macmillan Co., 1915), pp. 33 ff.

[6] Hobson was undoubtedly well aware of this point (on p. 162, for instance, he says that probably the greater part of our present national income is produced and

of socialism solved when they are convinced that superior brains would continue to function energetically in the absence of profit-making—forgetting that the problem of economizing the supply of ability and of making it satisfy the most urgent wants first would still remain.

The other sweeping criticism, which would be made by some psychologists,[7] concerns the scientific status of the social organism theory. The ancient realist-nominalist controversy gradually developed some aspects of this problem, showing, for instance, that a triangle is not quite the same thing as merely three lines, and that any whole adds at least an organizational form to the sum of its parts considered separately. Society (meaning our fellows) undoubtedly influences our characters, gives us rewards and punishments, and exacts from us sacrifices in part through the interest in posterity which it has helped to develop in us. In these and other matters the social-organism metaphor is interesting and useful. But Mr. Hobson's "real live Society" is more than a metaphor. It is supposed to use us mortals, its members, much as we use the cells of our bodies, for its own half-conscious ends. Whether society exists in this superorganic sense seems at present a metaphysical question, since we have even more difficulty in establishing communication with our oversoul than we have in conversing with the cells which make up the marrow of our bones. In Hobson's later work indeed, this ghostly entity does not seem to figure.

Let us now examine, from the more prosaic scientific point of view, the theory of work and welfare sketched above. Several types of evidence might be brought to bear: historical, psychiatric, and psychoanalytic. But I shall limit myself to psychological evidence in a narrower sense, meaning studies which utilize laboratory control and employ statistical logic.[8]

On the relative inherent attractiveness of various occupations to various people, a technique called "interest analysis" has lately been widely

---

consumed according to sound social-welfare economy); but he does not develop it explicitly enough in the books we are considering.

[7] Notably, at present, by Professor F. H. Allport. See his *Social Psychology*, and article, "The Group Fallacy in Relation to Social Science," *American Journal of Sociology*, XXIX (1924), 688–703. [Cf. also his paper (with Hartman) in the present volume, analysis 22.—EDITOR.]

[8] Some general references indicating the sorts of Fabian tactics which experimental science employs in the field we are considering are: A. W. Kornhauser, "The Motives-in-Industry Problem," *The Annals*, November, 1923, pp. 105–16; E. S. Robinson, "Factors Affecting Human Efficiency," *ibid.*, pp. 94–104; E. S. Robinson, "Mental Work," *Psychological Bulletin*, XVIII (1921), 456–82; H. D. Kitson, "A Study of the Output of Workers under a Particular Wage-Incentive," *University Journal of Business*, I, (1922), 54–68.

used in research relating to vocational guidance in colleges.[9] Students and practitioners in engineering, medicine, business, and so on are asked to indicate on a printed blank whether they would like or dislike, apart from considerations of income or social esteem, the work in each of a long list of occupations (actor, architect, aviator, etc.). Then, by mathematical methods, the significant differences in preferences among vocational groups are computed, with the object of eventually helping young people to find their best vocation with a minimum of fumbling. Thus far I have not heard of anyone who has attempted to analyze such data in terms of creative versus routine work, but the techniques appears rather promising for the purpose, being in considerable measure objective and quantitative. It shows certainly that psychologists are making a beginning in the study of the inherent attractions of various types of work.

In another class of investigations the theory of individual differences in human qualities and quantities is applied to our question of joy in work. The technique of mental tests has been used in this direction by a considerable number of vocational students, and it has been shown conclusively that for a given job there is a zone of "intelligence" within which workers stay on that job more firmly than others who have too little or too much intelligence. (Incidentally, there is some evidence supplied in this way on the extent to which young people profess interest in work which they have not suitable capacities for doing.[10]) In one factory it is reported that, when all workers in a large department devoted to monotonous work were asked if they cared to try some other job, it was predominantly those of high intelligence (as measured by an army alpha type of test) who expressed desire for change.[11] Recently, British industrial psychologists hired a few individuals of varying "intelligence" to work under observation, primarily for the purpose of finding the effect on output and comfort of change of work, and rest periods, compared with continuous work at a routine task. They found the workers of low or moderate intelligence best able to maintain output and comfort in the monotonous and continuous work.[12]

[9] See, e.g., Max Freyd, "A Method for the Study of Vocational Interests," *Journal of Applied Psychology*, VI (September, 1922), 243–54, and articles by Freyd, Hubbard, Cowdery, and Strong in the *Journal of Personnel Research* (now the *Personnel Journal*).

[10] D. Fryer, "Predicting Ability from Interests," *Journal of Applied Psychology*, XI (June, 1927), 212–25.

[11] W. D. Scott and M. S. Hayes, *Science and Common Sense in Working with Men*. New York: Ronald Press Co., 1921.

[12] *An Experimental Investigation into Repetitive Work: Report No. 30* of the British Government's Industrial Fatigue Research Board (Isabel Burnett, investigator); also *Journal of National Institute of Industrial Psychology*.

Mr. Hobson was not unaware of this possibility. In his chapter on "Scientific Management" he gave a couple of pages to Münsterberg's pioneer work on vocational selection (then only lately published).

If, then, in every grade of workers there are to be found men who appear destined by nature for a rigidly mechanical task conducted under servile conditions, it may be thoroughly sound social economy to put them to perform all labour of such kind as is required for the supply of human needs. This is a problem of applied psychology, or of psycho-physiology [p. 212].

Lately, he has spoken with respect of industrial psychological experimentation. But differential psychology was so novel while his thought was forming (in spite of the long preparation already made by the schools of Galton and psychophysics) that he has failed to realize how many of his paragraphs need some revision in the light of statistical studies of individual differences in a vast number of "traits."

He is much better prepared to grasp the limitations of such work as I have cited, at least in its initial phases. Thus, it is an open question how much an individual's score in an intelligence test depends on his native ability, how much on the advantages he has had in the way of nutrition, education, and wholesome upbringing generally. It may be that the low-score people stick to routine jobs longer, and appear to find the work less irksome, than high-score people, mainly because the former come from poor homes, are accustomed to hard conditions, and realize they have little chance of finding better employment. In other connections Mr. Hobson makes this point:

It might appear superficially a sound human economy to place all the burden of the heaviest and most repellent muscular toil upon classes or races of men whose powerful bodies and insensitive minds seemed to indicate that they were best fitted by nature for such work.* But if the effect of such an economy were, as it would be, to keep considerable bodies of population in a low grade of animalism, as represented in coarse modes of living and brutal recreations, this one-sided view, by neglecting these organic reactions, would injure the personality of these lower grades of citizens, and through them damage the efficiency of the society of which they were members [p. 313; cf. chap. iv, sec. 5].

* Ruskin had a curious notion of this sort. . . . .

The mental-test workers, however, in alliance with Galton's other followers, have built up a good case for the view that success in their tests is influenced very powerfully by native abilities; and perhaps some presumption is really established that (at least until genetics-eugenics becomes an exact science and art) there will be a considerable number of persons who find a satisfaction in work which would strike other people as intolerably monotonous or otherwise "humanly costly." Such research tends to improve on Mr. Hobson's exposition mainly in that it furnishes fact in place of opinion on the vital question of *how many* natural hewers of wood and drawers of water we have with us.

In most of the foregoing discussion we have tacitly identified conditions which are voluntarily sought by workers with conditions which are favorable to their welfare. Obviously, this identity does not always hold. Whiskey and opium, though voluntarily sought, are ordinarily injurious; and similarly it is conceivable that workers should be prohibited from indulging in their fondness for either repetitive or creative work. As ethical teachers are fond of pointing out, people often voluntarily adopt the course of action which they know will bring them (directly, at least) discomfort rather than comfort. Criteria of welfare easily give rise to ultra-scientific questions, yet given the criteria, science can collect relevant data. One class of data which seems clearly relevant to welfare is the subjective states of people—their comfort, happiness, pain, consciousness of virtue, or whatever subclasses we may find manageable. The scientific study of work has made some beginning at collecting periodic reports from workers as to the degree of comfort of their consciousness; and these reports throw some additional light on the correlated data of output, staying-on-the-job, working conditions, etc., which are yielded by the experiments. All such matters are relevant to the economics of welfare.[13]

A word should now be added dealing more specifically with the newer doctrines contained in *Free Thought in the Social Sciences*. The main burden of this book concerns the tendency of a writer's practical zeal and class interests to warp his judgment with regard to social issues. In a sense, this onslaught does not establish many new errors in the theories of Hobson's opponents, yet considerations like these do administer a salutary check to our confidence in our own conclusions. Of special interest also are his remarks on the relations of instincts, reason, and welfare,

[13] Professor E. L. Thorndike has studied reports of comfort from subjects working under experimental conditions. See his "The Curve of Work and the Curve of Satisfyingness," *Journal of Applied Psychology*, I (1917), 265–67; and *Ventilation*: the *Report of the New York State Ventilation Commission*. More recently Dr. Elton Mayo has published studies of the "reveries" of industrial workers (e.g., in "Revery and Fatigue," *Journal of Personnel Research*, III [December, 1924], 273–81) which involve an unusual combination of psychiatric and factory-statistics techniques. He interprets his data as showing that monotonous work per se tends to produce "pessimistic revery" in the worker; but the data offered do not appear fully to support the conclusion, since other factors than monotony—particularly a strained posture—might be adequate to account for the discomfort, resentment, and labor turnover.

mostly contained in the Appendix on "Economic Utilitarianism" (pp. 167–73). In fine, the author attempts a reconciliation between instinct psychology and rationalism in a manner similar to that of Graham Wallas —assigning a large place in human affairs to the alleged instinct or disposition of curiosity or thought. The maximum of instinct satisfactions —making due allowance for "higher" and "lower" pleasures—is taken to be the practical content of welfare, and a modified hedonic calculus is thus defended. These views will seem too fully hedonistic to many of Hobson's allies, but to me the truth lies still closer toward the position of James Mill and Bentham. Instinctive-habitual reactions, pleasurable or painful consciousness, seem merely objective and subjective aspects of the same thing. Reasoning appears to be a succession of these reactions, not merely the operation of "the instinct of curiosity" or the work of some independent factor; and the criterion of welfare on which we can come closest to general agreement seems a long-run maximization of reactions associated with pleasant subjective states. This is almost precisely the utilitarian view.[14]

The upshot of my discussion is somewhat as follows: Mr. Hobson gave us, fifteen years ago, a masterly synthesis of economic, psychological, and philosophical subject matter, proposing a number of interesting and important psycho-economic hypotheses; and he supported his views with generally judicious arguments based on wide-ranging, well-chosen, and usually qualitative materials. These generalizations are so large and so elusive that the process of scientific nibbling at them by investigating, for instance, the effects of a specified subtype of work on such-and-such workers under given conditions and time, has not made great headway in proving or disproving them. Possibly his zeal for reform sometimes warps his scientific judgment—the wish is always, as he claims, in some degree father to the thought. Perhaps the most definite amendment we could now suggest to his psycho-economic work as a whole is in the direction of more qualification to allow for inborn differences of ability, temperament, and taste—humanity is scarcely so homogeneous as most of his discussion implies. In one vital respect his contribution is a model for psychological economists: its main materials are drawn from economic life rather than from psychological laboratories or psychiatric clinics. Only in a limited way can we experiment with economic affairs

[14] For a fuller exposition of the latter position see my *Economic Motives* (Cambridge: Harvard University Press, 1922), especially chap. xii; C. Judson Herrick, *The Brains of Rats and Men* (Chicago: University of Chicago Press, 1926); and especially Bertrand Russell, *The Analysis of Mind* (London: G. Allen & Unwin, Ltd., 1921), and *An Outline of Philosophy* (London: G. Allen & Unwin, Ltd., 1927).

under laboratory controls (though the child-study institutes now getting under way illustrate something of the sort which may have great ultimate significance). For the most part, we must depend upon analyses of practical affairs, assisted more and more by managers who can arrange actual experiments in economic behavior, which are of scientific significance. In either case, statistical methods of observation are increasingly feasible and useful.

Hobson made some use of the older type of economic statistics—such as national income, wages, hours, accidents—and he gave some recognition to Münsterberg and the scientific management movement; but we now see that most of the other topics he treated also may gradually be subjected to quantitative empirical tests—at least, those related to sensible phenomena, which probably do not include the social organism.[15]

[15] [This analysis was first written in December, 1928. The analyst's revised copy is dated March 2, 1929.—EDITOR.]

ANALYSIS 36

SOCIAL FORCES IN PERSONAL-BEHAVIOR SEQUENCES STUDIED BY THE JUDGE BAKER FOUNDATION[1]

By FLOYD N. HOUSE
University of Virginia

SYNOPSIS

This case study deals with the behavior and adjustment problems presented by a sixteen-year old boy (nearly twenty years old when last data were obtained) of Greek parentage and birth, referred to the Foundation by the Juvenile Court of Boston because of (a) his repeated truancy, begging, and stealing, and (b) because a child-placing agency which had dealt with him had been unable to find a foster-home in which he could get along, and felt that a thorough study was needed to determine whether he should be sent to a correctional institution.

The study includes factual data as to (1) family and ancestry of the boy; (2) available information as to his physical development since birth, and results of the physical examinations given on two occasions by the clinic of the Foundation; (3) home and neighborhood influences; (4) habits and interests of the boy as learned from others, mainly from his father (a widower); (5) his school history; (6) his court record; (7) his history in foster-homes during the two years immediately before he was first studied by the Foundation; (8) his performance on mental tests of different sorts; an estimate of his "mental balance" and of his "personality traits"; (9) the boy's own story. All of these data are paralleled on opposite pages by the comments and discussion of their significance which have been worked out by the editors.

Following this body of data and comment the study presents a brief summary of findings, a statement of probable "background" and direct causations, and prognosis and recommendations—all taken from the staff conference on this case.

The "subsequent history" of the case is then given. It involves the

---

[1] *The Judge Baker Foundation Case Studies*, ed. William A. Healy and Augusta F. Bronner (but not so designated on the title-pages), Series 1, Case Study No. 1. A pamphlet of 44 pp. published by the Judge Baker Foundation at Boston, Mass., September, 1922. (Factual data and discussion on opposite pages, numbered 1, 2a, 3, 4a, etc.)

findings of a new examination by the Foundation at the age nineteen years and eleven months, and excerpts from an autobiography written by the boy at that time, guided by questions supplied by the Foundation, as well as the record of his school, home, employment, and court history during the interval between the two examinations.

ORGANIZATION

A. THE CASE STUDY AS A RESEARCH PROBLEM

For the purposes of this methodological study, the central problem in this case study is assumed to be the determination, in a single case, of the factors or forces involved in the causation of certain types of conduct; and the interpretation of certain behavior sequences of a particular individual in terms of the interaction and consequent modification of the factors in his behavior. It must be noted in the beginning, however, that the study made by the Foundation was carried out primarily for the purpose of personal guidance to be given the boy, and advice to the agencies and persons seeking to deal with him. Consideration must be had also for the fact that the case study as published has been prepared for teaching and not primarily for scientific purposes.

In the Judge Baker Foundation case studies, considerable emphasis is placed upon the *individualization* of cases. This principle would seem to involve the denial of all possibility of applying science in the diagnosis and treatment of such cases, for science is in essence *generalized* knowledge. What is really implied by the attempt to use such case studies for the training of case-workers is that the cases may be resolved by analysis into elements which can be seen as manifestations of universal, or at least widespread, forces and mechanisms. Knowledge of these forces and mechanisms, it is implicitly assumed, can be gained by the study of certain cases, and subsequently used in dealing with other cases. It seems legitimate and proper in the present methodological study to describe the assumptions, the logical procedures, and the general conclusions which are implicitly present in the case study as published.

Hypotheses and assumptions.—It is difficult to discover any special hypothesis which this case study is designed to test. The editorial treatment has very much the character of open-minded exploration, recording whatever findings may appear, and indicating the applicability of whatever generalized knowledge may be available to the interpretation of the facts at hand. As suggested above, the implied scientific objectives may be said to be these: the identification and the characterization of the factors or forces affecting personal behavior in this type of case, and the description of the processes whereby these factors interact to bring about the behavior sequence. The language of the editorial comment on the factual data is such as to imply that this case is representative of many others. It may therefore be named as an *unconscious assumption,* or perhaps a conscious one, that the processes and forces involved in the determination of the behavior sequences in this case are in some degree the same as those involved in other cases.

One important *general methodological hypothesis* is visible in the treatment of this case; namely, that a concrete, long-period human-behavior sequence such as is here studied may best be made intelligible in terms of *subjective* factors and processes; that is, the wishes of the individual, his experiences as preserved in memory, and his definitions of the situations in which he finds himself. In other words, the method of this study is distinctly not "behavioristic" in the narrow and technical sense of the term. The physical traits and handicaps of the individual are regarded as indirect, rather than as direct, dynamic factors in his behavior.

B. THE FACTUAL INQUIRY

a) *Use of quantitative method.*—The present case-study makes use of quantitative measurements in a rather incidental way, in connection with mental tests. The intelligence quotient (I.Q.) is recorded, together with other quantitative measures of performance on special tests which are carefully named. The I.Q., however, is used only as an indication of "good average ability" as compared with other persons of like chronological age. It is also noted that the boy has "no striking special capacities," a judgment presumably arrived at by comparing his performance on special tests with the performance of others on those same tests. Use is made also of the concept "mental balance," which seems to have a roughly quantitative implication, and to be based on comparisons between this boy and other persons. The mental balance is apparently not calculated from definite figures. The editors include a brief comment on the lack of satisfactory quantitative tests of "personality traits." For the description of these they have relied upon purely qualitative methods, based on impressions gained by various members of the staff, on reports from foster-homes, and on an informal psychiatric analysis.

b) *Personal history.*—All facts of the boy's personal history that were available and seemed relevant have been noted. Sources most relied upon were the father, the reports of visitors for social agencies, the court records, and the reports of temporary foster-parents. For present purposes we shall regard the boy's own story as a body of factual data separate from his history, although the latter is used to supplement and check the former, as well as for purposes of psychological analysis.

c) *Physical and mental clinical examination.*—Such examinations appear to have been very carefully carried out, and the results of the mental tests made use of as noted elsewhere. The findings of the physical examination being largely negative, little use seems to have been made of them in the general analysis of the case.

d) *Boy's own story.*—Two types of procedures have been employed, as opportunity afforded, to get the individual's own story: (1) The dictation of the story as gained by a skilled person, immediately after a personal interview with the boy, from notes taken during the interview. Other investigators have experimented with the use of the dictaphone and of stenographers inconspicuously placed or concealed from the observation of the person examined, but neither of these devices was used in this case. (2) An autobiography, guided by questions provided orally or in writing. It is noted by the editors that the autobiography disclosed information as to the father's drinking which was previously unknown to the staff of the Foundation, but which was apparently verified from other sources.

C. FINDINGS—ANALYSIS OF THE DATA, EXPERIMENTAL PROCEDURE, FACTORS AND PROCESSES DISCLOSED

It may be said that two general types of methods were employed in this case study in reaching the general conclusions: (1) the interpretation and analysis of available factual data, and (2) a method which may be thought of as sociological experiment, beginning essentially after the boy was first seen by the Foundation, and involving the trying-out of certain treatment and subsequent observation and interpretation of the results of this treatment. Only to a very limited extent could the factors in this experiment be controlled; and, it may be added, the subjective processes assumed to be involved in the determination of the behavior could be observed to only a limited extent. The editors themselves emphasize strongly the limitations of the insights they were able to gain by the study of this case.

It is in the enumeration of "background" factors and "probable direct causations" that we should expect to find, in more definite formulation than in any other part of the case study as arranged for publication, the findings of most general significance. Here as elsewhere, however, the editors have adhered to a plan of stating their analyses and explanations in common-sense language, rather than in the formal terms that would be appropriate to a fundamental science.

METHODS OF DERIVING THE ENUMERATION OF FACTORS
A. BACKGROUND

a) Heredity.—The points under this heading were derived from such information about parents and parents' families as could be obtained without exhaustive inquiry. The general assumption is that the heredity was "normal."

b) Development.—The information obtainable was not exhaustive nor especially reliable; and the editors have simply assumed that development was more or less normal.

c) Home conditions.—The importance and conditioning effect of the early freedom in the homeland, followed by life in crowded city surroundings in America, is deduced in part from remarks made by the boy. The interpretation made of this factor is supported, by implication, by its common-sense plausibility, and, presumably, by knowledge of similar cases on the part of members of the staff of the Foundation. The influence of life for ten years in a motherless home is a hypothesis to explain (i) certain features of the boy's early delinquency, which showed lack of home training such as another child might have received; (ii) lack of habits of cleanliness and other traits, preventing successful adjustment in a foster-home.

d) Habits.—No particular evidence is adduced to show influence of "bad habits" upon other factors of the boy's behavior. In fact, attempts to get from the boy's own story, i.e., through an informal psychiatric examination, some indication of mental conflict growing out of masturbation or other sex excitation resulted quite negatively. The existence of "bad habits" is apparently noted here for the use of anyone who may be interested, and to suggest possible causations which could not be worked out in the analysis actually made.

B. PROBABLE DIRECT CAUSATIONS

a) Of earlier delinquencies.—(1) *Maladjustments through immigration:* This is adjudged to be a dynamic factor in the case, partly as a hypothetical explanation of facts in the personal history, its importance being indicated by remarks made by the boy himself. These maladjustments are also named as a factor in a hypothetical explanation of conflicts between the boy and his various temporary foster-parents concerning American ways and ideals. (2) *Excessive street life with* (3) *bad companions:* These are treated as factors in the boy's behavior; in part, as a matter of useful hypothesis to account for certain facts; in part, from knowledge of similar cases by the staff. In this instance there is some direct evidence of the influence of bad companions; in the boy's own story he tells that he began stealing with a certain boy. The reliability of this evidence is not discussed by the editors. (4) *Poor parental supervision and* (5) *poverty:* These are obviously taken as factors only in a negative sense.

b) Probable direct causations of later behavior difficulties.—(6) *Peculiarities and lack of early training:* This seems to designate a factor in the boy's behavior only in a negative sense, so far as "lack" of early training is concerned. "Peculiarities" in the early training refer to the (7) *fostering of argumentative habits* in the boy by his father. This factor is also implied under (8) *personality traits:* The enumeration of these "personality traits" seems to consist in making an abstraction of striking features of the boy's behavior and in naming them as "tendencies." The naming of (9) *adolescence* as a factor is apparently based on general theories of adolescence which have been current among contemporary psychologists. The factors enumerated as (8), (10), and (11); viz., *personality traits, sense of inferiority in foster-homes* (*reaction* to sense of inferiority?), and *irresponsibility* somewhat fostered by charity, granting that they can be derived from the data, may be regarded as direct or dynamic factors in the boy's behavior, if we grant also the validity of stating them in subjective terms. Grounds for naming these factors are found mainly in the boy's own story, and in the reports of foster-parents.

THE ANALYSIS OF THE BEHAVIOR SEQUENCES

Taking some liberties with the editors' own presentation of this case study, we may impute to them a method of analysis of the boy's behavior sequences somewhat like that described by Thomas and Znaniecki in *The Polish Peasant in Europe and America.*[2] That is, it is assumed that the person has a set of "attitudes," or behavior tendencies, any one of which is normally latent, and becomes active when evoked by some environmental object or situation of the type with which the attitude has been correlated through previous experience. "Values" is the term used by Thomas and Znaniecki for these environmental elements as defined or conceived by the person in question. The single experience, or, more accurately, the unit which is subjective experience and action at the same time, is conversely seen as the elemental process in which "attitudes" and "values"

---

[2] New ed., New York, 1927. See especially the "Methodological Note" in Vol. I, and the Introduction written for the "Life-Record of an Immigrant," which closes Vol. II of the new edition. [Cf. also the analysis of this work by Robert E. Park (analysis 8). Also frequent references thereto in other analyses (consult Index), especially that of Thrasher's *The Gang* by Young (analysis 37).—EDITOR.]

intersect and are modified. If the environmental object or the situation which evokes a certain behavior tendency differs markedly from what it was taken to be, the result of the experience-act is the formation in the personality of the individual in question of a new "value" and a new attitude corresponding to it. It should be particularly noted that in this view of the development of personality in behavior sequences, the *attitudes of other persons*—which of course are in large part matters of group custom—are *environmental* factors or "values" for the person primarily under consideration.[3] It is also to be noted that in this theory it is almost necessarily assumed that the individual starts out in childhood with certain original, innate behavior tendencies or "temperamental attitudes," which are usually assumed to be more or less the same for all human beings, but which may also be assumed to differ with race and other elements of heredity.

In the *Judge Baker Foundation Case Studies* the authors have not made use of any particular enumeration of original innate behavior tendencies or attitudes. In the particular case study under consideration, however, it is rather definitely assumed that the boy starts out with "normal" desires for play, adventure, and excitement, and for recognition or status in the social order in which he finds himself.

Assuming, then, the presence of these and other less definite or less clearly discernible attitudes and wishes, the Foundation has been able to work out more or less definite explanations of the behavior sequence involving (*a*) truancy and other school difficulties; (*b*) stealing; and (*c*) friction with foster-parents in several homes tentatively tried for the boy. An instance of this implied analysis of behavior sequences may be briefly outlined as follows:

Behavior sequence leading to habit of anti-American argumentation: (i) Primitive activities and wishes—talking (thinking?), desire for recognition and status. (ii) Habits of talking and thinking (temperamentally strong?) given direction and content by father's training of boy and boy's own reading. (iii) Values meaning "America" to the boy given a negative definition by the change from the freedom of Greek country life to the restriction and the poverty of the foreign quarter of an American city. (iv) Boy's desire for recognition encounters unfavorable attitude of foster parents (inferred by him from their unfavorable criticisms of some of his acts), the result being a feeling of inferiority on his part, and an attempt to compensate by the exaggeration of the argumentative attitude. (v) Argumentative habits and anti-American opinions disappear, for reasons not clearly shown. Disappearance of anti-American opinions due, in part, by the boy's own statement in his auto-

[3] Cf. also Florian Znaniecki, *Laws of Social Psychology* (Chicago, 1926).

biography, to the ultimate influence of contact with a better grade of American life in foster homes. In the editor's *Final Comment* on this case, it is stated that placement in foster homes, subsequent return to his own home, and a six-weeks cruise in a Navy Summer School which was arranged for him, each in turn contributed to the formation of socially acceptable habits and personality traits.

Why did this boy become delinquent, while his brother one year older, of presumably similar heredity and environment, did not? This question is never explicitly answered in terms of any facts obtained in the inquiry. It is pointed out, however, that "even two brothers do not come in contact with exactly the same environmental influences" (p. 13a). An investigation of the families of 1,000 repeated offenders, recorded in Healy's *The Individual Delinquent*, is cited for the finding that of 137 of these families in which there were 2 children, both were known to be delinquent in only 26 instances. In a similar investigation in Boston, out of 102 families of delinquents in which there were 2 children, the Foundation found only 16 cases in which both were delinquent. These statistical data, however, help only to emphasize the problem, not to solve it. What the editors have done, in discussing this question, is to point out a method of studying the problem, in the form of a hypothesis to be tested. This hypothesis is that the behavior tendencies found in an individual at a given time, and his personal history, in so far as it is different from that of his associates of nominally similar environment and heredity, can only be explained in terms of the interplay of individual and environment—never in terms either of "personality" alone or of environment alone (p. 13a).

It should be pointed out that, in so far as this case study illustrates the rôle of *social* forces in the determination of personal-behavior sequences, the term "social forces" should be applied primarily to the types of behavior found by the boy in his social environment—these being, of course, matters of *social custom* in some group or other—and to the attitudes of others toward him—these also being determined largely by social custom and tradition. His own attitudes and behavior tendencies may of course be regarded as "social attitudes" in so far as they represent the shaping influence of these social-environmental forces. Among the social forces in this case the following may be enumerated: (1) the "generosity," in the sense of loose property regulations regarding fruit in the orchards, existing in the country-village community in which the boy spent his early years; (2) the rigorous property claims in the fruit on sale in the markets in Boston; (3) the custom of the boys in the city neighborhood, tolerated by older persons, of gathering up empty boxes and pieces of lumber and bringing them home for firewood or selling them for spending money (tending to blur the boy's sense of property values); (4) more serious forms of disregard for property found by the boy among his companions in the city; (5) attitudes of the father as interpreted by the boy—relieving the latter of all responsibility for household labor, critical interest in national history and institutions, etc.; (6) the laws and standards enforced in the city, represented by the Juvenile Court; (7) the treatment the boy received from the child-placing agency to which his case was referred by the Court (said to have given him, for a time, a sense of having a claim to be taken care of); (8) attitudes of disapproval of his habits manifested by foster-parents; (9) foster-parents' standards of living; (10) the attitudes of the larger world as represented to him by the counselors at the Foundation; (11) the social patterns and attitudes encountered while on the summer cruise in the navy training school; (12) various attitudes met with in school from teachers and principals. Through all these forces, the analysis tends to show, the personality of the boy was formed and reformed; that is, his attitudes were shaped and his wishes defined.

EVALUATION

In general, the merits of this case study, when it is regarded as a research contribution to science, must be determined for the most part by quite different criteria from those which are frequently applied to research contributions. In this document we find no particular attempt at rigorous exactness in the ascertainment of facts, except perhaps in the mental tests; and no systematic criticism of the sources of data is attempted. There is scarcely a question of statistical "sampling," or of testing in any way the truth of any hypothesis expressible in the form "All A is B." The ultimate conclusions as to factors and forces involved in this case have been arrived at speculatively, or intuitively, on the basis of the previous knowledge, the experience, and the common sense of the members of the staff of the Judge Baker Foundation. The logical position taken is, apparently, that the validity of any such analysis as is here attempted must be measured, not primarily with reference to the procedure by means of which it has been arrived at, but with reference to its power to make the case intelligible, and to afford a basis for dealing in a practical way with this case and with other cases of more or less similar character.[4]

[4] [This analysis was first written in March, 1928. The analyst's final revision is dated February, 1929.—EDITOR.]

ANALYSIS 37

FREDERIC M. THRASHER'S STUDY OF GANGS[1]

By KIMBALL YOUNG
University of Wisconsin

I. SUMMARY OF THRASHER'S REPORT

The first division of this book deals with the "natural history of the gang" in Chicago—the area of Thrasher's investigation. This involves an account of the nature and the scope of "gangland." The regions in which it thrives are shown upon a base map and coincide with what the author terms "the interstitial" areas of the metropolitan city.

Thrasher writes:

The most important conclusion suggested by a study of the location and distribution of the 1,313 gangs investigated in Chicago is that *gangland represents a geographical and social interstitial area in the city.* Probably the most significant concept of the study is the term interstitial—that is, pertaining to spaces that intervene between one thing and another. In nature foreign matter tends to collect and cake in every crack, crevice, and cranny—interstices. There are also fissures and breaks in the structure of social organization. The gang may be regarded as an interstitial element in the framework of society, and gangland as an interstitial region in the layout of the city.

The gang is almost invariably characteristic of regions that are interstitial to the more settled, more stable, and better organized portions of the city. The central tripartite empire of the gang occupies what is often called "the poverty belt"—a region characterized by deteriorating neighborhoods, shifting populations, and the mobility and disorganization of the slum. Abandoned by those seeking homes in the better residential districts, encroached upon by business and industry, this zone is a distinctly interstitial phase of the city's growth. It is to a large extent isolated from the wider culture of the larger community by the processes of competition and conflict which have resulted in the selection of its population. Gangland is a phenomenon of human ecology. As better residential districts recede before the encroachments of business and industry, the gang develops as one manifestation of the economic, moral and cultural frontier which marks the interstice.[2]

[1] *The Gang: A Study of 1,313 Gangs in Chicago.* Chicago: University of Chicago Press, 1927. Pp. xxi + 571.

[2] Pp. 22–23.

Upon the foundation of this ecological background the author describes the process of gang-building. The gang grows out of the normal play life of children and adolescents, constricted and patterned by the nature of the surrounding social and economic life. Spontaneous at the outset, it early takes on the characteristics of an organized primary in-group, with its separation from other gangs, its loyalties, its codes, its conflict mores which arise when it meets with opposition.

Next comes the question "What is a gang?" There are many varieties, and it is difficult to bring the concept within a definite boundary. By descriptive pictures of sample cases, however, the author attempts to present some of their principal characteristics. The following tentative definition emerges:

The gang is an interstitial group originally formed spontaneously, and then integrated through conflict. It is characterized by the following types of behavior: meeting face to face, milling, movement through space as a unit, conflict, and planning. The result of this collective behavior is the development of tradition, unreflective internal structure, *esprit de corps*, solidarity, morale, group awareness, and attachment to a local territory.[3]

The author shows that at one extreme gangs are very diffuse and amorphous. At the other, they are highly integrated solidified groups with criminal habits, or else they become indistinguishable from athletic clubs and recreational organizations of more conventionalized sort. His study shows, moreover, that the clearly defined age limits which other observers have frequently assumed do not always prevail. Thus he shows that in three hundred and five gangs the age range was nine years, from sixteen to twenty-five.

Part II deals with "life in the gang." Its activities are leisure-time responses in lieu of more socialized opportunities for play. The quest for new experience[4] is a conspicuous factor. Adolescence is a period of escape from parental control and the finding of one's self in the larger world of adults. The gang offers a method of securing this new experience. Mobility, change of scene, gambling, athletic games, movies, dime novels, loafing, indulging in stimulants, and predatory actions of all sorts (stealing, flipping freights, vandalism) make up the leisure-time occupations of the gang boy.

The rôle of fantasy-thinking is important in this group. Imaginative characters and imaginative exploits lead to activities patterned upon

[3] P. 57.

[4] [Cf. Professor Park's discussion of this concept in the Appendix to his analysis 8.—Editor.]

them. The playgrounds of the gang are those regions affording the greatest amusement and the free play of fantasy as it expresses itself in various activities along the market streets, in the retail business section, in the forests and parks, and along the canals, the railroad tracks, and the docks, as well as in those mysterious but interesting places, newspaper alleys, and areas given over to "flophouses" and prostitution.

Junking along the railroad tracks brings many gangs into conflict with the municipal and the railroad police. When this activity is abetted by the parents, as it often is, it simply enhances the significance of such depredations for the boys. Behavior patterns of the gang become associated with open warfare with other gangs. The conflict between in-group and out-group is seen in rudimentary form. Gang warfare is not merely mischievousness or predatory behavior; it grows out of an issue, a crisis. Codes may develop and thus the conflict is put into a somewhat formal framework. The outside community may step in and determine the direction which this shall take, though usually the gang tends to organize its own social world, often into a somewhat attenuated sort of feudal order.

Gang activities also relate themselves to race and nationality groupings. In fact, in Chicago the gangs are intimately connected with the immigrant communities of the poorer type.[5] On the other hand, nearly 50 per cent of the gangs whose nationality backgrounds were known had members of mixed nationality. It is economic and social status in the community which determines gang formation fundamentally. The author remarks:

A superficial conclusion might easily be drawn from the statistics presented at the beginning of this chapter that the immigrant peoples of the city are responsible for gangs and all the problems related to them. Such an inference would be entirely erroneous. Native white American boys of the same economic and social classes as the children of immigrants enter into gangs just as readily, but their identity is lost because of the vastly greater number of the children of foreign-born parentage in the regions of life where ganging takes place. It is not because the boys of the middle and wealthier classes are native white that they do not form gangs but because their lives are organized and stabilized for them by American traditions, customs, and institutions to which the children of immigrants do not have adequate access. The gang, on the other hand, is simply one symptom of a type of disorganization that goes along with the breaking up of the immigrants' traditional social system without adequate assimilation to the new.[6]

[5] Cf. J. Landesco, "Prohibition and Gangsters: A Chicago Community Study," *Papers and Proceedings of the American Sociological Society*, XXIII (1928), 330.

[6] Pp. 217–18.

The final chapter in Part II deals with the problem of "sex in the gang," an interest which represents a decidedly secondary activity, although it appears in certain of the older adolescent groups. At times girls themselves become gang members or even leaders. With younger groups there is often distinct hostility toward girls. In a few cases gangs made up of both sexes were organized for the exploitation among themselves of sexual practices. In spite of a great deal of sex immorality associated with life in these groups as a whole, the social impetus to marriage and to more regular sex life constitutes in a great many cases a distinct factor in their disintegration.

In concluding this chapter Thrasher discusses the older explanation of gang behavior in terms of atavistic instincts and the theory of recapitulation. While he freely admits the biological and the psychological foundations of adolescent actions, he points out that the direction which these impulses take "depends upon the environment," which means the social and cultural situations and the physical configurations of the world of the adolescent to which he is exposed and in which he finds expression of his natural urges. One cannot explain gang activity by an appeal to a doctrine of instinct based on an outworn biology.

Part III deals with the "organization and control in the gang." Its whole tendency to take on certain types of social order and control is exposed. The social patterns of the surrounding adult environment abound in evidences of criminality, social immorality, and a variety of Old and New World customs which greatly influence its organization. The gang life leads among other things to distinctive nomenclature, to a special argot, to certain patterns of morality, which may be in sharp contrast to those of the politically organized community.

Legends and traditions, which have marked effect upon the morale of the gang, accumulate and help in the retention of its code and behavior patterns. Loyalty, mutual aid, solidarity, high sense of obligation to the group, co-operation, group planning—all these are part and parcel of the gang life. It is, in fact, a rudimentary primary in-group, with definite codes, purposes, and certain virtues.

The chapter on "Personality and the Action Pattern of the Gang" is an attempt at a psychological analysis of some of the factors which go into its formation. Thrasher shows how such factors as compensation for physical handicaps, individual differences in intelligence, and previous experience come to function here. Finally, one's rôle is often crystallized by nicknames and appellations which make status evident to all. Out of this selective process arises leadership.

The author points out that leadership is not something of universal, easily determinable traits, but that it arises out of the conditions found in the gang: its history, it function, its relation to age, and its physical and social surroundings. By presentation of actual cases he shows how "gameness," "cleverness," physical prowess, and bravery distinguish leaders in their respective groups. The leader, in short, grows out of the gang; it is seldom that he makes it, although he certainly influences its direction.

Part IV deals with the problem in its wider social, political, and economic aspects. The criminal gangs which infest many of our American cities are distinctly related to the cultural and social frontiers which are found there. Of the continuity from adolescent to adult criminal gangs Thrasher says:

The continuity of life from the younger gangs to the older is so unbroken, the passage from one stage to the next is so gradual, that the serious crimes of young adult gangs can hardly be understood apart from their origins in adolescent groups.[7]

The author first takes up the process of demoralization in the individual member. The gang invites truancy and facilitates delinquency because delinquencies bring prestige in the group.[8] It is here, in fact, that the boy learns the disintegrating personal habits, the technique of crime, and a philosophy of life, which go far toward making for adult criminality. Aside from ordinary criminal activities, the gangs appear in the conflicts between capital and labor. Strike-breaking, intimidation, slugging, rock-throwing, and dynamiting may be indulged in between rival unions and between capital and labor—each employing gangs and their methods. They may also be involved in politics in many ways, sometimes by the indirect link-up of protection, and sometimes directly, as tools of politicians.

In the concluding chapter the author summarizes his materials as a basis for a discussion of how to deal with the gang problem. Factors which underlie ganging rest in the community organization, in the family disintegration, in the failure of religion to penetrate the experience of the slum boys, and in the fact that the school does not deal with the boy in his social setting. There is still found among legal authorities much naïve belief in the magic of punitive treatment of the gang members as isolated individuals. But the effective attack lies in working with the gang

[7] Pp. 367–68.

[8] In this matter he disagrees with Healy, who imagines the gang of less importance in delinquency. Cf. pp. 384–85, especially the footnote.

as a unit and transforming it. There is a discussion of various organizations which attempt to do this: Boy Scouts, boys' clubs, social-settlement clubs, Y.M.C.A., brotherhood republics, and the like. Much sentimental and well-meaning effort is still being directed at the boy as an individual without reference to his group contacts. But we need to preserve the values, for the boy, of loyalty, of status among his fellows, along with an opportunity for expression of his love of action, adventure, and romance, if we are to carry him safely over into the social responsibilities of adulthood.

II. ANALYSIS OF STANDPOINT AND METHOD

A. STANDPOINT

The investigation of the gang is undertaken by what may be described as an amplification of the survey and the case-study technique. Stripped of interest in immediate improvement of social, economic, and political life, the community survey and the case study of groups and individuals within this community have become important tools in the analysis of the social and personality processes which are the joint concern of sociology and social psychology. We may summarize the standpoint of the present study as a multiple approach to the study of these processes. The approaches involve four factors: the ecological, the social psychological, the study of culture patterns, and the study of social organization and social control.

1. *Human ecology.*—Park and McKenzie have written extensively on this topic, and we shall quote from them to make clear the meaning of this term. McKenzie writes:

Let us tentatively define human ecology as a study of the spatial and temporal relations of human beings as affected by the selective, distributive and accommodative forces of the environment. Human ecology is fundamentally interested in the effect of *position*, in both time and space, upon human institutions and human behavior.[9]

Thus there develop certain "typical constellations of persons and institutions" in our rural or urban regions which must be dealt with in reference to each other upon the groundwork of the *Gestalt* of the geographical and community arrangements. As Park puts it:

Within the limits of any community the communal institutions—economic, political, and cultural—will tend to assume a more or less clearly defined and characteristic distribution. For example, the community will always have a center and a circumference, defining the position of each single community to each other. Within the area so defined the local populations and the local in-

---

[9] Robert E. Park, Ernest W. Burgess, and Roderick D. McKenzie, *The City* (Chicago: University of Chicago Press, 1925) pp. 63–64.

stitutions will tend to group themselves in some characteristic pattern, dependent upon geography, lines of communication, and land values. This distribution of population and institutions we may call the ecological organization of the community.[10]

Thrasher in his volume begins with the standpoint of ecology as developed largely by Park and Burgess at the University of Chicago. One of his fundamental premises is that the gang must be understood upon the groundwork or configuration of gangland and the slum, and cannot be understood aside from this. Other studies of gang life have pointed out that such groups operate along the docks, the railroad lines, in the slums, and so on; but the wider significance of this in reference to expanding urban life, in terms of the distribution of various areas and functions—business, industry, and residence—has not formerly been thoroughly recognized. The ecological approach to sociological and social psychological data is an important recent development in both standpoint and method.[11]

[10] *Ibid.*, p. 115. As Park points out, however, human ecology for the sociologist is not the same as it may be for the historian and geographer. He says: "Human ecology . . . . seeks to emphasize not so much geography as space. Geographers are probably not greatly interested in social morphology as such. On the other hand, sociologists are. Geographers, like historians, have been traditionally interested in the actual rather than the typical." Cf. "The Concept of Position in Sociology," *Papers and Proceedings of the American Sociological Society,* XX (1925), n. 2. That is, sociologists are concerned in the last analysis with uncovering the typical rather than the unique in social processes, and in this sense they differentiate themselves from the historian and the geographer. However, one should consult H. H. Barrows, "Geography as Human Ecology," *Annals of the Association of American Geographers,* XIII (1923), 1–14. [Cf. analyses 14, 15, and 16; also Introduction, pp. 11–12, especially n. 12.—EDITOR.]

[11] Space prohibits extensive reference to the history of this ecological standpoint and approach. It roots, in part, in the social survey which goes back for its inception, perhaps, to such work as Charles Booth's *Life and Labor of the People in London,* and to Rowntree's *Poverty,* a study of standards of living in York. The social survey in this country was fostered by the work of Lincoln Steffens in his *The Shame of the Cities* and Upton Sinclair's *The Jungle.* This muck-raking technique gave way to more objective studies as represented, especially, by the work of the Russell Sage Foundation in the *Pittsburgh Survey,* and others. It is interesting to note in this connection a somewhat similar, although restricted, survey movement in the field of pedagogy. Reference is made to the rise of the educational or school surveys beginning about two decades ago. Both the larger social surveys and the school surveys were somewhat handicapped by the fact that they were organized at the outset with practical reforms in mind.

In the rural field the work of C. J. Galpin was particularly suggestive. Cf. his *Social Anatomy of an Agricultural Community: Research Bull. 34* (Agricultural Experiment Station. University of Wisconsin, May, 1915). Cf. also J. H. Kolb, *Rural Primary Groups, Research Bull. 51* (Agricultural Experiment Station. University of Wisconsin, December, 1921); and Dwight Sanderson and W. S. Thompson,

2. *Social psychology.*—From the standpoint of social psychology the author discusses the spontaneous primary group life of the gang and attendant social attitudes of loyalty, mutual aid, co-operation toward one's own group, and antagonistic or conflict attitudes toward other gangs and the police. Moreover, use is made of the social psychological standpoint in the treatment of the fantasy life of the gang boy as it expresses itself in romantic conceptions of his rôle and in his adventuresome life. He also treats of the psychology of leadership in the gang and the interrelation of personality and social patterns in such a group.

The Social Areas of Oswego County, New York: Research Bull. 422 (Agricultural Experiment Station. Cornell University, July, 1923); and C. C. Zimmerman and Carl Taylor, *Rural Organization: A Study of Primary Groups in Wake County, North Carolina: Research Bull. 245* (North Carolina Agricultural Experiment Station, August, 1922).

We owe to R. E. Park and E. W. Burgess credit for the more comprehensive development of this survey method. Dominated by a larger perspective, not hampered by any immediate aims for social betterment, they recognized that we need, first of all, a very careful description and observation of the social realities about us. Without bias we must uncover the facts of social processes irrespective of any *isms* or utopian hopes. Furthermore, they conceived the whole problem as involving a thoroughgoing study of all aspects of community life—economic, social, and political. Their own work, of course, led them more directly into the sociological aspects. The ecological approach became increasingly clear to them as they went into the matter of the ground pattern or configuration on which the socio-economic and political structure of the urban community is reared. They began the construction of maps, charts, and tables to show the location of business, industrial, slum, and hotel areas; "better" residential sections; and the like. They exploited the "spot map" idea in many new ways. Upon these ecological foundations they felt that one might study neighborhoods, delinquency, gang life, family disorganization, poverty, dependency, and any number of topics bearing upon the social processes. Even institutional formulations and public opinion may be analyzed, in part, from this angle. Cf. also papers by Hughes, Hayner, and Park in the *Papers and Proceedings of the American Sociological Society*, XXII (1927), 120–22.

And yet, through all this the approach was empirical. The concept "human ecology" itself has had a gradual growth. It was not purely an a priori matter. The present writer in 1916 began perhaps the first of the series of studies which are associated with this standpoint. A study of the monographs already published, those in manuscript, and those still in preparation would reveal a picture of just how a scientific standpoint and methodology grow up out of empirical, trial-and-error attempts to investigate, not abstract ideas, but concrete materials through a direct approach to the field or situation itself. Zorbaugh's *Gold Coast and Slum* illustrates very well a number of methods attempted in securing data for this most interesting and valuable analysis of life in two contrasted but contiguous areas of Chicago. One may also find valuable methodological material in E. Mowrer, *Family Disorganization;* and in Ruth Cavan, *Suicide.* The series of papers edited by R. E. Park and E. W. Burgess in *The City (op. cit.,* n. 9) are methodologically important. See also *The Urban Community,* ed. by Burgess; R. E. Park, "Urbanization as Measured by Newspaper Circulation," and R. D. McKenzie, "Ecological Succession in the Puget Sound Region," in *Papers and Proceedings of the American Sociological Society,* Vol. XXIII (1928).

3. *Culture patterns.*—Thrasher shows the importance of previous culture patterns in the groups he studied—for instance, the persistence of various European culture patterns in the immigrant groups in reference to gang life and criminality.[12] So, too, he points out how new culture patterns arise with the standardization of certain frames of behavior within the gang.

4. *Social organization and social control.*—Finally, there is a discussion of the data with reference to the rise of certain institutional features in gang life. The place which these have with regard to social control within the gang itself, and to the matter of social control of the gang by the organized community, is revealed. Codes of the two groups—gang and state—come into conflict, and the whole problem of the place of the gang in the larger social order is involved.

In discussing these aspects Thrasher wisely keeps clear of the evils of particularism in describing and analyzing social phenomena.[13] Upon the foundation, then, of these four factors he predicates his analysis.

B. METHOD OF MAKING INVESTIGATION

In this section we shall discuss the collection and treatment of the data relating to the various rubrics just noted, including as an aspect, especially of the first, the statistical and graphic.

1. *The collection of data.*—Thrasher does not state specifically just how he collected his material. Its accumulation and interpretation occupied him for seven years, during which time he came to know many gangs intimately. Some of his case studies both of gang operations, as a unit, and of gang personalities were secured by direct observation, and by personal interviews with the boys themselves. Other material was obtained from the files of social agencies, schools, and the police department. Furthermore, individuals dealing with boy problems contributed a great deal of information by interview and through their own personal records. The study is essentially one of the broad survey sort, and the author is fully conscious of its limitations in accuracy and completeness.

The task of securing data in case-history and community-study investigation offers an important methodological problem. The materials are amazingly complex and in a state of constant flux. Quantitative and statistical treatments of social data seem to provide stability, merely because once the units of measurement are assumed and the data are collected the

---

[12] Cf. R. E. Park and H. A. Miller, *Old World Traits Transplanted.*

[13] On the handicaps of particularistic explanations in social science cf. W. I. Thomas, *Source Book for Social Origins* (Boston: R. Badger, 1909), pp. 22–26, 531–33, 734–35.

analysis is relatively easy. One may control statistical computations somewhat as the chemist, for example, controls his liquids or his gases in the apparatus of his laboratory. But at the present stage of technique, where social and personality processes or functions are in question, the statistical method does not furnish a complete picture.[14] That is to say, in dealing with personal and social mechanisms in a time perspective the statistical analysis either breaks down or is at present inadequate to reveal the factors.

Furthermore, the personal relation between the collector and the objects of study has an importance in social data which has little or no analogy in physical science. Neither is such relationship essential in much biological study, although it is of some significance in the study of the behavior of higher vertebrates as Köhler has shown in reference to apes. But in social and psychological data a certain insight, a *rapport* between subjects and observer, is necessary.[15] Such participation with the objects of investigation is illustrated by Thrasher's recent report of the beginnings of a study of a gang of boys in Greenwich Village in New York City.[16] He recounts the inception of his first contact with the gang, and how he secured their confidence. He describes his inclusion by the boys as a member of the group and shows how this led to opportunities to observe the inner workings of the gang. What he terms the "collective interview" is an enlightening and important piece of technique. In the collective situation, with all the members taking part, he was able to uncover much valuable information on personalities, likes and dislikes, the rôle of various members, and considerable detail regarding gang activities.

There arises from this matter of technique some further considerations on the collection of data which should be mentioned. First, the time element is important. There must be ample opportunity for the making of personal and friendly contacts leading to preliminary inquiries which grow out of natural situations. The good observer does not rush in with paper and pencil and ask gang members about themselves, nor does he get hoboes, delinquents, or members of small congenial groups to answer formal questionnaires. Such procedures would only end in failure. Often

[14] Cf. Kimball Young, "The Measurement of Personal and Social Traits," *Papers and Proceedings of the American Sociological Society*, XXI (1927), 92–105. This article will be found also in the *Journal of Abnormal and Social Psychology*, XXII (1928), 431–42.

[15] E. C. Lindeman, *Social Discovery* (New York: Republic Publishing Co., 1924), pp. 191–99.

[16] "How To Study the Boys' Gang in the Open," *Journal of Educational Sociology*, I (1928), 244–54.

there must be a kind of "fooling around," a leisurely taking of everything seen or heard. It is evident from this fact that all persons are not suited to make such field studies.

Hence arises a second item of importance—the type of personality best fitted for those surveys. Some persons are too rigid, too compulsive, and too impatient to make such investigations.[17]

Many attempts to secure "inside" information from social groups are futile simply because the person doing the work has no flair for the proper manner of approach. One must be able to endure unusual and sometimes unsavory social situations. One must be capable of entering into the life of the group which is the object of investigation. Such matters as dress, manner of speech, and vocabulary are highly indicative. The wearing of glasses, the use of cultivated English, the walk and the gesture of the academic man may easily betray one in situations where data on gangs, delinquents, immigrants, laboring men, drifters, slum residents, and other groups not of one's own kind are desired.

So, in the third instance, note-taking or any other obvious attempts to collect facts may be detrimental. The question of reliable witnesses and the validity of testimony arises at once. If situations have to be *lived* and if one's descriptions and observations have to follow the events after some lapse of time, the whole problem of reliability of recall becomes significant. Just how to check for reliability it is difficult to say. The use of several informants is valuable. Certainly all kinds of objective check-up should be employed. The records of the court, of the social agencies, and of the schools are essential.[18]

[17] Much the same problem has arisen in anthropological research wherein some men have remarkable facility in securing the confidence of native peoples and from this ability to participate in the native's world and thus be able to secure invaluable information on culture patterns and the daily life of the people in question. It should be pointed out that not only in this particular, but in the ecological, the socio-psychological, and in the cultural treatment, there is much in common in standpoint and method between the so-called "historical school of ethnology" with which the name of Boas and his students is so closely associated and the group of sociologists undertaking the ecological and socio-psychological studies of which Thrasher's volume is a sample. While there are differences between the students of *Kulturgeschichte* and ethnology, and sociology, there is a common ground of significance. Moreover, there is a distinct *rapprochement* between the anthropologists and the sociologists as to concepts, terminology, and method as well. See Bessie B. Wessel, "The Community Area as a Unit for the Study of Ethnic Adjustments," *Papers and Proceedings of the American Sociological Society*, XXIII (1928), 338–39. (On the contrasts of viewpoint between sociology and history, including anthropology, see R. E. Park and E. W. Burgess, *Introduction to the Science of Sociology* [Chicago: University of Chicago Press, 1921], chap, I, pp. 8–12, 16–24.)

[18] Cf. C. R. Shaw, *The Jack-Roller: A Delinquent Boy's Own Story* (Chicago: University of Chicago Press, 1930), for a life-history document supported by extensive

The whole matter, of course, goes even farther and raises the issue of the nature of social knowledge.[19] The use of imagination and insight into social processes is often more essential to the revelation of their significance and nature than is the employment of numerical measurement. Certainly Thrasher's study would never have shown us the mechanism of social processes in gang life if he had not participated in this life and been able to capture the spirit which dominates the gang member throughout his activity.

2. *Treatment of the data.*—This is partly a matter of technical procedure (e.g., statistical and graphic) and partly a question of analyses of less overt types.

a) *Statistical and graphic.*—Thrasher does not ignore the statistical analysis of his data where it can be used. While his materials do not lend themselves to any elaborate quantitative treatment, he presents valuable tables showing the size and the types of gangs, age limits therein, the nationality groupings, delinquency rates, and similar material.

Perhaps as important as the tabular materials is the spot map showing the location of the ganglands investigated. This map shows the relation of these regions to the industrial, the commercial, and the residential areas of the city. His entire analysis, in fact, rests upon the fundamental ecological layout which is graphically presented by his map. If one were to make more detailed studies of gang activities, the use of the graphic method could be extended in various ways. Thus, the localities where gangs commit delinquencies, the range of their daily activities, their relation to nationality groupings, and a number of other such correlations could be presented by the use of maps. The whole ecological concept of position as it relates to the arrangements of streets and alleys, to industrial, commercial, and residential regions in their functional relations, could be treated at the outset through the technique of the map.

But the ecological analysis though fundamental is not enough. It is necessary to go on to analyze the social psychological, the cultural, and the social control features of gang life. The mere portrayal of the distributive and accommodative aspect of populations would leave us ignorant of other invaluable information about factors which determine gang behavior.

---

objective checks from school, police and institutional records and from other informants. Further reference to this work is made in the appendix to this analysis. Cf. also Pauline V. Young, *The Holy Junipers of Russian Town* (in press), which illustrates the need to "know" intimately the group one is studying.

[19] Cf. C. H. Cooley, "The Roots of Social Knowledge," *American Journal of Sociology*, XXXII (1926), 59–79.

b) Social psychological analysis.—The method of securing data for such an analysis must be taken into consideration. There are no mental tests, no personality scales by which this information can be captured. One is reduced to living with these persons, so as to secure their confidence in order to get "on the inside" of their reality. Personality documents—letters, autobiographies, sympathetic interviews, social case records based on personal investigation—seem to provide the essential data. While it may be objected that such data are not scientific because they cannot be stated in statistical terminology, the fact still remains that these documents picture the personalities in interaction with one another as no other technique has been able to do. It is not to be gainsaid that a technique for encompassing this material in quantitative terms may be developed, but no such method will be valid which does not rest upon this exploratory investigation.

In view of two factors, one may legitimately raise the question as to whether such quantitative considerations can ever give the full picture desired. The first of these is the overwhelming number and complexity of the variables involved. These include attitudes and habits, and the large number of factors in the situation to which the person responds. The second is the fact that the socio-psychological mechanisms alone do not expose the processes. That is to say, not only the matter of stimuli and response, the mechanisms of imagery, of attitude, and of habit formation must be taken into account, but also the content of the whole of mental life and behavior. In other words, the investigator must not only know the *how* of human behavior, he must know the *what*. He wants to know, to put the matter in mechanistic terms, not only how the human machine works, but also what goes through the machine as it works. For illustration, take the matter of a fixed idea about the police which the gang member may develop. We know from psychology a great deal about the mechanism of obsessions and fixed ideas, yet the manner in which this operates can only be fully described when the content of this idea, as well as the stimulus-response mechanism involved in it, is understood.

Had we at hand the complete picture of the person from his birth to his death and a careful account of every situation (complex of stimuli) to which he responded, overtly or covertly, we should have at hand everything necessary to understand his present behavior and considerable ground for prediction of his future conduct, although perhaps we could not have complete predictability. But it is impossible to secure such a total picture. For this reason, the personal document, the interview, the cross-section of content of ideas, attitudes, and habits in the group situation, reveal to us the present behavior constructed out of all this rich past. If we could then follow the personality in his group setting over a period of time and through space, we might be able to state, in somewhat reliable terms, the mechanisms of his actions. While the quantitative measure of his behavior in time would be desirable, it seems to the analyst that this desideratum is remote. Hence, we are reduced to a methodology and a standpoint somewhat like that followed in the present study.

c) Analysis of cultural factors.—While the social psychological analysis reveals the rise of attitudes, of organization out of crises, and shows the place of leadership, of fantasy life and of adventuring, it does not furnish us with the complete picture. The content of behavior, the *what* of social life, is determined also by the development of certain standardized pictures of the world and certain codified, regularized methods of dealing with this world that may be called culture patterns. Such spontaneously formed groups as gangs develop, in the course of their history, certain standardized patterns. Not only do the gangs give birth to these frames of behavior, but they also borrow other frames of action from the world about them. Thus, Thrasher reveals the influence of the feudal political organizations of our cities upon gang activities. He touches also upon the influence of immigrant codes as a part of the boys' social environment.[20] These factors can only be revealed, at present, by a technique which gets at behavior through personal documents of the sort already mentioned.

Just as in social psychological data, so here we may in time develop other means of securing these materials and putting them into quantitative concepts, but for the present the case-study method seems the most adequate.

d) Analysis of factors of social organization and social control.—Not much can be added to what has already been said on this matter. Thrasher points out how institutionalization takes place and how, associated with this, various techniques for social control arise in the gang. And for an analysis of these factors we are reduced to the same methodology and standpoint as indicated above. As to material regarding conflicts between the gang and the state, there are, of course, the records of police officials, of court procedures, and possibly medical, psychological, and psychiatric investigations. Frequently, however, the last two of these are so artificial that the picture of the personalities in the gang is blurred because matters of status and rôle in the group are ignored or thought to be of no con-

[20] He strongly emphasizes, however, that the immigrant per se does not produce the gang.

sequence. The earlier tendency in psychology and psychiatry was to deal with the individual under examination as if he had grown up in a vacuum. To mention this approach is sufficient to indicate its limitations.

3. *Critical considerations.*—It seems necessary to take note of certain features of Thrasher's work when it is considered from the angle of social science rather than of social practice or social reform. The first is the injection of valuational judgments. Have these any place in scientific analyses? Thrasher has kept himself clearer from them than most writers on similar subjects. Yet he is not entirely free from this deeply laid habit of sociological writers. In the analyst's mind, value judgments have no more place in social science than in physical or biological science. They should be separated sharply from the presentation and the analysis of social facts. Thrasher's interpretative sections are less objectionable but might preferably have been allocated to a particular section as a unit.

III. SUMMARY AND CONCLUSIONS

The analyst may summarize his criticisms in a somewhat categorical order as follows:

1. The study is methodologically valuable because it employs, in principle, the natural-science technique in securing the data. It attempts to describe a complex social process in terms of its situation, its social and physical ecology. It deals also with the psychological processes of interindividual stimulus and response within this larger framework of ecological organization and adult culture patterns. Out of this matrix of ecological arrangement, older culture framework, and socio-psychological processes are developed codes and behavior patterns which become the foundation of social organization and the means of social control in the gang.

2. The study is superior to earlier studies of the gang in that its conclusions grow out of concrete material. They are not biased by a priori conceptions, whether by biological analogies or by psychological misconceptions of recapitulation, nor by misconceptions of instincts and emotions or the particularistic viewpoint of intelligence testing. In fact, the easy biologizing of boy problems by the eugenists or the equally easy psychologizing by the mental testers proves inadequate in the face of the complexities revealed by the present study.

3. It indicates clearly the relativistic approach to personality and conduct problems of delinquent or non-delinquent gang members. The effort to comprehend the adolescent boy as an entity independent of his rôle and participation in the group is shown to be totally inadequate. This

presents a definite challenge to many psychologists and psychiatrists who essay to measure personality without taking these social factors into account.

4. Some negative criticisms might be made because of the rather wide use of the term "gang" to include criminal groups, on the one hand, and spontaneously formed athletic clubs, on the other. Also the statistical analyses are limited to rather simple presentations of percentages and averages. No attempt was made to deal with the data by the statistics of variables or correlations.[21] There are no psychological measurements of any kind, except those incidentally found in case records. The fault here lies in the nature of the material. Valuable as intelligence and emotional measurements are, attempts to secure such data from the gangs directly would have shut off the investigation at once and destroyed the opportunity for making the other observations. We shall have to wait for more detailed studies before we can secure this sort of quantitative data. Ultimately such material ought to throw light on the problems of leadership, division of function, and social participation, as these correlate with individual differences in physique, intelligence, and emotion.

5. It must be recalled that the study is distinctly exploratory. It was one of the first studies of this type of material and it must be judged always with this fact in mind. It represents an advancement in the general-survey and case-study method. Its degree of precision and the limited extent of quantitative analysis arise out of the limitations in the nature of the data, and these deficiencies are correlated with the time involved in the study. The study occupied seven years. This raises a point for research. Would not a co-operative attack on such a problem be more satisfactory? Further analysis of such a complex problem would probably be enhanced by a co-operative study undertaken by sociologists, psychologists, and psychiatrists. Even the political scientist might be drawn into such a scheme to investigate the political aspects of gang activities.

APPENDIX: SUPPLEMENTARY BIBLIOGRAPHICAL NOTE

Since this analysis was first written (February, 1928) and revised (January, 1929) considerable valuable material in this general field has appeared.

Some important contributions to rural ecology are: E. A. Taylor and F. R. Yoder, *Rural Social Organization of Whitman County: Research Bull. 203.* (Agricultural Experiment Station, Washington State College, June, 1926) and *Rural Social Organization of Clark County: Research Bull. 225* (Agricultural Experiment Station, Washington State College, April, 1928). R. A. Polson is

[21] One may contrast this study, for example, with Slawson's *The Delinquent Boy*, which is largely a statistical analysis. [Cf. analysis 39.—EDITOR.]

making a re-survey of Walworth County, Wisconsin, after fifteen years. This study will constitute an important analysis of socal change since Galpin's first study (*vide supra*, n. 11).

In the urban field the work of Clifford R. Shaw has been outstanding. [Cf. Analysis 40.—EDITOR.] His *Delinquency Areas* (Chicago: University of Chicago Press, 1929) is "a study of the geographic distribution of school truants, juvenile delinquents, and adult offenders in Chicago." The method is three-fold-ecological, statistical, and historical-genetic (case study). The latter plays but a minor rôle since it is used largely for illustrative purposes only. The concentration of truancy, delinquency, and crime in certain city areas is clearly shown and the amounts and rates of delinquency are given. This work tends to confirm the general position of Thrasher's study that delinquency depends on the general community situation rather than on racial and other biological factors. Shaw and his associates are now preparing a report on delinquency areas in certain other American cities. These comparative studies will throw into focus differences as well as likenesses in the findings on delinquency and should throw additional light on the value of Thrasher's method and results. [See Niles Carpenter's suggestions in his paper, "Urban Growth and 'Transitional Areas'," *Papers and Proceedings of the American Sociological Society*, XXIV (1930), No. 2, 254, in which he points out possible variations in rates of ecological change.] Shaw's *The Jack-Roller: A Delinquent Boy's Own Story* is the first of a group of projected case records of individuals from these areas of high concentration of delinquency and ganging. Methodologically this dual approach of Shaw's is superior to Thrasher's broad, pioneer survey in his first gang study.

Another development of method in this field is illustrated by Thrasher's present study of juvenile delinquency, boys' clubs, and boys' gangs in certain areas of New York City. Aside from an elaborate amount of detailed material, he has worked out various novel means of collecting and treating such data. See, for example, his chapter, "Social Attitudes of Problem Boys as Reported by other Boys of Like Ages," in the volume, *Social Attitudes* (edited by Kimball Young) to be published by Henry Holt and Company.

ANALYSIS 38

THE MISSOURI CRIME SURVEY[1]

By E. H. SUTHERLAND
University of Minnesota

I. DESCRIPTION OF THE SURVEY

The Missouri Crime Survey was initiated and controlled by lawyers through the Missouri Association for Criminal Justice. This Association, which was little more than a paper organization, was composed of representatives of legal, commercial, civic, and welfare societies of Missouri and was formed for the purpose of supporting the contemplated survey. This is called the first state survey of criminal justice. The explanation offered for using the state as the unit was that the laws which define felonies are state laws, the courts which try are state courts, and the remedies which must be applied are state-wide remedies. For practical purposes a sample rather than the entire number of counties was taken for study. Two counties were selected from one judicial circuit and one from each of the other thirty-seven circuits. The year ended October 1, 1924, was taken as the time unit in St. Louis and in the two counties in which Kansas City and St. Joseph are located, and the two-year period ended October 1, 1924, in the other counties of the state.

This study is called a "crime survey" but the name was adopted for convenience in preference to "a survey of the administration of criminal justice," which would describe the actual content more accurately. The following were explicitly excluded from consideration: misdemeanors, federal crimes, juvenile courts, penal treatment except in connection with parole, laws defining crimes and their punishment, causes of crime, the relation of crime to the press and the church, the ethics of the bar, and the allocation of personal responsibility for failures in the administration of justice. The scope of the investigation and the organization of work

[1] Missouri Association for Criminal Justice, *The Missouri Crime Survey* (Raymond Moley, ed.). New York: Macmillan, 1926. Pp. xxvi + 587. Footnote references which follow, unless otherwise indicated, are to this publication.

[The first draft of Professor Sutherland's paper, completed in November, 1928, was submitted to several members of the research staff of the study examined, and while he is solely responsible for the present critique, account was taken of the criticisms received in making his revision. The latter was received in March, 1929. —EDITOR.]

are indicated by the titles of the chapters in the report. These, with the names of the authors, are as follows: (I) "The Metropolitan Police System," by Bruce Smith; (II) "The Sheriff and the Coroner," by Raymond Moley; (III) "Preparation and Presentation of the State's Case," by Arthur V. Lashly; (IV) "Judicial Administration," by Arthur V. Lashly and J. Hugo Grimm; (V) "Bail Bonds," by Raymond Moley; (VI) "Ten Years of Supreme Court Decisions," by J. Hugo Grimm; (VII) "A Statistical Interpretation of the Criminal Process," by C. E. Gehlke; (VIII) "Necessary Changes in Criminal Procedure," by Herbert S. Hadley; (IX) "Record Systems," by James E. Boggs and William C. Jamison; (X) "Mental Disorder, Crime, and the Law," by M. A. Bliss; (XI) "Pardons, Paroles, and Commutations," by A. F. Kuhlman. An Advisory Committee served with the author of each report; the Committee generally consisted of five or six men who had a professional interest in the field covered by that report. The entire survey was under the control of a Survey Committee, which was composed of seven lawyers. This general Survey Committee was also the Advisory Committee for three of the specific reports. This Survey Committee exercised rather rigorous control, restricting the scope of particular studies to those aspects of the problem regarded by them as desirable, excluding many recommendations presented by the authors, and writing in other recommendations. Final responsibility, therefore, rested upon this group of seven lawyers.

The principal sources of information were the original records of the police, the courts, and the penal institutions; the legal codes; and the personal experiences of officials. Information was secured from these sources by personal interviews, observation, questionnaires mailed to the various officials,[2] and schedules on which information from the records of the officials was transcribed by twenty-eight field men.[3] Information regarding approximately ten thousand felony cases was transcribed on these schedules and constituted the data for a large part of the statistical material in the report.

II. GENERAL METHODOLOGY

The basic objective of the Survey Committee in making this investigation was the reduction of crime. The president of the Association for Criminal Justice referred to the alarming increase of serious crimes.[4] The survey contains approximately one hundred specific recommendations for changes in the administrative system; the evident objective of these

[2] Copy of questionnaires, pp. 559–60, 569–78.
[3] Copy of schedules, pp. 537–39.   [4] P. 7.

recommendations is the reduction of crime. Appeals for public support, as reported in the newspapers, were largely in terms of the reduction of crime.

In order to reduce crime effectively they wished to "get the facts." The president of the Association explained that the proposal to "get the facts" came because of the confusion which existed regarding the responsibility for the increase in crime and regarding the remedies which should be applied.[5] They expected that a policy of getting the facts would assist in developing effective remedies. The important question is, What facts? The answer was made, with no apparent hesitation or analysis, The facts regarding the administration of criminal laws.

This answer excludes certain things which are often included in surveys which have the objective of reduction of crime, particularly the facts regarding the causation of crime. The causation of crime is frequently included in such surveys on the hypothesis that an understanding of the personal and social processes leading to crimes is essential for effective control of crime. The reason given by the Survey Committee for excluding the study of causes of crime was that a great amount of confusion exists regarding the causation of crime. But confusion regarding the facts was the reason assigned for making the survey, and confusion regarding causation would be a reason for including rather than excluding causation. Aside from this nominal reason, which is evidently not the real reason for limiting the scope of the survey, other reasons may be found. First, time and money were limited and a selection was therefore necessary. Second, the Survey Committee was composed of lawyers who had a professional interest in the administrative system. Efforts of some other groups, especially of social workers, to secure representation on the Survey Committee were repulsed. Third, many lawyers and some of the lawyer-members of the Survey Committee had a theory of the causation of crime which would lead them to identify the causes of crime with the defects of the administrative system. This may be called the loophole theory of crime—that crime is due primarily to loopholes in the administrative system through which criminals escape punishment. That theory received much publicity in the United States during the years 1923–26 when the Missouri survey was being developed and completed. During those years leaders of the National Crime Commission and committees of the American Bar Association were emphasizing this theory. Chancellor Hadley, who was both a member of the Survey Committee in Missouri and of the National Crime Commission, stated as his

[5] *Ibid.*

belief that "the large amount of crime in this country is due to the fact that those who are disposed to commit crime do not stand in awe of the law, and they do not do so because comparatively few are punished."[6] Statements by other members of the survey group give a basis for the belief that some of them held the same theory.[7] Moreover, it is significant that the Survey Committee excluded from the survey consideration of all penal treatment except the system of releases from penal institutions. The portion of the report on parole of which they took cognizance was that dealing with the early releases from penal institutions, by means of which offenders escaped part of their punishment. Thus, in general, the scope of the survey was determined by the interests and the preconceptions of the Survey Committee. Likewise, the scope of the remedies which could logically be recommended was determined by the interests and the preconceptions of the Survey Committee.

After limiting the scope of the survey to the administrative system, the Survey Committee was concerned with three things: the efficiency of that administrative system as a whole and of its constituent parts, the reasons for inefficiency, and the remedies for inefficiency. The problem in methodology which is raised here is, When is an administrative system efficient? What is the criterion of efficiency? Does the criterion lie inside of the administrative system or outside of it? Can an investigation which limits itself to the administrative system measure the efficiency of that system? A survey limited to an administrative system may describe that system but can it evaluate it? Is it necessary to take into account the people for whom the system exists and upon whom it works in order to evaluate it?

Specific illustrations of the methods used in measuring efficiency will be submitted later. It is sufficient here to state that two criteria of efficiency of administrative systems may be used: a traditional or philosophical criterion of what the system is supposed to do, and the comparative effects of contrasted policies upon people. The traditional criterion was used more frequently in this study; in a few cases the effects on people were taken into account.

Another general question that may be raised regarding the methodology of the Survey Committee is, By what method may recommendations or remedies be derived from facts regarding efficiency, assuming that efficiency is measured and that inefficiency is located at certain points? Some of the leaders in the Missouri survey proposed that they "get the facts" in order that by means of the facts they might be able to arrive at "certain

---

[6] P. 350.   [7] Pp. 15–16.

and lasting remedies." Apparently they expected that the remedies would flow automatically from the facts regarding the operation of the administrative system. They placed much emphasis, also, on securing as staff members and advisers men who were experts in their fields and "who have actually held public office and who have thus learned to test rules by the rigorous standards of experience."[8] The remedies would then grow out of the previous experience of these experts rather than out of the facts. It was explained, also, that the "best experience of other states was drawn upon" and that in many cases "methods and devices of value proven elsewhere" were recommended.[9]

III.   THE CENTRAL THEME OF THE SURVEY

This survey consists of eleven reports prepared by different authors. Though the Survey Committee exercised control over these specific investigations, the report actually consists of eleven different surveys bound together, with essential differences in methods and conclusions and without much co-ordination. So far as a central theme, which can be taken as representing *the* survey, can be located, it consists of a statistical study by Professor Gehlke, with two chapters of interpretations of this statistical study by Mr. Lashly and Judge Grimm and a chapter of conclusions from the statistical study by Chancellor Hadley. These chapters constitute about one-third of the entire report. A large part of the available funds was used in making the statistical study. The advisory committees on three of these four chapters were the members of the central Survey Committee. This was the portion of the survey in which the controlling group was especially interested and to which they devoted their personal attention.

The statistical chapter presents the results of the field investigation of about 10,000 felony cases. The particular problem was to determine the extent to which cases started by warrants were withdrawn before punishments were executed, and the points at which withdrawals occurred. The data are presented in tables called "mortality tables." A case "dies" when it ceases its legal existence; the survivors are those persons who are punished. Of 100 cases started by warrants, 26 were withdrawn in the preliminary hearing, 3 in the grand jury, 33 in the circuit court, 5 by probation, 1 in the appellate court, and punishment was inflicted in 32 cases. The information in the mortality tables is classified so that the method and the place of withdrawal are evident. The tables show separately the rates of withdrawal for urban and for rural counties, for each

[8] P. 4.   [9] P. 3.

type of felony cases, for various time intervals lapsing between the different steps in the process. From the data, generalizations are made regarding the quantitative relations between the nature of the charge against the prisoner and the type of sentence imposed upon him, and between the type of plea offered and the type of sentence imposed. The tables show the frequency of jury trials and the frequency of execution of various types of penalties. This statistical study is, in general, careful, and guarded in methods and conclusions, and is an admirable piece of research work. A few questions may be raised regarding minor points:

The mortality tables indicate significant differences between rural and urban counties in respect to the proportions of cases withdrawn at different stages. In rural counties 11 per cent of the cases are withdrawn in the preliminary hearing, 43 per cent in the circuit court; in urban counties 42 per cent are withdrawn in the preliminary hearing, 22 per cent in the circuit court. If "efficiency" is represented by a low proportion of withdrawals, this indicates that rural preliminary hearings are four times as "efficient" as urban preliminary hearings, but rural circuit courts are one-half as "efficient" as urban circuit courts. No question is raised in the report regarding the validity of the comparison, but a footnote gives a reason for doubting its significance. This footnote states, "Rural justices of the peace do not usually keep a record of cases which are not sent on to the circuit court."[10] If that practice is customary in rural communities and not in urban communities, the result would be a significant distortion of the rates in rural as contrasted with urban counties, and of earlier stages in the process as contrasted with later stages. Suppose that 100 felony cases are started by warrants in a rural county and that 40 of these are withdrawn in the preliminary hearing and 40 in the circuit court, and that no record is made of 20 of the cases withdrawn in the preliminary hearing. When an investigation is made later, 80 of these cases will be found recorded, and percentages will be calculated on 80 as a base. This will show 25 per cent of the cases withdrawn in the preliminary hearing, and 50 per cent withdrawn in the circuit court, instead of 40 per cent withdrawn in each court as would be shown if the record had been made of the entire group. Since the cases from rural counties are approximately one-half the entire number, this will also affect significantly the statistics for the state.

The method of sampling may involve a bias. When circuits contained more than one county, the one was selected which had the largest number of commitments of felons to penal institutions during the preceding six

[10] P. 293 n.

years. This county may have been the one with the smallest proportion of withdrawals of cases between the warrant and the execution of punishment. Consequently the average "efficiency" of the sample may be greater than the average "efficiency" of the state. No positive evidence of this bias has been found, but the report contains no assurance that efforts were made to prove that the method of selection did not involve a bias. If the bias exists, its effect would be to make the rural counties appear more "efficient" than they actually are in comparison with the urban counties, and the entire state more "efficient" than it actually is.

The cases classified in the mortality tables as "disposed of as misdemeanors" are excluded from the class defined as "punishment executed." Some of the cases disposed of as misdemeanors did result in punishment. Since only about 3 per cent of the cases are disposed of as misdemeanors, the effect of this is very slight but is in the direction of a minimization of the number of punishments inflicted.

The principal defects in this central portion of the survey are found in connection with the interpretations of and conclusions from the statistical data. Professor Gehlke states with reference to the fact that only 32 punishments were executed in 100 cases in which warrants were issued: "This is the average apparent *effectiveness* of criminal procedure."[11] Chancellor Hadley and President Hennings use this as a measure of the *efficiency* of the administrative system.[12] It may safely be inferred that the purpose of making this statistical study was to measure the efficiency of the administrative system. This evaluation of the statistical data makes it necessary to raise three questions: (*a*) Is punishment a suitable criterion of efficiency? (*b*) Is the warrant a suitable base from which to compute percentages in measuring efficiency? (*c*) Is responsibility for inefficiency located at the points at which withdrawals occur?

a) One of the fundamental controversies in criminology during the present generation is between the punitive and the non-punitive policies of dealing with offenders. Most states have made some provision for a non-punitive policy in the form of probation.[13] The Missouri Survey Committee started with a basic objective of reduction of crime. Can crime be reduced more effectively by a policy which is 100 per cent punitive or one which is 50 per cent punitive and 50 per cent non-punitive? In 1924 in somewhat similar courts the ratio of probations to executions of punishment was about 1 to 1 in Massachusetts, 1 to 6 in Missouri. Is the more punitive policy in Missouri more efficient than the less punitive

---

[11] P. 344. [12] Pp. 350 and 15–16.

[13] Probation is called "judicial parole" in Missouri.

policy in Massachusetts in reducing crime? A survey which seeks for remedies on the basis of a policy of 100 per cent punishments is taking a definite stand on one of the fundamental issues in criminology. But it is not primarily a question as to whether a particular policy shall be used at all; rather it is a question of the conditions under which that policy shall be used. When is it preferable that a person suspected of theft should not be arrested? When is it preferable that a person against whom a warrant has been issued should be discharged in the preliminary hearing rather than bound over to the grand jury? When is it desirable that a person convicted of crime should be placed on probation? The answers to such questions should come from investigations rather than from a philosophy.

The possibility of making concrete comparisons to determine when a policy should be used is shown in the study of the parole system of Illinois by Professor Burgess and others. Persons paroled from the state prison of Illinois were divided into nine classes on the basis of personality traits, criminal records, social situations, and other facts. Of those in the class at one extreme, less than 2 per cent were known to violate parole; of those in the class at the other extreme, 76 per cent were known to violate parole; the intervening classes had rates of violation of parole progressing regularly from one extreme to the other.[14] It is desirable to test every policy with reference to every type of person and situation by a similar method of concrete comparison of effects of the policy. A group which is interested in studying the facts in order to secure remedies that will reduce crime cannot logically neglect this method of comparing effects of policies.

b) Even if punishment is accepted as a criterion of efficiency, the ratio of punishments to warrants is a doubtful measure. Ideally, the punishments should be related to crimes committed. The gap between felonies actually committed and felonies reported to the police is probably very wide, and the gap between felonies reported to the police and warrants issued is obviously wide. If we assume a supposititious case, probably not far from reality, with 100 felonies committed, 5 warrants issued, and 2 punishments inflicted, the actual efficiency in terms of punishments would be 2 per cent, but if warrants are taken as the base, the efficiency would be reported as 40 per cent. It is true that the statistics of crimes

[14] A. A. Bruce, E. W. Burgess, and A. J. Harno, "A Study of the Indeterminate Sentence and Parole in the State of Illinois," *Journal of the American Institute of Criminal Law and Criminology*, XIX, No. 1, Part II (May, 1928), 304. [Attention is given in analysis 43 to this type of research, and to some of the methodological questions in it.—EDITOR.]

committed are not available anywhere, and that the Missouri survey included such statistics of crimes reported to the police as were available.

c) The explanation may be offered that the procedure which was used measured the efficiency of the administrative system from the time of the issuance of the warrant until the execution of the punishment. This assumes that the warrants were justified in every case both from the standpoint of actual guilt and of available proof of guilt. That assumption is clearly incorrect. Mistakes are made in issuing warrants. If the assumption were correct, punishment might follow automatically without a trial after the issuance of the warrant. This is the difficulty involved in the effort to locate responsibility for inefficiency. In the report, the prosecuting attorney was held to be responsible for a larger proportion of withdrawals than any other officer. The legal authority of the prosecuting attorney is certainly very great, but the statistics themselves do not show whether this officer used his authority wisely or unwisely, efficiently or inefficiently. A specific evaluation of particular cases would be necessary in order to measure the efficiency of any part of the administrative system, and at no point in this survey was this done except in the study of the Supreme Court and to some extent in the study of parole.

In general, this statistical analysis of the relation between warrants and punishments is of very great value as factual data. The reports of the courts of every state should contain similar statistics. The value of these data does not consist in the measurement of the efficiency of the system or of any part of the system or in locating points at which reforms should be made. The value consists in locating points at which research work can be done to advantage. This statistical survey outlined problems but did not solve problems of administrative reform.

IV.   OTHER METHODS OF ASCERTAINING THE EFFICIENCY OF THE ADMINISTRATIVE SYSTEM

Aside from the statistical study above described two methods of appraising the efficiency of the administrative system or of its constituent parts are used in this survey: one is statistical analysis, the other is general description. These methods are not in all cases presented as specific measures of efficiency but they, nevertheless, convey impressions regarding efficiency. These will be described and appraised.

A.   STATISTICAL MEASURES OF EFFICIENCY

1. Homicide rates of Missouri cities are compared with homicide rates of other cities of approximately the same size.[15] This comparison shows

[15] P. 20.

that St. Louis and Kansas City have higher rates than any other cities in their respective classes, and that St. Joseph stands next to the highest in its class. The population classes are grouped as follows: 500,000 and over, 250,000–500,000, and 70,000–80,000. It would be possible, by altering the class lines so as to include several southern cities, to change the position of Kansas City. By some oversight probably, Knoxville, Tennessee, and El Paso, Texas, each of which has a population almost identical in size with St. Joseph, are not included in the table; El Paso has a homicide rate more than twice as high as St. Joseph, and the rate in Knoxville is slightly higher than in St. Joseph. In a more general sense, the table can be used as an index of administrative efficiency only on the assumption that the populations are alike in other respects, such as race, literacy, nativity, and any other biological or cultural traits which might affect criminality. If other things are equal, administrative efficiency is inversely proportional to crime rates; but if other things are not equal, it is possible that a community may have both a more efficient administration and a higher crime rate than another community.

2. The percentages of bail bonds forfeited, reduced to judgment, and collected are presented.[16] In the counties studied 3.5 per cent of the bail bonds were forfeited; of the amount thus forfeited 8.8 per cent was reduced to judgment, and of this amount 6 per cent collected. In the three cities $150,000 was forfeited, $8,500 reduced to judgment, and not a cent collected. This is important information regarding the bail-bond system, and similar information should be included in the regular reports of all states. Professor Moley presents evidence which shows that the defendant who does not fulfil his obligation to appear before the court at the proper time is rewarded by a delay in the hearing.[17] In general, however, the author is disposed to deny that the percentages of bonds forfeited serve as a measure of efficiency, but insists that the failure to collect bonds reduced to judgment is an index of inefficiency.

3. A study of the cases before the Supreme Court during the ten-year period 1915–24 contains a table showing the number of cases before this Court on appeal, the proportions of cases affirmed, reversed and remanded, and reversed.[18] This shows 56 per cent affirmed, 36 per cent reversed and remanded, and 7 per cent reversed. This, also, is important information which should be contained in the regular reports of all states. This table shows a considerable degree of inconsistency in the lower courts and the higher courts, but is it evidence of inefficiency, and if so, of the lower courts or the higher courts? The statistical report, in itself,

[16] Pp. 198–99.   [17] P. 203.   [18] P. 222.

gives no indication regarding the place at which improvements should be made. This study, however, differs from the other statistical tables in the specific analysis of particular cases. The causes of reversal are shown, and this gives information regarding specific points of disagreement. The chief cause of reversals is errors in instructions by the lower court. One important source of these errors is that printed instructions, which have been disapproved by the Supreme Court, are still used by the lower courts. The precise occasion for disagreement is here located and a method of correction would be fairly easy.

4. A study of the parole system includes statistics regarding percentages of persons on parole who have violated parole.[19] This shows that 46 per cent of those paroled from the Missouri Reformatory violated their parole. Is this a measure of the efficiency of the parole system? The author explains that it is not a measure of the efficiency of the parole system alone but that the responsibility rests on a great variety of other agencies as well. Aside from that division of responsibility, it is not necessary that two parole systems which show different rates of violation of parole differ in efficiency in the same proportion. It would be easy, for instance, for a parole board to reduce the rate of violation of parole almost to zero by sufficient limitation of parole. It is not certain that the effect on prisoners or on crime rates would justify a claim of increased efficiency for that reason. Professor Kuhlman has utilized these statistics of success and failure of persons on parole to throw considerable light on the causation of crime, and also as a basis for the guidance of a parole board in selecting prisoners for parole and supervising them on parole. Here, again, it is not by the measurement of efficiency as such that assistance may be rendered to the administrative system but by the comparison of effects of policies on persons of different types. That is, Kuhlman here makes an approach to the method used in Illinois by Professor Burgess.

5. In the study of the parole system is included a table showing the growth of recidivism among prisoners committed to the Missouri Penitentiary.[20] Recidivism is reported to have increased 100 per cent from 1905 to 1924. But methods of identification have improved in this period and it is probable that the reported increase in recidivism is partially, perhaps wholly, the result of this. Even if the record is correct, an increase of recidivism would be evidence of decreasing efficiency of the administrative system only if other things, especially the efficiency of the criminal group and the incentives to criminality, remained constant.

[19] Pp. 447–49.   [20] P. 526.

B. DESCRIPTIVE ACCOUNTS OF EFFICIENCY

In addition to the statistical appraisals, which require original data sufficiently co-ordinate so that they can be used for quantitative purposes, the reports contain much miscellaneous material. Some of this miscellaneous material, also, is statistical but has to do with specific details. For instance, it was found that in 85 per cent of the counties the sheriffs kept no records of crimes committed, and that in only one-third of the homicide cases were autopsies performed.[21] These bits of statistical information are relatively incidental. In general, the method here considered consisted of getting acquainted with a situation and forming a judgment regarding efficiency, though without a definite criterion or measure of efficiency. The author after this experience describes what the defects are. He offers little evidence. There is little check on his objectivity or biases. Much of the report consists of explanations of or reasons for the inefficiency. For this purpose two types of evidence are used frequently: (a) the previous occupations, for example of sheriffs, or the lack of previous experience, for example of prosecuting attorneys; (b) administrative and other rules which impede efficiency—for instance, in St. Joseph the patrolmen are required to travel in couples though that rule has been abandoned in almost all other cities; in St. Louis the law requires that the police force be divided into three platoons of approximately equal numerical strength though a large proportion of felonies occur between 6:00 P.M. and midnight.

V. CONCLUSION

The Missouri Crime Survey contains two types of material: factual data and evaluations. The factual data are partly in the form of statistical charts and tables, partly in the form of general descriptive accounts. It was the intention of the Survey Committee that the evaluation of the administrative system and of the proposed changes in the system would grow out of the factual data. In order to evaluate an administrative system it is necessary to have the facts regarding that system, but it is necessary to have something more. The best instrument by means of which to evaluate an administrative system is a demonstration of the comparative effects of contrasting policies upon human beings. In the Missouri Crime Survey the use of this method was prevented when the study was restricted to the administrative system. This survey proposed to secure facts on which to base modifications of the methods used by the public in dealing with criminals, but excluded the public and the

[21] Pp. 75 and 93.

criminals entirely from the investigation. Is there any scientific method of measuring the efficiency of an administrative system or of modifying that system except in connection with the public for which it operates and the people upon whom it operates? The only human beings considered in this study were the public officials. Consequently, the Survey Committee was thrown back upon its philosophical preconceptions.

From the practical point of view the survey was not successful in accomplishing the results desired by the Survey Committee. Not one of the remedies recommended had been enacted into legislation at the time of present writing, several years after the report. Various reasons are given for the failure of these recommendations, but perhaps the most significant factor is that the active participation in the control and the management of the survey was restricted to lawyers. In several other states programs of reform were developed during these years with much less expense and with more immediate success in the legislature than in Missouri.

Nevertheless, as social surveys go, this survey should take high rank. The principal contribution of the survey is the accumulation of factual data regarding the operation of an administrative system in a state. The chapters on the coroner, bail bonds, the Supreme Court, the statistical analysis of the judicial process, and parole are especially valuable. Moreover, this investigation has outlined problems and located points at which intensive research work can be done to advantage later. Professor Robert E. Park states, "In the most limited sense of the word, I should say that a survey is never research—it is exploration; it seeks to define problems rather than to test hypotheses."[22] In order to arrive by scientific methods at remedies for defects in the administrative system it is necessary to supplement this crime survey by intensive comparisons of effects of various policies.

[22] Introduction to Emory S. Bogardus, *The New Social Research*, p. 14.

SECTION VIII

ATTEMPTS TO DETERMINE RELATIONS AMONG MEASURED BUT EXPERIMENTALLY UNCONTROLLED FACTORS

INTERRELATIONS OF STATISTICAL AND CASE METHODS: STUDIES OF YOUNG DELINQUENTS BY JOHN SLAWSON AND CYRIL BURT[1]

By ROBERT S. WOODWORTH
Columbia University

These studies are similar in several respects. Both are the work of psychologists, but both endeavor to take account of environmental factors, along with individual traits brought out by tests and other forms of psychological examination. Fundamental to both is the concept of multiple causation of delinquent behavior. The problem, as each of the two investigators sees it, is to bring to light the different factors in delinquency, to show how they are interrelated, and to reach some sort of estimate of their relative importance. Neither author has any idea that a single "cause of juvenile delinquency" can be discovered.

The results of the two studies are similar and in close agreement, up to a certain point. They agree in finding a considerable degree of "association" of delinquency with dull intelligence of the individual, but fully as close an association with emotional instability. And both assign about the same medium weight to "broken homes."[2]

Some findings of each author go beyond what was attempted by the other, yet without any noticeable disagreement. In regard to physical development, Slawson finds the delinquent boys just about on a par in height and weight with the general average of American boys of their respective ages; while Burt finds a slightly disproportionate number of undersized boys and girls, but also a slightly disproportionate number of oversized boys and girls, among his London delinquents. In regard to intelligence, Slawson, by the use of verbal, non-verbal, and mechani-

---

[1] John Slawson, *The Delinquent Boy* (Boston: Richard G. Badger, 1926); Cyril Burt, *The Young Delinquent* (New York: A. Appleton & Co., 1925).

[Cf. Appendix C, which contains a portion of a letter from Professor Woodworth. The comment upon Slawson's book in the last paragraph led to the present analysis. Burt's book was later added to the assignment at the suggestion of the analyst because of its comparable interest and value. The analysis was written in December, 1928, and was revised by the analyst in February, 1929.—EDITOR.]

[2] [For a criticism of the employment of such a concept as that of "broken homes" as a factor in establishing such associations as these cf. analysis 40, pp. 549–65.—EDITOR.]

cal aptitude tests, is able to show that the inferiority of the delinquent appears mostly in the verbal (or "abstract") intelligence. Burt, using educational tests in addition to intelligence tests, is able to show that delinquents, as a group, are characterized even more by educational retardation than by mental dulness. Both investigators infer from these findings that poor adaptation of the child to school is often an important fact in the history of his delinquency. Burt, besides stressing broken homes, makes special mention of defective parental discipline. The association of this factor with delinquency was, statistically, the closest of all. Burt also, besides noting the high incidence of general emotional instability among delinquents, finds a strong causative factor in the excessive strength of specific instincts, anger, sex, acquisitiveness, wandering, and assertiveness; in fact, taken all together, these overdeveloped instincts have a closer association with delinquency than any other factor except defective parental discipline.

The results of the two extensive studies, then, are in harmony; and the authors agree, further, in reserving judgment on any final evaluation of the causative factors examined. Neither of the authors regards the "associations" which he has measured as indicating the precise weights to be attached to the several factors in delinquency. There is a considerable degree of agreement between the methods of study adopted by the two investigators, though there are also some significant differences.

The guiding concepts of both Burt and Slawson—who worked in entire independence of each other, one in London and the other in New York—are very largely the same. The concept of multiple causation has already been mentioned. The notion here is much like that long adopted in medicine.[3] Under the head of etiology medicine treats of predisposing and exciting causes. A specific bacillus is the exciting cause of typhoid fever; yet the invasion of the bacillus does not produce the fever if the individual has a natural or acquired immunity. So, in studying delinquency, a certain exciting cause may seem potent; and yet it does not give rise to asocial behavior in all children where it is present. Other factors must also be operative.

Another concept common to the two authors is that of a continuous gradation between the extreme of asocial behavior and the mild degrees of naughtiness which are observed in nearly all children. The line drawn between delinquent and non-delinquent is not a true psychological distinction. Yet this cleavage is accepted by both for purposes of compari-

[3] [Cf. analysis 4 by Dr. Philip Klein.—EDITOR.]

son of those who have been classed as delinquents and those who have never been placed by social agencies within that class.

A third common concept is that of devoting attention to the offender and not to the offense. The concept, unlike the two preceding, dates back to Lombroso. The offense, the criminal act, is simply a symptom; the condition of the individual—the disease of which the crime is a symptom—is the important matter for study, both on the side of etiology and on the side of treatment.

The fourth common concept is that of treatment, in place of the concept of punishment. Punishment, in and for itself, has no interest to the scientific student; but treatment is important as a species of scientific experiment (provided the case is followed up), and also as a practical means of reclaiming the individual, if possible.

The similarity between the two studies extends beyond these guiding concepts to the techniques of investigation. Burt—occupying a position of such a nature that boys and girls were, on account of bad conduct, referred to him by magistrates, social agencies, schools and parents— gave mental examinations, applied tests, investigated home conditions, and finally compiled his studies of two hundred consecutive cases, and treated these data statistically. Slawson, while attached to the New York State Board of Charities, applied tests in four institutions for delinquent boys, to over fifteen hundred boys in all, and made use of institutional records of the boys' home conditions, etc.

Both investigators emphasize the need for a control group for comparison with the delinquent group. To discover a high incidence of a certain condition—such as the broken home—among delinquents proves nothing unless we also know the incidence of this same condition among non-delinquents. This elementary statistical requirement has often been overlooked by those who are contemptuous of statistics, with the result that misleading impressions have been accepted as having great significance.

Though both authors make use throughout of the principle of the control group, their procedure differs considerably in the management of this necessity. Slawson does not test a comparable group of non-delinquents, except for one or two limited purposes, while Burt bases nearly all his statements upon a direct comparison of his group of two hundred delinquents with a group of "four hundred non-delinquent children of the same age, of the same social class, living usually in the same street and attending the same school. Both delinquents and non-delinquents have been tested, medically inspected, and reported upon periodically by teachers and visitors, according to the same prearranged scheme" (Burt, p. 13).

In part, however, Burt compares his delinquent group with the general population as represented by the age norms of standard tests, and this is the method most used by Slawson. However, Slawson clearly recognizes the fallacy that may lie concealed in a simple comparison of the delinquent with the general population, in respect to intelligence, for example. The delinquent group does indeed give a decidedly lower average than the general norm, but Slawson urges that account needs to be taken of the social class from which the delinquent group is recruited, since it is now well established that the lower the social (or occupational) class of the fathers, the lower is the average intelligence of their children. Slawson, therefore, seeks to compare his delinquents with non-delinquent averages representing the same range of paternal occupation, and consequently reaches the conclusion that there is only a slight inferiority of the delinquent group when thus compared; from this he infers that low intelligence, apart from social status, is only a minor factor in delinquency. This mode of treatment, of course, does not reveal whether low social status operates simply as an environmental factor or is itself the result of low parental intelligence, and thus an index of low native intelligence of the children; but it does show that the two factors, intelligence and social status, have to be considered together with relation to the cause of delinquent behavior.

Burt, having a compact control group from which all the data are at hand for comparison with his delinquent group, is able to carry his comparisons farther and show the interrelations of different factors in more detail.

The chief difference in method between the two investigators is one of crucial importance, and hangs upon the question: Can a careful study of the individual case reveal the causation of that individual's delinquency? Burt, following Healy and others, believes that it can. Though he admits that a concurrence of various apparently causative factors—such as poverty, low social status, low intelligence, defective home discipline, example of comrades—is the typical situation, yet he says (pp. 600–601):

In any given case, amid all the tangle of accessory factors, some single circumstance not infrequently stands out as the most prominent or the most influential. Often, as we have seen, it can be definitely established that the child in question showed no delinquent tendencies until the year of some unfortunate event. An illness, a new demoralizing friendship, the death or the remarriage of a parent, the emergence within the growing child himself of some fresh interest or instinct—some dated crisis of this kind has often ascertainably preceded, and perhaps has plainly precipitated, his first violation of the law. At times, and with the same abruptness, so soon as the untoward condition has been removed, his perversity has diminished and his outbreaks have ceased. In other instances, some salient quality of the child's own mind, existing from birth or inherited from his parents, goes far to explain his misconduct—a strong sex instinct, a weak and suggestible temper, or a general deficiency of common sense. In many cases, however, to look for one paramount influence is a more doubtful and precarious business; and to sift causative conditions into major and minor may be little more than an arbitrary assortment, based, it is true, on long inquiries and on many consultations, but of value only for a rough and summary review.

Burt counts up from his case studies "more than one hundred and seventy distinct conditions . . . . every one of them conducive to childish misconduct"; and of these as many as seventy different conditions formed "in one instance or another the principal reason for some child's offence."

In sharp contrast with this procedure of Burt, Slawson argues that only objective facts, as free as possible from the subjective evaluation of the psychologist who examines the individual, are worthy of consideration in a study of causal factors and their relative potency. He writes (pp. 5–6):

In this connection it is appropriate to compare the relative merits of the case study method used widely by psychiatrists and workers with delinquents, which we did not employ, and the statistical method utilized in this study. With the former method, by which each case is individually analyzed, both objective and subjective factors are investigated, and the verdict as to antecedent factors responsible for the anti-social behavior is based largely upon the expert judgment of the psychiatrist or physician, who bases his diagnosis upon an estimate of the relative strengths of the symptoms (constitutional or environmental) discerned. Although the utilization of this method is commendable when used by expert diagnosticians for individual dispositions, it is inapplicable for the determination of causal relations or the contributory strengths of factors to delinquency, when the latter is considered as a general problem. . . . . The attribution of causal significance in any given case to the apparent detection of a conspicuous element in the life history or constitutional makeup of a delinquent boy is an act in gross disharmony with scientific procedure and logical methodology. And such errors are inherent in the case study method when used to determine etiological potency.

Slawson's strictures are less applicable to Burt's procedure than to that of most students who use the case-study method, partly because of the thoroughness of Burt's case studies, but chiefly because of his control group. As the control group was studied by the same examiner, the subjective evaluating element is more nearly equal than would otherwise be possible. Still, by Burt's own admissions, the majority of cases show such an interlacing of apparently causative factors that even the expert is unable to point to the major factor with any assurance. Where treatment consists in removing the apparently major factor and is followed by prompt cessation of delinquent conduct, there we have almost an experimental demonstration of the previous potency of the factor in question. But such a case is decidedly the exception.

For the present, judgment must be reserved between those students who insist that only careful causal analysis of the individual delinquent is going to throw light on the problems of delinquency, and those other students who insist that causal relations cannot be traced in the individual case; that, on the contrary, they are to be found only by study of relative incidence and correlations, and by other varieties of the comparative and statistical method.

HYPOTHESES AND VERIFICATIONS IN CLIFFORD R. SHAW'S STUDIES OF JUVENILE DELINQUENCY[1]

By STUART A. RICE

University of Pennsylvania

METHODOLOGICAL ELEMENTS TO BE CONSIDERED IN THIS ANALYSIS

The following methodological elements in the author's work will be singled out for special attention: (*a*) the development of hypotheses from observations and inferences during the author's "experience" as a probation officer; (*b*) the hypothesis of "diffusion" and its empirical value in prediction; (*c*) the statistical verification of certain hypotheses; (*d*) the effects of certain sociological concepts in directing attention, in selecting factual evidence, and in interpreting results; (*e*) the immediate relation of "case method" and "statistical method"; (*f*) the function of "life-history documents" in "case method"; (*g*) case method and statistical method in relation to the author's more general objectives and concepts; (*h*) the telic element as a selective factor.

THE DEVELOPMENT OF HYPOTHESES

Emergence of problems.—How did it come about that the author undertook the particular studies in which he is engaged? If the explanation were complete, it would include many complex considerations beyond the scope of the present analysis. We cannot here, for example, pay attention to the development of his interests during childhood and youth.[2]

The analysis begins with the author's graduate work at the University of Chicago. Here he first became interested in juvenile delinquency, as a

---

[1] At the time this analysis was written, in the spring of 1928, very little was in print concerning Dr. Shaw's work. The paper is based primarily, therefore, upon unpublished materials, observations of the author's procedure, and conferences with him. The following reference to printed work was available: "Correlation of Rate of Juvenile Delinquency with Certain Indices of Community Organization and Disorganization," *Papers and Proceedings of the American Sociological Society*, XXII (1927), 174–79. Available also were manuscript and research materials for *Delinquency Areas* (Chicago: University of Chicago Press, 1929; pp. xxi+214). In preparation for publication was *The Jack-Roller: A Delinquent Boy's Own Story* (Chicago: University of Chicago Press, 1930). Dr. Shaw is Research Sociologist at the Institute for Juvenile Research, Chicago. His work receives additional attention in analysis 37.

[2] As in the important description by Professor Wesley Mitchell appended to Clark's interpretation of Mitchell's methods, analysis 47, pp. 673–80.

result of courses offered by Professor Ernest W. Burgess. It was customary for graduate students of sociology to engage in specific activities,
related to the problems discussed in the classroom, which might also provide material for use in the preparation of theses. Hence, the author
procured work as a probation officer in the city courts, and thus took the
first step in his professional career. An attempt will be made below to
isolate from his experience some definable elements antecedent to his
subsequent inquiries.

It is obvious that an awareness of problems must precede the formulation of hypotheses, just as the latter must precede, logically at least, efforts
at verification. The problems engaging the author's attention grew out
of his practical day-by-day activities. The work itself required the constant formulation and the solution of problems concerning sequences of
experience and behavior in the life of *individual* delinquent boys. That
is, it required in each limited situation processes of observation, inferences, a recognition of inferences as hypotheses, and their verification.
Among the problems concerning individuals, the author, by a process of
abstraction amounting to definition, became aware of certain common
features, and thus of certain more general problems. These in turn led
to more general hypotheses and efforts at verification. Generalizations,
furthermore, were subject to constant modification as a result of the influence of new particulars arising from the daily work.

The comparative method.—If there had been any selection in the types
of cases investigated by the author, his observations and inferences would
necessarily have been biased. But he was at different times assigned to
various sections of the city. Habits and characteristics of different parts
of the population came to his attention. That is, he was safeguarded from
the influence of factors which might have been associated with single
districts. What is sometimes called the "comparative method" was thus
involved prior to the formulation of more general hypotheses and their
verifications. The term "comparative method" has little meaning in this
connection except in the sense that it connotes abstraction by the investigator from a wider variety of particular situations. Moreover, it is clear
that during this early period the distinction between "observation," "inference," and "formulation of hypothesis" was obscure. Hypotheses tended
to appear in consciousness as sudden flashes of illumination, or "hunches."
Several of these "hunches" will presently be described.

Initial concepts as determinants of evidence.—Confronted with evidence
concerning a particular delinquent, the author consciously or unconsciously sought among the apparent factors in the case one or more

which seemed to have causal significance. But his *concepts* concerning the causation of delinquency predetermined the factors which received attention. These concepts were those commonly accepted by social workers, sociologists, and others at that time. For example, Shaw relates that among the factors involved in one case was the separation of the delinquent's parents. He immediately classified this in his mind as "a broken-home case." That is, the factor "broken-home" was interpreted as the *cause* of the boy's delinquency. It was customary at this period to assume, by naïve a priori inference, that a "broken home" *would tend* to produce delinquency. When this condition appeared as a factor it was seized upon as an explanation. To put the matter in another way, among the many factors which might have received attention, this one stood out as *evidence*, to the neglect of others. Thus an a priori judgment—a common assumption—determined in advance the character of the data which were to provide the foundation for further inferences. Then how were the commonly accepted and naïve explanations replaced by new hypotheses?

The answer is that older explanations were found inconsistent or inadequate by inductive tests.—An illustration of the manner in which the author revised his explanatory concepts is given by him as follows: In a certain family there were two brothers whose ages did not greatly differ. One was delinquent, the other not. The social worker who interviewed the delinquent boy diagnosed the delinquency of the first as "a case of bad companions." When a thorough case study of the family and its social environment was made, it was discovered that the brothers had the same companions. Moreover, the author points out, they lived in the same family, had the same immediate heredity, and shared the same community environment. Hence the causal explanation first assigned appeared deficient. Other traditional explanations had similarly to be abandoned when an effort was made to apply them to individual cases of delinquency. It is clear that *the logical methods of difference and agreement,* unconsciously applied, were the instruments by means of which the abandonment occurred.

An important point in this connection concerns the author's mental training. This included university courses in several of the natural sciences and two years of work in medicine, in addition to work in the social sciences previously mentioned. Presumably because of mental attitudes established in connection with these courses he habitually sought "controls" (in the experimental sense) prior to formal attempts at drawing inferences.

How are "hunches" obtained?—This is a psychological question concerning which there has been much speculation. While the author's "moments of illumination" have appeared to be of an "intuitive" or non-rational character, he believes that the ideas so obtained actually represent inductive logical judgments. Their nature is obscure only because the induction takes place quickly, because the steps are not formulated overtly, and because only the result receives conscious attention. Such judgments grow out of intimate familiarity with complex situations. But "familiarity" includes the dim perception and weighting of factors which receive no verbal formulation or conscious appraisal but which are nevertheless employed inductively or deductively in thought. If this interpretation be correct, "hunches" should be "good" or "bad" according to the relative soundness of the individual's habitual reflective processes.

Several of the author's observations and "hunches" during the period of his employment as a probation officer will now be described:

1. *Cases of delinquency tend to be concentrated in small areas.*—This was the first tentative generalization derived from the observation of factors in numerous individual delinquencies. It seemed to hold within each of the districts in which the author worked. It became a hypothesis which he attempted to verify by means discussed below.

2. *Networks of relationship.*—In interviewing delinquent boys the author became impressed with the manner in which the individuals involved were interrelated. That is, in talking to one, he obtained the names of others, and so on. An initial interview with one boy gave him eventually the names of more than two hundred and sixty others, all delinquent, and all directly or indirectly related in their delinquency to the first. Their delinquencies covered a period of twenty years.

3. *The common factor among interrelated delinquencies.*—In a few such networks of relationship there appeared to be an immediate common origin in a single individual progenitor. For example, the author at various times interviewed five boys in a South Side neighborhood who were separately charged with shoplifting. In each case a sixth boy appeared to have been the incitant. This boy's history was traced to a Southwest Side neighborhood, and from there to a Near West Side neighborhood where he had been a member of a shoplifting gang. More frequently delinquencies could be traced back to a common area or neighborhood or gang rather than to a single individual.

4. *Delinquency is specific rather than general.*—It was observed that delinquent behavior tended to conform to typical patterns of specific character. It did not usually include a variety of delinquencies or represent tendencies toward delinquency in general.

5. *Localization of types of offenses.*—It was observed that the residences of boys charged with particular types of delinquencies were concentrated in small areas. That is, the concentrations previously noticed were each based upon a single type of offense. There were little "shoplifting" areas, little "jack-rolling"[3] areas, little areas of homosexual perversion, etc.

6. *Importance of the total situation.*—It was observed that the customary *simple* explanations of delinquent behavior had little meaning except when they were related to a total situation. As already suggested, an explanatory principle such as a "broken home" may appear to be a satisfactory explanation in one case but may not "work" (i.e., may not reconcile the facts) in another case. For example, if two delinquent boys are being reared by a step-parent, the situation of one may still be totally different from that of the other. The step-parent has one meaning for one boy and another meaning for the other boy. The existence of the step-parent as a factor cannot be regarded as a simple cause of the delinquency, for it is related to a complex of factors in a complicated situation. It is even possible that a step-parent may be of more aid than a natural parent in assisting a child to make his adjustments. The important factors are attitudes, any pattern of which may or may not be involved in particular instances of the broken-home or step-parent complex. Nor can attitudes themselves be readily classified as delinquent-producing, or non-delinquent-producing.

For example: Undernourishment and slight stature have often been naïvely regarded as "causes" of delinquency. On the surface this explanation seemed to fit the case of "Benny": When Benny was about ten years of age, he accompanied a gang of boys who were planning to rob a butcher-shop. Unexpectedly, the door which they wished to enter was locked and Benny was the only boy small enough to be pushed through the transom. In a playful mood, the older boys gave him a loaded revolver. This was the proudest moment of his life and gave delineation to his delinquent career. Thus the important factor antecedent to delinquency in this case was neither "undernourishment" nor "slight stature." It was rather this complex situation: boy in gang with certain set of group values and attitudes; attempt to rob butcher-shop; door unexpectedly found locked; only member of gang sufficiently small to enter through transom; ego enhanced by praise and award of loaded revolver by older boys; variety of other factors and sequences not stated.

The term "total situation" and its attendant concepts have been made

[3] Cf. *infra*, p. 556.

generally familiar by the *Gestalt* school of psychologists,[4] by the sociological writings of Miss Mary Follett and others, and they have been much used at the University of Chicago. Neither the term nor the theoretical concepts were familiar to the author at the time the observations and the inferences here discussed were made. They were later encountered in the classroom and appropriated to reinforce and define his own empirical hypotheses and conclusions.

HYPOTHESIS OF "DIFFUSION"

Among hypotheses developed by the author from early observations and inferences, some of which have been sketched in preceding paragraphs, one has been of particular value in reconciling evidence, and for explanation and prediction. While it was not so termed in his own thinking, it may be designated by an expression borrowed from the field of cultural anthropology and called the "diffusion" of delinquent habit patterns. The development of this hypothesis illustrates again the logical methods by which naïve, "common-sense" explanations of behavior have been replaced by newer concepts. This hypothesis will be discussed in connection with a particular delinquency pattern, that of stealing.

From an investigation of many cases of boys charged with theft, and a segregation from each of the factors involved, the author came to the inductive inference that the behavior had two distinctive types of origin. In some instances the boy had begun as a very small child to appropriate, without restrictions, whatever suited his fancy. The parents regarded the child's conduct as normal at his age. At a certain point in the boy's development, sometimes as a result of a particular incident embarrassing to the parents, this habitual behavior came to be regarded as stealing. Unable to change his habits immediately, the boy was presently regarded as a delinquent. In a larger number of cases, however, it was found that the boy had learned to steal from other boys. The first type of origin is largely a matter of definitions, while the second involves the transmission in a child group of a social pattern of behavior.

It would be expected in accordance with these inferences that instances of stealing having the first type of origin would be scattered generally over the city; and that there would be small concentrated areas of stealing having the second type of origin. Both of these situations were found. New cases of stealing usually occurred within these concentrated areas.

It is impossible to say whether the author's observations and inferences —his inductive thought processes—followed the precise sequences indi-

---

[4] Cf., as to the theoretical bases of this school, the interpretation by R. M. Ogden of *Structural Psychology and the Psychology of Gestalt*, analysis 5, pp. 109–117.

cated in the two preceding paragraphs. It is more probable that the various problems involved were approached simultaneously, or alternately, in a variety of ways. For example, at a particular time he attempted to discover the community factors in the causation of delinquency. The logical ideas then involved were somewhat as follows: The localization of delinquency is evidently related to its causation. What, then, are the factors in the localized areas that will account for the delinquencies? Are there common elements of race or nationality, common conditions of housing, a common absence of educational or other cultural advantages, or common elements of low economic status *within* a given delinquency area, and, conversely, the absence or the presence of any such factor in the low delinquency areas surrounding it? If so, by the logical *methods of agreement and difference,* the causal significance of such a factor would be suggested. The answer was negative, within the range of the author's observation. Hence he was compelled to conclude that factors of the type suggested were not of primary importance in the situation.

Another type of observed fact had an important part in both of the sequences of reasoning just described: New cases of delinquency frequently appeared which seemed to be "out of their expected setting" with respect to such delinquency areas and in which (in the case of stealing) the "childhood habit" explanation was ruled out by the evidence. In one example, a boy who lived seven or eight miles from the Loop (where stealing is most prevalent) was arrested for shoplifting. The physical, psychiatric, and psychological findings and the history of childhood showed nothing abnormal which might be presumed to have relationship to the boy's conduct. There was nothing in the character of the neighborhood to suggest an explanation, nor were there precedents within it for the boy's behavior. Investigation then disclosed that the family had removed at an earlier time from an area in another section of the city in which shoplifting among boys of this age was common.

To summarize: observations and other evidences accumulated; tentative hypotheses were set up in accordance with prevailing conceptions to explain these evidences; informal attempts at verification of hypotheses resulted in the discredit of some of them, together with the conceptions upon which they were based; the *hypothesis of diffusion* emerged as the most serviceable explanatory concept yet formulated. It reconciles, among others, the following facts and evidences otherwise inconsistent: the localization of types of delinquency; the absence of common environmental factors in the areas of localization, not appearing elsewhere, which would account for the delinquency therein; the persistence of delinquency areas in spite of changes in the racial, nationality, or religious composition of their populations; the personal transmission of delinquent habit patterns from a delinquency area to a non-delinquency area, and their propagation in the latter, thereby tending to create a new delinquency area; the evidence that environmental factors may be favorable or non-favorable to, but not determinative of, delinquent habits in a juvenile population.

The hypothesis itself may be described as follows: Delinquency among boys usually consists of group behavior, the pattern of which is learned by the individual delinquent. This behavior meets social approval within the juvenile group, and is considered delinquent only if it meets disapproval from the larger social group of which the former is a part. Habits of delinquent behavior may be retained even in a new social environment. Particularly if reinforced by personal qualities which give the possessor of the habits prestige in the new environment, they may be acquired through emulation and imitation by still other individuals, to whom the traits are thereby "diffused."

The opportunity for "diffusion" is most typically presented under three circumstances: (1) When boys within a delinquency area come in contact with boys from outside of the area at its fringe. Numerous special factors determining the direction and the character of these contacts will condition the diffusion process in this instance. (2) When the family of a delinquent boy moves to a non-delinquent area. (3) When boys are in contact within correctional institutions, where delinquent patterns of various types are exchanged as well as reinforced.

In natural science the verification of a hypothesis is usually found in its utility for *prediction*. This test has been applied by the author in the follows instance: In an area on West Madison Street, the juvenile practice of "jack-rolling," or attacking and robbing drunken men, was common. Assuming that the process of diffusion would be operative, the author "had a hunch" (predicted) that in a certain Italian area adjacent, not visited for some years, he would now find the practice of "jack-rolling" where it had not hitherto existed. He again visited this second area, and immediately witnessed boys leaving the school playground to hold up (jack-roll) a drunken man. It is of interest that the trait in this instance had been diffused across lines of nationality, but had been somewhat altered in the process. That is, the Italian boys would not jack-roll a man of their own nationality although no such restriction prevailed in the area of presumed origin on Madison Street. It is of interest, likewise, that the parents of some of the boys involved were also witnesses of the particular incident observed by the author. The approval or the disapproval of parents is another factor of which account must be taken, but which is not, however, inconsistent with the hypothesis.

In another way the hypothesis has demonstrated its utility for purposes of prediction. It has given to the author and to others who have employed his findings a *clue* to the probable existence in individual cases of important factors which might otherwise be overlooked. For example, parents themselves are frequently aware of the importance of the conduct patterns in particular areas in determining their children's behavior. They move to avoid these. The child's readjustment to the new environment is not immediately made. Hence his behavior may continue to be delinquent while the parents endeavor to conceal its origin. Without the clue given by the hypothesis in such instances, the investigator would be at a loss to discover the more important factors in the situation, which may be complicated by a resulting estrangement between the child and the parents.

STATISTICAL VERIFICATION OF CERTAIN HYPOTHESES

The first formal method used by the author to verify any of his hypotheses was the preparation of "spot maps." This method had been employed extensively by Professor Ernest W. Burgess, and was taken over from him. An opportunity was presented to Shaw in 1923 to ascertain whether the tendency toward *concentration* of delinquency, that had been observed in particular districts, prevailed over the entire city. At that time he entered his present position and gave first attention to the city-wide mode of distribution. The residences of all boys between ten and sixteen years of age who were brought into police stations on complaints of delinquency during the preceding year were shown by dots on a city map. Obvious concentrations of cases appeared, in particular in the areas immediately surrounding the Loop. In general there was progressive diminution in the number of cases as the distance from the Loop increased. However, there were concentrations in certain industrial areas at a distance from the Loop, particularly in the Stock Yards, in the South Chicago steel-mill district, and in the Lake Calumet industrial region.

Although adding to the author's confidence that the hypothesis would be verified, the spot map did not provide a safe basis for conclusions because of inequalities in the distribution of the population itself. When census material became available *rates* of delinquency were calculated. Two series of geographic units were employed in these calculations: first, arbitrary square-mile areas into which the city as a whole was divided; second, census enumeration districts, approximately one-quarter of a square mile each in extent. The rates applied to individuals, not to complaints, and duplications were eliminated. In the areas immediately surrounding the Loop the rates varied between 20 per cent and 30 per cent. That is, between one-fifth and three-tenths of all boys resident in these areas were charged with delinquency during the year. The rate was at a minimum of 0.2 per cent in one of the more distant areas upon the so-called Gold Coast.

Having calculated rates of delinquency, and having observed the concentric manner in which rates appear to decline with distance from the Loop as a focus, a series of "radials" were drawn upon a map outward from the Loop in various directions. The delinquency rate within each unit area crossed was noted on the radial. This was another graphic device (the spot map being the first) for emphasizing the form of the distribution. The concept involved at this point will be discussed in the next section.

The author next proceeded to calculate coefficients of correlation between the rate of delinquency and various others which might be assumed to have direct or indirect relationship with it. For the same unit areas, rates relating to family dependency were calculated in three series, each being correlated with delinquency. When square miles were used as geographical units the correlation coefficients for the three pairs of series were each positive and in excess of 0.60. The same was true of the correlation between delinquency and the percentage of foreign-born. However, when the rates for enumeration districts were correlated, the coefficients were diminished in magnitude. This seems contrary to expectation if it is assumed that a genuine causal nexus exists between the factors. But such an assumption, so far as it concerns the causation of delinquency, is of the "common-sense" or naïve type already found to be inadequate for explanation in the course of the author's detailed experience. The fact that lower correlations between delinquency and dependency are found when smaller unit areas are employed as bases for rates seems to support the inductive inference already suggested that greater specificity in the definition and correlation of factors such as these is desirable. In other words, the author's correlations are not so much between pairs of factors as between pairs of aggregates or complexes of factors. On the other hand, the fairly high coefficients obtained appear to support the view that certain areas are simultaneously hospitable to the development of dependency and to the reception of habit patterns of delinquency.

The author's graphic comparisons and statistical calculations have been kept in close relationship, on the one hand, to his data, and on the other, to certain sociological conceptions which have guided the direction of attention. His statistical correlations have meaning to the author in terms of particular situations with which he is intimately familiar. That is, they provide a certain shorthand quantitative expression for relationships concerning the nature of which the author had already reached definite and convincing conclusions. Statistical method was thus employed in a confirmatory rather than in an exploratory manner.

THE PART PLAYED BY CERTAIN SOCIOLOGICAL CONCEPTS

The interaction between the data and certain sociological concepts can be clearly traced in at least one instance: Having made a graphic distribution of delinquencies upon a spot map, and having calculated rates which indicated concentration around the Loop, with diminishing incidence outward therefrom, the author was on the alert to obtain a concept in terms of which this concentric distribution pattern might be explained. At about this time Professor C. M. Child, of the University of Chicago, a biologist, addressed the Social Research Society, a local University organization. He discussed his hypotheses concerning the importance of "gradients" in the development and control of the biological organism.[5] Professor Robert E. Park, a sociologist, remarked that there were analogous gradients in the *city*.[6] The notion that gradients might be found in the city as well as in the individual organism seemed to be in harmony with an idea previously developed by Professor Ernest W. Burgess concerning the development, typically, in a growing city of "zones" or "natural areas" of defined character. These would "normally" be of concentric character.[7]

The author attended the meeting addressed by Professor Child. After further discussion with Park and Burgess, he took over the concept of gradients and sought to apply it to the delinquency rates which he had calculated for the city of Chicago. This was responsible for his map of "radials," and for certain statistical correlations related thereto. Whether the newer concept of "gradients" was more than a new name for the earlier concept of "zones" seems doubtful. The data are in accord with the expectation which the Park-Burgess theory of zones would call for, and seem to require at present no further explanatory concept, such as is implied

[5] These hypotheses, carried over from the biological to the social realm, are presented by Child in "Biological Foundations of Social Integration," *Papers and Proceedings of the American Sociological Society*, XXII (1928), 26–42.

[6] Park's subsequent reflections upon this notion are presented in a 1927 bulletin of the Social Research Society.

[7] Cf. E. W. Burgess, "The Growth of the City: An Introduction to a Research Project," *Papers and Proceedings of the American Sociological Society*, XVIII (1923), 85–97.

in the use of the biological term "gradient." Moreover, as used by Child, the term "gradient" refers to a mode of biological *control* exercised over the growth and the functions of certain parts of the body by other parts. The analogue of such control seems lacking in the present connection. It is clear, however, that Child's address and the discussion following gave direction to the author's attention. He had not hitherto given particular attention to the so-called radial tendencies appearing in the data, or to their possible sociological meanings.

THE USE OF STATISTICAL RESULTS IN CASE STUDIES

The author does not regard his statistical studies and findings as ends in themselves. They would not have been undertaken except for the belief that they might contribute to the better understanding of individual boys. From this immediate standpoint, therefore, statistical method as used by Dr. Shaw is subordinate to case method.[8] His observations and inferences suggested the great importance, in shaping habits and directing individual behavior, of social patterns and social norms. The character and the distribution of the latter can best be described with the aid of statistical analysis and summarization.

A "community analysis chart" will exhibit for all unit areas in the city various series of rates, each of which will serve as an index of one or more of the social patterns impinging upon the individual boy. These rates may be incorporated in the individual case record of a delinquent in the same manner, and employed for the same general purpose, as data concerning the boy's physical history or intelligence quotient. These community data have been hitherto unavailable to court officers except in the form of vague and inaccurate verbal appraisals. Attention has necessarily been focused by individual officers and social workers upon the individual rather than upon the community in which he resides. The rates in the community analysis chart are derived from a variety of current census reports, commercial indexes, and city records. They relate, in addition to juvenile delinquency, to Boys' Court cases (seventeen to twenty-one years inclusive), truants, and adult criminals.

The practical utility of the "community analysis chart" is readily apparent. If, for example, a boy is charged with stealing from a railroad box car, the social diagnosis and the judicial disposition of his case may both be modified if it is learned that he resides in an area in which conduct of this kind bears no stigma of social disapproval, as evidenced by the various rates and collateral evidences that have been assembled.

[8] Cf. analysis 39.

THE "LIFE-HISTORY DOCUMENT" AND ITS FUNCTION[9]

All of the author's observations, inferences, and verifications have tended to show the complexity of problems of human behavior, and the dangers of oversimplification in attempts to interpret or explain them. Moreover, his work has shown what in ordinary terms may be called the "subjective" character of the important factors. Objective factors have been found important only in relation to *meanings* placed upon them by individuals. It is evident that no manipulation of objective factors, quantitative or otherwise, will wholly disclose these meanings. An important question facing the author, therefore, has concerned the most efficient manner of ascertaining the subjective attitudes and meanings behind the more tangible evidences.

The traditional method of conducting such a search has been the *interview*. Answers are elicited from a subject to queries propounded by a questioner. Questions may be formal and stereotyped, or may depend upon the prior answers given. In any event, they tend to be directed by governing concepts concerning the probable value for explanation of the factors about which the subject is questioned. The subject, taking an explanatory cue from the questioner, is likely to be influenced. A defect of the interview for the purposes of fact-finding in scientific research, then, is that the questioner *takes the lead*. That is, the subject plays a more or less passive rôle. Information or points of view of the highest value may not be disclosed because the direction given the interview by the questioner leads away from them. In short, data obtained from an interview are as likely to embody the preconceived ideas of the interviewer as the attitudes of the subject interviewed.[10]

While the pertinency of this criticism depends to no small degree upon the skill of the questioner, a technique which by its very form would enable the subject to take an active rather than a passive rôle in the inquiry would be a useful supplement to the traditional interview. Some aspects of such a technique have been developed in the course of clinical experience by psychoanalysts. Another opportunity for the subject to play an active rôle is presented by the so-called life-history document. The purpose here is to note the general character of the life-history document and

[9] Cf. Shaw, *The Jack-Roller: A Delinquent Boy's Own Story*; Part II and the appendix of Young's analysis of Thrasher's *The Gang*, analysis 37, especially "Social Psychological Analysis" (pp. 523–24); Park's analysis of Thomas' and Znaniecki's *The Polish Peasant*, analysis 8. House's analysis 36 has especial relevancy to this section.

[10] Cf. Stuart A. Rice, "Contagious Bias in the Interview," *American Journal of Sociology*, XXXV (November, 1929), 420–23.

its relation to other methodological elements involved in the author's work, in particular to case method.

The life-history document is described essentially by its name. It consists of a detailed narrative by the subject himself and in his own language, of his history, experiences, and attitudes. If it is a sincere account, it will necessarily portray those elements and factors in his situation upon which he himself has placed the highest importance. Not to be taken literally in its explanatory efforts, it will nevertheless exhibit causal sequences in the mental life of the individual which might not be detected in the organized interview. By its exhaustive character it presumes to show his life in its historical development as well as in its social setting at each stage.

It portrays the individual's own conception of his rôle in society. It is obvious that such a document is of a lower order of generality than a case study of the same individual by the investigator. The former is essentially a part of the material employed for the purpose of the latter.

The relationship between a life-history document and a comprehensive case study is illustrated by the author's monograph devoted to a single delinquent boy. As outlined in manuscript, the first chapter upon "Behavior Difficulties" includes a résumé of official records of arrest, work records obtained from employers, and a statement of personality difficulties disclosed by the evidence. The second chapter contains an analysis of the community life surrounding the boy, his family contacts, and his relationships with other boys, play groups, and gangs. The author profits here from the concepts and findings of such other investigators as Healy and Bronner (cf. analysis 36) and Thrasher (cf. analysis 37). The third chapter presents a study of the medical, the psychiatric, and the psychological findings. The ten chapters which follow contain the life-history document proper. A final chapter presents the author's summary analysis of the case, including a synthesis of all of the evidence as related to the totality of the boy's life.

It is not to be supposed that the individual's own story should always be given the same importance which it receives in this outline. The methodological point to be observed is the subordinate part played by the life-history document to "case method" so called. Case method represents no precise steps of procedure. It stands rather for an effort to secure all possible data concerning a single unit of inquiry and to obtain from these data a unified, coherent concept concerning the part played by a variety of influences in determining the character and the experiences of this unit in its existence as a whole.

CASE METHOD, STATISTICAL METHOD, AND THE AUTHOR'S MAIN OBJECTIVES

It could be inferred from what has been said that the ultimate scientific form of the author's work is to be a more thoroughgoing type of case study. This is, indeed, the expectation of some persons engaged in comparable research by the use of comparable methods. Certain groups of social scientists have been contrasted by the statement that one exemplifies the use of statistical method while the other upholds the use of case methods. In such a comparison, Shaw would doubtless be classified with the exemplars of case method. The statement itself implies divergence between the objectives of the groups compared.

The author, however, would object to being classified within either of the categories mentioned, as he would also object to the principle of the classification itself. He feels the need of no such distinction in method or objectives with respect to his own research problems. He views his methodological procedure as an alternation, without defined termination, of case method and statistical method. He began with case study, which seems to be a necessary preliminary to statistical procedure. That is, before units can be counted they must first be identified, and identification is a process more and more equivalent to case study as the units become more complex. In the author's work, for example, before any statistical summaries of delinquency were made, it was first necessary to determine whether or not each individual boy was or was not a delinquent. This involved a collection of evidence by court officials and others concerning each boy, both as to the offense charged and his responsibility therefor. To determine responsibility and other related questions, study was made of the personality and the environmental factors in the boy's life.

With the accumulation of a number of such case studies, it became possible to abstract from each study certain factors which could then be given statistical treatment. As pointed out above, the results of the statistical inquiries are being utilized to throw further light upon the case studies. Nor does the process end here. The author conceives it to be possible and probable that the more extensive and elaborate case studies now being made, including the boys' own stories embodied in life-history documents, will again be the basis of further statistical analysis. With the accumulation of a sufficient number of case studies of the more elaborate type, it will again be possible to abstract certain factors, patterns, complexes, behavior sequences or relationships, which can presently be summarized by statistical means; and among which, it may be anticipated, certain regularities and modalities will appear.

To summarize, the author views case procedure and statistical procedure as interacting tools of analysis, alternating in the emphasis placed upon them by the investigator of phenomena, but never wholly unrelated to each other. They do not represent opposing, contrasting, or even alternative methods of securing truth; but rather supplementary and mutually consistent processes.

THE TELIC ELEMENT AS A SELECTIVE FACTOR

The teleological element frequently found in "social science" appears in a typical manner in the work here analyzed. The problems to which the author devoted his attention arose in the course of telic endeavor. That is, the desire to prevent delinquency and to change the behavior of boys now delinquent was the presumptive social *raison d'être* of his activities. In order to accomplish these and other humanistic aims more adequately, additional knowledge of the nature of delinquency, and of the processes involved in its causation, became necessary. The ultimate purposes for which the results of his inquiries would be used were thus replaced in the author's individual interests by more immediate aims of a scientific and factual character. It is unknown and irrelevant to what extent interest in the latter has been or is shared in the author's mind with telic interests of the more ultimate character. He himself would doubtless be unable to say. There is general agreement with the view that the two interests, if both exist, should not be allowed to interact in such a way as to affect the actual procedure employed in a given inquiry. Moreover, when once engaged upon the scientific study of relationships, any desire for the discovery or demonstration of particular kinds of relationships should be rigidly restrained or set aside.

The telic character of the ultimate objectives of his work, whether they exist in the mind of the author himself or whether they remain among the purposes of those who are responsible for his project, do not appear, however, to render that work less scientific. It seems probable that all scientific inquiry, whether in the physical or in the social sciences, has a telic origin, and is never wholly divorced from its possible utilization for practical ends. Nor does it seem possible for either the natural scientist or the social scientist to be altogether *disinterested* in the particular outcome of his inquiries. Without such an interest, much or all of the "drive" necessary for prolonged scientific effort would be lacking. It seems, rather, that he should be more interested in obtaining an unbiased outcome than in obtaining any particular outcome. There is every evidence that the author has been motivated in his work by the same "scientific disinterestedness" (in the paradoxical sense just noted) that would be felt by a scrupulous scientist or scholar in any other field. The influence of telic elements, if it exists, is to be found in connection with factors immediately involved. For instance, there might have been a hiatus between the purely scientific objectives of the author and the immediate telic interests of persons who collected the data which he has been compelled to use. The author has been unable to reach a personal decision concerning the applicability of the term "delinquent" to all of the boys involved in his statistical summarizations. These summarizations have rested, on the contrary, upon definitions in the minds of a large number of persons, and still more remotely, at least in part, upon telic interests which they may have in view.

Again, the immediate requirements for data which will comport with a given routine court procedure, or which will support a particular policy toward a case in hand, may limit or predetermine the types of data secured. These may not be the data which are most essential for the author's scientific inquiries. Selective influences of this character may play a rôle in the author's work similar to that of the governing conceptions within his own mind.[11]

Thus, telic interests may play a part in the selection of data, and in the selection for examination of particular questions of relationship among them. But once again, comparable instances of possible selective influence may readily be obtained from the natural sciences.

[11] This point is raised again in analysis 43 under the heading "Availability of Data as a Factor."

MATHEMATICAL TREATMENT BY DOROTHY SWAINE THOMAS OF SOCIAL DATA ARRANGED IN TIME SERIES[1]

By HUBERT R. KEMP

University of Toronto

The study here examined is an interesting example of the application of mathematical methods to sociological problems where long series of statistical data are available for analysis. It exemplifies both the merits and the limitations of the mathematical approach. That the alternations of prosperity and depression have important social consequences outside of the purely economic sphere has long been recognized. The distinctive contribution of the present research is that it contains a comprehensive survey of the British statistical evidence bearing on the problem, with similar data in many cases from the United States; an adequate uniform mathematical technique has been used for the analysis; the conclusions are stated in precise form and interpreted, in many cases, with considerable ingenuity.

The main problems dealt with may be briefly stated. On the basis of statistical observations collected in England and Wales from 1854 to 1913, the author has tried to find and measure the relations between business cycles and the more important social phenomena for which statistical measurements are available. The social phenomena thus examined include: (1) marriage, prostitution, divorce; (2) births (legitimate and illegitimate), maternal mortality, premature births; (3) crude death-rates, infant mortality, deaths from phthisis, suicides; (4) pauperism (indoor, outdoor, and casual); (5) alcoholism, as indicated by the consumption of beer and spirits, prosecutions for drunkenness, and deaths attributed to alcoholism; (6) crimes (which are classified into various groups according to the likelihood that they will be affected by economic conditions); (7) emigration.

[1] *Social Aspects of the Business Cycle.* First published in London: Routledge & Sons, 1925; printed in New York: A. A. Knopf & Co., 1927.

[Following the preparation of Professor Kemp's analysis of this work in December, 1928, and its revision by him in March, 1929, a penetrating self-analysis by the author of her own methods in making the study appeared in the *American Journal of Sociology* (cf. n. 2). Advantage has been taken of this unusual opportunity to place side by side these two analyses of the same inquiry. The relevant portions of Professor Thomas' paper are reprinted by permission as an appendix, following Professor Kemp's interpretation.—EDITOR.]

This list indicates the social importance of the inquiry, the different branches of social science which it touches, and the probability of fruitful results. In the field of vital statistics, for example, all students of population are looking for evidence to show exactly how prosperity and depression react upon the supply of population.

A few typical conclusions may be quoted. Marriage-rates showed a high positive correlation with business conditions, both in England and in America, while birth-rates showed a moderately high correlation in both countries. In England the correlation between business conditions and the marriage-rate was diminishing, while the correlation between business conditions and the birth-rate was increasing. This fact is consistent with the belief that people's reaction to economic pressure is tending more and more to take the form of voluntary limitation of the family rather than mere postponement of marriage. Illegitimacy shows a tendency to increase in times of depression (when marriage-rates are lower), and to decrease in times of prosperity. It is thus shown to be in part an economic phenomenon. In both countries a higher death-rate is found in periods of prosperity. Among the suggested explanations are: increased consumption of alcohol in prosperous times (though not all the deaths so caused are attributed in the death certificates to alcoholism); increased industrial employment of mothers; and, in the case of England, the extensive emigration of the young and vigorous members of the community during prosperous times, which has produced a less favorable age distribution and raised the crude death-rate among those who have remained behind. These tentative explanations might well be supplemented by medical research, and by further statistical research into the mortality from various specified causes. The research shows further that the correlation between crime and business depression is low, and even when the comparison is confined to the particular crime of larceny, the correlation remains surprisingly low. If the original data are reliable, it appears that hard times are only a minor factor in increasing the prevalence of crime.

The methods employed in the study have been largely borrowed from the armory of the business-cycle economists, especially Professor W. C. Mitchell and Professor W. M. Persons. Since it was desired to correlate social phenomena with the business cycle in England, it was first necessary to decide upon a statistical index to represent the typical movement of British business cycles throughout the period. Both annual and quarterly series were used. The annual series was obtained by averaging figures showing the cyclical movements of export trade, wholesale prices, unemployment (inverted), production of pig iron and coal, railway freight-traffic receipts, and provincial bank clearings. The quarterly series was based upon practically the same economic phenomena. In the choice of these series to represent the fluctuations of business in general, the author was following a well-trodden path, since these economic phenomena are generally recognized as criteria of prosperity in manufacturing and trading countries. It is also shown graphically, however, that the respective maxima and minima of these series are closely synchronized throughout the entire period; in other words, they are consistent with one another.

For isolating the cyclical fluctuations of all data employed, the author has used the method familiar to students of the Harvard Economic Service. Parabolas, mostly of the third degree, have been fitted to represent the various secular trends, which are found in practically all the social statistics under consideration. Trends have been eliminated by computing for each year the percentage deviations of the original items from the line of trend. In dealing with quarterly indices, "normal" seasonal fluctuations have been calculated by the median-link-relative method and eliminated by subtracting the quarterly indices thus obtained from the percentage deviations of original items from secular trend. The residuals thus obtained, expressed in terms of their standard deviations, have been taken to represent the cyclical fluctuations of the original data.

The indices of cyclical fluctuation for the various social phenomena were finally compared with the business-cycle indices both graphically and by means of the Pearsonian coefficient of correlation. Wherever it has seemed desirable, coefficients of correlation have been calculated for synchronous data and for lags of different lengths. Coefficients have also been calculated in the same way for various subintervals of the sixty-year period under investigation, with the result that the author has been able to show progressive changes in several of the relationships which have been discovered. The amount of arithmetic involved in the work is prodigious; but, as the author observes, optical comparisons usually confirm whatever preconceived notions the investigator may have, and the Pearsonian coefficient provides an impersonal and objective test of agreement which will give the same results in the hands of any investigator. The labor of computing the coefficients thus appears to be justified.

The practical application of the Harvard technique to so many social problems suggests some examination into the methodological problems and assumptions involved, the validity of the results obtained, and any light which the whole experiment may throw on the possibility of obtaining exact quantitative results in this field of social science. The methodological problems have to do with definition and measurement of the phenomena under investigation, analysis of the time series thus obtained, and interpretation of the results.

All statistical investigations are based upon measurement or counting, and hence the invention of valid and consistent methods of measurement and counting is of fundamental importance in both the physical and the social sciences. In the physical sciences, it is true, counting sometimes plays a subordinate part. One observation would suffice if it could be known that all disturbing influences and possible sources of error had been excluded from the experiment. Even in the social sciences, the generalizations of "common sense" are often reached from limited experience and without any conscious or unconscious balancing of statistical evidence.

Measurements in the physical sciences commonly depend upon the property of extension in space, and can be reduced to the comparison of magnitudes in space. Thus distance may be directly measured by a comparison of the length to be measured with that of the unit: weight may be measured by the position of a pointer on a scale; temperature is measured by the length of a column of mercury; the pitch of a musical note may be measured by counting the oscillations of a wavy line on a piece of smoked paper; and the strength of an electric current may be measured by the angular deflection of a needle or the rotation of a wheel. Units of physical measurement may be simple (like the foot or the pound) or complex (like the units of velocity, acceleration, and power). Physical measurements may be described as direct or indirect, the term "direct" being applied to those which involve merely a juxtaposition of two objects in space (as when we measure a distance with a foot-rule) and the term "indirect" when we measure things, not by immediate juxtaposition, but by observing other things which themselves depend upon what we are trying to measure. Such indirect measurements may be illustrated by triangulation to determine the distance between two inaccessible spots, the use of the log to determine a ship's speed, the use of the spectroscope to determine the dimensions of an atom, or the use of the barometer to determine altitude. Many of the advances of physical science have followed directly upon the invention of new units or techniques of measurement.

Inaccuracies in physical measurements may arise from impurities of the thing measured; from defects in the instruments employed, or in the motor and sense organs of the observer; and, in the case of indirect measurements, from errors in deducing the relation between the thing to be indirectly measured and the measurable thing from which its magnitude is deduced. Thus, altitude can be determined from barometric pressure only if we know the true relation between them.

Problems of measurement in the social sciences are in many ways analogous to those in the physical sciences. In the social sciences, units of measurement are more often complex than simple; thus, rates and percentages are usually more significant than absolute numbers. Measurements are more often indirect than direct. The objects, qualities, or actions in which social scientists are interested are often beyond the range of direct observation, but their presence is inferred from visible phenomena and their intensity is measured by counting or measuring the visible phenomena. It is often necessary to rely upon the counting or measuring of a sample. Much of the recent pioneer work in the social sciences has consisted in the invention of new and ingenious methods of measurement such as index numbers and scales for measuring intelligence.

In making a statistical study of the social consequences of the business cycle, it was necessary to define and measure phenomena which lent themselves to the purpose in varying degrees. The calculation of birth-, death-, and marriage-rates, though not free from pitfalls, need not be considered here. It was much more difficult to define and measure such things as prostitution, alcoholism, and crime, and even to decide upon a single index by which to measure prosperity over a long period. As the author of the study well shows, it is quite possible that the prevalence of prostitution itself is at a minimum when arrests (the visible and measurable index of it) are at a maximum. The extent of alcoholic indulgence may be fairly well judged in England by the official excise statistics: but in prohibition countries where such records would be useless, it would be necessary to deduce the fluctuations in consumption of alcohol indirectly from such data as arrests for intoxication, the number of deaths officially attributed to alcoholism, and the prevalence of alcoholic psychoses. Nobody knows how far these external evidences are correlated with alcoholism itself. For administrative purposes, it would be valuable and perhaps sufficient to be able to predict the number of arrests likely to take place in a given condition of business; but if the object of the investigation were to determine whether prohibition promoted sobriety, such indirect measurements would probably be inadequate. The prevalence of crime, like that of intemperance, can only be measured indirectly through police statistics, which may show either the number of offenses reported, the number of prosecutions, or the number of convictions. These statistics, too, are useful and valid for administrative purposes; but taken by themselves, they do not tell us whether antisocial conduct is becoming more or less prevalent. Our power of measurement of social activities or tendencies is limited to their external and visible manifestations; and this limitation restricts the scope of the questions that a social statistician may fairly be expected to answer.

If social phenomena are to be correlated with prosperity, it is necessary to decide upon an index of prosperity—or an index of the position of the business cycle, if that more noncommittal term is preferred. In the present study, use is made of a composite index based upon export trade, wholesale prices, employment, production of pig iron and coal, railway freight-traffic receipts, and provincial bank clearings. This composite index is supported by the fact that its various components are highly correlated with one another and with indices of prosperity used by other economists. The general concept of prosperity has been made familiar by many recent writings on business cycles, but it would be difficult to give a precise definition of it, and the word does not have exactly the same connotations for all who use it. For the purpose of the present study, the most precise definition would be to state that prosperity is the condition of business which exists when the composite index is above its average position. Such a definition, though not very expressive, would be adequate; and it involves no implication as to which social class is prosperous during the phase of the business cycle that is known as prosperity.

When this definition is kept in mind, the results of correlation will be interpreted with some reservation. Mathematical processes tell us the correlation between this particular index and the external evidences of alcoholic indulgence or whatever other social activity we choose to study. It does not follow that the same correlation exists between prosperity as defined by each reader and alcoholic indulgence itself, as distinguished from the number of arrests for drunkenness. This distinction is emphasized, not for the purpose of criticizing the present work, but rather as an obvious illustration of the limitations common to such studies. In interpreting results, it is necessary to bear in mind exactly what is being measured, and how the measurement is performed.

The familiar procedure which Miss Thomas has employed for isolating cyclical fluctuations from the raw data involves three steps: curves have been fitted by the method of least squares for the purpose of isolating secular trend; the median-link-relative method has been employed to determine the typical seasonal fluctuation; the residuals obtained after elimination of these two types of fluctuation are regarded as cyclical movements, and these are correlated. These three steps may be considered successively.

The method of least squares has been taken over from the physical sciences. Errors of observation due to a multiplicity of causes tend to be arranged on either side of the true reading in a certain pattern called the "normal distribution," which can be approximated by a binomial expansion or more adequately described by means of a Gaussian curve. The most probable value of the true reading is that which makes the sum of the squares of the deviations from it a minimum. This distribution of errors, and the least-squares criterion, have been deduced from the theory of probability on the hypothesis that the errors are due to a multiplicity of independent causes, without a predominance of biased errors on one side or the other. A similar distribution about a central tendency has been experimentally found in many other variables affected by a multiplicity of independent causes, as in anthropometry and even in records of temperature and precipitation over long periods. It is found in price changes from one year to the next; but, speaking generally, this type of distribution is not very common in economic variables.

In the process of curve-fitting by the method of least squares, we commence by postulating that the curve to be fitted shall be of a certain type such as a straight line, a third-degree parabola, or an exponential curve. While this introductory postulate is usually based upon ocular inspection of a scatter diagram, it assumes from the beginning the principal characteristics of the curve to be fitted. In assuming a straight line, we assume constant growth or decline; in assuming a second-degree parabola, we assume that the curve may have at most one maximum or one minimum (but not both); and in assuming an exponential curve, we assume growth or decline at a constant rate. The curve obtained in the process of fitting will necessarily have those characteristics which we have put into it. Miss Thomas states that, from a fairly wide experience in fitting trends to economic and social data, she has found that the series most often conform to the shape taken by third-degree parabolas. A third-degree parabola is a curve which may have a maximum followed by a minimum or a minimum followed by a maximum. The selection of this or any other type of curve to be fitted is arbitrary.

After a particular type of curve has been selected, the method of least squares assumes that the best formulation of the trend is a curve of this type representing the central tendency of the observations, which are supposed to be grouped about the trend in accordance with the "normal law." In other words, it is assumed that deviations from the trend are distributed in the same way as errors of observation due to a multiplicity of independent causes. Only on these assumptions can the method of least squares be justified. In using this method, the extreme deviations (which an instructed judgment might discard as unique abnormalities) are actually given the greatest weight in determining the position of the curve.

The interpretation of trend equations obtained by the method of least squares will of course be influenced by recognition of the fact that the type of curve has been taken for granted and that it has been assumed that deviations from the curve will be distributed according to the normal law. Lines of trend may be considered either as the expression of tendencies which may be used for prediction or merely as brief summaries of the movements during the period studied, useful for interpolation. In the book under discussion they are quite properly regarded in the second way. It is obvious that a curve valid for prediction cannot be fitted until we know that sufficient time has passed to disclose fully the law (if any) governing the series. Moreover, the preliminary hypothesis concerning the type of curve to be fitted determines the shape of the curve not only within the range of points fitted but also beyond that range.

The chief object in fitting a line of trend is to separate trends from cycles. In short series there is some difficulty in the separation, and the type of curve selected may be unduly influenced by the investigator's judgment as to whether a particular undulation pertains to the trend or to a cycle. For these various reasons the trend lines fitted by the method of least squares must be accepted with some reservation. Their construction is not independent of private judgment, and they cannot be taken at more than face value.

The median-link-relative method of isolating typical seasonal fluctuation, while probably as good as any other method of attaining the same object that could have been employed, makes the assumption that seasonal fluctuations of social phenomena remain unchanged throughout the period, an assumption contrary to fact in most cases. The residuals sometimes loosely called "cyclical fluctuations" are affected by this assumption of constant seasonal fluctuations. The result of this assumption would be to produce in the residuals many small fluctuations which have nothing to do with "cycles" in the common understanding of the term.

In connection with the interpretation of results it has already been shown that extrapolation is not legitimate. The analysis of time series by these methods is valid within limits for the period covered, but is not available for prediction. Nor is the "economic law" so obtained for Great Britain necessarily applicable to other countries. It is valid only for the time, the place, and the circumstances in which it was derived. This may seem to leave very little in the concept of economic law, but it is only a more precise formulation of the limitations which were recognized before economic laws were expressed in mathematical form.

When we find, as in these cases, that the "laws" discovered for one country do not hold true in another, we usually conclude that some of the "other things" are not equal. Is it possible to devise any statistical technique to overcome this difficulty? In physics, genetics, and some other branches of science, it is sometimes possible to make use of multiple or partial correlations in order to take into account the effect of a complex of influences. Even in economic statistics, some attempt has been made to apply these methods. In dealing with such phenomena as the ones considered in the present study, would these techniques be applicable? Can we resolve complex social phenomena into their simpler component parts, and ascertain invariable relationships among these parts?

There are at least two difficulties in the way of such attempts. In the first place, the data are rarely sufficiently extensive for such treatment. Our ancestors did not have such ample means of collecting statistics as we now enjoy, nor did they have sufficient reverence for statistics to collect even those which might quite easily have been obtained. Even our price statistics cover a regrettably short period, while most of the useful social statistics are of more recent date. This is, of course, no argument in favor of postponing sociological research for a century or two, until our statistical series becomes longer. We must do our best with what we have, and thus the correlations which Miss Thomas has calculated on the basis of eighteen pairs of items become justified.

The use of multiple or partial correlation for deducing social "laws" is, however, accompanied by a more formidable difficulty. It is shown in the present work that there is, in England, a close connection among prosperity, alcoholism, and arrests for prostitution—three variables, which might perhaps be further analyzed into a larger number of simpler factors. If the technique of partial correlation were permissible, Miss Thomas might have been able to show that the correlation between prostitution and alcoholism (holding prosperity constant) was x, while the correlation between prostitution and prosperity (holding alcoholism constant) was y. But if it is true that, in actual life, these three phenomena (and others) are usually found in an indissoluble complex, then such a formula as we have suggested would possess very doubtful validity. In social phenomena the "effects" of several "causes" operating together may be very different from the sum of their separate effects.

Readers accustomed to the fairly high correlations that are common in biometrics, and even in economic statistics, will find the socio-economic correlations of the present study rather low. This fact is perhaps largely due to the existence of other disturbing factors whose effects cannot be eliminated by any experimental or statistical technique. It is probable that, just as a "normal distribution" cannot be postulated of the coefficient of correlation with socio-economic data, so too lower coefficients may be regarded as typical and significant in studies of such data as compared with those where greater control is possible.

While considerable space has been given to the discussion of the methodological problems of measurement, analysis, and interpretation exemplified in this study, it would be unfair to suggest that the author has fallen short in recognizing these problems. Most of the points here elaborated have been at least suggested in the book itself, and the interpretation has been enriched with suggestions drawn from original thought and from the studies of other writers. The work has been fruitful in suggestions for further research. Additional discussion of these and of the very interesting conclusions reached by Miss Thomas is, however, beyond the scope of this study.

APPENDIX: THE AUTHOR'S OWN ANALYSIS OF HER METHODS[2]

In my study of the social aspects of the business cycle[3] my aim was to get an objective expression of the relationship between the cyclical movements in business and in social series. There was reason to believe that economic influences played an important part in determining fluctuations in certain social phenomena. The marriage-rate had long been held to be an indication of the prosperity of any community, and had been shown to be correlated strongly with fluctuations in trade and employment. There was some evidence, of a fragmentary sort, that crime, particularly theft, increased when the price of grain rose sharply. "Bad years," with their unemployment and business failures, called for greater relief of the poor. "Good years" were marked by a higher rate of consumption generally, and, as certain associated phenomena indicated, particularly of alcohol. Tuberculosis and some deaths from other causes had been shown to be strongly associated with poverty. There was then a great deal of a priori evidence that social phenomena reflected business conditions. But there had been no clear-cut attempt to get a great many of these data in a form in which an adequate statistical comparison could be made.

Certain preliminary problems arose. If such an investigation were to be made, how should the data be limited? Where could adequate data

[2] Excerpted from Dorothy Swaine Thomas, "Statistics in Social Research," *American Journal of Sociology*, XXXV (July, 1929), 1–17. Reprinted by permission of the author, the editors of the *Journal*, and the University of Chicago Press. Cf. n. 1.

[3] *Op. cit.*

be obtained? The first limitation, of course, was that the region for which the correlations were to be made should have had well-developed business cycles over a considerable period of years. It was known that business cycles took a number of years to complete their course from crest to trough and it would, therefore be necessary to have data extending over several cycles in order to feel reasonably secure that a relationship found to exist over some one or two cycles might not be due to some interfering fortuitous factor. Many interfering factors would probably also be ruled out if the region had a homogeneous population. Finally, the data to be used must have had a requisite and consistent degree of accuracy over the period of investigation.

A study of the possibilities of American data showed them to be unsatisfactory. Although the United States had had well-developed and sharply defined business cycles over a long period, the population is heterogeneous, there is no centralized source of most of the statistics, and the statistics of the individual states were found to be, with few exceptions, inaccurate and inconsistent. England, on the other hand, had had well-developed business cycles over a long period, with relatively homogeneous population, a well-developed centralized collection of statistics, and a tradition and practice of relatively great accuracy. After a preliminary study of the data of certain of our states,[4] in which the problem became more clear-cut and the results were sufficiently promising to make further investigation desirable, I decided to use English data.

Now the problem arose as to what index of "the business cycle" should be accepted. For the fluctuations do not occur simultaneously nor consistently in all series of economic or business statistics, although the general movement in quite similar in many of them. Since modern analysis of the business cycle seems to place such emphasis on price factors, I decided to use the best available series of price statistics as the standard and include only such other series as fluctuated in general concurrence with prices. The reason for including other series at all was to iron out minor irregularities peculiar to any one series. Data for exports were taken because of the importance of foreign trade in the economic life of England. Freight-traffic receipts complemented these by representing internal trade. Pig-iron and coal production were taken as representatives of the major industries. Bank clearings represented trade in general and credit facilities. Finally, unemployment data represented the direct re-

[4] W. F. Ogburn and D. S. Thomas, "The Influence of the Business Cycle on Certain Social Conditions," *Journal of the American Statistical Association* (September, 1922).

sponse of labor conditions. The index of the business cycle was composed of an average of these series. While aiming at representativeness, it was obviously composed of strongly "selected" rather than "random" series, and this selection was determined, ultimately, by my judgment of the data and theories of the economists.

The series of social phenomena were accepted on the a priori basis outlined in the foregoing. No series was utilized if there was no independent evidence that led to an anticipation of a relationship. (This independent evidence was, however, often of a scanty and inadequate sort.) The reason for this restriction was that the interpretation of the correlation coefficients with data of this sort must be made in the light of other evidence—the correlation coefficients alone will tell little.

The selection was also based on the a priori probability of any particular social series being influenced by the business cycle. Thus, there is a certain amount of evidence that tuberculosis is most prevalent among the poorer sections of the community. One might, therefore, suppose that deaths from tuberculosis (the only available index of the disease) would vary directly with pauperism and inversely with the business cycles, and the series should be tested by the correlation method. But, in the case of deaths from cancer, the causes are more complex, and the medical researches too limited to give the basis for any supposition of a connection with the business cycle. Examination of the series showed the connection, if any, to be slight—and, since a correlation coefficient between such a series and the business cycle would be practically uninterpretable, the series was discarded.[5]

The time period was determined entirely by the exigencies of the data. It was desirable to have as long a period as possible. Because of changes in classification, data for exports before 1854 were not comparable with later data. Since few of the social data were reliable before this date, I accepted this as the earliest possible year, and 1913 as the latest, because of the complications of the war and post-war inflation.

The next problem involved the removal of as many interfering factors as possible, antecedent to the actual correlations. All of these series, extending over a period of years, showed a secular trend. In the economic series this was almost continuously upward, representing the general growth of industry. In the social series it was frequently upward also, owing to the growth of population. But even after the social series had been expressed as rates in terms of population there was a residual trend, representing various different factors. In the birth-rate, for instance, there was a sharp downward trend, probably owing largely to the spread of the birth-control movement. The trend in marriage-rates changed its

[5] *Social Aspects of the Business Cycle*, pp. 15–16.

direction in the middle of the period, owing to the changing age-groupings in the population, and the like. Obviously, these trends must be removed or allowed for before we can measure the cyclical relationships.

The measuring of trends, which has played a large part in economic statistics, cannot be considered as other than an empirical process. The data may be plotted on a chart and a line drawn in a way that seems to the observer to give a good fit. A moving average may be used, with varying periods. Straight lines and parabolas may be fitted by the method of least squares, or curves of the compound-interest type, logistic curves, exponential curves, and so forth. Their computation will give much gratification to the investigator—particularly the more complicated ones, which are expressible in formulas of many terms—but he should not fail to admit that the determination of the "best" trend is largely subjective. It is not known how the "true" trend can be discovered, and in this investigation the problem of finding the true trend did not arise. My interest lay in approximating this trend in order that it might be eliminated. The line resulting from any of the calculations, therefore, would be regarded merely as an interpolation and as representing my idea of the "best" trend. It seemed inadvisable to draw the lines free-hand because of the possible intrusion of bias. The moving average was also inadvisable because these series were frequently convex, and a good fit could be obtained only by making a cumbersome correction. I used second- and third degree parabolas simply and solely because some such arbitrary procedure would result in cycles less dependent on my bias than free-hand drawing, and because these parabolas gave technically "good" fits to the particular series I was analyzing.

After the various trends were measured the next statistical problem was to eliminate them. This was done by taking the percentage deviations of the original items from the corresponding ordinates of the secular trend. Before correlations were computed it was considered desirable to examine the data with great care in order to eliminate any further "interfering causes." A great deal of the preliminary investigation, of course, had been concerned with learning everything possible about the nature of the data. Vital statisticians were consulted and government reports carefully gone over. I was in a position, therefore, to evaluate the data. Their inadequacies and inaccuracies were studied in order to avoid computing correlations in cases in which the data themselves would vitiate the study.

Series that were merely inadequate representatives of a given social phenomenon were not discarded for that reason alone, provided no better series could be found. Thus, it was necessary to take for the crime data series representing "total convictions for indictable crimes" because this series was the most consistent over a period of time. "Crimes known to the police" would on a priori grounds have been considered a more adequate index of crime in general, but actually this series was inconsistent over a period of time and had serious sources of irregular error.

Among the factors discovered which would undoubtedly have complicated the interpretation of correlations were: (1) a two years's periodicity in birth-rates and infant-mortality rates, noted previously by a number of investigators but unexplained. This periodicity was arbitrarily eliminated (by interpolation) from the groups of years in which it occurred. (2) Epidemic diseases tended to cause the death-rates to move in cycles that were probably unrelated to the business cycle. They were therefore eliminated from the general death-rate in order that the other cyclical movement might show an uncomplicated relation to the business cycle, if any such existed. Likewise, the etiology of diarrheal deaths suggested a close dependence on rainfall and temperature (which probably move in cycles not closely related to the business cycle), and such deaths were eliminated from the infant-mortality data. (3) Changes in laws and sudden changes in "policy" regarding crime and pauperism were determined from government data and reports. The years immediately contingent to these breaks were omitted from the correlations.

The simplest method of showing correlation is graphic. But my series were in no form for simple graphic comparison, since some of them had very large fluctuations and others very slight ones. A series might not vary much from year to year and yet move in cycles, just as consistently as a series showing great fluctuations. In a graphical comparison, it would be difficult to recognize the cyclical movement in those series in which the percentage deviations were small. Each series was therefore divided by its standard deviation, thus expressing it in terms of relative rather than absolute percentage deviations. Charts were then drawn showing each of the social series in relation to the average of the business series, and it was possible to estimate probable relationships from these charts. It was not desirable to omit further statistical calculations however, and write a book on the relationships observed between the social and business curves, for even if by much diligence I managed to bring to light and allow for my particular biases regarding these relationships, most of these charts could have been given very different interpretations by very many different readers. It was desirable to be able to discriminate quantitatively between the varying degrees of relationship.

Now the correlation coefficient has a definite meaning if computed for normally distributed data. For time series it has no such clear-cut meaning, except for perfect correlation ($r = \pm I$) or complete absence of correlation ($r = 0$). Recognizing this, I yet decided to compute correlation coefficients, for my problem seemed determinate. It was obvious that I could not differentiate exact amounts of correlation between these various series. But my aim was to compare each of the social series in turn with the average of the business series. The social series were roughly similar in form. Assuming that there were no specific strong interfering forces playing upon any of them, the correlation coefficients could be considered comparable among themselves (although they could be given no absolute meaning) and were, therefore, computed. There was much evidence of a high correlation between marriage-rates and the business cycle, and this evidence was strengthened by a correlation coefficient that would be considered high and well established under almost any circumstances. It was therefore assumed that this was a "high" correlation, and all the other coefficients were interpreted in the light of this assumption.

Some of the coefficients were what would be considered distinctly low under any circumstances except strict normality of distribution. It therefore seemed desirable to have a further check-up on my interpretation. The probable error seemed to have little meaning with correlations of this sort, so I computed the standard deviations of the correlation coefficients. These also have no strictly interpretable meaning with data of this sort, but they are valuable in that they are direct functions of the size of the coefficient and the number of cases used in its computation. I used them as a rough check on my interpretations, but they could not be considered as giving my interpretations any real security; they merely made my inferences more reasonable.

This somewhat detailed analysis of my own work is given here because I wish to indicate the uncertainties that complicate a statistical investigation. It is difficult to tell by reading the results of another person's investigations just what assumptions he has made; just how his interpretations can be made in the light of the particular application of statistical methods to particular data; just how often convenience has dictated procedure. In my own case, I am aware of at least some of the limitations of the methods I used. I know that they can have strict meanings only if used with data conforming to their premises and that my data do not and cannot conform to the premises.

In order to give my results the most definite possible meaning, therefore, I bring my data into a form in which my interpretations will not depend on "discoveries" arising through the manipulation of techniques. The most that I can show is the relative relationships of various social phenomena and the business cycle. In order to bring my data to that point I use what seem to be complicated techniques: trends fitted by the method of least squares, Pearsonian correlation coefficients, and standard errors. I have used these techniques, while realizing fully that my interpretations cannot be made clear-cut, because my data cannot fulfil the premises that these techniques demanded. But the use of these techniques has given me results that are objective and comparable within their context. It has been more convenient for me to eliminate my bias by these methods than by the more cumbersome and less certain ways of induction uncomplicated by statistics.

But my interpretations will still have to be considered highly inferential. None of my results can be expressed simply and quantitatively. I cannot, for instance, quote odds in showing that these coefficients could not have resulted from chance alone. The most that I can say in any specific case, for instance suicide-rates, is that suicides are correlated inversely with the business cycle and that the coefficient is —0.50. This series is, so far as I know, uncomplicated by any serious "interfering factors." It is statistically similar to the marriage-rates series, whose correlations with the business cycle (0.67) *I have assumed to be high.* The numerical value of this coefficient is high enough in comparison with this to lead to the inference that suicides are closely related to business conditions. This interpretation is strengthened by the fact that the coefficient is five times its standard deviation. The difficulties surrounding the use of correlation coefficients, as suggested by this study, are that they will rarely have a clear-cut meaning with sociological data. The advantages are that if interpreted within the context of the data they give a useful summary expression of relationship in an objective form.

ANALYSIS 42

THE CONCEPT OF RACE IN THE LIGHT OF FRANZ BOAS' STUDIES OF HEAD-FORMS AMONG IMMIGRANTS[1]

By FAY-COOPER COLE
University of Chicago

Physical anthropology appears, at first glance, to be out of place in a volume devoted to the social sciences. Minute physical measurements are supplemented by careful description of living man and his skeleton, and out of these observations comes the concept of race.

It is unnecessary to state that the term "race" is often based on less scientific data. The evident differences between black, white, and yellow, and the equally evident social and cultural differences between these physical groupings, have suggested a distinct correlation between physical and mental types. National pride and religious prejudice have likewise set certain groups apart and to them the term "race" is often applied. Differences—physical, linguistic, cultural, and national—lead to group consciousness, aversion, and hate. But it is easy to demonstrate that national boundaries often include people of quite diverse physical types, while a language or culture may extend far beyond national boundaries, or physical groupings. Apparently there is no correlation between race, language, nationality, or religion.

The physical anthropologist uses the term "race" to designate a group of people who have certain physical characteristics in common which distinguish them from all other groups; who now do or formerly did occupy the same or adjacent territory; and who have common descent. Once such a classification is adopted, there is a tendency to characterize a race by its most extreme or obvious traits and to ignore others which may be of equal importance biologically, while individuals who possess certain characteristics of two or more groupings are often classed as hybrids.

It must be recognized at once that there are today no pure or unmixed races. Apparently there has been mixture of physical types as far back as Aurignacian times, perhaps earlier, while in later epochs movements of people, slavery, warfare, and other causes have led to a thorough

[1] *Changes in Bodily Form of Descendants of Immigrants* (report of the United States Immigration Commission, Washington, 1910).

fusion in many regions. In such groups we find frequent reversions to type; individual variations also produce deviation, so that we find great extremes within each race, subrace, and even families. Nevertheless, if we consider many criteria and a large number of individuals we can describe a race or type so that it will include most of its members.

Archaeological material from early neolithic times onward indicates that physical types closely resembling the present races have existed in Europe for long periods. Long heads and short heads and other characters seem to have persisted with surprisingly little change, and this has led many to assume the permanence or stability of race. On the other hand, careful observation has led to the conclusion that environment, mutations, and inbreeding have brought about the establishment of new types. It is asserted that wherever man has gone and remained isolated for a time, there he has developed physical types. Apparently, then, we are met with two conflicting statements: first, that race is fixed and permanent; second, that it has undergone modification wherever the environment has been changed and inbreeding has been long continued.

Equally diverse views are held in regard to the subject of race mixture. One student holds to the idea that there is a limit to racial amalgamation, and that the mixed group becomes sterile after the fifth generation. Another asserts that hybrid groups are even more fertile than pure racial strains. It is claimed that physical weaklings and monstrosities may result from the crossing of diverse stocks. Again we are frequently met with the assertion that physically, mentally, and morally the half-blood inherits the worst elements of both ancestral lines. Denial, backed by many exceptions, has not succeeded in overcoming this oft-repeated charge. Many semipopular writers, drawing analogies with the performance of single traits in animals, have assumed that the various characteristics by which we define race are unit characters which follow simple Mendelian heredity, yet certain studies of race mixture indicate that while some characters do act as dominants and recessives, others produce a blend. It is now recognized that while in the relatively pure groups certain traits tend to cluster together, yet in race-crossing they do not always behave in the same manner. From a Negro-white mixture we may secure a mulatto who has the characteristic hair of the Negro combined with the thin lips and narrow nose of the Caucasian.

Thus it appears that while we can define race in a broad way, we are still vastly ignorant concerning this term which plays such an important part in our social and national consciousness.

It is evident that man's body undergoes certain modifications as a result of change in environment, yet it is uncertain to what extent this adaptation is limited by heredity. This uncertainty is in part due to the fact that we do not have control conditions; that we cannot put man into a laboratory and watch him through several generations. Physical anthropology has for the most part dealt with groups rather than with family lines because of the many difficulties in securing even that degree of control represented by a study of subjects from more than one generation.

The anthropometric study which most closely approaches control conditions, which offers most toward the solution of the problems raised, and which also best illustrates methodology is that of Franz Boas to which this paper relates. The purpose of the study was to ascertain the effects of American environment on the physical types of immigrants. Before embarking on the larger study, a preliminary test was made to see if the promise of results was sufficient to warrant the continuation of the investigation. This survey seemed to show remarkable differences in type among the children of immigrants according to the length of time elapsed between the arrival of the parents in this country and their own birth. Hence the more extensive study was undertaken.

The thirteen observers used in the work made a considerable number of control measurements in the schools to insure uniformity of method and to be certain that the individual differences were comparable. From time to time during the investigation these observers were required to measure one another, and since the deviations were consistently small the material gathered can be considered as sufficiently accurate.

The results of the preliminary study had been so peculiar and so unexpected that it seemed indispensable to control them by direct comparisons between the children and their own parents. Hence an extended series of measurements of whole families was taken. For the purposes of this study only a few of the most distinct European types were selected, and these were studied as nearly as possible in the same type of environment—namely, the congested districts of New York City. Only certain traits considered relatively stable were investigated; should they prove variable, then presumably other characteristics both physical and mental would likewise be subject to change.

When it was established that differences did exist, it became necessary to determine whether they increased with the time which had elapsed between the immigration of the parents and the birth of the children. By comparing parents with their own children influences due to changes in the composition of the immigrant population in different years were eliminated. The various measurements obtained for children born ten years or more after the arrival of the mother were compared with the corresponding measurements for children born less than ten years after the mother's arrival. Comparisons were also made with the foreign-born children. The differences between the respective averages of each of these three groups and the general average was determined. The results showed that the differences between the foreign-born and those born less than ten years after the arrival of the mother are greater than the differences between the two American-born classes, but that there are definite differences between the latter. It appears, then, that the effect of the American environment takes place immediately after the arrival of the parents, but that it is also cumulative.

The most significant results deal with differences in head- and face-form, but the study also gives data relating to pigmentation, stature, growth, and size of families. The measurements of families likewise make it possible to attack the problem of heredity and intermixture in a strictly scientific manner.

Our intention has not been to summarize the results of the study but rather to indicate the methods employed. However, it should be noted that the results argue for great plasticity of human types under new environmental conditions—a fact of great practical importance in a country like America where peoples of such diverse types are already present in considerable numbers.[2]

[2] [This analysis was written in December, 1928, and was revised by the analyst during the following spring.—EDITOR.]

ANALYSIS 43

BEHAVIOR ALTERNATIVES AS STATISTICAL DATA IN STUDIES BY WILLIAM F. OGBURN AND ERNEST W. BURGESS

By STUART A. RICE

University of Pennsylvania

I. INTRODUCTION

Social science may be expected to grow with the accumulation of its data. A contribution is made when data are assembled or recorded systematically in such forms that generalizations or inferences become possible. A contribution is also made when it is demonstrated that existing records, compiled for one purpose, may lead to new types of inference. The present analysis relates to three contributions of this second type. Each has derived scientific generalizations from public records compiled in the first instance for political or administrative ends. In form, these records consist essentially of classifications of human behavior in accordance with two or some other small number of alternatives. A characteristic form of such a record is a summary of *votes*.

The act of voting is a form of behavior. Its material consequent, a marked ballot let us say, is objective. The recorded vote or ballot may be regarded as an *index* of an attitude or opinion by which the voting behavior has been motivated.[1] The former will be an imperfect reflection of the latter, and the degree of correspondence will be variable.[2] But this is by no means a unique situation. A dollar, for instance, is meaningless apart from the subjective values which it ultimately represents, and its relationship to these is fluctuating. It can be contended that most if not all of the objective data of social science are indices of more essential but less tangible entities which are represented with varying degrees of exactitude. The relationships of data employed as indices to the general objects of inquiry, to the less tangible entities behind them, and to the conclusions drawn are in themselves important subjects of methodological research.[3]

---

[1] This is not the place in which to discuss concepts of attitude and opinion, or to take sides in controversies over consciousness and behavior. Cf. analysis 52.

[2] As this is written, "wets" and "drys" are quarreling over the "real" intentions and attitudes of those who voted for "modification" among three alternatives in a poll on prohibition conducted by the *Literary Digest*.

[3] Cf. Stuart A. Rice, *Quantitative Methods in Politics* (New York: A. A. Knopf & Co., 1928—transferred to F. S. Crofts & Co.). In chap. vii of this work it is con-

Behavioristic indices of attitudes and opinions are usually in the form of language symbols or their equivalent. When this is the case the problem of classifying verbal behavior in such a manner as to permit quantitative treatment is difficult. This is true not only because of the symbolic character of language, but also because of the indefinitely large number of combinations and permutations of verbal units by means of which the attitude may be expressed. The dangers of subjectivism enter in the interpretation. For example, when confronted with statements of attitude upon the same subject, investigators would have difficulty in agreeing upon the precise position to be assigned each in any systematic and detailed classification. The subjective interpretations of the statements by each investigator would affect his judgment of the appropriate classification. However, he may formulate a series of statements, each of which is presumed to be typical of a distinct variation of attitude or opinion.[4] A subject may then check that statement which seems to him to be the most representative of his opinion or attitude. His checked schedule may then be regarded as a vote.[5] The vote in such circumstances represents in effect the mid-point of a class artificially segregated in a continuum of possible opinions or attitudes.[6]

---

tended that the social scientist is almost always in search of "objective indices of subjective variables." What was sought was a position permitting rigid adherence to behaviorism in method without acceptance of its theoretical claims, concerning which one may remain skeptical. The present statement is modified to render it less objectionable according to the viewpoints of physical science. That is, such terms as "opinion," "attitude," and "intelligence" stand for pure concepts. Their existence (at least in other persons) is inferred from behavior, and they are not measurable directly by any known means. At this point we encounter "the operational character of concepts" (cf. P. W. Bridgman, *The Logic of Modern Physics*, pp. 3 ff.) in accordance with which "the concept is synonymous with the corresponding set of operations" required for its measurement. From this standpoint "attitudes" and "intelligence" could mean nothing more than the set of operations by means of which their results or manifestations are measured—which seems to bring them strictly within the behavioristic sphere.

[4] Professor L. L. Thurstone has devised an ingenious technique for securing a series of statements each with a scale value on a linear scale of attitude on a given topic. The scale value represents the interpolated median judgment of a group of judges as to its position, and is to be distinguished, in consequence, from a mere rank-order arrangement. Cf. L. L. Thurstone and E. J. Chave, *The Measurement of Attitude*, etc. (Chicago: University of Chicago Press, 1929). Cf. also a critique of this technique by the analyst, with an appended commentary by Professor Thurstone, in *Statistics in Social Studies*, Stuart A. Rice (ed.) (Philadelphia: University of Pennsylvania Press, 1930), pp. 171–96.

[5] The use of the term *vote* will henceforth be confined to the objective record which results from the act of voting.

[6] Cf. Rice, *Quantitative Methods in Politics*, chap. vi.

Votes which can be identified with individual voters may be related to various social and personality characteristics.[7] But if the ballot is secret, the voter and his vote are non-identifiable. Moreover, in a public election, which from an experimental standpoint is relatively uncontrolled, the continuum of attitudes upon an issue is expressed only by the two discrete indices of an affirmative or negative vote.[8] The propositions voted upon may be quite irrelevant to attitudes in which the investigator is interested. It will be apparent that when such limiting conditions are present, which is almost always the case, the task of drawing inferences concerning opinions and attitudes from summaries of votes offers special difficulties.

Two of the three studies here examined employ summaries of votes as their data and achieve considerable success in overcoming these special difficulties. In both of them Ogburn was a senior collaborator, in the first with Peterson, in the second with Goltra.[9] Both papers utilize election returns in the state of Oregon, and in particular popular votes on initiative and referendum measures. The third paper by Burgess has for its basic data records of parole violations among men released from certain penal institutions in Illinois.[10] Certain aspects of its methodology are the same as those of the Ogburn-Peterson paper. Finally, the analyst will refer to some of his own publications in which the same type of methodology has been used or criticized.[11]

[7] As in Thurstone and Chave, *op. cit.*

[8] I will not complicate the argument by reference to votes for candidates, but will confine it to votes on propositions only.

[9] William F. Ogburn and Delvin Peterson, "Political Thought of Social Classes," *Political Science Quarterly*, XXXI (June, 1916), 300–317; William F. Ogburn and Inez Goltra, "How Women Vote," *Political Science Quarterly*, XXXIV (September, 1919), 413–33.

[10] Ernest W. Burgess, "Is Prediction Feasible in Social Work? An Inquiry Based upon a Sociological Study of Parole Records," *Social Forces*, VII (June, 1929), 533–45.

[11] The Burgess paper is criticized in "Some Inherent Difficulties in the Method of Prediction by Classification" appearing in the same issue of *Social Forces*, VII, 554–58; chap. xv of *Quantitative Methods in Politics* contains a brief résumé of the theory underlying measurements of "group cohesion" and "group likeness" by means of votes, which owed much in its development to the Ogburn-Peterson paper, and which was first set forth in *Farmers and Workers in American Politics*, "Studies in History, Economics and Public Law" (New York: Columbia University, 1924). "The Verification of Social Measurements Involving Subjective Classifications," in collaboration with Wallace W. Weaver, *Social Forces*, VIII, 16–28, bears upon the present analysis to the extent that it examines the inevitable presence of subjectivism in certain types of so-called measurement.

II. SYNOPSES OF STUDIES ANALYZED
THE OGBURN-PETERSON PAPER

Five "social classes" in the state of Oregon were compared with respect to their "political thought." These were: (1) city dwellers, represented by the voters of Portland; (2) rural population, represented by the voters in 20 counties containing in 1910 no town of as many as 3,000 population; (3, 4, 5) upper class, middle class, and laboring class, represented respectively by the voters in selected groups of precincts in the city of Portland. The distribution of negative and affirmative votes within each of these samples of the electorate upon each of 103 initiative and referendum proposals, 1910–14, when reduced to a comparable percentage basis, provided the necessary indices of "political thought."

The percentage of a given sample voting in favor of a proposal was regarded as an index of the willingness of the corresponding social class to accede to social change in the direction indicated. The arithmetic difference between two such indices indicated the extent of the difference of opinion regarding the proposal between the respective classes. Composite indices of difference between classes were obtained by averaging the differences upon individual proposals. Six series of comparisons of this kind were made, the largest differences being between the upper and the laboring classes, and the next largest between the middle and the laboring classes. Among the 103 proposals there were selected 26 having greater importance, or having a definite "progressive" or "radical" character. These selected proposals disclosed greater average differences between classes, although the order of paired classes with respect to the magnitude of differences remained very nearly the same. Upon these selected proposals the laboring class showed the highest average favorable vote (52 per cent), thus indicating the greatest disposition to favor change. The upper class showed the lowest average favorable vote (37 per cent).

A number of conclusions were drawn concerning class opinions and differences between classes upon particular issues. The authors believed their chief contribution to be contained in the following generalization: "The differences between the social classes are not so great as many have been led to suspect. . . . . The figures . . . . point toward harmony and show a considerable ability on the part of the social classes to get along together."

THE OGBURN-GOLTRA PAPER

This study employed the statistical method of partial correlation as a means of ascertaining "how women vote" in comparison with men. For

each of 319 precincts in Multnomah County, including the city of Portland, Oregon, the following data were calculated: (1) the percentage
of affirmative votes upon each of 26 initiative and referendum measures
in the general election of 1914; (2) the percentage which women constituted of all persons voting in the same election; (3) an "index of
conservatism" consisting of the average percentage of the vote cast on
the conservative side of 6 conservative, progressive, and radical measures
in the election of 1912, prior to the enfranchisement of women. The
factor of comparative conservatism in the various precincts was then held
constant, while the relationship between the proportion of women voters,
on the one hand, and the favorable vote for each of the 26 initiative and
referendum proposals, upon the other, was determined. It was then inferred, for example, that if the vote on a proposal tended to be relatively
high in those precincts in which the proportion of women voting was
relatively high, that women were supporters of the proposal in greater
ratio than were men. Women, as compared with men, were found to be
"more opposed to the eight-hour day for women, to a single tax, to
proportional representation, to the abolition of the state senate, to extending certain functions of government, and perhaps to spending public
money."

THE BURGESS PAPER

One thousand consecutive records of paroled men from each of three
penal institutions in Illinois were examined. Each man was classified
as having either observed or violated parole.[12] In addition, each man
was reclassified twenty-one times in accordance with twenty-one different
sets of criteria. These included such objective social and psychological
data as age, residence, mental age, number of associates in the crime
resulting from conviction, and punishment record within the institution;
and such psychiatric or semi-subjective appraisals as social type, psychiatric personality type, and psychiatric prognosis of outcome. Within
each class, in each of the twenty-one classifications, the percentage of
parole violators was termed a "violation rate." For example, the violation rate for all of the 1,000 men paroled from Joliet was 28.4 per cent;
but for those of this number who were under twenty-one years of age at
the time of parole the violation rate was 16.7 per cent. With respect
to the age classification alone, 16.7 per cent may be viewed as the expectancy, or most probable ratio of parole violators, among men under twenty-

[12] Since the attitudes and behavior of these 3,000 individuals with respect to their
paroles were actually variable, it will be seen that the classification into simple alternatives of observance or violation is analogous to the classification of variable opinions into two discrete classes of affirmative and negative votes.

one years of age who may be paroled from Joliet in the future. In obtaining a composite expectancy rate based upon all of the twenty-one classifications, however, account was not taken of the precise violation rate for each of the twenty-one groupings in which each man was placed. Instead, each man was given a number of "points" varying from 0 to 21, corresponding to the number of classes to which he belonged in which the violation rate was less than the rate for all men paroled from his institution. Thus among 68 men paroled from Joliet and having between 16 and 21 "points," the violators of parole constituted 1.5 per cent; while among 25 men having from 1 to 4 "points" only, the violation rate was 76.0 per cent. By determining the number of "points" which any prisoner possesses in advance of his parole, the probability of violation may be established. The method, moreover, is applicable to a wide variety of other problems in which traits of personality and behavior are involved.

III. THE INFLUENCE OF PRECONCEPTIONS AND INTERESTS UPON THE CHOICE OF SUBJECT

The motives and interests which lead particular individuals to undertake particular tasks of research are in any instance various, and difficult to ascertain.[13] Sometimes they may be inferred, in connection with the preconceptions made evident in the work itself.

In the Ogburn-Peterson paper there is some evidence of the preconceptions and interests which underlie the procedure. A concept, the heterogeneity of modern society, is central to the inquiry. Without this the investigators' problem could not have arisen. Heterogeneity—the existence of social classes—is *assumed* in the introductory paragraphs of the author's paper, and is illustrated rather than established logically. Its acceptance is a priori.[14]

The senior collaborator had been a student of Franklin H. Giddings, of Columbia University, whose advocacy of quantitative methods in the social sciences has left a deep impress upon his followers. Giddings had

---

[13] Cf. analysis 12, the appendix to analysis 47, and Introduction, pp. 6–7.

[14] Thus Herbert Spencer is cited as having stressed "this fact" (of modern social heterogeneity) in his formula of evolution. "In very early times," the authors say, following Spencer, "the social group was the single undifferentiated horde." Since the date of publication of the author's study (1916) much discredit has been thrown upon the Spencerian formula in its social applications. The senior collaborator has himself been among the most outspoken critics of it. In the present instance, the Spencerian formula is logically unessential to the authors' argument. It has been introduced unnecessarily. Moreover, their position is essentially more defensible than they make it appear, for they are seeking to justify their central hypothesis. But the dangers of dependence upon non-empirical "authority" for a premise are nevertheless indicated.

developed the idea of heterogeneity from the psychological side, showing the principle of grouping to be a "consciousness of kind," and showing the dependence of collective effort upon like-mindedness. Leaning upon the authority of Giddings, and with the aid of illustrations, the authors indicate the importance of like-mindedness in the operation of government. "Peculiar difficulties for the governments of the future" may flow from unlike-mindedness among three classes in particular, the capitalist, the middle class, and the working class, established by the industrial revolution. Measurement of the extent of the differences actually existing among these classes is therefore desirable.

At the time of their inquiry, the authors were connected with Reed College, in the city of Portland, Oregon—a city and state in which public discussion of political and economic questions has been singularly acute and well informed. Hence an initial interest in such questions on the part of the authors was probably reinforced by the social milieu. Moreover, it was in this particular state alone that a relatively large number of initiative and referendum measures had been passed upon by popular vote; hence, in which data of the kind employed were available.

So far as the interests and preconceptions of the major collaborator were concerned, therefore, at least three influences upon the choice of subject matter may be discerned: (1) A set of concepts; some of them traceable to Giddings, and back of Giddings to Spencer; some, in addition, growing out of the philosophy of economic determinism. From all of these there emerged a concrete scientific *problem*. (2) A scientific bias, having its own conceptual roots, but again associated with Giddings, in accordance with which it was assumed that a scientific solution of the problem must be *quantitative*. (3) The circumstance of personal location, quite fortuitous from the present standpoint, that provided *available data*. Whether any one of these influences was essential—whether, for example, the study would have been undertaken had the senior collaborator resided in some other state—it is of course impossible to judge. Nor can account be taken of the other more personal factors, both subjective and environmental, which were present.

The preceding comments and queries would also apply with only minor variations to the Ogburn-Goltra study.

IV. AVAILABILITY OF DATA AS A FACTOR

The purpose of research may be so well defined in a given instance that data which are nonexistent may be conceived, and steps taken to procure them.[15] But research does not wait for the development of types of data that would be theoretically desirable. It utilizes whatever facts are available. The availability of data, then, will be a factor in determining the objectives of research, its detailed direction, and the conclusions reached.

Burgess classified paroled men in accordance with twenty-one sets of factors. But why did he employ these particular twenty-one and not some others? For example, each inmate was classified according to the nationality of his father. Inmates whose fathers were of certain nationalities showed lower rates of violation than did inmates having fathers of some other nationalities. Why was classification not made likewise according to the nationality of the mother? There would be some ground for assuming that the folk ways and mores of the mother would play a greater part in molding the character of the child, and hence in conditioning his later response to parole regulations, than would those of the father.

The answer seems to be that the datum concerning the father's nationality was more available, in the prison records or otherwise, than that concerning the mother's nationality. Certain facts about each prisoner were secured in connection with judicial and penal routine. The investigators made use of these facts as they were found.[16] The prediction of parole observance or violation was based to this extent upon data gathered for totally irrelevant purposes.

A similar situation is encountered in the Ogburn-Peterson study. The purpose here was to discover the kind and the extent of differences in the thought of social classes. It is inferred that differences are not large. But the authors were dependent for data upon a limited number of legislative proposals that had been voted upon by the electorate. There is no assurance that these particular proposals presented issues upon which the greater differences in thought exist, actually or potentially. Advocates of measures which would be most productive of social conflict may have been unable or unwilling to place them upon the ballot. For ex-

---

[15] For example, there are no uniform national data, collected periodically, with respect to unemployment in the United States. But the need for them has long been recognized, and periodic index numbers of unemployment will undoubtedly be perfected. The need, in fact, was recognized in the schedules of the fifteenth census.

[16] The fact here assumed is not altogether clear, since the investigators found the records which they employed in much disorder and confusion. Cf. Andrew A. Bruce, Albert J. Harno, John Landesco, and Ernest W. Burgess, *The Workings of the Indeterminate-Sentence Law and the Parole System in Illinois* (a Report to the Hon. Hinton G. Clabaugh, Chairman, Parole Board of Illinois, 1928), pp. 67 ff., 73 n., and *passim*.

ample, large numbers of migratory workers throughout the Northwest are deprived of votes because of legal qualifications respecting residence. In coincidence with this fact, it was part of the rationale of the Industrial Workers of the World during the period involved to refrain from participation in politics and to wage revolutionary activities by economic means. It seems questionable, then, whether the issues involved in the measures actually voted on were a representative sample of the issues upon which members of various classes would tend most to differ.

The same consideration applies in the Ogburn-Goltra study. The authors constructed an index of conservatism from a record of votes upon measures that *chanced* to have been presented to the electorate in 1912, in the last election preceding the introduction of woman's suffrage. However, with respect to the measures before the electorate in 1914, they avoided a precedent of the Ogburn-Peterson study. Instead of inquiring into the "political thought of women," they sought an answer to the more behavioristic question as to "how women vote." It is possible that the availability of data had a part in determining the choice of conservatism, as the particular factor to be held constant in the partial correlations. It seems more probable, however, that this choice depended upon preconceptions concerning relationships among factors. This will be considered in the next section.

V. THE INFLUENCE OF PRECONCEPTIONS UPON THE
CHOICE OF DATA

It has been noted that some of the factors which provided Burgess with the bases of twenty-one classifications of paroled men were selected because the data were available. What determined, then, the choice of the remaining factors? Obviously, the investigator's belief that they would have predictive value. In other words, the choice depended upon preconceptions concerning relationship among the possible factors involved in the total situation of parole violations. These preconceptions were based upon the author's extensive familiarity with personality analysis, especially in connection with delinquent behavior. Before beginning his work Burgess had a "feel" for the problem. That the preconceptions were justified is shown by the results of classification. That is, each assumption that a given factor was related to parole violation thereby became a hypothesis, tested and supported by the actual classification. He may have had preconceptions, set up as hypotheses, which failed to meet the test. If so, these were eliminated quite properly from further consideration.

The question remains, nevertheless, whether the *most significant* factors were discovered. The investigator was compelled to employ data either because of their availability or because his preconceptions concerning the subject led him to believe that certain significant relationships existed. In either event, the results of the research are not conclusive with respect to other, unperceived, and possibly more important relationships.

In the partial correlation study by Ogburn and Goltra, the part played by preconceptions is even more pronounced. It will be desirable at this point to illustrate the logic underlying the procedure by reference to a particular set of relationships which the authors examined.[17] We may consider for this purpose the votes upon a measure calling for an eight-hour day for women in industry. In the absence of a separation of the votes of men and of women, the authors sought to learn whether women as a class were more or less in favor of this proposal than were men.

When 319 precincts were distributed in a simple correlation table, first, according to the proportion of women voting, and, second, according to the percentage of all votes cast for the measure, a negative relationship between the two variables was disclosed. The coefficient of simple correlation was -0.408. That is, a tendency existed for those precincts in which women were most numerous to cast proportionately smaller numbers of votes for the measure. May the varying support given to the measure be attributed to the varying proportions of women among the voters? An affirmative answer assumes that men as a class and women as a class were each divided on the question in the same ratio in all precincts. This would not, of course, be *exactly* the case. The percentages of favorable votes among either sex class would be now higher and now lower. If the factors determining these latter variations were of an unrelated or "chance" character only, then the "errors" which resulted would tend to "cancel," leaving the simple correlation as a true indication of a tendency for the sexes to differ in the manner suggested. But if there be some other variable factor or factors related in some definite manner to either of the two variables, then all or part of the simple correlation may be due to the new variable or variables.

The authors find such an additional factor in the attitude variable of conservatism or radicalism. That is, although the vote for the measure was higher in precincts where the proportion of women voting was lower, these precincts are more likely to appear in working-class districts where

---

[17] No effort is made here to discuss the technical statistical procedure, for which the reader is referred to standard texts.

attitudes toward political and economic questions are comparatively radical. The authors obtained an index of conservatism by averaging the percentages conservative on six measures in an election two years earlier, in which men only participated. It was found that the more conservative precincts have larger percentages of women voting, the simple correlation being + 0.29. The conservative precincts voted against the eight-hour day for women, the simple correlation being − 0.77. The coefficient of partial correlation in which the variable factor of conservatism is held constant is − 0.30. This shows that women, proportionately, voted against the measure more numerously than did the men, even apart from the fact that the women in conservative districts were more numerous or more likely to vote than were the women of the working classes. That is, among men and women who were presumed to be of the same cultural background, the women were relatively more opposed to the measure than were the men, although their opposition was not as great as indicated by the simple correlation coefficient first secured, namely, −0.408.

Upon each of the remaining twenty-five measures, conservatism-radicalism was employed as a third variable, and held constant, in obtaining partial correlation coefficients between the proportion of women voters and the percentage of affirmative votes. Conservatism-radicalism, that is, was assumed to be the all-important variable affecting the validity of the simple correlations between the other two. Its significance was demonstrated in the case of the eight-hour-day measure. On the other hand, its introduction did not alter the simple correlation in the case of a proposed consolidation of the city of Portland and Multnomah County. In the latter instance, r_{xy} and $_zr_{xy}$ each amounted to + 0.18. The corresponding simple and partial correlation coefficients differed but little with respect to prohibition and a number of proposals of administrative type.

It is apparent that other variable factors might have shown a higher association with woman's vote than did conservatism-radicalism upon some of the twenty-six initiative and referendum measures. For example, some of the proposed laws may have been favorable to one of the major political parties and not to the other. In this event, the distribution of party strength among the 319 precincts would have been an important variable to hold constant. The authors themselves recognize that conservatism has a fluctuating meaning according to the field of interest that is involved. They recognize, moreover, that each of the twenty-six measures should have been considered separately with respect to the possible third or more variables to be controlled statistically. The use throughout of a single third factor must be attributed, first, to a preconception concerning its importance in *some* of the twenty-six sets of voting records; second, to the non-conception or the non-availability of indices of other important variables.[18]

It is contended by cultural determinists that the general direction of scientific inquiry at a given time depends upon the "culture base," or the state of culture then existing. This position has been supported by much data respecting the independent invention of the same devices by different persons. Be this as it may, the considerations advanced in Sections III–V of this analysis suggest that the formulation of *particular* problems of inquiry and the choice of specific research data are largely dependent upon the chance conjoining of many factors.

VI.   SOME QUESTIONS CONCERNING GENERALIZATION AND THE CONTROL OF VARIABLES

The three inquiries purport to discuss, respectively, *social classes, women,* and *men paroled from three penal institutions.* Burgess is particularly cautious in disclaiming an intent to generalize beyond the confines of his data. In all three studies, nevertheless, the actual subject matter is more restricted than the universe for which conclusions are drawn. The questions of methodology raised by this fact may be viewed as questions of sampling, discussed more fully in a following section. However, they transcend sampling in its more usual sense as a process of random selection to represent a whole. They concern the extent to which inferences regarding a whole may be drawn from one of its *segments.* Thus Ogburn and Goltra seek to answer the question as to "how women vote" with data relating to women voters of Portland, Oregon, in a certain election. The women to which the data relate were a part or segment of the larger-class "women" or "American women," rather than a random sample of the latter. The problems involved may be illustrated by particular reference to "Political Thought of Social Classes."[19]

---

[18] Some of the assumptions involved in constructing the index of conservatism may be mentioned at this point. This was based, it will be recalled, upon votes by men only upon the conservative side of six measures at an election two years earlier. The determination of the "conservative side" is a subjective procedure. It is assumed, further, that women and men residing in the same precinct tend to have similar social or cultural status, and hence to reflect similar attitudes of conservatism or radicalism. It must also be assumed that these attitudes, as distributed among precincts, remained constant over a period of two years.

[19] The authors safeguard their conclusions with the statement: "Only to the extent that western society is like Oregon will the class differences be like those of Oregon."

"Society," a pure concept, may be further conceived as *divided* into "social classes." The particular classes resulting from division are again wholly conceptual. The authors find "no agreement among writers in defining the social classes." In their own inquiry they recognize *upper, middle, working, urban,* and *rural classes.*[20] The first three result from the application of economic criteria; the fourth and fifth from a demographic criterion. Society is thus twice divided, and each voter (if the two classifications were complete) would belong at the same time within two social classes. Analogously, Burgess placed each paroled man in twenty-one classes. The application of other criteria by Ogburn and Peterson might have resulted in the identification of other classes, in addition to those found. Thus, Ogburn and Goltra employed a sex criterion.

Assume that Ogburn and Peterson had sought to compare the political thought of western Americans with eastern Americans. A priori, it is probable that differences in political thought between these two additional classes exist. If the authors' method of procedure were employed in comparing them, however, the differences between economic classes, and between urban and rural classes, would be neglected. Hence, it would be impossible to say how much of the difference, hypothetically discovered, was essentially regional, and how much was due to the association of the respective regions with differing proportions of the economic or the urban-rural differentials.

It will be apparent that the validity of simple comparisons between or among classes which have been distinguished on the basis of one criterion depends upon the assumption that other factors are constant. Regional differences will be constant provided the universe of discourse is confined to a single region. But if data are taken from one region

---

[20] Cf. Robert S. and Helen M. Lynd, *Middletown: A Study of Contemporary Culture* (New York: Harcourt, Brace & Co., 1929), p. 23 n. In this middle western American city of approximately 38,000 population these authors distinguished two classes only. "In so far as the traditional threefold classification might be applied to Middletown today, the city would have to be regarded as having only a lower and a middle class; eight or nine households might conceivably be considered as an upper class, but these families are not a group apart, but are merged in the life of the mass of businessfolk. R. H. Gretton, while pointing out the difficulty of separating out any group in present-day industrial society as 'Middle Class,' defines it as precisely that group here called the business class: 'The Middle Class is that portion of the community to which money is the primary condition and the primary instrument of life. . . . . It . . . . includes merchant and capitalist manufacturers . . . . [and the] professional class.'—*The English Middle Class,* (London: Bell, 1917), pp. 1–13."

only (in this case the state of Oregon), may conclusions as to class differences be applied to a larger area of which the region is a part (let us say the United States)?

An affirmative answer is possible, but only if there is reason to assume that all of the other factors which may be associated with one or another of the classes compared remain substantially constant while the region is varying. If this condition should exist, the urban and rural classes, for example, should *differ* in "social thought," each from the other, to about the same extent throughout the United States as in Oregon; although an absolute measure of thought for either class would vary with the region. The assumed situation may be illustrated quantitatively: If rural and urban thought in Oregon were expressed on a linear scale of conservatism-radicalism by the indexes 50 and 40, respectively, the rural-urban difference in Oregon would be 10. In Ohio a rural-urban difference of 10 might still be expected, although the respective positions of the two classes on the absolute scale might have dropped to 45 and 35. The accuracy of the expectation would depend upon the constancy of all factors associated with urban and rural, other than that of region. A similar situation and a similar inference were presented by the analyst in his attempts to compare the political attitudes of farmers and workingmen.[21] It was contended in that instance that *differences* between farmers and workingmen in one state might be equated with differences between the same classes in another state, even though the attitudes of the two classes in the first state were more nearly identical, by any common standard, than were the attitudes of either class in one state when compared with those of the same class in another state.

The employment by Burgess of rates of parole violation for prediction involves assumptions similar to those just discussed. His rates are based upon the observance or non-observance of parole in 1,000 consecutive cases from each of three institutions. For a spatial or regional variable we here have substituted a time variable. That is, the use of these rates for prediction assumes that no factors related to observance or non-observance will be attached to changes in the time period. It is quite possible, even probable, that secular, cyclical, or seasonal influences upon parole behavior exist. In this event, however, and in the absence of contradicting evidence, it may still be assumed that the Burgess rates will point to the *relative* strength of factors in "success" among those which he has taken into account.

[21] In *Farmers and Workers in American Politics.*

VII.   SOME QUESTIONS OF SAMPLING ARISING IN THE
USE OF VOTES AS DATA

The Ogburn-Peterson study will alone be considered at this point. A complete enumeration of the members of the several social classes, even within the state of Oregon or any of its subdivisions, was an obvious impossibility. Still more difficult would have been a complete enumeration of "political thought." Samples of class membership consisted of voters, while samples of political thought were provided by votes. Many problems of definition and identification were thereby avoided but numerous questions remained. The objectivity or subjectivity of the sampling process will first be examined.

Members of the various classes have no invariant characteristics to distinguish them. The samples actually selected provided the best indication of the authors' concepts concerning the classes themselves. Essentially, then, the selection of samples to represent the various classes was a subjective process, a matter of opinion dependent upon the author's concepts.

In *form*, however, some of the samples were given pseudo-objectivity. For example, the sample of rural population consisted of voters in certain counties with defined population character as indicated by the United States Census of 1910. An arbitrary selection of individual counties was in this case merely replaced by an equally arbitrary definition of the counties *en bloc*. If the reader, wishing to repeat the investigation, were dissatisfied with the counties selected he would be free to set up another definition of "rural" which would produce a different selection, and this definition would be as valid as that employed by the authors.

Neither objective nor pseudo-objective criteria governed the selection of precincts to represent the upper, middle, and working classes in the city of Portland, but objective data and the subjective opinions of others were used as checks. The choice of Portland to represent city dwellers was also frankly subjective, although pseudo-objectivity might have been obtained. That is, the authors could have taken as their sample of city dwellers the voters in "all cities having a population in excess of" a certain number, say 100,000, which would have included the city of Portland alone.

Criticism of the manner in which samples were selected might be of two forms: the first would concern the consistency of the concepts of the various classes held by the authors. The second would concern the consistency between the concept and the sample. That is, it would deal with the representative character of the sample. In addition there might be criticism of the manner in which a class was conceived, but this would not be a criticism of the sampling procedure. No inconsistencies among the concepts of class have been noted, and attention may next be directed, therefore, to questions regarding the representative character of the samples.

As a first question of representation it may be asked, Are votes samples of political thought? The authors assume without discussion that they are, although they take note of the possibility that votes may be cast according to "chance," and that they may be affected by "ignorance and lack of awareness" with regard to the questions on the ballot.

The belief among politicians that chance is a factor in voting is evidenced by the frequent endeavor of candidates to secure first place upon a ballot.[22] Ignorance of the intent and probable effect of a proposal may result in any one of various reactions to it: the voter may reject it from motives of caution, or approve it on the assumption that it would not have been placed before him without adequate reason; or his decision may turn upon irrelevant details of phraseology in the title.

An even greater cause to question the authors' assumption is the consideration, advanced at the outset of this analysis, that a vote is a discrete and therefore crude index of an attitude variable. Crude though a vote be as an index of individual attitude, however, an aggregate of votes provides an indication of the modal attitude. For example, if the votes are cast overwhelmingly on one side of an issue, it may be safely assumed that the modal attitude falls within the continuum extending on that side from the point at which the issue is drawn, but at some distance from the latter. As a hypothetical case, assume that a referendum is conducted upon a proposal to establish the death penalty as a punishment for all felonies, and that the vote is in the ratio 45 for to 55 against the proposal. Although the proposal would be defeated, it could still be inferred that the modal attitude of the voters was one of considerable severity toward the punishment of crime. If, on the other hand, the vote were 5 for to 95 against, it would be apparent that the modal attitude was one of less severity, although it could not be inferred that it represented disfavor to *all* capital punishment. The relationship between the distribution of affirmative and negative votes in a dichotomous division, on the one hand, and the location of the modal attitude, on the other, has not been

---

[22] A quantitative test of this belief would offer no special difficulties. Non-coercion and an accurate count of ballots are here assumed. The possibility of quantitative tests for these conditions is suggested in Rice, *Quantitative Methods in Politics*, pp. 107–115.

adequately explored. Yet it is evident that the former is an index of the latter, however lacking in precision.[23]

A second question concerns the employment of voters as samples of a class. While the latter has not been defined, it is clear that it would include non-voters. Are the attitudes of non-voters represented by those of voters who have the same economic and social characteristics? The authors' implicit assumption of the affirmative may be questioned. Those who vote may be "selected" by one or more factors associated with opinions concerning the issues involved in the election.

Again it may be asked whether the geographical units were so selected as to contain fair samples of the respective classes. The American system of voting is by geographical districts, rather than by occupations or by some other basis of division of population. Hence the authors were compelled to include or reject in their samples *aggregates* of voters grouped together geographically. The chief difficulty here was that class divisions do not coincide with political boundaries. Each aggregate, in consequence, inevitably contained voters who did not belong in the class represented by the majority. The problem was to find areas showing the maximum possible coincidence with class character. Hence, *random* sampling was impossible, and was replaced by what might be called *selected* sampling. The discovery of sample areas to represent classes depended upon various evidences which must be considered separately.

City dwellers were represented by the voters of Portland, a city containing about one-third of the state's population of 670,000. "The next largest town contains only 14,000 inhabitants. There are only five towns in the state with a population each of between 5,000 and 10,000." The term "city" was not defined. If the authors meant by it "large city" they made the only available selection of a sample. On the other hand, if the next larger "towns" were also populated by city dwellers, the latter may not have been adequately represented by the voters of Portland.[24]

Another procedure with respect to the class of city dwellers is the re-

---

[23] "We might even be willing to weight the opinion which represented strong conviction, relative to the opinion which was weakly held and very near the point of indifference. According to any one of the possible lines of classification, an average opinion might theoretically be obtained, in which each opinion was weighted according to its place along the scale in the entire distribution" (*ibid.*, pp. 75–76. Also, *passim*, other references to votes as indexes of attitudes).

[24] It must also be noted that "city," in the sense of incorporated municipality, is not always coterminous with "urban area." For example, the built-up area of Philadelphia extends much beyond its corporate limits on the west, while the corporate limits are drawn several miles beyond the urban area on the northeast. Thus, persons of rural habitat may cast votes as residents of the city, and conversely.

verse of sampling. The authors observe: "The vote of a growing city is not necessarily typical of urban thought, because many of the inhabitants of the city have migrated from the country where the lasting impressions of childhood were fixed. The social thought of Portland is thus modified strongly in the direction of rural thought." Thus they recognize city dwellers as of two types, city bred and rural migrants. The authors' interest is essentially with the political thought of the former, but the data which they employ as indices are based upon the thought of both. Now a sample consists of less than a whole, so chosen if it is representative that it will exhibit in the same proportions all of the variations to be found in the given universe or whole. In the present situation, a complete enumeration within a universe is accepted as representative of one of its parts. This is valid if the characteristics of the part are imparted to the larger whole.

The rural population was represented by the voters of twenty selected counties. The concept "rural population" was again not defined. While the definition of the United States Census Bureau has frequently changed,[25] it now designates as "rural" the population outside of incorporated places of 2,500 or more inhabitants. The authors allowed the inclusion of some municipalities of 2,500 to 3,000 inhabitants, although the relative number of voters in such places was apparently not large. The indefiniteness of the concept contributes to two possible, though antithetical, objections to their sample.

1. The rural population of counties containing municipalities larger than 3,000 was excluded. This must be regarded as an important limitation upon the representativeness of the sample, provided there was association between social attitudes and factors which promoted or retarded the growth of larger communities. Among such possible factors the authors examined "isolation" and "non-isolation." They concluded that in Oregon, which in 1920 had thirty-six counties, a selection of twenty could not be markedly isolated. But other factors may have existed. For example, the heavily timbered western section of the state tends to contain the larger towns, built up by the lumber industry. At the same time the strictly rural population in these western counties tends to be concentrated upon smaller holdings and to employ different agricultural methods than those of the farmers in the semiarid eastern and central sections. It seems possible, then, that the rural population of the western counties (which tended to be excluded from the sample) possessed differ-

[25] Cf. analysis 11.

ent attitudes than those of the rural population in the eastern and central counties.[26]

2. Small towns were contained within the twenty selected counties, raising the question whether their presence affected the character of the sample of rural population. The authors believed that the attitudes of the villagers were dominated by those of the surrounding countrymen. Since the time of their writing, considerable evidence has accumulated to discredit this belief. The residents of small villages at times hold political opinions in sharp contrast to those of the farmers in the adjacent countryside.[27] The need of adequate definition of the concept "rural population" is again indicated.

The samples of the upper, middle, and laboring classes consisted of the voters in selected precincts in Portland. In making the selections a series of steps was involved: (1) a tentative selection of areas having the desired class characteristics—this depended upon familiarity with the city, a state of mind which includes remembered observations, information obtained from others, and inferences; (2) a choice of precincts from within the more indefinite class areas—maps were of technical assistance in making the necessary comparisons; (3) checks upon the precincts that had been selected, to verify the hypothesis that they were representative. Three types of check were employed. There was, first, further observation of superficial evidences concerning the wealth and social standing of the residents. A second check was secured by classifying the occupations of registered persons.[28] This classification was inexact, inasmuch as uniformity and control were lacking in recording the occupations of registrants.[29] Moreover, the occupation of a person does not alone establish his social status. A "lawyer," for example, might have belonged to any of the three social classes, if his status had been measured by income, interests, or associations. Much overlapping of occupations among the respective samples of classes was found to exist. A third check consisted of estimates from real estate operators concerning the average value and the range of values of homes within each group of sample precincts.

---

[26] The analyst has found that the voters of the sparsely settled, semiarid wheat counties of eastern Washington, the neighboring state to the north, are conservative; while the farmers in the river valleys adjacent to the cities of western Washington are radical. Cf. *Quantitative Methods in Politics,* chap. xi.

[27] Cf. *ibid.,* chap. xii.

[28] "Registered persons" is more inclusive than "voters" but less inclusive than "citizens" and still less inclusive than "residents."

[29] For example, three persons in the precincts used as representative of the upper class gave their occupations as "railroad"—which might mean anything from section hand to railroad president.

Similar estimates were procured from business men concerning the incomes of the residents.[30]

In size, the sample of city dwellers approached a complete enumeration of the voters in this class. The sample of rural voters, moreover, was a substantial part of the whole. The samples of voters of upper, middle, and laboring classes varied in each case from 1,300 to 1,400 in 1914 to between 600 and 700 in 1910. Although the size of the samples seems to have been adequate, certain alterations of precinct boundaries placed further limitations upon the choice of precincts in order to maintain comparability as between the two elections. The authors do not discuss the question whether adequacy in size of sample was dependent upon the number of precincts as well as upon the number of voters.

The problem of comparability was present in various other ways. The authors say: "In 1914, women voted, increasing the vote by approximately one-half. The period studied covers four years only, because a longer period would have shown a changed complexion of the precincts." It could not be assumed that the same voters went to the polls in each of the four elections, especially in view of the enfranchised women voters in 1914. Hence, it was necessary to assume that the class character of the precincts remained the same throughout the four-year period; that the voters in each election constituted a fair sample of the residents of the precincts; hence, that the several samples were fairly comparable with one another. Since none of these assumptions was strictly true, the authors were unwilling to make them for a period longer than four years.[31]

VIII.   SOME QUESTIONS RELATING TO COMPARISONS AMONG GROUPS BY THE
USE OF VOTES AS INDICES

The Ogburn-Peterson study will again receive primary attention in the consideration of this topic.[32]

---

[30] Several incidental problems of procedure are involved here: How were the real estate and business men selected? What were the methods of questionnaire or interview by means of which their estimates were elicited? Upon what grounds of inference were their estimates based?

[31] A comparison of the vote upon two measures in the same election involves similar assumptions, which are not strictly true. Voters often fail to mark ballots in the case of certain measures, which will differ in individual cases. Hence a different group of voters decides upon each measure in the same election. Even if the voters marking their ballots for each measure were exactly the same, assumptions somewhat alien to the facts would be necessary when the votes on separate measures were compared. For the vote is but an index. The extent to which it is an index of "thought," and the extent to which it is the result of snap judgment, of chance, or some other factor, will vary with each measure.

[32] Having described their processes of sampling, the authors refer to the samples as if they were the respective classes themselves. This mode of expression is convenient, and will be employed here.

The indices of thought, by means of which classes are compared, consist of "the average number of voters, out of one hundred of each class, voting in favor of the measure. Thus the first question is that of woman suffrage and the table shows that the rural class voted 46 out of 100 in favor, the city people 32 out of 100 in favor. . . . . " These "average numbers" are merely "percentages." The need of care in employing the term "average" is illustrated again in the Burgess paper. The author there says: " . . . . The simple method was adopted of grading each man as falling below or above the average of the 1,000 cases in each institution on all twenty-one points." But the concept of "average" pertains to variables, while the greater number of Burgess' classifications were based upon attributes. For example, in his Table XVII the percentages of parole violators who were "ego-centric," "socially inadequate," and "emotionally unstable" were presented. An average individual or an average value does not appear in such a classification, for the concept of average does not apply.[33]

A further ambiguity is introduced into the Ogburn-Peterson paper by a terminology representing the survival of a concept known to its critics as "the group fallacy." This appears in such expressions as "what each class thinks," "the upper class is more eager to support," etc. As a mode of shorthand expression of facts pertaining to individuals grouped together in classes, this language may be both permissible and useful. Yet to say of a class that "it favors" a measure more than another class may convey either of two meanings. It may mean "the voters of this class are more favorable" or "more voters of this class are favorable." These two propositions are by no means equivalent. The first implies that attitudes may be favorable or unfavorable in varying degrees, and that some kind of average has been obtained of the attitudes of the individuals in each class. The second implies that attitudes are of two discrete types, "favorable" and "unfavorable," and that the percentage of the former is larger among the individuals in one class than among those of the other. Hence, one of the propositions might be true and the other remain false, although it is probable that if one is true the other will be true also. That is, if the proportion of the membership favorable is larger in one class than in

---

[33] What is meant is that the violation rate in each group of each classification is compared with the rate for "all persons." The latter represents a standard of reference, and is the value which the author terms the "average." It is indeed possible to conceive of this rate as an average or mode, and it has been so presented by the analyst in the analogous situation of a division of votes (cf. *Quantitative Methods in Politics*, pp. 224–26). That is, the rate for "all persons" represents the normal or typical rate to which the average rates of subgroups, or of repeated random samples of the whole, would be expected to approximate.

the other, the average of favorable tendency (considered as a variable) is likely also to be higher in the first than in the second. But it is possible that more intense support within the relatively smaller group of favorable members of the second class might make both the average and the total "favorability" within the latter class the larger.

The authors' data will support statements of the type "more voters of this class are favorable." When the percentage of favorable votes in one class is deducted from the percentage of favorable votes in another, the difference provides a numerical index of the difference in thought between the two classes. For example, 46 per cent of the rural population and 32 per cent of the city dwellers were favorable to woman suffrage. The index of difference between these two classes was consequently 14.

Another type of comparison among classes concerned their willingness to change. Such a willingness was indicated in the case of any class and with respect to the subject matter of any particular measure by the percentage of affirmative votes among those cast. A composite index for a given class of its willingness to change was procured by averaging the percentages of affirmative votes cast upon a number of measures. That is, a relatively low average percentage affirmative was assumed to indicate conservatism, while a corresponding high average was taken to indicate radicalism.

The use of such an index assumed that each of the various proposals was expected to achieve some innovation. The authors recognized that "an occasional measure was placed in the ballot for the purpose of preventing change." The assumption was verified to the authors' satisfaction, however, in the case of 26 among 103 proposals. All of these

related to the larger social movements and are either progressive or radical. Unfortunately several of the measures were crudely drawn, one or two might be called foolish, and several could have attempted the same end by a more practical method. . . . . They include such topics as woman suffrage, single-tax, prohibition, eight-hour laws, employers' liability, reorganization of the state government, government ownership, sterilization of criminals and insane.[34]

The selection was neither objective nor pseudo-objective, but subjective. It depended upon concepts in the minds of the investigators. Other investigators might have omitted some measures which were included, such as "three-fourths verdict in civil cases" or "government inspectors and official magazine," and included some which the authors excluded, such as "classification of property for taxation" and "abolition of the death penalty."

[34] Ogburn and Peterson, op. cit., pp. 314–15.

IX. FURTHER SUGGESTIONS AND APPRAISAL

Perhaps the chief value of all of the three studies has been to suggest leads for further inquiry. Some of these have already been discovered and followed by other investigators, including the analyst. Others have been pointed out in the preceding pages.

A further interesting suggestion occurs in connection with an endeavor by Ogburn and Peterson to explain their comparison of classes by means of percentages of favorable votes. They say: "If 100 inhabitants of the city were placed in a room with 100 farmers, on the average 14 pairs would disagree on woman suffrage and 86 pairs would agree." The meaning of this assertion is obvious. It is based upon the fact that 46 per cent of the rural voters and 32 per cent of the city voters favored this particular issue. The difference between these percentages is 14 per cent. Yet the statement is essentially ambiguous, for it would be equally correct to say that on the average 78 pairs would disagree and 22 pairs would agree. The correct statement would depend upon the particular pairs that were established. Each voter would have 100 possibilities of being placed with a voter of the opposite class, and the total number of possible arrangements of individual pairs would be 100 × 100 or 10,000. In a random pairing of city voters with farmers it would be mathematically probable that 51.44 pairs would be in agreement and 48.56 pairs in disagreement.[35]

While not so intended by the authors, their illustration suggests the possibility of mathematical statements concerning the interplay of social relationships, which so often seem to be infinitely varied. If 100 members each of two social classes were placed together, and a favorable or unfavorable attitude in each person postulated, potential relationships of agreement or disagreement would be in existence concurrently between each member and every other. These potential relationships would be finite in number. The extent to which they became conscious, and therefore real, would depend upon many factors, and would thus be indeterminate. The number of potential relationships would depend upon the combinations of two, between and within the various groupings. The questions involved here seem to offer a promising field of inquiry. Some further suggestions concerning it appear in the following appendix.

The method of partial correlation as a means of analyzing public opinion through the use of votes has received further exemplification by Ogburn in a more recent article, in which is examined the relative strength of factors operating in the choice between presidential candidates in the

[35] Cf. the appendix to this analysis.

election of 1928.[36] The possibilities of the method as a tool for the investigation of public opinion seem to be limited less by scarcity of data than by the general unfamiliarity with it of workers in this field.

The methods of prediction based upon classification which Burgess has developed have already been used by a number of other investigators, and seem destined to considerable extension of use when their nature and their limitations have become familiar.[37]

The considerations that have been advanced in the preceding analysis represent a selection among possible topics of methodological discussion in the three papers examined.[38]

APPENDIX: PAIRING VOTERS OF TWO CLASSES

If 100 farmers, 46 of whom favored woman suffrage, and 100 city dwellers, 32 of whom favored it, were placed together, what would be the numbers of pairs in agreement and in disagreement? Ogburn and Peterson assert (for the purpose only of illustrating a step in procedure) that 86 pairs would agree and 14 pairs would disagree.

But members could be paired together in a large number of ways. The authors have based their statement upon arrangements which would produce the maximum possible number of agreeing pairs. The corresponding minimum of agreement would be secured if 32 city dwellers who favored the measure were paired with an equal number of rural dwellers who opposed it; and 46 rural voters who favored it were paired with 46 city dwellers who opposed it, the total number of opposing pairs being 32 plus 46, or 78.

[36] William F. Ogburn and Nell Snow Talbot, "A Measurement of the Factors in the Presidential Election of 1928," *Social Forces*, VIII (December, 1929), 175–83.

[37] Professor George B. Vold, of the University of Minnesota, in a manuscript entitled "Factors Involved in the Violation or Non-violation of Parole in a Group of Minnesota Adult Males," still unpublished at the time of this writing, has subjected Professor Burgess' study and several others of similar type to a keenly critical analysis. Vold pays particular attention to the problem of reliability, to which none of these studies, or any of those examined in this analysis, has devoted attention. In his own study of Minnesota paroles, Vold has endeavored to test the reliability of his classifications in a variety of ways. These include reclassification by another investigator and by himself at a subsequent date. Several statistical devices are employed for comparing the results of these several classifications. Vold concurs with the view expressed elsewhere by the analyst that existing statistical methodology for the testing of the reliability of measurements based upon subjective classifications cannot at best be regarded as satisfactory. It still awaits development. Vold's own work probably represents the most definite attempt yet made to face this question. Cf. Rice and Weaver, *op. cit.*, n. 1.

[38] An outline analysis of the Ogburn-Peterson study, purporting to approach completeness of methodological exposition, was completed in November, 1927. Its length greatly exceeded that of the present paper. The Ogburn-Goltra paper was examined

The probability that both voters in a pair, each selected at random, would be favorable to the measure would be found by multiplying the probabilities of a favorable attitude in each separately; i.e.:

$$46/100 \times 32/100 = 1,472/10,000 .$$

The probability of both being opposed would be

$$68/100 \times 54/100 = 3,672/10,000 .$$

Agreement can occur by both members being in favor or by both members being opposed. To find the total probability of agreement, therefore, the foregoing may be added. The probability of agreement becomes

$$5,144/10,000 .$$

for a single pair. Similarly, the probability of disagreement is found to be

$$4,856/10,000 .$$

If there is a random pairing among 100 voters of each class, then it is probable (in a mathematical sense) that 51.44 pairs will be in agreement and 48.56 pairs in disagreement.

But in any pairing of the 200 voters, each voter would have 100 possibilities of being placed with a voter of the opposite class. The total number of combinations or arrangements of individual pairs, therefore, would be 100×100 or 10,000. Each of these arrangements is equally probable. That is, in 10,000 pairings of the 200 voters all together each arrangement would be expected to occur once. But each arrangement will produce some ratio of agreement (as well as disagreement) having as its denominator 100 and having as its numerator some even whole number between 22 and 86 inclusive. That is, there will be 33 possible ratios of agreement of which the two already mentioned, namely, 22/100 and 86/100, are the extremes. The distribution would tend to be such that in the aggregate 51.44 per cent of the individuals paired would be in agreement and 48.56 in disagreement.

It would be possible to construct a probability table showing the number of pairings together of the 100 voters of each class, among 10,000 of such pairings together, which would produce each of the 33 possible ratios of agreement. The extreme ratios (one of which has been made

---

less exhaustively in 1928, in a separate analysis. Some of the questions raised here were among those discussed in these earlier papers. The present analysis was completed in June, 1930.

the basis of conclusions by Ogburn and Peterson) would occur less frequently than the intermediate ratios, the whole taking the form of a frequency curve with a mode near the center of the range of values.

This may be illustrated empirically with a smaller number of cases: Ten farmers were represented by square bits of cardboard of uniform size. Four of these were presumed to vote affirmatively, and 6 negatively. Each was marked accordingly and the entire 10 placed in a hat. Similarly, 10 city voters of which 3 voted affirmatively and 7 negatively were represented by octagonal cardboard counters and placed in a second hat. Ten pairs were drawn simultaneously from the two hats and the number of agree-

TABLE I

Number of Pairs In		Number of Drawings of Ten Pairs Each	Number of Individual	
Agreement	Disagreement		Agreements	Disagreements
3	7	8	24	56
5	5	21	105	105
7	3	19	133	57
9	1	2	18	2
Totals.....	....	50	280	220

ments recorded. The process was repeated fifty times. The probable number of agreements between individual pairs was

$$[(3/10 \times 4/10) + (6/10 \times 7/10)] \times 10 \times 50 = 270.$$

The probable number of disagreements was

$$[(3/10 \times 6/10) + (4/10 \times 7/10)] \times 10 \times 50 = 230.$$

The results of the experiment appear in Table I. They are very close to the "expectation," or probability. The possible ratios of agreement were in this case 3/10, 5/10, 7/10, and 9/10, the odd numerators resulting from the complementary character of the numbers in each class favorable and unfavorable.

In a similar series of trials with the rural voters divided as before, but with the city voters divided 2 in favor and 8 opposed, the expected number of individual agreements was 280, and of individual disagreements 220. Precisely these numbers were obtained, in the distributions shown in Table II.

If the authors were to follow in these two cases the same type of argument which they have used in their hypothetical illustration, they would say that nine pairs and eight pairs, respectively, were in agreement, neglecting the fact that these proportions of agreement appeared in the first case but two times in 50, and in the second case but seven times in 50.

The number of combinations of n things taken r at a time may be found from the formula

$$C_{nr} = \frac{n(n-1)\ (n-2)\ \ldots\ (n-r+1)}{r!}$$

in which $r!$ is factorial r or $1 \times 2 \times 3 \times \ldots r$. The application of this formula to the present supposed situation will give the number of combinations or pairs among the members of each class separately, and

TABLE II

NUMBER OF PAIRS IN		NUMBER OF DRAWINGS OF TEN PAIRS EACH	NUMBER OF INDIVIDUAL	
Agreement	Disagreement		Agreements	Disagreements
4	6	17	68	102
6	4	26	156	104
8	2	7	56	14
Totals.....	....	50	280	220

also among the entire number of voters in the room. The sum of the first two figures deducted from the third will give the number of combinations in which one voter of each class enters, or this latter number may be procured directly.

The possible number of combinations will be as follows:

Pairs of city voters with city voters............... 4,950
Pairs of rural voters with rural voters............. 4,950
Pairs of city voters with rural voters.............. 10,000
                                                        ————
                                                        19,900

The possible number of combinations under each of the three categories just named is also the possible number of agreeing pairs within it (to be obtained in case all voters entering the given category of combinations voted alike).

It may then be asked in the case of either class of voters, whether city or rural: If a voter of this class is paired at random with another voter of the same class, what is the probability of agreement upon the question of woman suffrage? How does this probability compare with the probability of agreement if paired at random with a voter of the second class?

Answers to these questions appear to be mathematically possible in any given case, although they involve difficulties of logical character. For example, answers to the first question depend upon the numbers of voters in the class as well as upon the ratios of affirmative and negative votes within the class. The probability expressed as a percentage will be different, that is, when the division is 60–40 and when it is 120–80. Moreover, the probability of agreement declines but at a decreasing rate as the percentage of favorable or unfavorable votes declines from 100.0 to 50.0 and again increases and at an increasing rate as the percentage continues to decline from 50.0 to 0.0. It follows as a corollary that there is a minimum below which the number of agreeing pairs within a class cannot fall, at the point when the division on the question reaches 50–50. When the number of voters in the class is 100 this possible minimum of agreement is approximately 49.5 per cent, or, in other words, there must be, whatever the division, at least 2,450 pairs in agreement among the aggregate 4,950 pairs which are to be found among the 100 voters of a class. When 100 voters of one class are paired with 100 of another, however, the number of agreements may range from 0 to 10,000.

The procedure suggested here, if amplified, might provide indices of the extent to which the voters of each class were cohesive as a class. The cohesion of two classes could then be compared. But this comparison would not indicate anything with respect to the comparative thought of voters of the two classes upon the measures voted upon, because it would take no account of the *direction* of the votes, whether favorable or unfavorable. A technique developed along the lines here suggested, however, would avoid the use of the group concept by employing direct comparisons between the votes of individuals.

THE INDUCTIVE TESTING OF AN ECONOMIC DEDUCTION: A METHOD ILLUSTRATED BY ANALYSES OF MARGINAL PRODUCERS AND REPRESENTATIVE FIRMS, BY ALFRED MARSHALL, HORACE SECRIST, AND KEMPER SIMPSON[1]

By RAYMOND T. BYE

University of Pennsylvania

Prior to the present century, the method of study pursued by economists was almost wholly one of deduction from a few simple premises, the premises being derived from common experience and observations of a very casual sort. It was assumed, for instance, that men are governed by motives of monetary loss or gain, and that labor and capital are mobile enough to shift readily from one employment or investment to another. Out of such assumptions it was possible to arrive, by chains of logical reasoning, at a body of principles which constitutes the bulk of economic theory as we know it today. This method of analysis was attacked by the writers of the historical school, who sought to build up a new body of economics by undertaking a series of historical studies of economic institutions; but their constructive achievements were disappointing, and so, in spite of their criticisms, the deductive method continued to prevail. Within the past two or three decades, however, the growth of statistics has shown the possibility of applying a new technique to the study of economic phenomena, and a number of zealous workers have applied themselves diligently to its exploitation. Again, the method of deduction is being denounced, and the truth of the economic doctrines developed by its means is being seriously questioned. We are being told that the older body of theory must be thrown into the discard, and a different set of scientific principles built up by new methods, in which statistical induction will play an important part.[2]

---

[1] The first draft of this paper, written in July, 1928, was submitted to Professors F. S. Deibler, of Northwestern University; R. Opie, of Harvard University; and H. Secrist, of Northwestern University. I have been able, in the revision, March, 1929, to improve on the earlier version by adopting a number of their suggestions. On some of their criticisms I shall comment in the footnotes.

[2] Professor Opie objects to the contrast here drawn between "deduction" and "induction," which he says is "unfortunate and both historically and philosophically unsound." In this connection he refers to the excellent article on "Statistics and

It can hardly be denied that the increasing use of statistics is a move-ment of the greatest significance for economic theory. No science which deals with concrete phenomena can progress very far until it is able to make precise, quantitative measurements of its data. So long as the econ-omist was forced to rely upon casual observation for his facts, his con-clusions were necessarily of a tentative, and often of a vague, character. At best they could be no more than qualitative. At their worst they could be positively erroneous. Statistics afford inductive information which, when carefully handled, can be used to give quantitative precision to economic analysis, and to detect inaccuracies in deductive generalizations. But it is not to be concluded that all of the existing principles of economics are false, merely because they have been reached by deductive analysis, nor that these principles are to be replaced by an entirely new set of generalizations arrived at by inductive means. Like induction, deduction is a powerful tool of thought when employed with discretion. Many of the great truths of science are the result of reflective analysis, rather than of experimentation or fact-gathering. The Einstein theory of relativity, which has so revolutionized the thinking of physicists, is a conspicuous illustration of this. If such results can be obtained by deduction in a science so peculiarly suited to the use of laboratory research and induc-tion as physics, it is not unreasonable to suppose that the method may not be entirely fruitless in economics. It is quite probable that the economic principles arrived at by several generations of able thinkers, checking and correcting one another's results as they did, will prove to be of some validity when the last word has been said about them. But the new tech-nique should make it possible to refine and complete them, to detect such

Economic Theory," by Warren E. Persons, which appeared in the *Review of Economic Statistics*, VII (July, 1925), 179–97. He objects also to my use of the phrase "a priori" in a later part of this paper.

It should be stated, perhaps, that the difference between "deduction" and "in-duction" in economics is largely one of emphasis. Economic theory has not been built up by pure deduction without reference to actual experience—nor have I said that it has. I have explained that the older writers drew upon *casual* observation and experience for much of their data. Moreover, they recognized the value of inductive study and expected it to occupy a position of increasing importance in the future; but they were compelled to rely mainly on deduction because of the lack of available statistical material. Hence, it is correct to describe their work as mainly deductive in character.

As to the phrase "a priori," I have used it in its broader sense, as a synonym for "deduction." Professor Opie is correct in observing that it cannot properly be applied here in its strictly philosophical meaning, for this would imply that the premises from which economic theory proceeds are purely abstract assumptions not based on *any* actual experience.

errors in them as exist, and to supplement them with fresh generalizations made possible by data not at the disposal of the earlier economists.

Henceforth, then, deductive analysis and statistical observation in the field of economics must go hand in hand. There are at least three complementary relations between them which await development. In the first place, the generalizations of deductive theory must be tested and corrected by statistical studies. Deductive theory will thus suggest problems for the statistical economist to attack. The results of his work will serve to verify or refute the theory. Frequently, perhaps usually, it will be found that the theory is neither wholly true nor wholly false, but that it has not been sufficiently qualified or refined to fit the facts of the actual world. The recorded data will indicate the limitations and the discrepancies, and further reflection will then make possible the restatement of the doctrine in such a way as to conform accurately to the known phenomena. The revised theory will be the perfected development of its somewhat less accurate predecessor. In the second place, statistical work will make possible the statement in quantitative terms of propositions which deductive economics could develop only qualitatively. This will enable economic principles to be applied to the solution of economic problems which would otherwise be insoluble. For instance, economic theory can tell us that if the demand for cotton increases, the price of this commodity is likely to rise; but it tells us merely the direction, not the amount, of the price change. Not until we are in a position to construct actual demand curves, and measure the supply and the costs of production of cotton, can we use our knowledge of the laws of demand and supply for practical purposes, such as forecasting future changes in, or controlling, the price of cotton.[3] The growth of statistical work of this sort is proceeding at a very satisfactory rate, so that we may be encouraged to believe that the time is not too far distant when economics may fairly pretend to be a quantitative science. Finally, statistical work in various fields may give rise to entirely new theories where none existed before, or where older theories are shown to be clearly inadequate. Induction of this sort may yield generalizations which will constitute premises for further deductive analysis, leading to a new body of theory. The literature on business cycles, of which so much has appeared in the last decade and a half, and which owes its existence largely to the leadership of Professor Wesley C. Mitchell, is an excellent illustration.

[3] An interesting attempt to forecast the price of cotton by the construction of demand curves on the basis of statistical data has actually been made by Professor H. L. Moore, of Columbia University. See his *Forecasting the Yield and the Price of Cotton* (1917). [Cf. also analysis 46.—EDITOR.]

In the remainder of this paper, it is proposed to consider an example of the first of these three sorts of relations between deductive and inductive work, viz., the statistical testing and refinement of an abstract economic theory. The theory chosen for analysis is that connected with the concepts of the marginal producer and the representative firm, which figure in contemporary economic doctrine (especially in the writings of Alfred Marshall), and upon which certain recent statistical studies (notably those of Professor Horace Secrist, of Northwestern University) shed considerable light.[4]

It is in connection with the theory of value that the concepts of the marginal producer and the representative firm are found. According to this theory, the value of a commodity tends to settle at a point which equals the cost of producing a unit of it. This proposition is supported by a chain of logical reasoning which runs somewhat as follows: It is assumed that producers will not permanently continue to supply a commodity to the market if its price is less than their unit-costs, for in that case they would suffer losses, and sooner or later they would withdraw from the industry. A decrease in the supply of the commodity would result from this withdrawal, and its price would consequently rise, for it is taken as a law of the market that the smaller the amount of a commodity offered for sale at a given time, the higher will be the price which it can command. In the long run, then, value cannot remain below the cost of production of the commodity concerned. Neither, it is argued, can it remain above it; for if it rose higher than cost for a time, producers would then be enjoying more than the normal returns to capital and management. This would encourage them to increase their output, and would attract new enterprises into the industry. The attendant increase in the supply of the commodity would force its value down until it no longer exceeded costs. Thus, by showing that value will always return to costs if it is temporarily forced below or above them, the conclusion is established that cost of production determines its "normal" position. It is apparent that this theory is based very largely on deductive logic.

[4] This essay is not at all to be construed as an analysis of the writings of Marshall and Secrist as a whole. It is not a "case study" of these writers, but of a particular phase of economic theory. I have made use of such portions only of the work of these men as serve to illuminate this particular theoretical problem, and I have selected these portions because, taken together, they constitute an excellent illustration of my general thesis. In addition. I have made use of certain supplementary material taken from an article by Kemper Simpson, which will be noted in its proper place.

[The place occupied by the present analysis in relation to Professor Bye's concepts of the methodological problems of economics is indicated in Appendix D.— EDITOR.]

The theorists recognize, however, that this statement of the matter is far too simple, for account must be taken of two circumstances, characteristic of actual industrial conditions, which somewhat modify the foregoing analysis. In the first place, most theorists point out that, if the market situation is against the producers, they will accept a price less than their unit-costs, and will even continue producing *for a short period*, provided it does not fall below the prime costs of production. Marshall stresses this fact especially.[5] He points out that enterprisers usually have a considerable quantity of durable capital, in the form of buildings, machinery, and the like, which occasions certain fixed costs that run on whether their plants are operated or not. Any price that can be obtained above the prime costs of operating reduces the loss suffered on account of these fixed charges, and makes it worth while to continue operations. Hence, at a given time, it might be found that some firms would be selling at less than their total unit-costs of production. In the second place, it is to be expected that the costs of the various producers engaged in the production of a given commodity will differ considerably. Some enjoy greater advantages than others, and some are more efficient in management. To whose costs, then, do values tend to conform? It is here that the concept of the marginal producer is found useful. It is reasoned that the output of those plants which have the lowest costs will not be adequate to satisfy a given demand. Some of the producers with higher costs must, therefore, be induced to contribute to the supply. They will do this only if the price is high enough to cover *their* costs of production. Price must, therefore, be established at a point which will bring into the market precisely enough output to meet the demand. There will be certain producers who just consider it worth while to produce at that price, because the latter just covers their costs of production. It is they who constitute the *marginal producers*, and their costs are spoken of as *marginal costs*.[6]

[5] Alfred Marshall, *Principles of Economics* (5th or subsequent edd.) ; Book V, chap. v., esp. § 6.

[6] Marshall lays more stress on the concept of marginal *costs*, and less on that of marginal *producers*, than do some other writers. He thinks of all the producers as putting out a part of their product at or near the level of marginal costs, it being to their interest to take on additional business at high unit-costs so long as costs do not exceed the selling price. He recognizes, however, the existence of some producers who are "wholly on the margin." See his *op. cit.* (7th ed., 1916), p. 373.

It should also be pointed out that a different concept of the marginal producer is to be found in economic literature. He is sometimes conceived of as the producer who uses the poorest land that it pays to cultivate, and who is thus on the "margin of cultivation." In the present essay the phrase is used to refer only to those producers whose unit-costs (including the rent of land) are just equal to the selling price. These are not necessarily (and will not usually be) the producers who are employing marginal, or no-rent, land.

This situation can be illustrated nicely by Figure 1, which is similar to the diagrams which Marshall and other economic theorists employ. Here quantities of the commodity are measured along the line OX, beginning at the point O, and prices along the line OY. DD' represents the demand to which the supply is temporarily adjusted. It indicates that, as the quantity offered on the market increases (as, e.g., from OM to OM') the price that can be got for a unit of it must fall (from OP to OP'), in accordance with the well-known law of demand. SS' is what Marshall

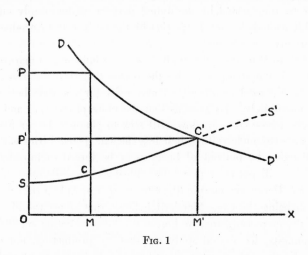

Fig. 1

calls a "particular expenses curve." It indicates the different levels of expense at which different units of the commodity are supplied to the market; it therefore measures the differences in the unit-costs of the different producers.[7] Thus we assume that some of the commodity (such as the Mth unit on the diagram) is produced at a low cost (such as MC), because the producers of that portion of the supply are favorably circumstanced, while other portions (such as the M'th unit) are produced at higher costs (such as $M'C'$), because they come from plants with a less economical position. In this situation, a low price will be likely to exclude from the market those producers who have high costs, because they cannot then dispose of their product without loss. A high price, on the other hand, will attract the producers with high costs into the market, thereby increasing

[7] This curve should be carefully distinguished from Marshall's "normal supply" curve, which measures the unit-costs at which a representative firm could produce given quantities of the commodity if it were organized with a plant of appropriate size and technique for handling the requisite output. See *ibid.*, Appendix H, § 4, n. 2 (pp. 810–12).

the supply. But, as supply increases, the price which buyers will pay, as shown by the demand curve, falls. There is a point of equilibrium where the falling demand-price meets the rising costs of production. Here price tends to settle, for quantity demanded then exactly equals quantity supplied. In Figure 1 this price is represented by OP', quantity demanded and quantity supplied being equalized at OM'. The producer of the M'th unit is here the marginal producer, and $M'C'$ indicates the marginal costs, which are just equal to the selling price. Potential producers with still higher costs, represented by the dotted portion of the supply curve, are presumably excluded from the market by their inability to produce profitably at the price established.[8]

According to Marshall's theory, however, the influence of marginal costs upon values is only temporary, for the reason that such differences in the costs of the different producers as may exist for the time being cannot continue indefinitely.[9] He reasons that the more progressive and efficient enterprisers, whose costs are low, will seek to obtain a larger proportion of the business by underselling their less efficient rivals. Firms with higher costs will either be put out of business or be forced to introduce economies, which will put them in a class with their erstwhile more successful competitors. Hence, the marginal producers occupy only a transitory position. Such being the case, Marshall believes that if we would ascertain what are the more enduring, or long-run influences acting on the supply of a commodity, we should study the costs of production, not of those firms which are on the margin, but of those which may be thought of as typical of the trend in the industry as a whole. It is here that he employs the device of the representative firm. In describing this somewhat elusive concept he says:

[8] This diagram, as Marshall draws it, is assumed to represent the equilibrium that would be reached in a stationary state, where all temporary differences in costs may be presumed to be eliminated. It can be used to represent a temporary situation, with temporary differences in costs prevailing, however; and it is in that sense that I shall employ it for purposes of comparison with Figs. 2, 3, and 4 below. I have already pointed out that Marshall regards prime costs as of more significance, for short periods, than total unit-costs. He would not argue that, in actual industry, at a given time, price would necessarily equal marginal total unit-costs. The significance of this will be made apparent later in the discussion. See p. 626.

[9] The only permanent differences in costs which Marshall recognizes are those due to permanent differences in the quality of lands. But for our problem these differences may be expected to disappear also; for they will be absorbed by compensating differences in the rents which users of land must pay, and these rents will be included in the expenses of production represented by our supply curves. This is in accord with the tendency of modern theorists to include land rents in the costs of production.

We shall have to analyse carefully the normal cost of producing a commodity, relatively to a given aggregate volume of production; and for this purpose we shall have to study *the expenses of a representative producer* for that aggregate volume. On the one hand we shall not want to select some new producer just struggling into business, who works under many disadvantages, and has to be content for a time with little or no profits, but who is satisfied with the fact that he is establishing a connection and taking the first steps towards building up a successful business; nor on the other hand shall we want to take a firm which by exceptionally long-sustained ability and good fortune has got together a vast business, and huge well-ordered workshops that give it a superiority over almost all its rivals. But our representative firm must be one which has had a fairly long life, and fair success, which is managed with normal ability, and which has normal access to the economies, external and internal, which belong to that aggregate volume of production; account being taken of the class of goods produced, the conditions of marketing them, and the economic environment generally.[10]

It is by watching the expenses of such a firm, in his opinion, that the long-run influences acting on the prices of commodities are to be observed. It is to the expenses of such a firm that values, in the long run, tend to conform. The reasoning at this point is exceedingly subtle. It is not supposed that the effect of competition is actually to level the costs of all producers; nor should we expect to find, by investigation, that the costs of production in any given industry, at a given time, are the same. We have already seen that he expects them to differ in any given situation. It is merely assumed, on logical grounds, that the influence of competition exerts a *tendency* to reduce differences in costs, and if we were to examine the costs of the various firms in an actual case over a series of years, we should expect to find them moving toward a common center. That center, says Marshall, is exemplified by those firms which maintain themselves over a period of years, and which are, therefore, representative of the industry at large.

But how can we speak of a leveling tendency among costs, if, in fact, their differences always remain as great as they were before? Marshall reasons in this way: While the more efficient firms are moving toward low costs, new ones are springing up whose costs are high during the period of their immaturity; and old, slowly dying ones are still in existence, whose costs are also high during the period of their senescence. The process is everlasting. Hence the center is only a focal point, exemplified, according to Marshall, by those firms which maintain themselves over

---

[10] A. Marshall, *op. cit.*, Book IV, chap. xiii, § 2, p. 317. See also Book V, chap. v, § 7, and Book V, chap. xii, §§ 2 and 3.

a period of years, and which are, therefore, representative of the industry as a whole.

All this, it must be repeated, is established chiefly by deductive reasoning. We are asked to accept it from the logic of the argument, rather than by any appeal to inductive evidence. No confirmation of the conclusions is presented from the facts of industry, other than such verification as may be adduced by the reader from his casual observation of industrial phenomena. Its validity rests, therefore, on the truth of the premises from which it proceeds, and on the inexorableness of its logic. But in a chain of reasoning so long, dealing with phenomena, some factor important to the argument is likely to be overlooked; modifying circumstances may easily be disregarded, and false conclusions can be arrived at. One cannot be sure of the correctness of the theory without verification from experience, and casual observation cannot be relied upon for such verification. The doctrine must be tested with scientific tools of another sort. Here is an opportunity for the inductive economist, who uses the methods of statistics.

It is to this problem that Secrist has applied himself in a series of studies in statistics upon which he has recently been engaged. He believes that by the proper use of statistical methods it is possible to detect laws— or "uniformities," as he prefers to call them—which reveal constant tendencies in the apparently varied, complex, and changing phenomena of competitive industry. He has devoted himself to the discovery of such laws in three industries: the retail distribution of clothing, the retail distribution of hardware, and banking.[11] His work in the retail distribution of clothing is particularly pertinent for the purposes of the present inquiry, for it deals specifically with the evidence bearing upon the existence or nonexistence of marginal and representative firms in this industry. I shall, therefore, devote the remainder of this essay primarily to it, supplementing the analysis with certain data from other sources. It will furnish an excellent illustration of the possibilities offered by statistics for the testing and the refinement of economic theory.

Secrist's study was based on figures obtained from one hundred and

[11] See Horace Secrist, *Competition in the Retail Distribution of Clothing—a Study of Expense or "Supply" Curves* (1923) ; *Expense Levels in Retailing—a Study of the "Representative Firm" and of "Bulk-line" Costs in the Distribution of Clothing* (1924) ; *The Widening Retail Market and Consumers Buying Habits* (1926) ; *Margins, Expenses and Profits in Retail Hardware Stores* (1928) ; and *Banking Standards under the Federal Reserve System* (1928). These studies have been published for the Bureau of Business Research, Northwestern University, of which Professor Secrist is the director. The present analysis is mainly concerned with the first two of the titles named.

seventy identical retail clothiers, for the five consecutive years from 1916 to 1920, inclusive. These firms were so distributed both in size and in geographic location as to be fairly typical of the industry as a whole in this country. As the business is an actively competitive one, it affords a good basis for testing the accuracy of Marshall's reasoning.[12] It was possible to ascertain, for all of these dealers, their expenses (or monetary costs) per unit of product (the product in this case being a service— the *sale* of merchandise, and the unit a hundred dollars of such sales). How did these costs compare among the various enterprises? Considerable differences in costs were clearly shown, so that the dealers could be arranged in series, beginning with those of low expenses and ending with those of highest. If these were then plotted in the form of a graph, the curve resulting was very much like the "particular expenses" curve of Marshall's theory. The curve for stores in cities of 40,000–120,000 population, for the year 1916, is reproduced in Figure 2. In this drawing, the figures on the vertical scale (OY) represent expenses per one hundred dollars of sales, those on the horizontal scale (OX) showing the percentage of the total supply contributed by each dealer. The broken line SS' is thus a supply curve, indicating the costs at which successive increments of the product were contributed to the market. It differs from the supply curve of Figure 1 only in that, since it deals with finite numbers, it is a broken line, whereas the curve of Figure 1 is a purely conventional, continuous line, intended to represent infinitesimal differences in the costs of the different producers. All of Professor Secrist's curves have the same general shape as the one here reproduced, and so have the similar curves constructed by other investigators for other commodities from time to time.[13]

[12] Deibler points out that there are two respects in which Secrist's data do not exactly represent the situation which Marshall had in mind. In the first place he shows that, while the industry concerned is a competitive one, not all of the firms included were in *direct competition with one another*, being scattered, as they were, in different cities and towns. Indirectly, however, they are competitors of one another, and the samples taken are so representative that it might not be unreasonable to assume that they show approximately what the situation would be among all the stores of a given community. Nevertheless, Deibler is justified in advising caution in the matter of drawing conclusions.

In the second place, he states: "I think recognition should be made of the fact that the data had to do with firms that remained in business throughout the period. It gives no information concerning the expenses of firms that may have failed, to see how close these figures were to those that remained in business. According to Marshall's mode of reasoning, the margin of difference would not be great. Here, again, I see no reason for pressing unduly the information that we have; hence, I think some recognition should be given to the limits of this inductive data."

[13] In Secrist's studies of banks and retail hardware stores, cited in n. 11, costs were found to follow the same general pattern. See also the curves in F. W. Taussig,

So far, the facts seem to accord fairly well with the theory. There are clearly some producers with high costs, who may perhaps be described as marginal,[14] and others with lower costs who enjoy a position of differential advantage. But the study affords a more precise knowledge of the nature of the supply curves, and the relation of marginal producers there-

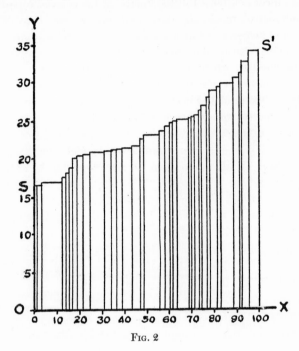

FIG. 2

to, than could have been established by deductive reasoning. On the basis of the data, the *exact shape* of the cost curve for this one product, and the differences in the curves for different years and different places, are made known. Here is quantitative information in place of the merely qualitative information afforded by the a priori analysis. The study also reveals an interesting fact about the changing positions of the various producers on the curves which, while it might have been inferred from Marshall's reasoning about the leveling effects of competition, is much more clearly

---

"Price Fixing as Seen by a Price Fixer," *Quarterly Journal of Economics*, XXXIII (February, 1919), 205–41; and P. G. Wright, *Sugar in Relation to the Tariff* (1924), esp. pp. 108 and 111.

[14] See further comment on this on p. 625.

shown by the statistical study.[15] By tracing the relative expenses of identical producers in successive years, Secrist found that there was a great deal of shifting going on. Producers whose costs were great at one time, and who might be described as marginal, often (in fact, usually) succeeded in reducing their expenses in the succeeding period, other firms meanwhile receding (through a rise in their costs) to the marginal position. They were continually exchanging places with one another. Thus few dealers, if any, could be described as marginal producers for any extended period of time, and any firm might find itself on the margin occasionally. This raises the question whether it is advisable to stress the concept of the marginal producer is a significant one for value theory, or whether it is not better to speak of the margin (as Marshall usually does) simply as a level of expense, rather than to apply this term to any individual; for, as Secrist says, "There do not appear to be marginal producers who hold their positions year after year, although marginal conditions are always present." Here is additional light on the theory made possible by the use of statistics.

Can we go farther and apply the statistics to that part of Marshall's theory which holds that there is a tendency for values to conform to marginal costs? Here we run into difficulties. To begin with, Secrist's data do not include any figures showing the prices (or "mark-ups") at which the retail clothiers sold their services during the period covered by his study.[16] But there is a more serious obstacle. Marshall reasoned that, for short periods, value tends to settle at prime, not total, unit-costs of production. It is reasonable to infer that, if he were drawing a "particular expenses" curve to represent a market situation in a dynamic

[15] Marshall's discussion is so largely devoted to the tracing of normative trends that it is difficult, sometimes, to know just what his views regarding a given dynamic situation would be. He appears, however, to have pictured a somewhat uniform progression of each firm through three stages: (1) the period of infancy, when costs are high, and the firm somewhere near a marginal position; (2) the period of maturity, when it occupies a typical, or "representative" cost position (or, if unusually successful, a position of marked differential advantage); and (3) the period of old age, when it is again near the margin. This is different from the continual shifting backward and forward which Secrist describes.

[16] He does give some evidence upon this point in his hardware and banking studies, especially in the former, where he compares the profits of hardware dealers with their expenses and their "margins of gross profit" (mark-ups). The findings confirm those of Simpson, in that they always show some firms operating at a loss, and selling, therefore, at less than cost. They have the same defect as Simpson's data for the present purpose, in that they deal with total unit-costs instead of prime costs, and they are even less satisfactory than his for checking the theory of value, in that "gross margins of profit" are not quite the same as the prices of the theory.

state,[17] it would be a curve showing only the prime costs of the different producers. The curves for retail clothing show only the total costs per unit of sales. Nor is it likely that statistics of prime costs, suited for the present purpose, could be secured for any other industry, for it is doubtful whether business men now keep their accounts in such a manner as to yield the requisite information. For the present, therefore, any attempt to test this part of the theory inductively must be abandoned.

It may not be altogether fruitless to inquire, however, what may be the relation between the price of a commodity and the *total* costs of producing a unit of it, at a given time, or over a given short period. Some instructive information on this problem is contained in an interesting article by Simpson, giving a statistical analysis of the relation between the costs and the prices of certain commodities which came within the purview of the Federal Trade Commission.[18] Simpson secured figures on the costs and the prices of book paper, newsprint paper, salmon, red salmon, copper and sugar beets, for various years ranging between 1913 and 1918. Although the graphs of his data, as he presents them, are not arranged in the form of the usual supply curves, they are capable of being cast into that form. One such drawing, showing the cost of production and price of book paper in 1916, is given in Figure 3. Since it is fairly typical of all the other cases, it will be sufficient to illustrate what appears to be the general situation. In this figure, the spaces along the base line OX represent not absolute quantities, but percentages, of output; those along the line OY indicate dollars of cost per ton. The curve thus shows the average costs at which various percentages of the total supply of book paper were brought to the market in the year 1916. The average net price for the year is shown by the heavy dotted line. It was $82.33. It is to be noted that this is considerably below the costs of a few of the mills, these costs in some case ranging close to one hundred dollars. In fact, more than 10 per cent of the total production in this year must have been disposed of at a loss. Approximately the same thing was found to be true of *all* the commodities, in *all* the years covered by Simpson's study. In every case some producers were found whose costs were above the prevailing price, the amount sold at a loss usually ranging around 10 per cent of the total production—sometimes more, sometimes less. This would appear, therefore, to be a common—perhaps the usual—situation in industry.

[17] It was pointed out in n. 8 that the curve was used by him only to represent the equilibrium that would be reached in a stationary state.

[18] Kemper Simpson, "A Statistical Analysis of the Relation between Cost and Price," *Quarterly Journal of Economics*, XXXV (February, 1921), 264–87.

How does this compare with the theoretical situation represented in Figure 1? If the supply curve of that diagram is constructed as depicting total unit-costs, it obviously portrays accurately the facts of industry, as Simpson found them.[19] In that diagram, the supply was represented as being so balanced with demand as to make the price exactly equal to the costs of the marginal producer, with no one selling at a loss. In the actual market, however, there appear to be producers whose costs exceed the selling price. This raises some question as to just how the term

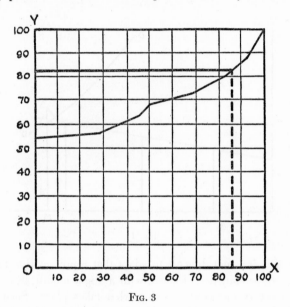

FIG. 3

"marginal producer" (or marginal costs) is to be defined. If the marginal producer is the one with the highest costs in the market, it cannot be said that price necessarily coincides with marginal costs. We would then need a new term to denote those firms whose costs are just equal to the price. It has been suggested that the term "bulk line producers" might be employed to designate those firms whose output is just needed to make up the bulk (80–90 per cent) of the supply. Price might then be presumed to be high enough to equal the "bulk line" costs, thereby insuring a profit to the bulk of the producers, though not to those who contribute that small proportion of the total supply which is produced at especially high costs. But the exact position of the "bulk line" is

[19] If the curve is construed as depicting prime costs, it might or might not conform to reality. This is the point on which no evidence is available.

too vaguely defined for scientific analysis, so that this is hardly a satis-factory term. A better procedure is to distinguish between "marginal" and "extra-marginal" producers, meaning by the former those firms whose costs are just covered by the price, and by the latter those firms which are selling at a loss. We will then have the corresponding terms "marginal costs" and "extra-marginal costs." However, the relation be-tween marginal costs and value in a given situation will not be quite as it was represented in Figure 1.

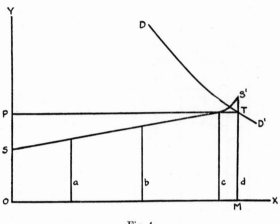

Fig. 4

Nevertheless, it is not difficult to adapt that representation to the facts revealed by these statistics. Indeed, with a slight modification, it affords a very satisfactory means of showing what takes place. Such a modifi-cation is incorporated in Figure 4.[20] Here the demand is indicated by the curve DD', and the supply (based on total unit-costs) by the curve SS', as in the previous drawings. The vertical lines a, b, c, and d repre-sent the costs of producers at various levels, ranging from low (at the left) to high (at the right). The combined output of all the producers being OM, price is fixed at OP (this being the marginal demand-price for that supply), instead of at the intersection of the two curves, as it was in Marshall's representation. Producer c is here the marginal pro-ducer, whose costs just equal the price, and d is an extra-marginal pro-ducer, selling at a loss. It will be observed that this drawing differs

[20] A substantially similar diagram has previously been employed to represent such a situation by Norman J. Silberling, in an article entitled "Graphic Illustration of the Laws of Price," which appeared in the *American Economic Review*, XIV (Sep-tember, 1924), 428.

only slightly from that of Figure 1. The earlier graph was constructed to picture a hypothetical and purely abstract situation. Yet it has helped in the analysis of an actual market phenomenon revealed by inductive study. Deduction and induction have again gone hand in hand.

So far, the statistical analysis has been confined to the relation between marginal costs and values at a given time (or over a short period), without reference to Marshall's "long-period normal" theory, in which he maintains that there is a tendency for the differences in costs between producers to be eliminated,[21] and for values to approach the costs of a representative firm. Can this doctrine also be tested by inductive means? Is it possible for statistics to reveal so subtle a thing as a competitive *tendency* toward an equalization of costs which is admittedly never attained? Many of the critics of economics have ridiculed the very concept of such a tendency as quite untenable. A long-run tendency is a meaningless fiction, they argue, for it is only the short run that can ever truly exist. Yet Secrist believes that statistics can show even so elusive an influence as this. And, with great ingenuity he has succeeded in demonstrating that the leveling *tendency* of competition upon costs can actually be discerned.

Attention has already been called to the fact that the positions of different retail clothiers on the expense curves shift considerably from year to year. Closer scrutiny of these changes reveals that they move toward a common point. It is found that those producers whose costs in any one year are above the average for that year succeed in moving closer to that average in the following year. Likewise, producers whose costs in any one year are below the average will be found to have higher costs in the year which follows. Thus there is a general tendency toward a central level. This is most clearly shown by a series of interesting charts, one example of which is reproduced in Figure 5. Here are shown, for five consecutive years, the movements of identical retail clothing stores from each year to the next, as well as for the five years as a whole. The heavy lines represent groups of firms which moved from high to slightly lower, or from low to slightly higher, cost positions. The dotted lines represent more extreme shifts, indicating firms which crossed the average line, moving from positions above the average to positions below it, or vice versa. If we consider the second column of the chart for illustration, the first solid sloping line at the top shows that the expenses of nine firms which were 40 per cent or more above the average

[21] This statement should be interpreted in the light of the explanation given in n. 9.

in 1916 were only from 30 to 40 per cent above the average in 1917. The bottom solid line, which slopes upward, represents two firms with expenses 40 per cent or more below the average in 1916, which had attained a position only 30–40 per cent below the average in 1917. The

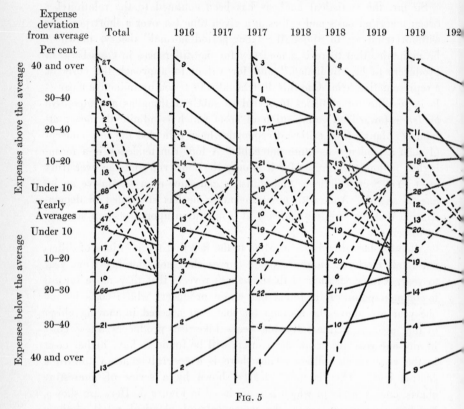

Fig. 5

general movement toward a common center from each year to the next, and for the five years as a whole, is clearly evident. For this industry, therefore, Marshall's belief that there is a tendency toward an equalization of costs appears to be correct. Statistical induction confirms the deductive theory completely. By similar methods, Secrist has succeeded in showing that this tendency exists also in hardware retailing, and in banking—two other competitive industries.[22]

[22] In his later studies Secrist has proved that similar tendencies, which he calls "regression to type," are characteristic, not only of costs, but of many other phases of competitive industry. Thus, businesses which, in any given period of time, show high or low extremes in almost any aspect of their operations, will be found to move toward the general average in subsequent periods.

What about the representative firm? Can its supposed existence, also, be verified? In approaching this problem, Secrist has recourse to the statistical concept of a mode. If we array the costs of producers in an ascending or a descending series, and find that there is a considerable concentration or grouping of these costs at any one level, we may think of this level of costs as being fairly typical, or representative, of the industry as a whole. These modal costs, therefore, may be taken as corresponding fairly closely with the costs of a representative firm.[23] The expenses of retail clothiers do reveal the existence of such a modal level or area. Secrist found that, if he plotted the expenses of such clothiers on a graph in an ascending scale, the resulting curve always had the general shape of the line *AB* in Figure 6.[24] It will be noted that there are a few producers with very low costs at one end of the scale (*Aa*), and a few with very high costs at the other (*bB*), but that the greater number fall closer together on the distinctly modal portion of the line (*ab*).[25] This modal area was found to lie between 20 per cent above and 20 per cent below the average of the costs of all producers. This area Secrist regards as constituting the level of representative costs for this industry. From 65 to 75 per cent of the entire retail clothing business, he found, was done at this level of costs. When we couple these findings with the proof of the leveling effects of competition already described, we have considerable objective confirmation of Marshall's doctrine, at least for this industry.

But so far we have spoken only of a representative *cost area;* we

[23] With reference to the discussion here and immediately following, Opie observes that "the relation of Marshall's 'representative firm' to cost and to value raises difficulties which are avoided here by assuming that the representative firm is the mode. Marshall is not clear on this point, but he defines that firm in terms of access to internal and external economies—one with its 'due' or 'fair' share of these." While there is perhaps some reason to be cautious in treating a modal firm as equivalent to Marshall's representative firm, the two concepts are at least not inconsistent. Marshall emphasizes as one charactertistic of a representative firm that it has fairly long life and fair success. Certainly a firm which occupies a modal position over a number of years is in harmony with such a description. Moreover, the very use of such words and phrases as "representative," "managed with fair ability," and the like, which Marshall uses in this connection, suggests the idea of the mode. Perhaps the chief merit of Secrist's identification of the representative firm as a modal firm lies in the fact that it does give definite meaning to a concept which hitherto has been decidedly vague.

Opie also suggests that the concept of an "equilibrium firm," which Pigou uses as a substitute for Marshall's concept, may contribute something of value to this problem. See Pigou's article in the June, 1928, issue of the *Economic Journal.*

[24] See his *Competition in the Retail Distribution of Clothing*, Charts 3 and 4.

[25] Simpson's cost figures did not always show so distinct a modal area.

have not proved the existence of that supposed representative *firm* which is just able to maintain itself in the business over a considerable period of years. In view of the fact, previously noted, that there is a continued shifting of positions in regard to costs among the various firms from year to year, it might be expected that none would remain in a modal position long enough to be considered truly representative. It is true that the identity of the firms lying within the representative area changed considerably from year to year. Indeed, nearly all of the firms succeeded in getting within this area at least one year in five. But it is interesting

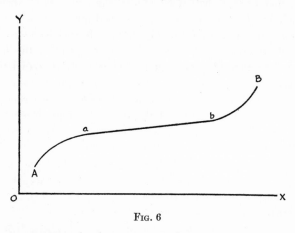

FIG. 6

to note that about 29 per cent of the businesses were stable enough to remain within the area for the five consecutive years covered by the study. Here, perhaps, is the actual embodiment of Marshall's representative firm. But we cannot be sure that these enterprises would have been able to maintain their modal position over a longer period; and five years is almost too short for a test.[26] In view of the fact that the modal area is distinctly existent, and that the identity of the firms within it does fluctuate at least to a considerable extent, it would appear more appropriate to speak of *representative costs* than of the costs of a *representative firm*. This is in line with the previous conclusion, in which the superiority of the concept of marginal costs over that of the marginal producer was established. Once more the definite knowledge of industrial conditions made possible by objective facts gives us a more precise

[26] However, Secrist had data for 120 identical stores over a seven-year period, and he found 21.7 per cent of these within the representative cost area in each of the seven years.

understanding of phenomena than deductive analysis afforded, but the general outlines of the theory are confirmed.

Unfortunately, data are lacking to test that portion of Marshall's doctrine which asserts that, in the long run, there is a tendency for values to conform to, or fluctuate about, what we are now disposed to designate as representative costs. Perhaps we could infer this conclusion from what has already been established, but positive inductive verification is not, for the present, forthcoming. On this point, therefore, we must wait for more light.

We may now be able, perhaps, to draw some conclusions from the material which has been presented. It will be borne in mind that our interest is not primarily in the findings concerning the validity of the concepts of the marginal producer and the representative firm. Those findings have been much more carefully stated and elaborated by the writers whose works have been cited than it has been possible to do in this paper. Our interest is rather in the significance of these studies as illustrations of a certain method in the development of economic science. We are concerned with the way in which induction has here been combined with deduction to test, refine, and modify a theory. Statistics have here been employed to check a generalization arrived at by reflective thinking, much as the astronomer checks the Einstein theory of relativity by observing the aberration of light from a star at the time of the sun's eclipse. In the present case, deductive theory suggested a study to the statistician and set him a problem to solve. The data brought to bear upon the problem illuminated it in a very helpful way. They not only served to verify those parts of the theory which were found to be in accord with the facts, and to refine and reformulate those portions which the evidence indicated were in need of modification, but they suggested a new way in which one aspect of the theoretical problem (that dealing with the relation between values and total unit-costs for short periods) could be formulated. It justifies us in placing confidence in both the deductive and the inductive methods; for deduction was not only the basis for the study, but its findings were to a considerable extent confirmed, while induction served to verify and perfect those findings. As a result, we have now a knowledge concerning the nature of marginal and representative costs—at least in certain types of competitive industry—on which we can really rely.[27]

    [27] Deibler has suggested that it would be well to include in this paper some consideration of "the limits of the quantitative method in testing deductive reasoning." Such a discussion has interesting possibilities, but I feel that it would be unwise to undertake it here. If my essay succeeds in illustrating one way in which deduction

It is interesting to note, too, that it was found possible, through ingenious statistical devices, to work out means of checking some very subtle, abstract conceptions—conceptions so abstract, indeed, that not a few contemporary critics have laughed them out of court as existing only in the imaginations of armchair philosophers. The very notion of the representative firm, as Marshall conceived it, was such an abstraction; yet Secrist has succeeded in giving very tangible evidence of the reality of representative costs, if not of the representative firm itself. And what could be more elusive than the theory that the costs of different producers in the long run tend to equality, though they are never equal at any one time? Yet this tendency, too, was shown by these studies to be capable of statistical demonstration. It is apparent, therefore, that abstract theory and inductive analysis are excellent partners, which, when appropriately united, lead to successful results. Studies of a similar nature may be expected to multiply in the future, and they should prove extremely fruitful in enriching the science of economics.

---

and induction can be used effectively in advancing economic theory, it will have served its purpose. It is not intended as an exhaustive analysis of the relation between these two methods, but merely as an example.

ANALYSIS 45

STATISTICAL MEASUREMENTS OF THE OPERATION OF THE LAW OF DIMINISHING RETURNS BY MORDECAI EZEKIEL AND OTHERS[1]

By JOHN D. BLACK
Harvard University

The law of diminishing returns as first stated about 1815 by Edward West, David Ricardo, and Thomas Malthus was deemed neither by them nor by their successors to require experimental or statistical proof. Everyday observation seemed indisputably to confirm it. Those who did rise up and deny it were thinking of effects over a long period during which other circumstances intervened and offset the operation of the law. They were speaking of what we now call the "secular law of diminishing returns." But although no proof of the law of diminishing returns has been needed, there is very great value in determining the rate at which it operates with any given set of productive agents or in any given set of circumstances. It is difficult to conceive of a kind of information any more valuable than this to a world profoundly bent on understanding and controlling its own processes and development. Yet only recently have economists set about securing such information. The following is a brief report on one line of such effort.

No doubt the first work done on the relation between amounts of the elements of production used and the resulting product was in experiments in the use of varying amounts of fertilizer, feed, and the like. But such experimentation was seldom clearly related to the economic law of

---

[1] [The genesis of the present analysis is explained in Appendix F. A number of contributions receive attention in following pages, references being supplied at the appropriate points. The most significant, in the analyst's judgment, is the *University of Wisconsin Research Bull. 79: Practices Responsible for Variations in the Physical Requirements and Economic Costs of Milk Production on Wisconsin Dairy Farms* (August, 1927), by P. E. McNall, F. B. Morrison, and Mordecai Ezekiel. Of it Professor Black says: "This is the best developed of a series of input-output studies in agriculture begun with the publication of *United States Department of Agriculture, Department Bull. 1277: Input as Related to Output in Farm Organization and Cost-of-Production Studies* (September, 1924), by H. R. Tolley, John D. Black, and Mordecai Ezekiel. These studies represent the most forward step that has been taken in research in production economics as well as a new development in technique." The analysis was first written in December, 1928. It was reviewed by Dr. Ezekiel and was revised by the analyst in January, 1929.—EDITOR.]

diminishing returns. In fact, the soil chemists affirmed, and still teach for that matter, a law which is partly contrary to the economists' law— Liebig's law of the minimum, which states essentially that production is proportional to the supply of that plant-food element which is present in the soil in least quantity. Out of the feeding experiments with live stock were slowly established some sets of "standards" by use of which could be estimated the feed intake required for a given amount of gain in weight, milk, or butterfat production. No doubt, most of those engaged in such experiments recognized at least vaguely the existence of some connection between what they were doing and the idea of diminishing returns, which had become common property; but if so, it was more often to question the law than to substantiate it. In general, their manner of presentation was in terms of production and gains in weight proportioned to feed intake in excess of maintenance requirements. The economic law as generally stated provides for an increasing stage before the decrease sets in. Moreover, all such analyses were in terms of purely physical inputs and outputs, whereas the economic law has always been associated somehow or other with value, income, and profits.

In farm-management analysis, and in engineering analysis for the most part, a concept of "unit requirements" has been accepted, of definite quantities of the various elements of production which are "required" in order to obtain a product. Such a concept is in essence a contradiction of the principle of diminishing returns.

Before much progress could be made with research in this field, the economists had to develop their qualitative analysis. The statements found in some of the standard textbooks in economics—Ely and Seager, for example—even as late as 1915 were far from clarifying on the subject. At its best qualitative analysis of the problem distinguishes first between a law of physical inputs and outputs and a law of costs and profits in value terms. It provides another distinct statement of the law as relating to the size of a business unit; another as relating to a given industry as a whole at any given time; and still another for an industry, or all industries, over a period of time—the secular law previously mentioned. As for the physical law, there are four possible statements of it: in terms of (a) total outputs, (b) marginal or additional outputs, (c) average outputs per unit of the varying input element, and (d) ratios of increases in outputs to increases in inputs—essentially Alfred Marshall's method of statement. All of these are capable of being stated as reciprocals of the foregoing. Present qualitative analysis also provides a statement of the law for combinations including more than one of the fixed or the varying elements, or both of them.[2]

Later experimental work with fertilizers by German soil chemists[3] has proved the falsity of Liebig's law of the minimum and has brought experimental results more closely in accord with the deductive economic analysis. However, Mitscherlich's formula, developed about 1910, and Spillman's formula[4] state that with one factor varying at a time the increments in product decrease from the start. Both propound a mathematical statement of the law. Since the two statements are mathematical equivalents, they can safely be repeated in Spillman's version alone, as follows: The successive increments of product accompanying equal increments of a varying input decrease in a geometric ratio—each being the same percentage of the preceding increment. Spillman finds the same sort of geometric ratios to maintain for feed and animals. It will be apparent that such a formula provides for no diminishing total outputs. Lang and Spillman attempt to explain away this difficulty by saying new conditions enter into the phenomenon at this point—reverse osmosis in the case of fertilizers, perhaps indigestion in the case of feeding. Lang's essay also includes Baule's explanation of results when several inputs are increasing simultaneously. Spillman in his essay makes an attempt at converting his formula into an economic law of diminishing returns or profits.

Dr. F. Lester Patton in his Columbia University dissertation, *Diminishing Returns in Agriculture* (1926), takes issue with Spillman and Lang on the score of their failure to provide for diminishing total outputs (p. 40); but he himself asserts that "there is no evidence of the general existence of an initial stage of increasing marginal physical returns in agriculture" (p. 47). The increasing stage, says Patton, is a phase of the economic law of diminishing returns, which he calls the "law of anticlinal profits." Patton also provides a mathematical solution for the problem of isolating the marginal increment occurring with the last fraction of the dose of input rather than for the dose as a whole.

The further explanation needed to reconcile the foregoing statements with each other and with the present qualitative analysis of economists is as follows: The diminishing geometric increments of Mitscherlich, Lang, and Spillman are true for any one discrete process; such as a

[2] John D. Black, *Introduction to Production Economics* (New York: Henry Holt & Co., 1926); see chap. xi, xii, xxi, and xxx.

[3] For an account of these see Emil Lang, "The Law of the Soil," as translated by W. J. Spillman in his *Law of Diminishing Returns*, Part II.

[4] In his essay published in 1924 as Part I of *ibid.*, by Spillman and Lang.

plant drawing food from the soil by osmotic action, or sunlight causing water to rise in plant stems and to be breathed out through the stomata of the leaves, or sunlight manufacturing plant food in the leaves by photosynthesis, or food being digested in a stomach, or absorbed into the blood stream, or converted into milk or tissue, or water being converted into steam in a boiler, or steam pressure being converted into motion of a piston in a cylinder. But almost any form of production is a complex of several such discrete processes. Even plant growth is a complex of processes, some of which are especially dependent on soil conditions, others on sunlight, etc. As the plants grow in size, they begin to shut the sunlight from one another—a new process enters the picture. The dense foliage may permit plant disease to develop—still another process. If the foliage grows too large, the plants may bend over and lodge—still another process. Foliage growth and seed production are surely to be interpreted as different processes. Any one of these processes operates according to some mathematical function. The work of Mitscherlich and Spillman would suggest that many of them obey a rule of geometric decrease in increments. But the same set of processes is not likely to be operating in all different combinations of the elements of production. The new increment of output accompanying any new increment in input is the sum, or possibly the product, of the mathematical functions of the different processes operating at that point. The reason that Mitscherlich, Spillman, and others have found decreases occurring with such regularity is that they have experimented with proportions of productive agents which result in functions running closely together for the major processes involved.

But some of the new processes which enter as more and more fertilizer is added to soil and seed as fixed elements do not have functions running so closely alike. When reverse osmosis begins to appear, the function is an increasing one—increasing decrements. If soil and fertilizer are fixed and seed is increased, there is a late stage when more plants are started than can mature their seed, and the increments of seed are negative. At an early stage when very little seed is planted, the weeds choke out crops sown broadcast, and increasing increments will appear for a while. One cannot say that reverse osmosis begins definitely at the point of diminishing total outputs; nor the overcrowding of plants for seed production. The chances are that they both begin operating considerably earlier, but that their decrements are offset by the increments still associated with the other processes. Diminishing total outputs begin at the point where the increments and the decrements exactly cancel each other. Diminishing additional outputs similarly occur at the point where decreasing increments of some processes exactly offset the increasing increments of others.

The significance of the increasing portion of a curve depends upon how many and how important are the processes giving increasing increments. Very small increments of fertilizer or water may show increasing increments of product. Many productive processes of the maintenance-ration type show such increments just before the point where the maintenance ration is provided. Thus a cow will produce increasing increments of milk just before the maintenance point is reached; machines, just before power enough is applied to enable them to carry a light load; machines or plants, in the stage when they are operating very short-handed.

It follows from the foregoing that the shape of the curves of physical outputs at any point is a composite result of the mathematical functions of the set of processes that are operating at that point.

The reason that the increments and the decrements follow mathematical laws is not difficult to see. The crowding of plants, like other forms of crowding, produces results according to the law of squares. As more units of a varying element are added, each unit has a smaller fractional part of the fixed elements to work with, and the fixed factors in turn have more of the varying elements to work with. Possibly a geometric function describes most of them; but surely more analysis is needed before this is affirmed.

One other aspect of the foregoing relationships is of great importance —the effects of the various productive elements on the product are *joint*, and not *additive*. That is, adding more irrigation water or more sunlight makes more effective the fertilizer, the labor of cultivation, and all of the other inputs, up to the point where it sets decremental processes in operation. This circumstance undoubtedly affects the form of the appropriate mathematical function in each case. If the effects of the various inputs multiply into one another, this would furnish a presupposition in favor of a general order of geometric increments and decrements.

In interpreting the experiments of Mitscherlich, one must bear in mind that he used sterile soil as a fixed factor, whereas most of the fertilizer experiments reported upon start with soil fairly well supplied with plant food. Also Mitscherlich took the weight of the whole plant as his measure of product, whereas the usual experiments take the weight of the seed or other valuable product. The curves resulting are bound to be greatly different in the two cases.

The first piece of work to appear in the United States which used the statistical method on this problem was *Input as Related to Output in Farm Organization and Cost-of-Production Studies* (see n. 1). The project out of which this report grew was outlined by Black in the summer of 1922 while serving as consulting specialist for the Bureau of Agricultural Economics of the United States Department of Agriculture, and was carried out by Ezekiel the following winter at the University of Minnesota under the direction of Black and Tolley. The difficult statistical problem involved was to isolate the effect of variations in several input elements probably affecting the product non-linearly. The line of attack which Ezekiel followed was that of endeavoring to determine the shape of the curve by plotting the residuals from a linear regression line obtained by multiple-correlation analysis. Out of his work along these lines he developed presently the full technique for multiple curvilinear analysis which is described in his series of articles in the *Journal of the American Statistical Association.*[5] Three sets of data were analyzed in this project: one consisting of survey data concerning potato growing from three hundred farms in New York, another of data from sixty-seven droves of beef cattle in Nebraska, and another of survey data relating to the wheat enterprise on sixty-seven farms in western Minnesota. None of these sets of data was collected with a view to their use in such analysis, and the original records were far from being accurate. Nevertheless, results were obtained such as the following:

Potatoes—with increasing applications of manure, increments of products as follows: 3.2, 3.1, 2.9, 2.7, 2.4, 2.1, 1.9; with increasing seed planted per acre: 9.0, 7.5, 5.5, 4.5; with additional depths in plowing: 2.5, 1.7, 0.3, −1.0, −3.0, −3.0.

Beef cattle—with additional grain fed per day, increments of grain in weight per day as follows: 0.35, 0.31, 0.14, 0.15; with additional roughage fed per day: 0.20, 0.17, 0.17, 0.15, 0.13. These results were strongly affected by the circumstances that with the lighter rations droves took longer to fatten and got more of their feed from pastures.

Wheat—with additional inputs of man-labor per acre, increments of yield per acre as follows: 0.0, 0.50; 0.24; 0.09; 0.33. Analysis of the labor records showed them to be very crude measures of labor input.

[5] "A Method of Handling Curvilinear Correlation for Any Number of Variables," *op. cit.,* December, 1924, pp. 431–53; "The Assumptions Implied in the Multiple Regression Equation," *ibid.,* September, 1925, pp. 405–8; "The Determination of Curvilinear Regression 'Surfaces' in the Presence of Other Variables," *ibid.,* September, 1926, 311–20. Cf. also *Methods of Correlation Analysis* (New York: John Wiley and Sons, Inc., 1930).

The economic analysis in the report is wholly of the synthetic type. Prices of the input elements and of the product prevailing in the market were combined with the data of physical inputs and outputs to see what combinations under various price situations would give least-cost and highest-profit production.

A much more significant contribution, so far as the actual quantitative results are concerned, is the 1927 study, *Practices Responsible for Variations in the Physical Requirements and Economic Costs of Milk Production on Wisconsin Dairy Farms* (see n. 1). In this, Ezekiel made use of data collected under Professor P. E. McNall's direction, while in the natural-science aspects of the problem he had the assistance of Mr. F. B. Morrison, then assistant director of the Wisconsin Experiment Station, and co-author of the standard work on feeds and feeding in the United States. Two sets of data were available, survey data from 180 farms and 95 route records, obtained by visiting the farms at frequent intervals and measuring feed and production. It later developed that 45 of these route records had been more carefully taken than the others, and in the final stage of analysis, only these 45 were used. The relative accuracy of the survey and the route records may be judged from the coefficients of multiple linear correlation, .709 ± .072 and .476 ± .148, respectively. The indexes of correlation were .860 ± .038 and .545 ± .135, respectively. A coefficient of .860 means that 74 per cent (.860 squared) of the variations in milk production were explained. The 45 records gave a multiple correlation of 0.83, linear, and .874, curvilinear, using only the five principal variables in place of the nine used with the 95 records. The other variables were omitted in the last analysis because their net coefficients were too small to be significant with so few observations. The variables used in the analysis of the 95 route records, with their coefficients of determination, were as shown in Table I.

An important departure in this study is that all of the variables are stated in terms of their logarithms. This makes the use of multiple correlation possible while adhering to the assumption that the variations in the inputs have a multiplying effect on the product; for example, that if a higher ratio of protein to non-protein in the ration adds 150 pounds or 5 per cent to the production of a cow at 3,000 pounds butterfat, it will add 200 pounds, or 5 per cent, to the production of a cow at 4,000 pounds butterfat. The method of stating the variables used in the first study reported would have assumed an absolute amount added in each case.

No doubt this second assumption is the more valid, but that it does not completely provide for the existing functional relations is indicated by the fact that curvilinear adjustments had to be made for most of the variables. For any one cow, as the point of maximum capacity is approached, the multiplying factor is likely to change considerably. The data used are averages of herds made up of animals differing widely in capacity. The multiplying factor may be different for different capacities. The results are presented in terms of multiplying effects (percentages of the average production) for an average cow fed an average ration, etc.—everything constant at the average except the one thing varying at the time.

The foregoing assumptions and several others are carefully stated by Ezekiel in the section named "Hypothesis Employed in the Analysis" (pp. 8–14). That the element of jointness in the effect of the different factors

TABLE I

Factors	Coefficients of Determination
X_1—Total digestible nutrients except pasture	15.2
X_2—Nutritive ratio*	23.4
X_3—Per cent of protein "good"	3.9
X_4—Per cent of lime	0.7
X_5—Per cent of summer feeding	7.0
X_6—Per cent of nutrients fed as silage	2.6
X_7—Fat test of milk	18.6
X_8—Per cent of herd fall-freshening	8.2
X_9—Value per cow	3.6
All factors	74.0

* "Nutritive ratio" is the name for the ratio of the digestible protein to the non-protein digestible nutrients, expressed as 1 protein to whatever non-protein.

has not been provided for in the set-up of the equation is explicitly stated. The method of handling this, outlined by Ezekiel in the September, 1926, *Journal of the American Statistical Association,* was not applicable here because of the limited number of observations.

The comparison of the results with those obtained by applying experimentally derived standards to the data of inputs is illuminating. The experimental results run much higher, as one would expect, since they do not exclude pasture food; but they show a larger absolute increase in the nutrients required for 3,000 additional pounds of milk per year, 1,610 as compared with 957 for the Savage standards, and 1,556 as compared with 900 for the Morrison standards. Ezekiel explains this by the fact that the correlation results indicated diminishing returns from the higher rates of feeding for the herds of this study, while the feeding standards are built up to include herds whose inherent capacities are much greater than the range of the production indicated by this study. These conclusions, of course, are true only for cows of the average ability of those in this area. As has already been indicated, cows of superior ability might not show decreasing returns until a much higher production had been reached.

The foregoing suggests one important advantage of statistical results. They obtain data which fit actual conditions in place of highly artificial laboratory conditions. It is seldom possible to reproduce in the laboratory all the variations in conditions found in actual affairs. But unless this can be done, the laboratory results are often not true enough to the realities to be especially useful.

As to one of the variables, butterfat in the milk, the statistical data indicate nearly twice as much additional feed as the experimental standards for an extra pound of butterfat per hundredweight of milk. Moreover, two other statistical studies made by Ezekiel check the Wisconsin results very closely. Here would seem to be a case where the statistical method is indicating the need of improved experimental technique on a problem.

One important assumption in this study has not been clearly stated: namely, that the different herds all consume the same relative amounts of pasture nutrients. It seems probable that the herds with high inputs of non-pasture feed and with high percentage of feed fed during the summer obtained less feed from pasture. If this is true, it will affect many of the regression curves, especially the one for the effect of summer feeding. It may help account for the excess of nutrients required for heavier production according to the statistical analysis.

Any study that includes correlation analysis of sampled observations raises several sorts of questions, one as to how well the results obtained describe the units taken as the sample, and another as to how well they would describe another sample taken from exactly the same universe. In samples from an area there is the further question as to how well they fit the periphery and the areas beyond that which was sampled. If the correlation is of the curvilinear type, these questions take on a special significance, for it is possible to bend the curve of relationships at will in any direction that seems needed in order to increase the apparent degrees of concomitant variation. That the curvilinear method can be so used has been demonstrated by uses already made of it in published studies. The conventional mathematical devices—probable error coefficients and the like—indicate only in a general way the extent to which dependence can be placed on correlation results when applied to the other units in the exact universe sampled; they are less valid for applications to other areas, and of uncertain meaning when the correlation is of the curvilinear type. Dr. Ezekiel calculates the probable errors of the several correlation and regression coefficients, and discusses their validity to some extent in the report of this study. He has also discussed elsewhere the general problem involved. It could well be analyzed very much further.

This study like the other one introduces the strictly economic aspects only synthetically. In any limited area prices vary so little that they furnish no basis for analysis. Data over a wide area or over a period of years will be needed before price factors can be introduced as variables. Or it may always prove best to be content with making such analyses in strictly physical terms, and then introducing such prices as maintain in any particular set of economic conditions.

It should be apparent that results such as outlined above have great social significance. They indicate to what extent increase in production is possible on our present farms and whether larger production will entail higher costs and at what rate, as well as point the way to more economical production generally. Until more of such studies are made, the part of Malthus' law which relates to the increase in the food supply is an approximation almost as wide as the heavens, and the secular law of diminishing returns is merely a historical record.

HENRY L. MOORE'S CONTRIBUTION TO THE STATISTICAL LAW OF DEMAND[1]

By HENRY SCHULTZ

University of Chicago[2]

I. DEVELOPMENT OF THE DEMAND CONCEPT

The statistical law of demand is a beautiful illustration of the frequent necessity of restating an economic principle if it is to admit of verification by the quantitative method.

A century ago the law of demand—or rather, the law of price which embraces it—was commonly stated as follows: "The price of goods varies directly as the quantity demanded and inversely as the quantity supplied."[3]

If it be permissible to take these words in their precise mathematical meaning, the law is

$$P \propto \frac{D}{S}, \tag{1}$$

where P stands for price, D for quantity demanded, and S for quantity supplied.

But what meaning can we give to the term "quantity demanded"?

---

[1] Professor Moore's path-blazing contributions to demand theory, arranged in chronological order, are as follows: *Economic Cycles: Their Law and Cause* (New York: Macmillan Co., 1914), chap. iv, "The Law of Demand"; *Forecasting the Yield and Price of Cotton* (New York: Macmillan Co., 1917), pp. 100–115, and chap. v, "The Law of Demand for Cotton"; "Elasticity of Demand and Flexibility of Prices," *Journal of the American Statistical Association*, XVIII (March, 1922), 8–19; "A Moving Equilibrium of Demand and Supply," *Quarterly Journal of Economics*, XXXIX (1925), 357–71; "Partial Elasticity of Demand," *ibid.*, XL (1926), 393–401; "A Theory of Economic Oscillations," *ibid.*, XLI (1926), 1–29; *Synthetic Economics* (New York: Macmillan Co., 1929), chap. iii.

In the first two references there are full and suggestive comparisons between his approach and that of Alfred Marshall (the neo-classical approach). In the last two references there are comparisons between his approach and that of Leon Walras.

[2] I wish to thank the University of Chicago Press for permission to quote from my *Statistical Laws of Demand and Supply with Special Application to Sugar* (1928).

[3] Thus, Jean-Batiste Say: "Le prix d'une marchandise ne baisse-t-il pas en proportion de ce qu'elle est plus offerte, et ne monte-t-il pas en proportion de ce qu'elle est plus demandée?" (*Catéchisme d'économie politique* [7th ed.; Brussels, 1837], chap. xi, p. 84). The *Catéchisme* is also reprinted in *Œuvres diverses de J. B. Say* (Paris, 1848); see p. 44. The first edition of the *Catéchisme* was published in 1817.

Obviously, "the quantity of a commodity *at a certain price.*" And what do we mean by the term "quantity supplied"? Obviously, "the quantity supplied *at a certain price.*" A consumer cannot tell how much he will purchase, and a producer cannot tell how much he will sell, unless the price of the commodity in question is specified. The foregoing "law" taken at its face value[4] now assumes this meaning: "Price varies directly as the quantity demanded, which depends on price, and inversely as the quantity supplied, which also depends on price"—clearly an ambiguous statement.

In 1838 Cournot brushed aside such "meaningless and sterile statements" as the foregoing, and stated the law of demand in the following unambiguous terms: "Let us admit," said he, ". . . . that the sales or the annual demand *D* is, for each article, a particular function *F(p)* of the price *p* of such article. To know the form of the function would be to know what we call the *law of demand or of sales.*"[5]

Mathematically, Cournot's law is

$$D = F(p). \tag{2}$$

Alfred Marshall developed this concept at great length and popularized it. It may, therefore, be called the "neo-classical law of demand."

But how can we obtain the form of the function $F(p)$? *Conceptually* this appears easy. We can ask a group of potential buyers how much of a given commodity each one of them would buy if the price were p_1; how much each would buy if the price were p_2; and so on. We can then add up all the quantities that would be purchased at each price, and thus obtain a "demand schedule." The mathematical formula which describes or summarizes this schedule, or which expresses the relation between changes in price and corresponding changes in the quantity taken, is the function $F(p)$ of the price p of the article in question.

It is generally assumed that $F(p)$ is a decreasing function of p; that is, that more will be bought when prices are low than when they are high.

In this hypothetical deduction of the law of demand we have tacitly assumed that each purchaser can tell us readily the amount of the commodity which he would purchase at each price in a unit of time. Is this

---

[4] It is admitted that the *explanations* which accompany this "law" sometimes remove something of its ambiguity. This is especially true of the explanations found in the modern texts in which the inexact statement is repeated more as a traditional formula than as a reasoned proposition.

[5] Augustin Cournot, *Mathematical Principles of the Theory of Wealth,* Bacon's trans. (New York: Macmillan Co., 1927), p. 47.

in accordance with the facts? If, for example, our hypothetical potential buyer be a poor housewife, and if she be asked how many pounds of porterhouse steak she would buy in a week if the price were, say 60 cents a pound, will she not also want to know the prices of the various cheaper cuts of meat, as well as the prices of potatoes, beans, and other meat substitutes? In general, is it possible for any buyer to make up his demand schedule for a commodity without knowing the prices of competing commodities? To ask these questions is to answer them. In general, a purchaser cannot decide how much he will buy of a given commodity, unless he knows not only the price of the commodity in question, but also the prices of competing (theoretically, of *all*) goods.

In mathematical terms, this means that the quantity of any commodity purchased in a given interval of time must be expressed as a function not only of its price, but also of all other prices, or

$$D = f\ (p_1, p_2, \ldots, p_n), \tag{3i}$$

where D is the quantity of the commodity demanded, p_1 its price, and $p_2, p_3, \ldots, p_n$ the prices of all other commodities.[6] Owing, however, to the modifications to which this equation will be subjected later, it is more convenient to write it as follows:

$$x_0 = f\ (x_1, x_2, \ldots, x_n), \tag{3ii}$$

where $x_0 = D$, $x_1 = p_1$, $x_2 = p_2$, etc.

Equation (3i) is due to Leon Walras, who, in 1873, was the first to write the demand for any commodity as a function of the prices of all commodities.[7] It is the law of demand of the mathematical school.[8]

[6] Cournot, Walras, Pareto, and most other mathematical economists make the price of the commodity (or the system of prices considered) the independent variable in the demand equation. This practice is convenient in the treatment of general equilibrium and it has the merit of suggesting that, *to the individual purchaser*, price fluctuations are independent of any action that he can take; all he can do is to adjust himself to them. However, Marshall and most English and American economists do not follow this practice. They make the quantity the independent variable in the demand equation. For the purpose of this exposition we shall follow the practice initiated by Cournot.

[7] *Eléments d'économie politique pure* (ed. definitive, 1926), pp. v–vii and esp. p. vii, n. 1. See also pp. 122–33.

[8] On the difference between the neo-classical and the mathematical statement of the law of demand, see Vilfredo Pareto, "Economie mathématique," *Encyclopédie des sciences mathématiques,* Tome I, Vol. IV, Fascicule 4, pp. 593–94, 614–21, and esp. pp. 628–30; *Manuel d'économie politique,* pp. 579 ff.; Leon Walras, *Eléments d'économie politique pure* (4th ed., 1926), pp. 122–24, 208–16; Gustav Cassel, *The Theory of Social Economy,* chap. iv, "The Mechanism of Pricing"; Henry L. Moore,

It is only through such a general formulation that all prices may be determined by a system of simultaneous equations and that an insight may be had into the tremendous complexity of our price economy.

To realize the importance of this achievement it is only necessary to recall that textbooks on economics are still being written by authors who are greatly troubled by the so-called problem of "circular reasoning" in price theory. Knowing that a change in the price of one commodity may bring about a change in the price of a second commodity, and that the change in the price of the second commodity may in turn bring about a change in the price of a third commodity, and so on, these authors ask, "If the price of coal is a cause of the cost of transportation, how can the cost of transportation in turn be a cause of the price of coal?" To them the problem of pricing in thus insoluble. They do not seem to know that over fifty years ago Walras showed that the pricing problem is perfectly soluble and that the concept of mutual determination must replace that of mechanical causation.

The law of demand of the mathematical school (3i) includes the neoclassical law of demand (2) as a special case. To obtain the latter from the former, we make use of the only valid non-experimental method for keeping the "other things" constant, which may be stated as follows: First, take all the factors (variables) into consideration; second, assign constant values to all the variables except the price and the quantity of the commodity in question. This means that we must first determine the equation connecting the quantity demanded and all the prices, and then assign constant values to all of the variables except the two under consideration. And it may well be that the demand curve thus obtained will depend upon the magnitude of the constants which are assigned to the other variables.[9] Thus the demand curve for wheat when the price of rye is kept constant at seventy-five cents a bushel may be considerably different from what it is when the price of rye is kept constant at a dollar and a half a bushel.

To derive the ordinary (neo-classical) demand curve as a special case

---

"A Theory of Economic Oscillations," *Quarterly Journal of Economics*, XLI (1926), 1–29. For a criticism of Pareto's *Manuel* which has a bearing on his treatment of the law of demand see Knut Wicksell, "Vilfredo Pareto's *Manuel d'économie politique*," *Zeitschrift für Volkwirtschaft, Sozialpolitik und Verwaltung*, XXII (1913), 132–51, and esp. p. 138.

The relation between the distribution of income and the law of demand is discussed by Pareto in "La legge della domanda," *Giornale degli economisti*, X (January, 1895), 59–68.

[9] This will be true, for example, when the general demand function—see equation (3i)—contains product terms in two or more of the variables.

of the general demand function of the mathematical school by assigning constant values to all of the variables in the general demand function except the price and the quantity under consideration is to effect an improvement over the neo-classical approach. The neo-classical economists only talked about the other variables, without troubling themselves first to introduce them into their demand equation and then to assign them constant values. True, Marshall considered (in general terms) the problem of substitutes, and the shifting of the demand curve from time to time. But he never faced the problem of the level at which each of the "other things" must be kept constant. The *ceteris paribus* postulate of classical fame must not, therefore, be confused with the method of mathematical ignoration described before.

The means by which we were led from the vague and indefinite statement of the law of demand represented by (1) to the general formulation represented by (3i) is the *operational procedure* of hypothetically asking each prospective purchaser in a given market: "How much will you buy of this commodity?" and of analyzing the probable replies. In this procedure, we have assumed that all of our "subjects" can give ready answers to our question, under the conditions explained above. As a matter of fact, this assumption is not generally valid. Many if not most, of our "subjects"—a term which may be stretched to include ourselves —will not be able to tell how much of a given commodity they would buy under given price conditions. And if they were compelled or induced to give an answer, it would not be a safe guide to the actual conduct. Most persons simply *do not know* how their consumption of a given commodity would be affected if prices were to move much above or below their accustomed range, and even within the accustomed range there may be considerable uncertainty. They must *experience* a given set of price relations in its proper institutional setting in order to make up their minds as to the quantities they will purchase. In short, there is only one way to deduce the demand functions for a commodity, and that is to observe the behavior of consumers in the market in masses.[10]

But each market transaction represents a unique combination of circumstances—a "point" on our demand "curve" or surface. To obtain the probable form of the demand function, we must have numerous observations; and in order to obtain the requisite number of observations, data covering a considerable period must, as a rule, be used. During the interval, however, important dynamic changes take place in the market. The

[10] This is not to be understood as excluding scientific experiments in the study of demand.

pragmatic approach must, therefore, deal with variables which are functions of *time*. Our law of demand then becomes

$$x_0 = \psi\ (x_1, x_2, \ldots, x_n, t)\ , \tag{4}$$

where the x's have the same meaning as in (3ii), and t stands for time
—a catch-all for all other disturbing factors. If, in this dynamic law of
demand, we give t a fixed value, t_0, representing the particular date (or
small interval of time) in which we happen to be interested, we obtain
the Walrasian statical law of demand (3i) as a special case. If we also
give constant values to all the x's except x_0 and x_1, we obtain the neo-
classical statical law of demand as another special case. In any inductive
investigation, however, the statical law of demand may only be approached, but never realized, since it is impossible to keep all the "irrelevant" factors fixed.

By continuing to ask the question, How much will you buy of this
commodity? and by analyzing the answers that may be given to it, we
have thus been compelled to abandon the earlier statements of the law
of demand and to reach its most general formulation as represented by
(4).

The method employed to deduce (4) serves as an illustration of what
Professor P. W. Bridgman in his stimulating book on *The Logic of
Modern Physics* (chap. i) has called "the operational procedure," which
he defines as follows:

If a specific question has meaning, it must be possible to find operations by
which an answer may be given to it. It will be found in many cases that the
operations cannot exist, and the question therefore has no meaning. For instance, it means nothing to ask whether a star is at rest or not . . . . [p. 28].
If the concept is physical, as of length, the operations are actual physical
operations, namely, those by which length is measured; or if the concept is
mental, as of mathematical continuity, the operations are mental operations,
namely those by which we determine whether a given aggregate of magnitudes
is continuous [p. 5].

Economists will do well to study the implications of Professor Bridgman's distinction between concepts which are defined in terms of operations, and those which are defined in terms of properties of things. Some
of the most important of the concepts with which they work are of the
latter variety. Thus, utility is defined as the *property* which a good has
to satisfy a want. As long as a concept remains in this category it is
vain to hope that it will yield to the quantitative approach. The restatement and extension of the earliest concept of demand into forms which
have meaning in terms of operations which was attempted in the fore-

going pages is the first step in the direction of the derivation of concrete, statistical laws of demand.

II. THE STATISTICAL STUDY OF DEMAND: PROFESSOR MOORE'S SOLUTION OF THE PROBLEM

"Economic theory," says Professor Young, "has never professed to
deal with the temporal succession or the spatial distribution of unique
combinations of circumstances, while statistics has to deal, in the first
instance, with nothing else."[11] This, in a nutshell, is the problem of
the statistical law of demand. If the form of the function

$$x_0 = \psi\ (x_1, x_2, \ldots, x_n, t)$$

and the interrelations of x_1, x_2, ... , x_n and t were known, the difficulty
to which Professor Young refers could be overcome; but they are not
known.

The procedure that Professor Henry L. Moore introduced is the treatment of the problem statistically by the method of multiple correlation.
As a preliminary step, he finds it convenient not to introduce time as an
explicit variable into the demand equation, but to make such adjustments in the other variables as are presumably due to time. The practice
of reducing the quantities consumed or produced to a per capita basis;
the use of first (or higher-order) differences, link relatives, trend ratios,
etc., are examples in point. When the data are so adjusted, the dynamic,
statistical law of demand becomes

$$X_0 = \phi\ (X_1, X_2, X_3, \ldots, X_n)\ , \tag{5i}$$

where the X's are the x's of (4), adjusted for time changes. Thus, if the
adjustment is by the method of trend ratios, to be explained later,
$X_1 = x_i/f_i(t_i)$, where t stands for time.

Professor Moore then experiments with the different types of function
ϕ and of interrelations of X_1, X_2, X_3, ... , X_n, and selects those types
which enable him to determine X_0 with the degree of accuracy sufficient
for the problem in hand.

As a first approximation he chooses the simplest possible function

$$\left.\begin{aligned}X_0 &= \phi(X_1, X_2, X_3, \ldots, X_n)\ , \\ &= a_0 + a_1 X_1 + a_2 X_2 + a_3 X_3 + \ldots + a_n X_n .\end{aligned}\right\} \tag{5ii}$$

As both the form of the function ϕ and the interrelations of the X_1, X_2,
. . . . , X_n are assumed to be linear, the method of multiple correlation

---

[11] Allyn A. Young, "English Political Economy," *Economica*, VIII, No. 22 (March,
1928), 10.

immediately suggests itself for determining the values of a_0, a_1, ... , a_n and the correlation between X_0 and the right-hand members of (5ii).

An excellent illustration is afforded by Professor Moore's derivation of the dynamic law of demand for cotton in the United States for the period 1890–1913.[12] It is:

$$X_0 = 7.11 - 0.97X_1 + 1.60X_2,$$

where X_0 is the percentage change in the price of cotton, X_1 the percentage change in the amount produced, and X_2 is the percentage change in the index of general prices. (The changes are measured from the corresponding values for the preceding year.) This formula enables us to say what the probable change in the price of cotton will be when we know the probable changes in the production of cotton and in the level of general prices.

The degree of accuracy with which this formula enables us to predict changes in the price of cotton is measured by the standard error $S = \sigma \sqrt{1 - R^2}$ (where R is the coefficient of multiple correlation), which shows the limits within which approximately two-thirds of the observations will fall. Professor Moore's computations show that

$$R = 0.859 \text{ and } S = 13.56$$

"This is a very high coefficient of correlation, and consequently the forecasting formula makes possible the prediction of the changes in the price of cotton with a relatively high degree of precision" (p. 158).

Should the linear function (5ii) fail to give good results, that is, should the error S involved in estimating X_0 from the linear function turn out to be too large for the problem under consideration, we must either include more factors in (5ii), or else take as a second approximation to our function ϕ some more general equations, as

$$\left.\begin{array}{l} X_0 = \phi(X_1, X_2, X_3 \ldots, X_n) = \\ A_{00} + a_{01}X_1 + b_{01}X_1^2 + c_{01}X_1^3 + \ldots, \\ \quad + a_{02}X_2 + b_{01}X_2^2 + c_{01}X_2^3 + \ldots, \\ \quad + a_{03}X_3 + b_{03}X_3^2 + c_{03}X_3^3 + \ldots, \\ \quad + \ldots \ldots \ldots \ldots \ldots \ldots, \\ \quad + \text{ terms involving products of} \\ \quad \quad \text{the variables,} \end{array}\right\} \quad \text{(5iii)}$$

[12] *Forecasting the Yield and Price of Cotton*, pp. 155–61. I have taken the liberty of modifying some of the symbols used by Professor Moore.

and determine the parameters of this equation and the correlations between X_0 and the right-hand members of (5iii).

If more variables are to be included, the function may become quite complicated, and the question arises: How can we deal with very complicated functions in any practical problem? The answer is that, although *in theory* it is necessary to deal with the demand function in all its complexity in order to show that the price problem is soluble, *in practice* only a small advantage is gained by considering more than the first few highly associated variables.[13]

Both (5ii) and (5iii) are examples of what Professor Moore calls a "dynamic law of demand in its complex form." These equations, however, also include an approximation to the *static* law of demand as a special case. Thus, if in these equations we single out X_1 as the important variable in relation to X_0 and assign constant values to all the other variables, we have examples of approximations to the *static* (neo-classical) law of demand. When the variables are all expressed in *percentage changes*, then the constant values which must be assigned to X_2, X_3, ... , X_n to obtain the static law are all equal to zero, since "the general hypothesis in mind when the static law of demand is formulated is that there shall be no changes in other economic factors."[14]

As an illustration of this procedure, we may cite Professor Moore's solution of the problem: "What is the relation between the changes in the price of cotton and the changes in the amount demanded when there are no changes in the purchasing power of money?"

Since in his formula

$$X_0 = 7.11 - 0.97X_1 + 1.60X_2,$$

the variables are all percentage changes, Professor Moore puts $X_2 = 0$, and thus obtains an answer to his problem. "The equation $X_0 = 7.11 - 0.97X_1$ expresses the relation between the changes in the price of cotton and the changes in the amount of cotton demanded *when the purchasing power of money remains constant*" (pp. 158–59). The standard error of the forecasts by means of this formula is $S = 15.38$, as compared with $S = 13.56$ by the three-constant formula.

The result is not the static law of demand in the Marshallian sense, since only one disturbing factor—the general level of prices—is held constant. If, however, the more important (theoretically, *all*) factors

[13] See Henry Schultz, "Mathematical Economics and the Quantitative Method," *Journal of Political Economy*, XXXV, No. 5 (October, 1927), 702–6.

[14] H. L. Moore, *Forecasting the Yield and Price of Cotton*, p. 152.

influencing X_0 were taken into account in the complex form of the law of demand, the foregoing procedure of assigning constant values to all of the variables except the price and the quantity under consideration would give us the statical neo-classical law of demand as a special case.

In fact, the foregoing is the *only procedure* by which the neo-classical law of demand may be deduced either conceptually or statistically. This becomes clear if we recall two fundamental assumptions in the neo-classical (and current) treatment of demand. First, there is the assumption that *all other things being equal,* an increase in the supply of the commodity will lead to a corresponding fall in the price. Second, there is the assumption that the concrete problem of the relation of price and supply of commodity will be simplified by attacking first the constituent elements of the question rather than by attacking the problem in its full concreteness.

Neither assumption is satisfactory nor indeed admissible. The "other things" that are supposed to remain equal are seldom mentioned and are never com pletely enumerated; and consequently the assumption that, other unmentioned and unenumerated factors remaining constant, the law of demand will be of a certain type, is really tantamount to saying that under conditions which are unanalyzed and unknown, the law of demand will take the supposed definite form. *The burden of proof is upon anyone using this method to show that the assumption does not at least involve a physical impossibility* [italics inserted].

The second of the above two assumptions is not more satisfactory than the first. It reproduces the defects of the first assumption with others superadded. The movement of prices results from changes in many factors: According to the statical method, the method of *caeteris paribus,* the proper course to follow in the explanation of the phenomenon is to investigate in turn, theoretically, the effect upon price of each factor, *caeteris paribus,* and then finally to make a synthesis! But if in case of the relation of each factor to price the assumption *caeteris paribus* involves large and at least questionable hypotheses, does one not completely lose himself in a maze of implicit hypotheses when he speaks of a final synthesis of the several effects?[15]

By adopting the general or Walrasian instead of the neo-classical statement of the law of demand; by modifying it so as to take into consideration the changes which the variables undergo in time; by showing that the parameters of the adjusted demand function and the interrela-

---

[15] H. L. Moore, *Economic Cycles: Their Law and Cause,* pp. 66–67. A fuller and even more suggestive analysis of the limitations of the statical, neo-classical law of demand is found in *Forecasting the Yield and the Price of Cotton,* pp. 147–51.

A fuller discussion of the relation between the neo-classical and the statistical demand curves is to be found in H. Schultz, *Der Sinn der statistischen Nachfragekurven* (Bonn, Kurt Schroeder, 1930), chap. iii, and in the references therein given.

tions of the various factors admit of being determined by the method of multiple correlation; and by actually determining for the first time concrete, statistical demand curves for several commodities, Professor Moore has accomplished what to Edgeworth seemed the impossible, and has paved the way to further progress.

Though the method of multiple correlation, is, as we have just seen, the best method for dealing with "disturbing factors" in the study of demand, it is not always a convenient method for eliminating long-time disturbing factors. To handle these in a simple, effective manner Professor Moore has invented two statistical devices: (1) the method of relative changes, and (2) the method of trend ratios.

The method of relative changes consists of finding the functional relationship, not between the absolute prices and the absolute quantities, but between the relative change in the price of the commodity and the relative change in the quantity demanded.

By taking the relative change in the amount of the commodity that is demanded, instead of the absolute quantities, the effects of increasing population are approximately eliminated; and by taking the relative change in the corresponding prices instead of the corresponding absolute prices, the errors due to a fluctuating general price level are partially removed. If the observations should cover the period of a major cycle of prices, and the commodity under investigation should be a staple commodity, ... the above method of deriving the demand curve will give an extremely accurate formula summarizing the relation between variations in price and variations in the amount of the commodity that is demanded.[16]

As measure of relative change we may take either the *percentage change* in the value from one year to the next, or the *ratio* of the given year's value to that of the preceding year (link relatives).

Using the method of percentage changes, Professor Moore deduced, for the first time (in 1914), the laws of demand for corn, hay, oats, and potatoes.[17]

The method of trend ratios derives the demand curve, not from the absolute prices and corresponding absolute quantities, but from the ratios of these prices and quantities to their respective trends. The rationale of this method rests on the following considerations.

If, during the period when our observations were taken, "all other things" had remained equal as theory demands, we should have no secular trend either of prices or of quantities. The existence of a secular trend in either series is prima facie evidence that "all other things" did not

[16] H. L. Moore, *Economic Cycles*, pp. 69–70.
[17] *Ibid.*, chap. iv.

remain equal, that there was one or more disturbing factor or element. It is the disturbing elements which give rise to the trend and which create a different "normal" from time to time. Hence it follows that by taking the ratio of the actual (observed) prices to normal or trend prices, we eliminate, to a first approximation, the effect of the long-time disturbing elements on the price of the commodity under consideration. Likewise, by taking the ratio of the corresponding quantities to their trend, we eliminate approximately all the long-time disturbing factors influencing the supply. By taking the ratios of our variables to their respective trends we are practically overcoming the chief difficulties which, according to Edgeworth and others, lie in the way of deriving statistical laws of demand. For our data, when thus adjusted, though extending over a period of years, may be conceived of as approximately representing observations taken at a given point in time—at least when the commodity in question is a staple farm product.

The first use of the method of trend ratios in the study of demand was in 1922, when Professor Moore applied it to deduce the demand curve for potatoes and to illustrate the application of his "typical equation to the law of demand."[18]

The various methods—multiple correlation, relative changes, and trend ratios—are not mutually exclusive. The competent statistician will know how to combine them to the best advantage. Nor is one of them necessarily superior to all of the others. They must all be valued according to their efficacy in enabling us to lay bare the true relationship between the phenomena under consideration.

An important consequence of Professor Moore's dynamic approach to the problem of demand is that the concept of *static equilibrium* gives way to the concept of *moving equilibrium*. This may be illustrated by reference to a concrete example.

Using the method of trend ratios, the analyst found the law of demand for sugar to be[19]

$$X = -0.4683Y + 1.468 . \tag{7}$$

In this equation $X = x/T_x$, and $Y = y/T_y$, where $x =$ observed per capita consumption; $y =$ observed real prices; $T_x =$ trend of per capita consumption; and $T_y =$ trend of real prices. The statistics on which this formula is based are for the period 1890–1914. Professor Moore has

[18] H. L. Moore, "Elasticity of Demand and Flexibility of Prices," *op. cit.*

[19] Henry Schultz, *Statistical Laws of Supply and Demand* (Chicago: University of Chicago Press, 1928), pp. 84–87.

shown,[20] however, that a simple transformation makes it possible to derive the law of demand for any one year in terms of *absolute quantities*. All that we have to do is to substitute for X and Y in (7) their values as given above. We obtain

$$x = -0.4683\ (T_x/T_y)y + 1.468T_x\ .\tag{8}$$

In order, therefore, to obtain the law of demand for any given year, it is necessary to find the values of T_x and T_y for that year and to substitute these values in (8).[21] Substituting the values of T_x and T_y for 1894 in (8), we obtain

$$x = -5.160y + 91.33\ .$$

The corresponding equations for 1904 and 1914 are

$$x = -6.843y + 107.19$$

and

$$x = -9.696y + 124.22\ ,$$

respectively. That is, a rise or a fall of one cent per pound would have decreased or increased the per capita consumption of sugar by 5.2 pounds in 1894, by 6.8 pounds in 1904, and by 9.7 pounds in 1914.

These equations—and they may be derived for the other years between 1890 and 1914—provide a quantitative measure of the degree to which the demand curve has shifted from year to year as a result of dynamic changes.

Similarly, a measure may be obtained of the shifting of the supply curve. Also, it can be shown that the two curves pass through the point whose co-ordinates are the "normal" (trend) figures of production and price. It follows, therefore, that the demand for the commodity and the supply for the commodity are in *moving equilibrium* about the trends of production and prices.[22]

The graphical representation of this moving equilibrium calls for a diagram in three dimensions—the first for price, the second for quanti-

[20] "Elasticity of Demand and Flexibility of Prices," *op. cit.*, p. 16.

[21] These values are given on p. 216 of the work referred to in n. 19 above.

[22] See H. L. Moore, "A Moving Equilibrium of Demand and Supply," *Quarterly Journal of Economics*, May, 1925, pp. 368–71, and H. Schultz, *Statistical Laws of Supply and Demand* (1928), pp. 165–67.

A more satisfactory method of measuring the shifting demand for sugar than that given by (8) is to be found in H. Schultz, *Der Sinn der Statistischen Nachfragekurven*, chap. iv, esp. Figs. X and XV.

ties, and the third for *time*. The diagram will resemble a long, inclined, slightly undulating wire, around which are fastened, at their centers, pairs of pins roughly perpendicular to each other. The long wire represents the ratios between the computed trends of prices and the corresponding trends of the quantities. It is about this line—the trend of the ratios —that the pairs of pins, the short-time demand and supply curves, fluctuate.

This moving equilibrium, however, is a *particular*, or *partial*, equilibrium. It deals with only two of the several equations which determine the general economic equilibrium. Furthermore, these equations are functions of only two variables, price and quantity, a feature which enables the moving equilibrium to be represented in a diagram of only three dimensions. However, in a paper published in November, 1926,[23] Professor Moore develops the concept of a *general* moving equilibrium, which embraces not only the complex formulation of the law of demand—see equation (3)—but also all of the other complex functions which constitute the Walrasian system. He shows how we can pass "from a statical, hypothetical equilibrium to a realistic treatment of an actual, moving equilibrium." A consideration of this achievement is beyond the scope of this paper. It is mentioned in this connection simply for the purpose of emphasizing the fact that Professor Moore's statistical studies of demand do not suffer from the lack of sound, theoretical inspiration.

III. UNSOLVED PROBLEMS IN THE STATISTICAL STUDY OF DEMAND

Two problems have arisen in the statistical study of demand for which solutions are greatly to be desired. First, there is the problem of the form of the equation representing the demand functions (3i), (4), or (5). Second, there is the problem of the demand for producer's goods, or the problem of the positively sloping demand curve.

Neither the statical statement.

$$x_0 = f\ (x_1, x_2, \ldots, x_n) \tag{3ii}$$

nor the dynamical statement

$$x_0 = \psi\ (x_1, x_2, \ldots, x_n, t) \tag{4}$$

of the law of demand is a *quantitative* formulation, for neither the form of the function nor the interrelations of the several variables are known. To expand (4) or its equivalent (5i) in a Taylor series and neglect

---

[23] "A Theory of Economic Oscillations," *op. cit.* The concept has since been developed more fully in his *Synthetic Economics* (1929).

terms involving second- and higher-order derivatives, and thus obtain the linear demand function (5ii), is not a safe procedure. Pareto has shown[24] that a linear supply-demand function for more than two commodities is incompatible with the assumption that the consumptions of the commodities are independent of one another. Yet this assumption is at the basis of the reasoning which leads to the negatively sloping demand curve.[25] Although the demand function (4) is not quite the same as Pareto's supply-demand function, nevertheless his proof ought to be a warning against the uncritical use of the linear function (5ii). Researches on the best forms of the demand function will be exceedingly useful to the statistical economist. As Pareto puts it: "Il serait fort utile de continuer des recherches de ce genre et de tâcher de mettre ainsi en rapport tous les faits qui nous sont connus au sujet de l'échange des marchandises."[26]

The second problem may be put in the form of a question: How can we distinguish statistically between a supply curve and a positively sloping demand curve when both relate to the same commodity?

That a demand curve of the positive type may arise under conditions of static equilibrium has been proved by mathematical economists.[27] It may arise when account is taken of the fact that the more a person spends on any one thing, the less power he retains of purchasing more of it or of other things, and the greater is the value of money to him; or it may arise whenever the utility derived from the consumption of a good also depends on the consumption of another good (as in the case of several courses of a dinner). Professor Moore argues, however, that the positively sloping demand curve is the typical demand curve for producers' goods in a dynamic society,

because if we assume that all demand curves are of the same negative type, we are confronted with an impossibility at the very beginning of our investigation. Upon the assumption that all demand curves are of the negative type, it would

---

[24] "Economie mathématique," *op. cit.*, p. 616.

[25] Pareto also shows that Marshall's constant-elasticity demand curve $yp^n = c$, where $y =$ quantity, $p =$ price, and n and c are constants, cannot be assumed for a market in which several commodities are exchanged, except in the special case when $n = 1$.

[26] *Ibid.*, p. 620.

[27] See Vilfredo Pareto, *Cours d'économie politique*, II (1897), § (974); *Manuel d'économie politique* (Paris: Giard & Brière, 1909), pp. 579–91; and his paper on "Economie mathématique," *op. cit.*, pp. 628–31; Antonio Osario, *Theorie mathématique de l'éxchange* (Paris: Giard et Brière, 1913), pp. 285–95; Wl. Zawadzki, *Les mathématiques appliqués a L'économie politique* (Paris: Ruiere et Cie, 1914), pp. 110–16. For a non-technical statement, see Jacob Viner, "The Utility Concept in Value Theory and Its Critics," *Journal of Political Economy*, XXXIII (August, 1925), 379.

be impossible for general prices to fall while the yield per acre of crops is decreasing. In consequence of the decrease in the yield per acre, the price of crops would ascend, the volume of commodities represented by pig-iron would decrease, and upon the hypothesis of the universality of the descending type of demand curves, the prices of commodities like pig-iron would rise. In a period of declining yield of crops, therefore, there would be a rise of prices, and in a period of increasing yield of crops there would be a fall of prices. But the facts are exactly the contrary.[28]

Taking pig iron as a representative producers' good, he finds that the correlation between the percentage change in the product and the percentage change in the price is $r = + 0.537$, and that the law of demand is $y = + 0.5211x - 4.58$, thus showing that the price rises with an increase of the product, and falls with its decrease.

An important series of questions now present themselves: If this is a demand curve, how may we deduce statistically the corresponding supply curve? If this is a supply curve, brought about by the shifting of the demand curve to the right (as some economists believe), how may we deduce statistically the corresponding demand curve? If the demand curve and the supply curve are both positively inclined, how is stable equilibrium reached?

It is not for nothing that all statistical economists, with the exception of Professor Moore, have confined their studies of demand to foodstuffs. The problem of the demand for producers' goods calls for a re-examination of accepted theory as well as of the statistical technique by which concrete demand curves are deduced. Let us hope that Professor Moore will throw more light on this problem.

IV. SUMMARY AND CONCLUSIONS

The most general formulation of the dynamic law of demand is that the quantity of any commodity consumed is a function not only of its price but also of all other prices and of *time*. To obtain the form of this law we must observe the *market behavior* of purchasers, though useful hints may be had from the accepted theory of utility. Human behavior is a rather complex phenomenon. To isolate the routine of human behavior as it operates under the stimulus of price changes, to summarize it in the "mental shorthand" of a mathematical formula—this is the object of a law of demand. ˙

Each market transaction represents a single observation, a "point" on the demand surface, subject to systematic and accidental "errors."

[28] H. L. Moore, *Economic Cycles: Their Law and Cause* (1914), pp. 110–16. See also his *Forecasting the Yield and Price of Cotton* (1917), p. 150.

Though these "errors" or "deviations" introduce many difficulties in the study of demand, yet they also enable us to deduce the probable demand "curve" about which they fluctuate. Without them it would be impossible, or extremely difficult, to deduce the short-time demand curve.

There are many methods for deducing demand curves from data of consumption and prices. In the examination of conclusions reached in any statistical study of demand, it is well to keep in mind the fact that the *results* of a method cannot be separated from the method itself. The fine differences between the various methods—differences which sometimes can only be felt but not explained—produce differences in the results obtained with their aid. Thus the elasticity of demand derived in an investigation may depend to a large degree on the particular method of curve-fitting employed.

The first economist to deduce concrete, statistical laws of demand was Professor Henry L. Moore, of Columbia University. By adopting the operational point of view, he succeeded in restating the hypothetical, statical law of demand in a form admitting of concrete, inductive treatment. By devising ingenious statistical devices for handling the time variable, and by adapting the method of multiple correlation to the same end, he succeeded in deducing for the first time the statistical demand curves for corn, potatoes, hay, rye, and cotton, and in measuring the elasticities of demand of these commodities. He thus opened a new, difficult, and useful field for research, in which considerable work is being done at present.

His work is not empirical. Possessing a mastery of the finer points of economic theory of which few can boast, he has used his knowledge of theory to formulate problems for statistical verification, and has used his mastery of statistical technique to provide "a statistical complement" to pure theory. If he has not given us a complete solution of the problem of the positively sloping demand curve, he has given us the grand conception of a moving general equilibrium, which has raised economic theory to a new level.

They used to say of Claude Bernard, "Il est la physiologie." It may with equal justice be said of Henry L. Moore, *"He is* the statistical law of demand."

WESLEY C. MITCHELL'S CONTRIBUTION TO THE THEORY OF BUSINESS CYCLES

By JOHN MAURICE CLARK
Columbia University

I. INTRODUCTION

If a single study can be selected as the "formative type" of the present movement of quantitative research in American economics, that distinction undoubtedly belongs to Wesley C. Mitchell's study of business cycles. It has already had a transforming effect on our ways of conceiving and approaching one major economic phenomenon, while it has implications for general economic theory and method which may be even more far reaching.

The material embodiment of this research is already voluminous. In 1913 appeared the quarto volume *Business Cycles,* published by the University of California. The method used is set forth and carried through its various stages to the culminating interpretation. The book carries no claims of completeness, but is permeated with a sense of the need for better and more comprehensive data; it is a logical preface to the author's subsequent work as research director of the National Bureau of Economic Research. The studies of this bureau may be largely oriented by the problem of cycles; but, if so, their scope indicates that this problem is hardly narrower than the whole of economic life. (Witness the studies of national income and of trade-union membership.) A rewriting of Mitchell's own work is in preparation, and the first volume has appeared, corresponding to the first of the three main divisions of the original treatise.[1] To this revision the Bureau has contributed, not only its studies already made, but additional data, analyses, and expert advice in the technique of statistical treatment.[2] For added light on Mitchell's conceptions of method, one must turn to other papers, especially his presidential address to the American Economic Association,[3]

[1] *Business Cycles: The Problem and Its Setting* (New York: National Bureau of Economic Research, 1927); referred to hereafter as "2d ed."

[2] Preface, *ibid.*

[3] "Quantitative Analysis in Economic Theory," *American Economic Review,* XV (March, 1925), 1–12.

and his essay in the collaborative volume, *The Trend of Economics*, edited by R. G. Tugwell.

In discussing research such as this, our major concern will naturally be with the larger matters of scientific strategy, rather than with details of statistical technique which might well constitute a separate study. It is noteworthy that such an outstanding statistical economist has developed his technique in the actual handling of problems, not by formal classroom training in the craft. The first edition makes little use of the more elaborate technical devices of statistical rendering. The second edition contains a fairly extended exposition of these methods, indicating a much larger use of them in the forthcoming volume. But Mitchell is no slave of these techniques, and repeatedly refrains from refinements of analysis and presentation where these are not justified by the adequacy and the accuracy of the data. In the original volume he makes free use of the theories, the data, and the organized indices produced by other students and agencies. Indeed, he gathers in an unprecedentedly wide range of material, both factual and theoretical. In the second edition the material is greatly enriched by the studies of the Bureau. The aid it has rendered in the actual preparation of the book is described as having been volunteered; nevertheless the outcome is a product, not of individual research, nor of the collaboration of independent students, but of organized staff work. As a result the statistical material is rounded out in a more systematic way than would otherwise be possible and contributes much to the comprehensiveness of the treatment; though for this result, considerable credit must also be given to the general development of statistics in the past fifteen years.

In spite of the fact that the original volume was the most comprehensively grounded treatise in its field, its statistical basis was limited. Its "annals of business,"[4] as well as its thoroughgoing statistical analyses, were confined to the period 1890–1911, and to the four countries: England, France, Germany, and the United States. International comparisons, even in the well-explored field of price movements, were handicapped by lack of comparability of data; and the elimination of noncomparable data reduced the size of the sample. In numerous fields other than that of prices, little international comparison was possible. In some matters, notably in physical production, consumption, and sav-

---

[4] The term "business annals" is applied to connected summaries of general business conditions built upon the summaries of contemporary financial writers. They are condensed into time-charts which simply designate the periods of prosperity, recession, depression, and recovery. Their only strictly quantitative feature is the duration of the periods.

ings, the data were extremely scant, or of an indirect character requiring much resort to inference.

For the first volume of the second edition far more complete data are available. Use is made of the Bureau's own series of business annals, compiled by Dr. Willard Thorp.[5] This series covers the United States and England from 1790, France from 1840, Germany from 1853, Austria from 1867, and twelve other countries from 1890, all concluding with the year 1925. These data provide observations upon a sufficiently large number of different cycles to permit the use of statistical methods in studying the annals themselves. They permit a sort of second-power statistical study which arrays the cycles and studies their characteristics by accepted methods of group analysis, including frequency curves of the main characteristics. The typical length and the departures therefrom are shown in frequency tables, both for the whole cycle and for its different phases; and notice is taken of the long-run trend of change in length, the relation of long-run price trends to the lengths of the different phases of the cycle, the relation of the length of the cycle to the relative length of its different phases, etc. International relationships are studied by the aid of a large chart of parallel spectrum-like bands.[6] The reliability of the "annals" is checked by comparisons with statistical indices of business conditions running back to 1875 for the United States, and to 1855 for England.[7] Use is made of the annals compiled by Dr. W. R. Scott, of St. Andrews, covering the period 1558–1720, to shed light on the question as to when the modern type of business cycles originated—those recorded by Scott being clearly a different variety.

On the statistical side, various indices of physical production are now available; and the Bureau itself has compiled, and is soon to publish, a series of social statistics for England, France, Germany, and the United States. In short, clear promise is given that the factual basis of the second edition will be far more complete than that of the first.

The end sought in the continuance of such inquiries is to make negligible the probability that the limitation of data has any material effect on the conclusions drawn. In some cases, this probability can perhaps be treated by quantitative methods; in others, it can only be estimated in general terms by the exercise of "judgment." In the field of prices the goal is either attained or closely approximated, while much improvement has been made in other directions. By its contribution to this result, staff re-

[5] Willard Long Thorp, *Business Annals* (New York: National Bureau of Economic Research, Inc., 1926). The volume contains an Introduction, "Business Cycles as Revealed by Business Annals," by Wesley C. Mitchell, pp. 15–100.

[6] 2d. ed., pp. 444–45.   [7] *Ibid.*, pp. 367–74.

search appears to have justified itself; while the work of independent investigators is also justified by the assistance they have rendered toward the same end.

II. THE DEVELOPMENT OF MITCHELL'S IDEAS OF METHOD

For an understanding of this study from the standpoint of method one fact is so vital as to call for somewhat detailed development. This is not, like so many superficially similar studies, a detached investigation of a special problem representing an exception to the general theory held by the author or devoid of important implications as to the existence or the truth of such a general theory. The method is not chosen merely because it seems appropriate to the handling of this type of special problem without reference to the methods appropriate to general theory. This may have been the case with Mitchell's earliest descriptive studies, but he was even then a rebel against deductive method in theory. Long before the writing of *Business Cycles* he had reached the conviction that general theory should be built on the results of the quantitative-descriptive type of method.

One may say that the interest which was focused in his early descriptive studies broadened—the problem of the business cycle playing an important part in the broadening process—until it grappled with the problems of general theory. With the resulting perspective, the factual interest narrowed again to the business cycle as a problem of practicable scope forming an integral part of the groundwork of the general structure. The fact that he set a new standard in the treatment of this problem is definitely an outcome of this broadening and subsequent refocusing. Because he has viewed the business cycle in its broadest relationships and lent a hospitable ear to all of the rival theories, he has in mind an unusually wide range of categories, in terms of which the business cycle may be described. Because his general theory is not a simple explanation of equilibrium, he could not be content with a simple conception of business cycles as departures from equilibrium (usually vaguely and inadequately conceived), but he is moved to drive toward as full a description as possible.

But enough of such generalizing! A more vivid picture is afforded by Mitchell's own words in a letter which he has, against his inclination, permitted to be published with this essay. In passing, one may note that his recollections cast doubt on some of the positions taken by Professor Homan in his very competent study.[8] Some modification is clearly called for in

[8] Paul Thomas Homan, *Contemporary Economic Thought* (New York: Harper & Bros., 1928), essay on Mitchell, pp. 375–436.

Homan's assumption that Mitchell brought to college only the common mental equipment of a well-brought-up, middle western boy of superior intelligence. The influence of Dewey and Veblen seems to have fallen in with and developed his previous leanings rather than to have planted the first seeds. Witness further the fact that, of various influences he might have received from Laughlin, he appears to have selected those which paralleled his own bent toward objectivity, rejecting others equally prominent. The evidence indicates that Mitchell felt himself to be influenced at least as much by those things he reacted against as by those with which he was in sympathy. And his statement that he regarded his first edition as an approach to general theory negatives Homan's surmise on this point.[9] Homan's suggestion that Mitchell's method of work has colored his conclusions[10] can hardly be other than true, but it does not follow that the basic character of his views is a mere rationalization of the bent of statistical workmanship.

The pyrotechnics of Veblen's battle with the orthodox left Mitchell not simply dazzled and confused, but grappling with the stubborn question: How important were the factors which Veblen emphasized and orthodox theory circumnavigated, compared to those which orthodox theory emphasized and Veblen slighted? A question of quantitative potentialities! One may conjecture that Mitchell's natural leanings received aid and comfort from Veblen's doctrine of replacing assumed harmonies by an observed sequence of matter-of-fact cause and effect. For, while Veblen preached this doctrine, Mitchell practices it—as nearly as may be and with reservations as to the meaning attached to "cause and effect" which will appear later.

It is quite natural that Mitchell refuses to subordinate quantitative economics to the function of verifying the conclusions of traditional deductive theory, or to be worried by the fact that, as yet, quantitative economics has not gotten far with this task.[11] In his view, traditional theory suggests problems and hypotheses, but they are likely to be recast in the process of adapting them to the test of observed behavior; while observation will itself suggest other problems whose standing is in no way inferior merely because traditional "theory" may ignore them. "Traditional theory," in this connection, means primarily the central theory of value and distribution, or the general theory of economic equilibrium; but the same proposition holds true in less degree of the

[9] *Ibid.*, p. 393.

[10] *Ibid.*, pp. 428–29.

[11] Cf. "Quantitative Analysis in Economic Theory," *op. cit.*, esp. 3.

special theories which have been set forth to explain, for instance, the business cycle. We shall see in a moment how these theories are utilized in Mitchell's study.

III. THE ORGANIZATION OF THE TREATISE

In organization and order of presentation, the method of the first edition is substantially followed in the second. Both studies start with a review of existing theories, the chief difference being that climatic theories are mentioned only in footnotes in the first edition, and receive more adequate attention in the second. There follows a survey of general features of the economic order, so far as they bear on the problem in hand. This is the author's closest approach to a formulation of his own economic philosophy. Next comes, in the first edition, a survey of "economic annals," or accounts of the sequences of prosperity and depression of business in general, by expert observers writing in financial journals and similar publications. Then follows a detailed statistical analysis of the behavior of different phenomena: prices of different classes of commodities, wages, interest rates of different classes, stock prices, physical production and consumption, unemployment, currency, banking conditions, savings, and profits. (Only the average amount of savings is studied, data being inadequate to reveal their variations.) In the second edition, this material is reserved for a later volume; but the first volume includes, with its lengthy exposition of methods of statistical analysis, enough sample tables and charts to give a very fair picture of the general form of the phenomenon as revealed by this method of attack.[12] Finally comes the author's own interpretation, which he characterizes as "analytic description" rather than causal explanation. He concludes that the modern type of business cycle is a phase of a well-developed "money economy," defined as a system in which the bulk of the people live by getting and spending money incomes, and production is guided by the pursuit of money profits.[13] In the second edition, this conclusion is based in part on a historical sketch of the development of the money economy (which reveals Mitchell as vastly more than a statistical analyst) but mainly on a detailed study of the "annals" reaching back to a period in which the present form of the phenomenon was clearly absent. This study constitutes a well-marked bit of "evolutionary economics," and is fulfilled by the conclusion that further changes are to be expected. The bulk of the "analytic description" is a picture of the typical course of cycles based on the common features of those observed but recognizing different degrees of variation from type.

[12] 2d ed., pp. 66–82.   [13] *Ibid.*, pp. 63 ff.

IV. THE TREATMENT OF EXISTING THEORIES

In the Preface to the first edition one finds the phrase: "To determine which of these [current] explanations are really valid. . . . . " This is to be taken, not as a formulation of the central problem, but as a device to aid the mind in approaching it. The various theories are not separately verified.[14] They suggest classifications of data as significant for the statistical part of the study, for instance, the distinction between producers' and consumers' goods, or between "organic" and "inorganic" products. They suggest causal relationships at numerous points in the ultimate interpretation; but clearly none contains the sole cause and none by itself contains a sufficient cause of all the features of the phenomena. Mitchell entertains the question whether practical reasons justify singling out one or more conditions as "the cause" or "the causes," but he himself makes no such selection.[15] If made, it would seem almost necessarily to imply as a point of departure some theory of normal behavior, lapses from which may then be explained by single (additional) causes; and this Mitchell might well regard as hypothetical rather than realistic economics.

While recognizing the value of the various theories, he finds them open to the general criticism that they take too readily for granted the nature of the phenomenon they undertake to explain, and that they tend to view cycles as special problems of abnormal behavior, by focusing attention on "explanations of" the crisis—Why need anyone explain prosperity?[16] Mitchell's fuller description of the cycle, aided as it is by the special theories, in turn develops and alters the nature of the problem which the special theories attack. Incidentally, in the second edition he takes up the definition of the term "cycle" and defends his use of it, distinguishing between periodicity, which implies regular intervals, and cycles, which may be of varying length.[17]

V. MITCHELL'S CONSPECTUS OF THE ECONOMIC ORDER

In summarizing the leading features of the economic order, Mitchell selects those which seems significant for the purpose in hand. As to the methods used in making this selection, the author himself would probably have difficulty in formulating them on paper. He deals in part with economic motives, but mainly with the economic machinery which forms the framework in which these motives work. In the first edition, he deals mainly with such matters of common knowledge as the ordinary economic theorist has at his disposal; while in the second edition, considerable

---

[14] *Business Cycles,* p. 20; 2d ed., p. 58. [16] *Ibid.,* pp. 2, 451–55.
[15] Cf. 2d ed., pp. 54–55. [17] *Ibid.,* pp. 464–69.

quantitative matter is introduced, utilizing the results of his own statistical researches. Even without this indication, it seems clear that the order in which this part appears in the published volume is not necessarily the order in which the work was done.[18] Presumably this section was formulated and reformulated as the statistical studies and interpretation progressed, the author having consciously undertaken to include such things, and only such things, as played a part in his final interpretation.

It is no contradiction of this statement to say that one finds symptoms of Veblenian influence: particularly in the distinction between technical and pecuniary occupations, in the subordination of technical to profit-making considerations, in the emphases on the motive of profit-making and the planlessness of production, without corresponding emphasis on the checks and the ordering influences of the "natural economic laws" of the traditional economics. Competition is mentioned, but not "normal competitive price," and the "law of supply and demand" is conspicuously absent.[19] There is also a decided kinship with the type of theoretical approach originated by Walras and used at present by Cassel, insofar as they substitute the idea of a multitude of interacting functional relationships for that of single or ultimate "causes" but Mitchell, of course, does not follow them in focusing attention on the conditions of a theoretical equilibrium in these relationships.

VI.   ANNALS AND STATISTICS

In the second edition, Mitchell pays careful attention to the relative advantages and limitations of business annals and statistics, attempting to gain whatever light can be secured from each. The main uses of the annals have already been indicated. Statistical studies play the larger part, since it is through them that he is able to trace the complicated order of events of which the cycle is made up. He finds, for instance, that retail prices vary more than wholesale; those of production goods more than those of consumption goods (even at wholesale) ; those of raw materials more than those of finished products; and wage rates less than any class of prices.[20]

With reference to the timing of different related phenomena, the indications are for the most part less clear and more difficult of interpretation. Perhaps the clearest cases are those of bond yields in relation to short-

[18] Contrast Homan's assumption that this section was first in formulation as in presentation (op. cit., p. 399).

[19] 2d ed., pp. 154–57.

[20] Business Cycles, p. 458; cf. charts of coal and iron production (pp. 231–36) in connection with price charts (pp. 97–126).

time interest rates, and the loans, the deposits, and the reserves of banks. The conclusion is also reached that the physical volume of production revives ahead of prices, sometimes by as much as two years.[21] The preliminary material included in the first volume of the second edition indicates that these time-sequences are to be treated far more elaborately, with the aid of statistical methods of gauging leads and lags, using the results of recent studies in this field.[22] Some of the indications in the first volume—for example, as to coal and iron production and wages—are complicated by the merging of cyclical and secular trends, and raise the question whether the earlier upturn of production is due to the secular trend rather than to the purely cyclical movement. Yet the isolation of secular trends and cyclical-irregular movements may raise more problems than it settles—as Mitchell clearly realizes. Indeed, he has already formulated a series of penetrating queries as to the interactions of secular and cyclical trends.

He may be counted on to determine whether the isolation makes any difference in the timing of the cyclical-irregular upturn. He will probably assume that for certain purposes—perhaps for explaining effects on prices and related processes—the actual upturn is the significant thing, while for other purposes analysis into components is necessary. His factual bent would naturally lead him to recognize that these components are theoretical abstractions and cause him to be on his guard against assignments of causal responsibility to such abstractions—assignments which might be as doubtful in their way as those of traditional deductive theory.

VII.   THE FINAL INTERPRETATION

Perhaps the most interesting questions as to Mitchell's method arise in connection with his final synthesis, or "analytic description," of the typical business cycle. Certain features of this are obvious enough. The facts revealed by his statistical studies are recombined in the order in which they occur, showing what is happening at each stage of the cycle and how each stage leads to the next. The emphasis is on "how" rather than "why," and the whole result is not characterized as a causal explanation; yet the description is not merely empirical—it must accord with reason.[23] In the same spirit is his cautious treatment of coefficients of correlation. Yet he is willing to speak of causal relations at particular points—this being the form in which the mind habitually frames some of its most fruitful hypotheses; but he insists on the recognition that these relationships are manifold and interacting—that causes are at the same time ef-

---

[21] 2d ed., p. 115.   [22] *Ibid.*, p. 233.   [23] Cf. *ibid.*, p. 470.

fects and effects are also causes. Apparently the things to which he chiefly objects are: (1) the idea of an absolutely necessary sequence where modifying conditions are too numerous to justify such an inference,[24] and (2) the conception of causation as a single chain running in one direction and anchored somewhere to a cause which is ultimate—"the" cause—rather than one of an indefinitely large network of conditioning factors. And Mitchell's work should do much to help consign this obsolete chain-and-anchorage notion of cause to the museum of historical antiquities.

But what is meant by a description which accords with reason? An example or two may help us here. If dealers buy more goods (in physical terms) than they are selling, their stocks must increase; conversely, if they increase their stocks, they must be buying more than they sell; and if they increase their stocks at a time when their sales are increasing, their purchases—and the sales of those who supply them—must increase more than their sales. Here we have the quasi-mathematical "reason" that deals with physical quantities. But when do dealers increase their stocks? It is natural for them, in the pursuit of maximum profits and minimum losses, to attempt to reduce them when they expect dull trade, and increase them when there is prospect of increased sales, and especially of increased prices; and the most available sign of such a prospect is the beginning of an actual upward movement. But here we are in the realm of human expectations and reactions whose behavior is notoriously variable even when most of the significant conditions are apparently the same. A movement toward "hand-to-mouth buying" might start for reasons outside the business cycle, or for reasons arising from it, and in either case might alter permanently the typical habits of stock-keeping. Here it is unsafe to reason from conditions to conduct and make a priori predictions; but given the conduct, one may see that it accords with the customary operation of known motives as conditioned by the given circumstances, and is, in this sense, "explained."

The most obvious difference between this method and that of traditional theory is that Mitchell reasons from conduct to conditioning motive and circumstance, while traditional theory, in appearance at least, reasons from motive and circumstance to "normal" conduct. Mitchell insists that he would not trust himself to use his analysis of motive and circumstance as a basis for predicting conduct without constant check by observations of actual behavior. Theory, being interested in "normal" behavior, has no such hesitation; variations of behavior from normal are merely the re-

[24] *Ibid.*, pp. 262–70.

sults of other than normal causes. The normal behavior of equilibrium theory is highly simplified and differs from actual behavior. But is not Mitchell simplifying also, to a less extent, in picturing the normal cycle and giving separate recognition to variations from it? At certain points in his analytic description he notes alternative versions of behavior, while every cycle has some features which are unique. His picture of determining conditions is comprehensive, including many of the "disturbing factors" of traditional theory. It is also too complex to permit the mind to deduce a result which is uniquely determined and exact. And it is the lack of this quality, in all probability, which causes some readers to miss the feeling of definite explanation which they get from more traditional methods.

Here is a very great difference. Relying on the deductive methods, traditional theory simplifies to the point at which this method can secure definite results; and this definiteness, though abstract rather than actual, is apparently held by John Stuart Mill to be the criterion of scientific character in economic thinking. Such thinking proceeds ostensibly from premises to resulting behavior.

Much could be said on both sides as to whether this is the order in which the thinking is actually done, or whether the (hypothetical) results are themselves assumptions actually determining the "premises" selected to explain them. Since the method is limited to such premises as are capable of yielding definite deductive results, there is ground for holding that the available premises of this character really limit and determine the results it can attain. On the other hand, from the fact that the whole structure is the outgrowth of the search for the "natural levels" of price and its "component parts" (shares in distribution), one may make at least a reasonable claim that the assumed result—normal prices and distributive shares—comes first and the apparent premises are derived from it, a selection of conditioning motives and circumstances which are sufficient to "explain" the result. To the inductive student, the whole structure is one hypothesis, with its implications somewhat elaborated and the emphasis on its own internal consistency, as Mitchell points out, rather than on the resemblance of the whole to the observed facts.

And it is this whole hypothetical state of normal equilibrium, of which Mitchell finds no evidence in the facts as he observes them.[25] There is no level of prosperity of which he can say: "Whenever business is above this level, economic forces are acting to bring it down, and whenever it is below, they are acting to bring it up." Economic forces act upward from

[25] *Business Cycles*, p. 86; 2d ed., p. 376.

trough to crest, downward from crest to trough; near the turning-points a conflict of forces may appear, but hardly at the mid-point. Each stage tends to bring its successor into being and not to return to an equilibrium level. Yet even Mitchell speaks of profits in a way which implies a long-run normal relation of prices to costs on the average of the ups and downs.[26] So far as there are forces that act in this way, some approach to the theorist's "normal" seems to find justification. On the other hand, the theorist's abstract normal implies no unemployment; and such a normal is obviously not the average of the periods of prosperity and depression, in the same way that the normal price may represent the average of high and low periods. Evidently different parts of the static norm bear different relations to reality.

An assimilation of Mitchell's results should certainly challenge the most orthodox theorist to produce some modifications in the traditional analysis, other than a slight lengthening of the chapter on business cycles in that part of the theorist's treatise labeled "special problems" or "applied economics." Shall we ever see the general economic theory which would be the logical outcome of an approach to the whole subject via Mitchell's study of cycles? Or will the effects of Mitchell's study be merged with the results of growing knowledge in many other realms of economic phenomena and motives?[27]

APPENDIX: THE AUTHOR'S OWN ACCOUNT OF HIS METHODOLOGICAL INTERESTS

EDITOR'S NOTE

In making their interpretations of an author's methods, analysts were encouraged to secure the co-operation of the author himself whenever circumstances permitted. In the present instance, Professor Clark was singularly fortunate in eliciting from Professor Mitchell an intimate and revealing account of the development of his research interests and methods. This was contained in a personal communication, unaffected by thought of publication. In addition to its value for Mr. Clark's analysis, it was found to represent a type of methodological inquiry which would otherwise not appear in the volume,[28] and Mr. Mitchell was asked to permit its publication in connection with Mr. Clark's analysis. The proposal

---

[26] *Ibid.*, pp. 182, 187–88.

[27] [This analysis was first written in September, 1928. After some negotiations concerning the inclusion of the correspondence between the analyst and Mr. Mitchell, it was given final revision by the former in April, 1929.—EDITOR.]

[28] Cf. the Introduction, pp. 6–7.

was personally distasteful, but he gave reluctant consent, yielding to an appeal to his loyalty to the Council[29] and its project, and to the editor's contention that an illustration of this kind of methodological analysis was needed in the volume.

Professor Clark concurred in the proposal to publish the correspondence, and commented as follows:

It may not be out of place to express my gratitude to my friend and colleague [Professor Mitchell] for the thought and effort embodied in the very revealing letter he produced; as well as to assure the reader that the sole reason for suggesting its publication is its value as a document bearing on the development of Mitchell's basic ideas and methods. From that standpoint there is reason to regret the amount of space occupied by a purely technical discussion of the minor matter of the index of price dispersion. If the inclusion of this technical discussion is justified (aside from presenting the correspondence as it was), it is because it exhibits one of the qualities which helps explain Mitchell's achievements: namely, a scientific humility and readiness to assimilate criticism. It may thus serve as an offset to his own avowal of youthful "intellectual arrogance," an avowal which an arrogant man would hardly have made!

The two letters below are reproduced as written, except for the omission from both of the technical discussion of price dispersion, to which Clark refers in the preceding paragraph.

LETTER FROM JOHN M. CLARK TO WESLEY C. MITCHELL

41 WRIGHT ST., WESTPORT, CONN.
Aug. 2, 1928

DEAR MITCHELL:

I have been persuaded to undertake one of these case studies of method in the social sciences, about which you undoubtedly know. Having side-stepped one assignment, I find myself committed to trying to handle your study of business cycles. I hesitate to discuss a colleague's work; and if you see any impropriety in my doing it, perhaps it is not too late to change. If not, there are some things I should like to discuss with you.

First as to the choice of the problem. Is there any use in raising the question whether you are drawn to this problem because you prefer the methods of quantitative and analytic description to those of abstract theorizing, or whether you develop these methods because you are interested in problems that require them? At any rate, others have dealt with the same problem of cycles in the abstract way. It seems reasonable to me to suppose that you are naturally interested in problems of concrete behavior; that you reacted against your early theoretical teaching because it did not come to grips with many such problems,

[29] Mr. Mitchell has been chairman of the Social Science Research Council since August, 1927.

among which that of business cycles stood out like the proverbial sore thumb. But your reaction is more fundamental than most in that it extends to the whole matter of method. And your choice of a problem seems part of a method of attacking the general interpretation of economic life, as the problem of equilibrium is to a different school.

In this I suppose it is fair to say that you were influenced by Veblen, despite obvious differences. I learn from Homan's book that Veblen's earliest study was more like your type of work than anything he has done since.

Your general survey of leading features of economic life involves, of course, the selection of those that are significant for the problem in hand. Can one say anything about the method by which this selection was made or guided? In some cases you are using facts of common knowledge, and your selection *could* be the result of the same kind of mental processes as produced the special theories of earlier writers. But, even if that is the case, I naturally assume that you would check the significance of such facts by the part they play in the final analytic description. Other facts are more detailed and quantitative in character (especially in the second edition) and seem clearly the outgrowth of your quantitative studies, as well as of at least a partial working out of your ultimate interpretation. Could you say anything as to the order in which the various parts of the work were done? Or am I trying to dissect mental processes that are unanalyzable or "intuitive"?

As to your final interpretation, I have often wondered, to no great purpose, over the difference between this kind of treatment and others more definitely "causal." As it looks to me now, the key of your treatment seems to consist in presenting each situation so that the behavior leading to the next step appears as the natural result of business motives under the given situation of market prospects, behavior of costs, etc. That seems to be the crucial part of the proposition that the description must square with reason, and distinguishes it from mere empiricism. Perhaps there are other features that have escaped me.

[Here follow two paragraphs devoted to details of the method of measuring price-dispersions.]

Pardon me for inflicting this on you. Possibly this letter will fail to reach you, in which case you will escape.

With best wishes;
John M. Clark

LETTER FROM WESLEY C. MITCHELL TO JOHN M. CLARK

Huckleberry Rocks, Greensboro, Vt.
August 9, 1928

DEAR MAURICE:

I know no reason why you should hesitate to dissect a colleague for the instruction, or amusement, of mankind. Your interest in ideas rather than in personalities will be clear to any intelligent reader. Nor is the admiration I feel for your skill as an analyst likely to grow less warm if you take me apart to see how I work. Indeed, I should like to know myself!

Whether I can really help you is doubtful. The questions you put are questions I must answer from rather hazy recollections of what went on inside me thirty and forty and more years ago. Doubtless my present impressions of how I grew up are largely rationalizations. But perhaps you can make something out of the type of rationalizations in which I indulge.

Concerning the inclination you note to prefer concrete problems and methods to abstract ones, my hypothesis is that it got started, perhaps manifested itself would be more accurate, in childish theological discussions with my grand aunt. She was the best of Baptists, and knew exactly how the Lord had planned the world. God is love; he planned salvation; he ordained immersion; his immutable word left no doubt about the inevitable fate of those who did not walk in the path he had marked. Hell is no stain upon his honor, no inconsistency with love. . . . . I adored the logic and thought my grand aunt flinched unworthily when she expressed hopes that some back stairs method might be found of saving from everlasting flame the ninety and nine who are not properly baptized. But I also read the Bible and began to cherish private opinions about the character of the potentate in Heaven. Also I observed that his followers on earth did not seem to get what was promised them here and now. I developed an impish delight in dressing up logical difficulties which my grand aunt could not dispose of. She always slipped back into the logical scheme, and blinked the facts in which I came to take a proprietary interest.

I suppose there is nothing better as a teething-ring for a child who likes logic than the garden variety of Christian theology. I cut my eye-teeth on it with gusto and had not entirely lost interest in that exercise when I went to college.

There I began studying philosophy and economics about the same time. The similarity of the two disciplines struck me at once. I found no difficulty in grasping the differences between the great philosophical systems as they were presented by our text-books and our teachers. Economic theory was easier still. Indeed, I thought the successive systems of economics were rather crude affairs compared with the subtleties of the metaphysicians. Having run the gamut from Plato to T. H. Green (as undergraduates do) I felt the gamut from Quesnay to Marshall was a minor theme. The technical part of the theory was easy. Give me premises and I could spin speculations by the yard. Also I knew that my "deductions" were futile. It seemed to me that people who took seriously the sort of articles which were then appearing in the *Q. J. E.* might have a better time if they went in for metaphysics proper.

Meanwhile I was finding something really interesting in philosophy and in economics. John Dewey was giving courses under all sorts of titles and every one of them dealt with the same problem—how we think. I was fascinated by his view of the place which logic holds in human behavior. It explained the economic theorists. The thing to do was to find out how they came to attack certain problems; why they took certain premises as a matter of course; why they did not consider all the permutations and variants of those problems which were logically possible; why their contemporaries thought their conclusions were significant. And, if one wanted to try his own hand at constructive theorizing, Dewey's notion pointed the way. It is a misconception to suppose that consumers guide their course by ratiocination—they don't think except under stress. There is no way of deducing from certain principles what they will do, just because their behavior is not itself rational. One has to find out what they do. That is a matter of observation, which the economic theorists had taken all too lightly. Economic theory became a fascinating subject—the orthodox types particularly—when one began to take the mental operations of the theorists as the problem, instead of taking their theories seriously.

Of course Veblen fitted perfectly into this set of notions. What drew me to him was his artistic side. I had a weakness for paradoxes—Hell set up by the God of love. But Veblen was a master developing beautiful subtleties, while I was a tyro emphasizing the obvious. He did have such a good time with the theory of the leisure class and then with the preconceptions of economic theory! And the economists reacted with such bewildered soberness! There was a man who really could play with ideas! If one wanted to indulge in the game of spinning theories who could match his skill and humor? But if anything were needed to convince me that the standard procedure of orthodox economics could meet no scientific tests, it was that Veblen got nothing more certain by his dazzling performances with another set of premises. His working conceptions of human nature might be a vast improvement; he might have uncanny insights; but he could do no more than make certain conclusions plausible—like the rest. How important were the factors he dealt with and the factors he scamped was never established.

That was a sort of problem which was beginning to concern me. William Hill set me a course paper on "Wool Growing and the Tariff." I read a lot of the tariff speeches and got a new side-light on the uses to which economic theory is adapted, and the ease with which it is brushed aside on occasion. Also I wanted to find out what really had happened to wool growers as a result of protection. The obvious thing to do was to collect and analyze the statistical data. If at the end I had demonstrated no clear-cut conclusion, I at least knew how superficial were the notions of the gentlemen who merely debated the tariff issue, whether in Congress or in academic quarters. That was my first "investigation"—I did it in the way which seemed obvious, following up the available materials as far as I could, and reporting what I found to be the "facts." It's not easy to see how any student assigned this topic could do much with it in any other way.

A brief introduction to English economic history by A. C. Miller, and unsystematic readings in anthropology instigated by Veblen reënforced the impressions I was getting from other sources. Everything Dewey was saying about how we think, and when we think, made these fresh materials significant. Men had always deluded themselves, it appeared, with strictly logical accounts of the world and their own origin; they had always fabricated theories for their spiritual comfort and practical guidance which ran far beyond the realm of fact without straining their powers of belief. My grand aunt's theology; Plato and Quesnay; Kant, Ricardo and Karl Marx; Cairnes and Jevons, even Marshall were much of a piece. Each system was tolerably self-consistent—as if that were a test of "truth"! There were realms in which speculation on the basis of assumed premises achieved real wonders; but they were realms in which one began frankly by cutting loose from the phenomena we can observe. And the results were enormously useful. But that way of thinking seemed to get good results only with reference to the simplest of problems, such as numbers and spatial relations. Yet men practiced this type of thinking with reference to all types of problems which could not be treated readily on a matter-of-fact basis—creation, God, "just" prices in the middle ages, the Wealth of Nations in Adam Smith's time, the distribution of incomes in Ricardo's generation, the theory of equilibrium in my own day.

There seemed to be one way of making real progress, slow, very slow, but tolerably sure. That was the way of natural science. I really knew nothing of science and had enormous respect for its achievements. Not the Darwinian type of speculation which was then so much in the ascendant—that was another piece of theology. But chemistry and physics. They had been built up not in grand systems like soap bubbles; but by the patient processes of observation and testing—always critical testing—of the relations between the working hypotheses and the processes observed. There was plenty of need for rigorous thinking, indeed of thinking more precise than Ricardo achieved; but the place for it was *inside* the investigation, so to speak—the place that mathematics occupied in physics as an indispensable tool. The problems one could really do something with in economics were problems in which speculation could be controlled.

That's the best account I can give off hand of my predilection for the concrete. Of course, it seems to me rather a predilection for problems one can treat with some approach to scientific method. The abstract is to be made use of at every turn, as a handmaiden to help hew the wood and draw the water. I loved romances—particularly William Morris's tales of lands that never were—and utopias, and economic systems, of which your father's, when I came to know it, seemed the most beautiful; but these were objects of art, and I was a workman who wanted to become a scientific worker, who might enjoy the visions which we see in mountain mists but who trusted only what we see in the light of common day.

Besides the spice of rationalizing which doubtless vitiates my recollections—uncontrolled recollections at that—this account worries me by the time it is taking, yours as well as mine. I'll try to answer the other questions concisely.

Business cycles turned up as a problem in the course of the studies which I began with Laughlin. My first book on the greenbacks dealt only with the years of rapid depreciation and spasmodic wartime reaction. I knew that I had not gotten to the bottom of the problems and wanted to go on. So I compiled that frightful second book as an apparatus for a more thorough analysis. By the time it was finished I had learned to see the problems in a larger way. Veblen's paper on "Industrial and Pecuniary Employments" had a good deal to do with opening my eyes. Presently I found myself working on the system of prices and its place in modern economic life. Then I got hold of Simmel's *Théorie des Geldes*—a fascinating book. But Simmel, no more than Veblen, knew the relative importance of the factors he was working with. My manuscript grew—it lies unpublished to this day. As it grew in size it became more speculative. I was working away from any solid foundation—having a good time, but sliding gayly over abysses I had not explored. One of the most formidable was the recurring readjustments of prices, which economists treated apart from their general theories of value, under the caption "Crises." I had to look into the problem. It proved to be susceptible of attack by methods which I thought reliable. The result was the big California monograph. I thought of it as an introduction to economic theory.

This conception is responsible for the chapter on "Modern Economic Organization." I don't remember precisely at what stage the need of such a discussion dawned upon me. But I have to do everything a dozen times. Doubtless I wrote parts of that chapter fairly early and other parts late as I found omissions in the light of the chapters on "The Rhythm of Business Activity." Of course, I put nothing in which did not seem to me strictly pertinent to the understanding of the processes with which the volume dealt. That I did not cover the field very intelligently, even from my own viewpoint, appears from a comparison of the books published in 1913 and 1927. Doubtless before I am done with my current volume, I shall be passing a similar verdict upon the chapter as I left it last year.

As to the relation between my analytic description and "causal" theory I have no clear ideas—though I might develop some at need. To me it seems that I try to follow through the interlacing processes involved in business expansion and contraction by the aid of everything I know, checking my speculations just as far as I can by the data of observation. Among the things I "know" are the way in which economic activity is organized in business enterprises, and the way these enterprises are conducted for money profits. But that is not a simple matter which enables me to deduce certain results—or rather, to deduce results with certainty. There is much in the workings of business technique which I should never think of if I were not always turning back to observation. And I should not trust even my reasoning about what business men will do if I could not check it up. Some unverifiable suggestions do emerge; but I hope it is always clear that they are unverified. Very likely what I try to do is merely carrying out the requirements of John Stuart Mill's "complete method." But there is a great deal more passing back and forth between hypotheses and observation, each modifying and enriching the other, than I seem to remember in Mill's version. Perhaps I do him injustice as a logician through default of memory; but I don't think I do classical economics injustice when I say that it erred sadly in trying to think out a deductive scheme and then talked of verifying *that*. Until a science has gotten to the stage of elaborating the details of an established body of theory—say finding a planet from the aberrations of orbits, or filling a gap in the table of elements—it is rash to suppose one can get an hypothesis which stands much chance of holding good except from a process of attempted verification, modification, fresh observation, and so on. (Of course, there is a good deal of commerce between most economic theorizing and personal observation of an irregular sort—that is what has given our theories their considerable measure of significance. But I must not go off into that issue.) . . . .

[Here follow two paragraphs on the measurement of price-dispersions, dealing with the points raised by Mr. Clark and referring to a discussion of the same points in F. C. Mill's *Behavior of Prices*, pp. 279 ff. esp. p. 283 n.]

I did not intend to inflict such a screed upon you when I started. Now that I have read it over, I feel compunctions about sending it. Also some hesitations. I don't like the intellectual arrogance which I developed as a boy, which stuck by me in college, and which I shall never get rid of wholly. My only defence is that I was made on a certain pattern and had to do the best I could —like everybody else. Doubtless I am at bottom as simple a theologian as my grand aunt. The difference is that I have made my view of the world out of the materials which were available in the 1880's and '90's, whereas she built, with less competent help than I had, out of the materials available in the farming communities of the 1840's and '50's. Perhaps you have been able to develop an outlook on the world which gives you a juster view than I had of the generations which preceded me and of the generation to which I belong. If I did not think so, I should not be sending you a statement so readily misunderstood.

Ever yours,

WESLEY C. MITCHELL

SECTION IX

ATTEMPTS TO DETERMINE QUANTITATIVE RELATIONS AMONG MEASURED AND EXPERIMENTALLY CONTROLLED FACTORS

ANALYSIS 48

EXPERIMENTAL DETERMINATIONS BY S. WYATT AND J. A. FRASER OF THE EFFECTS OF REST PAUSES UPON REPETITIVE WORK[1]

By STUART A. RICE

University of Pennsylvania

SYNOPSIS

The Industrial Fatigue Research Board of Great Britain has made a number of studies designed to show the influence of rest pauses upon the output of workers in repetitive occupations. Some of these studies, as in their Report No. 25, were based upon ordinary records made at the time the rest pause was introduced. Hence they were not free from the influence of important uncontrolled variables. That is, it was difficult to ascertain the extent to which there was uniformity throughout the experiment in working conditions other than the presence or absence of the rest period. Various laboratory experiments in which the "work" performed was of non-economic character were also made. But it cannot be assumed that laboratory results will be reproduced in a factory or in a shop. The present study was carried on in actual working situations, and under conditions such that a much higher degree of experimental control was secured. Moreover, during the entire periods covered in two of the three experiments, the workers involved were under the immediate observation of the investigators.

The study involved sixteen workers in four factories over periods of fifteen weeks. These workers were engaged in three separate processes: namely, folding handkerchiefs, hand ironing handkerchiefs, and stamping out tin lids of cigarette containers at mechanical presses. Handkerchief folders were observed for six weeks during the afternoon shifts only. These shifts were continuous (without rest pause) in the first three weeks. In the second three weeks no change in working procedure occurred except the introduction of a ten-minute rest period from 3:30 P.M. to 3:40 P.M. The rest period was already in existence in the morning shift so that the afternoon period alone was altered. Eight girls were the subjects in this series of observations.

---

[1] *Studies in Repetitive Work with Special Reference to Rest Pauses: Great Britain Industrial Fatigue Research Board Report No. 32* (1925; iv+43 pp.).

The second set of observations concerned four girls who ironed the folded handkerchiefs in the same room as the first eight, and whose general working conditions were the same. The observations extended over four weeks, including the period before and after the introduction of the rest pause. In the stamping process, observations were made over a period of three weeks following the introduction of pauses of ten minutes each, introduced at 11:00 A.M. and 4:00 P.M. These were compared with results recorded in a preceding period of equal length.

Throughout the entire period of six weeks the average time taken by each of the first eight girls to fold twelve handkerchiefs was recorded in seconds during each quarter-hour. Similarly, "the time taken to iron a dozen handkerchiefs was noted as frequently as possible throughout each afternoon spell." A correction was necessary here to allow for time taken to dampen the handkerchiefs before ironing. In the case of the stamping-press operatives, the number of sheets from which twelve lids each were stamped out was noted for each worker during every half-hour, together with the average duration of stoppages due to various uncontrolled causes.

In each of these three situations the introduction of the rest pauses was concomitant with an increased average *rate* of output by the individual workers. This increased rate pertained to the portions of the shift both before and after the rest pause. Moreover, the *total* per diem output increased except for the afternoon shift with the pressing machines where a decrease in total output occurred. The morning shift in this occupation showed a slight increase.

In connection with the results of their immediate inquiries, the investigators summarize earlier evidence collected by the Board, and by other investigators in both England and America. The increased rates and totalities of output here observed are shown to be general, following the introduction of rest pauses, and a threefold explanation, both physiological and psychological, is attempted.

A number of collateral observations and conclusions growing out of the experiment are included by the investigators in their report. These relate to such matters as the following: General characteristics of the work curves of rates of production in each occupation; individual differences among operators; the effects of "aggregation," i.e., the influence of workers in physical proximity upon one another; the time required for adaptation to modified conditions of work. Further laboratory experiments on rest pauses are recorded.

THE ELEMENTS TO BE CONSIDERED HERE

Two elements of the inquiry will be singled out for special attention in this analysis. These are: (1) the conditions involved in the experiment with respect to handkerchief folding, so far as this applies to rates and totality of output; (2) problems involved in the summarization of evidence to support general conclusions concerning the effects of rest pauses in repetitive work upon rates and totality of output. Detailed attention will not be given to the data with respect to hand ironers, because of the similarity of methodological elements to those with respect to folding; nor to data concerning the stamping-machine operators, because of the lesser degree of experimental control that was exercised. Furthermore, the collateral observations and conclusions mentioned above will be regarded as irrelevant and receive no further attention.

CONDITIONS OF THE EXPERIMENT IN HANDKERCHIEF FOLDING

In setting up an experimental situation, the primary requirements were to hold all factors constant except one, and to measure the changes in output which followed a defined change in the single variable. This defined change was the introduction, at the end of three weeks, of a stated ten-minute rest period at a given time in each shift. Thus two questions arise: Were all of the additional variables actually held constant? Were units so chosen and defined as to make measurements possible and accurate?

Some possible variables may be noted, together with comments upon the evidence concerning them: (1) The gross periods and duration of the working shift. By explicit statement these were constant. (2) The equipment and the relations of workers thereto, such as the work tables and the individual assignments of working space. By inference, no change occurred. (3) The process of folding. Mr. Wyatt states:[2] "The same kind of fold was maintained throughout the experiment." (4) The process of exchanging folded for unfolded handkerchiefs with the forewoman. This involved the distance which the folder must go from her working position, and the necessary time required for making the exchange. By inference both were constant, while by explicit statement the exchange occurred at the completion of each twenty-five dozen. (5) Size of handkerchiefs. A priori, this is important, for the spatial magnitudes of hand movements, affecting in turn the time required to complete an operation, would be a function, in part, of the size. My. Wyatt states that uni-

---

[2] In a letter to the analyst. The point was not made conclusive in the published report.

formity existed here throughout the experiment.[3] (6) Quality of hand-kerchiefs. Again, a priori, this seems important, since the weight and other aspects of quality may affect the muscular expenditure required for creas-ing the material. Once more, uniformity existed.[4] (7) Condition of hand-kerchiefs. This is admittedly an uncontrolled variable, for account is taken of time lost by the necessity of "special treatment," consisting of "stretching and smoothing some of the handkerchiefs before folding." This is "due to defective calendering." There appears to be no reason to assume, on the other hand, that a general improvement or alteration in this preceding process took place in the second three-week period. Mr. Wyatt says: "An average equality in the condition of the handker-chiefs may be assumed in the two experimental periods."[5] (8) Change in the season. This was of course inevitable. By inference, the experiment was made in the spring of the year, presumably in the months of March and April. The question is, Was seasonal change associated with altera-tions in the duration of daylight within the working shift; or with alter-ations of mean daily temperature, humidity, or other atmospheric condi-tions? If so, were any of these alterations associated in turn with factors related to working output? Mr. Wyatt's statement here is convincing: "Work was carried out under daylight conditions and there were no significant variations in the atmospheric conditions. Wet and dry bulb temperature readings were taken at hourly intervals throughout the day."[6] (9) Fortuitous changes in the weather, not functions of the advancing sea-son. That is, for example, did bright or humid weather predominate in either of the three-week periods, as compared with the other? Mr. Wyatt's statement with respect to the preceding possibility of variation seems equally determinative here. (10) The workers' ages and experience. The change in the former was obviously negligible. Since all workers were "experienced" at the outset, any change here may also be regarded as negligible. (11) Subjective interest by workers in the results of the ex-periment. Little evidence is provided in the report concerning the atten-tion given by the workers to the observers, or their interpretation of the observers' objectives. The distorting effects of such an interest are appar-ent if, combined with an understanding of the experiment and its implica-tions, one postulates a desire among the workers to procure the permanent introduction of the rest period. Such a desire might result from hope of reward, personal convenience, or other reasons. In any case, it might lead

[3] Ibid.

[4] Mr. Wyatt says in his letter: "The handkerchiefs folded represented a standard line and the same quality was maintained throughout."

[5] From his letter.   [6] Ibid.

to conscious or unconscious "speeding up" during the second three weeks. Since the piecework system of payment prevailed, no penalization would be involved. Or, as another possibility, friendliness toward the investigators might be a biasing factor. To negative such possibilities, it must be assumed (though quite unproved) that the piecework system of payment had already induced the maximum output that was to be expected in view of all of the surrounding circumstances.[7] (12) Time required for the introduction of a rest period to make its effects felt. The investigators contend that the full effects will not be reached for a considerable length of time. If this be the case, the question arises whether a negative factor, *retardation of adjustment to the new conditions,* is not to be regarded as an uncontrolled variable in the experiment. If so, it would lead to understatement of the real comparisons. Theoretically, at least, this might be controlled by allowing a period of time to intervene between the two three-week periods compared. In addition to the practical difficulties that may have existed, this expedient would increase the possible errors due to other uncontrolled variables that have been mentioned. In modified form the expedient has been utilized as a check, however, in that measurements were again taken at a period three months after the initiation of the experiment. The authors' contentions in the matter result in part from these subsequent measurements and in part from a priori explanations of the manner in which the rest period affected the workers.[8]

The foregoing enumeration of possible variables, and of the extent to which they were controlled and uncontrolled, will illustrate the great variety of factors which must be taken into account in such an inquiry as this. Much dependence must be placed upon *chance* in relation to the several individual workers. For example, periodic physical functions and variations in health may have affected the productivity of individuals

---

[7] Mr. Wyatt comments in his letter upon this possibility of variation as follows: "Constant motivation is notoriously difficult to control but every possible precaution was taken to minimise variations in this respect. Whenever operatives are paid on a piece-rate basis, the introduction of a rest-pause tends to create the belief that earnings will be proportionately reduced, and the operatives may attempt to overcome this possibility by increasing their rate of working, quite apart from the beneficial effects of the pause. When, however, they realise that earnings are maintained or even increased by the pause, the normal attitude is restored.

"A more satisfactory method of procedure would be: (i) the payment of a time-rate for the time spent in rests; (ii) to experiment with operatives who are paid according to time worked."

[8] Mr. Wyatt, in his letter, says: "Whenever possible, it is advisable to allow a period of some weeks to elapse between the introduction of the pause and the recording of observations of its effects, providing that other variables remain approximately constant."

more favorably in one period than in the other; but it may be assumed, barring evidence to the contrary, that these variations were distributed by chance, and hence that they tended to neutralize each other in the case of eight workers in an aggregate period of six weeks. Moreover, the possible range of error due to certain uncontrolled variables may be determined. This was done in the case of (4) by noting the actual time consumed in making the exchange of materials in certain test intervals. Furthermore, when the work is under continuous and immediate observation, any important variable which had escaped attention in devising the experiment would be likely to disclose itself to careful investigators. Acceptance of their results, therefore, involves reliance to some degree upon the skill and acumen of the investigators as observers.

SELECTION OF UNITS AND QUANTITATIVE COMPARISONS

The average time in seconds to fold twelve handkerchiefs during each quarter-hour was made the unit of comparison. For all workers combined this was 141.1 on the average for the "continuous period" (the first three weeks). The corresponding figure for the "rest-pause period" (second three weeks) is 134.2. This represents an average increase in working rate of about 5.0 per cent, the variation being from 2.7 to 6.5 per cent in the case of individual workers. The improvement appears throughout all parts of the working shift and is not confined, as might be assumed, to the hours following the rest pause.

The measurement of variability in the working rate required another unit. This was obtained by noting the time in seconds required to complete each successive dozen handkerchiefs. It was apparent that variability was much less after the introduction of the rest pause; moreover, that variations were less when the rate of work was in general at its maximum.

A separate calculation was required to determine the comparative total productivity per shift in the two periods, inasmuch as the introduction of the rest pause involved a corresponding reduction in the actual working time.

THE AUTHORS' EXPLANATION OF THE EFFECTS OF A REST
PERIOD UPON PRODUCTION

This is threefold, in part psychological and in part physiological. (1) The fear or expectation that the introduction of the rest period would decrease total earnings is thought to have been an incentive to greater activity. This explanation is supported by the fact that the increased rate of production occurred before as well as after the rest period, and is supported further by statements made by the operators in response to questions. This incentive is said to have decreased as the operators realized that they would be able to equal their former output in spite of time lost. To the authors it seems apparent, then, that the increased output was due in some degree to conscious effort on the part of the operatives. (2) The rest created a more buoyant attitude toward the work, which enabled the task to be performed with greater interest and ease. This explanation is supported by the girls' testimony. This is a psychological explanation, but does not refer necessarily to a conscious factor in the workers' minds. (3) Physiological recuperation was regarded as a partial explanation. It is supported by the fact that the increase in the rate of working was greater after the rest periods than prior thereto.

In part these explanations are factual, drawn by the investigators from their observations, and from direct testimony by the workers. In part they are logical inferences from their own quantitative measurements (as in the third explanation) and from the findings of other inquirers.

METHODOLOGY INVOLVED IN THE COMPARISON WITH OTHER SIMILAR STUDIES

In all three units of the inquiry (folding, ironing, and stamping press) "the introduction of the rest-pause causes in each case a distinct increase in the rate of working." The results "are very consistent and are strikingly confirmatory of those already obtained by previous investigators." Several American and English inquiries are cited in support of this statement. Moreover, the total output is said to be increased in most cases: "Of 89 American employers reported to have tried regular rest periods, in only one instance was it stated that they had led to a decrease in total output." The English inquiries cited tend further to support this second conclusion.

It will be seen that the authors regard the three parts of the present experiment as units in a series of evidences tending to show that the introduction of a rest pause in repetitive work increases the rate of output and the total product. These conclusions are drawn with much assurance. We will next examine the logical implications involved in reaching them from the particular evidences. First of all, it must be considered whether the units employed in the several inquiries are sufficiently similar to have comparability.

The inquiries summarized, from which the generalizations obtain support, appear to relate for the most part to work in which heavy muscular exertion is not involved. That is, the work is light but repetitive, or substantially continuous in the amount of muscular and nervous expenditure. This is at least the case in the three occupations involved in the present experiments. It may be assumed that such work is *monotonous,* and that the influence of the rest period is directed in some manner to the counteraction of the physiological and psychological effects of monotony. It may be assumed, on the other hand, that monotony of the *same kind,* producing similar physiological and psychological effects, is absent in much non-repetitive work.[9] It may be, moreover, that in the latter an equivalent of a formal rest pause is to be found in a series of informal pauses of indeterminate duration between moments of severe exertion.

It is a generally accepted principle of logic that generalizations can be made only within a given universe of discourse. In the present instance the universe of discourse clearly relates to repetitive occupations. Hence, any evidence pertaining to other than repetitive occupations would be of no value in this summary which the authors present.[10] It is not clear whether or not such irrelevant evidence is included among the reports to which they refer.

To state the matter in somewhat different form, if a number of inquiries within differing occupations are to be regarded as comparable, there must be reason to assume that the effects of a rest period are translated into working rates and total product through the same or similar intermediate factors. For example, a formal rest period of ten minutes introduced into the work of a dock-laborer might have *immediate results* very dissimilar from those which were observed in the case of handkerchief folders. Hence the "effects" of the pause upon output (a later stage in the causal sequence in each instance) could not be compared for purposes of generalization. In the case of handkerchief folders, the authors

[9] Mr. Wyatt disagrees with these assumptions. He writes: "I doubt if it is justifiable to assume that light repetitive work is monotonous, while non-repetitive work is not monotonous. Monotony is largely determined by subjective factors, and although it is more likely to arise in connection with repetitive work, it is not necessarily absent even in the most varied occupations. This view is based upon unpublished results which have been collected during the last four years."

[10] Since this analysis was written, P. Sargant Florence has made the identical point in *The Statistical Method in Economics and Political Science* (New York: Harcourt, Brace & Co., 1929), pp. 166–67: "In obtaining indices of work capacity the operations where the output was actually observed were all of a repetitive nature, otherwise no units of output would have been obtainable. But it would be a mistake to conclude that the curve or other variations observed in the output of measurable repetitive operations were representative of the curve or other variations of less measurable operations; and no amount of weighting the different types of repetitive operations can overcome this difficulty."

have concluded that the rest period is effective for increased production because of three physiological and psychological factors which are intermediate in the causal sequence between the experimental variable and the measured result. It may therefore be asked whether the same intermediate factors appear in the other experimental units.

One of these three factors was an increased buoyancy of attitude toward the work, which was consequently performed with greater interest and ease. This factor, or resultant of the introduction of the experimental variable, emerged from a given working situation, one of the characteristics of which was the comparative absence of involuntary stoppages. In the case of the machine-press operatives, on the other hand, stoppages because of factors beyond the control of the workers averaged some 88.2 minutes in a day of 9 hours, exclusive of rest periods. In both cases the piece-rate system of payment prevailed. Hence, according to the authors, the response of buoyancy among the handkerchief workers was replaced by an absence of enthusiasm among machine-press operatives. One may even suspect that the response of the latter was at times one of positive annoyance.

A similar differential might be expected with respect to another of the authors' three "explanations" (or intermediate causal factors), namely, physiological recuperation. It is evident that occupations will vary in the extent to which they are "repetitive," and hence monotonous, in character; also, that they will vary in the proportion of the working time covered by involuntary stoppages or informal pauses. Perhaps even more important, they will vary in the amount of muscular or nervous expenditure required by the tasks performed. Hence they will vary in the extent to which an increment of physiological recuperation is acquired in a formal rest pause.

The third of the authors' "explanations," namely, the spur to greater activity because of the fear of loss of earnings, was, according to their evidence, a transient factor in the case of folders, which disappeared with accommodation by the workers to the new element in working conditions.

It will be clear, therefore, that in comparing the effects upon productivity of the introduction of rest pauses in separate repetitive occupations, the authors are not comparing simple effects. They are comparing, rather, the derived composite resultants of a variety of intermediate factors of variable and sometimes contradictory character. The preponderance of the evidence that output increases with the introduction of a rest pause indicates, therefore, a preponderance of intermediate effects favorable to the end result, for these intermediate factors may be expected to combine to some degree according to chance. The logical foundation for the generalizations reached is therefore of the same nature as that which underlies criteria of statistical reliability and significance. Each additional piece of evidence is not additive in the support which it gives to the generalization. It strengthens the latter, rather, at a geometrical rate corresponding to the rate by which the enlargement of a sample increases the probability that it represents its universe.

METHODOLOGICAL IMPORTANCE OF THE INQUIRY

It is sometimes questioned whether experimentation within social science carries the same meaning and implications as experimentation within "natural" science. In the study here examined, a positive answer may be given. A given set of working conditions is made up of a large number of potential variables. In such a set of conditions, certain workers were carrying on certain tasks with certain measured end results in output. By introducing a single determinate change in the working conditions, all other potential variables being so far as possible held constant, determinate differences in the end results were observed. By universal scientific custom, the change in conditions may be regarded as having "produced" the change in end results.

It may be objected that in spite of all precautions certain variables were uncontrolled. This is probably true, as has been pointed out above. The experiment assumed that but for the introduction of the rest period, the same output would have appeared in the second three weeks as in the first. It is sure that this would not have been the case *precisely* because of these uncontrolled factors.

Nevertheless, the assumption made is less subject to error than any other. Uncontrolled variables cannot be wholly eliminated from experiments in the natural sciences, and in consequence a margin of error must always be taken into account. No quantitative determination of the magnitude of this error has been made by the authors, and the effort would no doubt prove difficult if not insuperable. Common-sense judgment appears to replace quantitative expression in support of the probability that the possible error would not equal or exceed the numerical differences attributed to the experimental variable. Yet there is no difference in principle between this experiment and one in physics or chemistry.

The first importance of the study from the standpoint of method, then, is perhaps to be found in its successful employment of experimentation in a natural-science sense. This cannot be stated dogmatically, for "importance" is a matter of valuation. In the present analysis the study has also served to illustrate some problems entering into the process of employing comparative results to support conclusions drawn from a particular experiment. The study also has value in reference to the immediate economic and humanistic ends which led to the establishment of the Industrial Fatigue Research Board. But since scientific method is non-teleological, consideration of these ends is here excluded. Because of concentration of attention upon the more prominent experimental aspects, a number of subsidiary aspects of the inquiry have been more or less neglected.[11]

[11] This analysis was first prepared in the winter of 1928–29, at the suggestion of Dr. Walter V. Bingham, of the Personnel Research Federation. It was revised in 1929 in such a manner as to give the central emphasis to the problem of experimentation in social science.

ANALYSIS 49

EXPERIMENTAL DETERMINATION BY FLOYD H. ALLPORT OF GROUP INFLUENCES UPON MENTAL ACTIVITY[1]

By L. L. THURSTONE

University of Chicago

Allport's problem was to reduce to a measurable experimental setting the influence of the group on various types of mental activity. For this purpose he arranged his subjects in two groups: those who worked alone, and those who worked together. The groups consisted of three to five subjects. The same subjects participated in the experiments under both conditions, "alone" and "together"; and the two conditions were alternated in such a way that practice effect, fatigue, or boredom so far as possible influenced the results equally in the two conditions. The subjects were asked to avoid rivalry or competition, but Allport does not believe that the effect of rivalry was entirely eliminated.

In one of the experiments the subjects wrote free chain associations starting from the same stimulus word. The groups consisted of three subjects, and there were weekly alterations of the two conditions "alone" and "together." The experiment was conducted for one hour each week. Total time required for one hundred word associations constituted the measure of speed of work. The results indicate a higher speed of free association when working together than when working alone. The subjects did not communicate during the experiment. They merely sat at the same table and they knew that the other members of the group were doing the same task.

Further experiments were conducted with the time-limit method, in which the speed of work was measured by the number of free associations written in constant time. The two conditions, "together" and "alone," were again alternated. The rooms of the subjects when working alone were interchanged from day to day in order to obviate the effect of the peculiarities of any one room upon the work of the subject. The initial records, which were lower than any following record, were omitted from the data in order to rule out practice effect. In these experiments fourteen out of the fifteen subjects produced more associations when working in the group than they produced while working alone.

[1] "The Influence of the Group upon Association and Thought," *Journal of Experimental Psychology,* III (June, 1920), 159–82.

694

The mean variation of the records for the fifteen subjects is higher relative to its mean for the group condition. The conclusion seems to point to increased variability of performance accompanying the social influence.

Allport analyses the data further with the following conclusions. The superiority of the group condition in speed of associations exists throughout the test, but it is greatest in the first minute and least in the last minue of the three-minute test. Further analysis of the data reveals that 80 per cent of all the subjects wrote more personal associations when alone than when together. Words suggested by the immediate surroundings appear to be more numerous in the group than in the solitary condition. Words suggested mainly by the stimulus word are more numerous in the solitary than in the group condition.

The excess of performance in the group condition shows a high correlation with subjectively estimated consciousness of rivalry. This indicates that rivalry is at least partly responsible for the difference in performance for the two conditions.

A variation of the foregoing experiment consisted in having part of the group write associations to the word "summer," while the rest of the group gave associations to the word "winter." The speed of writing the associations under these conditions was compared with the speed when all the subjects were writing words bearing upon the *same* topic. Although a slight advantage was seen in the situation where all wrote on the same subject, there were too few trials to establish definite conclusions.

In still another experiment the nature of the task was altered so as to involve more complex and abstract reasoning. It is generally believed that mental work of a more complex nature is better performed in solitude than in a group. The experiment was planned as a test of at least one aspect of this general belief. Short passages were selected from the works of Epictetus and Aurelius, which admitted of considerable argument for and against. The task of the subjects was to write down the arguments which they could think of, as many and as strong as possible, to disprove the point made in the passage given. At the beginning of the group test it was emphasized that all of the subjects were writing replies to the same statement. The replies were scored subjectively with a range from 1 to 3. It is assumed that those who scored the papers did not know under which of the two experimental conditions the papers were written. The replies were also scored as to the number of ideas involved. This is of course a rather unreliable method of scoring, but the nature of the task hardly allows a simple scoring method.

Eight of the nine subjects had higher idea scores in the group condition. This score consisted merely in counting ideas. On the other hand, six out of seven subjects had a higher proportion of ideas designated as superior or exceptionally effective in the solitary condition than in the group condition. The experiment thus points toward discursive reasoning for the group condition and toward the possibility of superior intellectual value or relevance for the ideas produced in the solitary condition.

The principal contribution that Allport has made with these experiments is to point the way toward the experimental study of the influence of the group on mental activity. If the same general plan of experimentation is carried out on larger groups, it should be possible to establish more conclusively the social psychological laws that are indicated in these experiments.[2]

[2] [This analysis was written in April, 1928. At the request of the analyst it was reviewed by Professor Allport, the analyst's final revision being dated in February, 1929.—EDITOR.]

HAROLD F. GOSNELL'S EXPERIMENTS IN THE STIMULATION OF VOTING[1]

By GEORGE E. G. CATLIN
Cornell University

THE PROBLEM AND ITS SIGNIFICANCE

Gosnell's study *Getting Out the Vote* is a continuation of the investigation into the causes of non-voting begun in Chicago by Merriam and Gosnell in connection with the mayoral election of 1923. It is based upon observations of the voting behavior of 6,000 persons in Chicago during the presidential election of November 4, 1924 and the aldermanic election of February 3, 1925, and of their action in registering as electors prior to these elections. Twelve selected districts, of which eight were voting precincts, were canvassed as completely as practicable. The districts were chosen from parts of Chicago differing in the wealth and the national origins of the inhabitants. The residents of each district were divided into two approximately equal groups, one for experimentation and one for control. The experimental groups were stimulated to register by a nonpartisan mail canvass for the election of president, United States senator, and governor on the two assigned registration days. The canvass took the form of a notice in English and, in some cases, in Polish, Czech, and Italian before the first registration day; and an informative notice, as before, together with a cartoon notice in English, before the final day of registration. Specimen ballots were sent out to the experimental groups before the presidential election; and a cartoon notice urging voting, with instructions in English for voters, was sent to them before the aldermanic election.

Certain questions of general interest in the working of democracy and of technical interest in connection with the machinery of elections were present in the minds of those engaged on the study. E.g., Are agencies of information, exhortation, and propaganda effective in getting out the

[1] H. F. Gosnell, *Getting Out the Vote: An Experiment in the Stimulation of Voting* (Chicago: University of Chicago Press, 1927). Cf. also C. E. Merriam and H. F. Gosnell, *Non-Voting: Causes and Methods of Control* (Chicago: University of Chicago Press, 1924); Ben A. Arneson, "Non-Voting in a Typical Ohio Community," *American Political Science Review*, XIX (November, 1925), 816–25. Page references in the text are to *Getting Out the Vote*, except as noted.

eligible voter? Is a non-partisan mail canvass a measurably effective stimulus for this purpose? What is the quality of the vote thus got out? Is the apathy of the non-voter "one of the greatest menaces to an intelligently governed democracy," or does "the fact that a man does not care enough about politics to vote indicate that he is probably not equipped to choose wisely among the issues and candidates?" An inquiry into the value of the non-voter as a citizen was obviously outside the scope of the investigation.

The object of the study was to give a specific answer to the question whether the non-voter is such by a deliberate act of will (i.e., whether he may be intelligent but lacking in public spirit) or whether he is a non-voter from ignorance. Thus the supply of information will alter the latter condition but not the former. The study was also designed to show the relation between certain specific conditions and voting or non-voting. The non-partisan appeal was presumed to disarm suspicion.

The important earlier study, *Non-Voting*, by Merriam and Gosnell, was more purely descriptive and informative. Information was obtained variously: The opinions of expert politicians were collected. Direct inquiry was made of 6,000 non-voters, classified according to age, sex, color, country of birth, nationality, economic status, occupation, length of residence at address and in state, and voting experience. This inquiry immediately followed the mayoralty election in Chicago of 1923, and the persons interviewed were intended to be a fair sample of the 700,000 non-voters in this election. The details thus gathered were checked against data from the books of the Election Commissioners concerning 5,000 registered voters in the same areas of the city, and by studies of particular precincts and groups. Two problems were considered: first, psychological and practical causes of non-voting; second, administrative remedies. As touching the first (and indicating remedial possibilities as well), an endeavor was made to discover the relative importance of such causes as "disgust with politics," "disbelief in women's voting," "fear of loss of business," and "poor location of polling booth."

Non-Voting is in the nature of a general report upon the basis of which practical action by well-disposed politicians would be possible, e.g., by amending the acts which require declaration of voter's age on each registration, repeated registration, etc. (chap. ix). The situation portrayed is on the whole typical, although limited in some respects to the special case in question. Gosnell's *Getting Out the Vote* is of greater scientific interest. However, its meaning is illuminated by the earlier portrayal of factors operating positively and negatively upon voting.

Arneson's study (*op. cit.*, n. 1) differs from that of Merriam and Gosnell in four essential respects: (1) All individuals within the universe of attention were included, so far as possible. (2) Both voters and non-voters were interviewed. Hence, the population of voters provided a control group with which to compare the population of non-voters. (3) The information sought from persons interviewed was primarily objective rather than subjective in character; i.e., an effort was made to relate non-voting to a variety of social "factors" rather than to a variety of "reasons" advanced by the non-voters themselves. (4) The non-voter's situation was studied under conditions other than those which may happen to be local to Chicago.

THE DATA

The following information concerning the 6,000 persons tabulated is provided in *Getting Out the Vote:* their district, with its general economic and nationality significance; whether they belonged to the experimental or the control group; whether they registered after the first or the second notice for the presidential election or after the notice for the aldermanic election; and whether they voted at either election. Furthermore, the following data were provided: nationality; sex; whether native-born or naturalized; voting experience; length of residence in the district; economic status; literacy; conditions of schooling; response to a test of general knowledge of government; and political party affiliation. The foregoing data were not obtained in all cases, but they were procured, when at all, for both the experimental and the control groups.

THE OBJECTIVITY OF THE DATA

Literacy was given objective connotation by tests as, for example, the reading of English. Economic status was determined by the monthly rental of house or apartment. Rentals were divided into three classes. Whereas the mail notices were sent to all persons canvassed, replies to such questions as economic status and the nature of party affiliation depended upon the responsiveness of the person interviewed. Hence, experience in the experimental group can only be compared with that in the control group on the probable assumption that reluctance to give information would be a factor equally operative in both cases.

The word "ignorant," moreover, used in the above fashion, may lend itself to misunderstanding. It may include those who fail to respond to a literacy test or to a test of their knowledge of government, and also some of the wealthy, who remain uncanvassed by party agents. Both were "ignorant" of necessary information so far as registration and voting were concerned (p. 51 n.). In Arneson's study, the objective nature of the information sought may have had the effect of ruling out automatically factors of high psychological importance. For example, it may be that varying attitudes of conservatism or radicalism are closely associated with voting and non-voting; but since attitudes are subjective and difficult to ascertain, this relationship would not be disclosed by the data selected for study by the author. It does not seem probable, however, that it would be difficult to devise a technique for recording objective manifestations which could reasonably be associated with these attitudes and which would give precision to the meaning which the investigator was attaching to the terms.

RESULTS

Stimulation by a non-partisan canvass was found in one instance only (aldermanic election, p. 70) to be negative in effect compared with the control group. The possibility of measuring the effects of this stimulation was proved. The need of the voter for the information supplied and the inadequacy of his present information were to this extent demonstrated.

In the aldermanic election the response to stimulation was most marked among the wealthiest (p. 91) and among the Italian and the Polish groups. The response in the presidential registration was marked among such overlapping groups as the wealthiest, the Negroes, the illiterates, those schooled abroad (short schooling period) (pp. 95–100), those naturalized by marriage, habitual non-voters, and women. Registration within the control groups, however, showed the interest of the wealthy to be high for the presidential election; while the interest of certain national groups was high for the aldermanic election. In the latter, the well-to-do districts, the native white districts, and the university districts yielded a low voting response.

Stimulation by cartoon was relatively successful with women; but stimulation of habitual non-voters among the women by a sixty-page copy of the election number of the *Illinois League of Women Voters' Bulletin* was neutral (p. 34). The increase in the vote in presidential elections as compared with mayoral elections was proportionately higher among women than among men (Gosnell, p. 43; Merriam and Gosnell, p. 251). The common supposition that women are likely to be interested merely in the politics of their own street and neighborhood was not borne out. Imagery rather than calculations of advantage may be the basis of an effective appeal. However, stimulation was proportionately more effective in the aldermanic election than in the presidential election.

TECHNIQUE OF INVESTIGATION

The assumption that voting actually took place as recorded is based upon the evidence of the pollbooks. This was, however, checked by trained observers at the polls, and the risk of serious statistical error due to tampering with the votes was guarded against (pp. 21–22, 58). Control and experimental areas were carefully chosen in the selected areas so as to expose them to the same influences of nationality, sex distribution, economic conditions, and stimulus from party organizations. In some cases, however, influences seem to have operated unequally in the control and the experimental areas (pp. 19, 52–53, 57, 60, 67, 70). This does not, however, vitiate the experiment as touching other districts. In a few cases (Chart VII: "Negroes") the number of control and experimental groups were not equal. In the grouping by economic status, the "$100 and over" rental group is only a ninth of the "under $10" group in proportion to the size of these groups in the total population. Hence, less confidence can be felt in conclusions drawn from figures concerning the wealthy than from other data. There seem to be indications that the mail service operated unevenly during the aldermanic election (p. 72).

METHODS OF DEDUCING RESULTS

Certain conclusions are drawn which, although possessing a measure of probability, cannot be said to be established. The superior response of women to a cartoon appeal (pp. 32, 63, 65)—a matter of high importance were it established as a psychological and not a cultural fact— may be due not solely to the emotional psychology of the women voters but also to special conditions. A "hortatory appeal" with cartoon (pp. 38–39) was more successful with men than with women for the aldermanic election (p. 44; cf. p. 60). It is stated that three men vote to every two women (registered electors for aldermen). This may be due to lack of special education or to national custom.[2] The figures seem to be available for an inference concerning the latter possibility but are not given (pp. 66, 87). Merriam and Gosnell's study (p. 26) indicates that cultural conditions and practical difficulties may have more to do with indifference to voting on the part of women than any permanent factor of feminine psychology. Voting is more frequent among younger women, the native-born, and those of the higher economic status, i.e., among those less dependent on the more conservative cultural influences.

The non-partisan nature of the stimulus may be said to have induced

[2] [Cf. H. F. Gosnell, *Why Europe Votes* (Chicago: University of Chicago Press, 1930). This work has appeared since the preparation of the present analysis.— EDITOR.]

many habitual non-voters to vote who, by deliberate decision, would not have voted under partisan appeals; i.e., the nature of the stimulus may have reduced the non-voting of well-informed citizens (pp. 54–55, and *vide supra*, II, "The Object," [*b*]). Further, the emotional nature of the cartoon stimulus may be held to have been such as to bring about a change of mind and to have led the informed voter to register and vote. Hence, the test ceases to be the precise, scientific one of whether non-voting is due to ignorance (control group) or to apathy and extraneous causes (non-voting in educationally stimulated group). It becomes merely the practical test as to whether or not a non-partisan appeal is likely to have any positive effect.

The study has established that a non-partisan mail-canvass stimulus can induce registration and "get out the vote": (*a*) especially among the more ignorant or indifferent sections of the population, e.g., Negroes, Italians, illiterates, and women; (*b*) in elections about which there is indifference, and to the extent to which the customary poll falls short of the plenum,[3] e.g., in aldermanic elections, especially in the case of the wealthier and the native-white groups; (*c*) among those little affected, or avoided, by party canvassers, e.g., LaFollette voters, and residents in wealthy neighborhoods (pp. 48, 73, 75, 91). But it has not been established that the result is due to the non-partisan stimulus and not to the novelty of that stimulus (p. 102) administered in one presidential and one aldermanic election in 1924–25.

Theoretically, the experiment should be repeated and the results compared with those of the present study. Allowance should be made, especially, for the result of the cartoon (novelty stimulus). This is needed to give a satisfactory basis for a judgment upon how far the elector will fail to vote, though wanting to do so, from lack of necessary information, or from apathy or preoccupation with other interests. The twelve selected areas permit a mutual check to be established in terms of the local conditions during these particular elections. But the experiment must be repeated in order to establish a check in terms of temporal changes (pp. 28, 63) and to allow for a possible variation in response as men became accustomed to this stimulus.

SIGNIFICANCE OF THE STUDY FROM THE STANDPOINT OF METHOD

The study has resulted in many highly interesting observations, such as the voting interests of particular national groups, e.g., Czechs (pp.

[3] [The term "plenum," which is somewhat unfamiliar in American political discussion, is defined by Professor Catlin in a letter as "the full vote of qualified electors."—EDITOR.]

63, 81); the low voting interest of native-white and of English and Scandinavian groups; the interests of various groups in national affairs as contrasted with their interests in municipal affairs. These are, however, only by-products of the investigation to the extent that this is an endeavor to give a scientific answer to certain questions. These results might have been reached by other methods of investigation designed *ad hoc.*

A *scientific experiment* is defined by Wundt[4] as involving exact observation and such control as admits of the isolation and the variation of conditioning factors. Professor J. Arthur Thomson[5] points out the importance of measurement in connection with exact observations and indicates that the significance of experiment, as distinct from mere observation, lies in its facilitation of verification and in its readier means of isolating causes. Professor Garner[6] shows how politics permits of *experimenta fructifera,* i.e., general improvements by experimental legislation. The problem is whether *experimenta lucifera* are possible, upon which scientific generalizations may be based.

The present study conforms to the scientific requirements of exact observation, statistical measurement, and isolation and variation of the conditioning factors (p. 12), save possibly the time factor. Sex, nationality, etc., being known, a stimulus was applied to persons of X sex and A nationality. The stimulus was not applied to others of the same sex, nationality, etc., in a control group. The same stimulus was applied to persons of Y sex and A nationality, and to persons of X sex and B nationality in other experimental groups, but not to persons in corresponding control groups. The results of these various units of the general experiment were compared. Apart from various by-products of the investigation, the net return is perhaps more generally enlightening than specifically decisive.

The method is entitled on the whole to be termed scientific in a precise sense. If repeated, the experiment might demonstrate that a nonpartisan mail-canvass stimulus increases the registration and the vote—perhaps in inverse ratio to the nearness to a plenum vote; and that it brings out the "ignorant" voter (illiterate, Negro, short-schooling voter) (pp. 96–98, 109), and short-residence voter (p. 88). It might also show

[4] W. Wundt, *Logik der exacten Wissenchaften* (Stuttgart: Ferdinand Enke, 1907), p. 357.

[5] J. Arthur Thomson, *Introduction to Science* (New York: H. Holt & Co., 1911), pp. 64, 69–71.

[6] J. W. Garner, *Political Science and Government* (New York: American Book Co.. 1928), p. 19.

the proportion of "ignorant" to deliberate non-voters. The stimulus used would not of itself show whether the non-voter, despite information, was such from fear, indolence, philosophic skepticism, lack of organization, or other cause; i.e., whether he was of the "intelligent" or of the merely cowardly or preoccupied members of a democracy (p. 64). Professor Gosnell's study only incidentally throws light on this.

Although it may lose some of the qualitative character which may appear to make other studies more fruitful and worth while, an exact study of the vote as an expression of support is of the highest significance for political science. As a unit of "will" or "opinion," the vote provides one of the few cases where "the political act" lends itself to exact measurements and statistical treatment. And, as J. Clerk Maxwell has said, for the scientist at least, "aspirations after accuracy in measurement" are to be coupled with "justice in action" as among "the noblest attributes in man."

The same use of control groups and experimental groups, in districts of such varying conditions that factors are isolable, may yield strictly scientific results in other fields of politics, involving such behavior as the vote or the quantitative expression of opinion. In the present study, the light stimulus of voluntarily provided and received information was applied. A stronger stimulus is that of industrial regulation or of coercive law. Where similar types of industrial regulation or of social legislation are adopted in different factories or communities, or diverse types of regulation are adopted in like communities, the requisite conditions of scientific experimentation are at hand. In such a case it should be possible to find measurable expressions of support, as in voting; or measurable factors making for support and favorably advertising a policy; or measurable infractions of the regulations, indicating non-support. Such a study should yield an estimate of the effect of a given type of stimulus in terms of different social conditions; and an estimate of the suitability to a given combination of social conditions of different types of regulations. This approach seems to be a fruitful one for further thought.

It may be concluded that experiment in the fields of politics and sociology is possible. The term "experiment" is here used in its strict scientific sense, as a process from which confident deductions can be drawn about measurable changes and uniformities. This conclusion has been so frequently denied that it is worth while reinforcing. We must not permit our minds to be confused by the rarity and the difficulties of such experiments or by the modest results at present to be expected from them while our technique is undeveloped. The greatest results of science have frequently sprung from the final demonstration of small points. The crux of the matter lies in exact observation, preferably quantitative such as we have in these vote studies; and in changes so designed as to test hypotheses, with unobserved alteration by other concurrent factors excluded. It will be noted that the isolation of the experimental field required for scientific purposes need not be absolute, but need only be adequate, as in financial theory, to convince us that changes ascribed to variation in one factor are not indeed due to the undetected variation of another. "Laboratory conditions" are relative. Nor need the observing scientist be the person who introduces the crucial change.[7] What distinguishes the experimental from the observational sciences is the power of some agency to act upon the subject in such a fashion as to test hypotheses by change and control.[8] The means of obtaining such scientific results in the social field are well indicated by the careful precautions taken and by the methods of random sampling and of control groups adopted in the present investigation by Gosnell. It has the high merit of being, precisely, a scientific social experiment.

The hypothesis "those who do not vote refrain from doing so by deliberate choice" has been shown by Gosnell's method to be false for ascertained percentages (under various conditions) of non-voters; but possibly true for the remainder. A further experiment with a purely informative notice and (for the experimental group) with a hortatory notice or cartoon, plus information, might test the hypothesis that "the non-voter is (in a percentage of cases) not such from lack of information but only from lack of adequate incentive," and might discover whether this hypothesis were true for any percentage under repeated experiments and varying conditions. Already Gosnell has indicated that this is true for that large percentage of non-voters in the stimulated group *not* induced to vote, despite his notices. We might conceivably end by testing the proposition, "non-voting is a normal condition, due to the rivalry of groups (civil, industrial, domestic) marketing rival advantages, in their claims upon the individual." A domestic or an industrial advantage may be so important that we cannot afford, for the sake of what a party has

---

[7] Claude Bernard, *Introduction to the Study of Experimental Medicine,* trans. Greene and Henderson (New York: Macmillan Co., 1927), p. 13: "Two things must, therefore, be considered in the experimental method: (1) The art of getting accurate facts by means of rigorous investigation; (2) the art of working them up by means of experimental reasoning, so as to deduce knowledge of the law of phenomena. We saw that experimental reasoning always and necessarily deals with two facts at a time: Observations, used as starting point; experiment, used as conclusion or control. . . . . "

[8] *Ibid.,* p. 9.

to offer, to risk a declaration of political support which might jeopardize this advantage. It may be that further research will point to the conclusion that non-voting can only be checked in proportion to the extent to which the advantages derived from civil government, national or municipal, are brought vividly to consciousness as worth expenditure of energy in gaining them, even to the point of risking other "goods." A recognition may be necessary that absence of willingness to display public spirit means in the end loss of solid advantages in the shape of the "goods" of civil order.[9]

[9] [This analysis was first completed in September, 1928. After several interchanges of correspondence between the analyst and Professor Gosnell, with respect to some of the points involved, it was given final revision by the former in March, 1929.—EDITOR.]

ANALYSIS 51

THE QUANTITATIVE MEASUREMENT OF HIGHER MENTAL PROCESSES IN THE PIONEER STUDIES OF H. EBBINGHAUS

By J. E. COOVER

Stanford University

Ebbinghaus is regarded as the pioneer in "the application of precise scientific method to the study of the 'higher mental processes.'" In this signal achievement he transcends the measurement of correlated physical stimuli or physiological process and attends to the psychical process itself. In his Preface to *Über das Gedächtnis* (Leipzig, 1885) he says:

In the realm of mental phenomena experiment and measurement have hitherto been chiefly limited in their application to sense perception and to the time relations of mental processes. By means of the following investigations I have tried to go a step farther into the workings of the mind and to submit to an experimental and quantitative treatment the manifestations of memory.

Ebbinghaus then reviews what is familiarly known of memory, of its effects, and of the conditions upon which it depends. Mental states once in consciousness and later disappeared from it are not forever lost, even though we cannot discover them at the moment by introspection: (1) Some we can recall by an exertion of the will. (2) Some return spontaneously and involuntarily after years of absence, occasioned by immediately present images, in accordance with the "laws of association." (3) Vanished mental states give proof of their continued existence even when they do not return to consciousness at all; they subsist in the boundless domain of the effect of accumulated experience, the effect that facilitates the occurrence of similar processes. We also know something of the conditions upon which the vitality of inner survival and the fidelity and the promptness of reproduction depend. But the deficiencies in our knowledge of memory are very great. Everything we can say retains the indefinite, general, comparative character of popular aphorisms and anecdotal evidence. To express our ideas concerning the physical basis of reproduction and association we use different metaphors—stored-up ideas, graven images, well-beaten paths. The only thing certain about these figures is that they are not suitable. If we crave specific information on the inner structure of the dependencies of memory we find no answer.

"How does forgetfulness depend upon the lapse of time? What proportion does the increase in certainty of reproduction bear to the number of repetitions?"

To improve our knowledge we must make it quantitative by introducing measurement into our study of memory. That this has not been done is evidence of its difficulty. The method of obtaining exact measurements of the inner structure of causal relations has been so elaborately and successfully developed in the natural sciences that it is sometimes identified as *the* method of natural science. But "its logical nature makes it generally applicable to all spheres of existence and phenomena" and, indeed, necessary for defining accurately and for comprehending the course of any process whatever. The mass of conditions causally related with a certain result is kept constant; one of these conditions (x) is isolated and quantitatively varied; the accompanying change (y) on the side of the effect is measured. The result is $y = f(x)$.

In order to find a measurement of the mental processes of memory, Ebbinghaus inspects the *conditions* of retention and reproduction upon which the vitality of that inner survival as well as the fidelity and the promptness of reproduction depends: (1) the individual person, (2) the content, (3) intensity of attention and interest, (4) number of repetitions, and (5) lapse of time. Of these, he finds two that permit a numerical determination, and a numerical variation: (4) the number of repetitions necessary to make a series of ideas reproducible, and (5) the time elapsed between impression and reproduction.

Of the *effects* (voluntary recall, spontaneous reproduction, subliminal facilitation of like processes), he found nothing measurable. Reproduction is possible and takes place, or it is impossible and it does not take place. It is taken for granted that with repetition the series comes closer and closer to reproduction, so that in its subliminal existence it possesses graded differences, masked from our direct apprehension.

Ebbinghaus discovered an indirect means of forcing these subliminal graded differences into the open. *The grade of latency of the series may be determined by the number of repetitions of the original stimulus required for a just possible reproduction of the latent series.* The difference between the number of repetitions required to learn a new like series and this number is the *measure of the inner energy in the latent series.* The temporal interval between impression and reproduction, and between successive reproductions, may be measured, and may be varied in measurable units.

The method of natural science is now available: phenomena on the side of the effects are clearly ascertainable; they vary in accordance with the varied conditions, and are capable of numerical determination. Two conditions must be fulfilled: (1) Certainty of determination of the repetition that is the just possible reproduction. This is readily recognized by absence of hesitation or error, and by a feeling of confidence. (2) The number of repetitions to bring a series of given length to reproduction must be a constant. The inevitable and ever fluctuating mental conditions must be brought sufficiently under control to reduce fluctuations to a value which permits the constancy presumed in causal relations to become evident. This is the first crux of the problem.

Trial by experiment had to be made. Under controlled conditions (to be noticed later) Ebbinghaus in 1879–80 had learned 92 tests, each consisting of 8 series of 13 syllables; and in 1883–84, 84 tests, each consisting of 6 series of 16 syllables. The means and probable errors of observation were 1,112 $\pm$ 76 sec. and 1,261 $\pm$ 48.4 sec., giving a relative variability ($2PE_{obs}/M$) of 13.6 and 7.7 per cent. Five other sets of smaller numbers gave 19.2, 14.2, 14.4, 9.6, and 12.2 per cent. These values are compared with some in the natural sciences: Helmholtz and Baxt, in determinations of speed of nervous transmission, attained 5 per cent; this was especially exact. Helmholtz' earlier determination gave 50 per cent. The first determinations of the mechanical equivalent of heat by Joule gave 23 per cent. Ebbinghaus, encouraged, decided that the deviations of the single results from their average are sufficiently small in ratio to their mean to permit the determination of significant differences between means.

Although the means are found to be sufficiently constant, are they *constants of natural science,* resulting from a single constant causal combination (like the determination of the position of a star, or the coefficient of expansion of a metal), or are they *statistical constants,* resulting from a multiplicity of causal combinations of very different sorts (like the count of the number of suicides in a month, or of pedestrians who pass a certain street corner in a day)? These two constants "are constant from different causes and with entirely different significance for the knowledge of causal relations" (p. 13).[1] This is the second crux of the problem.

Now, the fluctuations of determinations of the effects of a known single causal system, in natural science, are found to follow the law of errors in their graduated and symmetrical distribution about their mean. It is possible that fluctuations about a statistical constant might do so, but

[1] Page numbers refer to Hermann Ebbinghaus, *Memory: A Contribution to Experimental Psychology,* trans. Ruger and Bussenius (New York: Teachers College, Columbia University, 1913).

they have not yet been known to do so. Therefore, it is highly probable that if our fluctuations follow the law of errors, the constant about which they fluctuate is a constant of natural science and results from a single system of causal combinations which is as yet unknown to the psychologist.

Ebbinghaus tabulated the deviations, in the sets of data referred to above, within certain ranges from their mean and compared their frequency by count with the theoretical frequency calculated from the law of errors; and from a portion of the same data tabulated separately the deviations above and below their mean, in order to test for symmetry. The aggregate results follow:

PE_{obs}	¼	½	1	1.5	2	2.5	3
Law of errors	59.9	118.6	224.5	309.0	368.7	407.3	428.8
By count	56	124	231	301	368	408	430
Above M	14	37	67	86	106	115	121
Below M	15	32	69	88	109	121	128

With respect to both graduated amount and symmetry, "the grouping of the deviations comes as near as could be expected to the one demanded by theory."

These quantitative tests of the separate determinations (time or repetitions required to learn a series of nonsense syllables) assured Ebbinghaus of sufficient constancy of the causal conditions in the experimentation. They met his criterion that

the average values of several observations [be] approximately constant and at the same time we may assume that the separate cases belong to the same causal system, whose elements, however, are not limited to exclusively constant values, but may run through small cycles of numerical values symmetrical around a middle value [pp. 14–15].

Justification naturally rests with consistent experimental results in the succeeding investigations. To make experimental conditions as constant as possible, Ebbinghaus considered carefully one by one the conditions upon which retention and reproduction were known to depend, and met each one with characteristic ingenuity.

1. *The individual person.*—He himself was the subject; his own mental processes were the object of investigation.

2, 3. *The content, and the intensity of attention and interest.*—Constancy was provided for by inventing content material as meaningless and homogeneous as possible (nonsense syllables), and as little likely as possible to arouse variability in attention or interest. Periods of work were arranged with respect to the avoidance of fatigue and to the diurnal rhythm of attention.

4. *The number of repetitions.*—That repetitions should be equal, the rate of reciting was made constant at one hundred and fifty syllables per minute (provided by a clockwork metronome, or ticking of a watch), either three or four syllables were united in a rhythm, the first one of the group being accented by the voice. The separate series were always read through from beginning to end. There was free interchange between reading and attempts at reproduction, and any series partly recited was completed by reading, the reading beginning at the point the first hesitation in recitation occurred. Special associations of the mnemonic type between syllables were debarred, so that learning was carried on solely by the influence of the mere repetitions upon the natural memory. Upon the first unhesitating and confident reproduction, marking the completion of learning of a series, a pause of fifteen seconds was made to record the result, and the next series of the test was immediately begun. The result was recorded in time (convertible into repetitions through the factor of 0.4 sec. for each syllable) or in number of repetitions determined from a string of wooden beads held in the hands, one bead of which had been moved forward at the beginning of each repetition.

General conditions favorable for uniformity of mental process were adopted: intent to reach the goal as soon as possible, working with maximum concentration; care to keep away all outer disturbances, and to avoid the smaller distractions caused by carrying on the test in various surroundings; care to control the objective conditions of life during the period of the tests so as to eliminate too great changes or irregularities. When too great changes in the outer and inner life occurred, the tests were discontinued for a length of time. Their resumption was then preceded by some days of renewed training varying according to the length of the interruption.

The invention of the nonsense syllables was a stroke of genius.[2] All conventional material is highly variable in content and would have aroused highly complex and highly variable psychical processes. Out of 19 single consonants and 11 vowels and diphthongs 2,300 syllables of two consonants with an intervening vowel sound were formed. The series of syllables were made up by chance, except that some care was given to avoid a too immediate succession of similar sounds. Syllables

---

[2] [Cf. the subsequent use of this device by Ach as described by Professor Fearing in analysis 52, esp. n. 21 and accompanying text, *passim.*—EDITOR.]

used were each time laid aside until all had been used and then the whole number was again mixed together for the forming of new series.

In order to illustrate the type of problem, the method, and the nature of the results, two researches are selected, the first one widely quoted, the second not so well known. In both, the "savings method" was used. The score of a test was the saving in amount of work required to bring the latent series to reproduction over the amount of work required for learning a new series, finally expressed in per cent of the latter. It measured the energy remaining in the persisting hidden dispositions laid down in the first learning. A number of tests were made for each variable and the constants reported are averages with relatively small probable errors.

I. RETENTION AND FORGETTING AS A FUNCTION OF TIME

If syllables are learned and left to themselves, how will the process of forgetting go on under the influence of time or the daily events of life which fill it?

Ebbinghaus made 163 double tests, each consisting of 8 series of 13 syllables. Each test series was learned on one day and relearned after an interval that was varied as is shown below. The results were as follows:

Interval (in hours)	.33	1	8.8	24	48	6×24	31×24
No. of tests	12	16	12	26	26	26	45
Forgotten: per cent (v)	41.8	55.8	64.2	66.3	72.2	74.6	78.9
Retained: per cent (b)	58.2	44.2	35.8	33.7	27.8	25.4	21.1
Calculated from formula	57.0	46.7	34.5	30.4	28.1	24.9	21.2
Residuals	+1.2	−2.5	+1.3	+3.3	−0.3	+0.5	−0.1
PE_M	1.	1.	1.0	1.2	1.4	1.3	0.8

One hour after the learning approximately 56 per cent had been forgotten; after 8 hours, 64 per cent; after 24 hours, 66 per cent; after a week, 75 per cent; after a month, 79 per cent.

The amount retained varies inversely with the logarithm of the time. The calculated values above are from the formula

$$b = \frac{100k}{(\log t)^c + k},$$

in which $c = 1.25$ and $k = 1.84$. The fit is sufficiently close to warrant the general formula.

$$\frac{b}{v} = \frac{k}{(\log t)^c}.$$

The constants probably vary with individual subjects.

II. RETENTION AS A FUNCTION OF THE ORDER OF SUCCESSION
OF THE SYLLABLES IN A SERIES

The inner mechanism of one of the most generally accepted laws of "the association of ideas" was the subject of this research. "Ideas experienced in immediate succession mutually reproduce each other, and with greater ease in the direction of the original succession."

One investigation revealed the fact that a syllable is tied not only to the next in succession but also to the 2, 3, and 7 in succession after it: the per cent of savings being 10.8, 7.0, 5.8, and 3.3, which show the relative strengths of the tie. If the series number is recorded in Roman notation, and the successive syllables in Arabic, the method may be readily shown:

Normal order ..I(1)   I(2)   I(3) ....I(8)   I(9)   I(10)   I(11) ....I(16)
Derived order ..I(1)   I(3)   I(5) ....I(15) I(2)   I(4)   I(6)   ....I(16)

On one day 11 series of 16 syllables in normal order were learned; 24 hours later the same syllables in derived order were relearned. The derived order illustrated above was arranged for measuring the tie to the second syllable in succession (by skipping the immediate successor). It had been determined that the series in normal order could be learned after 24 hours with a saving of 33.3 per cent of the work in the original learning. And it was found that relearning in chance order of the same syllables that had been learned in original order is done with a saving of only 0.5 per cent. Hence the saving of 10.8 per cent in relearning the series derived by skipping one syllable is not accounted for by familiarity with the syllables, but by the latent dispositions that tie each syllable with its second successor. The generalization drawn by Ebbinghaus is that each syllable becomes tied with decreasing strength to all its successors in the series.

But the question of ties to antecedent syllables, reverse associations, had often been questioned, and never measured. Ebbinghaus by this same method of derived series measured the strength of the ties to the first and second preceding syllables. The syllable immediately preceding another was not much more closely associated with it than the second one following it, the second preceding scarcely as firmly as the third following. He also found that repetition of the odd-numbered syllables in the learning of a derived series indirectly increased the reproducibility of the even-numbered syllables in another derived series; that is, when syllables had been learned in sequence (1, 2, 3, 4, etc.), the relearning of alternate syllables (1, 3, 5, etc.) strengthened the latent associations between the alternate omitted syllables (2, 4, 6, etc.).

Although Ebbinghaus introduced measurement into the higher mental processes, he confined himself to the inner dispositions upon which memory depends. He stripped the content of all meaning, in order to avoid uncontrollable fluctuations in the mental processes, and sought the effect of repetition upon sensory functions, the natural memory. His method was taken over bodily from natural science, utilizing measures of dispersion to test the constancy of causal combinations and the significance between means. He discriminated his constants from statistical constants and inferred homogeneity of causes from approximations of his distributions to the Gaussian law. He regarded statistical constants as scientifically artificial, since they do not measure causal relations but result from heterogeneous causal combinations. He grants that although "they are of no direct value for the setting up of numerically exact relations of dependence, they are preparatory to this" (p. 14).[3]

[3] [This analysis was written in October, 1928, and was revised by the analyst in February, 1929.—EDITOR.]

THE EXPERIMENTAL STUDY OF ATTITUDE, MEANING, AND THE PROCESSES ANTECEDENT TO ACTION BY N. ACH AND OTHERS IN THE WÜRZBURG LABORATORY

FRANKLIN FEARING

Northwestern University

Thomas Hobbes in 1651 wrote that the "trayne" of our thoughts or "mental discourse" was of two sorts: unguided and regulated by desire and design. In the latter type of process the idea of end regulates the course of our mental activity and the action which results from it. The idea of end is, for Hobbes, directive in character. "And because the end, by the greatness of the impression, comes often to mind, in case our thoughts begin to wander, they are quickly again reduced into the way . . . . this is to say, in all your actions, look often upon what you would have, as the thing that directs all your thoughts in the way to attain it.[1]

Hobbes, preceding the development of the experimental psychology of the thought processes and action by two hundred and fifty years, anticipated in some degree the modern statement of the problem of the conditions antecedent to action. These conditions are expressed in the English terms *attitude, determining tendencies, mental set*,[2] and in the German terms *Aufgabe, Einstellung, Bewusstseinslage, Zielvorstellung, Richtungsvorstellung*, and the like. They refer in general to the preparation of the organism for action and stress those internal factors which determine responses.

The study of the movements of the organism is of interest to all the scientific disciplines which are concerned with the behavior of living forms. With the physiologist this study has taken the form of an analysis of the operations of the nervous, muscular and tendinous mechanisms; with the sociologist the concern is with the organized expression of action in the form of institutions. The aspect of these studies which deals with the factors preliminary to and essential for action has led to controversies in psychology, biology, and sociology. The tropistic theory

[1] *Leviathan* (Oxford: Clarendon Press, 1909), Part I, chap. iii, p. 20.

[2] There are also the less exact terms *purpose, motive*, and *belief*, which are employed in the contexts of social psychology. These terms have the same general connotation as those whose definitions are based upon experimentation.

of Loeb[3] and the "physiological states" of Jennings[4] are examples of opposing interpretations with reference to the conditions preliminary to movement in the field of the behavior of the lower organisms. In the case of the more complex animals and man the study of action in the past centered about speculations regarding the nature of the hypothetical "power" or faculty of the will. More recently the rise of objective psychology has pointed the interest of the investigators in the direction of the study of the innate factors which determine the responses of the organism. These factors in the form of inherited patterns represent a continuous preparation of the animal for adjustment to its environment.

The factors preliminary to the less stable types of action—called "voluntary" or "impulsive" action in the older psychology—have not been so readily analyzed. The result has been an oversimplification in the form of stimulus-response interpretations. The stimulus-response formula has represented an attempt to escape in part at least from metaphysical and speculative concepts of the power or faculty of the will.

The purely overt aspects of action have commanded attention somewhat out of proportion to their importance. It is one of the consequences of the general acceptance of the stimulus-response formula in psychology and the social sciences that the twitch of the muscle, the movement of the arm, the turning of the head, or the pronunciation of the word have come to be regarded as complete acts—acts initiated by external stimuli.

The total act—as the term is used in experimental psychology—has a history within the organism, a beginning, a climax, and an end for which the stimulus is more or less incidental, and for which the purely muscular part is but an easily observable aspect. All those factors involved in the readiness or preparedness of the organism to respond are referred to under the terms which we have used, i.e., determining tendencies, mental set, and attitude. These include all the processes preceding and determining the motor side of the act, not excepting those processes which antedate the stimulus itself. The latter becomes merely a releasing mechanism.

That these factors may be more aptly described in neural terms than in mental terms does not materially modify the concept of attitude or determining tendency. Nor is it material that some of them are native to the organism. These latter have the characteristic of persistency. Some of them may have conscious correlates—a fact which renders them

[3] J. Loeb, *Forced Movements, Tropisms and Animal Conduct* (Philadelphia: J. B. Lippincott Co., 1918).

[4] H. S. Jennings, *The Behavior of the Lower Organisms* (New York: Macmillan Co., 1906).

more accessible to observation. It should be pointed out that not all of these tendencies result in overt motor response. A determining tendency may control and guide processes to which the term "thinking" may be applied. In this case the overt action, if it occurs at all, is much delayed.[5]

It is the attitude which determines for the individual the characteristics of the situations to which he responds. In this sense, then, attitudes confer meaning on the stimulus or stimulus patterns. The situation is defined and the environment is organized from the point of view of the individual by the attitudes and predispositions with which he confronts his world. The stimulus is significant as a stimulus only as it is correlated with and serves as a releasing mechanism for the predispositions to action.

The experimental study of the factors of preparation for action does not begin until the beginning of the present century. In the hands of Wundt, Külpe, and their students the reaction-time experiment became a technique whereby the preparatory and other phases of action were subjected to analytical study. The physiological, the psychophysical, and the psychological periods of the history of the reaction-time experiment are treated adequately elsewhere.[6]

Külpe, in 1893,[7] discusses the "simple reaction" in the following terms: "The reaction is simply the exact type of all actions, as they are called in the psychology of everyday life, which are initiated by an external stimulus. The reaction experiment, therefore, presents many points of interest aside from the question of its duration." This marks the development of the reaction experiment[8] as a psychological technique for the study of action in general.

Külpe discusses the external and the internal factors in the reaction and points out that the latter are of greater psychological importance. In this connection he stresses the significance of the *preparation* of the

[5] E. Faris notes that the term *instinctive* is frequently applied to those acts in which the response occurs without delay. See *American Jour. of Sociol.*, XXXIV (1928), 275.

[6] Cf. E. B. Titchener, *Experimental Psychology, Instructor's Manual, Quantitative* (New York: Macmillan Co., 1905), pp. 356 ff.

[7] O. Külpe, *Outlines of Psychology*, trans. E. B. Titchener (London: Swan Sonnescheim & Co., 1895), pp. 407 ff.

[8] The reaction may be defined as movement made in response to a sense impression. The reaction experiment consists objectively in the measurement of the time elapsing between the stimulus and the reaction movement. For a discussion of the technique of the experiment see Külpe, *op. cit.*, pp. 406 ff. and Titchener, *op. cit.*, pp. 326 ff.

subject for the reaction. On this basis two types of reaction are distinguished: the sensory, in which the expectation is directed toward the sense impression; and the muscular, in which the expectation is directed toward the execution of the movement. The differences in expectation result in differences in the reaction times; the sensorial reaction being in general about a tenth of a second longer than the muscular type.

The use of the technique of the reaction-time experiment for the more detailed study of the factors involved in preparation of the subject reaches its most elaborate expression in a series of experimental studies of the higher thought processes and action carried out by Külpe and his associates in the laboratory at Würzburg. With this development are associated the names of Marbe,[9] Orth,[10] Watt,[11] Ach,[12] Messer,[13] and Bühler.[14] The reaction technique had been used previously as a method for psychological analysis by investigators working in Wundt's laboratory, but it remained for the Külpian group to elaborate the method[15] and to attack the problems of thinking and action.

These studies were notable for the simplicity of the apparatus employed, the type of problems which were attacked, the use of the reaction technique, and for the systematic development of the method of self-observation.[16] The introspective method finds its most thorough-

[9] K. Marbe, *Experimentelle-psychologische Untersuchungen über das Urteil, eine Einleitung in die Logik* (1902).

[10] A. May and J. Orth, "Zur qualitativen Untersuchung der Association," *Zeit. für Psych. und Physiol. d. Sinnesorg.*, XXVI (1901), 1–13.

[11] H. J. Watt, "Experimentelle Beiträge zu einer Theorie des Denkens," *Arch. für d. ges. Psych.*, IV (1905), 289–436.

[12] N. Ach, *Über die Willenstätigkeit und das Denken* (Göttingen, 1905); *Über den Willensakt und das Temperament* (Leipzig, 1910).

[13] A. Messer, "Experimentell-psychologische Untersuchungen über das Denken," *Arch. für d. ges. Psych.*, VIII (1906), 1–223.

[14] K. Bühler, "Tatsachen und Probleme zu einer Psychologie der Denkvorgänge: 1. Ueber Gedanken," *ibid.*, IX (1907), 297–365. Reference should be made also to the important contributions of A. Binet in France, A. Michotte at Louvain, and R. S. Woodworth, T. V. Moore, and R. H. Wheeler in America.

[15] Not all of these investigators used the reaction technique exclusively. Watt, Ach, and Messer made the most extensive use of this technique, and employed the more elaborate types of exposure and time-measuring apparatus.

[16] For critical discussions of the methods and results of these investigations the reader is referred to E. B. Titchener, *Experimental Psychology of the Thought Processes* (New York: Macmillan Co., 1909), Lecture, III; M. Bentley, *The Field of Psychology* (New York: D. Appleton & Co., 1924), chaps. xii and xv; M. F. Washburn, *Movement and Mental Imagery* (New York: Houghton Mifflin Co., 1916), chap. viii; and R. H. Wheeler, *The Science of Psychology* (New York: Thomas Y. Crowell Co., 1929), chap. xii. See also E. B. Barrett, *Motive Force and Motivation*

going application in the hands of these investigators. The objective conditions of the experiment—apparatus, instruction to the subjects, etc.—become in these studies merely a means for the systematic control of the situation for the purpose of permitting self-observation.

The investigation by Marbe of the psychology of judgment was particularly simple from the point of view of instrumentation. A description of one of the experiments is as follows:

In the first experiment, I placed before the observer . . . . two objects of the same size and shape but of different weight, and instructed him to lift them in turn to the same height with the same hand, and then to invert the one that he found the heavier. The act of inverting the weight was evidently right if the objectively heavier, and wrong if the objectively lighter weight was chosen. It was therefore, so far as it came to the observer's consciousness, a judgment. As soon as the observer had inverted the weight which he took to be the heavier, he was required to report the conscious processes that he had experienced after lifting the second weight. He was instructed not to confine himself to the experiences which ran their course coincidentally with the perceptions that took on the character of judgment, since it might possibly be of interest to know what conscious processes introduced the act of judgment. The experiment was performed three times with each observer, one or both of the weights being changed in the repeated trials.[17]

This description illustrates an important characteristic of the methods of this group, namely, the reliance on introspective reports. The method as here used consists in causing the observer (subject) to *judge, compare,* or *will* under controlled conditions, and then requiring him to describe the conscious experiences which occurred.

The work of Ach and Watt was more elaborate as to methods and instrumentation. Watt made use of the words "association method" in which stimulus words were given to the subject with the instruction that he respond with words bearing the relation of superordinate, co-ordinate, and subordinate to the stimulus. The time between the presentation of the stimulus word and the response was measured. For purposes of introspective observation, Watt marked off four stages: the preparatory stage, the appearance of the stimulus word, the search for the reaction word, and the appearance of the reaction. Messer made use of the same general technique, particularly emphasizing the introspective reports.

Tracts (New York: Longmans Green & Co., 1911). The latter investigation was carried out under the direction of A. Michotte at Louvain University. It employs in general the technique of the Würzburg school. For a repetition of Ach's experiments see K. Lewin, *Psych. Forsch.*, I (1922), 191–302; II, 65–141.

[17] Quoted by Titchener, *Experimental Psychology of the Thought Processes,* p. 81.

While Marbe, Watt, and Messer attacked the problems of thinking, judging, and the like, it is in Ach's studies of action that we find a development of method and a statement of results of particular interest to the student of attitudes and the conditions antecedent to action.

In the study of 1905, Ach makes extensive use of the reaction technique. The experimental study may be divided into two parts. In the first part, it is the purpose of the experimenter to study those reactions in which there is a predetermined relationship between the stimulus and the reaction movement which the subject is to execute. In the second part, this relationship is not definitely predetermined for the subject; in one series he is permitted to choose the stimulus to which he will respond, and in another he is permitted to choose between several possible reactions to a given stimulus.

Ach makes constant use of the technique of controlled self-observation (introspection), a method which he terms *systematische experimentelle Selbstbeobachtung*. The general purpose of this process is a complete description and analysis of the experience to be undertaken immediately after the experiment (or given experience) has run its course. To facilitate this analysis the reaction experiment is divided into the fore-, mid-, and after-period. The fore-period is the time from the preliminary or "ready" signal until the stimulus for the reaction, the mid-period is the time between the appearance of the stimulus and the reaction, and the after-period is the time from the reaction until the conclusion of the experiment. Ach makes it clear that the method of systematic self-observation is useful only under conditions of experimental control. These conditions of control include both the arrangement of the experimental sequences, i.e., the control of the stimulus, the arrangement of the different series, etc., and the nature of the instruction given the subject. From this point of view the objective controls and the objective measures obtained form a check on the introspective data; that is to say, a reciprocal relation exists between the two types of data. They are to be regarded, however, as being of equal importance.

In the first series of experiments, that is, those in which there was a predetermined relationship between the stimulus and the reaction, the complexity of the experimental conditions was varied. In certain experiments the situation was that of a simple reaction in which the subject was instructed to "react as quickly as possible when the stimulus comes" or to "react when the stimulus is fully apprehended." In other experiments the instructions ran, "A white or a red card will be exposed. Release the finger as soon as the card is apprehended." A more complicated form of instruction ran, "A card with either E or O will be shown; press down both fingers. If E is shown release the right finger, if O is shown release the left finger." The reaction time was obtained by means of the Hipp chronoscope in units of one-thousandth of a second (sigma). The subjects were all highly trained; they included Külpe and the members of the Würzburg laboratory.

The second section of the investigation involved the study of those situations in which there was no definitely predetermined relationship between the stimulus and the reaction. For example, cards were exposed on which were printed the letters r x or x r, and the subject was instructed to react *either* to r with the left finger or to x with the right finger, but always to react with one or the other. In the series in which the stimulus was determined but the reaction was undetermined, a card was exposed to the subject on which were two digits separated by a vertical line. The subject was instructed to divide, multiply, add, or subtract the figures. A highly significant series from the point of view of method is described in which post-hypnotic suggestion was used. In this series the subject was put into deep hypnosis and instructed that cards would be exposed on which would appear pairs of digits; in the case of the first card, the subject was to give the sum of the digits immediately upon their exposure; in the case of the second card, he was to give the difference. On being awakened the cards were exposed in succession and the subject carried out the instructions given in hypnosis without error. On being questioned, the subject was unable to say why he had given the figure which expressed the sum of the digits. He could only state that he felt the "need" *(Bedürfnis)* to give the correct figure and that he did not go through the arithmetical processes.

These experiments are designed to indicate the importance of the instructions in setting the task and fixing the type of preparation of the subject in his reaction to the stimulus. The study of the introspective reports reveals the presence of factors which determine the course of action and which may be described under the general term of determining tendencies. Among these factors is the *Aufgabe*, which is especially important.

It is the difference in the *Aufgabe* which determines the differences between the "muscular" and "sensorial" reaction types. The *Aufgabe* is reported as represented in consciousness by visual images of the stimulus, by inner speech ("I must react as quickly as possible" or "I must be sure of the stimulus"), by intentional movement sensations in the reacting muscles, by unanalyzable awarenesses *(Bewusstheiten)*, etc. In the case of the rapid "muscular" reaction, the subject had the *Aufgabe* or preparatory set of reacting as quickly as possible; in the case of the slower "sensorial" reaction, the *Aufgabe* is toward a careful discrimination of the stimulus.

The effectiveness of the *Aufgabe* is indicated in the experiments in which pairs of digits were exposed to the subject with the indeterminate instruction that he was to add, divide, subtract, or multiply. The *Aufgabe* —in this case not determined by the instruction—determined the character of the response. These determining tendencies become effective through the instructions, the *Aufgabe*, the influence of suggestion, etc., and may operate independently of the stimulus. They are regarded also by Ach as being independent of the processes of associative reproduction and perseverative tendencies; that is, they constitute a unique factor which enters in and controls the course of thought and action.

The analysis of the introspective material obtained from the fore-period of the reaction indicates that these factors of anticipation are present before the appearance of the sensory impression of the stimulus. On the side of the objective results (reaction times were obtained for each experiment in all the series), we find an increase in the length of the time between the stimulus and the reaction; the results ranging from values in the neighborhood of one hundred and fifty sigma in the case of the reactions *mit einfacher Zuordnung* to durations of twice that time in the experimental situations in which the subject was permitted to choose between stimuli or between one or more possible responses. That is to say, in the more precisely determined situations the reaction time was shorter.

The consciousness of these determinations is represented by imageless processes which appear in the form of unanalyzable conscious contents designated by Ach as *Bewussheit* or awareness. By this he means that we have awareness of meaning and relation in terms which may not be described as visual, auditory, kinaesthetic, or other sensory imagery. The meaning of a term or a word is simply present, for example, as an unanalyzable content. We may have awareness of determination in the sense that we are immediately aware that the on-going course of our action and mental processes are determined or directed by some purpose or instruction or task. These awarenesses are reported by the observers in the after-period of the reaction experiment. "These dispositions," says Ach, "unconscious in their operation, which take their origin from the meaning of the idea of end and look towards the coming perception of the object,—these dispositions that bring in their train a spontaneous appearance of the determined idea, we call determining tendencies."[18]

In 1910 Ach published the second monograph on the motivating factors in volition[19] which is marked by an extension of method and results. In this investigation it was the general purpose of the author to determine the *primaren Merkmalen*, and the strength or the effectiveness of the volitional action. The latter purpose involves the quantitative determination of the strength of the will act and the former a phenomenological description of the action process. To realize this aim, Ach pointed out[20] that it is necessary (1) to determine the temporal course of the will action and to compare it under different conditions, (2) to investigate the factors of determination of the act, (3) to call forth the will act in its most strongly marked form and to isolate its conscious aspects, and (4) to make quantitative determinations of the strength of different will acts which proceed from the same determination.

Ach makes use of the reaction technique again and, in addition, combines it with the use of nonsense syllables as stimulus material.[21] The method consisted in the establishment of associations of known strength between nonsense syllables, determined by the number of repetitions, and then in opposing the reproductive effects of these associations by setting up certain determining tendencies by means of instructions. The series of nonsense syllables consisted of three types: a list (four pairs) in which each syllable rhymed with the succeeding syllable (the *r* series); a list in which the beginning and end consonants of alternate syllables were reversed (*u* series); and a list in which there was no connection between the syllables in a given list (the *g* series).[22] The associative connections were established between these syllables by means of repetition of the pairs, and the strength of such association was measured by the number of repetitions. In opposition to the reproductive tendencies of these associations, the subjects were given the first member of the learned pairs and instructed to respond *not* with the associated syllable

---

[18] *Op. cit.* (1905), p. 228; quoted by Titchener, *Experimental Psychology of the Thought Processes*, pp. 127–28.

[19] *Über den Willensakt und das Temperament.*

[20] *Op. cit.* (1910), pp. 13–14.

[21] H. Ebbinghaus, *Über das Gedächtniss* (1885). The details of the technique employed by Ebbinghaus in this classical study are discussed in the preceding analysis by Professor J. E. Coover. The use of this method by Ach and others is a nice illustration of the fact that the story of the development of a science is essentially the history of the techniques of that science.

[22] Examples of the *r* syllables: *sol mol, sup tup;* examples of the *u* syllables: *dus sud, rol lor.* Cf. Ach (1910), pp. 25 ff.

but with one of the alternative syllable types. For example, in one experiment three types of syllables (*r*, *u*, and *g* lists) were learned over a period of six days (on the sixth day the number of repetitions was seventy for each list of eight syllables); on the seventh day, the first members of all the pairs in the lists were exposed to the subject and he was instructed to react by giving a syllable *which had no connection with* the stimulus syllable. On the eighth day, the procedure was repeated except that the instructions were to respond to the stimulus syllable, but with syllables in which the *beginning and end consonants were reversed*. On the ninth day, the instruction was to respond with syllables which *formed rhymes with the stimulus syllable*. It will be observed that these instructions are so arranged that on each day they are in effect a support for the already existing associations in *one* of the lists of nonsense syllables, while they are in opposition to the associations of the two remaining lists. The former situation Ach terms the *homogene Aufgabestellungen*, and the latter he terms the *heterogene Aufgabestellungen*.

On the quantitative side Ach obtained the reaction times under the two types of *Aufgabe*. That is, he obtained the times between the exposure of the stimulus syllable and the subject's response. This furnished a measure of the effectiveness of the various *Aufgaben* in overcoming the strength of the associative tendencies artificially established by repetition. We have also a measure of the strength of the determining tendency or *Aufgabe* in terms of the number of repetitions necessary to form an associative disposition which is just sufficient to overcome a determining tendency. If the associative disposition secured through practice is weak, i.e., the number of repetitions is small, the determining tendencies secured through instructions will control the course of the action. If the associative disposition is strong, the determining tendency will be ineffective. This value, i.e., the number of repetitions, Ach calls the *associative equivalent of the determination*.

The results from this long study, involving scores of reaction times and the presentation of hundreds of lists of nonsense syllables, is difficult to summarize. Ach discusses his conclusions under two general headings: the phenomenological results and the dynamic aspects of action. The phenomenological characteristics of the volitional action viewed as the adoption of a problem idea consist in the following: (1) the *anschauliche* or image moment, which consists of strain sensations primarily; (2) the *gegenständliche* or objective moment, which consists of the awareness of the idea of end, and of the means; (3) the *aktuelle* moment, which involves the consciousness phrased in the statement "I will" or "I really will," thus excluding every other possibility; (4) the moment of effort *(zuständliche)*. These generalizations are based by Ach on the interpretations of the introspective reports of his observers during the course of the investigation.

The quantitative results, which throw light upon the dynamic aspects of volitional action, relate in general to the statement of the effectiveness of the determining tendencies in overcoming the artificially established associations. They are stated in the longer reaction times observed in the "heterogeneous" *Aufgabe* and the shorter reaction times found in the "homogeneous" *Aufgabe*. This may be stated in a "law of special determination,"[23] i.e., that a fully determined problem is performed with less resistance and less effort than a less clearly determined problem with a consequent reduction in time. This was consistent with the results in both the 1905 and 1910 investigations.

It is safe to say that the analyses of the Würzburg school—particularly the work of Watt on judgment and Ach on action—have made necessary the re-writing of the pyschology of the higher thought processes and action. The concepts of *Aufgabe*, determining tendencies and imageless awareness are offered as a result of experimental investigation in a field in which systematic experiment had not ventured hitherto. These interpretations were not accepted without controversy.[24] But the principle of the determination of consciousness and of action has been accepted implicitly or explicitly by the majority of those who have attempted to deal systematically with the problem of motivation. Titchener in his review, favorable on the whole, of the work of the Würzburg school says:

The notion of an external and precedent determination of consciousness is, of course, familiar enough; we speak of command, of suggestion, of instruction, of the influence of surroundings, of classroom atmosphere and laboratory atmosphere, of professional attitude, of class bias, of habit and disposition, of temperamental interests and predilections, of inherited ability and inherited

---

[23] Cf. *ibid.*, p. 255.

[24] It is not the purpose to review the controversies over imageless thought, the nature of the "goal idea," etc. For these discussions reference may be made to Bentley, *op. cit.*, pp. 533 ff.; Titchener, *Experimental Psychology of the Thought Processes* (1909), Lecture V; R. S. Woodworth, *Jour. Phil. Psy. and Sci. Method*, IV (1907), 170; M. W. Calkins, *Amer. Jour. Psych.*, XX (1909), 269 ff.; T. V. Moore, *Psych. Monog.*, XXVII (1919), 67–305, and *Dynamic Psychology* (Philadelphia: J. B. Lippincott Co., 1924), Part VI, chap. iii; Wheeler, *op. cit.*, pp. 332 ff.; and E. G. Boring, *A History of Experimental Psychology* (New York: Century Co., 1929), pp. 393 ff.

defect; and in all these cases we imply that the trend of a present consciousness, the direction it takes, is determined beforehand and from without, whether
in psychophysical or in purely physiological terms. But a thing may be a
commonplace of the text-books, yet have escaped experimental study. Thus
laboratory psychology has, until very lately, looked askance at hypnosis as a
method of psychological investigation. . . . . Things are changing; Ach and
Martin have employed hypnosis in the laboratory. Things will change still
more, now that experimental results in general are seen to be functions of the
instructions given.[25]

The investigations of the Würzburg school are unique because of
the type of problems attacked, the development of experimental techniques, and the thoroughgoing use of the introspective method. This
method is based on the assumption that thinking and the antecedents to
action involve psychical processes—an assumption which implies a psychophysical theory unacceptable to the dogmas of objectivism. In this
connection it should be pointed out that Ach makes use of both the
objective data (reaction-time measurements, number of repetitions, etc.)
and the introspective data. The reaction times under varying *Aufgaben*
become an objective index of the subjective changes.

The problem of the objective indices of subjective states has not been
solved. In the recent work of Thurstone on attitude, we find the distinction between the objective index (statement of opinion) and the "inferred subjective inclination of the person" which Thurstone calls the
"attitude variable."[26] Thurstone's discussion of this problem is interesting.

There comes to mind the uncertainty of using an opinion as an index of
attitude. The man may be a liar. If he is not intentionally misrepresenting his
real attitude on a disputed question, he may nevertheless modify the expression
of it for reasons of courtesy, especially in those situations in which frank expression of attitude may not be well received. This has led to the suggestion
that a man's action is a safer index of his attitude than what he says. But
his actions may also be distortions of his attitude. . . . . Neither his opinions
nor his overt acts constitute in any sense an infallible guide to the subjective
inclinations and preferences that constitute his attitude. Therefore we must
remain content to use opinions, or other forms of action, merely as indices of
attitude. It must be recognized that there is a discrepancy, some error of
measurement as it were, between the opinion or overt action that we use as an
index and the attitude that we infer from such an index.

---

[25] *Experimental Psychology of the Thought Processes* (1909), pp. 161–62.
[26] L. L. Thurstone, *Amer. Jour. Sociol.*, XXXIII (1928), 532 ff.

Thurstone's technique is designed to "catch" the attitudes in the form of verbal opinion; Ach experimentally establishes associative connections and then tests their strength by attempting to overcome them by the use of *Aufgaben* set up by instruction. The general purposes of the two investigations are divergent, but there is a similarity in the incidental problems faced in the two cases. Thurstone implies that there *is* a "subjective" attitude—the "real" attitude—of which the opinion is merely an indication, and that either the action or the word (objective indices) are the only aspects which his method may reach. The necessities of measurement involve the use of indirect methods.[27] It is difficult to see, however, how a technique which involves the indication of one's position on an attitude scale is scientifically more satisfactory than a technique which involves the reporting by highly trained subjects of their attitudes which appear in consciousness under conditions of careful experimental control. The recent discussions of Faris[28] and Bain[29] are pertinent to these problems.

The preparations for action—the *Aufgabe* and determining tendencies —are significant not only as determinants of action but as conferring meaning on the situation. The concept of the organism's preparation for action involves an anticipation of the stimulus—the stimulus becomes effective, i.e., has meaning—in that it fits in with the state of preparedness of the organism. Mead's recent papers[30] present this point of view. Mead points out that objects of immediate experience exist and are dependent on their relation to "biologic and social" individuals. Attitudes and conduct function in the sense of drawing lines about objects in experience.[31] For Mead the environment "arises for an organism through the selective power of an attention that is determined by its impulses that are seeking expression." He continues:

This peculiar environment does not exist in the consciousness of the form as a separate milieu, but the consciousness of the organism consists in the fact that it outlines and defines its objects. In so far as the organization of one

[27] When the spoken word and overt action are used as *indications* of attitudes, it is important that statements regarding the attitudes be properly safeguarded. Recent studies in motivation do not seem to have observed due caution in this regard. For example, in the study of Merriam and Gosnell, *Non-Voting* (1924), reference is made to the "mental operations" of the non-voter on the basis of front-door interviews with untrained subjects. [Cf. analysis 50.—EDITOR.]

[28] *Op. cit.*, p. 273 ff.

[29] R. Bain, *Amer. Jour. Sociol.*, XXXIII (1928), 944 ff.

[30] G. H. Mead, *Jour. of Phil.*, XIX (March, 1922), 157–63; *Internat. Jour. of Ethics*, XXXV (1925), 251–77.

[31] Cf. Mead, *Jour. of Phil.*, pp. 158 ff.

individual differs from that of others, it will have a private environment, though these differences may be called those of standpoint. . . . . The most fundamental phase of these differences is found in the determination of what the relativist calls a "consentient set," i.e., the selection of those objects which may all be considered as "here" with reference to the individual.[32]

The common attitudes taken by the group toward objects define these objects for the group. Values consist in the fact that a number of individuals take a common attitude toward certain objects, principles of action, etc. When the individual assumes the same attitude toward himself which others assume toward him, he has become self-conscious, according to Mead's point of view. For example, we assume the same attitude toward our property and life that we expect the community at large to take. This is the psychological basis of a "right." Social control consists in the degree to which the individual "does assume the attitude of those in the group who are involved with him in his social activities."

Washburn in her monograph on the motor aspects of consciousness discusses the physiological interpretation of determining tendencies. She suggests[33] that in problem ideas the motor excitation in which the idea is based is associated with an "internal static movement system." A movement system of this type is a prolonged muscular contraction, e.g., postural reaction. This, together with the appeal on the part of persistent determining tendencies, accounts in physiological terms for the persistence of the problem idea and attitudes. The connection of the attitude with fundamental needs and drives of the organism also points to the strong affective elements which are observed in persistent and intense individual attitudes. The problems of the affective aspects of attitudes and their physiological correlates still await solution.

It is a far cry from the speculative concept of the control of the course of thought voiced by Hobbes to the experimentation of the Würzburgers and the concepts of Mead, Faris, and others. It has been a long, rough road and the end is not yet. Techniques have been suggested, however, which may serve as guideposts along a difficult way.[34]

[32] *Internat. Jour. of Ethics*, XXXV (1925), 256.

[33] *Op. cit.*, pp. 159 ff.

[34] [This analysis was submitted in December, 1928, and was revised by the analyst during the following spring.—EDITOR.]

APPENDIXES

APPENDIX A

HISTORY AND ORGANIZATION OF THE *CASE BOOK*

By THE EDITOR

Participants have frequently observed that the project resulting in this volume contained in itself a significant exemplification of method. This is apparent when the *Case Book* is examined in the light of criteria set forth in the Introduction. Taken as a whole, the preceding series of analyses represents an inductive approach to the study of methods in social science. Yet pure induction is an impossibility, apart from some conceptual organization of subject matter, and so it was here. The subject matter could not be distinguished and analyzed until concepts of "method" were formulated. It was essential that the meaning attached to the term be sufficiently clear and consistent to permit the establishment of a plan of procedure. The dependence of procedure upon concepts was especially apparent because of the participation of a large number of individuals whose conflicting viewpoints it was necessary to reconcile. With a starting-point once established the concepts tended to develop, thereby altering procedure as the work continued. An account of the history and organization of the *Case Book,* therefore, will have something of the character of another case analysis, with the *Case Book* itself providing the subject matter and with the collective participation of many scholars representing the authorship. Such an account follows:

An interest in methodology was shown by the Social Science Research Council at its very inception. At its second meeting, May 17, 1923, Professor Horace Secrist was appointed a committee of one to prepare a plan for a study of the aims and methods of research agencies. The recommendations in his report in the following November were accepted and the Committee was enlarged. Efforts to secure funds, however, were unavailing, and during the years 1924 and 1925 the Committee confined its activities to correspondence and to occasional discussion as opportunity permitted.

Meanwhile the Committee's functions were gradually changing, as the task of the Social Science Research Council became clarified. The latter was expressed by Professor Charles E. Merriam, its chairman, in his 1926 report as follows:

731

A broad view of the special research projects under way, approval of significant plans, bringing together of unrelated works, stimulation of research where now neglected, emphasis on the vital importance of more severely scientific methods, these will, it seems to me, constitute the chief work of the Council. This is of itself a large and difficult task in view of the multiplicity of research projects, the inadequacy of methods often employed, and the neglect of many important fields altogether.

Recognition of the "vital importance of more severely scientific methods" left the Council, presumably, with two alternatives: It might rely for its ideas of scientific methods upon the undebated preconceptions of its members, or it might sponsor a study of the problems of scientific method in the social sciences which would define, illustrate, and clarify the issues at stake. Such a study, while consistent with the changing interests of the Committee, seemed to require some reorganization in its membership, especially since its original task—a study of the aims and methods of research agencies—was presently included within the scope of an inquiry undertaken by the American Council of Learned Societies.[1] Early in 1926, therefore, the Committee was reconstituted and renamed the Committee on Scientific Method.[2]

The first important step taken by the new Committee was to arrange a conference of its members and a few invited guests, under the aegis of the Social Science Research Council and in connection with the annual meeting of the latter at Hanover, New Hampshire. This conference, held in August, 1926, was of one week's duration. Its object was to formulate a definite project of methodological study.

In opening the sessions, the chairman expressed the need for a clearcut statement of the central theme of method as it applies to the social sciences. No such statement, he said, existed. The methodology of the physical sciences had been stamped with rules applicable to them, and there was a tendency for social scientists to think in terms of these concepts, which were possibly unsuited to them. A formulation was needed for the Council, for students in the colleges, particularly in graduate work, and for the use of all those engaged in social research. This formulation should show what scientific method means to the social scientist, and it should illustrate how the methods are carried out in each of the

[1] Cf. Foreword, n. 1.

[2] Professor Horace Secrist remained as chairman of the new Committee, and retained this position until his departure for California in the summer of 1928 to undertake a special research assignment for Claremont colleges. On July 1 of that year he was succeeded as chairman by Professor Robert M. MacIver, of Columbia University.

disciplines. It should be a synthesis and integration of methods so far developed. Two projects were before the Committee: first, a book which should undertake to outline the methods now used in the various social sciences represented in the Council; second, a study of the techniques of fact-gathering.

It was subsequently agreed that the first would be more fundamental than the second. The notion of a "case book" was evolved. It was conceived as an inductive study of the methods *actually used* in significant contributions to social science. While it might not indicate new methods for the future, it would show where the social sciences stand at the present time with respect to their methodology.

This was but one among a number of possible enterprises to which the Committee at various times gave consideration. Some of these, together with the objections to which they were subject, were the following:

1. A general treatise upon the nature of scientific method in social science, by some prominent specialist with a broad philosophic outlook. It was objected that this proposal would be too dependent upon the capacities and viewpoints of a single individual. Such a treatise would necessarily be biased, and largely speculative.

2. Quotations from various contributions to show social science in the making. Had this procedure been followed, the reader himself would have been left to discover the methodological issues and principles involved.

3. A symposium by specialists upon the state of the respective disciplines. This was ruled out because of its duplication of other studies now available.

4. Autobiographical versions of the growth of their scientific interests from distinguished scholars who have contributed to the development of social science. While the Committee saw advantages in such a venture, it was regarded as impracticable because of the probable length to which such a series, if sufficiently comprehensive, would run.

5. Republication of past contributions to methodological theory. Many valuable discussions are imbedded in the voluminous works of half-forgotten scholars, or are otherwise inaccessible to the present student. This plan, however, would not have served to the best advantage the Committee's desire to portray the *present state of methodology* in the social sciences.

6. An extensive bibliography of works on scientific method. This was open to the same objection as the preceding proposal.

A case book seemed to have the special advantage, in comparison with these alternatives, that it would keep theoretical considerations closely related to the particular. The project was recommended to the Council, was approved, and obtained the necessary appropriation of funds.

Specific planning was begun on June 15, 1927, by Professors Robert M. MacIver, of Columbia University; Stuart A. Rice, of the University of Pennsylvania; and Hubert R. Kemp, of the University of Toronto, who were engaged as "investigators." Their reports formed the basis of discussion at a second conference arranged by the Committee at Hanover in August, 1927. While numerous differences in viewpoint among those present were uncovered, the plans for the *Case Book* submitted by the investigators were approved and Professor Rice was asked to proceed with the preparation of case analyses. Subsequently, during the first six months of 1928, Professor Harold D. Lasswell, of the University of Chicago, was associated with the work as coinvestigator.

Although much time and discussion had gone into the preparation of plans, the magnitude of the undertaking and many of its complexities were not foreseen at the end of August, 1927. They quickly began to appear. The meanings previously applied to the term "method" were insufficiently precise. Differences of opinion concerning the nature of the inquiry were more far reaching than had been appreciated. These difficulties have been discussed in the Introduction. The solutions there described were evolved gradually, and in close relationship to an evolution in organization, which will be described below. The latter took place in direct response to the almost insuperable difficulties involved in the selection of the studies to be analyzed.

The purpose of the Committee was constructive. Assuming that the social sciences contain much good work, it sought to analyze the methods employed in the best among many genuine contributions to scientific knowledge. By exhibiting the means of achieving important results, emulation might be expected to raise the level of work which would henceforth be done. But how were these genuine scientific contributions to be identified? And how was the more limited number of "outstanding" contributions to be chosen? It was obvious that no single investigator could be equally familiar with all of the various specialties into which social science has become divided; nor could he be aware of the more important trends of development within more than a limited number of these. Moreover, selection necessitated some system of classification which would provide criteria.

With regard to the latter requirement there were various possibilities. Classification might be based upon methods as such, or upon divisions of subject matter; it might be explicit and set up with deliberation, or it might be implicit and unperceived. Contributions, for example, might be selected from *history,* from *economics,* from *anthropology;* or they might be selected to illustrate *case method, statistical method,* or the *method of questionnaire.* In the absence of a planned structure the investigators would have fallen back naïvely upon some pre-existing classification.

The earliest suggestion of a comprehensive structure which would depart from traditional categories was made by Professor MacIver during the summer of 1927. His suggested classification was as follows:

A. Studies in which a central hypothesis or theory is advanced in explanation of social fact. Here the analysis would be directed chiefly to the object of evaluating the methods by means of which the author has sought to establish or support the theory, and to the adequacy and relevance of the theory to the range of fact to be "explained."

B. Studies in which an exposition of a particular subject or situation is presented, giving a descriptive account of its character and conditions. Here the analysis would be directed chiefly to assessing the accuracy, comprehensiveness, relevance of selection, validity of inference, and sense of proportion shown in the collection, arrangement, and treatment of the data.

C. Studies of applied social science, in which a social problem is presented with a view to the discovery, formulation, or corroboration or rejection of a solution. Here the analysis would be directed chiefly to examining the adequacy and relevance of the diagnosis, and the validity of the grounds of inference from the diagnosis to the solution.

D. Excerpts from works on social science. Here the analysis would be directed to testing the validity of a particular argument or chain of reasoning, or of some short application of a particular method of enquiry, such as the case method, the canons of induction, various statistical methods, non-mathematical considerations of probability, and so forth.

The first classification actually employed in case analysis, likewise during the summer of 1927, was based upon the concept of method as *logic.* An experimental analysis was made of a single chapter in a recent investigation,[3] to determine the grounds, sequences, and logical types of inference contained. While the result seemed to have value in testing the validity of conclusions reached by the author, the type of analysis

[3] Ben. M. Selekman, *Postponing Strikes* (New York: Russell Sage Foundation, 1927), chap. iii, "The Operation of the Act," pp. 62–95. The author's manuscript, prior to its publication, was employed. This analysis is not included in the present volume.

illustrated seemed of limited significance. Moreover, it had been employed recently and adequately by other writers.[4]

A collection of studies of ingenious techniques, found mainly in monographic and periodical literature, was widely favored. Actually, considerable attention has been given to techniques in the analyses above, and some were designed primarily to bring out technical considerations. However, an organization of the entire project based upon differences in technique was not practicable, for reasons sufficiently indicated in the Introduction.

Realizing the urgent need for aid in the all-important problem of selection, the Committee adopted the obvious course of calling upon the various societies represented in the membership of the Social Science Research Council for assistance. Each society was asked to appoint an advisory committee of three members which would select and recommend for analysis the contributions which it regarded as of outstanding significance in its field. This request, presented at the December, 1927, meetings of the societies, was in all cases granted, and led to the appointment of the following committees:

American Anthropological Association: Robert H. Lowie, University of California; Professor Leslie V. Spier, University of Washington; Professor Alfred L. Kroeber, University of California

American Economic Association: John R. Commons, University of Wisconsin; Edmund E. Day, University of Michigan; Frank H. Knight, University of Chicago

American Historical Association: Sidney B. Fay, Smith College; William L. Langer, Harvard University; J. C. Green, Princeton University

American Political Science Association: Charles E. Merriam, University of Chicago; John A. Fairlie, University of Illinois; Harold D. Lasswell, University of Chicago

American Psychological Association: Margaret F. Washburn, Vassar College; Howard C. Warren, Princeton University; Donald G. Paterson, University of Minnesota

American Sociological Society: Kimball Young, University of Wisconsin; Robert E. Park, University of Chicago; William F. Ogburn, University of Chicago

American Statistical Association: Robert E. Chaddock, Columbia University; Frederick C. Mills, Columbia University and National Bureau of Economic Research; Leo Wolman, Amalgamated Clothing Workers, and National Bureau of Economic Research

[4] For example, Charles H. Patterson, *Problems in Logic* (New York: Macmillan Co., 1926); Daniel S. Robinson, *Illustrations of the Methods of Reasoning* (New York: D. Appleton & Co., 1927).

A change in the conception of the task of analysis was at the same time bringing another enlargement of organization. Largely as a result of Professor Lasswell's insistence, it was perceived that analyses would be authoritative only to the extent that each was prepared by a thoroughly competent specialist. "Collaborators" were authorized, thereby freeing the investigators from the responsibility of preparing the analyses themselves.[5]

The problem of classification, however, still remained. The criteria previously employed or suggested seemed inadequate. Thus, for example, some of the writers whose influence has been most far reaching in the development of social science have made no particular contribution to method in the logical or technical senses. The significance of their work is to be found elsewhere—perhaps in the breadth of their generalizations or in the new and vitalizing ways in which problems have been conceived. Logical or technical criteria for the selection of contributions for analysis, in consequence, would remove from view some of the most important work, as judged by its cumulative effects. Again, it was felt that a classification based upon the traditional divisions among the social sciences would help to perpetuate distinctions which are frequently the result of historical accident rather than contemporary utility. Some of the most vital contemporary research is overlapping these habitual boundaries, a conclusion which is supported in Appendix H.

The investigators sought to establish a framework in which these most significant contributions would find an obvious place, and which would include all of the principal ways of conceiving their tasks which social scientists have adopted. They asked themselves, What are the principal tasks of social science, as they have been conceived by those who have provided its present structure? An assured answer to this question would have been rash, and would have violated the inductive spirit of the project. Nevertheless some answer was required as a working guide. The framework or outline with which the investigators answered their question tentatively was under continual revision as the collection and editing of analyses proceeded. One stage of this development, representing the particular contribution of Professor Lasswell, is reproduced in Appendix B. Another, that which has been employed in the arrangement of analyses

---

[5] The view of the investigators' functions which gave them this responsibility was held as late as the end of December, 1927, and a number of their analyses had by that time actually been prepared. A selected number of these appear in the present volume. From the spring of 1928 onward, however, they were occupied almost exclusively in formulating plans, in consulting members of the advisory committees and other scholars, and in conducting extensive negotiations in person and by correspondence with prospective analysts.

in this volume, is defended in the Introduction. Both of these, with the modified forms which intervened, were designed to aid, first, in the selection of significant contributions to social science; second, in the selection of crucial methodological issues to receive attention in the analyses; third, in the grouping of analyses for publication.

In their work, however, the investigators were confronted on every hand with the existing lines of demarcation among the social sciences. Members of the Council, members of the Committee, the special advisory committees by virtue of their appointment, the prospective analysts, and all other participants, including the investigators themselves, were identified with one or another of these existing divisions. It was necessary to work within molds, from which at the same time the workers were trying to escape. For each of the special disciplines, therefore, an outline was prepared, analogous to that which was evolving with respect to social science as a whole. One of these, that for psychology, is reproduced in Appendix C. The contributions to be analyzed were selected in consultation with the advisory committees, and with the further aid of these special outlines. By this means the more important methodological standpoints and issues in each of the social sciences were given recognition in the selective process.[6] When the collection of analyses had been completed in this manner, the separate papers were then rearranged in accordance with their contents and in conformity with the more general scheme.

The various enlargements of plan and organization by means of which the project had reached a definitive stage were ratified by the Council at a meeting in April, 1928. The remainder of that year was devoted to the co-operative work of those who had been drawn into the enterprise. Although a great deal of time was spent in negotiations which proved fruitless, the first drafts of all of the papers here presented had been procured by the end of 1928. The Committee on Scientific Method, regarding the task assigned it as completed with the submission of these manuscripts to the Council in a bulky report on December 31, 1928, voted to disband as of that date. At the request of the chairman of the Council, however, the chairman of the Committee continued as the responsible authority in control of the project until the annual meeting of the Council in April,

---

[6] At one time no less than ninety-seven separate analyses were in hand, in preparation, or in process of negotiation or planning. A few which were undertaken were not completed by analysts. A few others were discarded by the investigators when received. The chief reason for failure to represent particular interests in the volume was the inability to procure analysts within the recurring time limitations under which the investigators worked. Moreover, not infrequently analysts directed their chief attention to questions other than those the investigators had anticipated and suggested in the preliminary negotiations. Cf. Appendix G.

1929. The Committee was then discharged with grateful appreciation for its long and arduous services. At the same time publication of the *Case Book* was authorized, the present writer being asked to assume the editorial labor and responsibility involved.[7] This additional task, except for unavoidable interruptions and delays, has continued until the date of publication.

While numerous difficulties, administrative as well as theoretical, have beset the project throughout, these have been more than offset by the cordial response secured from the larger number of those called upon to co-operate. The willingness of so many scholars not merely to participate but to set aside their own work in order to do so seems to offer evidence of the importance with which methodological study is regarded by a substantial number, at least, of contemporary social scientists.

[7] His indebtedness to a number of advisers during this final period is acknowledged in the Foreword.

APPENDIX B

PROFESSOR HAROLD D. LASSWELL'S CLASSIFICATION[1]

The contributions to social science which have been recommended for inclusion in this volume may be divided into three major categories. Certain studies have defined an abstract object of investigation, others have revealed special skill in the discovery of historical facts, and most of them have envisaged social change in ways which are sufficiently distinctive to deserve extended consideration.

A. IDENTIFYING OBJECTS OF INVESTIGATION

Objects of study may be conceived with varying degrees of abstractness. It is possible to describe "Paris in the Middle Ages," "The Medieval City," or "The Urban Community." The first term, "Paris in the Middle Ages," specifies a relatively definite time-space setting for a particular object. "The Medieval City" is more abstract, which is to say that its time-place reference is more free. "The Urban Community" is a concept which describes a "type relation," for it does not bear on its face a specific time-place limitation. Certain contributions to social science have been influential because they clearly defined general aspects of social phenomena, thus throwing open for comparative study a range of hitherto-unrelated facts. Sumner's treatment of the "folk ways" and the "mores" has become classic.

I. IDENTIFICATION OF A TYPE RELATION

Among the cases see especially:

ANALYSIS 8 "The Methodology of William Graham Sumner in *Folkways*, etc.," by Robert E. Park

ANALYSIS 23: "The Section and the Frontier in American History: Methodological Concepts of Frederick Jackson Turner," by Merle E. Curti

---

[1] [Although the two investigators of the Committee on Scientific Method, Messrs. Rice and Lasswell, worked together upon the problem of classification, the content and phraseology of the present memorandum were almost wholly those of the second. It seems appropriate, therefore, that it should carry his name. This draft was perfected while a majority of the analyses were under negotiation with prospective contributors. Hence, it has important bearing on the collection obtained, while its relationship to the final organization of papers in the Table of Contents will be apparent by a comparison of the two. Cf. Appendix A, p. 737.—EDITOR.]

B. DISCOVERING HISTORIES

This section is intended to include cases which are important because of the way in which they infer specific temporal orders.[2]

II. FIXING A TEMPORAL SEQUENCE IN THE ABSENCE OF WRITTEN RECORDS AND LIVING WITNESSES

ANALYSIS 18: "A Determination of Sequences among Prehistoric Cultures in the Old World by Hugo Obermaier," by Robert H. Lowie

ANALYSIS 19: "Stratigraphic Technique Employed by N. C. Nelson in the Determination of Prehistoric Sequences in America," by Leslie Spier

C. ENVISAGING SOCIAL CHANGE

Most of our cases fall in this section, which is planned to emphasize the various ways of conceiving social change which influence the statement of scientific problems and results.

III. CHANGE CONCEIVED AS A SERIES OF STAGES THROUGH WHICH OBJECTS PASS

These stages, in turn, may be conceived in at least two distinct ways:

IIIa. SOCIAL CHANGE AS A PHASE OF A WORLD-HISTORICAL PROCESS WHICH IS PASSING THROUGH A NON-REPETITIVE SERIES OF PHASES

There have been studies of marriage institutions which treated monogamy as the most recent stage in a series of marital institutions reaching from the supposed promiscuity of a hypothetical primitive horde to the present. Writers on government have sometimes completed a retrospective analysis of this kind and then projected a forthcoming "desirable" stage as the culmination of "evolution."

IIIb. SOCIAL CHANGE AS AN ASPECT OF A WORLD-HISTORICAL PROCESS IN WHICH SEVERAL CULTURES PASS THROUGH COMPARABLE STAGES (CYCLES)

This mode of conceiving change breaks up history into separate movements which pass through the same phases. Spengler's *Decline of the West* treats history as the record of successive cycles of this kind.

[2] Since social science is concerned with the conditions of typical social change, most of the direct and widely recognized contributions to it go beyond the discovery of historical facts. However, certain chronological problems have been so skilfully handled that the inclusion of representative instances has been urged. A large proportion of the factual bulk of the social sciences is found in such "purely historical" monographs. Most of the technical problems which arise in the determination of different orders of fact will be considered in connection with cases which offer something more than "historical" interest. Hence no cases will be noted here which infer facts from written records, from the testimony of living witnesses of events, or from observations made directly by an investigator of "original" events.

Cultures may exist at the same time, but in different phases of cyclical development.

IV. CHANGE CONCEIVED AS A FUNCTION OF INTERRELATED VARIABLES

The idea of "relation" is that one object varies in terms of other objects and not simply in terms of past or future states of itself.

IVa. NON-EXPERIMENTALLY CONTROLLED FACTORS OF A CULTURAL, PSYCHOLOGICAL, GEOGRAPHICAL, OR BIOLOGICAL TYPE REGARDED AS CAUSES OF SOCIAL CHANGE, AND NON-MATHEMATICALLY TREATED

1. Complexes of two or more of these factors handled simultaneously
2. Cultural factors handled separately
3. Psychological factors handled separately
4. Geographical factors handled separately
5. Biological factors handled separately

IVb. NON-EXPERIMENTALLY CONTROLLED FACTORS OF A CULTURAL, PSYCHOLOGICAL, GEOGRAPHICAL, OR BIOLOGICAL TYPE REGARDED AS CAUSES OF SOCIAL CHANGE, AND MATHEMATICALLY TREATED

The same variety of combinations among factors of different types is to be found here as under IVa. The mathematical form of treatment increases the precision of statement.

IVc. EXPERIMENTALLY CONTROLLED FACTORS OF A CULTURAL, PSYCHOLOGICAL, GEOGRAPHICAL, OR BIOLOGICAL TYPE REGARDED AS CAUSES OF SOCIAL CHANGE, AND MATHEMATICALLY TREATED

The same variety of combinations among factors of different types is to be found here as under IVa and IVb. This heading includes studies in which there is an approach to the degree of control exercised by the physical scientist.

APPENDIX C

CLASSIFICATIONS OF METHODS IN PSYCHOLOGY[1]

Reference has been made in Appendix A to the problem of classification encountered by the investigators in working out the *Case Book* project. In addition to the "framework" which was evolved with respect to social science as a single coherent field (Appendixes A and B) an attempt was made to set up an analogous classification within each of the special social sciences (p. 738). While these minor classifications were in many respects inconsistent with the general framework, they served the practical purpose of securing representation among the projected analyses for all of the more important "schools" and points of view within the special disciplines. In this Appendix the evolution of the classification for the field of psychology alone will be sketched. The editor feels that this account will illustrate to advantage the nature of some of the problems encountered in working upon the project, as well as the methods employed by the investigators in meeting these problems.

By many, psychology is regarded as a "natural" and not a "social" science. So far as the organization of the *Case Book* project was concerned, this view seemed to beg a question already settled, inasmuch as the American Psychological Association was among the seven affiliated organizations in the Social Science Research Council. But on what ground do psychologists regard themselves as social scientists? Is it only within that poorly defined middle area known as "social psychology"? Upon this latter assumption, aid was requested of Professor R. S. Woodworth, of Columbia University, in formulating the methods of *social psychology*.

In response to the request, four methods were outlined by Woodworth in a letter[2] from which the following quotation is taken:

I think the psychologist would be apt to approach the question of method in social psychology with the general feeling that much still remained to be done before the methods in this subject were on a scientific basis. In particular, we are hoping that the experimental line of attack may be shown to be applicable here. Some beginnings have been made. Allport has been a

---

[1] Except as noted, this Appendix was written by the editor.
[2] To Stuart A. Rice, dated October 30, 1927.

pioneer here,[3] and some of his papers are reviewed in his *Social Psychology.* I might mention also the dissertation of Ethel M. Riddle, *Aggressive Behavior in a Small Social Group*, which reports an experiment on poker playing. I believe that the experimental study of group games may prove to be a good lead in social psychology.

Besides the experimental attack, which controls the conditions under which the observed phenomena occur, we have the genetic method, in which, without being able to control the essential conditions, we may be able to know what they are, and to follow up the development. With this line of attack in view, one very promising lead in social psychology is the study of the social behavior of children, i.e., actual following of the development as it occurs. Watson's and Rayner's study of conditioned fears would be an example of the method, though the behavior studied is not specially social. There are many studies of the growth of the child's vocabulary that would come under the head of genetic studies. There is a recent book by Harriet Johnson of the Bureau of Educational Experiments which is based upon continued records of young children in a free school environment.

Where the investigation has not started before the important phenomena develop, we are driven from the genetic to the historical method, which in the psychological realm takes the form of the biographical or case-history method. Published biographies have not proved thus far of great psychological value: but case histories of psychotic, neurotic and delinquent individuals have often seemed very illuminating. The defects of the method are (1) that the observations are not made at the time the phenomena occur but derived from memory, in large measure, and (2) that the material is selected after the event and is likely to lead to a distorted picture, unless provided with a background of normal or unselected case histories, which are not so easy to obtain. Psychiatric material is of the case-history type, though here, as in studies of delinquents, the case history may be supplemented by follow-up of the further development of the case (i.e., the genetic method from the time when the case is first studied), and by treatment with noting of results (a form of the experimental method). Perhaps some of the best case histories are to be found in the *Judge Baker Foundation Case Studies*, published about 1922–23.[4] Other interesting ones have come from the Joint Committee on Methods of Preventing Delinquency, e.g., *Three Problem Children* (1924). Terman's studies of California gifted children are perhaps fully as instructive.

There is another psychological method, which I call the "comparative," that is perhaps the most used in psychological studies having a social bearing. Here the data are not treated as antecedent and consequent, as in the previous three methods, but simply as parallel series, in the effort to reveal correspondences and differences which may throw indirect light on causation. Studies of intelligence in different social and racial groups belong here, as also

---

[3] [Cf. analysis 49.—EDITOR.]   [4] [Cf. analysis 36.—EDITOR.]

comparison of delinquent with non-delinquent groups, etc. Brigham's studies of the mentality of the immigrant, Hirsch's study of natio-racial differences, and Slawson's *Delinquent Boy* (1926)[5] are examples of this line of attack. The last-mentioned book is an especially good example of judicious statistical handling of the intricate network of variables with which such investigation must deal.

It is apparent that these four methods named by Professor Woodworth —the experimental, the genetic, the historical, and the comparative—are not limited in their applications to social psychology; that on the contrary they may be used in widely separated fields. This would seem to evidence the generality of the classification, and suggest its utility for the *Case Book* planning. It was presently decided, however, to err on the side of greater inclusiveness in making the psychological selections, by abandoning the limitation to social psychology. Inquiries dealing with collective social phenomena and those which deal with the mental processes of the individual are closely related. They are reciprocal in influence, and were held to be inseparable for the purpose in hand. With this enlargement of scope, as concerned psychology, it was obvious that Woodworth's classification could not serve the end of selection, by pointing to the significant variants of purpose and viewpoint within the field. It referred to differing ways of obtaining or manipulating data, prior to inference. The differences which divide psychologists refer to the broader questions: *What do psychologists regard as their data? What principles of explanation do they employ?*[6]

The following outline was therefore developed tentatively (it was never wholly completed) and used as a basis for the selection of methodological contributions in psychology. Headings and topics were in some instances fitted to the names of individuals, rather than the reverse, although the attempt to carry out a logical scheme introduced repetitions among these names:

I. General explanatory concepts
   A. Emphasis on nature of the stimulus
      Watson or Pavlov: Singularity of response
      Sherrington: Integrative response

[5] [Cf. analysis 39.—EDITOR.]

[6] These distinctions were pointed out by Professor Margaret F. Washburn, chairman of the Special Advisory Committee of the American Psychological Association, with whom the classification which follows was discussed at length, and who contributed greatly to its construction, after it had been drafted by the investigators.

    B. Emphasis on nature of the organism
        a) Varied innate drives
           McDougall: Instincts
           Cannon: Emotions
        b) Acquired tendencies
           Freud: Complexes
           Mead: Attitudes

II. Conceptions of the fundamental nature of psychological data
    A. As momentary processes
        1. Conscious processes
           Titchener: Structural psychology
           Köhler: *Gestalt* psychology
        2. Movements
           Watson: Behaviorism
    B. As more or less permanent tendencies or traits (These may be regarded either as conscious or as purely motor.)
        1. Quantitatively measurable
           Ebbinghaus: Memory
           Thorndike: Testing
        2. Qualitatively analyzable
           Kretschmer: "Typology"

The Table of Contents will disclose not merely the extent to which the analyses sought on the basis of this outline were procured, but also the extent to which the outline itself was discarded, once it had served its purpose.

APPENDIX D

PROFESSOR RAYMOND T. BYE'S CLASSIFICATION OF METHODS IN ECONOMICS

As an outgrowth of discussion, Professor Raymond T. Bye, of the University of Pennsylvania, was asked to write out a classification of methods in economics as he conceived them. This was incorporated in a letter[1] from which the following itemization is extracted. Professor Bye is "quite sure" that it is "not yet complete," but sanctions its publication for "what it is worth."

1. Abstract deductive theory by non-mathematical analysis. This is well exemplified by J. B. Clark's *Distribution of Wealth* and many other works in economic theory.

2. Abstract deductive theory by mathematical analysis. Good illustrations of this are A. L. Bowley's *Mathematical Groundwork of Economics,* and much of the work of Irving Fisher.

3. Abstract deductive theory modified and refined by practical observation of a general sort. Alfred Marshall's *Principles of Economics*[2] with its elaborate qualifications seems to me to be of this type.

4. Statistical testing (verification, refutation, or refinement and modification) of abstract, deductive theory. Examples are Horace Secrist's studies of marginal and representative costs in the retail clothing industry,[3] Jacob Viner's analysis of *Canada's Balance of International Indebtedness,* and numerous other recent works.

5. Quantitative measurement of economic data, without interpretation (although much good work in theory may have to be done to ascertain just what is to be measured, and how). An excellent case of this is the National Bureau of Economic Research's studies of income in the United States. Also the various index numbers of prices.

6. Inductive analysis of economic phenomena (by statistical and historical analysis—mainly statistical) leading to theoretical interpretation. Wesley Mitchell's analyses of business cycles[4] are of this sort, though he has not gone very far in the theoretical interpretation of his data.

7. Historical analysis of economic institutions. For instance, F. W. Taussig's survey of the tariff history of the United States, the (Sidney and Beatrice) Webb's studies of the history of trade-unions, etc.

[1] To Stuart A. Rice, dated February 22, 1928.
[2] [Cf. analysis 2 and analysis 44.—EDITOR.]
[3] [Cf. analysis 44.—EDITOR.]   [4] [Cf. analysis 47.—EDITOR.]

These are all in the field of what I would call pure economics. When we get into the field of applied economics, by which I mean the application of economic principles to the attainment of desired ends in the way of economic reform, we have still different methodology. I shall not attempt to develop this fully, but the following occur to me as obvious aspects of it:

8. Ethical criticism of economic institutions. See, for instance, T. N. Carver's *Essays in Social Justice*, and R. H. Tawney's *The Acquisitive Society*. Such analyses, of course, are not strictly scientific, but they may make use of scientific data.

9. The application of scientific principles to the solution of practical problems of reform. Examples of this would be P. G. Wright's *Sugar in Relation to the Tariff* ("Institute of Economics Series"), much of the literature on money and banking, and some of the chapters in *Applied Economics*, written by W. W. Hewett and myself.

10. Pure economic theory growing out of the attempt to solve practical problems. This is closely allied to point No. 4 above. The theoretical analysis growing out of the controversy over proper methods of valuation in rate regulation is a case in point. The necessity of formulating a satisfactory definition of income for the purposes of income taxation (excellently illustrated by William W. Hewett's *The Definition of Income and Its Application in Federal Taxation*) is another.

As I have indicated, I believe that further reflection would make it possible to enlarge this list considerably, but perhaps I have given enough to show the general trend of my thinking on the problem.

APPENDIX E

REPORT OF THE ADVISORY COMMITTEE OF THE AMERICAN SOCIOLOGICAL SOCIETY[1]

Each of the advisory committees from the organizations affiliated with the Social Science Research Council (cf. Appendix A, p. 736) was asked to recommend ten outstanding contributions, suitable for analysis, within its field. Before a majority of these committees had met, the plans for the *Case Book* had been altered, particularly with regard to the proposed organization and arrangement of analyses. As a consequence, the aid given by the advisory committees took the more helpful form of continuing advice to the investigators. That is, the committees' functions of formal report were replaced by advisory participation in a growing plan of work. The committee representing the American Sociological Society, however, met more promptly than the others and submitted a formal report. It is of interest from several standpoints: It illustrates the diversity of subject matter within sociology, and the extent to which this subject matter overlaps the territory of other social sciences. Second, it gives evidence of the difficulty of making a selection of "outstanding contributions" unless criteria of "significance" or "importance" are themselves agreed upon in advance. These criteria will depend upon a point of view, and will be arbitrary. A third interest attaches to the classification that the Committee set up, while a fourth attaches to the selection of items themselves. Last, the report seems of some interest as a document bearing upon the developing methodology of the investigation itself. It is therefore reproduced herewith.

LIST OF BOOKS AND ARTICLES OF IMPORTANCE IN SOCIOLOGICAL METHOD AND STANDPOINT[2]

NOTE.—The following titles are chosen from a large number of possible items. The books and periodical materials are organized under certain headings for convenience. The first section on systematic treatises are important largely for standpoint although they are also methodologically suggestive in some cases. The Committee has indicated by an asterisk (*) the titles which they believe are the ten most important.

Some of the materials cited overlap into other fields, such as economics, psychology, and anthropology. Methodologically these are important for sociology as well as for the particular fields with which they are concerned.

[1] The introductory paragraph is by the editor.

[2] Submitted by the Advisory Committee from the American Sociological Society: Kimball Young (chairman), William F. Ogburn, and Robert E. Park.

A. SYSTEMATIC TREATISES

1. BOAS, F. *The Mind of Primitive Man.*

While this book gives rather the standpoint than the actual methodology of Boas and his school of historical ethnology, it is important as the one systematic treatise from this writer who has had such profound influence on both method and standpoint in the study of primitive social cultures. For a well-selected bibliography of his monographic writings consult Goldenweiser's chapter in *The History and Prospects of the Social Sciences,* ed. Harry Elmer Barnes, pp. 243–44 (footnote references).

2. *DURKHEIM, E. *De la division du travail social.*

Important in indicating the place which the division of social and economic functions has in regard to social solidarity and social processes.

3. GIDDINGS, F. H. *The Scientific Study of Human Society.*

Important in its emphasis, particularly, on the quantitative analysis of social data.

4. PARETO, V. *Traité de sociologie générale* (French ed.).

Presents a mechanistic, logical, systematic approach to social data which takes into account a group of measurable variables in the analysis of social phenomena.

5. SIMMEL, G. *Soziologie.*

Indicates a philosophical foundation of sociology as a science distinct in itself. Important in treatment of formal aspects of social processes.

6. SUMNER, W. G. *Folkways: A Study of the Sociological Importance of Usages, Manners, Customs, Mores and Morals.*

Shows the significance of cultural factors in sociological analysis. Contributes to comparative method.

B. HISTORY OF SOCIAL INSTITUTIONS

7. SOMBART, W. *Der moderne Kapitalismus.*

Analysis of historical background of capitalism with some social-psychological interpretations.

8. *WEBER, M. *Gesammelte Aufsätze zur Religionssoziologie.*

Represents Weber's method in the study of cultural materials with particular reference to sociological relativity.

9. WESTERMARCK, E. *The History of Human Marriage.*

Comparative method applied to an important institution.

C. CASE-STUDY METHODS: ECOLOGICAL AND SURVEY TYPES

10. *BURGESS, E. W. "The Growth of the City: An Introduction to a Research Project;" *Papers and Proceedings of the American Sociological Society,* XVIII (1923), 85–97.

Gives a statement of the study of the community from the angle of ecology and socio-economic expansion. References are given to various monographic studies underway in the concrete analysis of Chicago as a type example.

11. GALPIN, C. J. *Social Anatomy of a Rural Community: Research Bulletin of the Wisconsin Agricultural Experiment Station* (1916).

The first attempt to make a study of the functional groups in a rural community upon what is now called an ecological basis. A large number of studies have grown out of Galpin's beginning, both in the rural and in the urban field.

12. *HEALY, W., and BRONNER, A. F. *Judge Baker Foundation Case Studies,* Nos. 1–20.

Present a method of analysis of personality problems, with special reference to delinquency, projected upon group membership and certain community backgrounds.

13. PARK, R. E. *The Immigrant Press and Its Control.*

Study of the press as it relates to assimilation and accommodation of alien groups in American social life. Indicates an objective beginning in the analysis of organs of public opinion.

14. *SHAW, C. R. *The Jack-Roller: The Delinquent Boy's Own Story.*

Valuable as a case document, but especially so as revealing a method of objective checking-up from all sorts of sources on the autobiographical document. It contributes to method in showing a manner of correlating objective data—school records, intelligence measures, institutional records, etc.—with the person's conception of his rôle in society.

15. *THOMAS, W. I., and ZNANIECKI, F. *The Polish Peasant in Europe and America.*

Highly important both as to theoretical statement of methodology and standpoint and as to the concrete material presented.

D. STATISTICAL OR QUANTITATIVE METHODS

NOTE.—Placed as a separate category because these titles represent important methodological advances independent of the subject matter with which they deal.

16. BOAS, F. *Changes in Bodily Form of Descendants of Immigrants, Being a Partial Report on the Results of an Anthropological Investigation for the United States Immigration Commission: Senate Document* 208 (61st Congress, 2d session, 1910). *(Abstract of the Report on Changes in Bodily Form of Immigrants.* Washington, 1911).

Invaluable study of influence of change of environment on physical characteristics of individuals.

17. *EZEKIEL, MORDECAI. "A Method of Handling Curvilinear Correlation for Any Number of Variables," *Journal of the American Statistical Association* (N.S.), XIX, No. 148, 431–54.

Use of partial correlations when the interrelations are not to be described as linear.

18. GORING, C. *The English Convict.*

Valuable in showing use of statistics with proper reference to sampling of general population.

19. PEARSON, K. "Mathematical Contributions to the Theory of Evolution— Regression, Heredity and Panmixia," Philosophical Transactions of the Royal Society of London, A, CLXXXVII (1896), 253–318.

20. *SLAWSON, J. The Delinquent Boy.

Methodologically valuable in showing use of partial and multiple correlations in dealing with environmental and other factors in delinquency.

21. *THOMAS, D. S. The Social Aspects of the Business Cycle.

Presents the use of correlational methods in dealing with social data in reference to economic changes.

22. *WOODBURY, ROBERT MORSE. Causal Factors in Infant Mortality—a Statistical Study Based on Investigations in Eight Cities: U.S. Department of Labor, Children's Bureau Publication 142.

On correlation of factors affecting infant-mortality rates in the United States.

APPENDIX F

"GROWING POINTS" IN AGRICULTURAL ECONOMICS, AS APPEARING IN STUDIES ABSTRACTED FOR ANALYSIS BY PROFESSOR JOHN D. BLACK[1]

The Advisory Committee on Economic and Social Research in Agriculture of the Social Science Research Council made a thorough survey of the research within its field which was in progress in the United States.[2] The chairman of the Committee, Professor Black of Harvard University, was among the first persons asked to collaborate as analysts in the preparation of the present *Case Book*. In March, 1928, he submitted abstracts of thirteen proposed analyses of work which, in the aggregate, would portray the "growing points" of agricultural economics. He added, "Research in our field has taken on a lot of young wood in the last five years."

The first of Black's abstracts or synopses has been employed as the basis of analysis 45 above. The remainder, arbitrarily arranged and numbered, follow below. By isolating points for methodological examination, Professor Black shows the variety of technical considerations which are involved in a specialized field of inquiry.

No. 1

The Demand Side of the New York Milk Market. By HARRY A. Ross, Cornell University. Published as *Cornell Bull. 459* (May 31, 1927).

Sales of milk and cream in New York City from 1919 to 1924 are determined and variations are analyzed by districts in the metropolitan area, from year to year (trends if any), from season to season in the year, from day to day in the week and as influenced by holidays, and according to changes in temperature, in price, and other factors.

Points especially to be considered: (1) size and composition of sample needed for such a study, and for different sorts of variables examined; (2) methods of isolating the different variables; (3) significance of such analysis in relation to theoretical demand curves of economists; (4) the validity of such data as compared with that obtained from house-to-house canvasses.

This project should be included, partly because of its magnitude and

---

[1] Introductory paragraphs are by the editor.

[2] Published as *Research Method and Procedure in Agricultural Economics* in two mimeographed volumes (August, 1928). Pp. 468.

thoroughness in more superficial aspects, and partly because of its close connection with fundamental qualitative analysis.

Estimated length of methodological analysis: 2,000–2,500 words.

No. 2

Shifts in Farming in the Red River Valley. By B. F. ALVORD, University of Montana, and JOHN D. BLACK, Harvard University. Not entirely completed at time of this writing.

The objective of this study is to trace and measure the shifts that have taken place in four counties in the area since data have been available (principally since 1880), and then to account for the shifts by a quantitative analysis of the data. This has involved, first, collecting historical data on prices, production, expense factors, etc.; second, the developing of techniques of analysis suitable to such a problem; and third, the actual analysis and its interpretation. The study is an attempt at historical analysis in quantitative terms; choosing a problem, a period, and an area which lend themselves to such a trial.

The problems especially to be considered are the methodology of the analysis, and the inferences from the results.

Estimated length of analysis: 1,200 words.

No. 3

Geographical Delineation of Systems of Farming. By C. L. HOLMES and EDGAR HURD, Iowa State College. Study not entirely completed at time of this writing. (An alternative study is by F. F. ELLIOTT and J. W. TAPP, U.S. Department of Agriculture, Bureau of Agricultural Economics, and REX WILLARD, North Dakota Agricultural College, of systems of farming in North Dakota.)

The research problem here involved is essentially one of definition of systems of farming and of a way of determining from data of physical conditions and production the boundaries of a region that has geographic unity.

Estimated length of analysis: 1,000 words.

No. 4

Economic Aspects of Country Grain Elevator Organization. By HUTZEL METZGER, U.S. Department of Agriculture, Bureau of Agricultural Economics. Manuscript in process of publication at time of this writing.

Detailed organization and operation data from a survey of fifty country grain elevators in Minnesota are analyzed from the point of view of efficient organization and operation as measured principally by unit costs and net incomes of elevators.

Points especially to be considered: (1) methods of analyzing variations in costs as an exhibition of the law of variable proportions or diminishing returns. This calls for the handling of curvilinear relationships between variables; (2) methods of analyzing variations in net incomes in relation to the principles of size of the business unit.

This study is the most thoroughgoing analysis of its type thus far—a type of marketing organization study most commonly being made today. Marketing research has shifted at present from description of the marketing process to the explanation of variations in marketing efficiency, in which the efficiency of individual marketing units is figuring largely.

Estimated length of analysis: 1,500–2,000 words.

No. 5

Factors Affecting Progress of Settlers in the Cut-Over Region of the Great Lakes States. By L. C. GRAY, U.S. Department of Agriculture, Bureau of Agricultural Economics, and JOHN D. BLACK, Harvard University. In process of publication at time of this writing by the Bureau of Agricultural Economics.

This is a study of 1,891 survey records of settlers in the cut-over region of the Great Lakes states, the objective being to determine the rate of progress being made by these settlers and the circumstances producing variations in rates of progress between settlements and between individual settlers.

Points especially to be considered: (1) methods of sampling of a large area with widely diverse conditions; (2) measures of progress; (3) method of adjustment for different dates of settlement; (4) method of isolating the effect of a large number of influences, such as resources, farm and other occupational experience, nationality background, age, size of family, type of land, type of timber and clearing, conditions of purchase, aid and supervision by land company, improvements in advance of settlement, etc.; (5) accuracy of survey results.

Estimated length of analysis: 1,500 words.

No. 6

Factors Affecting the Price of Hogs. By G. C. HAAS and MORDECAI EZEKIEL, U.S. Department of Agriculture, Bureau of Agricultural Economics. *U.S. Department of Agriculture Bull. 1440.*

An analysis of available data relating to hog prices in the central markets of the United States with a view to isolating the factors affecting the same and determining their relative significance.

Points especially to be considered: (1) sampling and inference from time-series data; (2) separation of short-time movements from trends; (3) correlation with time-series data; (4) curve-fitting.

This is one of a considerable series of studies of prices of agricultural products that was begun with Dr. Holbrook Working's study of factors affecting the price of potatoes. They are important because on the one hand they represent a quantitative approach to the theory of price, and on the other hand they are laying the foundation for a better understanding of current price developments by operators in the market.

Estimated length of analysis: 2,500–3,000 words.

No. 7

Factors Affecting the Supply of Milk. By A. R. GANS and H. P. YOUNG, Vermont Agricultural College, and MORDECAI EZEKIEL, U. S. Department of Agriculture, Bureau of Agricultural Economics. Published as *Vermont Agricultural College Bull. 269.*

An analysis of the receipts of milk at a group of receiving stations in Vermont, with a view to discovering the effect of price of milk, price of feed, and other factors on the supply of milk.

Points especially to be considered: (1) measurement of lag; (2) separation of trends and short-time movements with lag present; (3) inference and sampling with such data.

It may prove advisable to substitute for the foregoing a similar study by F. F. Elliott of the United States Department of Agriculture, Bureau of Agricultural Economics, for hogs. It has the advantage of displaying a distinct cyclical movement.

This type of study represents another main line of development in the field of prices of agricultural products.

Estimated length of analysis: 2,000 words.

No. 8

Sampling Iowa Agriculture. By C. F. SARLE, U.S. Department of Agriculture, Bureau of Agricultural Economics. At the time of this writing not published, but being used as a basis for a plan for collecting data of current developments in production, prices, wages, rents, land values, etc.

The problem is to determine how large a proportion of the townships need to be surveyed each year in order to obtain a reasonably accurate statement of changes in conditions. This is important as relating to the problem of securing better source data for research in agricultural economics, and also as a problem in geographic sampling. A great deal of research in economics involves current observation of changes as a continuation of series already analyzed to date. The technique of collecting current data is therefore very important.

The problem involves empirical testing of the accuracy of different estimates of sampling for various crops of different degrees of erraticalness by checking the samples against actual state-census data of the same date. The results of such tests are compared with the conventional mathematical measures of sampling which assume pure chance in order to discover the usefulness of such tests with geographical data.

Estimated length of analysis: 1,200 words.

No. 9

How Minnesota Farm Families Spend Their Incomes. By CARL C. ZIMMERMAN, University of Minnesota. Published as *Minnesota Agricultural College Bull. 234.*

An analysis of the living and spending of 694 farm families in Minnesota. The initial objective is to describe accurately how Minnesota farm families actually live at present, and the final objective is to explain the variations in the content of living on Minnesota farms, and possibly to develop some generalizations concerning rural consumption.

Problems especially to be considered: (1) sampling; (2) measures of the content of living.

This study is highly significant because it represents a decided breaking-away from the usual method of attempting to measure content of living in a one-figure monetary expression called "cost of living."

Estimated length of analysis: 1,000 words.

No. 10

The Most Profitable System of Farming for an Area. By D. W. FORSTER and S. W. SAVILLE, North Carolina Agricultural College. Published as *North Carolina Agricultural College Bull. 1* ("Research Series").

The procedure in studies of the foregoing type is to assemble the data that determine net incomes; on the basis of these, to estimate the probable net incomes from a considerable number of possible combinations of products; and, finally, in a number of recent instances, to record in detail the operation of farms practicing the combinations promising to be most successful. This latter step is an approach toward the experimental method, especially in view of the fact that modifications of actual farming plans are likely to be necessary to obtain the exact combinations desired.

On the theoretical side, such projects represent application under actual conditions of the principle of comparative advantage.

Projects of this type are important as a departure from the method still commonly practiced of trying to isolate costs of different products and comparing them with selling prices to see which production should be expanded.

Estimated length of analysis: 1,500 words.

No. 11

Measuring Bias in Estimates from Reporters. By C. F. SARLE and OTHERS in the U.S. Department of Agriculture, Bureau of Agricultural Economics. Not published at time of this writing, but being used in connection with the administration of the Division of Crop and Livestock Estimates.

The problem is to make proper allowance for the bias in the reports of acreage and condition of crops. This bias arises partly from unavoidable selections among the reporters, and partly from overestimates or underestimates by those who report. It is proposed in this report to indicate briefly how the proper allowance is determined. This is important as throwing light upon technique for similar undertakings in other fields.

Increasing use will be made in research of reports of current development. Administration and research merge in many problems in the social sciences.

Estimated length of analysis: 800–1,000 words.

No. 12

The Effect of the Use of the Combine on Kansas Agriculture. By W. E. GRIMES, Kansas State Agricultural College, and RUSSEL KIFER, U.S. Department of Agriculture, Bureau of Agricultural Economics. Manuscript in process of publication at time of this writing.

The principal research problem here involved is a method of analyzing production data for an enterprise as a whole so as to estimate the long-run effect on farming in the area of a new development. Such projects are important as furnishing a basis for forecasting future developments. Will combines come into increasing use?

Estimated length of analysis: 600 words.

APPENDIX G

CONTRIBUTIONS OF PUBLIC ADMINISTRATION TO POLITICAL SCIENCE[1]

The investigators' success in procuring desired analyses varied among the several social sciences.[2] Political science provides an illustration of inadequate representation in the *Case Book,* resulting from a series of disappointments and failures in the negotiations with prospective analysts. Some of the neglected interests within this field are suggested by the following titles, recommended by the Advisory Committee of the American Political Science Association: Arthur N. Holcombe, *The Political Parties of Today;* Stuart A. Rice, *Farmers and Workers in American Politics;* Lent D. Upson, *The Government of Cincinnati and Hamilton County;* James Arthur Salter, *Allied Shipping Control: An Experiment in International Administration;* Thomas Reed Powell, "Indirect Encroachments on Federal Authority by the Taxing Power of the State"; A. Esmein, *Eléments de droit constitutionnel.*

In the field of law, similarly, it was hoped that three distinct methodological approaches might receive attention: (1) traditional legal method —represented at its best, perhaps, by the *Restatements* of the American Law Institute; (2) the newer legal viewpoint, which takes account of the actual social and cultural bases of judicial decisions, and which is most closely associated in the public mind with the names of Roscoe Pound and Thomas Reed Powell; (3) the legal method which queries whether or not there exists a substratum of natural law to which appeal can be made by judicial bodies in the adjudication of international disputes.[3] Only the third of these three interests receives specific attention in this *Case Book,*[4] the first and second having been reluctantly abandoned after the failure of persistent efforts to give them adequate consideration.

Within the general area of political and legal research, the absence from the *Case Book* of studies involving questions of public administration is especially regrettable. In consequence, it seems of value to append

[1] Introductory paragraphs were written by the editor.

[2] Cf. Appendix H; also Appendix A, n. 5.

[3] Professor John Dickinson, now of the University of Pennsylvania Law School, assisted the investigators in arriving at this threefold formulation of viewpoints and problems in the legal field.

[4] In analysis 6.

a statement[5] by Dr. Luther Gulick, director of the Bureau of Municipal Research, National Institute of Public Administration, New York, which suggests some of the contributions of public administration to political science. This statement follows:

"Contributions to American political science" in the fields of public administration have not been made by monographs, books, or surveys. They have been made by men who were at work with practical problems. Some of these have been recorded in written form, usually by observers rather than by those who have themselves made the contributions. In this regard, public administration is in a somewhat different position than are the exact sciences where many of the contributions are the result of analysis, experimentation, and discoveries, first made public through the written reports of those who have made the discoveries.

. . . . From my limited acquaintance with the field, it seems to me that there are a number of distinct advances which have been made, such as:

1. *The efficiency movement in government.*—This includes the reorganization of municipal and state governmental agencies to establish definite responsibility and authority and the introduction of budget systems, central purchasing, standardization and classification of salaries, double entry accounting, and the whole modern philosophy of control over expenditures, personnel, and material.

2. *The governmental research movement.*—With the increasing complexity of government and the introduction of technology in all branches of administration, independent citizen knowledge (and therefore control) of government can be maintained apparently only through the establishment of bureaus of government research. The research idea is thus a significant aid if not an indispensable adjunct of intelligent democracy.

3. *The governmental survey.*—The governmental survey has made a distinct contribution to political science because it involves an unbiased, scientific, and comprehensive examination of government administration and the interrelated environmental factors, made by men of experience who endeavor to test the factors of a given situation by established criteria.

Perhaps I should mention as distinct contributions to American political science the development of home rule for cities, of free public education, the rise of systems of state aid, and even such technical matters as traffic control and the technique of city planning and zoning, though these are more or less implicit in the matters to which I have already referred.

And now where shall we turn for the monographs which embody these contributions? Obviously the monographs are many and scattered, and represent written reflections rather than unique contributions in themselves. Undoubtedly President Taft's Efficiency and Economy Commission, with its many reports which were prepared under the direction of Dr. Frederick A. Cleve-

[5] Excerpted from a letter to Professor Harold D. Lasswell, dated May 14, 1928.

land, who was at that time director of this organization, form the most spectacular written material in the government efficiency field, though the early publications of the New York Bureau of Municipal Research and the studies published by the efficiency and economy commissions, as in Chicago and Massachusetts, deserve mention as well.

The governmental research movement was founded in 1906–1912 here in New York City by those who organized and directed the first Bureau of Municipal Research. There is no single document which was of particular influence in this. The history of this organization is recorded in numerous publications, the most recent of which are *The National Institute of Public Administration*, Little, Ives and Company, 1928, and *Twenty Years of Government Research*, Governmental Research Association, 1927.

Among governmental surveys, the best are naturally not the earliest; though it may perhaps be said that the earlier surveys made a greater contribution, as they were pioneer projects. Perhaps the more significant surveys are those of Newark, New Jersey (New York Bureau of Municipal Research, 1919); of the Counties of New York State (Legislative Committee on Taxation and Retrenchment, 1923); of Tokyo (Charles A. Beard, 1923); of New York State (New York Constitutional Convention, 1915); the New York City Government (Henry Bruere, 1913); the annual reports of the New York Legislative Committee on Taxation and Retrenchment (1920–1928); the Cleveland Survey of Criminal Justice (1922); the annual reports of the Boston Finance Commission.

APPENDIX H

CLASSIFICATION OF ANALYSES BY DISCIPLINES

By THE EDITOR

The personnel of social science is divided among a number of subdivisions or disciplines known collectively as *the social sciences*. As previously noted,[1] the organization of personnel for the creation of the *Case Book* was inevitably based upon these existing subdivisions, and for a time it was supposed that they would provide the classificatory headings for the analyses themselves.

Apart from other considerations, which were determinative, a classification of analyses by disciplines was found to be as difficult and as arbitrary as any other form of classification. The difficulties began to appear when contributions were recommended for analysis by the advisory committees from the respective social science organizations. Duplications among these recommendations were numerous. It became apparent that the professional labels which social scientists adopt for academic purposes have no necessary relationship to the subject matter and the significance of their work.

The list of "sociological" contributions presented in Appendix D, for example, includes contributions by Boas, an anthropologist; Sombart, an economic historian; Ezekiel, an agricultural economist; and Pearson, a biometrician. Several of these scholars are also statisticians. The *Judge Baker Foundation Case Studies* and Slawson's *The Delinquent Boy* were separately recommended both as sociology and as social psychology. The British studies of Rowntree and Booth respecting standards of living, often referred to as sociological, were included among the suggestions of the Advisory Committee of the American Economic Association. Rice's *Farmers and Workers in American Politics*, a Ph.D. dissertation in sociology, was among the studies recommended for analysis by the Advisory Committee of the American Political Science Association. All of the suggestions of the Advisory Committee of the American Statistical Association might have been allocated to one or another, or to more than one, of the other disciplines. Such a paper as that by Dr. Truesdell (analysis 11), interpreting the methods employed by the United States Census Bureau in taking the federal census of population, has significance for

[1] Appendix A. Cf. also Appendix G.

nearly all of the special social sciences, and does not fall clearly within the jurisdiction of any one of them.

In consequence of this tendency for subjects, authors, analysts, and analyses to have relationships with two or more disciplines, the following table makes no attempt to avoid overlapping among these. Its aim is to bring together by title, and thus facilitate comparison, all of the analyses which may have special interest for each group of teaching or research specialists. A majority of the analyses appear in more than one grouping.

Once more it may be noted that the inclusion or exclusion of any paper from a particular category has been wholly a matter of editorial judgment, entirely arbitrary, and therefore subject to all of the possibilities of criticism which beset individual opinions.

ANTHROPOLOGY

8. "The Sociological Methods of William Graham Sumner, and of William I. Thomas and Florian Znaniecki." By ROBERT E. PARK, University of Chicago.

17. "The Culture-Area and Age-Area Concepts of Clark Wissler." By A. L. KROEBER, University of California.

18. "Hugo Obermaier's Reconstruction of Sequences among Prehistoric Cultures in the Old World." By ROBERT H. LOWIE, University of California.

19. "N. C. Nelson's Stratigraphic Technique in the Reconstruction of Prehistoric Sequences in Southwestern America." By LESLIE SPIER, University of Washington.

21. "The Concept of Phonetic Law as Tested in Primitive Languages by Leonard Bloomfield." By EDWARD SAPIR, University of Chicago.

22. "The Prediction of Cultural Change: A Problem Illustrated in Studies by F. Stuart Chapin and A. L. Kroeber." By FLOYD H. ALLPORT and DALE A. HARTMAN, Syracuse University.

31. "Historical Interrelation of Culture Traits: Franz Boas' Study of Tsimshian Mythology." By LESLIE SPIER, University of Washington.

34. "A Hypothesis Rooted in the Preconceptions of a Single Civilization Tested by Bronislaw Malinowski." By HAROLD D. LASSWELL, University of Chicago.

42. "The Concept of Race in the Light of Franz Boas' Studies of Head-Forms among Immigrants." By FAY-COOPER COLE, University of Chicago.

ECONOMICS

2. "Relation of Utility Theory to Economic Method in the Work of William Stanley Jevons and Others." By FRANK KNIGHT, University of Chicago.

12. "A Device for Measuring the Size of Families, Invented by Edgar Sydenstricker and W. I. King." By WILLIAM F. OGBURN, University of Chicago.

14. "A Detail of Regional Geography: Objectives and Methods in Robert

S. Platt's Study of the Ellison Bay Community." By K. C. McMurry, University of Michigan.

15. "The Influence of Geology and Physiography upon the Industry, Commerce, and Life of a People, as Described by Carl Ortwin Sauer and Others." By V. C. Finch, University of Wisconsin.

16. "The California Raisin Industry: C. C. Colby's Study in Geographic Interpretation." By Raoul Blanchard, Université de Grenoble and Harvard University.

23. "The Section and the Frontier in American History: The Methodological Concepts of Frederick Jackson Turner." By Merle E. Curti, Smith College.

24. "The Work of Henri Pirenne and Georg von Below with Respect to the Origin of the Medieval Town." By Carl Stephenson, Cornell University.

35. "The Psychological Approach in Economics, Represented in the Work of J. A. Hobson." By Z. Clark Dickinson, University of Michigan.

41. "Mathematical Treatment by Dorothy Swaine Thomas of Social Data Arranged in Time Series." By Hubert R. Kemp, University of Toronto.

44. "The Inductive Testing of an Economic Deduction: A Method Illustrated by Analyses of Marginal Producers and Representative Firms, by Alfred Marshall, Horace Secrist, and Kemper Simpson." By Raymond T. Bye, University of Pennsylvania.

45. "Statistical Measurements of the Operation of the Law of Diminishing Returns by Mordecai Ezekiel and Others." By John D. Black, Harvard University.

46. "Henry L. Moore's Contribution to the Statistical Law of Demand." By Henry Schultz, University of Chicago.

47. "Wesley C. Mitchell's Contribution to the Theory of Business Cycles." By John Maurice Clark, Columbia University.

48. "Experimental Determinations by S. Wyatt and J. A. Fraser of the Effects of Rest Pauses upon Repetitive Work." By Stuart A. Rice, University of Pennsylvania.

HISTORY

1. "The Method of Auguste Comte: Subordination of Imagination to Observation in the Social Sciences." By McQuilkin deGrange, Dartmouth College.

3. "The Possibility of a Science of Politics: With Special Attention to Methods Suggested by William B. Munro and George E. G. Catlin." By W. Y. Elliott, Harvard University.

17. "The Culture-Area and Age-Area Concepts of Clark Wissler." By A. L. Kroeber, University of California.

18. "Hugo Obermaier's Reconstruction of Sequences among Prehistoric Cultures in the Old World." By Robert H. Lowie, University of California.

19. "N. C. Nelson's Stratigraphic Technique in the Reconstruction of Prehistoric Sequences in Southwestern America." By LESLIE SPIER, University of Washington.

20. "The Concept of Progress and Its Influence on History as Developed by J. B. Bury." By SYDNEY B. FAY, Harvard University.

21. "The Concept of Phonetic Law as Tested in Primitive Languages by Leonard Bloomfield." By EDWARD SAPIR, University of Chicago.

22. "The Prediction of Cultural Change: A Problem Illustrated in Studies by F. Stuart Chapin and A. L. Kroeber." By FLOYD H. ALLPORT and DALE A. HARTMAN, Syracuse University.

23. "The Section and the Frontier in American History: The Methodological Concepts of Frederick Jackson Turner." By MERLE E. CURTI, Smith College.

24. "The Work of Henri Pirenne and Georg von Below with Respect to the Origin of the Medieval Town." By CARL STEPHENSON, Cornell University.

25. "History and Nationalism as Portrayed by Sidney B. Fay." By WILLIAM L. LANGER, Harvard University.

26. "The Historical Method of Jules Michelet." By HENRY E. BOURNE, Western Reserve University.

27. "The Historical Method of Ernest Renan." By JEAN POMMIER, Université de Strasbourg.

28. "Spiritual Values in the Work of Ernst Troeltsch." By FRANCIS A. CHRISTIE, Lowell, Mass.

29. "Voltaire, Historian of Civilization and Exponent of Rationalism." By FERDINAND SCHEVILL, University of Chicago.

30. "What Are Historians Trying to Do?" By HENRI PIRENNE, Commission Royale d'Histoire, Académie Royale de Belgique.

31. "Historical Interrelation of Culture Traits: Franz Boas' Study of Tsimshian Mythology." By LESLIE SPIER, University of Washington.

32. "The Development of Rural Attitudes: A Semi-intuitive Inquiry by James Mickel Williams." By STUART A. RICE, University of Pennsylvania.

HUMAN GEOGRAPHY

11. "Methods Involved in the Federal Census of Population." By LEON E. TRUESDELL, Chief Statistician for Population, United States Bureau of the Census.

14. "A Detail of Regional Geography: Objectives and Methods in Robert S. Platt's Study of the Ellison Bay Community." By K. C. McMURRY, University of Michigan.

15. "The Influence of Geology and Physiography upon the Industry, Commerce, and Life of a People, as Described by Carl Ortwin Sauer and Others." By V. C. FINCH, University of Wisconsin.

16. "The California Raisin Industry: C. C. Colby's Study in Geographic Interpretation." By RAOUL BLANCHARD, Université de Grenoble and Harvard University.

17. "The Culture-Area and Age-Area Concepts of Clark Wissler." By A. L. KROEBER, University of California.

23. "The Section and the Frontier in American History: The Methodological Concepts of Frederick Jackson Turner." By MERLE E. CURTI, Smith College.

26. "The Historical Method of Jules Michelet." By HENRY E. BOURNE, Western Reserve University.

32. "The Development of Rural Attitudes: A Semi-intuitive Inquiry by James Mickel Williams." By STUART A. RICE, University of Pennsylvania.

POLITICS AND LAW[2]

3. "The Possibility of a Science of Politics: With Special Attention to Methods Suggested by William B. Munro and George E. G. Catlin." By W. Y. ELLIOTT, Harvard University.

4. "Mary Richmond's Formulation of a New Science." By PHILIP KLEIN, New York School of Social Work.

6. "Problems of Method in International Law: Alfred Verdross' Concept of the Unity of the Legal Order on the Basis of the International Constitution." By JOHANNES MATTERN, The Johns Hopkins University.

7. "The Sociological Methods of Vilfredo Pareto." By MAX SYLVIUS HANDMAN, University of Minnesota.

11. "Methods Involved in the Federal Census of Population." By LEON E. TRUESDELL, Chief Statistician for Population, United States Bureau of the Census.

23. "The Section and the Frontier in American History: The Methodological Concepts of Frederick Jackson Turner." By MERLE E. CURTI, Smith College.

24. "The Work of Henri Pirenne and Georg von Below with Respect to the Origin of the Medieval Town." By CARL STEPHENSON, Cornell University.

25. "History and Nationalism as Portrayed by Sidney B. Fay." By WILLIAM L. LANGER, Harvard University.

33. "The Comparative Method of James Bryce." By HAROLD D. LASSWELL, University of Chicago.

37. "Frederic M. Thrasher's Study of Gangs." By KIMBALL YOUNG, University of Wisconsin.

38. "The Missouri Crime Survey." By E. H. SUTHERLAND, University of Minnesota.

43. "Behavior Alternatives as Statistical Data in Studies by William F. Og-

[2] Cf. Appendix G.

burn and Ernest W. Burgess." By STUART A. RICE, University of Pennsylvania.

50. "Harold F. Gosnell's Experiments in the Stimulation of Voting." By GEORGE E. G. CATLIN, Cornell University.

PSYCHOLOGY[3]

5. "Structural Psychology and the Psychology of *Gestalt:* The Methods of E. B. Titchener Compared with those of K. Koffka, W. Köhler, and M. Wertheimer." By R. M. OGDEN, Cornell University.

9. "Typological Method: E. Kretschmer's Study of Physique and Character." By HEINRICH KLÜVER, Institute for Juvenile Research, Chicago.

10. "William McDougall's Methodological Concept of Instinct." By CALVIN P. STONE, Institute for Juvenile Research, Chicago.

13. "Testing and Scaling Methods: E. L. Thorndike's Measurements of Handwriting." By JOSEPH PETERSON, Jesup Psychological Laboratory, George Peabody College.

34. "A Hypothesis Rooted in the Preconceptions of a Single Civilization Tested by Bronislaw Malinowski." By HAROLD D. LASSWELL, University of Chicago.

35. "The Psychological Approach in Economics, Represented in the Work of J. A. Hobson." By Z. CLARK DICKINSON, University of Michigan.

36. "Social Forces in Personal-Behavior Sequences Studied by the Judge Baker Foundation." By FLOYD N. HOUSE, University of Virginia.

39. "Interrelations of Statistical and Case Methods: Studies of Young Delinquents by John Slawson and Cyril Burt." By Robert S. WOODWORTH, Columbia University.

48. "Experimental Determinations by S. Wyatt and J. A. Fraser of the Effects of Rest Pauses upon Repetitive Work." By STUART A. RICE, University of Pennsylvania.

49. "Experimental Determination by Floyd H. Allport of Group Influences upon Mental Activity." By L. L. THURSTONE, University of Chicago.

51. "The Quantitative Measurement of Higher Mental Processes in the Pioneer Studies of H. Ebbinghaus." By J. E. COOVER, Stanford University.

52. "The Experimental Study of Attitude, Meaning, and the Processes Antecedent to Action, by N. Ach and Others in the Würzburg Laboratory." By FRANKLIN FEARING, Northwestern University.

SOCIAL PSYCHOLOGY

8. "The Sociological Methods of William Graham Sumner, and of William I. Thomas and Florian Znaniecki." By ROBERT E. PARK, University of Chicago.

[3] Cf. Appendix C.

10. "William McDougall's Methodological Concept of Instinct." By CALVIN P. STONE, Institute for Juvenile Research, Chicago.

17. "The Culture-Area and Age-Area Concepts of Clark Wissler." By A. L. KROEBER, University of California.

21. "The Concept of Phonetic Law as Tested in Primitive Languages by Leonard Bloomfield." By EDWARD SAPIR, University of Chicago.

22. "The Prediction of Cultural Change: A Problem Illustrated in Studies by F. Stuart Chapin and A. L. Kroeber." By FLOYD H. ALLPORT and DALE A. HARTMAN, Syracuse University.

32. "The Development of Rural Attitudes: A Semi-intuitive Inquiry by James Mickel Williams." By STUART A. RICE, University of Pennsylvania.

34. "A Hypothesis Rooted in the Preconceptions of a Single Civilization Tested by Bronislaw Malinowski." By HAROLD D. LASSWELL, University of Chicago.

35. "The Psychological Approach in Economics, Represented in the Work of J. A. Hobson." By Z. CLARK DICKINSON, University of Michigan.

36. "Social Forces in Personal-Behavior Sequences Studied by the Judge Baker Foundation." By FLOYD N. HOUSE, University of Virginia.

37. "Frederic M. Thrasher's Study of Gangs." By KIMBALL YOUNG, University of Wisconsin.

39. "Interrelations of Statistical and Case Methods: Studies of Young Delinquents by John Slawson and Cyril Burt." By ROBERT S. WOODWORTH, Columbia University.

40. "Hypotheses and Verifications in Clifford R. Shaw's Studies of Juvenile Delinquency." By STUART A. RICE, University of Pennsylvania.

43. "Behavior Alternatives as Statistical Data in Studies by William F. Ogburn and Ernest W. Burgess." By STUART A. RICE, University of Pennsylvania.

48. "Experimental Determinations by S. Wyatt and J. A. Fraser of the Effects of Rest Pauses upon Repetitive Work." By STUART A. RICE, University of Pennsylvania.

49. "Experimental Determination by Floyd H. Allport of Group Influences upon Mental Activity." By L. L. THURSTONE, University of Chicago.

52. "The Experimental Study of Attitude, Meaning, and the Processes Antecedent to Action, by N. Ach and Others in the Würzburg Laboratory." By FRANKLIN FEARING, Northwestern University.

SOCIOLOGY

1. "The Method of Auguste Comte: Subordination of Imagination to Observation in the Social Sciences." By McQUILKIN DEGRANGE, Dartmouth College.

4. "Mary Richmond's Formulation of a New Science." By PHILIP KLEIN, New York School of Social Work.

7. "The Sociological Methods of Vilfredo Pareto." By MAX SYLVIUS HANDMAN, University of Minnesota.

8. "The Sociological Methods of William Graham Sumner, and of William I. Thomas and Florian Znaniecki." By ROBERT E. PARK, University of Chicago.

11. "Methods Involved in the Federal Census of Population." By LEON E. TRUESDELL, Chief Statistician for Population, United States Bureau of the Census.

12. "A Device for Measuring the Size of Families, Invented by Edgar Sydenstricker and W. I. King." By WILLIAM F. OGBURN, University of Chicago.

14. "A Detail of Regional Geography: Objectives and Methods in Robert S. Platt's Study of the Ellison Bay Community." By K. C. McMURRY, University of Michigan.

15. "The Influence of Geology and Physiography upon the Industry, Commerce, and Life of a People, as Described by Carl Ortwin Sauer and Others." By V. C. FINCH, University of Wisconsin.

16. "The California Raisin Industry: C. C. Colby's Study in Geographic Interpretation." By RAOUL BLANCHARD, Université de Grenoble and Harvard University.

17. "The Culture-Area and Age-Area Concepts of Clark Wissler." By A. L. KROEBER, University of California.

20. "The Concept of Progress and Its Influence on History as Developed by J. B. Bury." By SIDNEY B. FAY, Harvard University.

22. "The Prediction of Cultural Change: A Problem Illustrated in Studies by F. Stuart Chapin and A. L. Kroeber." By FLOYD H. ALLPORT and DALE A. HARTMAN, Syracuse University.

31. "Historical Interrelation of Culture Traits: Franz Boas' Study of Tsimshian Mythology." By LESLIE SPIER, University of Washington.

32. "The Development of Rural Attitudes: A Semi-intuitive Inquiry by James Mickel Williams." By STUART A. RICE, University of Pennsylvania.

36. "Social Forces in Personal-Behavior Sequences Studied by the Judge Baker Foundation." By FLOYD N. HOUSE, University of Virginia.

37. "Frederic M. Thrasher's Study of Gangs." By KIMBALL YOUNG, University of Wisconsin.

38. "The Missouri Crime Survey." By E. H. SUTHERLAND, University of Minnesota.

39. "Interrelations of Statistical and Case Methods: Studies of Young Delinquents by John Slawson and Cyril Burt." By ROBERT S. WOODWORTH, Columbia University.

40. "Hypotheses and Verifications in Clifford R. Shaw's Studies of Juvenile Delinquency." By STUART A. RICE, University of Pennsylvania.

41. "Mathematical Treatment by Dorothy Swaine Thomas of Social Data Arranged in Time Series." By HUBERT R. KEMP, University of Toronto.

42. "The Concept of Race in the Light of Franz Boas' Studies of Head-Forms among Immigrants." By FAY-COOPER COLE, University of Chicago.

43. "Behavior Alternatives as Statistical Data in Studies by William F. Ogburn and Ernest W. Burgess." By STUART A. RICE, University of Pennsylvania.
48. "Experimental Determinations by S. Wyatt and J. A. Fraser of the Effects of Rest Pauses upon Repetitive Work." By STUART A. RICE, University of Pennsylvania.
49. "Experimental Determination by Floyd H. Allport of Group Influences upon Mental Activity." By L. L. THURSTONE, University of Chicago.

STATISTICS

11. "Methods Involved in the Federal Census of Population." By LEON E. TRUESDELL, Chief Statistician for Population, United States Bureau of the Census.
12. "A Device for Measuring the Size of Families, Invented by Edgar Sydenstricker and W. I. King." By WILLIAM F. OGBURN, University of Chicago.
13. "Testing and Scaling Methods: E. L. Thorndike's Measurements of Handwriting." By JOSEPH PETERSON, Jesup Psychological Laboratory, George Peabody College.
22. "The Prediction of Cultural Change: A Problem Illustrated in Studies by F. Stuart Chapin and A. L. Kroeber." By FLOYD H. ALLPORT and DALE A. HARTMAN, Syracuse University.
39. "Interrelations of Statistical and Case Methods: Studies of Young Delinquents by John Slawson and Cyril Burt." By ROBERT S. WOODWORTH, Columbia University.
40. "Hypotheses and Verifications in Clifford R. Shaw's Studies of Juvenile Delinquency." By STUART A. RICE, University of Pennsylvania.
41. "Mathematical Treatment by Dorothy Swaine Thomas of Social Data Arranged in Time Series." By HUBERT R. KEMP, University of Toronto.
43. "Behavior Alternatives as Statistical Data in Studies by William F. Ogburn and Ernest W. Burgess." By STUART A. RICE, University of Pennsylvania.
44. "The Inductive Testing of an Economic Deduction: A Method Illustrated by Analyses of Marginal Producers and Representative Firms, by Alfred Marshall, Horace Secrist, and Kemper Simpson." By RAYMOND T. BYE, University of Pennsylvania.
45. "Statistical Measurements of the Operation of the Law of Diminishing Returns by Mordecai Ezekiel and Others." By JOHN D. BLACK, Harvard University.
46. "Henry L. Moore's Contribution to the Statistical Law of Demand." By HENRY SCHULTZ, University of Chicago.
47. "Wesley C. Mitchell's Contribution to the Theory of Business Cycles." By JOHN MAURICE CLARK, Columbia University.
51. "The Quantitative Measurement of Higher Mental Processes in the Pioneer Studies of H. Ebbinghaus." By J. E. COOVER, Stanford University.

INDEX OF ANALYSTS

INDEX OF PRINCIPAL AUTHORS DISCUSSED[1]

[1] This Index includes only authors whose work receives extensive attention in the analyses. Less extended citations, and exact page references, are contained in the General Index. Page references here are to analyses as a whole.

GENERAL INDEX[1]

Abilities: Galton's curve of, 221; heredity, environment, and, 365; native, in mental tests, 498

Abraham, J., 455

Abstraction: economics as, 82 f.; in science, 151 f.; in words, 9

Ach, N., 711 n., 715 ff.

Acheulean culture: Chellean and, 268; Chinese, 271; definition of, 273; origin of, in Europe, 266 ff.

Achievement: conditioning factors of, 7; cultural phenomena as indices of, 334; in education, scales measuring, 226

Act psychology: basis of, 116; experience in, 112 f.; *Gestalt* psychology and, 113; Titchener on, 113

Action: Ach's study of processes antecedent to, 715 ff.; conditions determining, 715, 720, 722; control of, 144; energy for, 191, 716; impulsive, 716; as index of attitude, 726; instinctive, 186, 190; introspective method in study of, 720 ff.; non-logical, 139 ff.; overt aspects of, 716 f.; patterns of, in gangs, 514 f.; "physiological states" of, 716; and reaction, 407; reaction technique in study of, 717 f., 720 ff.; stimulus-response in, 716; tropistic theory of, 715 f.; volitional, 716, 724 f. *See also* Behavior, Instincts, Psychology, Volition

Activity: areal, in regional geography, 237; and intellect, 50 n., 52; productive, division of, 494; reality of,

63 n.; stages of, 23 n. *See also* Action, Mental activity

Acts: complex, "instinctive" for, 191; functions of, 487; motor side of, 716; total, in experimental psychology, 716

Adams, Brooks, 86

Adams, Henry, 353

Adams, Herbert B., 353

Adams, John, 85 n.

Adler, A., 483

Administration: of criminal justice (*see* Crime Survey, of Missouri); political, and policy, 77; public contribution of, to political science, 759 ff.; social, of routine industries, 495. *See also* Political science

Admiration, McDougall on, 193

Adolescence, and behavior, 507, 515

Adrian, 408

Aesthetics, in development of mankind, 55 f.

Age, classification of, in census, 204 f. *See also* Mental age, Modern age

Age-area concept: in anthropology, 248 f.; applicability of, 248, 263 f.; appraisal of, 259 ff.; basis of, 263; biological method and, 263; coinage of, 248; culture-area concept and, 248; Dixon on, 257 f.; in Europe, 256; as historical concept, 259 f.; Kroeber's use of, 257; as method of inference, 248, 263; Müller's use of, 249; in natural history and biological sciences, 248, 282; Ratzel's use of, 248 f.; Wallis on, 256; Wissler's de-

[1] In projecting this *Case Book*, the Committee on Scientific Method hoped that a second, supplementary volume would *synthesize* the individual analyses with respect to their methodological implications (cf. Foreword, p. vi, and Appendix A). But since no specific plans for the second volume were formulated, the editor has sought to aid the user of the *Case Book* in making his own syntheses. To this end, particular efforts have been made to prepare an exhaustive and informative General Index. It is intended, when used in conjunction with the Table of Contents, the Introduction, the appendixes, and the special indexes preceding, to provide a tool whereby related methodological usages and ideas may be easily brought together and compared. The burden of its preparation fell upon Miss Rose Epstein, competently assisted, in the later stages, by Mrs. Bernece Shalloo.

fist-hatchet of, 270; origin of, in Europe, 266 ff.

Chemical science, physical and, 43 f.

Chemistry: behavior in, 309; method of building, 678; nomenclature in, 29

Child, C. M., 559

Child-study institutes, 501

Children: in measurement of food costs, 210; parents and, 459, 584

China, 131, 271, 417, 429, 440

Chinese writing, 258

Chipewyan language: as member of Athabaskan, 302 ff.; prediction of Hupa from, 304 f.

Chirol, 390

Choice, psychology of, 492

Chouan, Jean, 401

Christ, 411 ff., 419

Christianity, 143; asceticism in, 419; "brotherhoods" in, 413; Catholic church in, 419; censorship by, 456; church types in, 422; civilization and, 413, 418 ff., 423, 433, 442; classes first adopting, 413; clergy in, 413; dualistic tendencies in, 423; during eighteenth century, 421; during Middle Ages, 420 f.; essence of, 418 ff.; ethics of, 415, 420; in evolution of religion, 416; fusion of, with world, 419; group expressions of, 420 f.; Hildebrandine struggle in, 420; humanity in, 422; as individual totality, 423; individualism in, 418 f.; Judaism and, 406, 413; legalism and grace in, 421; Lutheranism and Calvinism in, 421 f.; malleability of, 413; Michelet on, 399; in modern society, 423; modernism in, 422; Montanist sect and mystical gnosticism in, 419; origin of, 407 f., 413, 418; as product of Jesus and Paul, 412, 419; reality of, 415; Reformation in, 422; Renan on, 405 ff.; sin in, 419; sociological forms in, 418 f.; spiritual life in, 419; stoic and platonic thought in, 419 f.; theological and religious factors in, 415; tolerance in, 422; trinitarian dogma in, 419; Troeltsch on, 423; Voltaire on, 427. See also Church

Chronology: cooking wares in, 276; establishment of, 282 f.; of New World, 255; of Pleistocene Europe, 266 ff.; of prehistoric cultures, 269; in South-

western America, 275 ff. See also Archaeology, Stratigraphic technique

Church, 87 f.; in community, 461; in French history, 399; Hildebrandine struggle for, 420; as institution of salvation, 421; institutionalized behavior in, 87; property of, taken by state, 400; as serving royal power, 420; unity of, 419; in world-history, 427. See also Christianity

Circular insanity, 185

Circulation of the élites, 147

Citizenship: in democracies, 475 f.; diversity of, 74

City: in Dark Age, 372; German Burg and, 374; gradients in, 559; political organization of, 524; Roman, origin of, 372; rural thought as influencing, 602 f.; and urban area, 602 n. See also Medieval town, Urban community

City-manager plan, 319 ff.

Civic equality, in scientific politics, 73

Civilization: description of, 429; differentiation in, 433; European, Spengler on, 75; family relations in, 476; indispensable elements in, 413; intelligence in, 432; man and, 294, 433; order in, 336 ff.; progress in, 287, 295; Roman, 76; Rousseau on, 295; social organization and, 24, 33 f., 418 f.; Voltaire on, 424 ff. See also Culture, History, Man, Society, etc.

Clabaugh, Hinton G., 593 n.

Clark, J. B., 59, 747

Clark, John Maurice, 7 n., 549 n.

Class opinions, indices of, 589. See also Attitudes, Opinion, Public opinion

Classes. See Social classes

Classification: of acts, 486; of areas of characteristic food, 251 f.; as based upon attributes, 606; of behavior, 586 ff.; Comte's law of, 42 f.; of cultures, 251, 271; of functions of experience, 113; of handwriting, 222 ff.; of historical documents, 430; of instincts and emotions, 191 ff.; in measurement of families, 215; mental, 221 f.; of Pareto's "derivations" and "residues," 140 ff., 143 f., 150 f.; of paroled men, 590 f., 606; by physical anthropologist, determining race, 582; in political science, 79; of population, 202 ff.; of pottery wares, 278 f.; pre-

Psychiatry, 56 n., 176. *See also* Personality, Psychoses, Types, etc.

Psychoanalysis: anthropological test of hypothesis of, 480 ff.; "complex" in, 482 f.; functional concept and, 487 f.; Jones on Malinowski respecting, 484 f.; Malinowski on Freudian theory of, 482 ff., 488; of myths, 455; personal-history documents in, 483 ff.; as product of European civilization, 483. *See also* Types

Psychological economics: definition of, 489; Hobson's contribution to, 489 ff., 495 ff., 500 f.; problems in, 489 ff.; utilitarianism in, 500

Psychological history: as possibility, 9 n.; Williams' study of rural attitudes as, 459 ff.

Psychology: analyses classified by subject of, 767; of attitude, 715 ff.; Austrian school of, 113; behaviorism and, 64; concepts, scope, and status of, 55, 64, 70, 110 f., 115, 149, 176, 220, 310 f., 489, 743 f., 745 ff.; Cousin's method in, 405; culture and, 349; group influences in, 694 ff.; of higher thought processes, 707 ff., 715 ff.; history and, 355, 435 f.; of judgment, 719; of learning process, 333; of meaning, 715 ff.; of myths, 449 ff.; 455 ff.; physiological, method in, 73 f.; stimulus-response formula in, 716, 745; of work, 497. *See also* Act psychology, Behavior, Comparative psychology, Experience, Existential psychology, *Gestalt* psychology, Habits, Instincts, Mental activity, Psychoanalysis, Psychological economics, Structural psychology, Testing methods, Typology

Psychopathology, 148, 176

Psychophysics, 498

Psychoses: alcoholic, 570; body build and, 178; endogenous, 178; normality and, 176

Ptolemaic system, 8 f., 290

Public administration. *See* Administration

Public opinion: diplomacy as reflecting, 385; ecology of, 518 n.; partial correlation in analyzing, 608; in political science, 74; press and, 389. *See also* Attitudes

Public policy, concrete comparisons as determining, 535

Pueblo Indians. *See* American Indians

Pueblos, Tanoan, 275

Pufendorf, Samuel, 121 f.

Pulsations, stylistic. *See* Stylistic pulsations

Punishment: and efficiency of administration, 535; warrants and, 532 ff. *See also* Crime survey

Pure science. *See* science

Pyknic type, 185

Pythagoras, 36

Quaife, Milo M., 366

Qualitative analysis: in agricultural economics, 636; of costs and profits, 636; in Marshall's law of demand, 646; in psychology, 220; and quantitative, 220, 615, 624. *See also* Deduction, Economics, etc.

Quality-points, in Thorndike's scale, 223

Quantitative-descriptive method, Mitchell on, 665

Quantitative methods: Cattell's use of, 222; Chapin's use of, 318; in delinquency studies, 504; 522 ff., 526; in economics, 747; in psychological economics, 501; in psychology, 220; and qualitative, 220, 615, 624; in treating social data, 222, 519 f., 591 f., 751 f. *See also* Business cycles, Case method, Induction, Normal curve of error, Statistics, Testing methods, etc.

Quantitative research: by Ebbinghaus, 707 ff.; "formative type" of, 662; and historical analysis, 754; identified with natural sciences, 708; in public administration, 319 ff. *See also* Economics, Psychology, Sociology, etc.

Quartzite, prehistoric artifacts of, 267 ff.

Quesnay, François, 676, 678

Questionnaire method, 735; informal use of, by Bryce, 471; Michelet's use of, in historical method, 401; in Missouri Crime Survey, 529; sampling in, 85, 463; in social diagnosis, 106; in study of rural attitudes, 462 ff.; in studying public opinion, 88; use of, by Arneson, 699, by Merriam and Gosnell, 698. *See also* Case method, Interview method

Quicherat, 403

Quinet, Edgar, 396

as existing from Neolithic period, 538, and mental, 582, mixture of, 582; of physique and character, correlated, 176 ff., 582; pyknic, 185; range of, from normality to psychosis, 176; of Stern, 184; verification of, 178 f. See also Typological method

Typological method: accomplishments of, 178 f.; in biological and social sciences, 184; Kretschmer's technique in, 177 f.; origin of, 180; phenomena isolated by, 179 ff., 182 f.; in prehistoric archaeology, 268, 283; in psychology, 180 f., 184; purpose and limitations of, 181 ff.; static elements in, 181; statistics in, 178; "type" concept in, 184

Uhle, on interrelations of cultures, 250
Unemployment, uniform data of, 593 n.
Unilinear evolution. See Evolution
United States Bureau of Labor Statistics, 218
United States Department of Agriculture, 754
Universe of discourse, 690
Upper class: criteria determining, 593; samples of, in vote analysis, 604. See also Social classes
Upper Paleolithic. See Paleolithic
Upson L. D., 319, 759
Urban area, city and, distinguished, 602 n.
Urban class, criteria determining, 598. See also Social classes
Urban community: as abstract object of study, 740; administration of justice in rural and, 533 f.; evolution of, 374. See also Medieval town
Urban and rural concepts: in census, 207 ff.
Utilitarianism, in psychological economics, 500
Utility: as capacity to satisfy want, 60, 650; consumption as related to, 490; economic method and, 59 ff.; effort and error in, 60 f.; as force or motive, 64 ff.; Jevons and others on, 59 ff.; magnitudes in, 66, 68; physical analogies to, 60 f., 66 f.; price as related to, 59 ff., 66; as "real value," 69; scientific status of, 62. See also Marginal utility

Values: attitudes and, 507 f.; civic equality as, 73; in creative work, 489, 493; as determined by faith, 148 f.; in economic theory, 68, 329, 617 f., 620, 625 f., 631 n., 636; in history, 355, 437; in philosophy, 71; in politics, 71, 89; prediction affected by, 326; in regional geography, 235; social, 102, 163 ff., 507 f.; in social science, 525; spiritual, 415 ff. See also Marginal utility, Price, Utility, etc.
Vanderkindere, L., 37
Vaux, Clotilde de, 40, 56
Veblen, T. B., 148, 494, 666 f., 675, 679
Verdross, Alfred, 118 ff.
Verdun, partition of, 372
Versailles, Treaty of, 132
Vesalius, 290
Vico, J. B., 396, 406
Victoria, on sovereignty, 121
Village, medieval, 369 f., 420
Viner, Jacob, 659 n., 747
Vinogradoff, P., 378
Viollet-le-Duc, 396
Virgil, 396
Vitalism, and logical determinism, 491. See also Determinism, Mechanism
Vocational guidance, 497
Vold, George B., 609 n.
Volition: Ach on motivating factors in, 723 f.; McDougall on, 193. See also Action, Behavior, Instincts
Voltaire, 9 n., 396, 401, 414, 424 ff.
Voters: pairing, of two classes, 609 ff., 612 f.; as samples of class, 602
Votes: Catlin's interpretation of, 84 f.; chance in casting, 601; comparability of, 605; in geographic areas, 602; as Hobbesian estimate of relative strength, 84 f.; identification of, 588; as indexes of attitudes, 587 ff., 601, 605 ff.; method of weighing, 85; Ogburn-Peterson study employing, as data, 586 ff.; samples of, 600 ff., 605; sectional groupings of, 87; of urban and rural classes, 586 ff.; of women, 586 ff.
Voting: Arneson's and Merriam and Gosnell's studies on, 699 f.; as behavior, 87, 586; compulsory, 89; Gosnell's experiments in stimulation of, 697 f., 701, 703 f.; marked ballot as material consequent of, 586; motives